IMAGES
of America

TEXAS GUNSLINGERS

IMAGES
of America

TEXAS GUNSLINGERS

Bill O'Neal

ARCADIA
PUBLISHING

Published by Arcadia Publishing
Charleston, South Carolina

Library of Congress Control Number: 2014943074

For all general information, please contact Arcadia Publishing:
Telephone 843-853-2070
Fax 843-853-0044
E-mail sales@arcadiapublishing.com
For customer service and orders:
Toll-Free 1-888-313-2665

Visit us on the Internet at www.arcadiapublishing.com

*For my sons-in-law: Rudy Martinez,
Drew Gormley, and Dusty Henderson*

CONTENTS

Acknowledgments   6

Introduction   7

1.   The Cradle of Old West Gunfighting   9

2.   The Deadliest Trio   19

3.   Gunfighter Gallery   29

4.   Texas Rangers   51

5.   Blood Feuds   69

6.   Gunfighter Towns   87

7.   End of the Trail   109

ACKNOWLEDGMENTS

This book was proposed to me by Jared Nelson of Arcadia Publishing, and I was delighted at the opportunity to apply the Arcadia treatment to a subject that I have researched and written about for more than 40 years. My editors for this project were Blake Wright and Jeff Ruetsche, who were unfailingly helpful and gracious. The Arcadia production team applied their customary expertise to faded images from the 19th century. *Texas Gunslingers* is my fifth title for Arcadia, and I continue to be impressed by the high quality of professionalism and creativity with which the staff embraces each new book.

Sherri Baker, interlibrary loan specialist at Panola College in Carthage, located obscure books and images for me with her usual zeal for detective work. My first book, *Encyclopedia of Western Gunfighters*, remains in print after 35 years and has been published in several foreign editions. I have written biographies about gunfighters and accounts of feuds and range wars. In putting together these books, I have accumulated a large collection of images, as well as boxes and file cabinets full of gunfighter research. Therefore, when Arcadia Publishing invited me to write about Texas gunfighters, I already had most of what I needed at my home office, and my various acknowledgements of debts have been listed and detailed in earlier books.

But Chuck Parsons, a noted researcher and writer in the field of Texas Rangers and outlaws, granted permission for me to use certain images for this project. My daughter, Dr. Berri Gormley, took needed photographs on short notice at the Texas Ranger Hall of Fame and Museum. On an impromptu trip to Timpson to find and photograph a gravestone, my wife, Karon, and I were given invaluable help by staff members at city hall. And Karon, as always, cheerfully provided a sounding board throughout this project, then prepared the manuscript for the publishers. I could not complete a book without her.

INTRODUCTION

The gunfighter is a compelling figure of the Western frontier. Nothing is more dramatic than life-and-death conflict, and the image of men in big hats and boots brandishing six-shooters and Winchesters has been portrayed in countless novels, movies, and television shows. Nowhere is the gunfighter image more deeply emblazoned than in Texas. Indeed, Texas may be considered the Gunfighter Capital of the West. After the cowboy—a Texas creation—the most colorful and romanticized frontier figure is the gunfighter.

Texas made an enormous contribution to gunfighter lore. The revolving pistol, key weapon of gunfighters, evolved in Texas. Early Texas Rangers, desperate for a repeating weapon that could be used from horseback against mounted Comanche warriors, adapted Samuel Colt's little five-shooter revolvers. Soon, Texas Rangers secured improvements for Colt's pistols, which became larger, more powerful six-guns. Armed with at least two of these six-shooters, mounted Rangers could fire 12 rounds without reloading. In Texas, the US Army learned from Ranger tactics how to combat horseback warriors. In the 1850s, a US Cavalry regiment was organized and stationed in Texas, and each trooper carried a cap-and-ball six-shooter. Soon, these tactics and weapons would be utilized by cavalry units against horseback warriors all over the West.

During the 1850s, these same six-shooters began to be used by Texans against each other. Ben Thompson of Austin became the first gunfighter of note, and many more Texas men began to blaze away at each other with deadly intent and increasing skill. Most Western states and territories saw widespread gunplay for only a brief number of years before law and order prevailed: Kansas, for example, during the cattle-town era; New Mexico during the murderous Lincoln County War; and Oklahoma during its lawless heyday as an outlaw refuge. But in Texas, gunslingers first unlimbered six-shooters against each other during the 1850s and continued to blaze away until past the turn of the century.

A survey of 256 Western gunfighters and 589 shootouts in which they participated (*Encyclopedia of Western Gunfighters*, University of Oklahoma Press, 1979) reveals that Texans dominated the tally sheet of frontier pistoleers. More of these gunfights—nearly 160—occurred in Texas than in any other state or territory. No other Western state or territory was the arena of even half as many shootings. In rating gunfighters according to the number of killings each, as well as the total shootouts participated in, 10 of the deadliest 15 spent most of their careers in Texas. The top 15, with those from Texas italicized, were *Jim Miller, John Wesley Hardin*, Harvey Logan, Wild Bill Hickok, *John Selman, Dallas Stoudenmire, King Fisher*, Billy the Kid, *Ben Thompson*, Henry Brown, John Slaughter, *Cullen Baker*, Clay Allison, *Jim Courtright*, and *John Hughes*. More gunfighters were born in Texas than in any other state or territory, and more died in Texas.

There were more blood feuds in Texas than in any other state. The Regulator-Moderator War of the 1840s introduced feuding to Texas, and for the next three-quarters of a century, there were vicious outbreaks of violence between families or factions. These feuds featured ambushes, street fights, lynchings, night riders, hired killers, and unforgiving vendettas. Dr. C.L. Sonnichsen, the first student of Texas feuds (*I'll Die Before I'll Run* and *Ten Texas Feuds*) made the observation: " 'Vengeance is mine!' saith the Lord. But in and out of Texas he has always had plenty of help."

7

Killin' Jim Miller was the West's premier assassin, more lethal than even the legendary Tom Horn. For a time, Miller specialized in killing Mexican sheepherders during the range troubles in Texas between cattlemen and sheep ranchers. Mannen Clements, an in-law of Miller, expressed the same professional outlook: "For three hundred dollars I'd cut anybody in two with a sawed-off shotgun."

Shortly before being hanged for murder in 1878, 27-year-old Bill Longley reflected: "My first step was disobedience; next whiskey drinking; next carrying pistols; next gambling, and then murder, and I suppose next will be the gallows." Dallas Stoudenmire, who repeatedly displayed ferocious courage during Civil War combat and in eight gunfights, confidently proclaimed: "I don't believe the bullet was ever molded that will kill me." But he was proved wrong during an 1882 saloon brawl in El Paso.

It was the deadly risk of gunfighting that attracted novelists and filmmakers. The life-and-death adventures of Western gunfighters captivated audiences, especially when they could see exciting fast-draw contests on the silver screen. In recent years, there has been excellent research into the lives of gunfighters, and today, there are fine books available about Texas gunmen, Texas Rangers, and Texas feuds. Throughout the Lone Star State, there are museums, gun collections, gunfighter sites, and tombstones that exhibit the captivating reality of gunslinging on the Texas frontier.

One

THE CRADLE OF
OLD WEST GUNFIGHTING

Early Texas was settled by pioneers who came mostly from states of the Old South. These Southerners brought to Texas their music, cooking, home crafts, and the institution of slavery. Southern men also brought a proclivity for violence, from eye-gouging, knife-wielding brawls to blood feuds and formal duels. The rough-and-tumble Texas society embraced knife-fighting and pistol duels and blood feuds. The popularity of Sam Houston among Texans was enhanced by an 1827 duel in which he shot and nearly killed his opponent and by an 1832 brawl in Washington, DC, in which he thrashed a congressman who pulled a pistol on him.

Beginning in the 1760s and 1770s, the breakdown of British authority led to bands of "Regulators" who tried to reassert order in Southern colonies through extralegal actions. When Regulators went too far, "Moderators" tried to check their activities. These Regulator-Moderator conflicts continued in the South for decades, resulting in the first and deadliest Texas blood feud.

By the 1840s, a few of Sam Colt's new revolving pistols reached Texas. Capt. Jack Hays of the Texas Rangers, desperately battling mounted warriors armed with repeating weapons—bows and arrows—realized that Colt's small, awkward handguns could give his men repeating weapons to use from horseback. In Texas, these handguns evolved into powerful six-shooters—the iconic weapon of Old West gunfighters.

When a tavern fight broke out, a single-shot pistol was good for only one round, after which men went to their knives. The most famous knife-fighter on the frontier was Jim Bowie, who earned widespread notoriety in 1827 during a duel that exploded into a general melee. Despite being shot, stabbed, and beaten, Bowie disemboweled Sheriff Norris Wright and slashed another assailant. The last several years of Bowie's life were spent in Texas, where he died at the Alamo. A gambler who aggressively engaged in a variety of altercations, Bowie, had he lived in Texas a few decades later, would instead have been a gunfighter of renown. (Author's collection.)

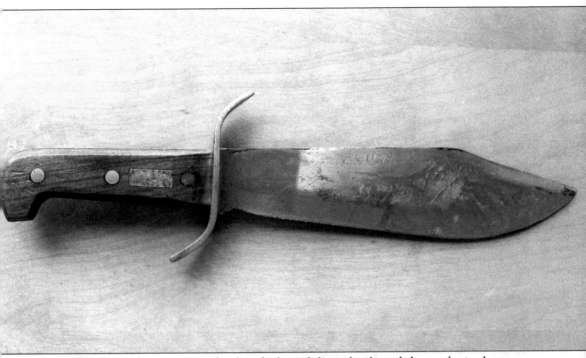

Brothers James and Rezin Bowie developed a large fighting knife, and the combative James was never without his weapon, even when fashionably dressed. The big, heavy blade often had a clip point on top, which held a cutting edge for backstrokes. When David Crockett first saw Bowie's famous weapon, he is said to have remarked that you could tickle a man's ribs a long time before drawing a laugh. In various models, the "bowie knife" became immediately popular in Texas. Other dangerous Texas knife-fighters include Henry Strickland, "The Bully of the Tenaha," who was slain during the Regulator-Moderator War. (Photograph by the author.)

Dueling was a common method of settling differences in the rugged frontier society of Texas. In 1837, Sam Houston, first president of the Texas Republic, directed the secretary of war, Gen. Albert Sidney Johnston (left), to take command of the 2,000-man Texas Army from temporary commander in chief Felix Huston, a newcomer who had no military experience. Although Johnston was a West Point graduate, Huston challenged him to a duel rather than surrender command. On February 5, 1837, Johnston was shot in the right hip. Occasionally, junior officers issued challenges to their immediate superiors, hoping to open a vacancy for promotion. (Both, author's collection.)

The first of many blood feuds in Texas was the Regulator-Moderator War, a vicious conflict that claimed nearly 40 lives during the 1840s. The killing began late in 1840 in the forested wilderness of newly organized Harrison County, where the Regulator leader was rugged William Pinckney "Hell-Roarin' " Rose. His soaring monument proclaimed, "He was Tower of Strength in War, in State, at Home." (Photograph by the author.)

In Harrison County, casualties included Sheriff John B. Campbell, Judge John Hansford, and Peter Whetstone, founder of Marshall, the county seat. Even more prominent was Robert M. Potter (pictured), attacked at his wilderness home by a posse led by William Rose. Potter had signed the Texas Declaration of Independence, served as secretary of the navy during the Texas Revolution, and, at the time of his death, was a senator of the Texas Republic. (Courtesy Jefferson Historical Museum.)

13

When fighting shifted into Shelby County, Regulator leader Charles Jackson and a companion were ambushed and slain. The new Regulator leader was "Colonel" Watt Moorman (pictured), a hard-drinking bully who wore a cutaway military jacket and carried a brace of pistols, a bowie knife, a bois d'arc cudgel, and a hunting horn to summon his men from the forests. (Courtesy Shelby County Historical Museum.)

After nearly four years of violence, in August 1844, Pres. Sam Houston issued a call for militia volunteers to gather in San Augustine. When Houston rode into town, he was met by 600 men, including officers who had campaigned with him in 1836. The old general quickly organized his men and sent the force marching into Shelby County. Regulators and Moderators promptly dispersed, and their leaders were taken into custody. (Author's collection.)

In the bitter aftermath of the feud, Watt Moorman was shotgunned and buried in a private family cemetery (pictured). In 1847, a young bride was given away by her Moderator stepfather into a Regulator family. The hateful stepfather poisoned the wedding cake, sending almost everyone into convulsions and killing several members at the tragic event. (Photograph by the author.)

Anglo pioneers first encountered horseback warriors in Texas. Comanche and Kiowa warriors were at their most dangerous as mounted archers, guiding their war ponies with their knees while firing arrows from three-foot bows. A quiver could hold 20 or more arrows, which gave the mounted, mobile warriors a repeating weapon against their Spanish, Mexican, or Texan adversaries. The bowman could fire 20 arrows at the gallop, while his enemy desperately tried to reload his single-shot rifle or horse pistol. The best riders had the smoothest firing platforms. Comanche warriors were regarded as the finest horsemen in the West, and they became the deadliest bowmen. (From *Comanche Giving Arrows to the Medicine Rock* by George Catlin, courtesy Smithsonian American Art Museum.)

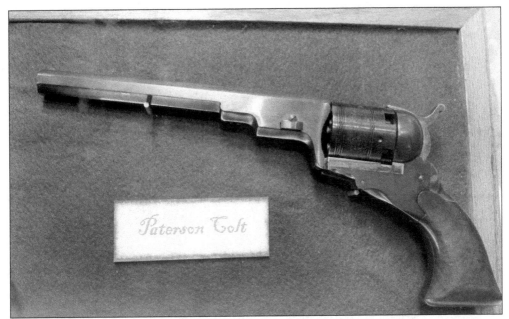

While working as a sailor in his teens, Sam Colt developed the idea of a revolving pistol by watching the operation of a ship's tiller drum. In 1836, Colt patented a .34-caliber, five-shot revolver known as a "Texas." The light, poorly balanced pistol had a troublesome trigger and was cumbersome to reload, but it was a repeating weapon that could be used from horseback. (Courtesy Buckhorn Saloon and Museum.)

Capt. Jack Hays recognized the potential of using Colt revolvers against Comanche warriors. Hays armed his Texas Rangers with a pair of five-shooters each and worked out tactics for employing them in combat. After using these weapons effectively against horseback warriors, Texas Rangers suggested various improvements. A statue of Hays brandishing a five-shooter is on the courthouse square in San Marcos. (Photograph by the author.)

Utilized by the Texas Rangers in horseback combat against Comanche warriors, Sam Colt's early five-shooters evolved by the 1850s into larger six-shooters with plow grip handles and hinged loaders, which rammed powder and shot into each of the six chambers in the revolving cylinder. Nipples behind each chamber were capped with fulminate of mercury percussion caps. Shown above is a Model 1851 Navy Colt of .36 caliber. Below is a .44-caliber 1858 Remington, with a backstrap above a removable cylinder. An extra cylinder, already loaded with powder, shot, and caps, rapidly increased the speed of reloading. Of course, these improved weapons could be used by Texans against each other. (Both photographs by the author.)

Two

THE DEADLIEST TRIO

The deadliest Texas gunfighters were Ben Thompson, John Wesley Hardin, and James B. "Killin' Jim" Miller. Thompson was the first Texas gunfighter of note. Born in England in 1842, he migrated with his family to Austin, Texas, in 1851. Following a quarrel with another teenager in 1858, Ben ran home, then chased his adversary with a single-barrel shotgun, peppering the fleeing youth with birdshot. The next year, an angry clash while geese hunting brought another adolescent face-off, this time with shotguns at 40 paces. Ben and his opponent were both wounded. Soon, Ben Thompson would be trading .45 slugs in his confrontations.

John Wesley Hardin was born in 1853 in Bonham. The son of a Methodist preacher, young Wes learned to handle firearms as a hunter and by shooting at effigies of Abraham Lincoln during the Civil War. In 1868, when he was 15, Wes pumped three pistol slugs into a former slave. During the next several years, the kill-crazy young outlaw was involved in one gunfight after another.

In 1867, when little Jim Miller was one year old, he moved with his family from Arkansas to Texas. Within a few years, the boy's parents died, and he was sent to live with his grandparents in Evant. When Jim was eight, his grandparents were murdered in their home. The boy was arrested, then released to live with a married sister on a farm near Gatesville. But the hot-tempered youngster clashed with his brother-in-law, and Jim shot him while he slept, setting the pattern for his life.

All three members of this deadly trio died violently. Killer Miller was lynched; Wes Hardin was shot dead in El Paso; and Ben Thompson was assassinated in San Antonio.

Ben Thompson was 19 when the Civil War began. He joined the Confederate army and served the duration of the war in Texas, New Mexico, and Louisiana. During an off-duty monte game at Laredo, trouble erupted, and Thompson shot two Mexicans to death. He injured a leg when his horse fell on him while he was smuggling whiskey, but while on medical furlough, he married Catherine Moore, daughter of a well-to-do Austin family. After the war, Thompson was jailed in Austin following gunplay with occupation troops. In 1868, he wounded his brother-in-law for striking his wife. During a saloon fight in 1876 in Austin, saloonkeeper Mark Wilson fired a shotgun at Thompson, who killed Wilson with three pistol shots, then wounded bartender Charles Matthews in the mouth. (Courtesy Western History Collection, University of Oklahoma Library.)

Billy Thompson, photo made in
Ellsworth, Kansas, 1872.

Billy Thompson was Ben's younger brother. He served alongside Ben during the Civil War, and he shared Ben's propensity for drinking, gambling, and gunplay. In 1868, Billy killed a US Army sergeant at Austin, and Ben helped him escape the state. Ben and Billy were in and out of Kansas cattle towns as gamblers during the early 1870s. In Ellsworth in 1873, a drunken Billy accidentally shotgunned Sheriff C.B. Whitney. "My God, Billy," exclaimed Ben, "you've shot our best friend!" Again, Ben helped Billy escape. In 1882, Billy hid in El Paso for several months to escape a murder charge in Corpus Christi. It was rumored that he was killed in Laredo about 1892. (Courtesy Western History Collection, University of Oklahoma Library.)

By the 1880s, Ben Thompson was well-regarded in Austin, where he quietly supported orphans and dressed well around town. In 1881, he was elected Austin's city marshal. The next year, he ventured into the Vaudeville Theatre and Gambling Saloon, the most notorious night spot in San Antonio. The Vaudeville was owned by Jack Harris, who for two years had nursed a grudge against Thompson over a gambling dispute. When told that Thompson had entered his building, Harris seized a shotgun and concealed himself behind venetian blinds. Spotted by Thompson, Harris raised the shotgun. But Thompson palmed a revolver and triggered a fatal round. Thompson surrendered himself, resigned as city marshal, and, following acquittal, was met in Austin with a spontaneous parade by well-wishers. (Courtesy Eakin Press.)

On March 11, 1884, Ben Thompson met his friend King Fisher, deputy sheriff from Uvalde, who was in Austin on official business. The two men had several drinks, then Thompson decided to travel by train with Fisher as far as San Antonio. On the train, the men continued to drink and were quite rowdy. In San Antonio, they saw a play in the evening, and at 10:30, they went to the theater where Jack Harris had been killed two years earlier. Thompson and Fisher had a drink, then were attacked by several friends of Harris. Thompson managed to get off one shot before dying with nine wounds. Fisher was struck 13 times. Most of the wounds were caused by shotgun and rifle fire, and there were powder burns on their faces. (Both, author's collection.)

After killing a former slave near Moscow in East Texas, Wes Hardin went on the run. Pursued by a trio of Reconstruction soldiers, he set an ambush near a creek crossing. There, two soldiers were shotgunned, and Wes killed the third man with a .44 revolver. Several former Confederates concealed the corpses while Wes, wounded in the arm, fled the scene. He began to drink and gamble, and there were other shootings. Early in 1871, he was arrested near Marshall, but he shot a guard and escaped. Soon, he left the state with a cattle drive, but, after reaching Kansas, he killed two more men. (Author's collection.)

In Texas in 1872, Hardin wounded members of the state police in two incidents, but he caught buckshot in the side. In Cuero in 1873, Hardin killed a deputy sheriff, and, later in the year, he killed Sheriff Jack Helm (pictured). The next year, Hardin celebrated his 21st birthday in Comanche. During an exchange of shots with Deputy Sheriff Charles Webb, Hardin was wounded in the side, but he drilled the lawman in the head. Hardin fled town ahead of an enraged mob, but his brother Joe and two other companions were captured and lynched. The State of Texas placed a $4,000 dead-or-alive reward on the head of John Wesley Hardin. (From Hardin's autobiography, *Life of John Wesley Hardin, As Told by Himself*, 1896; pen and ink drawing by J. Onderdonk.)

With Texas Rangers on his trail, Hardin passed as "J.H. Swain Jr." and moved his family to Florida and Alabama. His wife, Jane, bore him two daughters and a son. For three years, "Swain" lived quietly, but in 1877, Texas Ranger John B. Armstrong found him on a train in Pensacola. "Texas, by God!" shouted Hardin as the Ranger drew his long-barreled Colt .45. Hardin's revolver caught in a suspender, but, beside him, 19-year-old Jim Mann triggered a round that punched a hole in Armstrong's hat. The Ranger killed Mann with a bullet to the heart, then clubbed Hardin with his pistol barrel. Back in Texas, Hardin was sentenced to the penitentiary in Huntsville (pictured). (Author's collection.)

An 1870s scene in a Pecos saloon features what is believed to be Jim Miller in the white hat, seated at a gambling table. During part of his time in Pecos, Killin' Jim wore the badges of city marshal and of deputy sheriff. A feud broke out with Sheriff Bud Frazer, who twice opened fire on Miller in Pecos, in April and December 1894. Each time, Miller was hit in an arm or leg, but the deadliest rounds were deflected by a steel breastplate he often wore beneath his shirt. Frazer fled to New Mexico, but in 1896, Miller trailed him to a saloon in Toyah, west of Pecos. Killin' Jim blasted away most of Frazer's face, and when Bud's sister cursed the murderer, he threatened to shoot her, too. (Author's collection.)

By the 1890s, Jim "Killer" Miller was the West's premier assassin, often riding great distances afterward to establish an alibi. "I have killed eleven men I know about," he told a Fort Worth acquaintance, before adding with disdain, "I have lost my notch stick on sheepherders I've killed out on the border." In 1899, he ambushed and killed Joe Earp, who had testified against him during a trial. The murders continued into the 20th century. It took four rounds to finish Lubbock lawyer James Jarrott. "He was the hardest damn man to kill I ever tackled," admitted Miller. In 1904, Miller killed Frank Fore in a Fort Worth hotel, and two years later, he shotgunned lawman Ben Collins. Little wonder that when Pat Garrett was murdered in 1908, widespread blame was placed on Miller. (Courtesy Western History Collections, University of Oklahoma Library.)

Three

GUNFIGHTER GALLERY

More gunfighters operated in Texas than in any other state or territory. More gunfighters were born in Texas, and, in the Lone Star State, more shootists died—often violently. Gunmen who earned most of their notoriety elsewhere nevertheless engaged in their first gunplay in Texas: Doc Holliday, in Dallas; Bat Masterson, in Mobeetie; and Henry Brown, in a panhandle cow camp. There were Texas expatriates, men who took their deadly kills elsewhere. Tall Texan Phil Coe was drawn to booming Abilene, Kansas, where he was killed in a street fight with Wild Bill Hickok. Joe Horner, a fast-shooting Texas outlaw, fled the state and changed his name to Frank Canton. He was a hired gunman during Wyoming's Johnson County War. He later achieved high position and respectability in Oklahoma.

Of course, there were Texans who spent their entire careers in Texas. Pink Higgins was raised on the Texas frontier, and he used his preferred weapon, a Winchester, against adversaries for nearly four decades. Higgins, incidentally, was the father of nine children, more than any other Western gunman. King Fisher was the father of four daughters, but he used his guns on both sides of the law, and he was assassinated at the age of 30.

Twice, there were lynchings by gunfire, with gun barrels shoved between the bars of jail cells in Belton (1874) and Meridian (1878). Father and son Emmanuel Clements and Emmanuel Jr. were shot dead in Texas saloons about two decades apart. And, just as revolving pistols had evolved in Texas before the Civil War, after the war, Texan shootists utilized the latest revolvers, rifles, and gun rigs.

By the time he earned a DDS from the Pennsylvania College of Dental Surgery, young John H. Holliday had contracted tuberculosis. Hoping to prolong his life, Doc Holliday moved to the drier climate of the West. The 23-year-old dentist opened an office in Dallas, but he took an immediate interest in drinking and gambling. On the first day of 1875, Holliday exchanged shots with a saloonkeeper named Austin. No one was hit, but Holliday did better during the next several years, usually in saloon fights. He gunned down two men in shootouts in Las Vegas, New Mexico, and he shot four more antagonists in Tombstone and Tucson, Arizona, and in Leadville, Colorado. Most famously, he killed Tom McLaury at Tombstone's OK Corral. But the West's deadliest dentist first engaged in gunplay in Dallas, Texas. (Courtesy Kansas State Historical Society, Topeka.)

At the age of 19, William B. "Bat" Masterson was a member of the small party of buffalo hunters that fought off several hundred Comanche warriors at the Battle of Adobe Walls in the Texas Panhandle on July 27, 1874. Following this desperate battle, Masterson scouted for the Army for a time and hunted buffalo. On January 24, 1876, Masterson, 22, was involved in a wild saloon shootout in Sweetwater (later Mobeetie), near Adobe Walls. Masterson and saloon girl Mollie Brennan apparently were in each other's company at the Lady Gay when Cpl. Melvin King, from nearby Fort Elliott, roared into the saloon and fired his service revolver. Mollie and Masterson both were shot before Bat drilled King in the heart. King and Mollie died, but Masterson recovered from his hip wound. (Courtesy Kansas State Historical Society, Topeka.)

John King Fisher was a native Texan who had a troubled boyhood, being jailed for the first time at 16. As a young man, he cowboyed in south Texas, where he broke horses, chased Mexican bandits, and learned to shoot. A gaudy dresser, Fisher sported fringed shirts, crimson sashes, and bells on his spurs. He became a colorful and dominant figure in the nearby border town of Eagle Pass, and he was feared as a rustler, nailing up a celebrated crossroads sign that read, "This is King Fisher's Road—Take the other one." Fisher admitted to killing seven men, including four vaqueros in a blazing shootout on his ranch in 1875. The next year, he married, fathering four daughters. In 1884, Fisher, in the wrong place at the wrong time, was assassinated alongside Ben Thompson in San Antonio. (Courtesy Western History Collections, University of Oklahoma Library.)

John Calhoun Pinkney "Pink" Higgins was raised on his family's Lampasas County ranch during the 1850s and 1860s. The county suffered Comanche raids, and the only defense was neighborhood pursuit posses. Pink's father left his son, tall for his age and a good rifle shot, to defend the home while he rode with pursuers. But, by the time he was 14, Pink Higgins was riding with posses while his father stayed at home. Twice, Higgins was wounded in these combats. When he was 18, he helped chase down a rustler, then adjusted the noose around the man's neck. While still a teenager, he became a drover on trail drives, and he was a trail boss within a few years, ready to meet trouble with his Winchester. (Courtesy Standard Studio, Lampasas.)

With cartridge revolvers came cartridge belts, and holsters were made to fit over the gun belt. A man could wear his holster for a cross-draw (above), which was especially useful while in the saddle. When he dismounted, the gunman could slide the holster to his hip for faster access (below). (Both photographs by Karon O'Neal.)

To load a single-action Colt .45, pull the hammer back to half-cock, so that the cylinder will revolve freely. Open the loading gate and insert cartridges into the chamber. Since single-action Colts have no safety, it was considered prudent to carry only "five beans in the wheel," leaving the chamber beneath the hammer empty. (Photograph by Karon O'Neal.)

Some men shoved their pistols into their waistbands or hip pockets, while others preferred a shoulder holster beneath their coat. (Photograph by Karon O'Neal.)

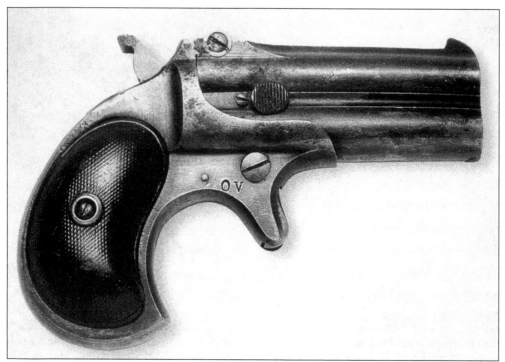

Many gunslingers carried a hideout gun as a backup. Perhaps a "belly gun"—a small, short-barreled revolver—was slipped into a coat or pants or vest pocket. More popular was the derringer, only a few inches long and easy to conceal. More than 150,000 of these .41-caliber Remington "Over and Under" hideout guns were sold. (Author's collection.)

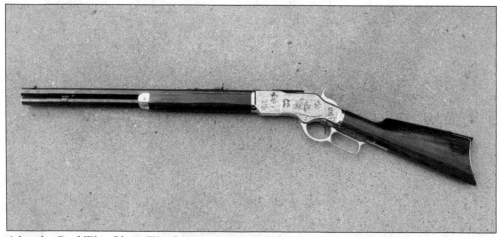

After the Civil War, Oliver Winchester reorganized the Winchester Repeating Arms Company, and the first Winchester, a lever-action repeater, was introduced in 1866. The Model 1873 became an immediate classic, the best-selling rifle in the West. The Winchester '73 (pictured) was so popular that Colt chambered its single-action Peacemaker for the same .44 cartridge so that a man could use interchangeable ammunition in his revolver and his shoulder gun. (Photograph by the author.)

Cullen Montgomery Baker was a vicious desperado of early Texas. At the age of four, in 1839, the boy moved with his family from Tennessee to the Republic of Texas. His father received a land grant in Cass County, where Cullen grew up to be quarrelsome and a problem drinker. In 1854, when he was 19, Baker killed his first man, and, two years later, he claimed his second victim. In 1861, he enlisted in a Confederate troop in Cass County, but he deserted, joined the Union army, then deserted again and joined a gang of bandit raiders. After the war, Baker organized a gang of thieves, and, after a number of depredations, he was chased down and killed in East Texas in 1869. On his corpse were found a shotgun, four revolvers, three derringers, and six pocketknives. Cullen Baker was buried at Jefferson's Oakwood Cemetery. (Photograph by the author.)

Born in 1851, native Texan William Preston Longley became known as "Bloody Bill" during the gunfighter era. He shotgunned Wilson Anderson for killing a relative. Bloody Bill murdered Rev. William Lay, who was milking a cow. He killed Lou Shroyer in a running fight, and two other victims brought his total to five before he was arrested by two Texas lawmen in 1877. The officers slipped into Louisiana and, at shotgun point, "extradited" Longley back to Texas. Jailed at Giddings, he was tried and convicted of murder. When Longley was hanged, five days short of his 27th birthday, he died with courage, although his knees dragged the ground and he had to be hoisted up and rehanged. (Left, courtesy Western History Collections, University of Oklahoma Library; below, author's collection.)

In 1879, actor Maurice Barrymore (right), father of Lionel, Ethel, and John and great-grandfather of Drew, brought his traveling troupe to Marshall for a performance at the Mahone Opera House. That night after the show, Barrymore and fellow thespians Ellen Cummins and Ben Porter traded insults in a restaurant with drunken railroad detective Big Jim Currie. Barrymore, an accomplished boxer, doubled his fists and approached Currie, but Big Jim produced a hammerless Smith & Wesson five-shooter, plugged Barrymore in the shoulder, and mortally wounded Porter. Eastern newspapers severely castigated Texas and Texans, especially after Currie won acquittal. But, as the local saying went, "Steal a hog, get sent to jail; kill a man, get set free." (Both, author's collection.)

Henry Newton Brown was orphaned as a boy, and at 17, he left his native Missouri to seek adventure in the West. Brown worked as a cowboy, and in 1876, he turned up in a cattle camp in the Texas Panhandle. Brown was outwardly courteous and soft-spoken, but a lethal ferocity lurked below the surface. In the camp, he quarreled with a fellow cowboy, then pumped three slugs into his adversary—the first of several victims. In New Mexico, Brown fought on both sides of the Lincoln County War and later ran with outlaw Billy the Kid. Back in Texas, Brown wore a deputy's badge in Tascosa. As city marshal of Caldwell, Kansas, he tamed the raucous cattle town. But Marshal Brown led a murderous bank robbery at Medicine Lodge, Kansas, and was lynched with his gang. (Courtesy Kansas State Historical Society, Topeka.)

Phil Coe, Texas gambler and saloon owner, had a long connection with Ben Thompson. The two men served together in the 2nd Mounted Texas Rifles in 1862. After the Civil War, Coe opened a saloon in Austin and installed Thompson as a house gambler. In 1871, Coe and Thompson owned the Bull's Head Saloon in Abilene, Kansas. An obscene sign at the Bull's Head attracted the ire of city marshal Wild Bill Hickok. Even though Thompson and Coe soon sold out, Coe continued to have trouble with Wild Bill, flooring him during a fistfight. On October 5, 1871, Coe went on a drunken spree with about 50 fellow Texans. When challenged by Hickok, Coe fired a shot, which missed, and Wild Bill drilled Coe in the stomach. Coe died four days later and was taken back to Texas for burial. (Right, courtesy Chuck Parsons; below, courtesy Kansas State Historical Society, Topeka.)

West Texan Barney Riggs drifted into Arizona Territory long enough to kill his employer and earn a life sentence in Yuma Territorial Prison. But during an attempted prison break, Riggs picked up a revolver and shot a convict, helping to save the warden's life and winning a pardon. Riggs returned to Texas, ranching west of Pecos. In 1896, Riggs was assaulted in a Pecos saloon (above) by John Denson and Bill Earhart. A round from Earhart's revolver grazed Riggs, who coolly drilled his assailant between the eyes. Denson fled the premises, but Riggs put a slug into the back of his head. In Fort Stockton six years later, Barney Riggs was shot dead by a step-grandson. (Both photographs by the author.)

Emmanuel "Mannen" Clements and his brothers, Gyp, Jim, and Joe, were brought up on a cattle ranch south of Smiley. During the Sutton-Taylor Feud, the Clements brothers—related by marriage to the Taylors—were involved in several ambushes and sieges. Their cousin, John Wesley Hardin, fought alongside them, and Mannen once broke him out of jail. In 1887, while drinking in Ballinger's Senate Saloon, Mannen was shot dead by city marshal Joe Townsend. (Courtesy Western History Collections, University of Oklahoma Library.)

Emmanuel "Mannie" Clements Jr. was as violence-prone as his father. Following an 1894 murder in Alpine, Mannie relocated to El Paso. For the next 14 years, he wore badges as a deputy constable, constable, and deputy sheriff. By marriage, Mannie became a brother-in-law of Killin' Jim Miller. Indicted for armed robbery in 1908, he was assassinated in El Paso's Coney Island Saloon. (Courtesy Western History Collections, University of Oklahoma Library.)

In 1871, when he was 18, A. John Spradley was twice wounded in a fight with two brothers named Hayes. But Spradley shot both brothers to death, fled from Mississippi to Texas, and, within several years, assumed the vacated sheriff's office of Nacogdoches County. During his long tenure, Sheriff Spradley sometimes had to defend himself; in 1893, he killed fast-shooting saloonkeeper Joel Goodwin. In 1884, Spradley was shot through the torso while trying to make an arrest. But a resourceful doctor used a ramrod to push a whiskey-soaked silk handkerchief through the wound to heal it, and Sheriff Spradley lived to be 87. (Author's collection.)

Dave Kemp was born in Hamilton County in 1862, and Comanche raiding parties remained active in the area throughout his boyhood. When Kemp was 15, a fight broke out on Hamilton's courthouse square. Young Kemp killed a man named Smith and turned his gun on the sheriff before being seized from behind. Sentenced to hang, he tore away from his guards and leaped from a second-floor courthouse window. He broke both ankles in the fall but somehow scrambled onto a horse before being subdued. Gov. Richard Hubbard commuted the teenager's sentence, then issued a pardon. Kemp moved to New Mexico, killed Sheriff Les Dow, and returned to Texas, where he lived out his days as a rancher—and peace officer! (Author's collection.)

After the Civil War, teenaged Texan Joe Horner began herding cattle up the Chisholm Trail for famed rancher Burk Burnett. By his early 20s, Horner had established a small ranch north of Jacksboro. But he stole horses from Indian reservations in Oklahoma, then began stealing livestock from fellow ranchers. In 1874, he engaged in a shootout with troopers from nearby Fort Richardson. There was other gunplay, and in 1875, he was jailed in Jacksboro. Within a week, Horner was broken out of a flimsy lockup, probably by his three brothers. In 1876, "the Horner Gang" robbed a bank in Comanche of $5,500, but after a furious shootout with a posse, Joe was cornered. Twice more he escaped custody, fleeing Texas in 1879. (Courtesy Jim Gatchell Museum, Buffalo, Wyoming.)

Joe Horner changed his name to Frank Canton and found a fresh start on the Wyoming frontier. He became sheriff of Johnson County, married, and became a father. Soon, Canton was a gunslinging operative of the powerful Wyoming Stock Growers Association (WSGA). In the infamous Johnson County War, the expatriate Texas gunslinger was a cold-blooded assassin. During the 1892 climax of the range war, Canton and his WSGA allies were reinforced by more than 20 gunmen from Texas. After being cleared by legal machinations, the Texans returned to Texas. But Canton/Horner stayed away from Texas, eventually becoming adjutant general of the Oklahoma National Guard. He is seen here, at center with gray mustache. (Courtesy Western History Collections, University of Oklahoma Library.)

Temple Lea Houston was Sam Houston's youngest child and the first baby born in the Texas governor's mansion. Temple was not yet three when his father died, and, at the age of 12, he rode off to become a Texas cowboy. At 13, Temple helped drive a herd of cattle to Dakota Territory. He clerked for two years in the US Senate, enrolled in the first class of Texas A&M College, and graduated from Baylor University at 19. A lawyer, Houston was appointed district attorney for the Texas Panhandle, working out of turbulent Tascosa and Mobeetie. He dressed flamboyantly and carried a white-handled Colt he called "Old Betsy." An expert shot, he frequently won money in shooting contests, and, during two gunfights in the 1890s, he drilled each of his adversaries. (Courtesy Western History Collections, University of Oklahoma Library.)

A native of Tennessee, Clay Allison served the Confederacy during the Civil War. Soon after Appomattox, he and most of the rest of his family moved to Texas. In 1866, he was one of 18 drovers who rode with Texas cattlemen Charles Goodnight and Oliver Loving, blazing the historic Goodnight-Loving Trail. Allison later became a trail boss before establishing a ranch in New Mexico. He engaged in gunplay in New Mexico and in Colorado, killing four adversaries. In 1887, while ranching about 40 miles from Pecos, he drove a wagon into town for supplies. On the way back, rumored to have been drunk, he fell from the wagon, fractured his skull on a front wheel, and died. He was buried in Pecos. (Right, courtesy Western History Collections, University of Oklahoma Library; below, photograph by the author.)

In 1872, a two-story limestone jail was erected in Belton, seat of Bell County. The western part of the county is hilly, broken country, which provided hideouts for rustlers and assorted fugitives. But, in the spring of 1874, the sheriff led a sweep of the outlaw haven. Soon, 10 criminals were tossed inside the big iron-slatted cage in the new jail. The worst of the lot was a man who had murdered his wife with an axe. On the night of May 26, with the sheriff out of town, a large lynch mob stormed the jail. As the prisoners cowered at the rear of the cell, rifle and revolver muzzles were fitted between the slats. Volley fire killed nine men. An ill prisoner had been isolated in another room; he was later sentenced to life in prison. The 1872 jail later was converted to a private residence. (Author's collection.)

Four

TEXAS RANGERS

The Texas Rangers are the most famous law-enforcement body in the world. The Ranger force was created to battle horseback warriors on the Western frontier and Mexican raiders on the border. For more than three decades, Texas Rangers fulfilled this military role, including notable service during the war with Mexico.

Texas was the only Confederate state with a frontier. But, during the Civil War, there was little military presence on the Texas frontier, and for two years after the war, Union troops functioned as a Reconstruction occupation force. Texas proposed to organize 1,000 Texas Rangers for duty on the frontier, but the last thing Reconstruction officials would permit was 1,000 armed Texans.

In 1874, however, with Texans back in charge of the state, the legislature authorized the Frontier Battalion of Texas Rangers. There would be six companies—A, B, C, D, E, and F—with 75 men each. Military organization prevailed: each company would have a captain, lieutenant, sergeants, corporals, and privates. Gov. Richard Coke appointed Maj. John B. Jones, a distinguished Civil War officer, as commander of the Frontier Battalion with the rank of major of Rangers.

For a year, the Frontier Battalion fought numerous engagements against war parties and border raiders. In 1867, the US Army returned to the frontier, and Texas Ranger companies soon were reduced in size. Major Jones now turned the efforts of the Frontier Battalion to law enforcement. Texas Rangers hounded killers and rustlers, intervened in blood feuds, and established a fearsome presence as fast-shooting lawmen.

A native of South Carolina, John B. Jones was born in 1834 and moved to Texas with his family when he was four. Well-educated for the time, he distinguished himself as a Confederate officer, rising to the rank of major. In 1874, he was appointed major in command of the Frontier Battalion of Texas Rangers. The Ranger reorganization was efficiently led by Major Jones, who also led his men in frontier combat against Comanche war parties. The Indian wars finally at an end, Jones focused attention on outlawry and feuds. He effected a truce in the Horrell-Higgins Feud and engineered the manhunt for Sam Bass. Appointed adjutant general of Texas in 1879, he simultaneously commanded the Frontier Battalion until his premature death in 1881. (Author's collection.)

Frank Jones was born in Austin in 1856. Enlisting in the Texas Rangers, Jones (first row, third from left) eventually rose to the command of Company D. He was active along the Mexican border, running to earth rustlers, train and bank robbers, and an assortment of dangerous criminals. On June 30, 1893, Captain Jones led five other officers in pursuit of several cattle thieves. Crossing the Rio Grande, there was a running fight, in which two of the rustlers were wounded. The gang holed up in an adobe building at tiny Tres Jacales. Captain Jones was shot off his horse, but he straightened his broken leg in front of him and fired his Winchester from a sitting position. Suddenly, a slug tore into his chest, and he gasped, "Boys, I am killed." (Courtesy Texas Ranger Hall of Fame and Museum.)

When John Hughes was a 15-year-old cowboy, during a brawl in 1872, he took a rifle bullet through his clothing, was nearly knifed, and was wounded in his right arm. The arm was permanently impaired, and he had to switch gun hands, becoming so skilled that most people thought he was a natural southpaw. After several years as a trail driver, Hughes acquired a small horse ranch near Liberty Hill. In 1886, six rustlers stole nearly 100 horses, including 18 belonging to Hughes. He tracked them for a year, twice shooting his way out of ambushes. Finally, with the help of a deputy sheriff, Hughes killed four of the rustlers and recovered the stolen herd. During his trek, he rode 1,200 miles, used up nine mounts, and spent all but 76¢ of the $43 with which he started. This Colt .45 revolver belonged to Hughes. (Courtesy Buckhorn Saloon and Museum.)

Soon after returning to his ranch, Hughes (seated, right) helped Texas Ranger Ira Aten track down escaped murderer Judd Roberts. When confronted by the two manhunters, Roberts reached for his guns, but he was riddled by six bullets. Shortly afterward, in August 1887, Hughes enlisted as a Ranger, beginning 28 years of service. Promoted to corporal by 1889, he uncovered an ore theft ring at the silver mines of Shafer. Setting a trap with two other officers, Hughes and his men engaged in an hour-long rifle duel, in which three of the thieves were killed. On Christmas night, 1889, Hughes led three other officers in setting an ambush at a Rio Grande crossing for rustlers Will and Alvin Odle. The Odle brothers tried to fight, but they were shot out of their saddles. (Courtesy Western History Collections, University of Oklahoma Library.)

In 1893, now a sergeant, Hughes (seated at far right) and two of his men encountered a trio of fugitives at a village on the border. When one outlaw tried to flee, Hughes and Lon Oden gave chase and killed the men. Also in 1893, Hughes was promoted to captain of Company D, following the death of Capt. Frank Jones in a border shootout. In 1896, Captain Hughes led a posse in pursuit of three horse thieves, who tried to make a stand on a hilltop. The posse advanced on foot, and when rustler Jubel Friar raised up to fire at Hughes, Ranger Thalis Cook drilled him through the chest with a Winchester slug. Friar's brother, Art, was twice wounded but fired his revolver at Hughes and Cook. The two Rangers pumped one bullet apiece into Art Friar, who fell dead. (Author's collection.)

Capt. John R. Hughes
Texas Ranger
1887 to 1915
Sun Bowl Carnival
Parade - El Paso
1938

Late in his career, Hughes was appointed senior captain of the Texas Rangers, with headquarters in Austin. He became chair of the board of directors of the Citizens Industrial Bank of Austin. When he retired, in 1915, he had served as a Ranger and as a captain longer than any other man. Hughes never married, and in retirement, he lived in El Paso, where Company D was based through the years. He traveled a great deal and enjoyed riding in parades and making other public appearances. When he reached his early 90s, he moved to Austin to live with a niece. In ill health, he committed suicide in 1947 at the age of 92. He was buried in the Texas State Cemetery in Austin. (Author's collection.)

In 1877 and 1878, Sam Bass (standing at left) led several desperadoes in robbing at least seven stagecoaches and five trains. Bass had left Texas in 1876 to trail a herd of cattle to booming Dakota Territory. Soon, Bass and his partner, Joel Collins, turned to outlawry. After looting stagecoaches in the Black Hills, Bass and his henchmen robbed a train of $65,000. But, within several days, Collins and two other outlaws were hunted down and killed. Bass escaped to Texas and organized another gang. In the spring of 1878, the Sam Bass Gang staged four train holdups in the Dallas area. But the robbers snared little loot, and a widespread manhunt ensued. Although Bass next intended to rob a bank in Round Rock, gang member Jim Murphy betrayed the plan to Texas Rangers in return for leniency. (Courtesy Western History Collections, University of Oklahoma Library.)

SAMUEL BASS

BORN
July 21,1851
DIED
July 21,1878
Age 27
Years

A brave man reposes in death here.

Why was he not true?

Round Rock was swarming with lawmen on Friday afternoon, July 19, when Sam Bass led Seaborn Barnes, Frank Jackson, and Jim Murphy from their camp west of town. The outlaws had already cased the town twice and decided to rob the bank on Saturday. Murphy dropped behind his companions, muttering something about his horse. Bass, Barnes, and Jackson entered a store near the bank, where two deputy sheriffs suspiciously accosted them. The outlaws gunned them down and headed for their horses. Texas Rangers and several citizens opened fire, and Barnes was killed by Ranger Dick Ware. Bass and Jackson galloped away, but Ranger George Harrell sent a slug through Sam's torso. The two outlaws escaped into the growing darkness, but Bass could not stay on his horse. Jackson rode on, while Bass was found on Saturday and died on Sunday, his 27th birthday. (Photograph by the author.)

CAPTAIN JOHN ARMSTRONG
Captain of State Rangers, and captor
of John Wesley Hardin.

John B. Armstrong was 25 when he enlisted in the Texas Rangers in 1875. Serving first under famed border captain L.H. McNelly, he accompanied violent forays into Mexico and became known as "McNelly's Bulldog." In 1876, Armstrong, by now a sergeant, conducted a patrol into King Fisher's territory. Jumping an outlaw camp at midnight, Sergeant Armstrong and his men gunned down all four fugitives; three of the outlaws died and the fourth was hit four times. Promoted to lieutenant, Armstrong and Ranger Leroy Daggs rode to the Wilson County ranch of murderous John Mayfield. When Mayfield went for his guns, the two Rangers killed him on the spot. (Courtesy Western History Collections, University of Oklahoma Library.)

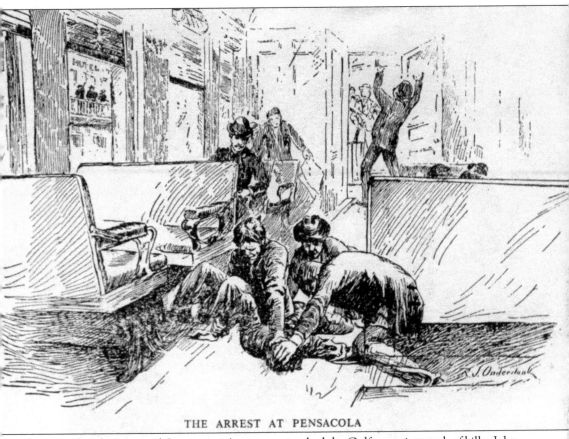

THE ARREST AT PENSACOLA

Attracted by a large reward, Lieutenant Armstrong combed the Gulf states in search of killer John Wesley Hardin, finally locating him in Florida. When the fugitive's train pulled into Pensacola, Armstrong—who held no legal authority in Florida—was waiting with a hastily assembled posse. Armstrong entered Hardin's coach and ordered Wes and his companions to surrender. Jim Mann, seated next to Hardin, pulled a revolver and shot a hole in Armstrong's hat. The Ranger coolly shot Mann in the heart. Hardin's revolver was caught in his suspenders, and Armstrong knocked him unconscious with his pistol barrel. Armstrong placed Hardin and three companions on a train to Texas. With the $4,000 reward, Armstrong left the Rangers and installed his large family on a 50,000-acre ranch in Willacy County. (From Hardin's autobiography, *Life of John Wesley Hardin, As Written by Himself*, 1896; pen and ink drawing by J. Onderdonk.)

James B. Gillett was born in 1856 and raised in Austin, where he learned to ride and shoot. At 17, he left home to become a cowboy, but two years later, he enlisted as a Texas Ranger. For more than six years, he was embroiled in fugitive manhunts and skirmishes with Comanche warriors. In January 1877, Gillett led five other Rangers in pursuit of outlaw Dick Dublin, who once had cowboyed with Gillett. Closing in on a ranch hideout, Gillett pursued Dublin into a ravine. After a warning, Gillett fired a round from his carbine, hitting Dublin above the right hip. The bullet coursed upward through his body, killing him instantly. After leaving the Rangers, Gillett built up a 30,000-acre ranch near Marfa. (Author's collection.)

In the late 1800s, Texas Ranger badges were not provided by the state, but many officers carved their own out of Mexican silver coins, tin cans, wood, or even leather. These badges always featured a star, often surrounded by a circle—the famous "wagon wheel badge." Some badges had a shield surrounding the star. The words "Texas Ranger" or "State Ranger" were usually cut into the badge. Rangers frequently worked under cover and kept their badges inside a pocket until it was time to reveal their identity. After 1935, when the unit became part of the Department of Public Safety, Rangers wore highway patrol badges. But in 1967, the DPS changed the Ranger badge to a traditional star within a circle. (Courtesy Eakin Press.)

Bass Outlaw, old time Texas
ranger, and all-round bad-man
who was killed by Selman.

In 1885, Baz Outlaw joined the Texas Rangers. At five feet, four inches, Outlaw was feisty and won rapid promotion to sergeant, although he proved to be a problem drinker. In 1889, while drinking heavily, Outlaw shot a Mexican to death when the mine worker pulled a knife on him. Later in the year, Outlaw was part of a four-man posse that ambushed and killed fugitives Alvin and Will Odle. (Courtesy Western History Collections, University of Oklahoma Library.)

Discharged from the Rangers for being drunk while on duty, Baz Outlaw secured appointment as a deputy US marshal. In El Paso as a court witness on April 5, 1894, Outlaw spent the afternoon drinking and visiting Tillie Howard's sporting house. When Texas Ranger Joe McKidrict tried to settle him down, Outlaw shot him in the head and back. Constable John Selman drilled Outlaw in the chest. Outlaw put two slugs in Selman's leg but died four hours later on a prostitute's bed. (Author's collection.)

Ira Aten joined the Texas Rangers at the age of 20, and he soon became known as a crack shot. During his rookie year, 1884, two rustlers wounded one Ranger and killed another, Frank Sieber. But Aten wounded both rustlers with his Winchester, and soon, they were in custody. In 1887, Aten twice exchanged shots with outlaw Judd Roberts before finally killing him at a ranch hideout. On Christmas night 1889, Aten and three other officers ambushed Alvin and Will Odle, killing the outlaw brothers in the moonlight. In Dimmitt in 1891, Aten, no longer a Ranger, was denounced in public by the McClelland brothers, Andrew and Hugh, who began shooting at Ira. Aten halted the fight by wounding both brothers. (Author's collection.)

William Jesse "Bill" McDonald was born
in Mississippi in 1852. His father was killed
during the Civil War, and the family moved
to Texas in 1866. As a young man, McDonald
worked as a merchant, supplementing
his income by serving as a peace officer.
He was a deputy sheriff in two counties,
deputy US marshal, and a special Ranger.
His performance in law enforcement was
impressive, and in 1891, Gov. James Hogg
appointed him captain of Company B of
the Frontier Battalion of Texas Rangers. In
1893, Captain McDonald and Sheriff John
Matthews, who despised the Ranger, had a
street shootout in Quanah. Both men were
twice wounded, and Matthews died. In 1906,
the year before he retired, Captain McDonald
and his men shot their way out of an ambush
near Rio Grande City. (Right, author's
collection; below, photograph by the author.)

A different law officer was the legendary Judge Roy Bean, popularly known as the "Law West of the Pecos." For two decades, Bean was a justice of the peace at Langtry, a hardscrabble village he named for singer Lily Langtry. He dispensed his version of the law from his saloon. During one inquest, a revolver and $40 were found on a corpse. Judge Bean fined the deceased $40 for carrying a concealed weapon and confiscated the pistol, for use by the court. Bean freed an Irishman accused of killing a Chinese railroad worker after searching his single law book and concluding that the statutes "did not say it was against the law to kill a Chinaman." (Both, author's collection)

Five

BLOOD FEUDS

There were more blood feuds in Texas than in any other state or territory. The Regulator-Moderator War in 1840–1844 produced almost 40 dead, setting a high standard for future Texas feudists. The Lee-Peacock Feud during Reconstruction was a vicious four-year conflict that resulted in the bushwhacking deaths of both faction leaders.

The large-scale Sutton-Taylor Feud featured the murder of Bill Sutton in front of his wife and baby daughter. But there apparently was little other Sutton involvement. Instead, the Taylor clan seems to have led a vast crime ring involving 200 criminals committing nefarious deeds across a 45-county area. For more than two decades, there were robberies, rustling, and gunplay.

In 1875, the Hoo Doo War, or Mason County War, pitted Anglos against German-Texans, with cattle rustling and shootings rampant until Maj. John Jones of the Texas Rangers arrived to quiet the difficulties. Major Jones was needed again two years later in nearby Lampasas County, arranging a truce to halt the Horrell-Higgins Feud. But vendettas were commonplace in the wake of feuds, and more men were killed after the "end" of the Horrell-Higgins conflict than were slain during the feud.

The Jaybird-Woodpecker Feud inspired superlative heroism from Tom Smith. And there was widespread feuding between cattlemen and sheepherders as they competed for use of Texas ranges. The last old-fashioned feud in Texas, the Johnson-Sims Feud that raged from 1916 to 1918, took place three quarters of a century after the Regulator-Moderator War of frontier East Texas.

The Lee-Peacock Feud erupted in 1867 in the vicinity of Pilot Grove. Lewis Peacock guided a faction of Reconstruction Union League gunmen against former Confederates led by Capt. Bob Lee. Wilderness bushwhackings produced three fatalities, and in April 1868, Peacock was wounded during a skirmish in Pilot Grove. Bob Lee led another ambush two months later that resulted in the death of three of Peacock's men. (Photograph by the author.)

In December 1868, Peacock rode at the head of a few of his men and a detachment of Union soldiers in a search for Bob Lee. Near Farmersville, however, Lee sprang another ambush. One of the soldiers was killed, a Peacock ally was wounded, and Peacock narrowly escaped. But in June 1869, Lee finally was ambushed and slain near his home. (Photograph by the author.)

Following the death of Bob Lee, there were further revenge killings, and Lewis Peacock began to spend most of his time in hiding. On June 12, 1871, however, two friends of Lee, Dick Johnson and Joe Parker, spotted Peacock sneaking back to his Pilot Grove home. Johnson and Parker set a vigil, which lasted throughout the night. At dawn, Peacock emerged to get firewood, and Johnson and Parker opened fire. Peacock was mortally wounded, and his assassins fled the scene. (Photograph by the author.)

In a case of feuding books, *The Sutton-Taylor Feud*, by veteran outlaw-lawman author Chuck Parsons (University of North Texas Press, 2009), and *The Feud That Wasn't*, by noted Reconstruction researcher James Smallwood (Texas A&M University Press, 2008), present opposing viewpoints about the long, murderous Sutton-Taylor "Feud." Parsons provides great detail about the factions and incidents of what he subtitles *The Deadliest Blood Feud in Texas*. Smallwood points out, however, that there was little Sutton involvement. He insists that there was a vast, loosely organized crime ring dominated by the large Taylor clan. Smallwood lists 197 men involved in the ring, including 11 Taylors and other desperados such as Wes Hardin, Bill Longley, and Killin' Jim Miller. Rustling, robberies, and other crimes occurred in 45 counties. (Photograph by the author.)

Bill Sutton (right) was a Confederate veteran who clashed with the Taylors. After several shooting incidents, Sutton decided to leave Texas. At the port of Indianola (below), Sutton, along with his wife, child, and a friend, Gabe Slaughter, boarded a steamboat bound for New Orleans. But brothers Jim and Bill Taylor hurried onto the boat and opened fire. Before his horrified wife, Sutton dropped to the deck with bullets in his head and heart, and Slaughter died beside him. The next year, Jim Taylor was shot to death. Other Taylors who died violently were Hays Taylor, slain in an 1867 ambush; Buck Taylor, killed the next year; Doboy Taylor, shot three times in an 1871 brawl; and Rufus Taylor, lynched in 1874. (Right, courtesy Chuck Parsons collection; below, author's collection.)

The Mason County War, also called the "Hoo Doo" War, erupted in 1875. Essentially a clash between Anglos and Germans, the conflict was aggravated by cattle thefts. There were several shootings, as well as mob violence. A key figure was Scott Cooley, a former Texas Ranger who had turned to farming and ranching. When a close friend was killed in Mason County, Cooley came to the area seeking vengeance, gunning down three men in separate incidents. John Ringo (pictured) also killed a man. Texas Rangers under Maj. John Jones intervened to arrange a truce. Cooley and Ringo were arrested but were then broken out of jail. Cooley died under mysterious circumstances, while Ringo later brought his guns to Arizona. (Author's collection.)

In Hood County, the Mitchell and Truitt families feuded in 1874 over a land dispute, and two of the Truitts died of wounds. The next year, county officials legally hanged patriarch Cooney Mitchell in Granbury. Mitchell's son, Bill, blamed the Reverend James Truitt (right), a young minister whose testimony was the key to the conviction. After nursing his grudge for more than a decade, Bill Mitchell murdered Truitt in 1886 at his home in Timpson. Truitt's grave is shown below. (Right, author's collection; below, photograph by the author.)

The Horrell-Higgins Feud swept across Lampasas County in 1877. The Horrell brothers were rustlers and chronic troublemakers, and in 1876, Merritt Horrell stole a yearling from the ranch of Pink Higgins. Higgins retrieved the stolen yearling and filed charges. When Horrell was exonerated, Pink vowed to seek justice with his Winchester. But Merritt arrogantly stole several more cattle. On Saturday, January 20, 1877, Pink found Merritt drinking in the same saloon (second door to the left) where the Horrells had gunned down four members of the Texas State Police in 1873. Pink Higgins leveled his Winchester and said, "Mr. Horrell, this is to settle some cattle business." Pink's first round knocked Horrell to the floor. Merritt stood up shakily, but Higgins triggered three more bullets into him. (Courtesy Standard Studio, Lampasas.)

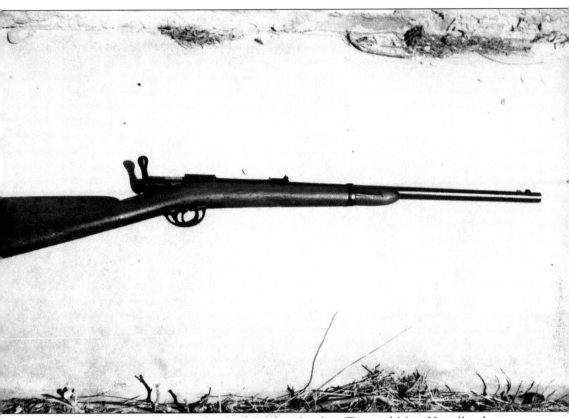

On March 26, two months after the death of their brother, Tom and Mart Horrell rode into Lampasas for a scheduled court appearance. Pink Higgins and a few of his men set an ambush about five miles east of Lampasas at a stream later called "Battle Branch." When Tom and Mart stopped to water their mounts, the hidden gunmen opened fire. Tom was knocked out of the saddle by a bullet in the hip, and Mart suffered a flesh wound in the neck. His horse bolted, but Mart controlled the animal and turned back to his fallen brother. Brandishing his Winchester, Mart drove off the ambushers with a one-man charge. Mart managed to carry Tom to a nearby house before galloping into town for help. (Photograph by the author of a Horrell rifle on display at the Keystone Square Museum in Lampasas.)

The Horrell-Higgins Feud climaxed with a battle on the Lampasas square on June 7, 1877. Higgins (seated, far right) and some of his allies had legal business in town. Members of his trail crew included feud allies Bob Mitchell (beside him) and Alonzo Mitchell (behind him). A large Horrell faction was in town, and Tom Horrell was first to spot the approaching Higgins riders. Bill Wren, a future sheriff, was wounded, and Bob Mitchell helped him inside a building. Bob's brother, Frank Mitchell, spotted Mart Horrell and Jim Buck Miller advancing. Frank drilled Miller in the chest, but he was killed by a return shot from Mart Horrell. With one fatality on each side, a cease-fire finally was arranged. (Courtesy Standard Studio, Lampasas.)

Maj. John P. Jones and a squad of Texas Rangers imposed a truce on the Horrell and Higgins factions. But vendettas often followed feuds, and for more than a year, night riders struck Horrell supporters in at least three violent assaults. And in May 1878, when a popular Bosque County merchant was robbed and murdered, Mart and Tom Horrell were implicated and jailed in Meridian. On December 15, 1878, a mob of more than 100 masked men broke into the jail and gunned down Mart and Tom in their cell. The brothers were buried in Lampasas. There were seven Horrell brothers. The oldest died in the Civil War, and five of the remaining six were killed by gunfire. (Photograph by the author.)

The Jaybird-Woodpecker Feud erupted in Fort Bend County in 1888, waged by political and racial factions that derisively called each other "Jaybirds" and "Woodpeckers." For several months, there were ambushes and brawls, and Texas Rangers were sent to quell the violence. But killings continued on both sides, and at dusk on August 16, 1888, the "Battle of Richmond" exploded in front of the courthouse (pictured). Sheriff J.T. Garvey was escorting a Jaybird prisoner to the courthouse when he was cut down by a volley of fire. Deputy sheriffs Tom Smith and H.S. Mason drew their revolvers, but Mason fell wounded. Smith opened fire, emptying his gun and then using the revolvers of his fallen comrades. Then, two Texas Rangers ran out of the courthouse, and one was hit while the fallen lawmen were carried inside. (Courtesy Fort Bend County Historical Museum, Richmond.)

The Battle of Richmond produced eight casualties, including four dead. The next day, Gov. Sul Ross (right) and two militia units arrived to restore order, staying in Richmond for several days. Tom Smith's heroic stand to provide covering fire established his reputation as a lethal shootist. He accepted the position of city marshal of Taylor, where he was reputed to have killed two men in the line of duty. Perhaps feeling that he could earn more money by collecting fees and rewards while working as a deputy US marshal, Smith left his family in Taylor and centered his professional activities in Paris, the location of the headquarters (below) of the Eastern Judicial District of Texas. (Right, author's collection; below, courtesy Aiken Regional Archives at Paris Junior College.)

Deputy US marshals and posse men stayed near the federal courthouse at Paris, hoping for the opportunity to serve warrants, thereby collecting arrest fees, travel expense, and rewards. In 1891, the highly regarded deputy US marshal Tom Smith was hired by the Wyoming Stock Growers Association to assist with the range difficulties. These problems soon exploded into the Johnson County War, the West's most notorious range conflict. Wyoming cattle barons decided to launch an expedition into Johnson County to kill or arrest rustlers. Deciding to import a number of Texas gunmen, they dispatched Tom Smith (standing at left, white shirt, dark hat) back to Texas to recruit men who were willing to use their guns in Wyoming. In Paris, Tom Smith recruited

more than a score of deputy marshals and posse members. Smith promised excellent wages, while suggesting that the intent of the expedition was to round up rustlers and place them into the legal system. Smith and his recruits traveled by train to Cheyenne, where they were presented with new rifles before marching north to Johnson County. The invaders were more than 50 strong, including big cattlemen, WSGA stock detectives such as Frank Canton (formerly Joe Horner from Texas), and the Texas gunmen. But following a four-day battle at the TA Ranch against 400 citizens, the invaders surrendered. In a famous group photograph, the Texans occupy the bottom two rows. (Courtesy Jim Gatchell Museum, Buffalo, Wyoming.)

The most heroic opponent of the Johnson County invaders was another Texas expatriate, cowboy-gunman Nate Champion. Cornered by more than 50 invaders at the KC Ranch, Champion courageously stood them off for hours. When his cabin was set on fire, he sprinted for safety with guns blazing, but he was gunned down by Texas adversaries, who were paid a bonus. (Courtesy Jim Gatchell Museum, Buffalo, Wyoming.)

Thanks to legal maneuvers by a superb team of lawyers, the Johnson County invaders were released from custody. In the melee, two Texans had died from gunshot wounds. The rest returned to Texas. Tom Smith resumed his duties as a deputy US marshal. But on a train in 1892, he was shot above the eye by a fugitive. Tom Smith was buried in Taylor. (Photograph by the author.)

There was trouble on Texas ranges between cattlemen and sheepherders. Sheep were cursed by cowmen as "hoofed locusts," "stinkers," "maggots," and "baaa-a-ahs." Cowboys liked to say, "There ain't nothing dumber than sheep except a man who herds 'em." Cowmen also derisively referred to sheepherders as "mutton punchers" and "lamb lickers." Killin' Jim Miller reportedly was hired by Texas cattlemen at $150 per killing. "I have killed eleven men that I know about," he admitted to a Fort Worth acquaintance, before adding with disdain, "I have lost my notch stick on sheepherders I've killed out on the border." (Author's collection.)

In Texas, there were at least 29 violent incidents by cattlemen against sheepherders. More than 3,200 sheep were killed, along with four sheepherders and two cowboys. In 1889, an out-of-work cowboy persuaded Burnet County sheep rancher Andy Feild to hire him as a herder. But the cowboy ignored his duties and was fired. Before leaving the ranch, the cowboy rode up to accost Feild. Dismounting, he cursed Feild, then drew his revolver and snapped off a shot. But Feild had taken the precaution of placing the Colt seen here in his waistband. Feild charged, shooting the cowboy in the elbow, chest, and head. When the Feild sheepdog licked the wounds, the cowboy moaned but soon died. (Courtesy Andy Field.)

Six

GUNFIGHTER TOWNS

Dodge City, Tombstone, and Deadwood attained notoriety as gunfighter haunts, complete with saloon shootouts and street battles. The most famous of all gunfights took place at Tombstone's OK Corral, in which the Earp faction killed three adversaries.

But in Lampasas, site of numerous gunfights during the 1870s, four members of the Texas State Police were gunned down in an 1873 saloon battle. It was the only Old West shootout in which four police officers were fatally wounded. There also were four fatalities in the 1886 Tascosa clash, which became known as "the Big Fight." The four victims were buried in Tascosa's Boot Hill, one of the most famous boot hills in the West.

Tascosa's red-light district was called "Hogtown," and there were fights and killings there. Fort Worth denizens enjoyed the illicit pleasures of "Hell's Half Acre," just south of downtown. Austin's "Guy Town" was just north of the Colorado River. The cowboys of Amarillo roistered in the "Bowery District," while the crown jewel of El Paso's red-light neighborhood was Tillie Howard's sporting house.

Gunplay was no stranger to any of these rough districts. Indeed, three officers were shot—two fatally—at Tillie Howard's. John Wesley Hardin, John Selman, and Dallas Stoudenmire also were killed in El Paso shootouts. There was a gunfight in Fort Worth between noted shootists Luke Short and "Longhaired Jim" Courtright. Ben Thompson and King Fisher were slain together in San Antonio. Early Waco saw enough gunplay to earn the nickname "Six-Shooter Depot."

Among the bloodiest shootouts in the West were bank holdups. In 1894, Bill Dalton and three confederates raided the First National Bank of Longview. During the robbery, five citizens were shot, including two fatally, and one outlaw was killed. Dalton was tracked down and shot dead. In many Texas towns, shootists needed to keep their guns loaded.

Tascosa's two-story rock courthouse was built in 1884, when the cattle town was known as the "Cowboy Capital of the Panhandle." Just as accurately, Tascosa could have been branded the "Gunfighter Capital of the Panhandle." During the 1880s, there were 10 gunfights in Tascosa. Billy the Kid, Pat Garrett, Henry Brown, and Temple Houston were among the lethal gunfighters who rode Tascosa's dusty streets. In addition to the adobe saloons along Main Street, a cluster of dives a quarter of a mile east became known as "Hogtown," featuring the charms of such sporting women as Homely Ann, Gizzard Lip, Rowdy Kate, Box Car Jane, Slippery Sue, and Frog Lip Sadie. There were at least four shootouts in Hogtown. (Courtesy Panhandle-Plains Historical Museum, Canyon.)

Tascosa's most famous saloon, the Equity Bar, stood on the north side of Main Street. In 1881, Sheriff Cape Willingham rounded the corner at left and blasted troublemaker Fred Leigh out of the saddle with both barrels of his shotgun. Inside the building in 1889, Sheriff Jim East killed gambler Tom Clark in Tascosa's final shootout. (Courtesy Panhandle-Plains Historical Museum, Canyon.)

The Howard and McMasters general store stood on the northeast corner of Tascosa's principal intersection. Jules Howard clashed with saloonkeeper Bob Russell, who was his own best customer. One morning early in March 1881, Russell, already inebriated, stalked into the Howard and McMasters store. Jules Howard stood with his gun drawn. Russell fumbled for his revolver and triggered one wild shot, but he was drilled in the chest, head, and trigger finger. (Courtesy Panhandle-Plains Historical Museum, Canyon.)

Tascosa's deadliest explosion of violence was an 1886 shootout known as "the Big Fight." There were hard feelings against cowboys from the nearby LS Ranch, and a post-midnight revelry resulted in an ambush at Tascosa's main intersection. One LS cowboy was shot dead in the street from the darkened Jenkins and Dunn Saloon. His three comrades charged into the saloon, but two of them were killed, along with a bystander. (Courtesy Panhandle-Plains Historical Museum, Canyon.)

The next day, four coffins were built and the corpses were dressed in new black suits. A mass funeral was held in the afternoon, and the entire populace of Tascosa, along with area cowboys, formed a half-mile procession to Boot Hill. The LS Ranch provided headstones for its three dead riders. (Photograph by the author.)

90

In the fall of 1878, Billy the Kid (pictured) and four other New Mexico fugitives moved a herd of stolen horses to the Tascosa area. During the next few weeks in Tascosa, Billy and his companions gambled and raced horses and shot at targets. During a money match, the Kid outshot Temple Houston. In November, the Kid and Tom O'Folliard returned to New Mexico, where they were later slain. (Author's collection.)

Three years after Billy the Kid returned to New Mexico, he was killed by Sheriff Pat Garrett. Garrett claimed his first shooting victim in the Texas Panhandle in 1876, while hunting buffalo. During a fistfight in camp, a skinner ran with an axe toward Garrett, who had to shoot him. In later years, Garrett ran a horse ranch at Uvalde and was a customs collector in El Paso. After Garrett's murder in New Mexico, the assassin was rumored to be Killin' Jim Miller. (Courtesy Arizona Historical Society Library.)

The frontier community of Fort Worth took shape around a military outpost founded in 1849. When the Army moved farther west four years later, the old parade ground became the town square. After the Civil War, Fort Worth was an important stop on the Chisholm Trail. Cowboys frolicked in saloons and gambling halls. In the south part of town, a red-light district developed, known as "Hell's Half Acre." There were numerous shootouts, including the classic face-to-face gunfight between Luke Short and Longhaired Jim Courtright. And Killin' Jim Miller moved to town. His wife ran a boardinghouse, which he left from time to time to go on lethal errands. Shown above is an 1876 street scene; below, the 1878 courthouse is on the skyline at center of the panorama. (Both, courtesy Fort Worth Courthouse.)

Timothy Isaiah "Longhaired Jim" Courtright served as city marshal of Fort Worth from 1876 to 1879. Later, he formed a private detective firm, the T.I.C. Commercial Agency. But the agency's primary activity was a protection racket by which Fort Worth's gambling joints were "policed" in return for a piece of the action. (Courtesy Western History Collections, University of Oklahoma Library.)

Luke Short was a professional gambler who killed Charles Storms in Tombstone's Oriental Saloon. Short had other gunfights in Dodge City and Leadville. A dapper dresser, Short had his right pants pocket lined with leather to hold his revolver. By 1887, he had bought an interest in Fort Worth's White Elephant Saloon, soon coming in conflict with Jim Courtright and his T.I.C. shakedown efforts. (Courtesy Kansas State Historical Society, Topeka.)

JIM "LONGHAIRED" COURTRIGHT
1845   1887
U.S. ARMY SCOUT, U.S. MARSHALL, FRONTIERSMAN, PIONEER
WAS A MAN OF A CLASS OF MEN NOW PASSING FROM TEXAS
WHATEVER THEIR FAULTS WERE, TYPE OF THAT BRAVE COURAGEOUS
HARDY MEN WHICH COMMANDS RESPECT AND ADMIRATION
ERECTED 1953
IN MEMORY OF HIM BY HIS DESCENDANTS

Trouble between Luke Short and Jim Courtright came to a head in Fort Worth on February 8, 1887, soon after Courtright threatened the gambler. Accompanied by Bat Masterson, Short encountered Courtright at a shooting gallery. Courtright pulled one of his revolvers and jammed it into Short's mid-section. But the hammer caught on Short's watch chain, and Short snapped out his own pistol. He emptied his gun rapid-fire: the first slug smashed the cylinder of Courtright's drawn six-gun; two shots went wild; and three bullets tore into Courtright's right thumb, right shoulder, and heart. Courtright collapsed and died within minutes. He was buried at Fort Worth's Oakwood Cemetery. (Photograph by the author.)

A gambling dispute drew Luke Short into his final gunfight in Fort Worth on December 23, 1890. Saloon owner Charles Wright ambushed Short with a shotgun blast from behind. Short was hit in the left leg, but he opened fire with his revolver. Wright managed to escape, but one of Short's bullets broke his wrist. Short died of dropsy in 1893 at the age of 39. (Courtesy author's collection.)

Luke Short was buried in Oakwood Cemetery, not far from Jim Courtright, his most famous victim. Several years later, Short and Courtright were joined at Oakwood by Killin' Jim Miller. (Photograph by the author.)

For more than two decades, Lampasas was the scene of saloon shootouts and street battles. In 1855, the year the new townsite was surveyed, Bob Willis fatally wounded a man named Nixon. Several years later, Willis was assassinated at his home, probably a revenge killing. Early shooting victims were buried in Pioneer Cemetery. (Photograph by the author.)

During the 1870s, a series of deadly shootings erupted in the saloons of Lampasas. In 1872, Sheriff Shade Denson tried to arrest the drunken Short brothers, Mark and Wash, but they grappled with him. Mark shot the sheriff in the side and escaped the scene with his brother. Denson survived but carried the bullet the rest of his life. Four years later, Denson's oldest son, Sam, encountered Mark Short in another Lampasas saloon and killed him with three revolver bullets. (Courtesy Keystone Square Museum, Lampasas.)

The cell shown above, from the 1870 Lampasas County jail, housed shootists as well as a succession of other troublemakers. In 1876, John Ringo and Scott Cooley, arrested during the Mason County War, were incarcerated in the Lampasas jail, but they were soon broken out by 15 armed riders. Also in 1876, county attorney B.F. Hamilton and Newton Cook traded shots on the town square. After shooting himself in the hand with his derringer, Hamilton darted for cover among the live oak trees. The square was also the scene of a pitched battle during the Horrell-Higgins Feud. Higgins began the feud by killing Merritt Horrell in Jerry Scott's Matador Saloon on the square, also the site of Sheriff Shade Denson's shooting. And, on March 4, 1873, four members of the state police entered the saloon to arrest the Horrell brothers. All four were slain. It was the only gunfight in which four Western lawmen were killed. The saloon table, chairs, and whiskey jug (below) are preserved by the Keystone Square museum. (Both photographs by the author.)

In April 1881, booming El Paso appointed a new city marshal. Tall, rangy Dallas Stoudenmire patrolled the teeming streets of El Paso with a brace of revolvers tucked inconspicuously under his coat in a pair of leather-lined hip pockets. He also carried a snub-nosed revolver as a hideout gun. Wounded in combat during the Civil War, Stoudenmire served as a Texas Ranger and was involved in at least three gunfights. On April 14, 1881, a gun battle exploded on an El Paso street. Marshal Stoudenmire charged onto the scene with two guns blazing. In the melee, three men died, two by Stoudenmire's guns. Three nights later, Bill Johnson, a drunken former city marshal, tried to ambush Stoudenmire. But Stoudenmire and his brother-in-law, Doc Cummings, pumped eight slugs into Johnson. (Author's collection.)

Marshal Stoudenmire soon proved to be a problem drinker, often firing his guns in the dead of night. Censured by the city fathers, Stoudenmire resigned after a year in office and was replaced by his deputy, Jim Gillett. Stoudenmire continued to drink and quarrel with the Manning brothers, Jim, Frank, Doc, and John. On September 18, 1882, trouble erupted in a saloon shootout. Doc Manning triggered the first shot, sending a bullet through Stoudenmire's arm and into his chest. Doc charged his reeling opponent, but Stoudenmire shot him in the arm with his belly gun. As the two men grappled, Jim Manning ran up and shot Stoudenmire behind the right ear. Dallas Stoudenmire was 36. (Author's collection.)

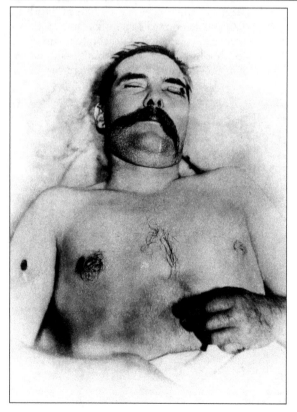

JOHN W. HARDIN Esq.

ATTORNEY AT LAW

OFFICE:
200½ El Paso
Wells Fargo Bldg.

PRACTICE IN
ALL COURTS

Wes Hardin served 17 years in the Texas State Penitentiary in Huntsville. While in prison, he studied for the bar. Sadly, less than two years before his release, his long-suffering wife died. Freed in February 1894, Hardin lived briefly in Gonzalez with his three children. He soon moved westward to Junction, where he married a young girl, who left him on the day of their wedding. Hardin opened a law office in El Paso. Drinking heavily, he quarreled with local lawmen John Selman and John Selman Jr. On August 19, 1895, while Hardin was gambling at the Acme Saloon, old John Selman stepped inside and shot him in the head. Selman walked to the fallen Hardin and drilled him twice more. John Wesley Hardin was 42. (Above, author's collection; left, courtesy Western History Collection, University of Oklahoma Library.)

When John Selman turned up in El Paso in 1888, he was pushing 50 and brought a reputation as a rustler and deadly gunman. In 1892, the formidable Selman won election as city constable of wide-open El Paso. At Tillie Howard's sporting house in 1892, Constable Selman killed a drunken Baz Outlaw, who had just slain Texas Ranger Joe McKidrict and wounded Selman. Selman was forced to use a cane for the rest of his life. In 1895, after a simmering feud, he killed legendary gunfighter Wes Hardin in the Acme Saloon. The following year, on April 5, 1896, a drunken Selman abrasively quarreled with noted lawman George Scarborough, who pumped slugs into his neck, hip, knee, and side. Selman was 56. (Right, courtesy Leon Metz; below, photograph by the author.)

JOHN HENRY SELMAN
BORN NOV. 10, 1839
DIED APR. 6, 1896
EL PASO CONSTABLE

In the 1860s and 1870s, Waco was dotted with saloons, gambling houses, and bordellos, and there was enough gunplay to give the town the nickname "Six-Shooter Depot." By the 1890s, the forces of civilization seemed to prevail. But within four months in 1897–1898, nine casualties resulted from shootouts triggered by combative Civil War veteran Judge George B. Gerald. (Courtesy the Texas Collection, Carroll Library, Baylor University.)

As a colonel commanding a Mississippi regiment, George Gerald was wounded four times in combat, permanently crippling his left arm. He moved his family to Texas in 1869, settling in Waco during the heyday of Six-Shooter Depot. He served eight years as county judge, once strapping on a gun belt to personally wreck a gambling hall. In 1897, Judge Gerald feuded publicly with newspaper editor J.W. Harris, a dispute that exploded in front of Waco's Old Corner Drug Store. (Courtesy Texas Collection, Carroll Library, Baylor University.)

Upper: Jim Harris pistol
Lower: Bill Harris pistol

On November 19, 1897, J.W. Harris was at the cigar counter of the Old Corner Drug Store, and his brother Bill stood across the street, when Judge Gerald drove up in a buggy. When Gerald approached the drugstore, J.W. shot him in his crippled arm, but the judge drilled Harris in the throat. Bill Harris shot Judge Gerald in the back. A policeman grappled with Bill, but Gerald reached in and shot him in the head. Both Harris brothers died, and Judge Gerald lost his crippled arm. (Courtesy Texas Collection, Carroll Library, Baylor University.)

Judge Gerald was a friend of William C. Brann (pictured), a controversial writer and lecturer from Waco. On April 2, 1898, Brann and his manager, W.H. Ward, were walking near the Old Corner Drug Store when a local lawyer, Tom Davis, stepped up and sent a .45 slug into Brann's back. Brann whirled and shot Davis with his .38. A furious exchange of shots put two more slugs into each adversary and wounded Ward and two bystanders. Both Brann and Davis died. (Courtesy Texas Collection, Carroll Library, Baylor University.)

Longview was founded in the early 1870s, when the Southern Pacific Railroad built westward into East Texas. When Gregg County was organized in 1873, Longview was designated the county seat. But the town was rough, and through the years, there were several gunfights between angry citizens. In 1894, Longview's First National Bank (pictured) was assaulted by a gang led by an infamous outlaw. (Courtesy Gregg County Historical Museum.)

The notorious Dalton Gang was decimated in 1892 at an abortive bank robbery in Coffeyville, Kansas. But another brother, Bill Dalton (pictured), was second-in-command of Bill Doolin's large gang of "Oklahombres." On the run in 1894, Dalton holed up on the Houston Wallace farm, 25 miles west of Ardmore. Jim Wallace, Houston's brother, had lived in Longview and told Dalton about the prosperous First National Bank. (Courtesy Gregg County Historical Museum.)

Riding together to Longview, Bill Dalton and Jim Wallace enlisted the Nite brothers, Jim and Big Asa. On May 23, 1894, Dalton and Jim Nite entered the bank, while Wallace and Big Asa waited in the back alley with the horses. Inside the bank, cashier Tom Clemmons (pictured) courageously clutched Dalton's revolver. Dalton pulled the trigger, but the hammer dropped onto the fleshy part of Clemmons's hand, between his thumb and his forefinger. Twice more, Dalton tried to fire, but each time, the only damage was a hole in the flesh of the cashier's hand. As Dalton and Clemmons grappled, Nite stuffed $2,000 into a burlap bag, while two men slipped outside to sound the alarm. (Courtesy Gregg County Historical Museum.)

As armed citizens hurried to the scene, Jim Wallace (above) began shouting war whoops and firing his brace of revolvers. He gunned down bartender George Buckingham, city marshal Matt Muckleroy, Charles Learn, and J.W. McQueen, and, with a single round, he nicked two bystanders. Buckingham and McQueen were fatally wounded. But from a window behind Wallace, J.C. Lacy squeezed off a Winchester round that instantly killed the crazed gunman. The surviving outlaws used Tom Clemmons and his brother Joe as hostages to escape town, then galloped away from a pursuit posse. Meanwhile, furious citizens hanged Wallace's corpse (right) from a nearby telegraph pole. (Both, courtesy Gregg County Historical Museum.)

Bill Dalton, in death.

The dead outlaw's hatband carried an Ardmore store label, and subsequent detective work sent a nine-man posse to Houston Wallace's farm. Dalton tried to flee, but he was shot dead. Dalton's embalmed body was identified by Tom Clemmons and the Gregg County sheriff, then was placed on display for five days. The Nite brothers surfaced three years later in West Texas. Big Asa was killed by a posse, which captured Jim. Tried in Longview, he was sentenced to 20 years in prison. Jim Nite was paroled in 1911, but in 1920, he was killed during an attempted robbery in Tulsa. (Courtesy Gregg County Historical Museum.)

Pecos was a cowboy town that claimed the world's first rodeo, a series of cowboy contests staged at the Fourth of July in 1883. In 1887, gunfighter Clay Allison died outside town, and he is buried beside a Pecos museum. During the 1890s, Killin' Jim Miller served a term as city marshal. Sheriff Bud Frazer feuded with Miller, and in 1894, those men twice traded shots on the streets of Pecos. In 1896, Miller killed Frazer in another town, and he also began a feud with Barney Riggs, an ex-convict who had earned a pardon by killing another inmate during a prison break. John Denson and Bill Earhart, two of Miller's henchmen from Fort Stockton, came after Riggs in a Pecos saloon. But Riggs killed both men. Today, the saloon is a museum complete with bullet holes. (Both photographs by the author.)

Seven

END OF THE TRAIL

Across the Old West, gunfighting was a lethal exercise largely of the 1800s. But in Texas, with its long tradition of frontier violence, gunfighters continued their deadly activities into the 20th century. Pink Higgins, who had used his guns against Comanche warriors, stock thieves, and personal adversaries since he was a teenager, clashed with fellow range detective Bill Standifer in 1902. Although in his 50s, Pink rode out to meet Standifer in a mano a mano rifle duel. Killin' Jim Miller, headquartering in Fort Worth, continued to shoot one victim after another until he was lynched in 1909.

In the second decade of the 20th century, the last old-fashioned Texas blood feud broke out between two ranching families. West Texans continued to embrace the values and attitudes of the frontier, even in a new century. They still bristled with the violent impulses of the pioneers who had settled the region only a generation earlier. And the most tragic victim of this feud was the oldest son of frontier feudist Pink Higgins.

Nostalgic remnants of the gunfighter era in Texas include Tascosa's Boot Hill, Fort Worth's Oakwood Cemetery, and El Paso's Concordia Cemetery. The Orient Saloon in Pecos offers the site of a fatal gunfight, complete with bullet holes. There are superb gun collections at Waco's Texas Ranger Hall of Fame and Museum and at San Antonio's Buckhorn Museum, as well as more modest collections at smaller museums around the state.

The gunfighter culture was exaggerated and transmitted by fiction and motion pictures. The fast-draw myth was invented by Hollywood, which filmed as many as 300 Western movies per year. In the 1950s and 1960s, television brought Western gunfighting into homes through weekly television series. The gunfighters of the 1800s all are gone, but Texans remain keenly aware of their state's gunfighting traditions.

Pink Higgins left Lampasas County for a job as stock detective with the vast Spur Ranch, which was being raided by rustlers. Pink's towering reputation as a gunslinger intimidated several known rustlers, who moved to New Mexico. "Cattle leakage" on the Spur Ranch sharply declined. Pink built a board-and-batten house for his family on his small spread, the "Catfish Ranch." (Author's collection.)

At the Spur Ranch, Pink Higgins clashed with his fellow stock detective, Bill Standifer. A native of Lampasas County and a one-time sheriff, Standifer nursed an old grudge toward Higgins. A challenge was issued, and on October 1, 1902, the two men met for a rifle duel near Pink's home. Pink's horse was mortally wounded, but Higgins drilled Standifer in the chest. Standifer was buried where he fell. (Photograph by the author.)

Hell's Half Acre, Fort Worth's notorious red-light district, continued to flourish into the new century. By December 1900, following a bold bank robbery in Winnemuca, Nevada, Butch Cassidy and several members of his "Wild Bunch" were in Fort Worth to vacation at Hell's Half Acre. While there, five gang members, dressed in party clothes, went to the photography studio of John Swartz, at 705 Main Street. The group photograph of the "Fort Worth Five" includes, from left to right, (seated) Harry Longabaugh (Sundance Kid), Ben Kilpatrick, and Butch Cassidy; (standing) Will Carver and Harvey Logan. The outlaws soon moved on to San Antonio's red-light district, while Swartz placed the handsome photograph in his studio window. Someone recognized the fugitives and sent the photograph to the Pinkerton Detective Agency. (Courtesy Western History Collections, University of Oklahoma Library.)

Hanging Jim Miller: Allen: Burwell and West, at Ada, Oklahoma.

Killin' Jim Miller's wife, Sallie, operated a Fort Worth boardinghouse, where he stayed between jobs. In 1909, he was employed by three Oklahoma cattlemen who had been feuding with Gus Bobbitt, whose spread was near Ada. On February 26, Bobbitt was driving a supply wagon toward his home when Miller blasted him with both barrels of his shotgun. Mrs. Bobbitt dashed out to hold her dying husband, while Miller fled to Fort Worth. Texas officials were happy to extradite Miller to Oklahoma, and Killin' Jim was thrown in jail with his three employers. On April 19, a lynch mob carried the prisoners to an Ada livery stable. After the nooses were fitted, Miller (above, far left) coolly asked for his hat to be placed on his head. Dead at 42, he was taken back to Fort Worth for burial. (Above, courtesy Western History Collections, University of Oklahoma Library; below, photograph by the author.)

The graves of three noted gunfighters, Luke Short, Jim Courtright, and Jim Miller, may be found at Fort Worth's Oakwood Cemetery. Oakwood, known as the "Westminster Abbey of Fort Worth," provides a walking history of lethal gunfighters, powerful cattle barons, local heroes, Confederate veterans, business tycoons, writers, and musicians. (Photograph by the author.)

When Oakwood Cemetery was established north of downtown Fort Worth, there were no bridges across the Trinity River. A funeral procession followed a horse-drawn hearse to a ford, which led to the cemetery. But when the river ran high, less devoted mourners would turn back at the ford. A saying resulted: "He is a good friend; he will follow you all the way across the river." (Photograph by the author.)

The Arizona Rangers were organized in 1901 to halt the rampant outlawry that was the main reason the US Congress would not grant statehood to Arizona Territory. The Arizona Rangers were modeled on the Texas Rangers, and several Texas Rangers migrated to Arizona Territory to pin on a badge. Sgt. Billy Old of the Texas Rangers became Lieutenant Old of the Arizona Rangers. Mounted at left, Old rode as an Arizona Ranger from 1904 to 1908. (Courtesy Arizona Historical Society.)

The maximum strength of the Arizona Ranger company was 26 men. During the life of the company (1901–1909), a total of 107 men served as Rangers, and 44 of them (41 percent) were from Texas. Texans with the instincts of a frontier manhunter could find plenty of wrongs to right in Arizona Territory. Capt. Harry Wheeler, standing at left, led this 1907 patrol. Next to him is Sgt. Rye Miles from Texas, and standing fourth from left is Texan Oscar McAda. (Courtesy Arizona Historical Society.)

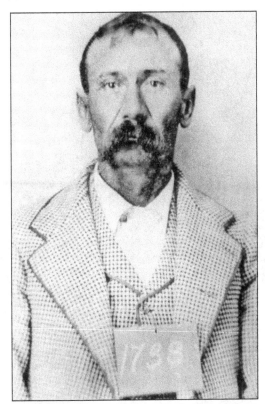

By 1908, the Arizona Rangers had killed or imprisoned or hounded out of the territory the worst of Arizona's criminals. The most troublesome badman remaining in Arizona Territory was Texan William F. Downing (right), and he was confronted by Texan Billy Speed (below), an Arizona Ranger since 1906. Downing, a convict, operated the Free and Easy Saloon in Willcox, where Ranger Speed was stationed. The Free and Easy became a nefarious dive, and Downing, who packed a revolver in his hip pocket, threatened Speed on multiple occasions. Capt. Harry Wheeler warned Speed to be ready to kill Downing. On August 5, 1908, following a drunken rampage, Downing met Speed in the street, groped for his hip pocket, and was mortally wounded by a Winchester bullet. (Both, courtesy Arizona Historical Society.)

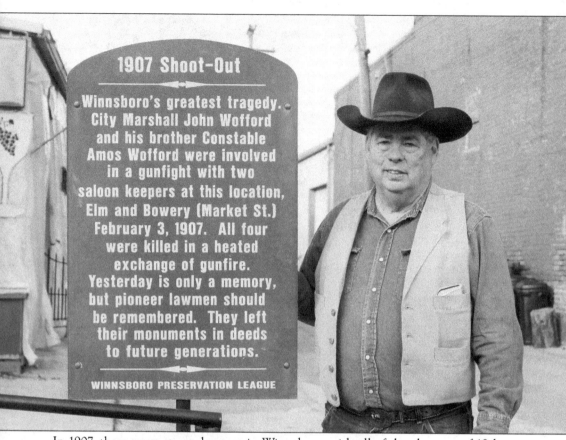

In 1907, there was a street shootout in Winnsboro, with all of the elements of 19th-century gunplay. City marshal Amos Wofford and his brother, Constable John Wofford, clashed with saloon owner Dick Milam and his son, Bud. The conflict came to a head on February 3 in the Bowery, Winnsboro's two-block district of saloons and dives. The explosion of gunfire rattled nearby store windows. All four adversaries were hit. The Wofford brothers died where they fell, and so did Dick Milam. Bud Milam survived the fight but died of his wounds nine days later. It was a classic Wild West gunfight: peace officers versus saloon men, with four shootists fatally wounded. The author stands at the site. (Photograph by Karon O'Neal.)

Billy Johnson was a teenaged drover on an 1878 cattle drive when he discovered a spring-fed creek on the open grasslands of northern Scurry County. Johnson built a large ranch on this prime frontier property. He married and raised three sons and a daughter on the ranch, teaching all four children to ride and shoot. (Courtesy Betty M. Giddens.)

Successful as a rancher, Billy Johnson also founded the First National Bank of Snyder and, in 1910, built a 16-room mansion on his ranch. He spoiled his daughter, Gladys, who became headstrong and hot-tempered. (Photograph by the author.)

In 1887, Dave and Laura Belle Sims brought their cattle herd and growing family to rugged, isolated Kent County. Dave acquired more than 25,000 acres and built this frame house, which still stands. Eventually, there were 10 Sims children. The oldest son, Ed Sims, fell in love with pretty Gladys Johnson, who lived on her father's ranch just 15 miles to the south. (Photograph by the author.)

In 1905, Ed Sims, 21, married 14-year-old Gladys Johnson. Billy Johnson helped the couple acquire a ranch south of Post City, seat of Garza County. Ed and Gladys had two daughters, but instead of the happy union of two ranching families, the marriage became turbulent and adulterous. In 1916, there was a contentious divorce. (Courtesy Charles Anderson Sr.)

Gladys moved back to her father's luxurious ranch house, but custody of the two young daughters became a bitter problem between the divorced couple. Hard feelings exploded into murderous violence on Saturday, December 16, 1916, when Gladys was supposed to deliver her daughters to Ed in front of the First National Bank (the two-story building). But Gladys shot Ed when he approached her car, and her brother Sid came from the bank and finished him with a shotgun. (Courtesy Scurry County Museum, Snyder.)

Ed Sims was buried in the Post City Cemetery, and the sentiment on his gravestone was heartfelt: "Our precious one from us is gone. A voice we loved is stilled, a place is vacant in our home, which never can be filled." It was the second decade of the 20th century, but both families were shaped by the frontier values of the 1800s, and an old-fashioned blood feud ensued. (Photograph by the author.)

Following the shooting, gunmen were hired and the violence escalated. Billy Johnson employed as bodyguards Harrison Hamer and his brother Frank (pictured). Frank Hamer and Gladys Johnson Sims fell in love and were married. Frank and Gladys had two sons and a happy marriage, and in 1934, the experienced lawman earned lasting fame by hunting down Bonnie and Clyde. (Author's collection.)

On October 1, 1917, Frank and Gladys Hamer, traveling with brothers Harrison Hamer and Emmett Johnson, were ambushed by gunmen led by Gee McMeans, a Sims son-in-law. The shootout took place in Sweetwater, at the left edge of this photograph. McMeans shot Hamer in the left arm and leg, but Frank, a southpaw, drilled his assailant in the heart with his right hand. Meanwhile, Gladys thwarted the advance of a second gunman with her automatic. (Courtesy Pioneer Museum, Sweetwater.)

Cullen Higgins, oldest son of Pink, was a former district judge and an excellent attorney whose office was on the second floor of Billy Johnson's bank. Cullen skillfully secured the exoneration of both Gladys and her brother in the murder of Ed Sims. A three-man hit team succeeded in assassinating Judge Higgins by shotgun. His death at 42 brought an enormous funeral crowd to Snyder. (Courtesy Samantha Usnick.)

The three-story Nolan County jail stood on the northeast corner of the Sweetwater square. Si Bostick, arrested soon after the assassination of Cullen Higgins, was brought to the jail's vacant third floor in the middle of the night. Coerced into revealing the location of the murder weapon and the identity of his confederates, Bostick was found dead in his cell the next morning. A highly improbable suicide was ruled. (Courtesy Pioneer Museum, Sweetwater.)

For those interested in the gunfighter lore of Texas, there is no more rewarding place to visit than the Texas Ranger Hall of Fame and Museum in Waco. There are superb displays of famous Texas Rangers and notable Ranger events. (Photograph by the author.)

The gun collection in the Texas Ranger Hall of Fame and Museum is magnificent. Rangers were instrumental in the evolution of the revolving pistol, an evolution made obvious by gun after gun. There is a vast array of shoulder guns as well, along with bowie knives. Every manner of 19th-century firearm is on display, as well as many historic guns of the 20th century. (Photograph by Dr. Berri O'Neal.)

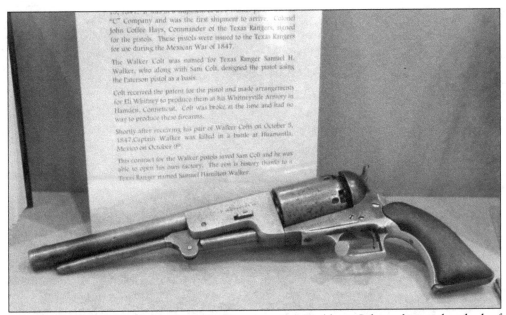

Another Texas Ranger museum, housed in San Antonio's Buckhorn Saloon, features hundreds of artifacts. The Buckhorn opened in 1881. No longer at its historic location, the Buckhorn Saloon today is two blocks from the Alamo and is a popular tourist destination. Among the variety of displays is an excellent collection of frontier weaponry. (Photograph by the author.)

In Pecos, the Orient Saloon still stands beside the Orient Hotel in front of the railroad tracks. In the saloon, bartender Barney Riggs killed John Denson and Bill Earhart, and bullet holes are prominently marked. The adjoining hotel utilizes 50 rooms for historic displays. Behind these buildings is the grave of Clay Allison, along with a replica of Judge Roy Bean's Jersey Lily Saloon. (Photograph by the author.)

Tascosa's Boot Hill is the final resting place of numerous 1880s gunfight victims, including the three LS cowboys and the luckless bystander who died in "the Big Fight" of 1886. (Photograph by the author.)

Concordia Cemetery in El Paso stands beside busy Interstate 10, with the Franklin Mountains as an impressive backdrop. John Wesley Hardin is Concordia's most famous inhabitant. John Selman, who killed Hardin, also is at Concordia, along with buffalo soldiers, Civil War veterans, and Chinese railroad laborers. Hardin's grave is shown here. (Photograph by the author.)

Gunfighting became a major element in Western fiction and motion pictures. The pulp magazine pictured here was published in April 1938 and featured short stories about fast-shooting Texas Rangers. (Author's collection.)

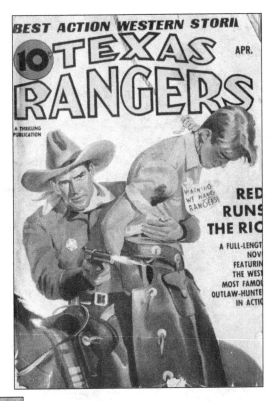

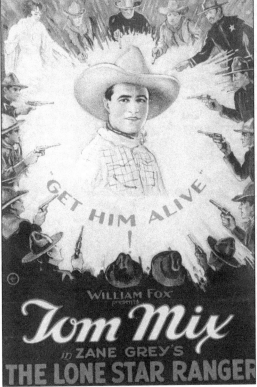

The enormously successful western novelist Zane Grey often centered his books on Texas Rangers. Grey's novels were filmed, frequently in multiple versions. In 1924, Tom Mix, the most popular Western star of the silent screen, starred in Grey's *The Lone Star Ranger*. In his publicity, Mix claimed to have served as a Texas Ranger. (Author's collection.)

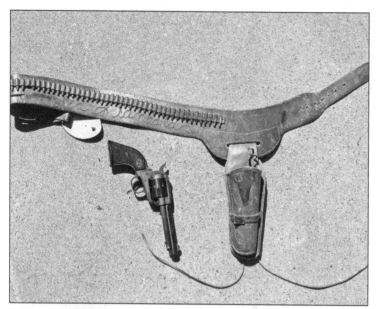

The buscadero rig was popularized by Hollywood Westerns, as fast-draw scenes added drama to the silver screen. Movie and television fast-draw rigs featured a dropped panel with a slot on the gun belt for a low-slung holster that was tied down above the knee. Sometimes, the holsters were tilted for even faster draws. Such gun-belt and holster combinations were unknown on the frontier. (Photograph by the author.)

PRC Pictures presents Tex Ritter and Dave O'Brien as the Texas Rangers in "ENEMY OF THE LAW"
with Guy Wilkerson.

Printed in U.S.A. 45/100

Dave O'Brien (left) played Texas Ranger Dave Wyatt in all 22 films of the "Texas Rangers" series (1942–1945). Tex Ritter (right) costarred in the last eight films, including *Enemy of the Law*. All three actors wear buscadero rigs, and Ritter's is handsomely tooled. Ritter starred in 60 Western films; in countless gunfighting scenes, he beat his opponent to the draw, often shooting the gun out of his hand. (Author's collection.)

Sunset Carson grew up in the Panhandle of Texas and became a rodeo star. Tall and good-looking, he starred in B-Westerns during the 1940s. With his fancy buscadero rig, he was a fast-draw artist in his films. (Author's collection.)

In *The Comancheros*, a major motion picture of 1961, John Wayne played a Texas Ranger, Capt. Jake Cutter. Skilled with firearms throughout the film, he outdrew and killed Lee Marvin during a saloon fight. (Author's collection.)

Visit us at
arcadiapublishing.com

'*International Law and Policy on the Protection of Civilians* is a masterful guide to the multiple legal, political and normative influences that are transforming our understanding of obligations to protect civilians from violence. The result is a rich depiction not only of sources of civilian protection, but of the complex ways in which expectations evolve in a decentralised international system. Casey-Maslen and Vestner have rendered an invaluable service by preparing a volume that will be indispensable to state officials, military leaders, non-governmental organisations and anyone who cares about protecting the innocent from the ravages of conflict.'

Mitt Regan, *McDevitt Professor of Jurisprudence, Co-Director, Center on National Security, Georgetown Law Center*

'In this wide-ranging and meticulously researched book, Stuart Casey-Maslen and Tobias Vestner explain with remarkable clarity the many ways in which international organisations, states and non-state actors protect civilians in and outside of armed conflict. From classical international law on the use of force and international humanitarian law to the evolving landscape of state protection policies or frequently overlooked topics, such as protecting older people and persons with disabilities, this book offers the most systematic treatment of the Protection of Civilians concept to date. It promises to be a go-to resource for academics and practitioners for years to come.'

Patryk I. Labuda, *Assistant Professor of (International) Criminal Law, University of Amsterdam*

'Anyone who has had anything to do with "PoC" will know how hard it is to translate sincere intentions into meaningful actions. This book by Stuart Casey-Maslen and Tobias Vestner makes a major contribution to building a better understanding of the topic and improving implementation. Easy to read and impressive in scope, it disentangles compartmentalised thinking on PoC and doesn't duck the issue of where still more clarity is needed. For those seeking more light on the grey area of Protection of Civilians, this publication will have enduring relevance and will serve them well.'

Adrian Foster, *Major General (Retd), CMG MBE, previous Deputy Military Adviser, UN Peacekeeping; Acting/Force Commander of the UN peacekeeping mission in the Democratic Republic of the Congo*

'This book is an insightful resource on civilian protection for everyone, from students to seasoned practitioners. The analysis of contemporary practice, focus on the normative legal frameworks, and discussion of different PoC approaches across international and regional organisations make it a definitive source on the topic. It provides a fantastic foundation from which political and military leaders, practitioners and the next generation of protection advocates can continue the vital work of further developing the ability to protect civilians in future conflicts.'

Marla B. Keenan, *Adjunct Senior Fellow, Strengthening NATO's Ability to Protect, The Stimson Center*

'This book is important. It brings together and explicates the legal and policy architecture for Protection of Civilians that has been coming into focus over recent years. It is an important added value for anyone seeking to understand that architecture, and is a most welcome contribution to the literature.'

Todd F. Buchwald, Professorial Lecturer in Law, George Washington University Law School, former Ambassador for Global Criminal Justice, US Department of State

INTERNATIONAL LAW AND POLICY ON THE PROTECTION OF CIVILIANS

This is the first comprehensive treatment of international law and policy on the protection of civilians in armed conflict. In addition to international humanitarian and human rights law, *jus ad bellum*, disarmament law, and international criminal law are all critical to civilian protection. The book offers in-depth analysis and explanation of the normative framework while also outlining and discussing the policies of concerned States and international and humanitarian organisations. The role of the United Nations as a key actor is considered along with regional organisations such as the African Union, the European Union, and NATO. Particular attention is given to those at direct risk of harm during armed conflict, including children, women, persons with disabilities, and LGBTI persons.

Stuart Casey-Maslen is the author of *The Right to Life under International Law* (Cambridge University Press, 2021), the first comprehensive treatment of this fundamental right. He has worked in dozens of conflict-affected countries over the last thirty years and teaches at the University of Pretoria in South Africa on the Freedom from Violence in Africa Programme.

Tobias Vestner leads the Security and Law Programme at the Geneva Centre for Security Policy (GCSP). He teaches and researches on the intersection between security policy and international law and is Honorary Senior Research Fellow at the University of Exeter, Fellow at Supreme Headquarters Allied Powers Europe (NATO), and reserve Legal Advisor at the Swiss Armed Forces Staff.

International Law and Policy on the Protection of Civilians

University of Pretoria

TOBIAS VESTNER

Geneva Centre for Security Policy (GCSP)

CAMBRIDGE
UNIVERSITY PRESS

CAMBRIDGE
UNIVERSITY PRESS

University Printing House, Cambridge CB2 8BS, United Kingdom

One Liberty Plaza, 20th Floor, New York, NY 10006, USA

477 Williamstown Road, Port Melbourne, VIC 3207, Australia

314–321, 3rd Floor, Plot 3, Splendor Forum, Jasola District Centre,
New Delhi – 110025, India

103 Penang Road, #05–06/07, Visioncrest Commercial, Singapore 238467

Cambridge University Press is part of the University of Cambridge.

It furthers the University's mission by disseminating knowledge in the pursuit of
education, learning, and research at the highest international levels of excellence.

www.cambridge.org
Information on this title: www.cambridge.org/9781316511442
DOI: 10.1017/9781009052757

First published 2022

A catalogue record for this publication is available from the British Library.

Library of Congress Cataloging-in-Publication Data
NAMES: Casey-Maslen, Stuart, author. | Vestner, Tobias, author.
TITLE: International law and policy on the protection of civilians / Stuart Casey-Maslen, University
of Pretoria; Tobias Vestner, Geneva Centre for Security Policy (GCSP).
DESCRIPTION: Cambridge, United Kingdom ; New York, NY : Cambridge University Press, 2022. |
Includes index.
IDENTIFIERS: LCCN 2022006081 (print) | LCCN 2022006082 (ebook) | ISBN 9781316511442
(hardback) | ISBN 9781009055901 (paperback) | ISBN 9781009052757 (ebook)
SUBJECTS: LCSH: Combatants and noncombatants (International law) | War – Protection of
civilians. | Humanitarian law. | International law and human rights. | Just war doctrine. | BISAC:
LAW / International
CLASSIFICATION: LCC KZ6515 .C39 2022 (print) | LCC KZ6515 (ebook) | DDC 341.6/7–dc23/eng/
20220526
LC record available at https://lccn.loc.gov/2022006081
LC ebook record available at https://lccn.loc.gov/2022006082

ISBN 978-1-316-51144-2 Hardback

Contents

Foreword by Ambassador Thomas Greminger   *page* xv

Preface   xvii

Introduction   1

I.1   Who are 'Civilians'?   2
I.2   What is 'Protection'?   6
I.3   Who Protects Civilians?   10
I.4   A Brief History of the Protection of Civilians   11

PART I   THE INTERNATIONAL LEGAL FRAMEWORK   17

1   *Jus ad Bellum* **and the Protection of Civilians**   19

   1.1   Introduction   19
   1.2   The General Prohibition on Inter-State Use of Force   20
   1.3   UN Security Council 'Authorisation' of Military Action   21
   1.4   UN Peacekeeping Operations and the Protection of Civilians   22
         1.4.1   Responsibility to Protect and the Protection of Civilians   24
   1.5   Humanitarian Intervention and the Protection of Civilians   27
   1.6   The Right of Self-Defence and the Protection of Civilians   29

2   **Protection of Civilians under International Humanitarian Law**   30

   2.1   Introduction   30
   2.2   The Protection of Civilians in the Conduct of Hostilities   32
         2.2.1   The Rule of Distinction   33
         2.2.2   The Rule of Proportionality in Attack   39
         2.2.3   The Rule of Precautions in Attack   40
         2.2.4   The Protection of Civilian Objects   41
         2.2.5   Protection of Civilians under Foreign Military Occupation   44
         2.2.6   Civilians in the Power of the Enemy   46

3   Protection of Civilians under Human Rights Law   50

     3.1   Introduction   50
     3.2   The Right to Life of Civilians in Armed Conflict   51
           3.2.1   Arbitrary Deprivation of Life   51
           3.2.2   The Duty to Investigate Suspicious Death   56
     3.3   The Right to Freedom from Torture and Other Ill-Treatment   60
           3.3.1   The Prohibition on Torture or Other Ill-Treatment   60
           3.3.2   The Duty to Investigate Ill-Treatment   61
     3.4   The Right to Freedom from Arbitrary Detention   61
     3.5   The Right of Peaceful Assembly   63
     3.6   The Application of Human Rights Law to Non-State Actors   64

4   The Protection of Refugees   67

     4.1   Introduction   67
     4.2   The Right to Seek and Enjoy Asylum   68
     4.3   International Humanitarian Law and Refugees   70
     4.4   The 1969 OAU Refugees Convention   72

5   Disarmament Law and the Protection of Civilians   74

     5.1   Introduction   74
     5.2   The 1992 Chemical Weapons Convention   75
     5.3   The 1997 Anti-personnel Mine Ban Convention   77
     5.4   The 2008 Convention on Cluster Munitions   81
     5.5   The 2013 Arms Trade Treaty   84

6   International Criminal Law and the Protection of Civilians   86

     6.1   Introduction   86
     6.2   War Crimes   87
     6.3   Crimes against Humanity   92
     6.4   Genocide   95

7   The Prohibition of Sexual and Gender-Based Violence   97

     7.1   Introduction   97
           7.1.1   The Work of the Special Representative of the Secretary-General
                   on Sexual Violence in Conflict   98
     7.2   The Prevalence of Sexual and Gender-Based Violence in Armed Conflict   99
     7.3   IHL Rules on Sexual and Gender-Based Violence in Armed Conflict   102
     7.4   Sexual and Gender-Based Violence as a War Crime   103
     7.5   Sexual and Gender-Based Violence as a Crime against Humanity   104
     7.6   Sexual and Gender-Based Violence as Genocide   106

PART II   SPECIFIC PROTECTION OF CERTAIN HIGH-RISK GROUPS   107

8   **Protection of Women in Armed Conflict**   109

8.1   Introduction   109
8.2   IHL Rules on the Protection of Women   110
8.3   Women and the Death Penalty   112
8.4   The Protection of Women in a UN Peacekeeping Mission   114

9   **Protection of Children in Armed Conflict**   115

9.1   Introduction   115
   9.1.1   The Definition of a Child   115
9.2   The Application of the Convention on the Rights of the Child
in Armed Conflict   116
9.3   IHL Rules on the Protection of Children   117
9.4   Enlistment in Armed Forces or Groups   118
9.5   The Six Grave Violations   122
9.6   Children and the Death Penalty   123
9.7   Child Protection in a UN Peacekeeping Mission   124

10   **Protection of Persons with Disabilities in Armed Conflict**   126

10.1   Introduction   126
   10.1.1   The Threats to Persons with Disabilities in Armed Conflict   127
10.2   The Global Normative Framework   130
   10.2.1   IHL Rules on the Protection of Persons with Disabilities   131
   10.2.2   Protection under International Human Rights Law   132
   10.2.3   IASC Guidelines on Inclusion of Persons with Disabilities
in Humanitarian Action (2019)   133
   10.2.4   Camp Coordination and Camp Management   138
   10.2.5   Food Security and Nutrition   138

11   **Protection of Older Persons in Armed Conflict**   140

11.1   Introduction   140
11.2   The Threats to Older Persons in Armed Conflict   141
11.3   Protection under International Human Rights Law   141
11.4   Older Persons and the Death Penalty   143
   11.4.1   The Death Penalty under IHL   143
11.5   Protection of Older Persons under IHL   144

12   **Protection of Medical and Humanitarian Personnel**   145

12.1   Introduction   145
   12.1.1   The Definition of Medical Personnel   145
12.2   The Protection of Medical Personnel   146
12.3   The Protection of Humanitarian Personnel   148

13   **Protection of Internally Displaced Persons**   151

      13.1   Introduction   151
      13.2   The Normative Framework   151
             13.2.1   The Guiding Principles on Internal Displacement   153
             13.2.2   The Kampala Convention   156

14   **Protection of LGBTI Civilians**   160

      14.1   Introduction   160
      14.2   Attacks against LGBTI Civilians in Armed Conflict   161
      14.3   LGBTI Persons and the Death Penalty   163

      PART III   STATE AND INSTITUTIONAL POLICIES ON THE PROTECTION
                  OF CIVILIANS   165

15   **The United Nations and the Protection of Civilians**   167

      15.1   Introduction   167
      15.2   The Protection of Civilians in UN Peacekeeping Missions   168
             15.2.1   The 2019 DPO Policy   171
      15.3   Protection of Civilians by UN Agencies and Bodies   181
             15.3.1   Protection of Civilians and the Global Protection Cluster 181
             15.3.2   The Role of the Office of the UN High Commissioner for
                      Human Rights   183
             15.3.3   The Role of UNICEF in Child Protection in Armed Conflict 184
             15.3.4   The UNHCR and the Protection of Refugees   185
             15.3.5   WFP and the Protection of Civilians   187

16   **NATO and the Protection of Civilians**   190

      16.1   Introduction   190
      16.2   The Policy Framework   191
      16.3   NATO and International Humanitarian Law   194
      16.4   NATO and International Human Rights Law   196
      16.5   Operation Unified Protector in Libya   197

17   **The African Union and the Protection of Civilians**   201

      17.1   Introduction   201
      17.2   'Tiered' Protection of Civilians under the AU Guidelines   201
      17.3   Mandates to Protect Civilians   203
      17.4   The Power of the AU to Intervene to Protect Civilians   207

18   **The European Union and the Protection of Civilians**   209

      18.1   Introduction   209
      18.2   The 2015 Concept on Protection of Civilians in EU-Led Military
             Operations   210

18.3   DG ECHO Thematic Policy Document on Humanitarian Protection   213
18.4   The European Union and International Humanitarian Law   215
18.5   The European Union and International Human Rights Law   216
18.6   The 2020 UN Security Council Debate on the Protection of Civilians   217

19   **The ICRC and the Protection of Civilians**   219

19.1   Introduction   219
19.2   ICRC Policy on Protection   219
   19.2.1   Guiding Principle 1: A Neutral and Independent Approach   220
   19.2.2   Guiding Principle 2: Dialogue and Confidentiality   220
   19.2.3   Guiding Principle 3: The Holistic and Multidisciplinary
        Character of ICRC Action   220
   19.2.4   Guiding Principle 4: Search for Results and Impact   221
   19.2.5   Ethical and Professional Standards for Protection   221
   19.2.6   The Principle of Humanity   221
   19.2.7   The Principle of Non-Discrimination   222
   19.2.8   The Principle of Impartiality   222
   19.2.9   'Do No Harm'   222
   19.2.10   Participation of Affected Communities   223
19.3   Particular Challenges for the ICRC   223

20   **Switzerland and the Protection of Civilians**   225

20.1   Introduction   225
20.2   The Swiss Strategy on the Protection of Civilians   225
20.3   The 2020 UN Security Council Debate on the Protection of Civilians   227

21   **The United Kingdom and the Protection of Civilians**   229

21.1   Introduction   229
21.2   The 2010 UK Strategy   230
   21.2.1   Policy Area 1: Political Engagement   230
   21.2.2   Policy Area 2: Protection by Peace Support Operations   231
   21.2.3   Policy Area 3: Humanitarian Action   231
   21.2.4   Policy Area 4: State Capacity   232
21.3   The Development of the 2020 Policy Paper   232
21.4   The 2020 Policy Paper   234
21.5   The 2020 UN Security Council Debate on the Protection of Civilians   238

22   **The United States and the Protection of Civilians**   239

22.1   Introduction   239
22.2   The US Department of Defense *Law of War Manual*   242
22.3   The 2016 Executive Order   244
22.4   The Army War College Military Reference Guide   245
22.5   The National Strategy on Women, Peace, and Security   246
22.6   The 2020 UN Security Council Debate on the Protection of Civilians   247

23 Brazil and the Protection of Civilians   249

    23.1 Introduction   249
    23.2 Responsibility While Protecting   250
    23.3 The 2020 UN Security Council Debate on the Protection of Civilians   252

24 India and the Protection of Civilians   254

    24.1 Introduction   254
    24.2 Responsibility to Protect   255
    24.3 The 2020 UN Security Council Debate on the Protection of Civilians   256

25 Norway and the Protection of Civilians   258

    25.1 Introduction   258
    25.2 The 2020 UN Security Council Debate on the Protection of Civilians   259

26 South Africa and the Protection of Civilians   262

    26.1 Introduction   262
    26.2 The 2020 UN Security Council Debate on the Protection of Civilians   263

27 The Future of Protecting Civilians   265

    27.1 Enhancing the Protection of Civilians through the Law   266
        27.1.1 Clarity and Normative Development of IHL   266
        27.1.2 Making Refugee Law More Protective of Those Fleeing Armed
                Conflict   269
        27.1.3 More Force or Less?   270
    27.2 Enhancing the Protection of Civilians through Policy   271
        27.2.1 State Policy on the Protection of Civilians   271
        27.2.2 Organisational Policy on the Protection of Civilians   272
    27.3 New Challenges to the Protection of Civilians   275
        27.3.1 Urban Warfare   275
        27.3.2 Cyber Operations   277
        27.3.3 Great Power Conflict and Hybrid Warfare   279
        27.3.4 Protection of the Environment   280

    Conclusion   282

Appendix 1 *Overview of Relevant International Law*   284
      A1.1 *Introduction*   284
         A1.1.1 *The Definition of a State*   284
         A1.1.2 *The Definition of an International Organisation*   285
         A1.1.3 *The Definition of a Corporation*   286
         A1.1.4 *The Definition of a Non-State Actor*   286
      A1.2 *The Sources of International Law*   287
         A1.2.1 *Treaties*   287
         A1.2.2 *Soft-Law Instruments*   288

	A1.2.3	*Customary International Law*	290
	A1.2.4	*General Principles of Law*	290
	A1.3	*Applicable International Legal Regimes*	291
	A1.4	*The Relationship between International and Domestic Law*	292
Appendix 2		*The Two Types of Armed Conflict under International Humanitarian Law*	294
	A2.1	*International Armed Conflict*	294
	A2.2	*Non-international Armed Conflict*	296
	A2.3	*Armed Conflicts May Exist in Parallel*	297
	A2.4	*The Key Differences in Applicable Rules in Armed Conflicts*	297
	A2.5	*The Prevalence of International and Non-international Armed Conflicts*	297
Index			300

Foreword

Protecting civilians in conflicts is both a legal and a moral duty. Too often, civilians pay a high price for military confrontation. Historic conflicts, such as World War II, were characterised by disaster and human casualty. Twenty-first-century conflicts, such as in Syria, Ukraine, and Yemen, tend not to be much, if at all, better. In the foreseeable future, warfare and the use of force will most likely remain a reality in many parts of the world. Therefore, it is crucial that we strengthen our efforts to protect those who suffer from violence and conflict.

The international community has come a long way and achieved major normative progress. The fourth Geneva Convention of 1949, for instance, is specifically dedicated to civilians, thereby representing a cornerstone of well-established international law governing the protection of civilians. By the early 2020s, many international and regional organisations had adopted new or revised policies on the protection of civilians, thereby committing themselves to this cause and guiding their action. Switzerland and the United Kingdom also adopted national policies.

These normative developments play an important role for effectively protecting civilians, but the task remains difficult. Most twenty-first-century conflicts are protracted civil wars, whose complexities, including fighting among the civilian population, pose significant challenges to the belligerent parties and to actors engaged in protection. Radical acts of violence are specifically targeted at civilian populations and often conducted during times of peace. While renewed great power rivalry carries the risk of large-scale war, confrontation with multiple military and non-military means below the threshold of war is already now a reality. Such forms of warfare and new technologies, including cyber capabilities, add further complexities and unknowns for the protection of civilians.

Given these challenges, this book aims to support those who work on the protection of civilians and related issues. It is the result of serious efforts to better comprehend, analyse, consult, reflect, and offer insights into the vast normative framework on the protection of civilians. We hope, therefore, that the book brings greater clarity and will prove to be an invaluable instrument to all those seeking to protect civilians better at the local, national, regional, and global level. We also hope that the book advances reflections and ideas on the improvement of the normative framework and related practice.

The Geneva Centre for Security Policy (GCSP) will continue its efforts concerning the protection of civilians. The GCSP aims to serve other institutions and persons who are dedicated to protect those who deserve protection, especially the most vulnerable. Protecting civilians from violence and harm constitutes an integral part of the international community's mission to advance peace, security, and international cooperation. More broadly, an individual's right to protection is underpinned by the global architecture established in 1945 to maintain international peace and security. The four pillars of the United Nations – peace and security, human rights, the rule of law, and development – must all be brought to bear to this end. We must not relent but increase our efforts in this regard.

Ambassador Thomas Greminger
Director, Geneva Centre for Security Policy

Preface

The 'protection of civilians' is essentially a concept consisting of a complex set of international law, policies, and practices by States, international organisations, and other key actors that aims to safeguard civilians against violence and other harm. At the same time, the protection of civilians (or PoC, as it is sometimes referred to) is also a political notion by which actors signal that they pay attention to civilian harm during armed conflicts and other disasters.

Protection of civilians is a longstanding concept that has undergone significant transformation in recent years. Since the first laws of warfare and even before, those engaged in fighting understood that the innocent should be spared (even if they did not always do so). More recently, the notion of the protection of civilians has broadened from the primary goal of not killing or injuring civilians during military operations to encompass efforts to actively protect them from suffering. Now more comprehensive in scope, protecting civilians has become an explicit goal of certain military and humanitarian missions conducted by States, international organisations, and non-governmental organisations (NGOs).

Today, there exists a swathe of international legal rules, policies, and practices that govern, guide, and aim to ensure the protection of civilians. The international legal framework has primarily been established in the post–World War II period. Practice on civilian protection has developed more recently, notably by increased efforts since the end of the Cold War, in particular by United Nations (UN) peace operations and humanitarian organisations. The last decade has brought several new or renewed policies on the protection of civilians, which guide the respective organisations' or States' actions.

In light of these developments, this book aims to expound and clarify the normative framework pertaining to the protection of civilians. In some ways, the concept was overshadowed in academic literature by debates on the related doctrine of responsibility to protect (R2P). Besides a few useful monographs, which, tend to focus on the protection of civilians in the framework of UN peace operations, existing literature largely sought to address specific legal questions, policies, or practices of specific organisations, or specific country cases. This was complemented by analyses of civilian casualties and civilian harm in warfare.

To fill the broader gap in scholarship, this book endeavours to offer an in-depth analysis and explanation of the existing normative framework on the protection of civilians. It scopes the existing international law along with specific policies. Thereby, it addresses key controversies and challenges as well as the most relevant practice from the last decades. The aim is to support policymakers, diplomats, the military, scholars, practitioners, and students to better understand, implement, and further develop the protection of civilians. Indeed, for people suffering from armed conflict and other disasters it does not matter which law or policy is applied – what matters for them is that they receive protection. Yet, to safeguard them, their families, and their communities effectively, it is crucial to grasp and master the nuances of the tools at our disposal.

This work has benefited significantly from the insights and guidance of others, for which the authors are very grateful. The authors would like to especially thank the following for their valuable comments on a draft manuscript in an expert meeting at the Geneva Centre for Security Policy: Dr Simon Bagshaw, Senior Policy Advisor, Policy Section, Operations and Advocacy Division, United Nations Office for the Coordination of Humanitarian Affairs (OCHA); Ms Danielle Bell, Chief, Human Rights Office, United Nations Assistance Mission for Iraq (UNAMI), and Representative, Office of the UN High Commissioner for Human Rights (OHCHR); Dr Robin Coupland, former war surgeon and advisor, Legal Division, International Committee of the Red Cross (ICRC); Ms Reka Dobri, Policy Officer, Directorate-General for European Civil Protection and Humanitarian Aid Operations, Unit C.1-Humanitarian Aid Thematic Policies, European Commission; Ms Regina Fitzpatrick, Protection of Civilians Team Leader, Policy and Best Practices Service, Policy, Evaluation and Training Division, UN Department of Peace Operations (UNDPO); Ms Alison Giffen, Director, Peacekeeping Program, Center for Civilians in Conflict (CIVIC); Mr David Haeri, Director, Division of Policy, Evaluation and Training, UNDPO; Mr Steven Hill, former Legal Advisor and Director, Office of Legal Affairs, NATO Headquarters; Ms Marla Keenan, Adjunct Senior Fellow, Transforming Conflict and Governance Program, The Stimson Center; Professor Patryk Labuda, Assistant Professor of International Criminal Law, Amsterdam Centre for International Law, Law School, University of Amsterdam; Mr Ralph Mamiya, Executive-in-Residence Fellow, GCSP, and Non-Resident Advisor, International Peace Institute (IPI); Ms Erin Mooney, Senior Protection Adviser, UN Protection Capacity (ProCap), United Nations in Yemen; and Professor Mitt Regan, McDevitt Professor of Jurisprudence and Director, Center on Ethics and the Legal Profession, and Co-Director, Center on National Security and the Law, Law Center, Georgetown University. The authors would also like to thank Ms Altea Rossi, Programme Officer, GCSP, and Ms Chiara Giaccari, Junior Programme Officer, GCSP, for project support.

All involvement in the project by the experts mentioned above was in a purely personal capacity, and the views expressed in the book do not necessarily reflect those of anyone who provided input to, or commented on, earlier drafts. Any errors remaining are the responsibility of the authors alone.

Introduction

Protecting civilians essentially means minimising the negative consequences of conflict for those who are not actively engaged in fighting or ancillary activities. One might assume that shielding civilians from harm is a global public good upon which consensus can readily be achieved. Yet the reality is more blurred. Already the notions of both 'civilian' and 'protection' are contested, for instance. So too are the interpretation and application of many of the legal obligations which intend to ensure that civilians are safeguarded. In addition, protecting civilians oftentimes is in tension with other stakes while also involving costs and trade-offs. As such, some justify civilian harm by national security imperatives or the exercise of a people's right to self-determination. Others perceive the concept as political cover for Western neo-imperialism.

This chapter begins by discussing key terms and concepts in the protection of civilians – 'civilian' and 'protection' in particular – while illustrating their unsettled and complex character. Key moments in history in international law, policy, and practice over the last century and a half are recalled. This aims to provide the context and conceptual clarity before delving into more details. Following this introduction, the book is divided into two parts.

Part I covers the international rules pertaining to the protection of civilians. It does so in two ways. First, the main branches of applicable international law are reviewed as they relate to the protection of civilians: *jus ad bellum* (the law on inter-State use of force), international humanitarian law, international human rights law, disarmament law, international criminal law, and refugee law. A separate chapter is dedicated to the prohibition of sexual violence. Then the protection of specific groups of civilians is addressed: women; children; persons with disabilities; older persons; the internally displaced; medical and humanitarian personnel; and lesbian, gay, bisexual, transgender, and intersex (LGBTI) persons.

Part II of the book reviews the institutional policies of certain key States and leading international organisations. The heterogeneity of the policies and practices within the United Nations (UN) system bear witness to the manifold challenges inherent in the protection of civilians. The fact that no UN-wide strategy on the protection of civilians yet exists is discussed. Some within the United Nations declare such a strategy unnecessary;

1

others believe its conclusion and adoption are practically unachievable. Within the UN Security Council, however, since the final years of the last millennium, the protection of civilians has been transformed from an issue of peripheral importance to one that lies 'at the core' of its work to maintain international peace and security.[1] That does not imply, however, that the permanent or non-permanent members of the Council agree as to either the nature of protection that should be afforded to the civilian population in countries of concern or the actors that should ensure its provision.

At regional level, the African Union (AU), the European Union (EU), and the North Atlantic Treaty Organization (NATO) have all played roles of significance in the protection of civilians, though not all have been equally protective. The same is true for Brazil, India, Norway, South Africa, Switzerland, the United Kingdom, and the United States. Their policies and practices are reviewed in turn. In the non-governmental realm, the International Committee of the Red Cross (ICRC) – also the subject of a dedicated chapter – is a critical reference. So too are the many local and international non-governmental organisations (NGOs) that seek to protect civilians on a systematic or ad hoc basis in the field: the Center for Civilians in Conflict (CIVIC), Geneva Call, the International Rescue Committee, Médecins sans Frontières, and Save the Children, among many others. Amnesty International, Bellingcat, and Human Rights Watch further seek to ensure accountability for violations of international law perpetrated against civilians. No single volume could possibly hope to describe in sufficient depth, much less to evaluate, the achievements and shortcomings in their work, whether considered individually or collectively.

1.1 WHO ARE 'CIVILIANS'?

If civilians are to be protected, who are civilians? This is a short and deceptively simple question, but one that is not readily capable of receiving a brief answer that is also comprehensive.[2] Modern conflicts, which tend to involve a multitude of non-State actors to the extent that observers have termed this the 'civilianization of conflict',[3] further complexify the answer. In general terms, however, civilians are *non-military* persons. This lay understanding, which dates back to the latter half of the eighteenth century of

---

[1] Statement by the President of the UN Security Council, UN doc. S/PRST/2015/23, 25 November 2015, at: http://bit.ly/2HTRqQN, p. 3.

[2] This is, in part, due to the complexities of the fragmentation of international law and its vernacular whereby specialised law-making often takes place with relative ignorance of legislative activities in adjoining fields and of the general principles and practices of international law. The result can be conflicts between rules or rule-systems. Fragmentation of International Law: Difficulties Arising from the Diversification and Expansion of International Law, Report of the Study Group of the International Law Commission, Finalized by Martti Koskenniemi, UN doc. A/CN.4/L.682, 13 April 2006, at: https://bit.ly/2NkHMvr, para. 8.

[3] See for example, A. Barros and M. Thomas (eds.), *The Civilianization of War: The Changing Civil–Military Divide, 1914–2014*, 1st ed., Cambridge University Press, Cambridge, 2018. See also A. Wenger and S. Mason, 'The Civilianization of Armed Conflict: Trends and Implications', *International Review of the Red Cross*, Vol. 90, No. 872 (2008), 835–52.

the current era (CE),[4] and based on the moral distinction that killing civilians is worse than killing soldiers,[5] persists to this day and is a helpful starting point. The true etymology of the notion of civilian, however, is of a 'citizen'. Derived from the Latin *civilus*, it was used in this sense in the Roman empire in the first century before the current era (BCE).[6] Julius Caesar, for instance, was writing of a 'civil' war, meaning one between citizens of Rome.

Ralph Mamiya has traced the modern concept of civilians, and the duty on belligerents to refrain from violence against them, to the laws and customs of war that evolved in the early twentieth century CE, especially in the period following the end of World War I.[7] Considered seminal is the 1923 article in the *International Review of the Red Cross* by Dr Frédéric Ferrière, the original French title of which translates as 'A draft international convention on the situation of civilians during war who have fallen into the power of the enemy'.[8] Already in Ferrière's article the complexity of the issue of civilians and their protection was laid bare. In advocating for international legal regulation of the issue, he declared that due distinction would need to be made between civilians who could be called up for military service and those who could not. This latter group, he said, comprised those civilians who 'deserve' to be accorded 'a certain level of security', identifying in this regard 'the infirm, the sick, those who were too old to bear arms and the elderly, children and youth who were not old enough to join the ranks of the military, [and] women and girls'.[9]

In 1929, a diplomatic conference of States was convened in Geneva to adopt for the first time an international convention on the status and treatment of prisoners of war.[10] The Final Act of the conference contained a unanimous recommendation that 'extensive examination be made with a view to concluding an international convention on the condition and protection of enemy civilians on the territory of a belligerent or on territory

---

[4] The sense of civilian as a 'non-military' person is said to be attested by 1766. 'Civilian', *Online Etymology Dictionary*, accessed 1 June 2019, at: http://bit.ly/2Kk2nxc.

[5] S. Lazar, *Sparing Civilians*, 1st ed., Oxford University Press, New York, 2017.

[6] In his *Commentarii de Bello Civili*, Julius Caesar was discussing the Roman Civil War of 49 BCE and 48 BCE. In late Middle English, the term 'civilian' described a practitioner of civil law: its origins for this sense were in the Old French *droit civilien*.

[7] R. Mamiya, 'A History and Conceptual Development of the Protection of Civilians', in H. Willmot, R. Mamiya, S. Sheeran, and M. Weller (eds.), *Protection of Civilians*, 1st ed., Oxford University Press, Oxford, 2016 (hereinafter, Willmot et al., *Protection of Civilians*), p. 65 note 6. In 1899, the Hague Convention II on the Laws and Customs of War on Land employed the term civilian but only in relation to espionage. In this regard, civilians who openly delivered 'despatches destined either for their own army or for that of the enemy' were not to be considered spies. Art. 29, Convention (II) with Respect to the Laws and Customs of War on Land; adopted at The Hague, 29 July 1899; entered into force, 4 September 1900. See similarly Art. 29, Convention (IV) respecting the Laws and Customs of War on Land and its annex: Regulations concerning the Laws and Customs of War on Land; adopted at The Hague, 18 October 1907; entered into force, 26 January 1910.

[8] F. Ferrière, 'Projet d'une Convention internationale réglant la situation des civils tombés à la guerre au pouvoir de l'ennemi', *International Review of the Red Cross*, 1923, 560–85, at: https://bit.ly/3sDm323.

[9] Ibid., pp. 566–7.

[10] In their earliest iterations in 1864, 1906, and 1929, the Geneva Conventions otherwise focused on alleviating the suffering of wounded or sick soldiers.

occupied by him'.[11] An important area of unfulfilled law-making had been identified. Following the call, the International Convention on the Condition and Protection of Civilians of enemy nationality who are on territory belonging to or occupied by a belligerent was drafted in Tokyo, although it was never formally concluded and adopted by States. The 1934 draft text defined civilians as persons 'not belonging to the land, maritime or air armed forces of the belligerents, as defined by international law'.[12] Separately, the same year, the Monaco Convention on 'sanitary cities and localities',[13] an instrument which also did not enter into force as binding international law, contained a section dedicated to the protection of the 'civil population'.[14] The Monaco Convention defined the civil population as including 'all persons who are not enlisted in the army'.[15]

The aftermath of World War II marked a milestone in international law with the adoption of the first legally binding instrument explicitly and exclusively dedicated to the protection of civilians in armed conflict. Thus, the Fourth Geneva Convention of 1949 is formally entitled the Convention relative to the Protection of Civilian Persons in Time of War.[16] The provisions are based on the text of the 1934 draft text elaborated in Tokyo, with the 1949 Convention thus focusing on the protection of civilians in occupied territory as well as of foreign nationals in the territory of a party to an international armed conflict.[17] While the four Geneva Conventions of 1949 do not, individually or collectively, explicitly delineate who are civilians, they do generally serve to reinforce the general distinction between the members of the armed forces (combatants) on the one hand and the civilian population (non-combatants) on the other.

The 1977 Additional Protocol I to the Geneva Conventions[18] would later use this bifurcation as the starting point for its *explicit* definition of civilians in a situation of international armed conflict. But the complexity of the definition also showcases the elements of nuance brought to the question by international humanitarian law (IHL).

---

[11] Final Act of the Diplomatic Conference, issued at Geneva, 27 July 1929, at: http://bit.ly/3iofHio, Recommendation VI.

[12] Art. 1(a), Draft International Convention on the Condition and Protection of Civilians of Enemy Nationality who are on Territory Belonging to or Occupied by a Belligerent; elaborated at Tokyo but not concluded, 1934.

[13] First Convention on Sanitary Cities and Localities; adopted in Monaco, 27 July 1934; never entered into force (hereinafter, 1934 First Convention on Sanitary Cities and Localities).

[14] The ICRC has observed that the text of the draft Convention was drawn up by a Commission of doctors and jurists that met in Monaco on 5–11 February 1934 in response to a wish expressed at the Seventh International Congress of Military Medicine and Pharmacy held in Madrid in 1933. ICRC, 'First draft Convention adopted in Monaco (Sanitary cities and localities), 27 July 1934', at: http://bit.ly/3sGDqPk.

[15] Art. 1, Chap. IV, 1934 First Convention on Sanitary Cities and Localities.

[16] Convention (IV) relative to the Protection of Civilian Persons in Time of War; adopted at Geneva, 12 August 1949; entered into force, 21 October 1950.

[17] In general terms, an international armed conflict is one occurring between two or more States, including where sovereign territory is occupied by a foreign State. The issue is discussed briefly in Chapter 2 and in further detail in Appendix 2.

[18] Protocol Additional to the Geneva Conventions of 12 August 1949, and relating to the Protection of Victims of International Armed Conflicts (Protocol I), 8 June 1977; adopted at Geneva, 8 June 1977; entered into force, 7 December 1978 (1977 Additional Protocol I). As of 1 April 2022, 174 States were party to the Protocol. See the ICRC list of States Parties, at: https://bit.ly/2Oe2Iin.

Thus, under its Article 50(1), the 1977 Additional Protocol I classifies a civilian in the negative, deeming him or her to be any person *other than* the following:

Members of the armed forces of a Party to the conflict,[19] including members of militias or volunteer corps that form part of such armed forces. This is so, whether or not the armed forces belong to a government that is recognised by the enemy.[20]

Members of militias and or volunteer corps, including organised resistance movements, which belong to a Party to the conflict but which are not part of its armed forces. This is so, as long as they are under 'responsible command'; bear a fixed distinctive sign recognisable at a distance; carry arms openly; and comply with IHL.[21]

Inhabitants of a non-occupied territory who, on the approach of the enemy, spontaneously take up arms to resist the invading forces, without having had time to form themselves into regular armed units (this is known as a *levée en masse*). They lose their civilian status (but gain the right to be considered and treated as prisoners of war, provided they carry arms openly and respect IHL).[22]

The notion of a combatant is thus cast widely in IHL. It is not limited to those who belong formally to the regular armed forces.[23]

The 1977 Additional Protocol I confirms that the civilian population 'comprises all persons who are civilians'.[24] In case of doubt whether a person is a civilian, the Protocol further stipulates, 'that person shall be considered to be a civilian'.[25] But there are different categories of civilian under IHL and varying levels of protection that this body of law affords to them, as Chapter 2 describes. In particular, when civilians participate 'directly' in hostilities – in any armed conflict – they lose the protections under IHL to which they were entitled as civilians, in particular that of immunity from direct attack.

The 1977 Additional Protocol I formally applies only in international armed conflict. Yet the concept of loss of immunity applies equally in all 'non-international' armed conflict, that is to say, where a State is engaged in sustained combat against an organised armed group. In such conflicts, however, a particular issue of dispute pertains to whether those who 'belong' to non-State armed groups are no longer to be considered civilians as a matter of law. In 2009, the ICRC averred in its controversial Interpretive Guidance on the notion of 'direct participation in hostilities' that organised armed groups constitute the

---

[19] 'The armed forces of a Party to a conflict consist of all organized armed forces, groups and units which are under a command responsible to that Party for the conduct of its subordinates, even if that Party is represented by a government or an authority not recognized by an adverse Party.' Art. 43(1), 1977 Additional Protocol I. Under paragraph 3 of the article, it is confirmed that paramilitary forces and gendarmerie may be incorporated within the armed forces, such as occurs in Belgium and France.

[20] Art. 4(A)(1) and (3), Convention (III) relative to the Treatment of Prisoners of War; adopted at Geneva, 12 August 1949; entered into force, 21 October 1950 (hereinafter, 1949 Geneva Convention III).

[21] Art. 4(A)(2), 1949 Geneva Convention III.

[22] Art. 4(A)(6), 1949 Geneva Convention III.

[23] That said, military medics and religious personnel belonging to the armed forces are 'non-combatants', meaning that they do not have the right to participate directly in hostilities. The contested interpretation and application of this notion is discussed in Chapter 2.

[24] Art. 50(2), 1977 Additional Protocol I.

[25] Art. 50(1), 1977 Additional Protocol I.

armed forces of a non-State party to a non-international armed conflict and consist of individuals whose 'continuous function it is to take a direct part in hostilities'.[26]

The ICRC concept of continuous combat function, which remains contested, does not appear in any IHL text. If, however, it does exist as a matter of law, it serves to deprive a person of civilian status, thereby potentially rendering him or her liable to attack under IHL at all times, including when unarmed and even when asleep. Indeed, 'continuous combat function' and its concomitant consequences could even apply even to child members of organised armed groups, including those recruited when under fifteen years of age, an act that is a serious violation of international law.[27] Only when rendered *hors de combat* by wounds or sickness or upon surrender are those who were until that time participating directly in hostilities fully protected from attack.

In sum, under IHL, civilians in a situation of international armed conflict are all those who are not members of armed forces of a party to such a conflict, members of an organised resistance movement (that meets certain criteria), or who do not engage in a *levée en masse*. In a situation of non-international armed conflict, civilians are ostensibly all those who are not members of regular (State) armed forces. It may be the case, however, that members of organised armed groups who have a continuous combat function are also not civilians for the purposes of the application of IHL. The approach of the United States, however, 'has been to treat the status of belonging to a hostile, non-State armed group as a separate basis upon which a person is liable to attack, apart from whether he or she has taken a direct part in hostilities'.[28] In this case, it is not clear how membership is to be determined, however. In peacetime – meaning any situation outside armed conflict[29] – civilians are all persons who are not members of State armed forces.[30]

1.2 WHAT IS 'PROTECTION'?

Just as the notion of civilian is difficult to define, so too is the notion of protection. There is no universally accepted definition in international law of 'to protect', 'protection', or 'protected' as these terms pertain to the safeguarding of civilians from violence and indirect effects thereof. Moreover, this is the case even though both terms are employed widely in international law, in particular in IHL and in international human rights law.

A range of attempts have been made to define protection outside the realm of treaty law. With respect to the United Nations and its relations with operational non-governmental

---

[26] N. Melzer, *Interpretive Guidance on the Notion of Direct Participation in Hostilities under International Humanitarian Law*, ICRC, Geneva, 2009, chapter II.

[27] Ibid., p. 60.

[28] United States (US) Department of Defense, *Law of War Manual*, June 2015 (updated December 2016), Washington DC, 2016, para. 5.8.2.1.

[29] See, for example, Art. 2, 1949 Geneva Convention III: 'In addition to the provisions which shall be implemented in peacetime, the present Convention shall apply to all cases of declared war or of any other armed conflict . . . '.

[30] This includes members of the police or of another law enforcement agency where the law enforcement agency is not incorporated within the armed forces.

agencies, the Inter-Agency Standing Committee (IASC)[31] has defined protection, based on years of prior work by the ICRC, as *'all activities aimed at obtaining full respect for the rights of the individual in accordance with the letter and the spirit of the relevant bodies of law (i.e. human rights law, IHL, refugee law)'*.[32] This sets ambitious aims for protection activities – nothing less than 'full respect' for the legal rights of individuals is sought – while at the same time being exceptionally broad in scope, encompassing 'all' activities that pursue such a goal.

The IASC definition's operational utility is, however, debatable. Indeed, in 2015, the report of an independent review of protection in humanitarian action, published on behalf of the Standing Committee,[33] concluded that the definition 'does not facilitate a clear, operational and robust system level approach to protection deficits'. This is because it is interpreted by 'humanitarian actors and other stakeholders, in many different ways'.[34] The Standing Committee's review argued that the lack of a common understanding of the UN definition of protection 'contributes to dysfunctional approaches that fail to identify, at the system level, the diverse range of actions required, including challenging imminent threats to life for at-risk populations'.[35] The views of many interlocutors cited in the report on the IASC are rather less flattering: 'dysfunctional', 'all over the place', and 'useless' were some of the descriptors they applied, or it was deemed to mean 'everything and nothing'.[36] Despite this criticism, the review report did not call for a new definition to be developed and agreed upon, although it did recommend that the existing IASC definition be 'unpacked' to make it 'accessible'.[37] So far, this has not happened.

Within civil society, the Core Humanitarian Standard, concluded by an array of international NGOs in 2014, also offers a definition of what constitutes 'protection'. In similar terms to the IASC definition, the Core Humanitarian Standard refers to *'all activities aimed at ensuring the full and equal respect for the rights of all individuals, regardless of age, gender, ethnic, social, religious or other background'*.[38] The Standard recalls that IHL, international human rights law, and international refugee law 'set out fundamental legal standards relating to the protection of individuals and groups'.[39] To

[31] Created by UN General Assembly Resolution 46/182 in 1991, the IASC is 'the longest-standing and highest-level humanitarian coordination forum of the UN system, bringing together the executive heads of 18 UN and non-UN organizations to ensure coherence of preparedness and response efforts, formulate policy, and agree on priorities for strengthened humanitarian action'. UN Office for the Coordination of Humanitarian Affairs (OCHA), 'The Inter-Agency Standing Committee', at: http://bit.ly/3izskXR.
[32] *IASC Policy on Protection in Humanitarian Action*, United Nations, New York, 2016, at: http://bit.ly/31yoqTg.
[33] N. Niland, R. Polastro, A. Donini, and A. Lee, *Independent Whole of System Review of Protection in the Context of Humanitarian Action*, report commissioned by the Norwegian Refugee Council on behalf of the Inter Agency Standing Committee and the Global Protection Cluster, Norwegian Refugee Council, May 2015, at: http://bit.ly/301dcUn.
[34] Ibid., p. 63.
[35] Ibid.
[36] Ibid., p. 23.
[37] Ibid., p. 63.
[38] *Core Humanitarian Standard on Quality and Accountability*, CHS Alliance, Group URD, and the Sphere Project, Geneva, 2014, Glossary, p. 19.
[39] Ibid., p. 8.

further emphasise the breadth of the concept, however, the definition clarifies that protection 'goes beyond the immediate life-saving activities that are often the focus during an emergency'.[40] The Standard is expressly said to be 'underpinned by the right to life with dignity, and the right to protection and security as set forth in international law, including within the International Bill of Human Rights'.[41]

Others have proposed different definitions of protection. In a major academic work on the protection of civilians published in 2016, its four editors suggested that the international community would be 'well served' by adopting a definition of the protection of civilians along the lines of the following:

> [T]he act of protecting from violence and minimising harm towards those not directly participating in hostilities, in conflict situations. Such acts are undertaken pursuant to the rights and responsibilities of national authorities, belligerents, and the international community, and are governed by a legal framework of positive and negative obligations based on the UN Charter, IHL, IHRL [international human rights law], and refugee law. In this context, the state of being protected manifests primarily as fulfilment of the rights to life and physical integrity, whether citizen or alien. Direct protection activities are those that have a proximate causal connection resulting in the immediate and direct physical protection of civilians. Indirect protection activities are those that have a less proximate causal connection vicariously resulting in the protection of civilians.[42]

This description of protection tends to be intricate and legalistic yet contains a number of significant elements. It describes the object of protection as those not directly participating in hostilities during an armed conflict, thereby denoting all so-called 'innocent'[43] civilians (meaning those not actively engaged in armed struggle in support of one party to an armed conflict against another, whether State or non-State). It is also, though, made explicit that the notion of civilian is restricted to situations of armed conflict. Thus, protection from acts of violence in peacetime, including against major terrorist attacks and even with respect to the commission of crimes against humanity or genocide, would not be encapsulated. This renders the proposed definition incomplete. For while policies on the protection of civilians do indeed focus on armed conflict, many also address protection measures in other situations of armed violence. A broader understanding is needed of the contexts in which civilians need to be protected. The proposition also does not say much about measures for protection.

Although there have been additional definitions and specifications of the concept,[44] some have suggested that the notion of protection is not one that is capable of universally

---

[40]   Ibid.

[41]   Ibid., p. 2.

[42]   Willmot et al., *Protection of Civilians*, Conclusion, p. 431.

[43]   The word comes from the Latin *innocens*, meaning one who does not harm others. H. Slim, 'Civilians, Distinction, and the Compassionate View of War', in Willmot et al., *Protection of Civilians*, p. 16.

[44]   DPO, *The Protection of Civilians in United Nations Peacekeeping*, Policy, New York, 1 November 2019, para. 23; NATO *Policy for the Protection of Civilians*, endorsed by the Heads of State and Government participating in the meeting of the North Atlantic Council in Warsaw, 8–9 July, para. 9; *Draft Guidelines for the Protection of Civilians in African Union Peace Support Operations*, African Union, Addis Ababa, 2012, para. 1; *Protection of Civilians Military Reference Guide*, 2nd ed., *Army Peacekeeping and Stability Operations Institute*, Army

applicable or acceptable definition. Perhaps, to coin the famous words of Justice Potter Stewart of the US Supreme Court (albeit with reference to a very different concept), 'one knows it when one sees it'.[45] Or alternatively, as one international public health expert, Robin Coupland, has suggested, it may be the case that 'protection' is just an 'unsatisfactory term'.[46] While both positions are defensible, this work does not endeavour to sustain either but proposes that:

> *Protection of civilians is the defence of civilians against violence and the alleviation of harm in conflict and other situations threatening their physical and mental integrity through the application of preventive and responsive measures.*[47]

As Coupland has observed, preventive measures in favour of civilians are executed through one of three avenues: by reducing *physical capacity* to undertake unlawful violence against civilians; by reducing *psychological capacity* to undertake unlawful violence against civilians; and by reducing the *vulnerability* of civilians to violence.[48] This categorisation leads to the following avenues for the protection of civilians:

Physical capacity to undertake violence against civilians is reduced, through a combination of arms control, the lawful use of force, and the prosecution and incarceration of perpetrators of criminal acts. Policies can provide for civilian harm mitigation measures that are not required by international humanitarian law, for instance a requirement that there be near certainty that civilians will not be harmed during an attack.[49]

Psychological capacity to undertake violence against civilians is reduced, by ensuring respect for domestic and international law and through the deterrent effect of effective investigation, apprehension, and prosecution of others as well as the lawful use of force and the threat thereof.[50] Training, codes of conduct, norms, and organisational culture are further means in this regard.

The *vulnerability of civilians to violence is reduced* through a combination of 'humanitarian' protection measures (such as through the provision of shelter and the

War College, Carlisle, PA, January 2018, p. 3. For details and discussions of these definitions or specifications, see the chapters on the respective institutions.

[45] US Supreme Court, *Jacobellis* v. *Ohio*, 378 US 184 (1964), at 197.

[46] Email from Robin Coupland to Tobias Vestner, 3 November 2020.

[47] The World Health Organization (WHO) has defined violence as 'the intentional use of physical force or power, threatened or actual, against oneself, another person, or against a group or community, that results in injury, death, psychological harm, maldevelopment or deprivation'. WHO, 'Definition and Typology of Violence', at: http://bit.ly/3sHfdZc. The definition was first expounded in 1996 in the WHO Global Consultation on Violence and Health publication *Violence: A Public Health Priority*, WHO doc. WHO/EHA/SPI.POA.2, Geneva, 1996. Complex emergencies are situations of disrupted livelihoods and threats to life produced by warfare, civil disturbance, and large-scale movements of people, in which any emergency response has to be conducted in a difficult political and security environment. WHO, *Environmental Health in Emergencies and Disasters: a Practical Guide*, Geneva, 2002, para. 1.6.

[48] Email from Robin Coupland to Tobias Vestner, 3 November 2020.

[49] For a differentiation of types of measures, see for example, M. Keenan and A. W. Beadle, 'Operationalizing Protection of Civilians in NATO Operations', *Stability: International Journal of Security & Development*, Vol. 4, No. 1 (2015), 1–13.

[50] This could mean placing military or police forces near vulnerable populations, conducting patrols, or proactively using force against those who might harm civilians.

assurance of safeguarded areas) and 'social' protection measures (e.g. forms of social welfare), which reduce the motivation for risk-taking.[51]

This understanding of protection as possessing an especially broad preventive nature is consonant with the duty to protect life under the right to life in international human rights law. Thus, as the Human Rights Committee has affirmed, the application of the right to life under the International Covenant on Civil and Political Rights (ICCPR)[52] demands that States must both respect and ensure the right to life, including by exercising due diligence to protect the lives of individuals against deprivations caused by persons or entities whose conduct is not attributable to the State.[53]

This further indicates another dimension of the modern understanding of the protection of civilians, namely that civilians are not only to be protected from one's own actions as a military actor but potentially also from the conduct of others. While IHL predominantly – though not exclusively – foresees that parties to armed conflict shall avoid harming civilians during combat, international human rights law and notably the UN and NATO protection of civilians or ('PoC') policies also foresee the latter. Humanitarian organisations' work obviously contributes to the more extensive approach to protection.

If measures to prevent civilian harm fail, measures to alleviate the harm should also be undertaken to assist and support civilians. The provision of health care to victims of violence, the provision of food and shelter to those in need, as well as assistance to refugees and internally displaced persons are just a few examples of such support. There must be judicial investigations into alleged criminal conduct against civilians. States, international organisations, and humanitarian organisations all provide such measures – and are in certain circumstances obligated to do so under international law.

1.3 WHO PROTECTS CIVILIANS?

This leads to an initial consideration of the range of actors and entities who are obligated under international law to protect civilians or do so by proper initiative. The proposed scholarly definition from 2016 identified a number of key actors who have such responsibilities under international law: governments, military forces (armed forces and armed opposition groups), as well as the international community more broadly. Falling within this broad notion are the United Nations and other international or regional organisations, which are required to protect civilians in particular by virtue of customary international law. The detail of the international legal obligations incumbent on these different actors as well as their policies are set out in the relevant chapters.

---

[51] World Bank, 'Social Protection: Overview', last updated 29 March 2019, at: http://bit.ly/2XNJHsF.
[52] International Covenant on Civil and Political Rights; adopted at New York, 16 December 1966; entered into force, 23 March 1976. A total of 173 of 197 States recognised by the UN Secretary-General, the depositary of the Covenant, were party to it as of 1 April 2022.
[53] Human Rights Committee, General Comment No. 36: Article 6: right to life, UN doc. CCPR/C/GC/36, 3 September 2019, para. 7.

The ICRC, NGOs, human rights institutions, and human rights defenders are typically critical in advocating for protection as well as executing protection measures. All such entities can, and should, also monitor the extent to which civilians are being protected in any relevant situation and, depending on their respective mandates, report on their findings publicly or in confidence. In addition, private military and security companies can play both positive and negative roles regarding the protection of civilians. Last, but by no means least, communities themselves can and do engage in self-protection.[54]

1.4 A BRIEF HISTORY OF THE PROTECTION OF CIVILIANS

To help understand the different perspectives on the protection of civilians that exist today, this final section offers a brief historical review of the protection of civilians. The idea of non-combatant immunity had already been developed by 'just war' theorists.[55] But no consensus yet existed on the principle of civilian immunity from violence.

Thus, for example, the 1863 Lieber Code, a document drafted by an academic of the time and promulgated by US President Abraham Lincoln to govern the acts of the Union armies in the American Civil War, affirms that a 'citizen or native of a hostile country' is 'an enemy'.[56] The Code did, though, go on to note that the 'principle has been more and more acknowledged that the unarmed citizen is to be spared in person, property, and honor as much as the exigencies of war will admit'.[57]

Although the fighting in the American Civil War was primarily between soldiers, a significant number of civilians not taking a direct part in the struggle were also casualties. Although all data should be treated with caution, estimates suggest about one in twelve of those killed in the Civil War was a civilian, totalling some 50,000 souls.[58] In July 1864, as Union forces prepared to take Atlanta from the Confederates, the commander of the Military Division of the Mississippi, General William Sherman, declared: 'If the people raise a howl against any barbarity or cruelty, I will answer that war is war and not popularity-seeking.'[59] That said, Sherman did seek to ensure the evacuation of Atlanta of all non-military citizens before launching the final assault.

A few years after the publication of the Lieber Code, the preamble to the 1868 Saint Petersburg Declaration,[60] one of the first modern treaties of the law of war (called today the law of armed conflict or, more popularly, IHL), declared that 'the only legitimate

---

54 See, for example, A. Gorur and N. Carstensen, 'Community Self-Protection', chapter 19 in Willmot et al., *Protection of Civilians*, pp. 409–27.

55 See, for example, M. Schulzke, *Just War Theory and Civilian Casualties: Protecting the Victims of War*, 1st ed., Cambridge University Press, Cambridge, 2017. See also M. Walzer, *Just and Unjust Wars: A Moral Argument with Historical Illustrations*, 1st ed., Basic Books, New York, 1992.

56 Art. 21, Instructions for the Government of Armies of the United States in the Field, General Order No 100 (hereafter, 1863 Lieber Code), promulgated by the US Department of War on 24 April 1863.

57 Art. 22, 1863 Lieber Code.

58 R. Coker, 'Historian Revises Estimate of Civil War Dead', *Discover-e*, Binghamton, 21 September 2011, at: http://bit.ly/2XaZvZL.

59 Cited in S. Foote, *The Civil War: A Narrative*, Vol. III, 1986 ed., Vintage Books, New York, p. 602.

60 Declaration Renouncing the Use, in Time of War, of Explosive Projectiles Under 400 Grammes Weight; adopted at St Petersburg, 11 December 1868; entered into force, 4 September 1900.

object which States should endeavour to accomplish during war is to weaken the military forces of the enemy'. While the term 'civilian' is not employed in the Declaration, the notion of civilian immunity from attack was clearly being espoused. It would be specifically reflected in treaty law a century later in the basic IHL rule of distinction, which requires that, in their military operations, parties to an armed conflict target only military objectives (military personnel or *materiel*) and not civilians or civilian objects.[61]

While the 1949 Geneva Convention IV sets out rules for the protection of civilians in the power of foreign forces, it does not specifically regulate civilian protection during the conduct of hostilities (the IHL term for combat). Yet this was already a matter of international legal concern prior to the outbreak of World War II in 1939. Thus, British Prime Minister Neville Chamberlain made a speech in the UK Parliament declaring that it was 'against international law' to bomb civilians and to make 'deliberate attacks' on the civilian population.[62] In 1938, he instructed Bomber Command in the following terms, were Britain to be engaged in war with Germany:

1. It is against international law to bomb civilians as such and to make deliberate attacks on the civilian population.
2. Targets which are aimed at from the air must be legitimate military objectives and must be capable of identification.
3. Reasonable care must be taken in attacking those military objectives so that by carelessness a civilian population in the neighbourhood is not bombed.[63]

A year earlier, the US Department of State had condemned the Japanese bombing of Chinese cities, stating that: 'Any general bombing of an extensive area wherein there resides a large population engaged in peaceful pursuits is unwarranted and contrary to the principles of law and humanity.' US President Franklin D. Roosevelt called civilian bombing 'inhuman barbarism'.[64] Yet, parties to the myriad of armed conflicts that made up World War II would little practice what they preached.

The 1945 Charter of the United Nations had pledged, at the very outset, 'to save succeeding generations from the scourge of war'.[65] But civilians oftentimes did not receive appropriate protection thereafter. In his outstanding 'moral history' of the twentieth century, entitled *Humanity*, Jonathon Glover observes that technology 'has made a difference', with the decisions of a few people potentially meaning 'horror and death for hundreds of thousands, even millions, of other people'.[66] Civilians were bombed, shot,

---

[61] Art. 45, 1977 Additional Protocol I.

[62] D. Siebert, 'British Bombing Strategy in World War Two', *BBC*, last updated 17 February 2011, at: bbc.in/2XaM100.

[63] See S. A. Garrett, 'The Bombing Campaign: The RAF', chapter 1 in I. Primoratz (ed.), *Terror from the Sky: The Bombing of German Cities in World War II*, Berghahn Books, Oxford and New York, 2014, pp. 19–38.

[64] Ibid.

[65] Charter of the United Nations; signed at San Francisco, 26 June 1945; entered into force, 24 October 1945 (hereinafter, UN Charter), first preambular para.

[66] J. Glover, *Humanity: A Moral History of the Twentieth Century*, 2nd ed., Yale University Press, New Haven and London, 2012, p. 3.

stabbed, strangled, hanged, and beaten in countless episodes of violence across every continent in each and every year that followed the end of World War II.

A few egregious examples serve to illustrate the point. In 1971, genocide was wrought by Pakistan's armed forces on civilians in East Bengal[67] (later to become independent Bangladesh). Up to two million men, women, and children died in Cambodia (Kampuchea) under the Khmer Rouge in 1975–9.[68] A further one to two million civilians died in Vietnam in the course of the Vietnam War,[69] with tens of thousands of others bombed and killed or seriously injured in neighbouring Laos.[70] Massacres of indigenous communities in Guatemala by the army in the 1980s and early 1990s are also widely characterised as acts of genocide.[71]

The horrors of the Vietnam War, in particular, led to the adoption of the two 1977 Additional Protocols to the Geneva Conventions with a view to better protect civilians in situations of armed conflict. Two decades later, the genocide in Rwanda in 1994 and a year later in Bosnia and Herzegovina would prove further watersheds in the level of international attention paid to the protection of civilians, particularly by the UN Security Council. Dramatic failures by the UN system in these two countries would lead to a sea change in the rhetoric of protection and increased efforts at the policy and practical level.

In 1994, the international community – and the UN peacekeeping force present on the scene – largely watched from the sidelines as genocide was wrought by Hutus on Tutsis across Rwanda. Hundreds of thousands were massacred. A year later, in eastern Bosnia and Herzegovina, Bosnian Serb forces summarily executed some 8,000 Bosnian Muslim men and boys after storming the designated 'safe area' of Srebrenica in July 1995.[72] The UN Secretary-General's report on Srebrenica concluded that the 'cardinal lesson' from the fall of the enclave was that 'a deliberate and systematic attempt to terrorize, expel or murder an entire people must be met decisively with all necessary means'.[73] It went on: 'Through error, misjudgement and an inability to recognize the scope of the evil confronting us, we failed to do our part to help save the people of Srebrenica from the Serb campaign of mass murder. No one regrets more than we the opportunities for achieving peace and justice that were missed.'[74]

[67] See, for example, S. Ganguly, 'Pakistan's Forgotten Genocide: A Review Essay', *International Security*, Vol. 39, No. 2 (2014), at: http://bit.ly/2KyfsVo.
[68] BBC, 'Khmer Rouge: Cambodia's Years of Brutality', 16 November 2018, at: http://bbc.in/3bYbJvD.
[69] BBC, 'Was My Lai Just One of Many Massacres in Vietnam War?' 28 August 2013, at: http://bbc.in/3c6sJQe. Though see also for a markedly lower estimate C. Hirschman, S. Preston, and V. Manh Loi, 'Vietnamese Casualties During the American War: A New Estimate', *Population and Development Review*, Vol. 21, No. 4 (December 1995), 783–812.
[70] BBC, 'Laos: Barack Obama Regrets "Biggest Bombing in History"', 7 September 2016, at: http://bbc.in/3bXNNsd.
[71] See, for example, A. Oettler, 'Guatemala in the 1980s: A Genocide Turned into Ethnocide?', German Institute for Global and Area Studies (GIGA), 2006, at: https://bit.ly/391wPHv; and Holocaust Museum Houston, 'Genocide in Guatemala', at: http://bit.ly/35Xek5f.
[72] See, for example, O. Bowcott and J. Borger, 'Ratko Mladić Convicted of War Crimes and Genocide at UN Tribunal', *Guardian*, 22 November 2017, at: http://bit.ly/2Kjrn7E.
[73] 'The Fall of Srebrenica', Report of the Secretary-General pursuant to General Assembly 53/35, UN doc. A/54/549, 15 November 1999, para. 502.
[74] Ibid., para. 503.

Also published in the final year of the millennium was the report of the independent inquiry on the United Nation's conduct in Rwanda. It stated that the 'failure by the United Nations to prevent, and subsequently, to stop the genocide in Rwanda was a failure by the United Nations systems as a whole'. It ascribed this 'fundamental failure' to a 'lack of resources and political commitment devoted to developments in Rwanda and to the United Nations presence there'. There was also, though, a sustained attempt to spread the blame, citing a 'persistent lack of political will by Member States to act, or to act with enough assertiveness'.[75]

The first UN Secretary-General's report bringing the protection of civilians to the attention of the UN Security Council was delivered by Kofi Annan in September 1999. Urging the use of force 'as a mechanism of last resort', he stated as follows:

> Protection mechanisms rely first and foremost on the willingness of State and non-State actors to comply with applicable international law. In situations where the parties to the conflict commit systematic and widespread breaches of international humanitarian and human rights law, causing threats of genocide, crimes against humanity and war crimes, the Security Council should be prepared to intervene under Chapter VII of the Charter. The use of coercive action should be seen as a mechanism of last resort to protect the civilian population from immediate threats to their lives and to ensure the safe passage of humanitarian convoys.[76]

Secretary-General Annan was effectively calling for threats and violence to civilians to be considered as a breach of international peace and security in certain circumstances, thereby paving the road for a significant ramping-up in Security Council practice. The commonly accepted barrier for UN-authorised or instigated intervention for humanitarian reasons was about to be lowered. Thereby, the protection of civilians would also start its ascension to become a standard task for UN peacekeepers as well as being embraced by regional organisations around the globe.

UN Security Council Resolution 1265, adopted on 17 September 1999, represented the first time the Council had dedicated a resolution to the protection of civilians as a subject of global importance to international peace and security in its own right. An ever more important normative development occurred the following month when the Council adopted Resolution 1270, in which it attributed an explicit mandate to its peacekeeping mission in Sierra Leone to protect civilians 'under imminent threat of physical violence', with concomitant powers to use force under Chapter VII of the UN Charter.[77] The mandate was limited in scope, but a significant precedent – dangerous to some,[78] but long overdue to others – had been set. The protection of civilians has since become

---

[75] Report of the Independent Inquiry into the actions of the United Nations during the 1994 genocide in Rwanda, UN doc. S/1999/1257, December 1999, p. 3.

[76] Report of the Secretary-General to the Security Council on the Protection of Civilians in Armed Conflict, UN doc. S/1999/957, 8 September 1999, para. 67.

[77] UN Security Council Resolution 1270 (1999), adopted unanimously on 22 October 1999, para. 14 [added emphasis].

[78] Kofi Annan, for instance, is said to have expressed grave concern about the mandate to protect civilians. E. Paddon Rhoads, *Taking Sides in Peacekeeping, Impartiality and the Future of the United Nations*, Oxford University Press, Oxford, 2016, p. 106. See also p. 129.

a mainstay for military operations, both in warfare and in peacekeeping, leading to new terms to describe UN peacekeeping, such as 'active impartiality' or 'robust' peacekeeping.[79]

Civilians continue to suffer, though. By June 2019, according to the Office of the UN High Commissioner for Refugees (UNHCR), an unprecedented seventy million people around the world had been forced from home by conflict and persecution. Among them were nearly twenty-six million refugees seeking sanctuary outside their own countries, more than half of whom were children.[80] A study by the International Institute for Strategic Studies (IISS) estimated that, in 2014 alone, 80,000 people were killed because of armed conflict, the largest number since World War II.[81] Wars in Syria and Yemen are notable conflicts that continue to be humanitarian disasters. The war between Russia and Ukraine that started on 24 February 2022, is also causing tremendous suffering and has provoked massive displacement of civilians.

'Never again!' is a regular refrain after acts of genocide are perpetrated. Yet, the 'crime of crimes' has continued in the twenty-first century CE. In Darfur, the Sudanese government employed Arab militia to murder and terrorise Black Africans across the region beginning in 2003.[82] The United States asserted the following year that genocide had occurred while the International Criminal Court indicted the president and two senior officials in the Sudanese government for genocide.[83] The Myanmar army is held to have engaged in genocide against the Muslim Rohingya since 2016;[84] the issue is being adjudicated before the International Court of Justice.[85] Most recently, in January 2021, the outgoing US Secretary of State claimed that China was engaged in genocide against Muslim Uighurs.[86]

In conclusion, the protection of civilians has become a well-established concept in modern international law and policy. In practice, however, its interpretation, application, and implementation remain challenging.[87] Indeed, as with any concept, the devil lies in the details. The following chapters address these details.

---

[79] See ibid., pp. 1, 5.
[80] UNHCR, 'Figures at a Glance', at: http://bit.ly/2MwHZsL.
[81] N. Redman and N. Inkster, *The IISS Armed Conflict Survey, 2015*, Routledge, New York, 2015.
[82] 'Darfur Genocide', World Without Genocide, at: http://bit.ly/3sJTqQL.
[83] ICC, 'Darfur, Sudan: Situation in Darfur, Sudan', ICC-02/05, at: http://bit.ly/3p3hlZm.
[84] Report of the detailed findings of the Independent International Fact-Finding Mission on Myanmar, UN doc. A/HRC/39/CRP.2, 17 September 2018, at: https://bit.ly/39X03tE, especially paras. 1390–433.
[85] International Court of Justice (ICJ), *Application of the Convention on the Prevention and Punishment of the Crime of Genocide (The Gambia v. Myanmar)*, at: http://bit.ly/2XWYrHy.
[86] See, for example, K. Manson, 'Pompeo Says China's Repression of Uighurs is "Genocide"', *Financial Times*, 20 January 2021, at: http://on.ft.com/2M7AjiW.
[87] For further analysis and discussion of related practice see, for example, H. Slim, *Killing Civilians: Method, Madness and Morality in War*, 1st ed., Oxford University Press, Oxford, 2007; J. Tirman, *The Death of Others: The Fate of Civilians in America's Wars*, 1st ed., Oxford University Press, Oxford, 2012; and B. Renz and S. Scheipers, 'Discrimination in Aerial Bombing: An Enduring Norm in the 20th Century?', *Defense Studies* Vol. 12, No. 1 (2012), 17–43.

PART I

The International Legal Framework

Part I identifies and explains the international legal rules that protect civilians against violence. These rules exist in a range of branches of international law: *jus ad bellum* (the law on inter-State use of force); international humanitarian law (which governs the use of force in situations of armed conflict); international human rights law (which protects all civilians from unlawful violence at all times); refugee law (which protects civilians fleeing persecution); and disarmament law (which prohibits the possession and use of certain weapons in all circumstances). International criminal law requires and governs the prosecution of individuals for the commission of international crimes. These branches of law are described in Chapters 1 through 6. Chapter 7 concerns the transversal prohibition of sexual violence in international law.

Particular protection is also afforded under international law to certain groups of civilians, as successive chapters recount. These groups include women, children, persons with disabilities, older persons, the internally displaced, medical and humanitarian personnel, and lesbian, gay, bisexual, transgender, and intersex (LGBTI) persons. Their protection is described in Chapters 8 through 14. Appendix 1 offers a primer of international law on which the existing rules are based. Appendix 2 describes in greater detail the classification of armed conflicts under international humanitarian law.

1

Jus ad Bellum and the Protection of Civilians

1.1 INTRODUCTION

Civilians can be protected from violence by avoiding wars. The branch of international law that governs and restricts use of force between States is widely known by its Latin moniker, *jus ad bellum*.[1] This chapter delineates the content and contours of the general prohibition on inter-State use of force, which was established by the Charter of the United Nations (UN) in 1945.[2] *Jus ad bellum* is not concerned with the use of force by a State within its own borders, for instance to quell an insurrection, unless it is targeted at a foreign force or leader on its territory. The legality of action to counter an insurgency is the preserve of the various branches of international law discussed in the following chapters.

Today, two main exceptions temper the general prohibition on inter-State use of force: when the UN Security Council authorises forcible measures by States to maintain or restore 'international peace and security' in a given context or when a State acts in self-defence against an armed attack. Otherwise, sovereignty and the associated legal principle of non-intervention[3] ordinarily act to prevent use of force by foreign States to protect civilians. This is so where force is applied without the consent of the territorial State.[4]

But, as this chapter describes, the UN Security Council's understanding of what constitutes a threat to international peace and security has broadened materially in

---

[1] The term *jus contra bellum* or 'law against war' is also sometimes used. See, for example, O. Corten, *The Law Against War*, Hart, Oxford, 2010; R. Kolb, *Ius contra bellum: Le droit international relatif au maintien de la paix*, 2nd ed., Helbing Lichtenhahn/Bruylant, Basel/Brussels, 2009.

[2] Charter of the United Nations; signed at San Francisco, 26 June 1945; entered into force, 24 October 1945 (hereafter, UN Charter). In addition to the 49 original States Parties to the Charter (see: http://bit.ly/325zqud), 144 States have subsequently been admitted in accordance with Article 4 of the Charter (see: http://bit.ly/2M8JKvL). Thus, as of 1 April 2022, there were 193 UN Member States.

[3] Also referred to as non-interference. International Court of Justice (ICJ), *Case Concerning Military and Paramilitary Activities in and against Nicaragua (Nicaragua v. United States of America)*, Judgment (Merits), 27 June 1986 (hereinafter, ICJ, *Nicaragua* judgment), para. 202; see also Art. 18, Charter of the Organization of American States; signed at Bogotá, 30 April 1948; entered into force, 13 December 1951; and Art. 4(g), Constitutive Act of the African Union; adopted at Lomé, 7 November 2000; entered into force, 26 May 2001; Art. 2(2)(e), Charter of the Association of Southeast Asian Nations; adopted in Singapore, 20 November 2007; entered into force, 15 December 2008.

[4] See on this issue, for example, S. Casey-Maslen, *Jus ad Bellum: The Law on Inter-State Use of Force*, Hart, Oxford, 2020, chapter 2.

recent decades to encompass conflicts and armed violence within a State,[5] in particular
where widespread attacks are being perpetrated against civilians.[6] In the case of forcible
action to protect civilians abroad from mass atrocities, some States argue that, in certain
circumstances, they have the unilateral right to intervene in foreign countries for
humanitarian purposes. Although States may use force to protect their own civilians
after an armed attack against them, when exercising their right of self-defence, States
generally do not use the term protection of civilians (PoC) to describe their actions.

1.2 THE GENERAL PROHIBITION ON INTER-STATE USE OF FORCE

The UN Charter does not refer specifically to civilians. That does not, however, mean
that the protection of civilians was not a concern for the drafters. As the Introduction to
this book recalled, the Charter's preamble begins with the express motivation and
determination 'to save succeeding generations from the scourge of war'.[7] Reflecting
the 'untold sorrow' inflicted on civilians and soldiers alike by World Wars I and II,
a primary aim of the Charter was thus to prevent further recourse to warfare as a means
of resolving disputes. The United Nations would endeavour to achieve this aim by
instituting a legal prohibition on the use of force between States and by obligating
a corresponding duty upon States to resolve international disputes by peaceful means.
The cornerstone of *jus ad bellum* is the general prohibition on the use of force by one
State against another. This includes instances when force is used by one State on
another's territory without the territorial State's valid consent. This is so even if the latter
State does not respond to that use of force with military action of its own. The general
rule is set out in Article 2(4) of the UN Charter: 'All Members shall refrain in their
international relations from the threat or use of force against the territorial integrity or
political independence of any State, or in any other manner inconsistent with the
Purposes of the United Nations.' While the concept of force is not explicitly defined
in the UN Charter, the drafters deliberately chose to employ the term 'use of force' in
Article 2(4), which is wider than the notion of 'war'.[8] The prohibition is, though, limited
to curbing a use of *armed* force. Accordingly, it does not apply to economic sanctions
imposed against another State, irrespective of whether or not those sanctions are licit.
Armed force may emanate from land, sea, air, outer space, or cyberspace. While it is
applied most obviously through bullets, bombs, and missiles, non-kinetic means of
warfare, such as chemical or biological weapons, electromagnetic weapons, or even
offensive cyber operations of significant vigour could also amount to a use of force under
international law.[9]

---

[5] H. Willmot, 'The Evolution of the UN Collective Security System', in H. Willmot, R. Mamiya, S. Sheeran,
and M. Weller (eds.), *Protection of Civilians*, 1st ed., Oxford University Press, Oxford, 2016, p. 123.
[6] Ibid., p. 124.
[7] UN Charter, first preambular para.
[8] C. Gray, *International Law and the Use of Force*, 4th ed., Oxford University Press, Oxford, 2018, p. 9. See
generally A. Clapham, *War*, Oxford University Press, Oxford, 2021.
[9] Casey-Maslen, *Jus ad Bellum: The Law on Inter-State Use of Force*, p. 22.

While not every forcible action by a State amounts to a violation of Article 2(4) of the UN Charter,[10] the minimum threshold is very low. The prohibition certainly encompasses 'all physical force which surpasses a minimum threshold of intensity'.[11] Thus, for example, bombardment of the territory of another State ordinarily violates the international legal prohibition on the use of force. Suggestions, occasionally made, that 'targeted' or localised bombardments are not encapsulated[12] are legally incorrect.[13] It is also sometimes suggested that attacks against non-State actors on the territory of another State do not fall within the general prohibition on inter-State use of force. This claim is also wrong, as such a use of force violates both the territorial integrity of the territorial State and its political independence.

1.3 UN SECURITY COUNCIL 'AUTHORISATION' OF MILITARY ACTION

The first exception to the general prohibition on the inter-State use of force under *jus ad bellum* is when the UN Security Council authorises to execute such action according to Chapter VII of the UN Charter. Under Chapter V of the Charter, UN Member States confer on the Security Council 'primary responsibility for the maintenance of international peace and security', and 'agree that in carrying out its duties under this responsibility the Security Council acts on their behalf'.[14] Chapter VII, which covers Articles 39 to 51 of the Charter, concerns 'Action with respect to threats to the peace, breaches of the peace, and acts of aggression.' Invariably, such threats, breaches, or acts will result in a need to take action – of a legal, political, social, and economic nature, as well as potentially military – in order to protect civilians.

The UN Charter had originally foreseen that military forces would be placed at the Security Council's disposal, albeit under the strategic direction of the Military Staff Committee.[15] This never occurred, in large part due to the divisions between States during the Cold War. The UN Charter had empowered the council itself 'to take such action by air, sea, or land forces as may be necessary to maintain or restore international peace and

---

[10] *Independent International Fact-Finding Mission on the Conflict in Georgia*, Report, Vol. II, p. 242; T. Ruys, 'The Meaning of "Force" and the Boundaries of the *Jus ad Bellum*: Are "Minimal" Uses of Force Excluded from UN Charter Article 2(4)?', *The American Journal of International Law*, Vol. 108, No. 2 (April 2014), 159–210.

[11] *Independent International Fact-Finding Mission on the Conflict in Georgia*, Report, Vol. II, September 2009, p. 242.

[12] In this regard, one commentator had proposed that the bombing by Israel in 1981 of an Iraqi nuclear research centre at Osirak did not affect Iraq's territorial integrity because no portion of Iraq's territory 'was taken away from Iraq by the bombardment', only a 'use of the territory – to construct a nuclear reactor – was interfered with'. A. D'Amato, 'Israel's Airstrike upon the Iraqi Nuclear Reactor', *American Journal of International Law*, Vol. 77, No. 3 (July 1983), 584–8, at: http://bit.ly/2CIfXFl, at p. 585.

[13] O. Schachter, 'The Legality of Pro-Democratic Invasion', *American Journal of International Law*, Vol. 78, No. 3 (July 1984), 645–50. Indeed, in its Resolution 487, adopted unanimously on 19 June 1981, the UN Security Council strongly condemned 'the military attack by Israel in clear violation of the Charter of the United Nations and the norms of international conduct'. UN Security Council Resolution 487, adopted by unanimous vote in favour on 19 June 1981, operative para. 2.

[14] Art. 24(1), UN Charter.

[15] Art. 47, UN Charter. See, for example, Willmot, 'The Evolution of the UN Collective Security System', p. 119.

security'.[16] In 1990, however, with the Cold War over, when the Security Council considered how to react to Iraq's invasion of Kuwait, it effectively interpreted the Charter as allowing it to 'authorise' Member States to take military action instead. Thus, acting under Chapter VII of the Charter, Resolution 678 authorised Member States co-operating with the government of Kuwait, to use 'all necessary means' to 'restore international peace and security in the area'.[17] The formulation *all necessary means* 'has become the common euphemism for employing force',[18] although also used on occasion has been the phrase 'all necessary measures'.[19] This was the case with respect to the use of force in Libya, which the Security Council authorised in 2011 to 'protect civilians and civilian populated areas under threat of attack in the Libyan Arab Jamahiriya, including Benghazi'.[20]

1.4 UN PEACEKEEPING OPERATIONS AND THE PROTECTION OF CIVILIANS

Although not necessarily always operating under a Chapter VII mandate, the UN has established numerous peacekeeping operations which have ultimately, if not initially, included the goal to protect civilians. Traditional UN peacekeeping operations, which are established with the consent of the parties to a dispute, operate under Chapter VI of the UN Charter. Such operations were typically limited in their ability to use force to instances where they were acting in self-defence.[21] With respect to the first armed UN peacekeeping force – the UN Emergency Force I (UNEF I), established in 1957, exceptionally, by the UN General Assembly[22] to secure and supervise the cessation of hostilities over the Suez Canal – the UN Secretary-General reported to the General Assembly that 'UNEF troops have a right to fire in self-defence. They are never to take the initiative in the use of arms, but may respond with fire to an armed attack upon them.'[23]

---

[16] Art. 42, UN Charter.

[17] UN Security Council Resolution 678, adopted on 29 November 1990 by twelve votes in favour (Canada, Colombia, Côte d'Ivoire, Ethiopia, Finland, France, Malaysia, Romania, the Soviet Union (now the Russian Federation, as successor State), the United Kingdom, the United States, and Zaire (now the Democratic Republic of Congo)) to two against (Cuba and Yemen) and one abstention (China), operative para. 2.

[18] Y. Dinstein, *War, Aggression and Self-Defence*, 6th ed., Cambridge University Press, Cambridge, 2017, para. 851.

[19] Indeed, Niels Blokker argues that this phrase even became the preferred formulation to authorise use of force between 2000 and 2012. N. Blokker, 'Outsourcing the Use of Force: Towards More Security Council Control of Authorized Operations?', chapter 9 in M. Weller (ed.), *The Oxford Handbook of the Use of Force in International Law*, Oxford University Press, London, 202–26, at p. 213.

[20] UN Security Council Resolution 1973, adopted on 17 March 2011 by ten votes in favour to nil, with five abstentions (Brazil, China, Germany, India, and Russia), operative para. 4.

[21] Willmot, 'The Evolution of the UN Collective Security System', p. 126.

[22] UN General Assembly Resolution 998 (ES – 1), adopted on 2 November 1956 by fifty-seven votes in favour to nil, with nineteen abstentions (Albania, Australia, Austria, Bulgaria, Byelorussian SSR, Czechoslovakia, Egypt, France, Hungary, Israel, Laos, New Zealand, Poland, Portugal, Romania, Ukrainian SSR, Union of South Africa, United Kingdom, and USSR). See, for example, Willmot, 'The Evolution of the UN Collective Security System', p. 121.

[23] Summary study of the experience derived from the establishment and operation of the force: Report of the Secretary-General, UN doc. A/3943, 9 October 1958, at: http://bit.ly/2MYvlBT, para. 70. See also B. Oswald,

By the time armed conflicts were raging in Bosnia and Herzegovina in the early 1990s, the consensual view of peacekeeping and limited scope for use of force was under significant political pressure. Following the UN Secretary-General's 1993 report, *An Agenda for Peace*, the President of the Security Council issued a statement in which he reaffirmed that the Council *may* authorise peacekeepers to use all means necessary 'to carry out their mandate'; this would be in addition to 'the inherent right of United Nations forces to take appropriate measures for self-defence'.[24] But proactive measures, in particular without the consent of the territorial State, would not be lawful. Thus, in early 1994, when the UN military force commander in Rwanda, Roméo Dallaire, sought permission to seize arms caches stashed in preparation for the genocide, the request would be denied on the basis that such action would be outside the Chapter VI mandate.[25] The extermination of hundreds of thousands of Tutsi and moderate Hutu civilians would follow.

In its seminal Resolution 1265 (1999) on the protection of civilians,[26] the Security Council expressed its 'willingness to consider how peacekeeping mandates might better address the negative impact of armed conflict on civilians'.[27] A month later, in Resolution 1270 on Sierra Leone, the Council, overtly acting under Chapter VII of the Charter, decided that, in the discharge of its mandate, UNOMSIL (the UN Observer Mission in Sierra Leone) was authorised to take the necessary action 'to afford protection to civilians under imminent threat of physical violence'.[28] The Rubicon had been crossed and a significant precedent set.[29]

At the same time, the UN acknowledges the challenges it typically faces in protecting civilians. These include operating 'in harsh conditions and in difficult terrain, with limited resources'; 'unrealistic' expectations that UN peacekeepers will be able to protect all civilians at all times; and the 'dynamic nature' of the places in which peacekeepers operate, meaning that the security situation can change very quickly.[30] In outlining the principles of UN peacekeeping, the UN cautions that:

> A UN peacekeeping operation should only use force as a measure of last resort. It should always be calibrated in a precise, proportional and appropriate manner, within the principle of the minimum force necessary to achieve the desired effect, while sustaining consent for the mission and its mandate. The use of force by a UN peacekeeping operation always has political implications and can often give rise to unforeseen circumstances.[31]

'Soldier Self-Defense Symposium: The Evolution of the UN Doctrine of Self-Defence in UN Peacekeeping', *Opinio Juris*, 1 May 2019, at: http://bit.ly/2pxfnGG.

[24] Statement of the President of the UN Security Council, UN doc. S/PV.3225, 28 May 1993, p. 3.

[25] See, for example, K. Shiffman, 'As Genocide Raged, General's Pleas for Help Ignored', CNN, 10 December 2008, at: http://cnn.it/2MSFqQJ. See also 'A Good Man in Hell: General Roméo Dallaire and the Rwanda Genocide', United States Holocaust Memorial Museum, 12 June 2002, at: http://bit.ly/2VTMZum.

[26] UN Security Council Resolution 1265 (1999), adopted by unanimous vote in favour on 17 September 1999.

[27] Ibid., operative para. 11.

[28] UN Security Council Resolution 1270 (1999), adopted by unanimous vote in favour on 22 October 1999, operative para. 14.

[29] Willmot, 'The Evolution of the UN Collective Security System', p. 129.

[30] UN, 'Protection of Civilians Mandate', undated but accessed 1 October 2021, at: http://bit.ly/2Bqhdf2.

[31] UN, 'Principles of Peacekeeping', undated but accessed 1 October 2021, at: http://bit.ly/2VTa7t6.

Indeed, while the tendency until recently has been towards more proactive and forceful implementation of mission objectives, it is likely that the trend will be reversed towards less use of force. Overall, UN peacekeeping has traditionally been and remains a major conceptual driver of the protection of civilians,[32] as is further analysed in Chapter 15 on the United Nations and the protection of civilians.

1.4.1 Responsibility to Protect and the Protection of Civilians

Distinct from UN peacekeeping, the UN Security Council may authorise the use of force specifically to protect civilians from mass atrocities under the doctrine of 'responsibility to protect' (R2P). In the 1990s, Dr Francis Deng and others began to recast the notion of sovereignty in international discourse in reaction to the failures by the international community to prevent the genocide against the Tutsi in Rwanda in April–July 1994[33] and then the genocide against Bosnian Muslims in the aftermath of the fall of Srebrenica in Bosnia and Herzegovina in July 1995.[34] They called for the notion of sovereignty to be viewed through a new lens: not as an impenetrable barrier to intervention but rather as a form of *responsibility* according to which the State is 'accountable to both domestic and external constituencies'.[35] The doctrine of R2P is a noted result of this reformulation.[36]

In this regard, in 2001, the International Commission on Intervention and State Sovereignty, an initiative formed the year before with the support of Canada, released its report entitled *The Responsibility to Protect*. The report advocated a re-characterisation of sovereignty as 'control' to sovereignty 'as responsibility in both internal functions and external duties'.[37] Then in 2004, the UN High-Level Panel on Threats, Challenges and Change issued *A More Secure World, Our Shared Responsibility*, a report that further endorsed the notion of R2P. It stated:

> Collective security institutions have proved particularly poor at meeting the challenge posed by large-scale, gross human rights abuses and genocide. This is a normative challenge to the United Nations: the concept of State and international responsibility to protect civilians from the effects of war and human rights abuses has yet to truly overcome the tension between the competing claims of sovereign inviolability and the right to intervene.[38]

---

[32] For a history of the protection of civilians in UN peacekeeping, see C. Foley, *UN Peacekeeping Operations and the Protection of Civilians: Saving Succeeding Generations*, 1st ed., Cambridge University Press, Cambridge, 2017.

[33] International Criminal Tribunal for Rwanda (ICTR), *Prosecutor v. Akayesu*, Judgment (Trial Chamber) (Case No. ICTR-96-4-T), 2 September 1998, para. 126.

[34] International Tribunal for the Prosecution of Persons Responsible for Serious Violations of International Humanitarian Law Committed in the Territory of Former Yugoslavia since 1991 (ICTY), *Prosecutor v. Krstić*, Judgment (Trial Chamber) (Case No. IT-98-33-T), 2 August 2001, para. 598.

[35] See, for example, F. M. Deng, S. Kimaro, T. Lyons, D. Rothchild, and I. W. Zartman, *Sovereignty as Responsibility: Conflict Management in Africa*, Brookings Institution Press, Washington, DC, 1 June 1996.

[36] See, for example, F. M. Deng, 'From "Sovereignty as Responsibility" to the "Responsibility to Protect"', *Global Responsibility to Protect*, Vol. 2, No. 4 (1 January 2010), available at: http://brook.gs/32yA4AR.

[37] International Commission on Intervention and State Sovereignty (ICISS), *The Responsibility to Protect*, Report, 2001, para. 2.14.

[38] *A More Secure World: Our Shared Responsibility*, Report of the High-Level Panel on Threats, Challenges and Change, UN, New York, 2004, para. 36.

As unanimously endorsed by the UN General Assembly in 2005,[39] the responsibility 'to protect populations from genocide, war crimes, ethnic cleansing and crimes against humanity' sees the use of force as a possible means to protect civilians, although it is envisaged only as a last resort and even then it will solely be lawful when exercised 'through the Security Council'. This means that if the Security Council is blocked, as it was in the case of Syria for example, the use of force other than in lawful self-defence remains illegal under international law. In its Resolution 1674 (2006) on PoC in armed conflict, the UN Security Council reaffirmed the provisions of paragraphs 138 and 139 of the World Summit Outcome document regarding the responsibility to protect populations from these crimes.[40]

While sometimes used or interpreted to mean the same thing, the R2P doctrine and the concept of protection of civilians are not synonyms. Indeed, in his report to the Security Council in 2012 on the protection of civilians, the UN Secretary-General expressed his concern about 'the continuing and inaccurate conflation' of the two concepts, noting that while they 'share some common elements, particularly with regard to prevention and support to national authorities in discharging their responsibilities towards civilians, there are fundamental differences'.[41] Thus, the Secretary-General wrote:

> First, the protection of civilians is a legal concept based on international humanitarian, human rights and refugee law, while the responsibility to protect is a political concept, set out in the 2005 World Summit Outcome … Second, there are important differences in their scope. The protection of civilians relates to violations of international humanitarian and human rights law in situations of armed conflict. The responsibility to protect is limited to violations that constitute war crimes or crimes against humanity or that would be considered acts of genocide or ethnic cleansing. Crimes against humanity, genocide and ethnic cleansing may occur in situations that do not meet the threshold of armed conflict. I urge the Security Council and Member States to be mindful of these distinctions.[42]

In 2009, the UN Secretary-General had released a report on the implementation of R2P in which he suggested a three-pillar approach: (1) emphasising the protection responsibilities of the State; (2) providing international assistance and capacity building; and (3) the exercise of a timely and decisive response to prevent and halt genocide, ethnic cleansing, war crimes, and crimes against humanity.[43] Following the publication of Secretary-General Ban Ki-moon's report, a UN General Assembly debate on R2P was convened. At this debate, Member States reaffirmed the 2005 commitment and in a consensus

---

[39] UN General Assembly Resolution 60/1 ('2005 World Summit Outcome'), adopted without a vote on 16 September 2005, paras. 138 and 139.

[40] UN Security Council Resolution 1674, adopted unanimously on 28 April 2006, operative para. 4.

[41] Report of the Secretary-General on the protection of civilians in armed conflict, UN doc. S/2012/376, 22 May 2012, para. 21.

[42] Ibid.

[43] 'Implementing the Responsibility to Protect', Report of the UN Secretary-General, UN doc. A/63/677, 12 January 2009, at: http://bit.ly/2MssoMb.

resolution (63/308) 'took note' of the Secretary-General's report. It is now generally accepted that R2P does indeed contain three 'pillars':

Pillar One: Every State has the Responsibility to Protect its populations from four mass atrocity crimes: genocide, war crimes, crimes against humanity, and ethnic cleansing.

Pillar Two: The wider international community has the responsibility to encourage and assist individual States in meeting that responsibility.

Pillar Three: If a State is manifestly failing to protect its populations, the international community must be prepared to take appropriate collective action, in a timely and decisive manner, and in accordance with the UN Charter.[44]

Perhaps the first time the concept of R2P firmly underpinned a UN Security Council authorisation to use force under Pillar Three was in relation to Libya.[45] In February 2011, Resolution 1970 recalled 'the Libyan authorities' responsibility to protect its population'.[46] The Council expressed grave concern at the situation in Libya, condemning 'the violence and use of force against civilians', deploring 'the gross and systematic violation of human rights, including the repression of peaceful demonstrators', and expressing 'deep concern at the deaths of civilians'.[47] As noted above, the following month, with the situation worsening, Resolution 1373 authorised Member States to take all necessary measures 'to protect civilians and civilian populated areas under threat of attack in the Libyan Arab Jamahiriya'.[48] The Libyan intervention would prove to be controversial for two reasons. First and foremost, there was concern that the Security Council authorisation to intervene to protect civilians was used to effect regime change.[49] Second, and following on from the first, the obligation to protect civilians and civilian areas under threat of attack seemed not to be implemented when forces challenging the Libyan leader Muammar Gadhafi were alleged to be attacking civilians.[50] Writing in the *Canberra Times* in September 2011, Ramesh Thakur said: 'The jury is still out on whether international military action in Libya will promote consolidation or softening of the R2P norm. The Libyan people's

---

[44] Global Centre for the Responsibility to Protect, 'About R2P', at: http://bit.ly/2IkhtR1.

[45] Though see, in this regard, Willmot, 'The Evolution of the UN Collective Security System', p. 128.

[46] UN Security Council Resolution 1970 (2011), adopted by unanimous vote in favour on 26 February 2011, ninth preambular para.

[47] UN Security Council Resolution 1970 (2011), first and second preambular paras.

[48] UN Security Council Resolution 1973 (2011), adopted on 17 March 2011 by ten votes in favour to nil, with five abstentions (Brazil, China, Germany, India, and the Russian Federation).

[49] In 2016, the American political scientist Micah Zenko questioned the Obama administration's claim that it was just trying to protect civilians, arguing that its actions revealed that in practice it was seeking regime change. He argued:

> In truth, the Libyan intervention was about regime change from the very start. The threat posed by the Libyan regime's military and paramilitary forces to civilian-populated areas was diminished by NATO airstrikes and rebel ground movements within the first 10 days. Afterward, NATO began providing direct close-air support for advancing rebel forces by attacking government troops that were actually in retreat and had abandoned their vehicles.

M. Zenko, 'The Big Lie About the Libyan War', *Foreign Policy*, 22 March 2016, at: http://bit.ly/33LcxfQ.

[50] See, for example, M. Gobush, 'The Libya Intervention: A Just War Unjustly Disowned', *Providence*, 19 April 2017, at: http://bit.ly/2pzhABg.

euphoria and NATO's relief over the successful military campaign to remove Gaddafi is likely to temper criticisms of the manner in which NATO rode roughshod over UN authorisation to protect civilians.'[51] Amid a series of strong Russian criticisms of the burgeoning NATO action, Russia's main State-owned television station aired a critical report in April 2011 describing the military campaign as 'aggression by the great world powers against a sovereign country'.[52] The motive, it was alleged, was to secure unfettered access to Libyan oil fields.[53] The American academic, Eric Posner, was also critical. Writing in *Foreign Policy* in October 2011, he claimed that: 'Both international and US law took a drubbing alongside Qaddafi's ragtag army, casting further doubt upon the already tenuous notion that international military actions can be conducted on a legal basis.'[54] But this is perhaps to disregard the changing political climate in the Security Council. The resolution was lawfully adopted and a potential genocide was averted: this had posed a clear threat to international peace and security, in the Council's assessment.[55]

1.5 HUMANITARIAN INTERVENTION AND THE PROTECTION OF CIVILIANS

If the Council does not authorise a use of force, few States assert that a unilateral right of humanitarian intervention by force of arms exists under international law, in particular where this is necessary to protect civilians.[56] This tends to be insufficient for the existence of a corresponding customary rule, which demands a general belief among States that a particular practice is either obligated or prohibited by international law, however.[57]

Humanitarian intervention thus remains a contested issue in international law.[58] Some argue that the notion is little more than a cover for Western imperialism.[59] Others

---

[51] R. Thakur, 'Has R2P Worked in Libya?', *Canberra Times*, 19 September 2011, text available at: http://bit.ly/2pzFnB6.

[52] Cited in H. VanHoose, 'Understanding the Russian Response to the Intervention in Libya', Center for American Progress, blog post, 12 April 2011, at: http://ampr.gs/2J2nhic.

[53] See, for example, O. Nwakanma, 'Libya: NATO's War of Aggression on Sovereign African State', *Pambazuka News*, 9 June 2011, available at: http://bit.ly/32spV8J.

[54] E. Posner, 'Outside the Law: NATO Intervention in Libya Made a Mockery of International Law', *Foreign Policy*, 25 October 2011, at: http://bit.ly/2J1k1Un.

[55] According to the twenty-first preambular paragraph of Resolution 1973 (2011), the Council '*Determin[ed]*' that the situation in the Libyan Arab Jamahiriya continues to constitute a threat to international peace and security.'

[56] This is the case with Belgium and the United Kingdom.

[57] Art. 38(1)(b), 1945 Statute of the International Court of Justice. See also Annex II of this book, at p. 290.

[58] There is also no consensual definition in international law of what constitutes humanitarian intervention. One academic definition proposes that the concept means a coercive, notably military action across State borders by a State or a group of States aimed at preventing or ending widespread and grave violations of human rights of individuals other than its own citizens, without the permission of the State in whose territory force is applied. J. L. Holzgrefe, 'The Humanitarian Intervention Debate', in R. Keohane and J. Holzgrefe (eds.), *Humanitarian Intervention*, Cambridge University Press, Cambridge, 2003, p. 18; see Independent International Fact-Finding Mission on the Conflict in Georgia, Report, Vol. II, 2009, p. 283. This definition should be slightly amended to exclude cases, according to the doctrine of R2P, where the use of force is grounded in due authorisation by the UN Security Council.

[59] See, for example, R. Bush, G. Martiniello, and C. Mercer, 'Humanitarian Imperialism', *Review of African Political Economy*, Vol. 38, No. 129 (September 2011), 357–65; J. Damboeck, 'Humanitarian Interventions:

disagree. Writing in 1990, W. Michael Reisman argued that where 'free elections are internationally supervised and the results are internationally endorsed as free and fair and the people's choice is clear', those 'confirmed wishes' may not be 'ignored by a local caudillo'. He claimed that a 'jurist rooted in the late twentieth century' can 'hardly say' that 'an invasion by outside forces to remove the caudillo and install the elected government is a violation of national sovereignty'.[60]

But under international law as it stands, forcible intervention for avowedly humanitarian purposes without due UN Security Council authorisation, tends to be perceived as illegal.[61] An autonomous right in international law of humanitarian intervention was most recently claimed in April 2018 by the United Kingdom as a lawful response to chemical weapons attacks in Syria. The United Kingdom stated that it is permitted under international law, on an exceptional basis, to take measures in order to alleviate overwhelming humanitarian suffering. The legal basis for the use of force is humanitarian intervention, which requires three conditions to be met:

(i) there is convincing evidence, generally accepted by the international community as a whole, of extreme humanitarian distress on a large scale, requiring immediate and urgent relief;

(ii) it must be objectively clear that there is no practicable alternative to the use of force if lives are to be saved; and

(iii) the proposed use of force must be necessary and proportionate to the aim of relief of humanitarian suffering and must be strictly limited in time and in scope to this aim (i.e. the minimum necessary to achieve that end and for no other purpose).[62]

But while there was indeed 'intense scholarly and inter-State debate' during and since NATO's intervention against the Federal Republic of Yugoslavia over Kosovo in 1999,[63] this has 'not yet led to a development of international law in favour of unilateral humanitarian interventions without a Security Council mandate'.[64] At the time, only Belgium and the United Kingdom advanced a right of humanitarian intervention to justify the use of force in Kosovo. And as has been observed, in the later case of Libya, 'It speaks volumes about the new state of mind prevailing in NATO that … there was no dissent from the view that any humanitarian intervention in Libya, in early 2011, must be firmly embedded in Security Council authorization'.[65]

Western Imperialism or a Responsibility to Protect?: An Analysis of the Humanitarian Interventions in Darfur', *Multicultural Education & Technology Journal*, Vol. 6, No. 4 (November 2012), 287–300.

[60] W. M. Reisman, 'Sovereignty and Human Rights in Contemporary International Law', *American Journal of International Law*, Vol. 84, No. 4 (1990), 866–76, at p. 871.

[61] Brownlie, *International Law and the Use of Force by States*, p. 301; Dinstein, *War, Aggression and Self-Defence*, 6th ed., para. 207.

[62] 'Syria Action: UK Government Legal Position', Policy paper, UK Prime Minister's Office, 10 Downing Street, Published 14 April 2018, at: http://bit.ly/2LT70wG.

[63] Independent International Fact-Finding Mission on the Conflict in Georgia, Report, Vol. II, 2009, p. 284.

[64] Ibid.; and see S. Chesterman, *Just War or Just Peace? Humanitarian Intervention and International Law*, Oxford University Press, Oxford, 2001, especially p. 226.

[65] Y. Dinstein, *War, Aggression and Self-Defence*, 5th ed., Cambridge University Press, Cambridge, 2011, p. 338; see also I. Henderson, *The Use of Force and International Law*, Cambridge University Press, Cambridge, 2018, p. 161.

1.6 THE RIGHT OF SELF-DEFENCE AND THE PROTECTION
OF CIVILIANS

As noted above, the right of a State to use force in self-defence has been safeguarded under the UN Charter. Thus, Article 51 provides in part that: 'Nothing in the . . . Charter shall impair the inherent right of individual or collective self-defence if an armed attack occurs against a Member of the United Nations, until the Security Council has taken the measures necessary to maintain international peace and security.'

Where the right of self-defence exists, its lawful exercise is subject to two principled constraints: necessity and proportionality.[66] These substantive elements dictate that the use of force must be both objectively necessary in the circumstances and the force employed must be proportionate to the aim of repelling the armed attack. According to the International Court of Justice, the targets of action in self-defence must also be lawful military objectives under IHL. In its 2003 judgment in the *Oil Platforms* case, the Court stated that: 'The United States must also show that its actions were necessary and proportional to the armed attack made on it, and that the [Iranian oil] platforms were a legitimate military target open to attack in the exercise of self-defence.'[67] If the Court is correct,[68] attacking the civilian population (or civilian objects) cannot be considered a necessary or proportionate act of self-defence. This is a further international legal protection for civilians in armed conflict.

---

[66] ICJ, *Nicaragua* judgment, para. 194; approved by the Court in: *Case Concerning Oil Platforms (Islamic Republic of Iran v. United States of America)* Judgment, 6 November 2003 (hereinafter, *Oil Platforms* judgment), paras. 43 and 51.

[67] ICJ, *Oil Platforms* judgment, para. 51.

[68] Yoram Dinstein criticises the Court's holding as a misreading of the applicable law. Dinstein, *War, Aggression and Self-Defence*, 6th ed., para. 490.

Protection of Civilians under International Humanitarian Law

2.1 INTRODUCTION

International humanitarian law (IHL), also known as the law of armed conflict or the law of war, was originally not created with a view to protecting civilians, but to care for wounded soldiers. A Swiss businessman, Henry Dunant, was shocked by the sight of thousands of wounded French and Austrian troops dying in agony, uncared for, after the Battle of Solferino in northern Italy in 1859. Describing their sufferings in his 1862 book, *A Memory of Solferino*, he called for the establishment of 'relief societies for the purpose of giving care to the wounded in wartime'.[1] This led to the establishment of the International Committee for Relief to the Wounded, which in 1876 became the International Committee of the Red Cross (ICRC). Dunant sent a copy of his book to the Swiss jurist Gustave Moynier, who would be instrumental in the elaboration, in 1864, of the first Geneva Convention for the Amelioration of the Condition of the Wounded in Armies in the Field.

Four years later, Tsar Alexander II invited States to Russia to discuss outlawing, in warfare, the anti-personnel use of newly developed exploding bullets. The resultant 1868 Saint Petersburg Declaration[2] is the first modern treaty governing the use of weapons in war. While devised with a view to protecting soldiers engaged in combat – it continues to do so to this day – wording in the Declaration's preamble would also serve to inspire the legal protection that IHL would, later, bestow on civilians. The affirmation that 'the only legitimate object which States should endeavour to accomplish during war is to weaken the military forces of the enemy' is the underpinning of the fundamental principle of distinction: the duty to target, during all military operations, only combatants and not civilians.

Thirty-one years after the adoption of the Saint Petersburg Declaration, States met in The Hague to negotiate a series of further treaties on warfare. Among those governing the 'conduct of hostilities' (the IHL term for combat), the 1899 Hague Convention II and

---

[1] H. Dunant, *Un souvenir de Solférino*, Geneva, 1862.
[2] Declaration Renouncing the Use, in Time of War, of Explosive Projectiles Under 400 Grammes Weight; adopted at St Petersburg, 11 December 1868; entered into force, 4 September 1900.

especially the Regulations on Land Warfare annexed to it[3] are particularly noteworthy. These regulations refer specifically to 'civilians' as such only once, but, for the first time under an IHL treaty, they do offer significant legal protection to the civilian population. Perhaps the most important of those rules governs the actions of a State whose military forces occupy territory in another State. Articles 42–56 of the 1899 Hague Regulations (repeated in the corresponding 1907 instrument)[4] prohibited the requisitioning of food, goods, and vehicles from inhabitants 'except for the necessities of the army of occupation', and made it unlawful to involve the population 'in the obligation of taking part in military operations against their country'.[5]

The thirty-one-year period between World War I and World War II saw little concrete development in international law offering protection to civilians. States rejected the ICRC's proposal that the draft 1934 International Convention on the Condition and Protection of Civilians of enemy nationality who are on territory belonging to or occupied by a belligerent, prepared in Tokyo,[6] be applied by the belligerents during World War II even though it had not entered into force.[7] In the aftermath of the war, the Convention Relative to the Protection of Civilian Persons in Time of War[8] (1949 Geneva Convention IV) lays down protection for civilians in occupied territories and for certain foreign civilians ('aliens') who find themselves in the territory of a party to an international armed conflict.

Part II of the 1949 Geneva Convention IV does offer 'general protection' to populations against 'certain consequences of war', but this protection is quite limited because it does not regulate the fighting ('conduct of hostilities').[9] Nonetheless, in a remarkable innovation for international law at the time, Article 3 of the 1949 Geneva Convention IV[10] refers to and regulates action in *non-international* armed conflict, meaning a conflict between a State and an armed group or between two non-State armed groups. Previously, such internal strife had been considered a purely domestic affair, beyond the reach of

---

3 Convention (II) with Respect to the Laws and Customs of War on Land and Its Annex: Regulations Concerning the Laws and Customs of War on Land; adopted at The Hague, 29 July 1899; entered into force, 4 September 1900.

4 The Hague Convention II was reviewed in 1907, and the result of negotiations was the adoption of the Hague Convention IV with the annexed Regulations on Land Warfare: Convention (IV) respecting the Laws and Customs of War on Land and its annex: Regulations concerning the Laws and Customs of War on Land; adopted at The Hague, 18 October 1907; entered into force, 26 January 1910. Little changed substantively compared with its 1899 antecedent.

5 Art. 52, 1899 Regulations Concerning the Laws and Customs of War on Land.

6 ICRC, 'Draft International Convention on the Condition and Protection of Civilians of enemy nationality who are on territory belonging to or occupied by a belligerent. Tokyo, 1934', at: http://bit.ly/2NpYS9i.

7 Ibid.

8 Convention (IV) relative to the Protection of Civilian Persons in Time of War; adopted at Geneva, 12 August 1949; entered into force, 21 October 1950.

9 A draft Convention for the Protection of Civilian Populations Against New Engines of War, which concerned the protection of civilians during the conduct of hostilities, was prepared by a committee of the International Law Association in 1938 but did not became a treaty. See, for example: http://bit.ly/2ZgaPov.

10 This provision is generally referred to as 'Common Article 3' because identical text is included as Article 3 in each of the four 1949 Geneva Conventions.

international law. And while this 'Convention in miniature' as Article 3 has been termed[11] does not explicitly protect civilians, its reference to 'persons taking no active part in the hostilities' certainly protects all civilians unless and for such time as they *directly participate in hostilities*.

It was not until 1977, however, and the adoption of the two Additional Protocols to the four 1949 Geneva Conventions that detailed, broad-based protection was afforded by IHL to civilians during combat in single treaties. The Protocols govern actions of parties to armed conflict both during the conduct of hostilities and when civilians have fallen into the 'power' of the enemy (for example, because they have been detained), significantly complementing the protection afforded by the 1949 Geneva Convention IV. The 1977 Additional Protocol I[12] protects civilians during international armed conflicts, while the 1977 Additional Protocol II[13] offers (less extensive) protection in certain non-international armed conflicts. The Protocol II applies where a non-State armed group is fighting State armed forces and it controls part of the national territory.

Together with customary international law[14] (which largely reflects the rules on the conduct of hostilities in the 1977 Additional Protocol I), IHL now offers an extensive platform for the protection of civilians in all armed conflicts. Thus, in May 2019, in the United Nations (UN) Security Council debate on the protection of civilians, UN Secretary-General António Guterres declared that: 'Chief among our challenges is enhancing and ensuring respect and compliance for international humanitarian law in the conduct of hostilities.'[15]

2.2 THE PROTECTION OF CIVILIANS IN THE CONDUCT OF HOSTILITIES

When IHL applies to a situation of armed violence, the 'hostilities' between the belligerents are regulated by a series of key principles and rules. These are effectively the same whether the conflict is international (i.e. between States) or non-international (e.g. between a State and an organised armed group). Appendix 2 to this work contains a more detailed explanation of these two classifications of armed conflict.

---

[11] The phrase was used at the time by a representative of one of the negotiating States and was cited in the ICRC's 1958 commentary on the provision. See the official commentary on Article 3 to the 1949 Geneva Convention IV under the aegis of Jean Pictet, the general editor of the ICRC's 1958 commentary, at: http://bit.ly/2HhToet.

[12] Protocol Additional to the Geneva Conventions of 12 August 1949, and relating to the Protection of Victims of International Armed Conflicts (Protocol I), 8 June 1977; adopted at Geneva, 8 June 1977; entered into force, 7 December 1978 (1977 Additional Protocol I). As of 1 April 2022, 174 States were party to the Protocol. See the ICRC list of States Parties, which is regularly updated, at: http://bit.ly/2Oe2Iin.

[13] Protocol Additional to the Geneva Conventions of 12 August 1949, and relating to the Protection of Victims of Non-International Armed Conflicts (Protocol II); adopted at Geneva, 8 June 1977; entered into force, 7 December 1978 (1977 Additional Protocol II). As of 1 April 2022, 169 States were party to the Protocol. See the ICRC list of States Parties, at: http://bit.ly/2m85zBr.

[14] Customary international law evolves through State practice combined with a generally held belief among States that the practice is legally binding. Once established, a rule applies to all States, irrespective of whether or not they have adhered to a particular treaty that reflects the content of any given customary rule.

[15] António Guterres, 'Remarks to the Security Council on the Protection of Civilians in Armed Conflict', UN, New York, 23 May 2019, at: http://bit.ly/2ZsLQyo.

The civilian population and individual civilians are entitled to general protection against 'dangers' arising from military operations.[16] This protection is enunciated in a series of core rules (also called 'principles'; the nomenclature does not materially affect its content). These are: the rule of distinction (including the notion of direct participation in hostilities); the rule of proportionality in attack; and the rule of precautions in attack. They are discussed in turn in the following sections.

2.2.1 *The Rule of Distinction*

This 'basic' IHL rule requires all belligerents ('parties' to an armed conflict, in legal parlance) to 'at all times distinguish between the civilian population and combatants and between civilian objects and military objectives' and to 'direct their operations only against military objectives'. This requirement to target only combatants and other military objectives means that it is unlawful to *deliberately target* the civilian population, for example by shooting at individual civilians or bombing areas populated by civilians. Such an attack is a 'direct attack on civilians'.[17] The rule also renders unlawful a military operation that does not seek to target a lawful military objective. Such an attack is *indiscriminate*.[18] For details of the corresponding war crimes under international criminal law, see Chapter 6.

It is not clear how accurate an attack must be to comply with the IHL rule of distinction, however. Bombs and shells often miss their targets but this does not mean that the rule has been violated. The judgments of international criminal courts and tribunals suggest that, depending on the weapon that is used, even missing by several hundred metres a lawful military objective in case of long-range artillery or aerial bombardment may not necessarily breach the rule.[19] Much smaller margins of error certainly apply to the use of rifles and even mortars.

The protection afforded to each civilian lasts for as long as he or she does not participate *directly* in hostilities.[20] The precise scope of this notion is one of IHL's most contested issues. This is a major concern because loss of protection means that, potentially, an individual civilian who is directly participating in hostilities may be targeted and even killed without warning.

2.2.1.1 Direct Participation in Hostilities

While the notion of direct participation in hostilities (DPH) certainly includes use of a weapon in combat against the enemy, it is clear that other acts by a civilian can also lead

---

[16] Art. 51(1), 1977 Additional Protocol I.

[17] Article 51(2) of the 1977 Additional Protocol I reiterates that the civilian population as such, as well as individual civilians, shall not be the object of attack.

[18] The basic rule protecting civilians is codified in Article 48 of the 1977 Additional Protocol I and is part of customary law, and therefore applicable to all States.

[19] See on this issue S. Casey-Maslen with S. Haines, *Hague Law Interpreted: The Conduct of Hostilities Under the Law of Armed Conflict*, Hart, Oxford, 2018, pp. 157–8 and 231–2.

[20] Art. 51(3), 1977 Additional Protocol I.

to loss of his or her immunity from attack. Indeed, a civilian does not even need to be personally armed to lose this legal protection. Other combat-related activities may also amount to DPH, such as gathering and transmission of operational intelligence or instructions; the production of weapons for operational use or their delivery to the front line; and the impeding of enemy operations (for example by physically blocking roads or clearing mines in an area of hostilities). This is so, as long as the act or acts serve to assist one party to an armed conflict in their struggle against another. According to the ICRC, in addition to the commission of the act or acts themselves, the temporal and geographical scope of participation includes both travelling to, and returning from, a relevant act or operation.[21]

Acts of *indirect* participation include making or storing weapons that are to support the war effort ('war-sustaining activities'), but which are not being dispatched to front-line operations. These do not result in a loss of civilian protection from attack. (The weapons themselves, however, remain a lawful target for military action, so nearby civilians may be incidental victims.) Support for the waging of war in the media and even propaganda are also forms of indirect participation that do not result in the loss of civilian immunity from attack. According to a broader interpretation of DPH, however,[22] which is advanced by the United States and has been endorsed by the Israeli Supreme Court, the notion also includes these and other war-sustaining activities.[23]

HUMAN SHIELDS. Acting as a 'human shield' may amount to direct participation in hostilities, depending on the circumstances.[24] This likely depends on whether the enemy's operations are physically constrained by the acts of individual civilians. Thus, blocking access on the ground to a military objective, by being physically interposed between a belligerent and the objective (person or object), amounts to civilians directly

---

[21] N. Melzer, *Interpretive Guidance on Direct Participation in Hostilities under International Humanitarian Law*, ICRC, Geneva, 2009, chapter VI.

[22] For an overview of the different stances, see, for example, D. E. Stigall, 'The Thickest Grey: Assessing the Status of the Civilian Response Corps under the Law of International Armed Conflict and the US Approach to Targeting Civilians', *American University International Law Review*, Vol. 25 (2010), 885–914, at pp. 894, 898. See also T. A. Keck, 'Not All Civilians Are Created Equal: The Principle of Distinction, the Question of Direct Participation in Hostilities and Evolving Restraints on the Use of Force in Warfare', *Military Law Review*, Vol. 211 (2012), 115–178, in particular at pp. 129–32, and 141–8. For a response to critiques by Kenneth Watkins, Michael Schmitt, William Boothby, and W. Hays Parks of the ICRC's interpretative guidance, see, N. Melzer, 'Keeping the Balance Between Military Necessity and Humanity: A Response to Four Critiques of the ICRC's Interpretive Guidance on the Notion of Direct Participation in Hostilities', *New York University Journal of International Law and Politics*, Vol. 42, No. 3 (2010), 831.

[23] For details of the US position on the notion of DPH, see US Department of Defense, *Law of War Manual*, 2015 (updated December 2016), Washington DC, 2016, §5.9.3. The US view is that DPH 'also includes certain acts that … effectively and substantially contribute to an adversary's ability to conduct or sustain combat operations'. The United States also takes a broader approach to the notion 'through the prism of self-defense'. See: Stigall, 'The Thickest Grey: Assessing the Status of the Civilian Response Corps under the Law of International Armed Conflict and the US Approach to Targeting Civilians', p. 896; and A. S. Janin, 'Engaging Civilian-Belligerents Leads to Self-Defense/Protocol I Marriage', *Army Law*, July 2007, 82, at p. 89.

[24] For an overview, see B. Van Schaack, 'The Law and Policy of Human Shielding', in W. S. Williams and C. M. Ford (eds.), *Complex Battlespaces: The Law of Armed Conflict and the Dynamics of Modern Warfare*, Oxford University Press, Oxford, 2019.

participating in hostilities, leading to loss of civilian immunity from attack. In contrast, those that are no physical impediment to a belligerent, such as when civilians are in or around a military objective that is going to be attacked from the air, do not amount to DPH. This means that the civilians retain their immunity from attack. The military objective, however, continues to be lawful to attack, subject to the rule of proportionality discussed in Section 2.2.2 below. This may be so regardless of whether civilians are voluntarily or involuntarily serving as shields.[25]

Others, however, make the distinction between the voluntary or involuntary nature of human shields. They consider that if civilians are forced to shield military objectives, they retain their protection, whereas those voluntarily shielding military objectives are deemed to take direct part in hostilities and as a consequence lose their protection from direct attacks for such time as they participate.[26] Those relying on the distinction between voluntary and involuntary human shields consider that voluntary human shields should not be included in the proportionality assessment as they have lost their protection against attack.[27] Yet, making a distinction between voluntary and involuntary action is difficult in armed conflicts because it is based on a perceived mental element.[28] It is often hard for a soldier to know whether a civilian seemingly shielding a military objective is doing so by choice or under duress.

That said, an armed force is prohibited from using the civilian population or individual civilians to seek to render certain points or areas immune from military operations. Belligerents may not move the civilian population or individual civilians 'in order to attempt to shield military objectives from attacks or to shield military operations'.[29] The use of human shields by armed forces and notably non-State actors remains a challenge in modern armed conflicts, however.[30]

2.2.1.2 Sieges

Although sieges may 'conjure up images of medieval warfare', armed forces and armed groups continue to encircle and besiege populated areas, in both international and

---

[25] See among others: R. Geiss and J. G. Devaney, 'Zealots, Victims and Captives: Maintaining Adequate Protection of Human Shields in Contemporary International Humanitarian Law', *Israel Yearbook on Human Rights*, Vol. 47 (2017); and see also Melzer, *Interpretive Guidance on Direct Participation in Hostilities under International Humanitarian Law*, pp. 56–7.

[26] Among others, Michael Schmitt is of the latter view: 'yet, concluding that in case of doubt as to whether civilians act as human shields directly or indirectly, they should be treated as acting involuntarily'. M. N. Schmitt, 'Human Shields in International Humanitarian Law', *Columbia Journal of Transnational Law*, Vol. 47 (2009), 292.

[27] Y. Dinstein, 'The Principle of Proportionality', in K. Larsen, C. Guldahl, and G. Nystuen (eds.), *Searching for a 'Principle of Humanity' in International Humanitarian Law*, Cambridge University Press, Cambridge, 2012.

[28] See Geiss and Devaney, 'Zealots, Victims and Captives: Maintaining Adequate Protection of Human Shields in Contemporary International Humanitarian Law'; and Melzer, 'Keeping the Balance Between Military Necessity and Humanity: A Response to Four Critiques of the ICRC's Interpretive Guidance on the Notion of Direct Participation in Hostilities', p. 873.

[29] Art. 51(7), 1977 Additional Protocol I.

[30] See T. Vestner, 'Addressing the Use of Human Shields', *Strategic Security Analysis Series*, 8, Geneva Centre for Security Policy, 2019.

non-international armed conflicts.[31] Indeed, the practice may even be increasing, as armed conflict in Iraq and Syria over the past decade (and most recently in Ukraine) have shown. Sieges typically lead to significant and prolonged civilian harm.[32]

It is not prohibited under IHL to besiege a city, town, or village as long as there are lawful military objectives (combatants or objects of military value) located within it. That said, among many States, there is less tolerance towards such tactics, as has been evidenced by discussions in the UN General Assembly and Security Council in recent years.[33] Moreover, conducting a siege of a city, town, or village in which there are only civilians and civilian objects is prohibited by the rule of distinction.

Starvation of civilians as a method of warfare is also prohibited.[34] This prohibition is also accompanied by the obligation to evacuate besieged areas and to provide humanitarian relief.[35] This means it is prohibited to prevent civilians from receiving the food and water they need to survive. Combatants, however, may lawfully be starved to death under IHL. With respect to the provision of humanitarian assistance, who is entitled (or required) to provide the consent to relief consignments continues to be debated.[36] Some contend that in case of cross-border consignments, which are destined for territory under the control of an armed group, only the consent of this latter is needed.[37]

2.2.1.3 Protection of Humanitarian Personnel

Humanitarian personnel are civilians protected from attack (unless and for such time as they participate directly in hostilities). Providing relief to civilians does not constitute direct participation in hostilities, nor does providing relief to combatants who are no longer fighting because of sickness or wounds. Such acts comply with IHL. In contrast, supplying combatants who are still engaged in hostilities could be direct participation in

---

[31] E.-C. Gillard, 'Sieges, the Law and Protecting Civilians', Briefing, International Law Programme, Chatham House, London, June 2019, at: https://bit.ly/39e6WEn, p. 1.

[32] See generally on sieges, S. Casey-Maslen, 'Protecting Civilians in Siege Warfare: Constraints on Military Action', Report, Ceasefire, London, March 2022.

[33] For an overview on legal constraints and the international community opinion on sieges with respect to the Syrian conflict, see: S. Watts, 'Under Siege: International Humanitarian Law and Security Council Practice Concerning Urban Siege Operations', 27 May 2014, available at SSRN: https://bit.ly/3m61nx6.

[34] Art. 54(1), 1977 Additional Protocol I.

[35] Watts, 'Under Siege: International Humanitarian Law and Security Council Practice concerning Urban Siege Operations', at p. 5. See also F. Hampson, 'Besieged Civilian Population: Is There Any Right to Evacuation and Humanitarian Assistance?', *Collegium*, Vol. 46 (2016), 100.

[36] On providing humanitarian assistance, see, among others, R. A. Stoffels, 'Legal Regulation of Humanitarian Assistance in Armed Conflict: Achievements and Gaps', *International Review of the Red Cross*, Vol. 86 (2004), 515; and Y. Dinstein, 'The Right to Humanitarian Assistance', *Naval War College Review*, Vol. 53, No. 4 (2000), 77–91, at p. 84; D. Akande and E.-C. Gillard, 'Oxford Guidance on the Law Relating to Humanitarian Relief Operations in Situations of Armed Conflict', UN Office for the Coordination of Humanitarian Affairs, 2016.

[37] See, for example, J. Dungel, 'A Right to Humanitarian Assistance in Internal Armed Conflicts Respecting Sovereignty, Neutrality and Legitimacy: Practical Proposals to Practical Problems' *The Journal of Humanitarian Assistance*, Blog entry, at: https://bit.ly/3idOyQa, para. 2.3.1.2. For a useful overview of the debate see Sassòli, *International Humanitarian Law: Rules, Controversies and Solutions to Problems Arising in Warfare*, p. 578, para. 10.206.

hostilities, depending on the type of goods supplied and the circumstances in which this aid is given.

Just providing food to an armed force is, ordinarily, indirect participation.[38] But providing food to combatants during a siege, in which they are close to surrendering because they are starving, might reach the threshold for direct participation in hostilities. Naturally, providing them with weapons or logistics certainly would.

2.2.1.4 Protection of Journalists

Journalists are also civilians protected from attack (of course, unless and for such time as they participate directly in hostilities).[39] Reporting on an international armed conflict is not direct participation in hostilities even where the journalist is sharply critical of the actions of one party or another. Only when the transmission of information of high military value reaches the threshold of harm for an act to amount to a direct participation in hostilities, may journalists' activities amount to DPH.[40]

Under the 1949 Geneva Convention III, journalists ('war correspondents') who are formally embedded within armed forces that are engaged in an international armed conflict are even entitled to prisoner-of-war status and concomitant treatment if they fall into the hands of the enemy (though they remain civilians before that, protected from attack).[41] However, according to one expansive interpretation of the notion of DPH, it is 'conceivable that journalists who are in direct support of modern military operations could lose their immunity like other civilians accompanying the force'.[42]

2.2.1.5 Acts of Terror

Acts of terror are defined differently under IHL than they are in treaties on terrorism. This is because certain acts considered as 'terrorist' in nature during peacetime are not prohibited by IHL during armed conflicts, the most obvious being the targeting of military

---

[38] Melzer, *Interpretive Guidance on Direct Participation in Hostilities under International Humanitarian Law*, p. 55.

[39] For an overview of the status of journalists and war correspondents under IHL as well as the legal framework applicable to them, see B. Saul, 'The International Protection of Journalists in Armed Conflict and Other Violent Situations', *Australian Journal of Human Rights*, Vol. 14, No. 1 (2008), 99–140 (text available on SSRN at: https://bit.ly/3m5iFKO); A. Balguy-Gallois, 'The Protection of Journalists and News Media Personnel in Armed Conflict', *International Review of the Red Cross*, Vol. 86, No. 853 (2004), at: https://bit.ly/2ZCrCnp.

[40] R. Geiss, 'The Protection of Journalists in Armed Conflicts', *German Yearbook of International Law*, Vol. 51 (2008), 289–320 at p. 296.

[41] Art. 4(3), 1949 Geneva Convention III.

[42] According to this view, which is supported by elements of the US military, a 'civilian entering the theater of operations in support or operation of sensitive, high Value [sic] equipment, such as a weapon system' has directly participated in hostilities and has lost his or her protection. See: Stigall, 'The Thickest Grey: Assessing the Status of the Civilian Response Corps under the Law of International Armed Conflict and the US Approach to Targeting Civilians', p. 896; and see also D. W. Moore, 'Twenty-First Century Embedded Journalists: Lawful Targets?', *Army Law*, July 2009, p. 21; and Memorandum from W. Hays Parks, Special Assistant for Law of War Matters, US Department of the Army, *Regarding the Law of War Status of Civilians Accompanying Military Forces in the Field*, May 1999, §3(a).

personnel or military buildings. Accordingly, the 1997 Terrorist Bombings Convention, which prohibits the bombing of government buildings (including the Ministry of Defence or a military garrison), excludes its application during armed conflicts for acts of belligerents that are governed by IHL.[43]

Acts of terror under IHL concern certain attacks – and also threatened attacks – that are perpetrated or made against the civilian population.[44] Thus outlawed are acts or threats of violence 'the primary purpose of which is to spread terror among the civilian population'.[45] Such acts may include, for instance, the systematic bombing of civilian areas. To be captured by the IHL prohibition on terror attacks, the *primary* – but not necessarily the exclusive – purpose of the acts must be to spread terror. The acts are prohibited even if the civilian population is not in fact terrorised as a result.

It is debated, however, whether such acts are to be deemed lawful if an attack is directed against military objectives, despite their primary purpose of spreading terror among the civilian population.[46] A similarly contested issue is whether terror attacks can encompass attacks intended to undermine civilian morale. Such attacks are those that affect the civilian support for the war, for example 'attacks intended primarily to induce the civilian population to rebellion or to overthrow its leadership' or 'to demoralize civilians and lead them to pressure their leaders to surrender'.[47] Often, however, they have been a euphemism for indiscriminate attacks on cities.[48] But from an operational viewpoint, attacks targeting civilian morale represent a longstanding feature of conflicts, whose effectiveness has been often advanced by senior military personnel.[49] From a legal

---

[43] 'The activities of armed forces during an armed conflict, as those terms are understood under international humanitarian law, which are governed by that law, are not governed by this Convention'. Art. 19(2), International Convention for the Suppression of Terrorist Bombings; adopted at New York, 15 December 1997; entered into force, 23 May 2001. As of 1 April 2022, 170 States were party to the Convention.

[44] There are very few instances where IHL governs threats to do something. A further case is with respect to threatened acts of terrorism against civilians by an enemy, such as when they have detained them or otherwise held them in their power. In the Sierra Leone conflict, for example, the non-State armed group, the Revolutionary United Front (RUF), were known for amputating the arms or hands of civilian women and children in villages they attacked.

[45] Art. 51(2), 1977 Additional Protocol I; Art. 13(2), 1977 Additional Protocol II.

[46] For a positive answer to this question see, ICTY, *Prosecutor v. Galić*, Judgment (Trial Chamber) (Case No. IT-98-29-T), 5 December 2003, para. 135; and Sassòli, *International Humanitarian Law: Rules, Controversies, and Solutions to Problems Arising in Warfare*, para. 8.303. See also Human Rights Watch, *Needless Deaths in the Gulf War: Civilian Casualties During the Air Campaign and Violations of the Laws of War*, Report, 1 June 1991, at: https://bit.ly/2ZNnrVY; and (for a contrary view) see I. Henderson, *The Contemporary Law of Targeting: Military Objectives, Proportionality and Precautions in Attack under Additional Protocol I*, Martinus Nijhoff, Leiden, 2009, pp. 116–17.

[47] Henderson, *The Contemporary Law of Targeting: Military Objectives, Proportionality and Precautions in Attack under Additional Protocol I*, p. 119.

[48] See, for example, with respect to the bombing of Nazi Germany: D. L. Miller, *Masters of the Air*, Ebury Press, London, 2021, pp. 5–6.

[49] The importance of targeting the civilian morale was stressed, for instance, with respect to provoking a coup against Saddam Hussein, in the context of the 1980 Iran Iraq war, during World War II with respect to the morale of the German people, or in the context of World War I. For a contrary view, however, see, among others, Dinstein, *The Conduct of Hostilities under the Law of International Armed Conflict*, 3rd ed., para. 390.

perspective, according to the view of a majority of authorities and commentators, they are unlawful.

2.2.2 *The Rule of Proportionality in Attack*

Even if an attack[50] is targeted at a lawful military objective in accordance with the rule of distinction, the decision to launch the attack must also respect the rule of proportionality. This rule is codified in the 1977 Additional Protocol I[51] and is also part of customary law applicable to all armed conflict.[52] Under the rule, an attack against a military objective will be unlawful where it 'may be expected' to cause incidental civilian harm that is 'excessive' compared with the projected 'concrete and direct' military advantage. Civilian harm is explicitly defined as encompassing deaths or injuries to civilians, destruction of or damage to civilian objects, 'or a combination thereof'.

Proportionality is thus not adjudged afterwards, depending, for instance, on the number of civilians harmed by an attack, but relates to the situation when the attack was launched. What does the commander know about the risk to civilians (or what should he or she reasonably know)? And based on that knowledge, is the attack justified because of the military benefit it is likely to bring? Would a reasonable commander come to a similar decision to proceed with the attack?[53]

The difficulty with proportionality is that its interpretation, and especially the notion of what is to be considered 'excessive' civilian harm, is unclear. In 2016, the ICRC convened an international expert meeting to seek to clarify the interpretation of the rule, but little headway was made on the issue.[54] What is clear is that IHL does not prohibit all incidental killing and maiming of civilians even though, as discussed further in Section 2.2.3, 'constant care' must be taken to 'spare' civilians and civilian objects.[55] The question remains as to how much civilian harm is legally permissible. Controversy encompasses both the components of the assessment as well as the criterion of excessiveness. As to the anticipated direct military advantage, a question concerns whether commanders may aggregate advantages deriving from different attacks.[56] A longstanding controversy on the rule of proportionality also revolves around including the protection of a State's own

---

[50] Under IHL, the term 'attack' is defined broadly to mean 'acts of violence against the adversary, whether in offence or in defence'. Art. 49(1), 1977 Additional Protocol I.

[51] Art. 51(5)(b), 1977 Additional Protocol I.

[52] The ICRC has expressed the customary IHL rule as follows: 'Launching an attack which may be expected to cause incidental loss of civilian life, injury to civilians, damage to civilian objects, or a combination thereof, which would be excessive in relation to the concrete and direct military advantage anticipated, is prohibited.'

[53] ICTY, *Prosecutor v. Galić*, Judgment (Trial Chamber), para. 58.

[54] See L. Gisel, *The Principle of Proportionality in the Rules Governing the Conduct of Hostilities under International Humanitarian Law*, Report of an International Expert Meeting in Quebec, 22–3 June 2016, ICRC, Geneva, August 2018, at: http://bit.ly/397bsor, Part III.

[55] Art. 57(1), 1977 Additional Protocol I.

[56] See on this, Capt. G. Keinan, 'Military Advantage and Ground Combat in Urban Areas', in *Urban Warfare, Proceedings of the 16th Bruges Colloquium, 15–16 October 2015*, pp. 109–17.

forces within the notion of concrete and direct military advantage as one limb of the assessment required under the rule.[57]

It is also unsettled whether elements such as mental harm to civilians, civilian illness, displacement, economic loss, or reverberating effects should be deemed relevant under the proportionality rule.[58] Another question concerns whether the determination of excessiveness is a subjective standard. Some are of the view that the rule cannot lend itself to a quantitative analysis or that it is not amenable to a mathematical tabulation.[59] Others consider that the excessiveness determination is an objective parameter because it is based on the assessment of the 'reasonable' commander.[60] This notion also raises questions, however.[61] As to the comparison between the two values, some have asserted that they are simply incommensurate factors.[62] We are left, therefore, with a critical rule, whose application is not denied but whose practical interpretation remains unspecified.

2.2.3 *The Rule of Precautions in Attack*

Underpinning the rules of distinction and proportionality in attack are the precautionary measures that an attacker must take. The general rule, evoking the entitlement of the civilian population and individual civilians to general protection against dangers arising

---

[57] For an overview on such debate, see: R. Geiss, 'The Principle of Proportionality: "Force Protection" as a Military Advantage', *Israel Law Review*, Vol. 45, No. 1 (2012), 71–89. Dinstein, for instance, supports the inclusion of force protection within the notion of military advantage, whereas Sassòli believes that force protection could be better achieved through the adoption of precautionary measures. Sassòli, *International Humanitarian Law: Rules, Controversies, and Solutions to Problems Arising in Warfare*, p. 363, para. 8.325. See also Gisel, *The Principle of Proportionality in the Rules Governing the Conduct of Hostilities under International Humanitarian Law*, pp. 23–31.

[58] Gisel, *The Principle of Proportionality in the Rules Governing the Conduct of Hostilities under International Humanitarian Law*; see also, L. Gisel, 'Relevant Incidental Harm for the Proportionality Principle', in *Urban Warfare, Proceedings of the 16th Bruges Colloquium, 15–16 October 2015*, pp. 121–3; and I. Henderson and K. Reece, 'Proportionality under International Humanitarian Law: The Reasonable Military Commander Standard and Reverberating Effects', *Vanderbilt Journal of Transnational Law*, Vol. 51 (2018), 835.

[59] ICTY, *Prosecutor v. Pavle Strugar*, Prosecutor's Pre-Trial Brief Pursuant to Rule 65 ter (E) (i) (Case No. IT-01–42), 27 August 2003, para. 152. See also the HPCR Manual, Rule 14, p. 98, para. 7; and US Department of Defense, *Law of War Manual*, 2016, para. 5.12.4.

[60] See, for example: Henderson, *The Contemporary Law of Targeting: Military Objectives, Proportionality and Precautions in Attack under Additional Protocol I*, p. 222; and Gisel, *The Principle of Proportionality in the Rules Governing the Conduct of Hostilities under International Humanitarian Law*, p. 52. See also 'The Conduct of Hostilities and International Humanitarian Law: Challenges of 21st Century Warfare', International Law Studies Series, US Naval War College, Vol. 93 (2017), 322–88 at p. 369.

[61] Gisel, *The Principle of Proportionality in the Rules Governing the Conduct of Hostilities under International Humanitarian Law*, pp. 53, 56, and 58–9. On the standard see also Henderson and Reece, 'Proportionality under International Humanitarian Law: The Reasonable Military Commander Standard and Reverberating Effects'. Generally, on a need to clarify the principles and different approaches in its application see B. Clarke, 'Proportionality in Armed Conflicts: A Principle in Need of Clarification', *Journal of International Humanitarian Legal Studies*, Vol. 3 (2012), 73.

[62] See, K. Anderson, 'The Ethics of Robot Soldiers?', Law of War and Just War Theory Blog, Post of 4 July 2007, at: https://bit.ly/3ibVsFI; 'The Conduct of Hostilities and International Humanitarian Law: Challenges of 21st Century Warfare', p. 368.

from military operations, holds that in the conduct of military operations, 'constant care must be taken to spare the civilian population, civilians and civilian objects'.[63]

The main precautionary measures incumbent upon an attacker are to do 'everything feasible' to verify that the objectives to be attacked are lawful military objectives. They must also take 'all feasible precautions' in the choice of weapons (and the way that they are used) so as to avoid, or at least minimise, incidental civilian harm.[64] The standard of feasibility is not, however, a demanding one in international law. It does not amount to an obligation to do *everything necessary* to protect civilians, and it is not even an obligation to do *everything possible in the circumstances* to protect civilians.

In practice, it is challenging to determine what the standards of doing 'everything feasible' and taking 'all the feasible precautions' entail.[65] For instance, with respect to the measure of target verification, the ICRC is of the view that the slightest doubt as to whether an object or person is a lawful military objective requires a search for additional information.[66] Many States and commentators, however, disagree with this proposition, considering it an overly demanding standard.[67] Similarly, different positions exist as to whether the obligation needs to be somehow limited depending on the military level of the individual(s) involved.[68] Overall, feasibility does not depend upon the resources and technology potentially available to the attacker, and the obligation of precautionary measures does not require the purchase of more advanced and precise targeting technologies.[69]

2.2.4 *The Protection of Civilian Objects*

The rule of distinction prohibits the targeting of civilian objects.[70] A civilian object is defined simply as an object which is not a military objective.[71] In turn, military objectives are objects whose nature, location, purpose, or use make an effective contribution to

---

[63] Art. 57(1), 1977 Additional Protocol I.

[64] Art. 57(2)(a)(i) and (ii), 1977 Additional Protocol I.

[65] For an overview of precautionary measures, see, for example, 'The Conduct of Hostilities and International Humanitarian Law: Challenges of 21st Century Warfare', p. 371.

[66] On the knowledge sufficient to carry out an attack lawfully from an operational perspective, see: E. J. Marchant, 'Insufficient Knowledge in Kunduz: The Precautionary Principle and International Humanitarian Law', *Journal of Conflict and Security Law*, Vol. 25, No. 1 (Spring 2020), 53–79.

[67] See, for example, G. Corn and J. A. Schoettler Jr., 'Targeting and Civilian Risk Mitigation: The Essential Role of Precautionary Measures', *Military Law Review* Vol. 223 (2015), 785–842, at pp. 803–4. For an overview of the different positions on this issue, see Henderson, *The Contemporary Law of Targeting: Military Objectives, Proportionality and Precautions in Attack under Additional Protocol I*, pp. 161–7.

[68] See for example, Switzerland's reservation stating that the 'provisions of Article 57, paragraph 2, create obligations only for commanding officers at the battalion or group level and above'. For an overview of selected State practice, see Henderson, *The Contemporary Law of Targeting: Military Objectives, Proportionality and Precautions in Attack under Additional Protocol I*, pp. 159–61.

[69] Sassòli, *International Humanitarian Law: Rules, Controversies, and Solutions to Problems Arising in Warfare*, p. 366, para. 8.331.

[70] Art. 52(1), 1977 Additional Protocol I.

[71] Ibid.

military action.[72] These rules are also of a customary nature applicable in all armed conflicts.

An objective that is military in *nature* is one that is inherently military, such as a weapon belonging to an army or a military facility. Thus, tanks, military aircraft, munitions, army trucks, and military barracks and other ancillary facilities are all, by nature, military objectives. So too is the Ministry of Defence's headquarters. An object may also be a military objective by virtue of its *location*. This includes an area of land that has strategic, tactical, or operational value to the enemy military.

An object that is ostensibly civilian in nature may become a military objective by virtue of its *use*. Thus, a home, a school, an office, or a religious building may become a military objective if it is used to store weapons, station military personnel, or to facilitate military communications. Finally, where there is firm evidence – not a mere suspicion or a possibility – that a building or facility will be used in the future for a military *purpose* (even if this is not the case currently), it may be targeted as a lawful military objective.

In distinguishing between civilian and military objects, it is contested as to whether war-sustaining capabilities, such as those that contribute merely economically to the enemy's ability to sustain the conflict, are lawful military objects.[73]

2.2.4.1 The Special Protection of Civilian Hospitals

Under IHL, the highest level of 'special' protection to objects is given to hospitals. Under the 1949 Geneva Convention IV, civilian hospitals 'may in no circumstances be the object of attack, but shall at all times be respected and protected by the Parties to the conflict'.[74] This is one of the very few provisions in the Geneva Conventions where the conduct of hostilities are regulated.

Nonetheless, a civilian hospital may lose its special protection if it is used to commit acts 'harmful' to the enemy.[75] Such acts concern use of the hospital to store weapons; to station active military personnel; or to facilitate military communications linked to operations.[76] Protection may, though, cease only after due warning has been given to end these acts and a reasonable deadline has been given for compliance. If this deadline expires and the enemy has not ended its unlawful behaviour, an attack may then be

---

[72] Art. 52(1), 1977 Additional Protocol I. The provision further requires that the object's total or partial destruction, capture, or neutralisation, in the circumstances ruling at the time, must offer a definite military advantage.

[73] For an overview on the different positions and practice and a suggested way forward, see, R. Goodman, 'The Obama Administration and Targeting War-Sustaining Object in Non-international Armed Conflict', *American Journal of International Law*, Vol. 110 (2016), 663. In support of the legal validity of the US practice in considering such objects as military objectives, see also 'The Conduct of Hostilities and International Humanitarian Law: Challenges of 21st Century Warfare', pp. 340–2. For a critique of this approach, see: I. D. King, 'The Legality of Attacking War-Sustaining Economic Objects', *Stanford Journal International Law*, Vol. 54 (2018), 61.

[74] Art. 18, 1949 Geneva Convention IV.

[75] Art. 19, 1949 Geneva Convention IV.

[76] Ibid. The fact that sick or wounded members of the armed forces are cared for in civilian hospitals, and the presence of small arms and ammunition taken from such combatants and which have not yet been given back to the armed forces, are not acts harmful to the enemy.

launched.[77] It will still, though, be subject to the rule of proportionality in attack. Only if an armed force is coming under direct fire from within a medical facility may these procedural measures be dispensed with and force used immediately.

Some have affirmed, however, that even if a hospital loses its special protection, it still benefits from the general protection as civilian object according to the rule of distinction. While the military use of the hospital may, however, render the hospital a military object, this must not occur automatically: a separate assessment according to Article 52(2) of the 1977 Additional Protocol I (definition of military objectives) needs to be undertaken.[78]

2.2.4.2 Other Objects Entitled to Special Protection

There is also special protection under the 1977 Additional Protocols for dams, dykes, and nuclear electrical generating stations. These objects may not be attacked, even where they are military objectives, 'if such attack may cause the release of dangerous forces and consequent severe losses among the civilian population'.[79] In international armed conflict, this protection only ceases if the objects are employed in 'regular, significant and direct support of military operations' and if attack is the 'only feasible way' to end that support.[80] If they are attacked, all practical precautions must be taken to 'avoid the release of the dangerous forces'.[81]

Cultural objects also attract special protection both under the Additional Protocol I and under other instruments of IHL. Under the 1954 Hague Convention for the Protection of Cultural Property, such objects may only be attacked in cases of unavoidable military necessity when they are being used for military activities incompatible with their civilian status.[82] The definition of what is a cultural object differs under the 1977 Additional Protocol I and the 1954 Hague Convention. Under Article 53 of the Geneva Convention IV, for instance, the definition is broader because it is not built on the 'importance' of the property[83] and includes also intangible heritage.[84] Debate has arisen also with respect to the interpretation of the relationship between the provision on

---

[77] Art. 19, 1949 Geneva Convention IV.

[78] Kolb, Nakashima, and Sassòli argue differently. R. Kolb and F. Nakashima, 'The Notion of "Acts Harmful to the Enemy" under International Humanitarian Law', *International Review of the Red Cross*, Vol. 101, No. 912 (2019), at p. 1177; and Sassòli, *International Humanitarian Law: Rules, Controversies, and Solutions to Problems Arising in Warfare*, p. 241, para. 8.29.

[79] Art. 56(1), 1977 Additional Protocol I.

[80] Art. 56(2), 1977 Additional Protocol I.

[81] Art. 56(2), 1977 Additional Protocol I.

[82] Arts. 9 and 11, Convention for the Protection of Cultural Property in the Event of Armed Conflict with Regulations for the Execution of the Convention; adopted at The Hague, 14 May 1954; entered into force, 7 August 1956. As at 1 April 2022, 133 States were party to the Convention. See the ICRC list of States Parties, at: http://bit.ly/2k7kXgy.

[83] S. von Schorlemer, 'Legal Changes in the Regime of the Protection of Cultural Property in Armed Conflict', *Art, Antiquity & Law*, Vol. 9 (2004), 43, at p. 47. For an overview on the applicable legal framework see also C. Johannot-Gradis, 'Protecting the Past for the Future: How Does Law Protect Tangible and Intangible Cultural Heritage in Armed Conflict?', *International Review of the Red Cross*, Vol. 97 (2015), 1253.

[84] Sassòli, *International Humanitarian Law: Rules, Controversies, and Solutions to Problems Arising in Warfare*, p. 564, para. 10.178.

cultural heritage protection under the Additional Protocols and that under the 1954 Hague Convention. It is debated whether the absolute protection under the 1977 Additional Protocols should be limited by the exceptions foreseen under the 1954 Hague Convention.[85]

THE PROTECTION OF SCHOOLS. Schools do not enjoy special protection under IHL.[86] They are civilian objects and are entitled to the same level of protection as other 'ordinary' civilian objects. However, under the Protocol, in case of doubt whether an object which is normally dedicated to civilian purposes, such as a school, is being used to make an effective contribution to military action, it shall be presumed not to be so used.[87]

In addition, a politically binding instrument, the Safe Schools Declaration, commits signatory States[88] to the Guidelines for Protecting Schools and Universities from Military Use During Armed Conflict.[89] These Guidelines, agreed upon in 2014, are not legally binding in themselves and do not affect existing obligations under international law.[90] They are, though, intended 'to lead to a shift in behaviour that will lead to better protections for schools and universities in times of armed conflict and, in particular, to a reduction in their use by the fighting forces of parties to armed conflict in support of the military effort'.[91]

2.2.5 *Protection of Civilians under Foreign Military Occupation*

Military occupation by a foreign State is a form of international armed conflict. Specific rules apply to such situations under the 1899/1907 Hague Regulations and the 1949 Geneva Convention IV. The rules represent customary law and therefore bind all States.

The fundamental principle underlying military occupation is that the occupying power does not acquire sovereignty over the territory.[92] Accordingly, occupation is only to be considered a temporary situation, and as a consequence the occupying power must generally respect the laws in force in the occupied territory. This is so unless and to the extent that these laws threaten its security or impede the application of IHL governing occupation.[93]

---

[85] Sassòli argues for the inclusion of the 1954 Hague Convention limitations to protection into the Additional Protocol regime. But see the contrary views he cites in ibid., footnote 371.

[86] On the protection of schools, see B. Sheppard, and K. Kizuka, 'Taking Armed Conflict Out of the Classroom: International and Domestic Legal Protections for Students When Combatants Use Schools', *Journal of International Humanitarian Legal Studies* Vol. 2, No. 2 (2011), 281–324.

[87] Art. 52(3), 1977 Additional Protocol I.

[88] As at 1 April 2022, 114 States had signed the Declaration. See the Norwegian government's list of signatories, at: http://bit.ly/2k3LOtS.

[89] Available at: http://bit.ly/2lY5ZtM.

[90] *Commentary on the Guidelines for Protecting Schools and Universities from Military Use During Armed Conflict*, at: http://bit.ly/2m6212t, p. 5.

[91] Ibid.

[92] See, for example, ICRC, 'Occupation and International Humanitarian Law: Questions and Answers', 4 August 2004, at: http://bit.ly/2Zn3Yu6.

[93] Art. 64, 1949 Geneva Convention IV.

The occupying power is required to take measures to ensure, as far as possible, public order and safety.[94] But in so doing, collective punishment and the taking of hostages are prohibited, as are reprisals[95] against protected persons or their property.[96] People accused of criminal offences must be treated humanely and in accordance with international human rights law applicable to a fair trial.[97]

To the fullest extent of the means available to it, the Occupying Power must ensure sufficient hygiene and public health, as well as the provision of food and medical care to the population under occupation. The occupying power should bring in the necessary food, medical supplies, and other articles if the resources of the occupied territory are inadequate.[98] Red Cross/Red Crescent personnel must be allowed to carry out their humanitarian activities.[99] The ICRC, in particular, must be given access to all protected persons, wherever they are, whether or not they are deprived of their liberty.[100]

Collective or individual forcible transfers of population from and within the occupied territory are prohibited. Nevertheless, the Occupying Power may undertake total or partial evacuation of a given area if the security of the population or imperative military reasons so demand.[101] Internment is only possible for imperative reasons of security.[102] Transfers of the civilian population of the occupying power into the occupied territory, regardless of whether this is forced or voluntary, are prohibited.

The confiscation of private property by the occupant is prohibited. As noted above, the civilian population in occupied territory cannot be forced to enlist in the occupier's armed forces.[103] Agreements concluded between the occupying power and the local authorities cannot deprive the civilian population in occupied territory of the protection afforded by IHL.[104] Similarly, protected persons can in no circumstances renounce their rights.[105]

One of the controversies as to the applicability of the protection regime under the law of occupation concerns the beginning thereof, including whether the so-called boots on the ground are necessary for the application of IHL governing military occupation to apply,[106] or, as a distinct question, whether it is applicable already during the invasion phase.[107] In

---

[94] Ibid.

[95] A reprisal is where one party to a conflict engages in what would ordinarily be unlawful conduct to seek to persuade an enemy to stop prior and serious unlawful conduct.

[96] Arts. 33, 34, 1949 Geneva Convention IV; Art. 75, 1977 Additional Protocol I.

[97] Arts. 71–5, 1949 Geneva Convention IV.

[98] Arts. 55 and 56, 1949 Geneva Convention IV.

[99] Art. 63, 1949 Geneva Convention IV.

[100] Art. 143, 1949 Geneva Convention IV.

[101] Art. 49, 1949 Geneva Convention IV.

[102] Art. 78, 1949 Geneva Convention IV.

[103] Art. 51, 1949 Geneva Convention IV.

[104] Art. 47, 1949 Geneva Convention IV.

[105] Art. 8, 1949 Geneva Convention IV.

[106] For a positive view, see, among others, Y. Dinstein, *The International Law of Belligerent Occupation*, Cambridge University Press, Cambridge, 2009, p. 44.

[107] For an overview on the opposite stances on this issue see, Sassòli, *International Humanitarian Law: Rules, Controversies, and Solutions to Problems Arising in Warfare*, p. 314, paras. 8.215 and 8.216; see also H. Cuyckens, *Revisiting the Law of Occupation*, Brill, Leiden, 2018, p. 54; and M. Zwanenburg, M. Bothe, and M. Sassòli, 'Is the Law of Occupation Applicable to the Invasion Phase?', *International Review of the Red Cross*, Vol. 94 (2012), 29.

the latter case, according to a functional approach, military occupation law would apply progressively, which implies that its rules would apply as soon as the objects they regulate fall under the control of the occupying party. This view is not unanimously shared.

2.2.6 *Civilians in the Power of the Enemy*

Civilians are also protected when they are in the 'power of the enemy', in particular because they are detained in connection with an international armed conflict. Of particular importance is Article 75 of the 1977 Additional Protocol I, entitled 'fundamental guarantees'. This provision mirrors many of the international legal protections afforded in peacetime by fundamental human rights. It applies insofar as greater protection is not afforded under another rule of IHL.

In non-international armed conflict, the protection afforded under Common Article 3 applies to anyone (fighter or civilian) who is no longer directly participating in hostilities (because they are sick or wounded or have surrendered or been captured) and to all civilians who are not directly participating in hostilities, including those formally detained.[108] This is so, even though the term 'civilian' does not appear anywhere in Common Article 3.[109] The application of the provisions in Common Article 3, it is stipulated, 'shall not affect the legal status of the Parties to the conflict'. This is to allay concerns among governments that application of the article might be seen as conferring legitimacy on a non-State armed group.

Those who are detained or interned must, to the same extent as the local civilian population, be provided with food and drinking water and be protected against the dangers of the armed conflict.[110] The wounded and sick must be treated and cared for.[111] They must receive a fair trial.[112] And at the end of hostilities, the authorities should consider granting the 'broadest possible amnesty to persons who have participated in the armed conflict, or those deprived of their liberty for reasons related to the armed conflict, whether they are interned or detained'.[113] This is not a strict legal obligation, but an earnest encouragement to act in this manner.

2.2.6.1 The Duty of Humane Treatment

The overriding duty on the State in whose power civilians find themselves is to treat them humanely in all circumstances. This duty must be implemented without any adverse

---

[108] The provision refers to 'active' rather than 'direct' participation in hostilities, but they are synonyms for this purpose. ICRC *Interpretive Guidance on Direct Participation in Hostilities under International Humanitarian Law*, pp. 43–5.

[109] As the ICRC observes, Common Article 3 'implies a concept of civilian comprising those individuals "who do not bear arms" on behalf of a party to the conflict'. Melzer, *Interpretive Guidance on Direct Participation in Hostilities under International Humanitarian Law*, p. 28.

[110] Art. 5(b), 1977 Additional Protocol II.

[111] Arts. 5(a) and 7, 1977 Additional Protocol II.

[112] Art. 6(1) to (4), 1977 Additional Protocol II.

[113] Art. 6(5), 1977 Additional Protocol II.

distinction based on 'race, colour, sex, language, religion or belief, political or other opinion, national or social origin, wealth, birth or other status, or on any other similar criteria'.[114]

The duty of humane treatment encompasses explicit prohibitions 'at any time and in any place' of murder; violence to life, health, or physical or mental well-being; rape, other forms of sexual assault, or enforced prostitution; and collective punishments.[115] Also explicitly prohibited are threats to commit any of those acts.[116]

2.2.6.2 The Treatment of Detainees

Specific provisions in the 1977 Additional Protocol I govern the treatment of civilian detainees.[117] Any person arrested, detained, or interned in connection with the armed conflict must be informed promptly, in a language he or she understands, of the reasons they are being detained or interned. Those interned must be released 'with the minimum delay possible' and in any event 'as soon as the circumstances' justifying the internment have passed.[118] Those being prosecuted are entitled to enjoy all minimum fair-trial guarantees, including the right to know the charges against them, the right to a defence, the right to impartial judgment, and the right to be considered innocent until proven guilty beyond reasonable doubt.[119] The right to appeal against conviction and/or sentence is not specified in the Protocol.

2.2.6.3 The Special Protection of Women

Under the 1977 Additional Protocol I, civilian women who are detained must be held in quarters that are separated from men's quarters and which are under the immediate supervision of women.[120] The exception to this rule is where entire families are detained or interned, where they may be quartered together in special family units.[121] All women must be protected against rape, any other form of indecent assault, and forced prostitution.[122]

Pregnant women and mothers with dependent infants who are detained in connection with the armed conflict must have their cases considered 'with the utmost priority'.[123] If

---

[114] Art. 75(2), 1977 Additional Protocol I.
[115] Art. 75(2)(a) to (d), 1977 Additional Protocol I.
[116] Art. 75(2)(e), 1977 Additional Protocol I.
[117] Art. 75(3) to (8), 1977 Additional Protocol I.
[118] Art. 75(3), 1977 Additional Protocol I.
[119] Art. 75(4), 1977 Additional Protocol I.
[120] For a comprehensive overview on protection of women in armed conflict, see C. Lindsey, *Women Facing War*, ICRC, Geneva, 2020. For a review of IHL protecting women and the comprehensiveness of the legal framework, see also, R. K. Dixit, 'Special Protection of Women During Armed Conflicts under the Geneva Conventions Regime', *Indian Society of International Law (ISIL) Yearbook of International Humanitarian and Refugee Law*, Vol. II (2002), 147.
[121] Art. 75(5), 1977 Additional Protocol I.
[122] Art. 76(1), 1977 Additional Protocol I.
[123] Art. 76(2), 1977 Additional Protocol I.

they are convicted of a serious criminal offence, they should not be sentenced to the death penalty. If they are condemned by a duly constituted court to die, the penalty must not be carried out.[124]

2.2.6.4 The Special Protection of Children

Specific provisions also govern the protection of children. Children must be provided with the 'care and aid they require' and must be protected against any form of sexual assault.

Children under fifteen years of age must not be recruited into the armed forces.[125] This is so whether they are conscripts or volunteers.[126] An Optional Protocol to the Convention on the Rights of the Child – a human rights law treaty not an IHL treaty – has raised the age of enlistment into the armed forces to at least sixteen, and the minimum age of conscription to eighteen.[127] It is only a war crime to recruit children under the age of fifteen years, as Chapter 6 describes.

The Parties to the conflict are required to take all feasible measures to ensure that children who have not attained the age of fifteen years do not take a direct part in hostilities.[128] Under the Optional Protocol to the Convention on the Rights of the Child, this minimum age is raised to eighteen years.[129] Yet controversy arises as to what participation is prohibited. International tribunals have affirmed that the prohibition does not only cover acts of direct participation in hostilities but all those activities that can put them in danger.[130]

Despite the outlawing of the recruitment of children, a question arises as to whether those nonetheless recruited or who take direct part in hostilities become legitimate targets and can therefore be treated as their adult counterparts. Some argue that the principle of humanity together with international human rights law requires resort to capture rather than killing if that option is available.[131] Others assert that

---

[124] Art. 76(3), 1977 Additional Protocol I.

[125] Art. 76(2), 1977 Additional Protocol I.

[126] See also Art. 8(2)(b)(xxvi), Rome Statute of the International Criminal Court; adopted at Rome, 17 July 1998; entered into force, 1 July 2002 (Statute of the International Criminal Court).

[127] Arts. 2 and 3, Optional Protocol to the Convention on the Rights of the Child on the involvement of children in armed conflict; adopted at New York, 25 May 2000; entered into force, 12 February 2002. As of 1 April 2022, 172 States were party to the Protocol. See the UN Treaty Section List, at: http://bit.ly/2k6fCWO.

[128] Art. 76(2), 1977 Additional Protocol I.

[129] Art. 1, 2000 Optional Protocol to the Convention on the Rights of the Child on the involvement of children in armed conflict.

[130] See M. Sassòli, *International Humanitarian Law: Rules, Controversies and Solutions to Problems Arising in Warfare*, Edward Elgar, Cheltenham, 2019, p. 284; and see ICC, *Prosecutor v. Lubanga*, Judgment (Case No. ICC-01/04-01/06), 14 March 2012, paras. 627–8.

[131] Sassòli, *International Humanitarian Law: Rules, Controversies and Solutions to Problems Arising in Warfare*, p. 259, para. 8.77. For support for the equal treatment of children and adult combatants see the citation in S. Bosch, 'Targeting and Prosecuting Under-Aged Child Soldiers in International Armed Conflicts, in Light of the International Humanitarian Law Prohibition against Civilian Direct Participation in Hostilities', *Comprehensive and International Law Journal of South Africa*, Vol. 45 (2012), 324.

considerations of humanity and the special protection accorded to children make it permissible to target them only in situations amounting to self-defence.[132] The argument of giving the interests of children more weight in the proportionality assessment vis-à-vis their adult counterparts has also been advanced.[133]

---

[132]   S. Pack, 'Targeting Child Soldiers: Striking a Balance between Humanity and Military Necessity', *Journal of International Humanitarian Legal Studies*, Vol. 7 (2016), 183; C. Roughley, 'Mind the Gap: Child Soldiers and the Law of Targeting', *Australian International Law Journal*, Vol. 23 (2017), 65.

[133]   Roughley, 'Mind the Gap: Child Soldiers and the Law of Targeting', 65.

3

Protection of Civilians under Human Rights Law

3.1 INTRODUCTION

International human rights law (IHRL) applies at all times to protect civilians, even though the status of civilian does not exist in the same way that it does under international humanitarian law (IHL). The law binds primarily States, which become party to human rights treaties. States are also bound by rules of customary human rights law. But the duty to respect fundamental human rights also applies to international organisations, including the United Nations (UN), and arguably also to armed groups and corporate entities.

In the past, it was sometimes questioned whether human rights law applied in situations of armed conflict. Especially since an Advisory Opinion by the International Court of Justice (ICJ) in 1996, that issue has been resolved.[1] The Court recalled that the protection of the International Covenant on Civil and Political Rights[2] (ICCPR) 'does not cease in times of war, except by operation of Article 4 of the Covenant whereby certain provisions may be derogated from in a time of national emergency'.[3] With regard to the right to life, the Court said that: 'In principle, the right not arbitrarily to be deprived of one's life applies also in hostilities.'[4] Thus, loss of civilian life in the context of fighting may, in certain

---

[1] The applicability of IHRL in times of armed conflict is often linked to the issue of IHRL's extraterritorial reach. Indeed, the mostly debated questions on the interplay between IHL and IHRL arise from situations of non-international armed conflicts fought extraterritorially or military occupation (extraterritorial by definition). A small number of States and commentators have rejected the extraterritorial applicability of IHRL based on a conjunctive reading of the jurisdiction clause under the ICCPR (within its territory and subject to its jurisdiction). See, for example, the Fifth Periodic Report of the United States under the ICCPR, UN doc. CPR/C/USA/5, 19 January 2021, para. 14. The vast majority of States, commentators, and international bodies, however, read the clause disjunctively. They conclude that States remain bound by IHRL during operations conducted extraterritorially when a certain level of jurisdiction, either over territories or over individuals, can be established. For a detailed overview on extraterritoriality, see I. Park, *The Right to Life in Armed Conflict*, Oxford University Press, Oxford, 2018, pp. 65–101. See also M. Milanovic, 'Norm Conflicts, International Humanitarian Law, and Human Rights Law', chapter 5 in *Extraterritorial Application of Human Rights Treaties: Law, Principles, and Policy*, Oxford University Press, Oxford, 2011.

[2] International Covenant on Civil and Political Rights; adopted at New York, 16 December 1966; entered into force, 23 March 1976. As of 1 April 2022, 173 States were party to the ICCPR.

[3] International Court of Justice (ICJ), *Legality of the Threat or Use of Nuclear Weapons*, Advisory Opinion, 8 July 1996, para. 25.

[4] Ibid.

circumstances, amount to a violation of the right to life. But despite the ICJ holding and subsequent human rights jurisprudence confirming the applicability of IHRL in armed conflict, it remains unsettled how, precisely, IHL and international human rights law interrelate during armed conflict. This may be problematic when an issue is regulated differently by the two bodies of law, such as with respect to deprivation of life or liberty, for instance.

In recognising that a debate on this issue among States and among international lawyers persists, this chapter describes how international human rights law acts to protect civilians during armed conflict. In doing so, it focuses especially on State implementation of four fundamental rights: to life; to freedom from torture and other inhumane treatment; to liberty; and to peaceful assembly. The interrelationship with IHL is considered in each instance. Then discussed is the contested application of international human rights law to non-State actors.

3.2 THE RIGHT TO LIFE OF CIVILIANS IN ARMED CONFLICT

The right to life applies to every person, whether he or she be a civilian or a combatant, a prisoner, or a person at liberty. The right to life is the 'supreme right' on which the enjoyment of all other rights depends.[5] The right to life comprises a core substantive prohibition – on 'arbitrary deprivation of life' – and a duty to protect life as well as a procedural obligation to investigate all suspicious, potentially unlawful death.

The right to life applies fully at all times: as the UN Human Rights Committee, which oversees the implementation of the ICCPR by the States Parties to the Covenant, has said: 'no derogation is permitted even in situations of armed conflict and other public emergencies which threaten the life of the nation'.[6] (The concept of derogation, which applies to certain other human rights but not the rights to life or to freedom from torture, allows a State to declare that, given extraordinary circumstances it is facing at a particular time, such as during armed conflict, it cannot fully comply with one or more given rights for a temporary period.)

3.2.1 *Arbitrary Deprivation of Life*

An arbitrary deprivation of life is one that occurs in a manner that is not according to law. During law enforcement (policing) actions during peacetime and in a situation of armed conflict, that may be, for instance, because the use of a particular weapon by a police officer (or a soldier, if he or she is engaged in law enforcement not fighting) is illegal[7] or

---

5　Human Rights Committee, General Comment No. 36: Article 6: right to life, UN doc. CCPR/C/GC/36, 3 September 2019 (hereinafter, Human Rights Committee, General Comment 36 on the right to life), para. 2.
6　Ibid.
7　As the UN Special Rapporteur on extrajudicial, summary, or arbitrary executions observed in his 2014 report to the Human Rights Council, 'The first step of securing the right to life is . . . the establishment of an appropriate legal framework for the use of force by the police, which sets out the conditions under which force may be used in the name of the State.' Report of the Special Rapporteur on extrajudicial, summary or arbitrary executions, Christof Heyns, UN doc. A/HRC/26/36, 1 April 2014, para. 26.

because the force used was either unnecessary or disproportionate under international rules governing law enforcement.

These law enforcement rules apply in all situations and to all use of force by the authorities other than to combat between two parties to an armed conflict. As Chapter 2 recalled, this fighting is known under IHL as the 'conduct of hostilities'. Civilians may be harmed by the fighting or, in certain cases, they may decide to join the fighting. When civilians do 'directly participate in hostilities', they lose their protection from attack under IHL unless and until that participation ceases. Whether human rights law offers any additional legal protection to such a civilian is a contested issue, and there is no settled answer under international law.

3.2.1.1 Use of Force in Law Enforcement

Law enforcement is the means by which States ordinarily enforce their domestic criminal law. The police arrest and detain criminal suspects, who may later be charged with a crime and brought before the courts. If convicted of a serious offence, they may be sentenced to a term of imprisonment. At all stages of the criminal justice process, international human rights law will apply: regulating all use of force by the State, as well as the legality of an arrest, the fairness of a trial, and the treatment and conditions of the person in detention. The use of force is regulated by three core principles: necessity, proportionality, and precaution (all quite distinct from their respective meanings in IHL). A violation of any of these three principles will usually mean that loss of life has been arbitrary and, therefore, that the right to life has also been violated.

THE PRINCIPLE OF NECESSITY. Under international law, the police (or any other security force, including the military, when it is engaged in law enforcement)[8] may use force 'only when strictly necessary'.[9] This is the principle of necessity. The principle of necessity holds that only minimum necessary force in pursuit of a legitimate law enforcement purpose is permissible. In addition, once the need for any force has passed (such as when a violent suspect has been handcuffed and is no longer resisting arrest), application of further force will be unlawful. Moreover, as the European Court of Human Rights has held, where injuries are caused by the police, 'the burden to show the necessity of the force used lies on the Government'.[10]

---

[8] In accordance with the 1979 UN Code of Conduct for Law Enforcement Officials, the term 'law enforcement officials' includes all officers of the law, whether appointed or elected, who exercise police powers, especially the powers of arrest or detention. In countries where police powers are exercised by military authorities, whether uniformed or not, or by State security forces, the definition of law enforcement officials shall be regarded as including officers of such services. Commentary to Article 1 of the Code of Conduct for Law Enforcement Officials; adopted at New York by UN General Assembly Resolution 34/169 (resolution adopted without a vote on 17 December 1979) (hereinafter, 1979 Code of Conduct).

[9] Art. 3, 1979 Code of Conduct.

[10] European Court of Human Rights, *Anzhelo Georgiev and others* v. *Bulgaria*, Judgment (Fourth Section), 30 September 2014, para. 67.

THE PRINCIPLE OF PROPORTIONALITY. Even if a certain degree of force is necessary in the circumstances, it must *also* be proportionate. According to Principle 5 of the 1990 UN Basic Principles on the Use of Force and Firearms, 'Whenever the lawful use of force and firearms is unavoidable, law enforcement officers shall ... act in proportion to the seriousness of the offence and legitimate objective to be achieved.'[11] The principle of proportionality in law enforcement sets an upper limit on when minimum necessary force may be lawful, based on a balancing between the threat posed by an individual or group of individuals and the harm inflicted on life or limb and to property by law enforcement officials seeking to repel the threat. Proportionality has thus a specific meaning in the law applicable to law enforcement that is quite distinct from its meaning in other branches of international law, such as in IHL on the conduct of hostilities[12] or in self-defence under the law on inter-State use of force (*jus ad bellum*).[13]

The principle of proportionality in law enforcement operations is particularly important in restraining the use of potentially lethal force, especially firearms. The general rule is that the police and other law enforcement officials may not use firearms against any person except in self-defence or defence of others against an imminent threat of death or serious injury, and even then only when less-lethal means are insufficient.[14] Use of a firearm by the police purely to defend property (whether movable or immovable) from theft or damage, or in order to disperse an assembly, is therefore unlawful.

An even stricter rule applies to the discharge of a firearm where the intent is to kill rather than to 'stop' a person. Under 1990 Basic Principle 9, 'intentional lethal use of firearms may only be made when strictly unavoidable in order to protect life'. This rule effectively limits the use of 'shooting to kill' to instances of a person who is on the point of detonating a bomb or killing a hostage and no other way reasonably exists to prevent this.

THE PRINCIPLE OF PRECAUTION. Buttressing these two principles on the use of force is the human rights principle of precaution. This principle requires that the authorities plan law enforcement operations in a manner that minimises the risk of the police having to resort to a potentially lethal weapon and thereby to lessen the possibility of death or serious injury to a member of the public or law enforcement official.

The principle was first enunciated by the European Court of Human Rights in its 1995 judgment in the *McCann* case, which concerned the killing of suspected terrorists by British military personnel in the course of a law enforcement operation. The European Court's Grand Chamber – its ultimate authority – stated that it was obliged to 'carefully scrutinise ... not only whether the force used by the soldiers was strictly proportionate to the aim of protecting persons against unlawful violence but also whether the anti-terrorist

---

[11]   Basic Principles on the Use of Force and Firearms by Law Enforcement Officials; adopted at Havana by the Eighth UN Congress on the Prevention of Crime and the Treatment of Offenders, 7 September 1990 (hereinafter, 1990 Basic Principles). In December 1990, the UN General Assembly welcomed the Basic Principles and invited governments to respect them. UN General Assembly Resolution 45/166, adopted without a vote on 18 December 1990, para. 4.

[12]   See Chapter 2 above.

[13]   See Chapter 1 above.

[14]   Principle 9, 1990 Basic Principles.

operation was planned and controlled by the authorities so as to minimise, to the greatest extent possible, recourse to lethal force'.[15]

Where the use of force is unavoidable, appropriate planning of a medical response is essential. The *Finogenov* case[16] before the European Court of Human Rights concerned the violent resolution by Russian Special Forces of a hostage crisis by Chechen separatists at a Moscow theatre. A narcotic gas was pumped into the theatre before it was stormed. The authorities impeded ambulances from accessing the scene afterwards and did not tell medical personnel what gas they had used. As a result of the effects of the gas, several hundred of the hostages died; many, if not most, unnecessarily. This led to Russia being found by the European Court to have violated the right to life of many of the victims.

3.2.1.2 Use of Force in the Conduct of Hostilities

As noted above, the International Court of Justice said in 1996 that 'the right not arbitrarily to be deprived of one's life applies also in hostilities'.[17] The Court continued its analysis by declaring that to determine what constitutes arbitrary deprivation of life during such combat, the relevant rules of IHL must be applied.[18] Thus, as the Human Rights Committee stated in 2019, during the conduct of hostilities: 'Use of lethal force consistent with international humanitarian law ... is, in general, not arbitrary.'[19]

That means that the two fundamental principles of IHL (distinction and proportionality in attack) must be duly complied with. Accordingly, as Chapter 2 explained, an attack must be directed against a lawful military objective (whether that is a person or an object) and the expected civilian harm must not be 'excessive' when compared to the 'concrete and direct' military advantage anticipated. In such a case, where the rule is fully complied with, not only IHL but also the right to life will *not* have been violated. The term civilian harm means civilian deaths or injuries or damage to civilian objects 'or a combination thereof'.

It is not certain how accurate an attack must be, nor how much civilian harm will be excessive, however. Indeed, interpretation of the rules of distinction and proportionality differs markedly among States. It is certain, though, that an aerial or artillery bombardment does not need to hit its target in order to comply with IHL. Honest mistakes in targeting are also not per se a violation of IHL. There is further no general IHL obligation

[15] European Court of Human Rights, *McCann and others* v. *United Kingdom*, Judgment (Grand Chamber), 27 September 1995, para. 194.

[16] European Court of Human Rights, *Finogenov and others* v. *Russia*, Judgment (First Section), 20 December 2011 (as rendered final on 4 June 2012).

[17] ICJ, *Legality of the Threat or Use of Nuclear Weapons*, Advisory Opinion, 8 July 1996, para. 25. For an overview on the interplay between IHRL and IHL with respect to the right to life, see, Park, *The Right to Life in Armed Conflict*; and L. Doswald-Beck, 'The Right to Life in Armed Conflict: Does International Humanitarian Law Provide All the Answers?', *International Review of the Red Cross*, Vol. 88, No. 864 (December 2006), 881–904. See also S. Casey-Maslen, *The Right to Life under International Law: An Interpretive Manual*, Cambridge University Press, Cambridge, 2021, chapter 5.

[18] ICJ, *Legality of the Threat or Use of Nuclear Weapons*, Advisory Opinion, 8 July 1996, para. 25.

[19] Human Rights Committee, General Comment 36 on the right to life, para. 64.

on a State to use precision-guided ('smart') munitions. The consequence is that civilians – potentially many civilians – may die and/or be seriously injured without IHL being infringed.

The International Committee of the Red Cross (ICRC) argues that in addition to the restraints imposed by IHL on specific means and methods of warfare, the force that can be used against anyone not entitled to protection against direct attack 'must not exceed what is actually necessary to accomplish a legitimate military purpose in the prevailing circumstances'. It also contends that 'while operating forces can hardly be required to take additional risks for themselves or the civilian population in order to capture an armed adversary alive, it would defy basic notions of humanity to kill an adversary or to refrain from giving him or her an opportunity to surrender where there manifestly is no necessity for the use of lethal force'. This norm would apply to civilians who participate directly in hostilities.[20] If correct, this would provide additional protection to civilians, and a violation of the rule would give rise to a corresponding human rights violation. The IHL rule has not yet, though, been generally accepted by States.

Some international lawyers argue that international human rights law as applicable to situations of law enforcement imposes additional restrictions over and above IHL rules. This, in particular in non-international armed conflicts and situations of military occupation,[21] would require that belligerents capture rather than kill an enemy where it is feasible to do so, and do not ordinarily shoot to kill.[22] This position has not, though, been generally endorsed by States.

3.2.1.3 Use of Force in Detention Facilities

The international legal situation is clearer in a detention facility. The duty upon the detaining State is to both respect and protect the life of all inmates in all cases, irrespective of whether they are detained under domestic law for an ordinary criminal offence or for unlawfully participating directly in hostilities. By 'respect' is meant that the authorities must not arbitrarily deprive a detainee of his or her life. To 'protect' a detainee is to prevent others (e.g. other inmates or other third parties) from killing or harming him or her. They must also be given food and water and, whenever necessary, appropriate medical treatment. These fundamental duties apply to all civilians detained during an armed conflict, whatever the reason for their detention.

A specific rule applies to the use of force against a person trying to escape from custody. Under what are known as the Nelson Mandela Rules, staff may use force in a case of

---

[20] N. Melzer, *Interpretive Guidance on the Notion of Direct Participation in Hostilities under International Humanitarian Law*, ICRC, Geneva, 2009, pp. 77–9 and 82. See also R. Goodman, 'The Power to Kill or Capture Enemy Combatants', *European Journal of International Law*, Vol. 24, No. 3 (2013), 819–53.

[21] On IHRL applicability during military occupation, see N. Lubell, 'Human Rights in Military Occupation', *International Review of the Red Cross*, Vol. 94, No. 885 (2012), 337.

[22] See, for example, Goodman, 'The Power to Kill or Capture Enemy Combatants'; see also the discussion in M. Milanovic, 'When to Kill and When to Capture?', *EJIL Talk*, 6 May 2011, at: http://bit.ly/2U79rBE. See further D. Kretzmer 'Targeted Killing of Suspected Terrorists: Extra-Judicial Executions or Legitimate Means of Defence?', *European Journal of International Law*, Vol. 16, No. 2 (2005), 171.

attempted escape from a prison, but that force must still be no more than is strictly necessary.[23] Shooting an escapee who does not pose an imminent threat of seriously injuring someone or a grave threat to life is unlawful and violates fundamental human rights. Even if the person survives, a violation of the right to life may have occurred.[24]

3.2.2 *The Duty to Investigate Suspicious Death*

In all situations, there is a duty on the State to investigate a suspicious death, including of all civilians. By suspicious is meant a death that may have been caused unlawfully, in particular as a result of violence. It does not matter whether or not the involvement of the State is suspected to have led in any way to the death.

The European Court considers the duty to investigate a potentially unlawful death to be a procedural component of the right to life.[25] The same approach is taken by the African Commission on Human and Peoples' Rights: 'The failure of the State transparently to take all necessary measures to investigate suspicious deaths and all killings by State agents and to identify and hold accountable individuals or groups responsible for violations of the right to life constitutes in itself a violation by the State of that right.'[26]

The duty to investigate exists where the authorities know or should have known of potentially unlawful deprivations of life.[27] This certainly encompasses any situation where it is alleged that excessive use of force has been used 'with lethal consequences'.[28] Moreover, a presumption of arbitrary deprivation of life by the State exists when loss of life occurs in custody in unnatural circumstances. This presumption can only be rebutted on the basis of an effective and impartial investigation that establishes that the State has complied with its obligations under the right to life.[29]

Such investigations of potentially unlawful deprivations of life should be undertaken in accordance with relevant international standards, in particular the *Minnesota Protocol on the Investigation of Potentially Unlawful Death* (2016), an expert document elaborated under the auspices of the Office of the UN High Commissioner for Human Rights.[30]

---

[23] Rule 82(1), UN Standard Minimum Rules for the Treatment of Prisoners (the Nelson Mandela Rules), adopted by UN General Assembly Resolution 70/175 (resolution adopted by unanimous vote on 17 December 2015).

[24] See, for example, European Court of Human Rights, *Makaratzis* v. *Greece*, Judgment (Grand Chamber), 20 December 2004, para. 38; European Court of Human Rights, *Acar and others* v. *Turkey*, Judgment (Fourth Section), 24 May 2005, para. 77.

[25] European Court of Human Rights, *Mastromatteo* v. *Italy*, Judgment (Grand Chamber), 24 October 2002, para. 89.

[26] African Commission General Comment on the Right to Life, para. 15.

[27] Human Rights Committee, General Comment 36 on the right to life, para. 27.

[28] Ibid.

[29] Ibid., para. 29.

[30] *Minnesota Protocol on the Investigation of Potentially Unlawful Death* (2016), The Revised United Nations Manual on the Effective Prevention and Investigation of Extra-legal, Arbitrary and Summary Executions, OHCHR, New York/Geneva, 2017. The duty to conduct an effective investigation as a procedural part of the right to life was first recognised in *McCann and Others* v. *United Kingdom*, Judgment (Grand Chamber), para. 161.

Investigations into any alleged violation of the right to life must be independent, impartial, prompt, thorough, effective, and transparent.[31]

The Minnesota Protocol recalls that, to be effective, investigations must, at a minimum, take all reasonable steps to:

- identify the victim or victims
- recover and preserve all material probative of the cause of death, the identity of the perpetrator or perpetrators, and the circumstances surrounding the death
- identify possible witnesses and obtain their evidence in relation to the death and the circumstances surrounding the death
- determine the cause, manner, place, and time of death, and all of the surrounding circumstances;[32] and
- determine who was involved in the death and their individual responsibility for the death.[33]

Of critical importance in the case of a death is the conduct of an autopsy. The Minnesota Protocol stipulates that: It will 'almost always be the case' that meeting the aims set out above 'will be materially assisted in some way by the performance of an autopsy'. A 'decision not to undertake an autopsy should', the Protocol declares, 'be justified in writing and should be subject to judicial review'.[34]

3.2.2.1 The Duty to Investigate during Armed Conflict

The human rights law duty to investigate continues during a situation of armed conflict.[35] In situations of international armed conflict, IHL explicitly requires that every death of, or serious injury to, a civilian internee that is caused or suspected to have been caused by a guard or another prisoner or indeed any other person, as well as any death the cause of which is unknown, 'shall be immediately followed by an official enquiry by the Detaining Power'.[36] In both international and non-international armed conflict, violence against detainees is prohibited by treaty and customary IHL 'and can amount to a war crime'.[37] As the ICRC has observed, the obligation under IHL to prosecute war crimes 'logically presupposes an obligation to investigate'.[38]

---

[31] *Minnesota Protocol on the Investigation of Potentially Unlawful Death* (2016), para. 22.

[32] In determining the manner of death, an investigation should distinguish between natural death, accidental death, suicide, and homicide.

[33] *Minnesota Protocol on the Investigation of Potentially Unlawful Death* (2016), para. 25; and see Inter-American Court of Human Rights, *Veliz Franco and others* v. *Guatemala*, Judgment (Preliminary objections, merits, reparations, and costs), 19 May 2014, para. 191.

[34] *Minnesota Protocol on the Investigation of Potentially Unlawful Death* (2016), para. 25.

[35] According to the Minnesota Protocol, the duty to investigate any potentially unlawful death applies to all cases during an armed conflict outside the conduct of hostilities, meaning that it concerns, in particular, cases of detention with sufficient nexus to the armed conflict. *Minnesota Protocol on the Investigation of Potentially Unlawful Death* (2016), para. 16.

[36] Art. 131, Geneva Convention relative to the Protection of Civilian Persons in Time of War; adopted at Geneva, 12 August 1949; entered into force, 21 October 1950 (hereinafter, 1949 Geneva Convention IV).

[37] ICRC, *Guidelines for Investigating Deaths in Custody*, Geneva, 2013, p. 12.

[38] Ibid.

A duty to investigate can be inferred also from the duty to respect and ensure respect for the 1949 Geneva Conventions in all circumstances.[39] In addition, the 1977 Additional Protocol I[40] obligates all States Parties to take measures necessary to suppress all breaches of the Geneva Conventions or of the Protocol 'which result from a failure to act when under a duty to do so'.[41] However, it is disputed by some whether this duty arises with respect to violations of IHL that do not seemingly amount to war crimes.[42]

Jurisprudence upholds that the duty under the right to life to investigate potentially unlawful death continues to apply during situations of armed conflict. In its judgment in one case, the Inter-American Court of Human Rights recognised the 'difficult circumstances' prevailing, given the armed conflict existing at the relevant time. The Court, though, stated that 'no matter how difficult' the conditions were, they 'do not release a State Party to the American Convention [on Human Rights] of its obligations'.[43]

In a later judgment, the European Court of Human Rights' Grand Chamber similarly acknowledged that where the death to be investigated under the right to life of the European Convention on Human Rights occurs 'in circumstances of generalised violence, armed conflict or insurgency, obstacles may be placed in the way of investigators'. Further, 'concrete constraints may compel the use of less effective measures of investigation or may cause an investigation to be delayed'.[44] Nonetheless, the Court concluded, 'even in difficult security conditions, all reasonable steps must be taken to ensure that an effective, independent investigation is conducted into alleged breaches of the right to life'.[45] In the *al-Skeini* case, one of the applicants was a colonel in the Basra police force whose son, Baha Mousa, was aged twenty-six when he died while in the custody of the British army, three days after having been arrested by soldiers on 14 September 2003. Baha

---

[39]   Art. 1 common to the four 1949 Geneva Conventions.

[40]   Art. 87, Protocol Additional to the Geneva Conventions of 12 August 1949, and relating to the Protection of Victims of International Armed Conflicts; adopted at Geneva, 8 June 1977; entered into force, 7 December 1978 (hereinafter, 1977 Additional Protocol I).

[41]   Art. 86(1), 1977 Additional Protocol I.

[42]   For instance, Schmitt is of the view that 'investigations are required only if there is reasonable suspicion or a credible allegation of a war crime having been committed', whilst, for the UN Special Rapporteur on the promotion and protection of human rights and fundamental freedoms while countering terrorism, the duty 'to conduct a prompt, independent and impartial fact-finding inquiry' exists in 'any case in which civilians have been, or appear to have been, killed'. On these and other views on the matter, see M. Lattimer, 'The Duty in International Law to Investigate Civilian Deaths in Armed Conflict', in M. Lattimer and P. Sands (eds.), *The Grey Zone: Civilian Protection Between Human Rights and the Laws of War*, Hart, Oxford, 2018, 41–72, at pp. 52–3. Lattimer finds that 'State practice more broadly supports the existence of a duty to report and perform some form of investigation in all cases of suspected violations', citing Australian, Canadian, UK, and US practice. He claims that this broad investigation duty exists under IHL independently, so that it is applicable even when IHRL does not apply or its applicability is disputed. See, Lattimer, ibid., at pp. 55 and 71. See also M. N. Schmitt, 'Investigating Violations of International Law in Armed Conflict', *Harvard National Security Journal*, Vol. 2 (2011), 31; and A. Cohen and Y. Shany, 'Beyond the Grave Breaches Regime: The Duty to Investigate Alleged Violations of International Law Governing Armed Conflicts' in M. N. Schmitt and L. Arimatsu (eds.), *Yearbook of International Humanitarian Law*, Vol. 14 (2011), 39.

[43]   Inter-American Court of Human Rights, *Case of the 'Mapiripán Massacre' v. Colombia*, Judgment (Merits, Reparations, and Costs), 15 September 2005, para. 238.

[44]   European Court of Human Rights, *al-Skeini and others v. United Kingdom*, Judgment (Grand Chamber), 7 July 2011, para. 164.

[45]   Ibid.

Mousa, who was found to have ninety-three identifiable injuries on his body, died of asphyxiation.[46]

The *Jaloud* case[47] concerned the shooting to death of a passenger in a car approaching a checkpoint that was jointly manned at the time by armed Iraqi Civil Defence Corps personnel and Dutch troops. The shooting took place during the foreign military occupation of Iraq led by the United States. A key issue was to determine who had fired the fatal shots: the Iraqi or the Dutch forces. It appears that the calibre of ammunition fired by each differed.[48] The European Court observed that an autopsy of the body seems to have been carried out in the absence of any qualified Dutch official and that nothing was known of the qualifications of the Iraqi pathologist who performed it.[49] Moreover, the Court noted, the pathologist's report 'had serious shortcomings; extremely brief, it was lacking in detail and there were not even any pictures included'.[50] More generally, no alternative arrangement appeared to have been considered for the autopsy even though the US or UK forces might have had facilities and qualified personnel available.[51] The Court found, therefore, that the investigation was deficient with respect to the autopsy.[52] The Netherlands had thereby violated the right to life in its procedural element.

Most recently, in its judgment on acts by Russia during the conflict in Georgia in 2008, the European Court reiterated that the duty to investigate applies to armed conflict and affirmed that the obligation to carry out an effective investigation under the dictates of the right to life protected under the European Convention 'is broader than the corresponding obligation in international humanitarian law'.[53]

However, a few commentators argue against the applicability of the IHRL duty to conduct investigation precisely because, they claim, it requires higher standards than does the corresponding obligation under IHL.[54] Notably, they criticise the requirement of transparency of investigations under IHRL, whose content, it is argued, contravenes the need for information to remain classified in the context of armed conflicts.[55] This is not persuasive. A human rights-compliant investigation may withhold information from the victim's family if the interests of justice warrant it, and national security considerations

---

[46]   Ibid., paras. 63, 66.
[47]   European Court of Human Rights, *Jaloud* v. *The Netherlands*, Judgment (Grand Chamber), 20 November 2014.
[48]   North Atlantic Treaty Organization (NATO) standard 5.56 mm rounds were fired by the Dutch soldiers, but 7.62 mm rounds were fired by the Iraqis.
[49]   European Court of Human Rights, *Jaloud* v. *The Netherlands*, Judgment (Grand Chamber), para. 213.
[50]   Ibid., para. 214.
[51]   Ibid., para. 215.
[52]   Ibid., para. 216.
[53]   European Court of Human Rights, *Georgia* v. *Russia (II)*, Judgment (Grand Chamber), 21 January 2021, paras. 325 and 328–337.
[54]   Notably, by relying on the *lex specialis* argument they argue that in a situation of armed conflict, in particular in the conduct of hostilities, IHL overrides IHRL. See, for instance, Schmitt, 'Investigating Violations of International Law in Armed Conflict', pp. 53–4.
[55]   On this and an alternative interpretation of *lex specialis* with respect to the obligation to conduct investigations in armed conflict, see Lattimer, 'The Duty in International Law to Investigate Civilian Deaths in Armed Conflict', pp. 62–5.

may also prevent disclosure. What is not lawful is the failure to disclose information on the basis that it is embarrassing to the authorities or identifies human rights violations.

3.3 THE RIGHT TO FREEDOM FROM TORTURE AND OTHER ILL-TREATMENT

3.3.1 *The Prohibition on Torture or Other Ill-Treatment*

The ICCPR stipulates that no one shall be subjected to torture or to cruel, inhuman, or degrading treatment.[56] Torture is defined in the 1984 Convention against Torture[57] as any act by a State official in which severe physical or mental pain or suffering is intentionally inflicted on a person, especially one who is in custody or detention.[58] In general terms, cruel treatment refers to pain or suffering that is applied wantonly, gratuitously, or sadistically; inhuman treatment is the inflicting of severe pain or suffering; while degrading treatment comprises acts intended to humiliate the victim. In contrast, torture is primarily committed when the victim is in the physical power of the perpetrator, whether or not he or she has been formally arrested by a law enforcement official[59] (or detained by an armed force or armed group).

The right to freedom from torture and other ill-treatment is, as is the case with the right to life, non-derogable. Thus, it applies in all situations, including in all armed conflict, and to all persons, whether civilian or not. This right is fully reflected in IHL. In any armed conflict, 'violence to life and person, in particular murder of all kinds, mutilation, cruel treatment and torture', is prohibited against any detainee held in connection with the conflict, as it is against any other civilian in the power of the enemy.[60]

Torture may involve threats as well as acts. In the 2003 *Urrutia* case, the Inter-American Court of Human Rights found that Ms Urrutia was subjected to very long interrogations during which she was shown photographs of individuals who had been

---

[56] For a critique on framing the prohibition of torture as 'absolute' see S. Greer, 'Is the Prohibition against Torture, Cruel, Inhuman and Degrading Treatment Really Absolute in International Human Rights Law?', *Human Rights Law Review*, Vol. 15 (2015), 101.

[57] Convention against Torture and Other Cruel, Inhuman or Degrading Treatment or Punishment; adopted at New York, 10 December 1984; entered into force, 26 June 1987 (hereinafter, CAT).

[58] Art. 1(1), CAT. On the different interpretations of the 'actor requirement' (i.e. the requirement that the perpetrator has to be 'a public official or other person acting in an official capacity') in the definition under CAT, see S. Sivakumaran, 'Torture in International Human Rights and International Humanitarian Law: The Actor and the Ad Hoc Tribunals', *Leiden Journal of International Law*, Vol. 18 (2005), 541 at pp. 546–55.

[59] S. Casey-Maslen and S. Connolly, *Police Use of Force under International Law*, Cambridge University Press, Cambridge, 2017, p. 153.

[60] Article 3 common to the four 1949 Geneva Conventions. See also Art. 4, Protocol Additional to the Geneva Conventions of 12 August 1949, and relating to the Protection of Victims of Non-International Armed Conflicts; adopted at Geneva, 8 June 1977; entered into force, 7 December 1978 (hereinafter, 1977 Additional Protocol II). Since there is no explicit definition of torture under IHL, international tribunals have applied the CAT definition. However, the question whether the CAT 'actor requirement' forms also part of the definition of torture under IHL has been the subject of debate within the jurisprudence of ad hoc tribunals. See Sivakumaran, 'Torture in International Human Rights and International Humanitarian Law: The Actor and the Ad Hoc Tribunals', pp. 542–6.

tortured or killed in combat and threatened that she would be found by her family in the same way. Guatemalan State agents also threatened to torture her physically or to kill her or members of her family if she did not collaborate. Ms Urrutia was obliged to appear in a propaganda video that was later broadcast by two Guatemalan television channels.[61]

Under international law, rape can amount to torture. The *Aydin* case before the European Court of Human Rights[62] concerned the brutal treatment of a seventeen-year-old Turkish woman of Kurdish origin in custody. She was blindfolded, beaten, stripped naked, placed in a tyre, and hosed with pressurised water, before being raped by a member of the security forces, and then beaten for about an hour by several people. The Court stressed that rape of a detainee by an official of the State is an especially grave and abhorrent form of ill-treatment, which leaves deep psychological scars on the victim. The Court found that both the accumulation of acts of physical and mental violence inflicted on the applicant while in custody, and the especially cruel act of rape to which she had been subjected, amounted to torture.[63]

3.3.2 *The Duty to Investigate Ill-Treatment*

As with the right to life, there is a duty to investigate whenever reasonable grounds exist to believe that an act of torture or other inhumane treatment has been committed, irrespective of whether a formal complaint has been received. In a prison, the prison director is obliged to report any serious injury that occurs in custody to an independent authority mandated to conduct prompt, impartial and effective investigations 'without delay'. The prison administration must cooperate 'fully' with that authority and 'ensure that all evidence is preserved'.[64] Details of how to conduct an effective investigation into suspected torture are set out in the Istanbul Protocol, an expert document from 1999 that was undergoing revision as of writing.[65]

3.4 THE RIGHT TO FREEDOM FROM ARBITRARY DETENTION

The risks of a civilian being arbitrarily arrested and detained during an armed conflict are exceptionally acute. Article 9(1) of the ICCPR stipulates that everyone has the right to liberty and security of person. This provision prohibits arbitrary arrest or detention. There

---

[61] Inter-American Court of Human Rights, *Maritza Urrutia v. Guatemala*, Judgment (Merits, Reparations, and Costs), 27 November 2003, para. 85.

[62] European Court of Human Rights, *Aydin v. Turkey*, Judgment (Grand Chamber), 25 September 1997.

[63] Ibid., paras. 82–4. For an analysis of the Committee against Torture's approach see F. D. Gaer, 'Rape as a Form of Torture: The Experience of the Committee against Torture', *City University of New York (CUNY) Law Review*, Vol. 15 (2012), 293. For a critique against reconceptualising rape as torture, see C. McGlynn, 'Rape as "Torture"?, Catharine MacKinnon and Questions of Feminist Strategy', *Feminist Legal Studies*, Vol. 16 (2008), 71–85.

[64] Rule 71(1), 2015 Nelson Mandela Rules.

[65] *Manual on the Effective Investigation and Documentation of Torture and Other Cruel, Inhuman or Degrading Treatment or Punishment* ('Istanbul Protocol'), 1999.

must be a clear legal basis for any deprivation of liberty, which may not be conducted on a discriminatory basis.[66]

However, in contrast to the rights to life and to freedom from all forms of inhumane treatment, the right to liberty is derogable in a situation of emergency.[67] This may allow a State to intern individual civilians without charge for the purpose of safeguarding national security. Once they have been detained for reasons connected to an armed conflict, civilians are at heightened risk of harm (as are all detainees).

In an important 2009 judgment,[68] the European Court of Human Rights' Grand Chamber held that the indefinite detention of non-nationals on suspicion of involvement in terrorism, on the basis of a decision by a UK Secretary of State for the Home Department, amounted to arbitrary detention. The derogating measures that permitted their indefinite detention were deemed to have discriminated unjustifiably between nationals and non-nationals.[69] The Court said that to avoid being branded as arbitrary, detention under the relevant provision of the European Convention on Human Rights[70] must be carried out in good faith; the place and conditions of detention should be appropriate; and the length of detention should not exceed that 'reasonably required' for the purpose for which the person is being detained.[71]

As the ICRC has observed, the relationship between IHL and international human rights law concerning internment[72] in non-international armed conflicts, in particular its admissibility and procedural guarantees, is more controversial than is the case in international armed conflicts.[73] In international armed conflicts, IHL permits the internment, under certain conditions and on an individual basis, of civilians. For instance, under the 1949 Geneva Convention IV, in a situation of foreign military occupation, if the Occupying Power considers it necessary, for imperative reasons of security, to take safety measures concerning civilians, it may subject them to internment.[74] No similar power, however, exists in non-international armed conflict. A basis for internment must therefore be found in domestic law insofar as it complies with international human rights law.

In its 2017 judgment in the *Serdar Mohamed* case,[75] the UK Supreme Court noted that the provisions in IHL pertaining to internment in international armed conflict 'do not apply to non-international armed conflict'. In such a situation, 'lawful authority must be sought elsewhere. Normally, it will arise under domestic law, but it may also arise out of

---

[66] Art. 2(1), ICCPR.

[67] In *Hassan v. United Kingdom*, the European Court of Human Rights has recognised that in international armed conflicts, it is not mandatory to derogate from Art. 5 of the European Convention on Human Rights, although administrative detention in not mentioned among the legitimate grounds listed by that article. European Court of Human Rights, *Hassan v. United Kingdom*, Judgment (Grand Chamber), 16 September 2014, paras. 101–3 and 107.

[68] European Court of Human Rights, *A. and others v. United Kingdom*, Judgment (Grand Chamber), 19 February 2009.

[69] Ibid., para. 190.

[70] Article 5(1)(f): of a person against whom action is being taken with a view to deportation or extradition.

[71] European Court of Human Rights, *A. and others v. United Kingdom*, Judgment, para. 164.

[72] Internment is detention without charge, especially when this is done for reasons of national security.

[73] ICRC, 'Internment', How Does Law Protect in War? at: http://bit.ly/2RW8TM3.

[74] Art. 78, 1949 Geneva Convention IV.

[75] United Kingdom Supreme Court, *Serdar Mohammed v. Ministry of Defence*, Judgment [2017] UKSC 2.

other branches of international law, as for example where it is conferred by' a resolution of the UN Security Council.[76] Controversially, the ICRC has affirmed that an 'inherent power' to detain exists in non-international armed conflicts though it acknowledges that some additional 'authority' is needed, which defines the grounds and process for internment. It identifies such potential 'authority' in domestic law, international agreements between the belligerent parties, or UN Security Council Resolutions.[77] An implied power to detain under IHL in non-international armed conflict, as proposed by the ICRC, has not been generally accepted by States.

3.5 THE RIGHT OF PEACEFUL ASSEMBLY

The right to demonstrate and protest is fundamental to any democratic society. As the Human Rights Committee has stated: 'Where they are used to air grievances, peaceful assemblies may create opportunities for inclusive, participatory and peaceful resolution of differences.'[78] Accordingly, under Article 21 of the ICCPR, it is stipulated that the right of peaceful assembly must be 'recognized'. Any restrictions on the exercise of the right of peaceful assembly must be legal and necessary for national security or public safety, public order, public health, or the protection of the rights of others.[79]

Demonstrations during armed conflict are especially hazardous. They may be suppressed by the State; participants may be attacked; violence may be stirred up by *agents provocateurs*; and members of non-State armed groups may seek to exploit an assembly in order to attack the security forces. These risks heighten the likelihood that civilians participating in an assembly may be harmed (or prevented from exercising their right of peaceful assembly).

The Human Rights Committee concluded its General Comment on the right of peaceful assembly in 2020. With respect to a situation of armed conflict, the General Comment recalls that, if not derogated from, the right of peaceful assembly continues during states of emergency, including in armed conflict. 'State parties must not rely on derogation from the right of peaceful assembly if they can attain their objectives by imposing restrictions in terms of article 21.'[80]

One of the most debated provisions in the General Comment concerns the use of force with respect to assemblies during armed conflict. The General Comment stipulates as follows:

> In a situation of armed conflict, the use of force during peaceful assemblies remains regulated by the rules governing law enforcement, and the Covenant continues to

---

[76] Ibid., para. 267 and compare also para. 274.

[77] ICRC, 'Internment in Armed Conflict: Basic Rules and Challenges', Opinion Paper, November 2014, at: https://bit.ly/39HHW84, pp. 7–8.

[78] Human Rights Committee, General Comment No. 37: Article 21: right of peaceful assembly, UN doc. CCPR/C/GC/37, 17 September 2020, para. 1.

[79] Art. 21, ICCPR.

[80] Human Rights Committee, General Comment 37 on the right of peaceful assembly, para. 96.

apply. Civilians in an assembly are protected from being targeted with lethal force unless and for such time as they take a direct part in hostilities, as that term is understood under international humanitarian law. In such a circumstance, they may be targeted only to the extent that they are not otherwise protected under international law from attack. Any use of force under applicable international humanitarian law is subject to the rules and principles of distinction, precautions in attack, proportionality, military necessity and humanity. In all decisions on the use of force, the safety and protection of assembly participants and the broader public should be an important consideration.[81]

As discussed in Chapter 2, the status of 'continuous combat function' is a term that was proposed by the ICRC in its 2009 interpretive guidance on direct participation in hostilities by civilians.[82] The notion whereby a civilian that joins a non-State armed group as a full military member is no longer a civilian has some support among States. The status-based approach to direct participation in hostilities, though, was implicitly rejected by the 2019 Commission of Inquiry on the protests in Gaza.[83]

3.6 THE APPLICATION OF HUMAN RIGHTS LAW TO NON-STATE ACTORS

The application of international human rights law to non-State actors remains controversial. Authorities question whether non-State actors are directly bound by international human rights law, since treaties are elaborated, adopted, signed, and ratified by States. In so doing, however, the situation under international human rights law is often distinguished from that in IHL where Common Article 3 to the four 1949 Geneva Conventions explicitly applies to 'Each Party' to a non-international armed conflict.

Others question whether non-State actors can ever 'contract' international legal obligations on the basis that they are not a 'subject' of international law in the same way States are. This is despite the fact that, for instance, States recognise that parties to a non-international armed conflict not only can but 'should further endeavour to bring into force, by means of special agreements', all or part of the other provisions of the 1949 Geneva Conventions beyond Common Article 3 (which explicitly governs non-international armed conflict).

In one of its judgments, the Special Court for Sierra Leone did not find that armed groups had sufficient 'international legal personality' to be able to conclude a binding agreement under international law, though it had no difficulty affirming that such groups are directly bound by IHL. Thus, in 2004, the Appeals Chamber held that 'it is well settled that all parties to an armed conflict, whether States or non-State actors, are bound

[81] Ibid., para. 109, citing UN doc. A/HRC/40/CRP.2, summary and para. 106.
[82] Ibid., pp. 33–4.
[83] This is despite the Commission claiming in its report that it did not 'opine on the recognition of CCF, nor its lawfulness as an IHL-based status'. Report of the detailed findings of the independent international Commission of inquiry on the protests in the Occupied Palestinian Territory, UN doc. A/HRC/40/CRP.2, 18 March 2019, paras. 105, 394, and 410. See also para. 399.

by international humanitarian law, even though only States may become parties to international treaties'.[84]

Notwithstanding this affirmation, it remains unclear as to how, as a matter of legal theory, non-State armed groups are bound by international law. As noted above, a widely advanced argument is that Common Article 3 explicitly states that the provision binds 'each Party to the conflict', a formulation understood to encompass non-State actors. A major drawback of this approach,[85] though, is that it implies that where a treaty does not use such express language, as is the case, for instance, with the 1977 Additional Protocol II, it would not bind a non-State belligerent in an armed conflict governed by the Protocol.[86]

More persuasive is the argument that non-State actors are bound by customary international law. Thus, with respect to Common Article 3 to the Geneva Conventions, the Special Court's Appeals Chamber asserted that insurgents 'are bound as a matter of customary international law to observe the obligations declared by Common Article 3 which is aimed at the protection of humanity'.[87] This is the best approach in legal theory as to how non-State armed groups are bound by IHL. That said, it is also not without its challenges, particularly with respect to the precise point in time at which the rules set out in Common Article 3 became binding as a matter of custom.

A similar approach can be envisaged with respect to the application of human rights law to non-State actors: that the law has become binding through the operation of customary law. This is the approach taken by the UN in its reports on the protection of civilians in Afghanistan:[88] 'While they cannot become parties to international human rights treaties, non-State actors, including armed groups, are not precluded from being subject to human rights obligations under customary international law. Non-State actors are increasingly deemed to be bound by certain international human rights obligations, particularly those actors exercising de facto control over some areas, such as the Taliban.'[89] A slightly different approach is to restrict the application of human rights law to non-State armed groups to peremptory (*jus cogens*) norms of international law,

---

[84]   Special Court for Sierra Leone (SCSL), *Prosecutor v. Sam Hinga Norman*, Decision on Preliminary Motion Based on Lack of Jurisdiction (Appeals Chamber) (Case No. SCSL-2004-14-AR72(E)), 31 May 2004, para. 22.

[85]   See, for example, D. Murray, *Human Rights Obligations of Non-State Armed Groups*, Hart, Oxford, 2016, p. 107.

[86]   Moir's argument is, primarily, that it would be 'bizarre' if Common Article 3 were legally binding but Additional Protocol II, which complements and supplements it, were not. See L. Moir, *The Law of Internal Armed Conflict*, Cambridge University Press, Cambridge, 2002, p. 97.

[87]   SCSL, *Prosecutor v. Kallon and Kamara*, Decision on Challenge to Jurisdiction: Lomé Accord Amnesty (Appeals Chamber) (Case Nos. SCSL-2004-15-AR72(E) and SCSL-2004-16-AR72(E)), 13 March 2004, paras. 45–7.

[88]   UN Assistance Mission in Afghanistan (UNAMA) Human Rights Service, *Afghanistan, Protection of Civilians in Armed Conflict: 2018 Annual Report*, UNAMA and OHCHR, Kabul, February 2019, p. 55.

[89]   See UN Secretary-General, *Report of the Secretary-General's Panel of Experts on Accountability in Sri Lanka*, 31 March 2011, para. 188. See also Report of the International Commission of Inquiry to investigate all Alleged Violations of International Human Rights Law in the Libyan Arab Jamahiriya, UN doc. A/HRC/17/44, 1 June 2011; the Report of the International Commission of Inquiry on the Situation of Human Rights in the Syrian Arab Republic, UN doc. A/HRC/19/69, para. 106; and UN Mission in the Republic of South Sudan (UNMISS), *Conflict in South Sudan: A Human Rights Report*, 8 May 2014, para. 18.

that is to say, customary rules that are binding on all States without exception and which cannot be derogated from by treaty.[90] Andrew Clapham, a leading authority on the issue of non-State actors, notes that within the UN 'perhaps the clearest' statement was made by a 2014 report on human rights in South Sudan:[91]

> The most basic human rights obligations, in particular those emanating from peremptory international law (*ius cogens*), bind both the State and armed opposition groups in times of peace and during armed conflict. In particular, international human rights law requires States, armed groups and others to respect the prohibitions of extrajudicial killing, maiming, torture, cruel, inhuman or degrading treatment or punishment, enforced disappearance, rape, other conflict related sexual violence, sexual and other forms of slavery, the recruitment and use of children in hostilities, arbitrary detention as well as of any violations that amount to war crimes, crimes against humanity, or genocide.[92]

---

[90] Such norms of *jus cogens* are universal in application and their respect is not limited to sovereign territory or territory controlled by an armed group. See, for example, African Commission on Human and Peoples' Rights, General Comment on the Right to Life, 2015, para. 5; Casey-Maslen, *The Right to Life under International Law: An Interpretive Manual*, para. 3.09.

[91] A. Clapham, 'Violations by Armed Non-State Actors', in S. Casey-Maslen, A. Clapham, G. Giacca, and S. Parker, *The Arms Trade Treaty: A Commentary*, Oxford University Press, Oxford, 2016, para. 7.73.

[92] UNMISS, *Conflict in South Sudan: A Human Rights Report*, 8 May 2014, para. 18. Interestingly, this paragraph is cited by the UNAMA report on the protection of civilians in Afghanistan.

4

The Protection of Refugees

4.1 INTRODUCTION

Refugees are a certain category of civilians who benefit from specific treatment and protection under international law. In 1948, the Universal Declaration of Human Rights decreed a right to seek and enjoy asylum from persecution.[1] The Declaration was, however, only a political commitment not a legally binding set of obligations. The right to protection as a refugee was established in treaty law by the 1951 Refugee Convention.[2] A cornerstone of the Convention is its definition of a refugee as a person who: 'owing to well-founded fear of being persecuted for reasons of race, religion, nationality, membership of a particular social group or political opinion, is outside the country of his nationality and is unable or, owing to such fear, is unwilling to avail himself of the protection of that country'.[3] Many commentators argue that the definition of a refugee in the 1951 Convention is too narrow insofar it does not encompass all people fleeing acute situations of violence or danger, such as armed conflicts or natural disasters. To overcome this, some States interpret broadly the persecution grounds of the refugee definition under that Convention. Regional instruments adopting a broader refugee definition have also been adopted, such the 1969 Organization of African Unity (OAU) Convention discussed in Section 4.4 below.[4]

The 1951 Refugees Convention was also limited to events occurring in Europe prior to 1 January 1951 (i.e. as a result of World War II and the subsequent 'iron curtain' descending over Europe), but the threat must be specific and not merely one resulting from armed conflicts. The temporal and geographical restrictions were removed in a 1967 Protocol on the status of refugees but not the substantive limitations.[5] In any event, the right to seek and

---

[1] Art. 14, Universal Declaration of Human Rights; adopted at Paris by UN General Assembly Resolution 217, 10 December 1948.

[2] Convention relating to the Status of Refugees; adopted at Geneva, 28 July 1951; entered into force, 22 April 1954. As of 1 April 2022, 146 States were party to the 1951 Refugees Convention.

[3] Art. I(A)(2), 1951 Refugees Convention.

[4] For an overview of this issue, see, for example, A. Pijnenburg and C. Rijken, 'Moving beyond refugees and migrants: reconceptualising the rights of people on the move', *International Journal of Postcolonial Studies*, Vol. 23, No. 2 (2021), 273–93, at pp. 277–9.

[5] Protocol relating to the Status of Refugees; adopted at New York, 31 January 1967; entered into force, 4 October 1967. As of 1 April 2022, 147 States were party to the Protocol. A State does not need to be a party to the 1951 Refugees Convention in order to adhere to its 1967 Protocol.

'enjoy' asylum from persecution on the stipulated grounds – though not necessarily the right to be *granted* asylum[6] – is also a rule of customary international law binding on all States.

A refugee must be distinguished, for the purpose of legal protection, from a migrant.[7] Under the 2018 Global Compact, it is noted that: 'Refugees and migrants are entitled to the same universal human rights and fundamental freedoms, which must be respected, protected and fulfilled at all times. However, migrants and refugees are distinct groups governed by separate legal frameworks. Only refugees are entitled to the specific international protection defined by international refugee law.'[8]

4.2 THE RIGHT TO SEEK AND ENJOY ASYLUM

The right to seek asylum exists for those who leave the country of their nationality and fear to return because of a well-founded fear of persecution. Persecution refers to serious harm, such as threats to life or liberty, of inhumane treatment, as well as of a serious act of discrimination.[9] This persecution must, though, be on one of five stipulated grounds: race, religion, nationality, membership of a particular social group, or political opinion. An asylum-seeker who has committed an international crime or a serious non-political crime is excluded from refugee status.[10]

It is noteworthy that neither the context of an armed conflict nor a person's gender is mentioned as a ground of persecution, though potentially persecution on the basis of gender is encompassed by the broad notion of a 'particular social group'. But ostensibly, fleeing fighting, even when groups of civilians are forced over an international border by parties to an armed conflict, is not in and of itself sufficient to guarantee refugee status under the global instruments. Thus, in its 1999 judgment in the *Adan* case,[11] the United

---

[6] R. Boed, 'The State of the Right of Asylum in International Law', *Duke Journal of Comparative and International Law*, Vol. 5, No. 1 (1994), at: http://bit.ly/2UcuDEN, p. 9.

[7] The International Organization for Migration (IOM) considers 'migrant' to be an

> umbrella term, not defined under international law, reflecting the common lay understanding of a person who moves away from his or her place of usual residence, whether within a country or across an international border, temporarily or permanently, and for a variety of reasons. The term includes a number of well-defined legal categories of people, such as migrant workers; persons whose particular types of movements are legally defined, such as smuggled migrants; as well as those whose status or means of movement are not specifically defined under international law, such as international students.

See A. Sironi, C. Bauloz, and M. Emmanuel (eds.), *Glossary on Migration*, IOM, Geneva, at: https://bit.ly/3EOO9NQ, p. 132.

[8] 'Global Compact for Safe, Orderly and Regular Migration, Intergovernmentally Negotiated and Agreed Outcome', 13 July 2018, para. 4.

[9] There is no explicit definition of 'persecution' in the Refugee Convention. It is argued that the drafters deliberately left the notion open to allow new circumstances to be covered as they arise. See A. Grahl-Madsen, *The Status of Refugees in International Law*, Vol. I, Sijthoff, Leyden, 1966, 193. For an overview of the notion of 'persecution' and its interpretation, see J. Hathaway and M. Foster, *The Law of Refugee Status*, 2nd ed., Cambridge University Press, Cambridge, 2014, p. 182.

[10] Art. 1(F), 1951 Refugees Convention.

[11] UK House of Lords, *Adan v. Secretary of State for the Home Department*, Judgment, 6 April 1998 [1999] 1 AC 293 (HL).

Kingdom (UK) House of Lords held, by majority, that while the 1951 Refugee Convention did not exclude group persecution, individuals fleeing armed conflict and seeking asylum needed to show they would be at risk of 'differential impact', over and above the normal risks to life and liberty inherent in the ordinary incidents of civil war.[12] Thus, while it is 'conceivable that civilians in a particular context could constitute a particular social group', it is 'likely that the group would have to be defined by more criteria than simply 'civilian' for it to constitute a particular social group in the sense of the 1951 refugee definition'.[13]

Only in Africa, under the 1969 OAU Convention (see Section 4.4), is fleeing armed conflict a general basis for the accord of refugee status.[14] Nonetheless, a paper published by the Office of the UN High Commissioner for Refugees (UNHCR) in January 2020 observes that the organisation 'unequivocally instructs' that the 1951 Refugees Convention is applicable to civilians displaced by armed conflict and violence, as the 'majority of these situations engender political religious, ethnic, social, or gender persecution'.[15] That said, while the 1951 Convention certainly applies during a situation of armed conflict its 'weaknesses' include, as Erin Mooney has noted, a lack of non-derogable provisions.[16] Indeed, the Convention explicitly provides that a State Party, 'in time of war or other grave and exceptional circumstances', may take provisional measures 'which it considers to be essential to the national security in the case of a particular person', pending a determination as to whether that person is in fact a refugee.[17]

---

[12] H. Storey, 'Armed Conflict in Asylum Law: The "War-Flaw"', *Refugee Survey Quarterly*, Vol. 31, No. 2 (June 2012), 1–32, at p. 6. The UNHCR, however, in its submission to *QD (Iraq)* v. *Secretary of State for the Home Department*, affirmed that: 'It would be incongruent if refugee law and non-refoulement law did not protect persons against being returned to places where they would be at risk of harm caused by breaches of IHL.' *QD (Iraq)* v. *Secretary of State for the Home Department*, Submissions by UNHCR, C5/2008/1706, p. 8. On the topic see also J.-F. Durieux, 'Of War, Flows, Laws and Flaws: A Reply to Hugo Storey', *Refugee Survey Quarterly*, Vol. 31, No. 3 (2012), 161–76. Similarly, some commentators claim that customary IHL can complement human rights law with respect to forms of harm that can amount to persecution (such as attacks directed against civilians), which may or may not relate to the 1951 Refugee Convention grounds. See V. Holzer, 'Persecution and the Nexus to a Refugee Convention Ground in Non-International Armed Conflict: Insights from Customary International Humanitarian Law' in D. J. Cantor and J.-F. Durieux (eds.), *Refuge from Inhumanity? War Refugees and International Humanitarian Law*, Brill, Leiden, 2014.

[13] V. Holzer, 'The 1951 Refugee Convention and the Protection of People Fleeing Armed Conflict and Other Situations of Violence', Division of International Protection, UNHCR doc. PPLA/2012/05, Geneva, September 2012, pp. 32–3.

[14] The 1984 Cartagena Declaration on Refugees for the Americas is not a treaty, though it certainly has normative force.

[15] S. Weerasinghe, 'Refugee Law in a Time of Climate Change, Disaster and Conflict', Legal and Protection Policy Research Series, Division of International Protection, UNHCR, Geneva, January 2020, at: http://bit.ly/3rfpZon, pp. 82–3.

[16] E. Mooney, 'Displacement and the Protection of Civilians under International Refugee Law', chapter 8 in H. Willmot, R. Mamiya, S. Sheeran, and M. Weller (eds.), *Protection of Civilians*, 1st ed., Oxford University Press, Oxford, 2016, p. 195.

[17] Art. 9, 1951 Refugees Convention. While some commentators believe that this exception should be applied individually, others uphold that it can be applied on a collective basis provided that it lasts until the individual screening is completed. A. Edwards, 'Temporary Protection, Derogation and the 1951 Refugee Convention', *Melbourne Journal of International Law*, Vol. 13, No. 2 (2012), 1–41, at p. 30.

The logical consequence of being granted refugee status is that you cannot be forced to return to the country of your nationality where you fear being persecuted.[18] This principle of *non-refoulement* is a rule of both treaty[19] and customary international law.[20] The rule also prohibits the authorities from turning away an asylum seeker at the border.[21] Moreover, the principle of *non-refoulement* is also argued to be a rule of *jus cogens* (a peremptory norm of international law), which is binding on all States and from which no derogation is possible, even in a situation of armed conflict.[22]

4.3 INTERNATIONAL HUMANITARIAN LAW AND REFUGEES

Additional protection for asylum seekers and refugees is contained in the instruments of international humanitarian law (IHL), although Mooney has observed a 'surprising' lack of enthusiasm among staff in UNHCR to use IHL instruments and provisions in practice.[23]

In the 1949 Geneva Convention IV,[24] which applies to protect civilians in international armed conflict, including to occupied territories, it is stipulated that in applying measures of control under the Convention, 'the Detaining Power shall not treat as enemy aliens exclusively on the basis of their nationality de jure of an enemy State, refugees who do not, in fact, enjoy the protection of any government'.[25] This is a logical measure since if

---

[18]   There are different views, however, as to whether, under the 1951 Refugees Convention, this protection is to be granted only to those already recognised as refugees according to Art. 1(A)(2) of the 1951 Convention or also to asylum-seekers waiting for such recognition and 'non-Convention refugees'. For an overview of this debate, see M. Jacques, *Armed Conflict and Displacement: The Protection of Refugees and Displaced Persons Under International Humanitarian Law*, Cambridge Studies in International and Comparative Law, Cambridge University Press, Cambridge, 2012, p. 180.

[19]   Art. 33, 1951 Refugees Convention.

[20]   Mooney, 'Displacement and the Protection of Civilians under International Refugee Law', pp. 194–5.

[21]   Ibid., p. 195.

[22]   International Law Commission, Fourth report on peremptory norms of general international law (*jus cogens*) by Dire Tladi, Special Rapporteur, UN doc. A/CN.4/727, 31 January 2019, paras. 123 and 131–4. Yet the *non-refoulement* principle in the 1951 Refugees Convention is not absolute. If there are reasonable grounds for regarding refugees and asylum seekers as a danger to the national security of the host country or if they have been convicted of a particularly serious crime so as to represent a danger to the community of that country, they can exceptionally be returned. Art. 33(2), 1951 Refugee Convention. This exception to the *non-refoulement* principle is, however, overridden by human rights law when there are reasons to believe that the person faces a danger of being killed, tortured, or otherwise brutally treated upon return. In addition, it is claimed that the exception in the Refugees Convention must be strictly interpreted. Jacques, *Armed Conflict and Displacement: The Protection of Refugees and Displaced Persons Under International Humanitarian Law*, p. 179; and see S. Lauterpacht and D. Bethlehem, 'The Scope and Content of the Principle of Non-refoulement: Opinion', in E. Feller, V. Türk, and F. Nicholson (eds.), *Refugee Protection in International Law: UNHCR's Global Consultations on International Protection*, Cambridge University Press, Cambridge, 2003, pp. 87–177, at pp. 133–4.

[23]   Mooney, 'Displacement and the Protection of Civilians under International Refugee Law', p. 195. She questions whether this is part of the institutional turf war competition between UNHCR and the UN Office for the Coordination of Humanitarian Affairs (OCHA). Ibid., p. 196.

[24]   Convention (IV) relative to the Protection of Civilian Persons in Time of War; adopted at Geneva, 12 August 1949; entered into force, 21 October 1950 (hereinafter, 1949 Geneva Convention IV).

[25]   Art. 44, 1949 Geneva Convention IV.

a person is fleeing persecution from its own government, it can hardly be considered an agent of that government.[26]

In addition, evoking the principle of non-refoulement, it is further provided that in non-occupied territories: 'In no circumstances shall a protected person be transferred to a country where he or she may have reason to fear persecution for his or her political opinions or religious beliefs.'[27] In occupied territories, refugees who are legally considered as protected persons[28] benefit from the protection against deportation and forcible transfer accorded by Article 49 of the 1949 Geneva Convention IV. Those who do not meet this status are given protection under Article 70(2) of the 1949 Geneva Convention IV.[29]

Under the 1977 Additional Protocol I,[30] which is applicable in all international armed conflict, protection as 'protected persons' under IHL is extended to all those who, before the beginning of hostilities, were considered as refugees under applicable international or national law in the State of refuge or State of residence.[31] This protection exists 'in all circumstances and without any adverse distinction'.[32]

There is, however, no corresponding protection for refugees during a situation of non-international armed conflict.[33] They remain, of course, civilians protected from attack. When detained or otherwise in the power of a party to the conflict, customary rules require humane treatment in all circumstances and without adverse distinction. Fundamental

[26] This does not bar States from applying measures of control, however. If a refugee, on the basis of their activities or political convictions, represents a danger to the security of the State, they can be subjected to the security measures, and in accordance with the procedures set forth under Geneva Convention IV. Pictet, Commentary on the 1949 Geneva Convention IV, 1958, pp. 264–5; see M. Jacques, 'The Protection of Refugees under International Humanitarian Law', p. 168. Still, the criticism is made that protection of refugees in armed conflicts puts too much emphasis on nationality. Ibid., p. 170.

[27] Art. 45, 1949 Geneva Convention IV.

[28] IHL accords the status of 'protected person' to certain individuals. According to Article 4 of the 1949 Geneva Convention IV, protected persons under that Convention are those who, during an international armed conflict, including a military occupation, 'at a given moment and in any manner whatsoever', find themselves in the hands of a Party to the conflict or Occupying Power of which they are not nationals. Nationals of a neutral or co-belligerent State are not protected persons if the State of which they are nationals has normal diplomatic representation in the State in whose hands they are.

[29] Nationals of the Occupying Power who, before the outbreak of hostilities, have sought refuge in the territory of the occupied State, shall not be arrested, prosecuted, convicted or deported from the occupied territory, except for offences committed after the outbreak of hostilities, or for offences under common law committed before the outbreak of hostilities which, according to the law of the occupied State, would have justified extradition in time of peace.

[30] Protocol Additional to the Geneva Conventions of 12 August 1949, and relating to the Protection of Victims of International Armed Conflicts; adopted at Geneva, 8 June 1977; entered into force, 7 December 1978 (hereinafter, 1977 Additional Protocol I).

[31] Art. 73, 1977 Additional Protocol I.

[32] Ibid.

[33] V. Muntarbhorn, 'Protection and Assistance for Refugees in Armed Conflicts and Internal Disturbances: Reflections on the Mandates of the International Red Cross and Red Crescent Movement and the Office of the United Nations High Commissioner for Refugees', *International Review of the Red Cross*, No. 265 (July–August 1988), pp. 351–66; H. Obregón Gieseken, 'The Protection of Migrants under International Humanitarian Law', *International Review of the Red Cross*, Vol. 99, No. 1 (2017), 121–52, at: http://bit.ly/2PAlx35, at pp. 139–40.

guarantees, which include the prohibitions on physical or sexual violence and the passing of sentences without a fair trial, must also be respected in all circumstances.[34]

4.4 THE 1969 OAU REFUGEES CONVENTION

In Africa, the 1969 OAU Refugees Convention[35] is the only regional treaty that grants refugee status to those fleeing armed conflict. Article 1(1) of the Convention repeats the definition in the 1951 Refugees Convention. According to Article 1(2), however, the term 'refugee' shall 'also apply to every person who, owing to external aggression, occupation, foreign domination or events seriously disturbing public order in either part or the whole of his country of origin or nationality, is compelled to leave his place of habitual residence in order to seek refuge in another place outside his country of origin or nationality'.[36] The principles of *non-refoulement* apply it to any person, not just any refugee: 'No person shall be subjected by a Member State to measures such as rejection at the frontier, return or expulsion, which would compel him to return to or remain in a territory where his life, physical integrity or liberty would be threatened for the reasons set out in [the definition of a refugee in] Article I, paragraphs 1 and 2.'[37] In an article in the *Forced Migration Review* in 2014, Judicial Officer Moses Okello considered whether, forty years after the OAU Refugees Convention came into force, the 'dismal state' in which refugees in Africa find themselves 'raises the question as to whether the Convention has lived up to expectations'.[38] Moses Okello, who had previously been the UNHCR Representative in Ethiopia, argued that 'the real value' that the Convention has added is the focus, in the definition, 'on the objective circumstances which compel flight and not linking the flight to the individual asylum seeker's subjective

---

[34] International Committee of the Red Cross (ICRC), 'IHL and the Protection of Migrants Caught in Armed Conflict', Geneva, 4 June 2018, available at: http://bit.ly/2wkcxYQ. The problem concerning refugee protection in non-international armed conflicts arises in particular for refugees who find themselves in territory under non-State actors' control. Jacques, 'The Protection of Refugees under International Humanitarian Law', p. 165.

[35] OAU Convention Governing the Specific Aspects of Refugee Problems in Africa; adopted at Addis Ababa, 10 September 1969; entered into force, 20 January 1974. As of 1 April 2022, forty-six of fifty-five African Union members were party to the Convention. Only Djibouti, Eritrea, Madagascar, Mauritius, Morocco, Namibia, the Sahrawi Arab Democratic Republic, Somalia, and Sao Tome & Principe were States not party to the Convention and all but Morocco were signatories. The UN Treaty Section, however, lists Morocco as having ratified the Convention in 1974. At: http://bit.ly/2Tfr9lD.

[36] Concerning the enlarged definition of 'refugee' under the 1969 Convention, a debate exists as to whether those who qualify under such Convention also benefit from the protection accorded by the 1951 Convention. For a discussion on this and other aspects of the relationship between the two Conventions, see M. Sharpe, 'The Relationship Between the 1951 and 1969 Conventions', chapter 4 in *The Regional Law of Refugee Protection in Africa*, Oxford University Press, Oxford, 2018. For a comparative overview on the two Conventions, see also UNHCR, 'Key Legal Considerations on the Standards of Treatment of Refugees Recognized under the 1969 OAU Convention Governing the Specific Aspects of Refugee Problems in Africa', *International Journal of Refugee Law*, Vol. 30, No. 1 (2018), 166–72.

[37] Art. 2(3), 1969 OAU Refugees Convention.

[38] Judicial Officer Moses Okello, 'The 1969 OAU Convention and the Continuing Challenge for the African Union', *Forced Migration Review*, November 2014, 70–3, at: http://bit.ly/2PCkFel, p. 70.

interpretation of danger arising from events around his or her person'.[39] But at the time of its conclusion, the 'primary concern' was the 'large number of Africans fleeing conflict arising from the struggles against colonialism'.[40]

That is no longer the case today. Indeed, as he observes, 'Since the rise of international terrorism, security has taken the prime position in the consideration of asylum for refugees. This development threatens the very survival of the institution of asylum in Africa.'[41]

He acknowledges, though, that despite the worrying overall trends, some African nations still strive to meet their obligations. He cites the example of Ethiopia, which practises an open-door policy towards refugees.

> Between 2009 and 2014 the country received nearly 450,000 refugees and in 2009 introduced an 'out-of-camp' policy according to which refugees are allowed to live outside camps provided they are able to support themselves. Originally applicable only to refugees from Eritrea, this policy is now applicable also to refugees of other nationalities who qualify. Ethiopia has admitted the refugees in the face of very difficult local challenges, such as the overwhelming impact on its fragile environment.[42]

---

[39] Ibid., p. 73.

[40] Ibid., p. 70.

[41] Ibid. It is argued that effective protection under the 1969 OAU Refugee Convention is also undermined by an existing gap between the black letter of its expanded refugee definition and its application in practice. Notably, Wood claims that despite the broader content of Article 1(2) of the 1969 Refugee Convention, in Kenya and South Africa, decision makers typically resort to the more conservative terms of the 1951 Convention refugee definition during status determination procedures. From another study focusing on South Africa's practice, it emerges that claims potentially falling under the enlarged protection of the 1969 Convention definition based on conflict, insecurity, or violence have been instead analysed under the 1951 Convention 'well-founded fear of persecution'. See T. Wood, 'Expanding Protection in Africa: Case Studies of the Implementation of the 1969 African Refugee Convention's Expanded Refugee Definition', *International Journal of Refugee Law*, Vol. 26 (2014), 555. See also R. Amit, 'No Refuge: Flawed Status Determination and the Failures of South Africa's Refugee System to Provide Protection', *International Journal of Refugee Law*, Vol. 23 (2011), 458–88, at p. 473. For an analysis of the gaps between textual and practical protection of refugees in South Africa, see T. Aluwa and A. Katz, 'Who is a Refugee?: Twenty-Five Years of Domestic Implementation and Judicial Interpretation of the 1969 OAU and 1951 UN Refugee Conventions in Post-Apartheid South Africa', *Indiana Journal of Global Legal Studies*, Vol. 27, No. 2 (2020), p. 129ff.

[42] Moses Okello, 'The 1969 OAU Convention and the Continuing Challenge for the African Union', p. 71.

5

Disarmament Law and the Protection of Civilians

5.1 INTRODUCTION

Civilians can be protected by eradicating and reducing the availability of weapons that would harm them. While international humanitarian law and international human rights law regulate the use of weapons, international disarmament law outlaws weapons entirely, notably those which tend to have indiscriminate effects and thereby are particularly dangerous for civilians.

Disarmament law is the branch of international law that governs the possession, production, transfer, and use of weapons (both weapons of mass destruction and 'conventional' weapons).[1] The law is directed towards the actions of States and their armed forces. Whereas during the Cold War the focus of disarmament law was on outlawing or at least greatly restricting weapons of mass destruction (i.e. biological, chemical, and nuclear weapons), since the 1990s, attention has turned also to conventional weapons. While all disarmament treaties contribute to the protection of civilians, many describe this as an objective. Indeed, avoiding and lessening harm to civilians has become a core rationale of modern disarmament treaties and of disarmament more broadly.[2]

This chapter addresses the three disarmament treaties that are most important to the protection of civilians: the 1992 Chemical Weapons Convention,[3] the 1997 Anti-Personnel Mine Ban Convention,[4] and the 2008 Convention on Cluster Munitions.[5] While the Chemical Weapons Convention was elaborated also to protect soldiers, the other two

---

[1] Conventional weapons are generally understood to be all weapons other than biological, chemical, nuclear, and radiological weapons.

[2] See, for example, S. Casey-Maslen and T. Vestner, 'Trends in Global Disarmament Treaties', *Journal of Conflict and Security Law*, Vol. 25, No. 3, 2020, 449–71; M. Finaud, '"Humanitarian Disarmament": Powerful New Paradigm or Naive Utopia?', *Geneva Papers Research Series*, 21, Geneva Centre for Security Policy, 2017.

[3] Convention on the Prohibition of the Development, Production, Stockpiling and Use of Chemical Weapons and on their Destruction; adopted at Geneva, 3 September 1992; entered into force, 29 April 1997. As of 1 April 2022, 193 States were party to the Convention.

[4] Convention on the Prohibition of the Use, Stockpiling, Production, and Transfer of Anti-Personnel Mines and on their Destruction; adopted at Oslo, 18 September 1997; entered into force, 1 March 1999. As of 1 April 2022, 164 States were party to the Convention.

[5] Convention on Cluster Munitions; adopted at Dublin, 30 May 2008; entered into force, 1 August 2010. As of 1 April 2022, 110 States were party to the Convention.

treaties were developed specifically to protect civilians. The Anti-Personnel Mine Ban Convention and the Convention on Cluster Munitions each incorporate innovative features on assistance to victims and on clearance of those weapons that have been used. The 2013 Arms Trade Treaty[6] is also relevant to the protection of civilians. While not a 'pure' disarmament treaty, the ATT impacts States' access to conventional weapons by establishing international standards on the legality of transfers.

5.2 THE 1992 CHEMICAL WEAPONS CONVENTION

A range of chemical weapons have been used in armed conflict, harming soldiers and civilians alike. Although globally there has been relatively little use over the last three decades, widespread use has been recorded in Syria, particularly of sarin and chlorine. Sarin is a highly toxic nerve agent that was developed for chemical warfare during World War II. Exposure can result in death, but may otherwise have short-term health effects, including seizures, paralysis, and difficulty breathing.[7] When liquid chlorine is released, it quickly turns into a gas. The gas, which is heavier than air, sinks, rendering people hiding in basements or underground bomb shelters particularly vulnerable to exposure. When chlorine gas comes into contact with moist tissues such as the eyes, throats, and lungs, acid is produced. When inhaled, chlorine causes air sacs in the lungs to secrete fluid, essentially drowning those affected.[8]

The use of chemical weapons in warfare was first outlawed in 1899 at the First Hague Peace Conference.[9] The 1899 Hague Declaration on the Use of Asphyxiating Gases did not, though, prevent massive use of chemical weapons during World War I (an estimated fifty million shells containing toxic chemicals were used by the different belligerents.

After the war, responding to the appalling toll those weapons took on the lives and long-term health of soldiers, States adopted the 1925 Geneva Gas Protocol.[10] The preamble to the Protocol noted the intention of States Parties to ensure that the prohibition of the use of 'asphyxiating, poisonous or other gases, and of all analogous liquids, materials or devices' would become 'universally accepted as a part of International Law, binding alike the conscience and the practice of nations'. (The Protocol also banned the use in warfare of biological weapons.) There were, however, two significant problems with the Protocol. First, it applied only in armed conflict between States but not to the use of chemical weapons in non-international armed conflict. Second, reservations to the Protocol by more than 20 States Parties effectively reduced it to only a ban on first use.

---

[6] Arms Trade Treaty; adopted at New York, 2 April 2013; entered into force, 24 December 2014. As of 1 April 2022, 111 States were party to the Convention.

[7] 'Sarin: Potential Long-term Neurological Effects', National Toxicology Program, National Institute of Environmental Health Sciences, United States, last updated on 29 November 2019, at: http://bit.ly/38UQQwN.

[8] N. al-Maghafi, 'How Chemical Weapons Have Helped Bring Assad Close to Victory', *BBC Panorama*, 15 October 2018, available at: http://bbc.in/3aOyUp7.

[9] Declaration concerning the Prohibition of the Use of Projectiles Diffusing Asphyxiating Gases; adopted at The Hague, 29 July 1899, entered into force, 4 September 1900.

[10] Protocol for the Prohibition of the Use in War of Asphyxiating, Poisonous or Other Gases, and of Bacteriological Methods of Warfare; signed at Geneva, 17 June 1925; entered into force, 8 February 1928.

To ensure that the prohibition on chemical weapons would be effective, it was clear that merely banning their use would be insufficient. Outlawing production and supply and ensuring the verifiable destruction of stockpiles already amassed would also be needed. On this basis began the negotiation of the Chemical Weapons Convention in 1980. It would take twelve years to finalise the text, which runs to 165 pages, largely because of the extensive verification mechanisms that States wished to incorporate. Adopted by the Conference on Disarmament in Geneva in 1992, the Chemical Weapons Convention entered into force on 29 April 1997 and has become the most universal of all the disarmament treaties so far. Only four States (signatory State Israel, and non-signatory States Egypt, North Korea, and South Sudan) were not yet party to the Convention as of writing.

While the Convention does not expressly mention civilians and their protection, its fifth preambular paragraph does note the aim of the States Parties to completely exclude the possibility of the use of chemical weapons 'for all mankind'. As such, the Convention prohibits all use of chemical weapons as a method of warfare. But while the use of riot control agents such as tear gas is specifically prohibited in warfare, the Convention makes an exception for their use for law enforcement, 'including domestic riot control'.[11] This means that tear gas can potentially be used to disperse riots or unlawful assemblies even during an armed conflict.

There are no other exceptions to the Convention's core prohibitions of chemical weapons: their development, production, stockpiling, and transfer are all unequivocally outlawed. It is also unlawful to assist others to violate the Convention. But the Convention does not specifically require clearance of chemical weapons that have been used (millions of artillery shells containing chemical agents fired during World War I remain unexploded under fields in Belgium and France). It also does not obligate assistance to the victims of chemical weapons attacks.

On 16 March 1988, Iraqi war planes and artillery dropped mustard gas[12] and sarin on the Kurdish town of Halabja in northern Iraq. Thousands of civilians, mainly women and children, died that day, and up to 12,000 are believed to have lost their lives since.[13] In March 2010, the Supreme Iraqi Criminal Tribunal recognised the attack, which took place within the al-Anfal campaign against the Kurds during the Iran–Iraq War, as an act of genocide.[14] Iraq adhered to the Chemical Weapons Convention in 2009.

Syria adhered to the Convention in October 2013 following an August 2013 attack on the outskirts of Damascus using sarin, which is believed to have killed more than 1,400 civilians. Syria is, however, alleged to have used chemical weapons on many occasions since.[15] Many attacks in Syria, including those perpetrated by the non-State armed group,

[11] Art. II(9)(d), 1992 Chemical Weapons Convention.
[12] Mustard agent is a 'vesicant', meaning that it has blistering effects on its victims. It damages DNA, especially in the bone marrow, but is fairly rarely fatal. Centers for Disease Control and Prevention, 'Facts About Sulfur Mustard', last updated 4 April 2018, at: http://bit.ly/2U50xaH.
[13] H. de Bretton-Gordon, 'Remembering Halabja chemical attack', *Aljazeera*, 16 March 2016, at: http://bit.ly/2tAfFir.
[14] United Press International (UPI), '1988 Kurdish Massacre Labeled Genocide', *UPI*, 8 March 2010, at: http://bit.ly/3aqXagL.
[15] Human Rights Watch, *Death by Chemicals*, United States, 2017, at: http://bit.ly/38P9xlj, Summary.

Islamic State, have employed chlorine gas.[16] In June 2018, after attempts by the United States and others in the UN Security Council to create a new mechanism to investigate chemical weapons attacks, a special meeting of States Parties to the Chemical Weapons Convention agreed to give the Organisation for the Prohibition of Chemical Weapons (OPCW) established by the Convention the mandate to identify responsibility for chemical weapon attacks.[17]

5.3 THE 1997 ANTI-PERSONNEL MINE BAN CONVENTION

Internal armed conflicts, especially in the 1980s and early 1990s, saw widespread use of anti-personnel mines. State armed forces and non-State armed groups alike used these weapons to protect their soldiers, channel the enemy, and inflict casualties. Often designed to maim rather than kill the enemy (so that additional human resources would be used to transport military casualties to a medical facility), in reality it is civilians who are often the innocent victims, sometimes years after the end of the conflict.

In 1994, at the height of the global landmine crisis, the International Committee of the Red Cross (ICRC) estimated, on the basis of its field data and that of other humanitarian organisations, that up to 2,000 people a month were being killed or injured by anti-personnel mines.[18] Beyond the direct humanitarian consequences were also the significant negative social and economic costs. Land could not safely be used for agriculture or grazing livestock; precious blood and medicines in health centres were rapidly exhausted, such were the needs of mine victims; and refugees and the internally displaced were impeded from safe return. In the early 1990s, Human Rights Watch and Physicians for Human Rights termed landmines 'weapons of mass destruction in slow motion'.[19] In a similar vein, in 1994 the UN Secretary-General called for anti-personnel mines to be placed 'in the same legal and ethical category as biological and chemical weapons'.[20]

---

[16] See, for example, K. Shaheen, 'Almost 1,500 Killed in Chemical Weapons Attacks in Syria', *Guardian*, 14 March 2016, at: http://bit.ly/2RZWLcT.

[17] On 27 June 2018, the Fourth Special Session of the Conference of the States Parties to the Chemical Weapons Convention adopted a decision on addressing the threat from chemical weapons use. The decision brought forward by the United Kingdom and supported by thirty States (Albania, Australia, Belgium, Bulgaria, Canada, Denmark, Estonia, Finland, France, Georgia, Germany, Iceland, Ireland, Japan, Latvia, Lithuania, Luxembourg, Malta, the Netherlands, New Zealand, Norway, Poland, Portugal, Republic of Moldova, Romania, Slovakia, Slovenia, Sweden, Turkey, and the United States), was adopted with 106 States Parties present and voting, of whom 82 voted in favour and 24 voted against (Belarus, Bolivia, Botswana, Burundi, Cambodia, China, Eritrea, India, Iran, Kazakhstan, Lao PDR, Myanmar, Namibia, Nicaragua, the Philippines, the Russian Federation, South Africa, the Sudan, Syria, Tajikistan, Uganda, Uzbekistan, Venezuela, and Vietnam). Decision C-SS-4/DEC.3, dated 27 June 2018, in Report of the Fourth Special Session of the Conference of the States Parties to the Chemical Weapons Convention, CWC doc. C-SS-4/3, 27 June 2018, at: https://bit.ly/36pWmZq, Agenda Item 3: Upholding the global ban against chemical weapons use, pp. 6–7.

[18] ICRC, 'Anti-Personnel Mines: Overview of the Problem', FAQ, Geneva, 2 November 2009, at: http://bit.ly/2TscIt7.

[19] Human Rights Watch and Physicians for Human Rights, *Landmines: A Deadly Legacy*, Human Rights Watch, Washington, DC, 1993.

[20] B. Boutros-Ghali, 'The Land Mine Crisis: A Humanitarian Disaster', *Foreign Affairs*, Vol. 73, No. 5 (September–October 1994), pp. 8–13.

International law regulated the use of landmines in a protocol annexed to an international humanitarian law treaty adopted under UN auspices: the 1980 Convention on Certain Conventional Weapons[21] (CCW). But the original Protocol on Landmines did little to protect civilians in practice.[22] The Protocol also did not apply to non-international armed conflict, which was the setting for the overwhelming majority of the use of anti-personnel mines by the early 1990s. Following an initiative by France, States Parties to the CCW revised the Protocol, adopting a new instrument in May 1996.[23] The amended Protocol requires all anti-personnel mines to be detectable while remotely delivered anti-personnel mines must self-destruct and self-deactivate to a high combined standard.[24]

By that time, however, many came to the conclusion that the only effective solution to the 'epidemic' of mine casualties would be a total prohibition of anti-personnel mines. In 1997, Canada led the negotiation of what would become the Anti-Personnel Mine Ban Convention – the first disarmament treaty outlawing a conventional weapon. The very first preambular paragraph links the Convention's rationale to the protection of civilians: 'Determined to put an end to the suffering and casualties caused by anti-personnel mines, that kill or maim hundreds of people every week, mostly innocent and defenceless civilians and especially children, obstruct economic development and reconstruction, inhibit the repatriation of refugees and internally displaced persons, and have other severe consequences for years after emplacement.'

The heart of the Convention is its Article 1(1), which is closely modelled around the corresponding provisions in the Chemical Weapons Convention:

Each State Party undertakes never under any circumstances:

(a) To use anti-personnel mines;
(b) To develop, produce, otherwise acquire, stockpile, retain or transfer to anyone, directly or indirectly, anti-personnel mines;
(c) To assist, encourage or induce, in any way, anyone to engage in any activity prohibited to a State Party under this Convention.

The emphasis placed on the ban on use reflects the fact that while the 1899 and 1925 treaties had outlawed the use of chemical weapons (at least in international armed conflict), there was no corresponding IHL treaty prohibition on the use of anti-personnel mines. The prohibition on use in the 1997 Anti-Personnel Mine Ban Convention is applicable in all circumstances, and to all situations, including peacetime as well as armed conflict. In contradistinction to the Chemical Weapons Convention, no exception is allowed for use for the purpose of law enforcement.

---

[21] Convention on Prohibitions or Restrictions on the Use of Certain Conventional Weapons Which May Be Deemed to Be Excessively Injurious or to have Indiscriminate Effects; adopted at Geneva, 10 October 1980; entered into force, 2 December 1983.

[22] Arts. 3(2) and (3), Protocol on Prohibitions or Restrictions on the Use of Mines, Booby-Traps and Other Devices; adopted at Geneva, 10 October 1980; entered into force, 2 December 1983.

[23] Protocol on Prohibitions or Restrictions on the Use of Mines, Booby-Traps and Other Devices as Amended on 3 May 1996 (hereinafter, 1996 Amended Protocol II).

[24] Arts. 4 and 5 and Technical Annex, paras. 2 and 3, 1996 Amended Protocol II.

The treaty prohibition on new use has been violated by at least one State Party to the Convention, Yemen,[25] while serious accusations have been levelled at South Sudan,[26] Turkey,[27] and Ukraine.[28] The 2019 Landmine Monitor published by the International Campaign to Ban Landmines (ICBL) reported that there had been no allegations of use of anti-personnel mines by States Parties over the last three years and that only two States not party (Myanmar and Syria) had used anti-personnel mines.[29] Extensive use of the weapons has, though, been documented by non-State armed groups over the lifetime of the Convention; most recently this has concerned groups in Afghanistan, India, Nigeria, Myanmar, Pakistan, and Yemen.[30] Previously, Islamic State forces (also called ISIS or Daesh) made massive use of anti-personnel mines in Iraq and Syria.[31]

The mines produced and emplaced by the non-State armed group Islamic State have given rise to renewed discussion about the definition of an anti-personnel mine under the 1997 Anti-Personnel Mine Ban Convention. Anti-personnel mines are defined in Article 2(1) as follows: 'a mine designed to be exploded by the presence, proximity or contact of a person and that will incapacitate, injure or kill one or more persons'.[32] The definition focuses on the victim-activated nature of the explosive device; accordingly command-detonated devices do not fall within the scope of (are not thus prohibited by) the 1997 Convention. But the method of production of the weapon (factory or artisanal) is not relevant; indeed during the negotiations, the question was asked as to whether improvised anti-personnel mines were covered and it was confirmed by the chair that they were; subsequent State practice has endorsed this position.[33]

---

[25] The first confirmed use of anti-personnel mines by a State Party occurred in Yemen in 2011–12 at Bani Jarmooz, a location north of Sana'a, during the uprising that led to the ousting of then-President Saleh. In November 2013, the office of Yemen's prime minister admitted that a 'violation' of the Convention had occurred in 2011. Human Rights Watch, 'Memo to Delegates: Yemen's Compliance with the Mine Ban Treaty: The Case of Bani Jarmooz', 8 April 2014, at: http://bit.ly/32D3zSA.

[26] ICBL, 'Concern at Reported Use of Antipersonnel Mines in South Sudan: South Sudanese authorities should confirm or deny the claimed use of antipersonnel mines', 31 March 2015, at: http://bit.ly/2JVspW3.

[27] See, for example, ICBL, 'Spotlight on Turkey', 19 February 2014, at: http://bit.ly/38cKB6L.

[28] In 2016, the Office of the UN High Commissioner for Human Rights (OHCHR) reported that the Ukrainian armed forces had used anti-personnel mines. OHCHR, 'Report on the Human Rights Situation in Ukraine 16 February to 15 May 2016', para. 14, at: http://bit.ly/2IldoNv. In contrast, the ICBL's Landmine Monitor stated in 2019 that it 'has received no credible information that Ukrainian government forces used antipersonnel mines in violation of the Mine Ban Treaty since 2014 and into 2019'. Landmine Monitor, 'Ukraine: Mine Ban Policy', last updated 7 October 2019, at: http://bit.ly/39O0330.

[29] *Landmine Monitor Report 2019*, ICBL – Cluster Munition Coalition (CMC), Geneva, 2019, at: http://bit.ly /2x1jSgr, p. 8.

[30] Ibid.

[31] See, for example, Landmine Monitor, 'Syria: Mine Ban Policy', last updated 24 September 2019, at: http://bit.ly/2Tx3LyC.

[32] In turn, a mine is defined as 'a munition designed to be placed under, on or near the ground or other surface area and to be exploded by the presence, proximity or contact of a person or a vehicle'. Art. 2(2), 1997 Anti-Personnel Mine Ban Convention.

[33] ICRC, 'Views and Recommendations on Improvised Explosive Devices Falling Within the Scope of the Anti-Personnel Mine Ban Convention', Working Paper submitted to the Fourth Review Conference of the 1997 Anti-Personnel Mine Ban Convention, Oslo, 25–9 November 2019, p. 2.

By far the most expensive and demanding obligations under the 1997 Anti-Personnel Mine Ban Convention are those upon each State Party to clear all emplaced anti-personnel mines on territory under its jurisdiction or control. A wide range of negotiating States and other parties were insistent that the future Convention must have a humanitarian component as well as a disarmament bent. States settled on an initial ten-year deadline with the possibility of securing additional deadlines of up to ten years at a time. Thus, according to Article 5(1) each State 'undertakes to destroy or ensure the destruction of all anti-personnel mines in mined areas under its jurisdiction or control, as soon as possible but not later than ten years' after becoming a party to the Convention.[34]

In the twenty years since the entry into force of the Convention, progress in mine clearance among States Parties can best be described as uneven, and often slow. That said, a total of at least 2,880 square kilometres of mined area has been cleared, equating in the words of the Mine Action Review published by Norwegian People's Aid to an area greater than the size of Nairobi, New York City, and Rome combined. Furthermore, demining operations have destroyed more than 4.6 million emplaced anti-personnel mines.[35] This transformed the problem from a humanitarian crisis to what is predominantly now a developmental challenge. Over the same period, thirty-two States Parties to the Convention[36] and one State not party (Nepal), as well as one other territory – Taiwan – have completed mine clearance on their territory.[37]

As of 1 April 2022, however, thirty-four States Parties to the 1997 Convention still had to fulfil their clearance obligations,[38] with many already into their second or third deadline extension periods. A further twenty-two States not party were also mine-affected.[39]

Mine Action Review estimates that global contamination from anti-personnel mines covers no more than 2,000 square kilometres in total.[40] The Third Review Conference of the Convention, held in Maputo, had set the objective of global clearance of anti-personnel mines by the end of 2025. As of mid-2022, though, relatively few States Parties

<hr>

[34] The notion of 'jurisdiction' over geographical area concerns, first and foremost, sovereign territory (whether metropolitan or non-metropolitan), whereas 'control' concerns other territory that a State occupies abroad. L. Pinches and S. Casey-Maslen, 'Clearance under the Anti-Personnel Mine Ban Convention', in *The Anti-Personnel Mine Ban Convention: Twenty Years of Saving Lives and Preventing Indiscriminate Harm*, UNODA Occasional Papers, No. 34, United Nations, New York, 2019, p. 44.

[35] Mine Action Review, *Clearing the Mines 2020*, Norwegian People's Aid, October 2020, p. 1.

[36] Albania, Algeria, Bhutan, Bulgaria, Burundi, Chile, Costa Rica, the Democratic Republic of the Congo, Denmark, Djibouti, France, The Gambia, Germany, Greece, Guatemala, Guinea-Bissau, Honduras, Hungary, Jordan, Malawi, Montenegro, Mozambique, Nicaragua, North Macedonia (previously known as the former Yugoslav Republic of Macedonia), Palau, Rwanda, Suriname, Swaziland, Tunisia, Uganda, Venezuela, and Zambia. See Mine Action Review, *Clearing the Mines 2021*, Norwegian People's Aid, October 2021, Overview: Table 3. Guinea-Bissau has since reported newly discovered mined areas.

[37] Mine Action Review, *Clearing the Mines 2020*, p. 1.

[38] Afghanistan, Angola, Bosnia and Herzegovina, Cambodia, Cameroon, Chad, Colombia, Croatia, Cyprus, the Democratic Republic of the Congo, Ecuador, Eritrea, Ethiopia, Guinea-Bissau, Iraq, Mali, Mauritania, Niger, Nigeria, Oman, Palestine, Peru, Senegal, Serbia, Somalia, South Sudan, Sri Lanka, Sudan, Tajikistan, Thailand, Turkey, Ukraine, Yemen, and Zimbabwe.

[39] Armenia, Azerbaijan, China, Cuba, Egypt, Georgia, India, Iran, Israel, Kyrgyzstan, Lao People's Democratic Republic, Lebanon, Libya, Morocco, Myanmar, North Korea, Pakistan, Russia, South Korea, Syria, Uzbekistan, and Vietnam.

[40] Mine Action Review, *Clearing the Mines 2019*, p. 1.

were on course to meet that objective. On average, a manual deminer can clear about twenty square metres of land a day.[41]

Victim assistance may be, in strict legal respects, one of the weaker substantive components of the 1997 Anti-Personnel Mine Ban Convention. This is despite the Convention's preamble, which records the desire of the States Parties 'to do their utmost in providing assistance for the care and rehabilitation, including the social and economic reintegration of mine victims'. Yet, there is no general obligation to assist mine victims under the Convention, despite calls for its inclusion in the lead up to the diplomatic conference in Oslo.[42] Instead, under Article 6(3), those States 'in a position to do so' are obliged to provide international cooperation and assistance for the care and rehabilitation of mine victims in other affected countries. These provisions do, though, complement States' obligations towards their own citizens,[43] in particular under international human rights law. Moreover, State practice and international support have combined to fill the legal gap in the treaty on assistance to victims.

Those who lose a limb from an anti-personnel mine blast will need life-long care: beginning with emergency medical care, most will require physical rehabilitation, including physiotherapy, prosthetics, and assistive devices, as well as psychological support and social reintegration. Thirty States Parties[44] have indicated that they have significant numbers – hundreds or thousands – of landmine survivors for which they must provide care. Many of these countries face significant challenges in fulfilling their responsibilities. As such, international assistance and implementation support remains crucial to advance further the elimination of landmines.

5.4 THE 2008 CONVENTION ON CLUSTER MUNITIONS

Cluster munitions were originally developed and used before World War II but it was their use on an unprecedented scale by the United States during the Vietnam War, especially during its bombing of Laos where 260 million submunitions were dropped over the country,[45] that marked the weapons as being especially hazardous to civilians. Soviet forces used air-dropped and rocket-delivered cluster munitions on a wide scale in Afghanistan in the 1980s, while Israel fired several million submunitions into Lebanon during its invasion of the country in 2006. These explosive munitions are designed to kill

---

[41] Mechanical clearance is far faster, but is expensive, often unwieldy, and can only be used in certain areas. Dogs and increasingly rats are also used for mine detection, but are also not cheap to secure or apply, largely because of the demanding training requirements.

[42] The reason for this omission is somewhat spurious: in response to calls from the ICRC for a provision on the duty to assist victims, representatives from one of the Western States in the 'core group' leading the negotiation of the Convention felt it would be insulting or at least upsetting to developing nations to include such a provision.

[43] ICRC, '1997 Anti-Personnel Mine Ban Convention', Fact Sheet, Geneva, September 2019, p. 2.

[44] Afghanistan, Albania, Angola, Bosnia and Herzegovina, Burundi, Cambodia, Chad, Colombia, Croatia, Democratic Republic of Congo, El Salvador, Eritrea, Ethiopia, Guinea-Bissau, Iraq, Jordan, Mozambique, Nicaragua, Peru, Senegal, Serbia, Somalia, South Sudan, Sri Lanka, Sudan, Tajikistan, Thailand, Uganda, Yemen, and Zimbabwe. Implementation Support Unit, 'Assisting the Victims', at: http://bit.ly/2PFpEuK.

[45] Also heavily affected were (and still are) Cambodia and Vietnam.

personnel or destroy vehicles, including tanks. Whereas anti-personnel mines are often designed to maim, submunitions are typically designed to kill.

In 1974, a group of countries led by Sweden had called for the prohibition of a number of anti-personnel weapons including 'cluster warheads', and these proposals were subsequently discussed in the diplomatic conferences that resulted in the two 1977 Additional Protocols and the Convention on Certain Conventional Weapons (CCW). When the CCW was adopted in 1980, however, it contained no measures on cluster munitions.

Renewed use of the weapons in Afghanistan in 2001–2, this time by the United States, and then in Iraq in 2003, underlined problems associated with the accuracy and reliability of a weapon intended to saturate areas with explosive force, and increased disquiet among national policymakers in a number of States Parties to the CCW.[46] Israel's use in Lebanon proved to be a tipping point.

In a process led by Norway, the Convention on Cluster Munitions was adopted in Dublin on 30 May 2008, entering into force on 1 August 2010. As was the case with the 1997 Anti-Personnel Mine Ban Convention, the 2008 Convention on Cluster Munitions was negotiated at an ad hoc diplomatic conference convened outside UN auspices, as agreement to prohibit those weapons within the global organisation's consensus-based framework proved impossible. As of 1 April 2022, 110 of the global total of 197 States in a position to adhere were party to the Convention on Cluster Munitions.

The Convention's preamble indicates its objective of protecting civilians. Its first two paragraphs reflect States Parties' deep concern that the civilian populations and individual civilians 'continue to bear the brunt of armed conflict' and their determination to 'put an end for all time to the suffering and casualties caused by cluster munitions'. The third preambular paragraph indicates the concern that cluster munition remnants 'kill or maim civilians, including women and children, obstruct economic and social development, including through the loss of livelihood, impede post-conflict rehabilitation and reconstruction, delay or prevent the return of refugees and internally displaced persons, can negatively impact on national and international peacebuilding and humanitarian assistance efforts, and have other severe consequences that can persist for many years after use'.

Consequently, similar to the 1997 Anti-Personnel Mine Ban Convention, States adhering to the Convention must never under any circumstances use, develop, produce, acquire, stockpile, retain, or transfer cluster munitions. They are also generally prohibited from assisting, encouraging, or inducing anyone to undertake any activity prohibited by its provisions.

The Convention on Cluster Munitions defines a cluster munition as 'a conventional munition that is designed to disperse or release explosive submunitions each weighing less than 20 kilograms, and includes those explosive submunitions'.[47] Cluster munitions are typically deployed by aircraft or artillery with a canister or dispenser that disperses explosive submunitions. The Convention applies also to explosive bomblets that are specifically

---

[46]   V. Wiebe, J. Borrie, and D. Smyth, 'Introduction', in G. Nystuen and S. Casey-Maslen (eds.), *The Convention on Cluster Munitions: A Commentary*, Oxford University Press, Oxford, 2010, paras. 0.21, 0.22.

[47]   Art. 2(2), 2008 Convention on Cluster Munitions.

designed to be dispersed or released directly from dispensers fixed to aircraft.[48] All mines are excluded from the scope of the Convention on Cluster Munitions, as are munitions or submunitions designed to dispense flares, smoke, pyrotechnics, or chaff, and munitions or submunitions designed to produce electrical or electronic effects.[49]

As with the 1997 Anti-Personnel Mine Ban Convention, the Convention on Cluster Munitions requires that clearance and destruction of unexploded submunitions be completed within ten years of its entry into force for the affected State, although in both cases it is possible to request extensions to the deadline from the other States Parties. In total, clearance operations around the world have destroyed at least 844,000 unexploded submunitions in 2010–19, returning more than 638 square kilometres of land to communities, enabling resettlement, reconstruction, and development to occur. In 2018 alone, more than 128 square kilometres of cluster munition-contaminated area were released through clearance, with the destruction of over 135,000 submunitions. This total was the highest ever recorded for a single year's clearance, bettering by nearly 35 per cent the previous high set in 2017 (95 square kilometres).[50]

As of mid-2022, twenty-five States and three other areas were confirmed or strongly suspected to have areas containing cluster munition remnants on their territory. Affected States Parties were Afghanistan, Bosnia and Herzegovina, Chad, Chile, Germany, Iraq, Laos, Lebanon, Mauritania, and Somalia. Signatory State DR Congo was also suspected to have still cluster munition remnants. Affected States not party to the Convention were Azerbaijan, Cambodia, Georgia, Iran, Libya, Serbia, South Sudan, Sudan, Syria, Tajikistan, Ukraine, Vietnam, and Yemen, along with the territories of Kosovo, Nagorno-Karabakh, and Western Sahara. Twelve States had completed cluster munition survey and clearance on their territory since 2010: Angola, Colombia, Croatia, the Republic of Congo, Grenada, Guinea-Bissau, Montenegro, Mozambique, Norway, Thailand, the United Kingdom, and Zambia. Croatia, Montenegro, and the United Kingdom all fulfilled their survey and clearance obligations in 2020. Angola was close to being removed from the list of affected States as of writing.

In the Convention on Cluster Munitions are set out the most detailed obligations on victim assistance of any disarmament treaty. Article 5 of the Convention allocates clear responsibility to each State Party to 'adequately' provide age- and gender-sensitive assistance to cluster munition victims in areas under its jurisdiction or control. The required assistance includes medical care, rehabilitation, and psychological support, as well as provision for their social and economic inclusion. Article 5 also sets out in detail how a State Party is to implement these obligations. Similar to the 1997 Anti-Personnel Mine Ban Convention, international assistance and cooperation continue to be necessary to enable further progress to be achieved. Broader adherence by States could also strengthen the Convention on Cluster Munitions' contribution to the protection of civilians.

---

[48] Art. 1(2), 2008 Convention on Cluster Munitions.
[49] Art. 2(2)(a) and (b), 2008 Convention on Cluster Munitions.
[50] Mine Action Review, *Clearing Cluster Munition Remnants 2019*, Norwegian People's Aid, London, 2019, p. 1, at: mineactionreview.org.

5.5 THE 2013 ARMS TRADE TREATY

Civilians can further be protected against harm by reducing access to conventional weapons by States and non-State actors which would use them in violation of international law. Traditionally, States have controlled their weapons transfers by national export controls. The Wassenaar Arrangement on Export Controls for Conventional Arms and Dual-Use Goods and Technologies as well as regional instruments have established standards for doing so, yet mostly without directly addressing the impact of conventional arms transfers on civilians. A motivation for the elaboration of the 2013 Arms Trade Treaty (ATT), in particular among civil society which lobbied for a 'bulletproof' Treaty,[51] was to prevent harm to civilians by setting international standards for the regulation of international arms transfers.

In this sense, the Arms Trade Treaty's preamble recognises the 'security, social, economic and humanitarian consequences of the illicit and unregulated trade in conventional arms' while bearing in mind that 'civilians, particularly women and children, account for the vast majority of those adversely affected by armed conflict and armed violence'. Article 1 defines the Treaty's purpose of reducing human suffering (among other aims).

Article 5 of the Treaty obliges States Parties to establish and maintain national control authorities, which includes national lists of items that are subject to transfer control. From a perspective of protecting civilians, however, the most important provisions are Articles 6 and 7 as they govern State Parties' national decisions on whether to authorise arms transfers to certain users.

Article 6 reiterates the prohibition on allowing a conventional arms transfer that would violate a States Party's 'obligations under measures adopted by the United Nations Security Council acting under Chapter VII of the Charter of the United Nations, in particular arms embargoes', as well as 'its relevant international obligations under international agreements to which it is a Party'. Paragraph 3 further prohibits a State Party from authorising an arms transfer if it has 'knowledge at the time of authorization that the arms or items would be used in the commission of genocide, crimes against humanity, [or] war crimes'. If these prohibitions are properly applied, arms transfers that manifestly lead to significant civilian harm can be prevented.

Article 7 establishes criteria that need to be fulfilled for authorising a proposed weapons export. If the export is not prohibited by the prohibitions in Article 6, an exporting State Party must assess the potential that the arms or ammunition would contribute to or undermine peace and security. If it is determined that the arms or items would undermine peace and security, the export must not be authorised. If, however, it is determined that the arms or items would contribute to peace and security, there must be further assessment of the extent to which they could be used to commit or facilitate a serious violation of international humanitarian law or international human rights law as well as to commit or facilitate an offence of terrorism or transnational organised crime.

If, after conducting this risk assessment and once available mitigating measures have been taken into account, the exporting State Party determines that an 'overriding risk'

---

[51] See, for example, the work and history of Control Arms, at: https://controlarms.org/att/.

exists of any of these negative consequences, it must not authorise the export. The precise meaning of the notion of 'overriding risk' is, though, debated.[52] The exporting State needs also to take into account the risk of the items being used to commit or facilitate serious acts of gender-based violence or serious acts of violence against women and children and the risk of diversion of the arms or ammunition.[53] Although these criteria do not address only harm inflicted upon civilians, they do encompass, to a large extent, civilian protection. Notably the references to IHL and international human rights law serve to reinforce and ensure respect for these bodies of international law.

The Treaty further provides mechanisms for the prevention and combating of diversion, notably unauthorised re-exports and illicit trafficking of weapons. In addition to requirements for recording, the ATT obliges its States Parties to report on their measures to implement the Treaty provisions as well as to submit annual reports on weapon imports and exports or authorisations for such imports or exports. The Conference of States Parties, the ATT Secretariat, and other institutional mechanisms further contribute to achieving the Treaty's object and purpose.

Among the Arms Trade Treaty's 111 State Parties (coming from all continents) and 35 signatory States are found many conflict-affected countries and arms exporters. China, France, and the United Kingdom, all permanent members of the Security Council, have all joined. While the United States had signed the Treaty in 2013, the Trump Administration declared that the United States would no longer seek to ratify.[54] Nonetheless, although major arms exporters and importers remain outside the Treaty, the ATT has become a regime covering many global arms transfers.

Given that few exporting States have significantly adapted their national legislation or export practices, the jury is still out regarding the Treaty's concrete impact on the protection of civilians, however. It is noteworthy that in the United Kingdom, judicial processes have been initiated against the government's exports of arms to Saudi Arabia, which could be used to commit war crimes in Yemen.[55] The Court of Appeal had found in 2019 that the UK Government had not properly assessed this risk.[56] A few months after the ruling, though, the government resumed its arms exports to Saudi Arabia. In April 2021, anti-arms trade campaigners were given permission to challenge the UK government's decision to resume the sale of arms to Saudi Arabia in the High Court.[57] Other, similar cases in States Parties to the Treaty may increasingly occur in the future.

---

[52] For a discussion of the controversy surrounding the meaning of 'overriding risk', see S. Casey-Maslen and A. Clapham, 'Article 7', in S. Casey-Maslen, A. Clapham, G. Giacca, and S. Parker, *The Arms Trade Treaty, A Commentary*, 1st ed., Oxford University Press, Oxford, 2016, paras. 7.90–95.

[53] Art. 7(4) and 11(2), 2013 Arms Trade Treaty.

[54] J. Abramson and G. Webb, 'US to Quit Arms Trade Treaty', *Arms Control Today*, Vol. 49, 2019.

[55] See, for example, J. S. Bachman, 'A "Synchronised Attack" on Life: The Saudi-Led Coalition's "Hidden and Holistic" Genocide in Yemen and the Shared Responsibility of the US and UK', *Third World Quarterly*, 2019.

[56] High Court, R *(On Application of the Campaign Against Arms Trade)* v. *The Secretary of State for International Trade*, Judgment, T3/2017/2079 (20 June 2019).

[57] D. Sabbagh, 'High Court to Hear Legal Battle Over UK Arms Sales to Saudi Arabia', *Guardian*, 22 April 2021, at: https://bit.ly/39IF2zQ.

6

International Criminal Law and the Protection of Civilians

6.1 INTRODUCTION

Both the physical capacity to undertake unlawful violence against civilians and, through the deterrent effect, the psychological capacity to do so are reduced by the effective investigation, apprehension, and prosecution of those who have attacked or ill-treated civilians. As Carsten Stahn has observed: 'Hardly any situation of armed conflict or atrocity can be settled without engagement with the question of accountability.'[1] In many instances, as this chapter illustrates, violence perpetrated against civilians is not only a crime under domestic law, but also an international crime.[2] This can allow its prosecution in an international criminal court or tribunal if domestic courts are unable or unwilling to do so.

A serious violation of the prohibition of inter-State use of force under *jus ad bellum* is an act of aggression, which is now capable of being prosecuted by the International Criminal Court (ICC) when perpetrated by a senior government or military official of a ratifying State. Such prosecutions are, in practice, very unlikely.[3] The last time an international tribunal successfully prosecuted 'crimes against peace' was in the trials of Nazi war criminals at Nuremburg after the end of World War II.[4] In March 2006, the United Kingdom (UK) House of Lords unanimously decided in R v. *Jones (Margaret)*, in the context of the invasion of Iraq in 2003, that although the crime of aggression existed under customary international law, there was no such crime under the law of England and Wales.[5] Given the relative improbability of a successful prosecution for aggression in the next decade, this chapter does not devote further attention to this international crime.

---

[1] C. Stahn, *A Critical Introduction to International Criminal Law*, Cambridge University Press, Cambridge, 2019, p. 3.

[2] See ibid., p. 21.

[3] See, for example, D. Ferencz, 'The Nuremberg Legacy and the Crime of Aggression: A Promise Betrayed or Merely Delayed?', Blog entry, Centre for Criminology, University of Oxford, 13 February 2015, at: http://bit.ly/365tKVg.

[4] Global Institute for the Prevention of Aggression, 'The Crime of Aggression: a Brief History', at: http://bit.ly/3c7DO3E.

[5] UK House of Lords, R v. *Jones (Margaret)* [2007] 1 AC 136.

What may be – and are – prosecuted, both domestically and at international level, are war crimes, crimes against humanity, and genocide.[6] This chapter summarises the main elements in international crimes against civilians and illustrates the prosecution of offenders. It must be acknowledged from the outset, though, that only a small percentage of the crimes actually committed are even properly investigated and that in a considerably smaller number of cases are the perpetrators prosecuted. This is despite the fact that the extent of unlawful violence against civilians could be reduced by substantially enhanced efforts to ensure respect for domestic and international law by holding individuals to due account for their illegal actions. In the words of the International Military Tribunal at Nuremburg, 'Crimes against international law are committed by men, not by abstract entities, and only by punishing individuals who commit such crimes can the provisions of international law be enforced.'[7]

This chapter addresses in turn the core elements of war crimes, crimes against humanity, and genocide as they pertain to the killing, maiming, and persecution of civilians. Those engaged in protection work at field level need to monitor whether such crimes are being perpetrated (and may even be called to testify in a trial of an individual accused of having committed an international crime), so it is important that they are aware of the principal contours of the main offences.

Also important to bear in mind is the fact that there are always two elements to any international crime that must be successfully established for a conviction to be secured: a culpable act (known by its Latin moniker, '*actus reus*') and a culpable state of mind ('*mens rea*'). This is the same as routinely occurs in domestic law. Thus for example, under the law in force in England and Wales, murder is where one person kills another unlawfully (the *actus reus* element) with the intention to cause either death or serious injury (the *mens rea* element).[8]

6.2 WAR CRIMES

War crimes are serious violations of international humanitarian law (IHL) whose commission in the context of an armed conflict is criminalised. In order to amount to a war crime a violation of IHL 'must be serious, that is to say, it must constitute a breach of a rule protecting important values, and the breach must involve grave consequences for the victim'.[9] There is a duty to prosecute (or to hand over to another State or international

6 W. Schabas, 'National Courts Finally Begin to Prosecute Genocide, the Crime of Crimes', *Journal of International Criminal Justice*, Vol. 1. (2003), 39.

7 *Trial of the Major War Criminals before the International Military Tribunal*, Vol. I, Nuremberg, 1947, 223.

8 See, for example, Crown Prosecution Service, 'Homicide: Murder and Manslaughter', updated 18 March 2019, at: http://bit.ly/3o8Wrqh.

9 International Committee of the Red Cross (ICRC), 'War Crimes', *How Does Law Protect in War?*, at: http://bit.ly/39ay33m. 'Thus, for instance, the fact of a combatant simply appropriating a loaf of bread in an occupied village would not amount to a "serious violation of international humanitarian law" although potentially in breach of Article 46, paragraph 1, of the Hague Regulations. In addition, the individual bears criminal responsibility if the violation entails, under customary or conventional law, the individual criminal responsibility of the person who has violated or participated in the violation of that rule. International

court for prosecution) all those reasonably suspected to have committed war crimes,[10] whether they acted as perpetrators or under other modes of liability (such as ordering the crime to be committed, or aiding and abetting its commission).[11]

For a prosecution of an alleged war crime to be successful, there must be a direct connection – a nexus – to a specific armed conflict. Thus, an accused's lawyer will often use as a first line of defence: 'There was no armed conflict.' Or, if that defence fails, he or she may argue that: 'My client's actions were not sufficiently connected with the armed conflict.' Only then may the approach turn to focus on arguing that the actions of the defendant do not meet the requirements of either the *actus reus* or *mens rea* for the offences with which he or she has been charged.

In the first case to come before the International Criminal Tribunal for the former Yugoslavia (ICTY) in the 1990s – *Prosecutor* v. *Tadić* – Mr Tadić's lawyers opposed and then appealed against the jurisdiction of the Tribunal to try their client for war crimes. Mr Tadić was alleged to have committed acts of murder and torture, but these occurred in and around three Bosnian Serb-run camps in 1992 in the Prijedor region of north-west Bosnia and Herzegovina, a considerable distance from the bulk of the fighting that was ongoing at the salient time. In its decision on the issue, the ICTY Appeals Chamber stated that:

> Even if substantial clashes were not occurring in the Prijedor region at the time and place the crimes allegedly were committed – a factual issue on which the Appeals Chamber does not pronounce – international humanitarian law applies. It is sufficient that the alleged crimes were closely related to the hostilities occurring in other parts of the territories controlled by the parties to the conflict. There is no doubt that the allegations at issue here bear the required relationship.[12]

Criminal Tribunal for the former Yugoslavia (ICTY), *Prosecutor* v. *Tadić*, Decision on Defence Motion for Interlocutory Appeal on Jurisdiction (Case No. IT-94-1-AR72), 2 October 1995, para. 94.

[10] International humanitarian law obligates States to search for and prosecute or extradite for prosecution (so-called universal jurisdiction) every individual alleged to have committed 'grave breaches' of the Geneva Conventions or Additional Protocol I anywhere in the world and regardless of the alleged war criminals' nationality (Art. 49, 1949 Geneva Convention I; Art. 50, Geneva Convention II; Art. 129, Geneva Convention III; and Art. 146, Geneva Convention IV). For war crimes that do not amount to grave breaches, States have instead the obligation to investigate and prosecute them when committed by their own nationals, members of their armed forces, or on their territory (ICRC, Customary IHL Rule 158: 'Prosecution of War Crimes', at: http://bit.ly/37FdYin) and the prerogative – but not the obligation – to exercise universal jurisdiction. See S. Casey-Maslen, with S. Haines, *Hague Law Interpreted: The Conduct of Hostilities under the Law of Armed Conflict*, Hart, Oxford, 2018, at pp. 344–5. See also G. Corn, K. Watkin, and J. Williamson, *The Law in War*, 1st ed., Vol. 1, Routledge, Abingdon, 2018, chapter 12: 'War Crimes and Accountability', 272–90, at p. 277.

[11] See Art. 25(3), Rome Statute of the International Criminal Court; adopted at Rome, 17 July 1998; entered into force, 1 July 2002 (Statute of the International Criminal Court). As of 1 April 2022, 123 States were party to the Statute.

[12] ICTY, *Prosecutor* v. *Tadić* (aka *'Dule'*), Decision on the Defence Motion for Interlocutory Appeal on Jurisdiction (Appeals Chamber) (Case No. IT-94-1), 2 October 1995, at: http://bit.ly/2YR8mzd, para. 70. In the *Kunarac* case, the ICTY Appeals Chamber made it clear that what distinguishes a war crime

> from a purely domestic offence is that a war crime is shaped by or dependent upon the environment – the armed conflict – in which it is committed. ... [T]he armed conflict need not have been causal to the commission of the crime, but the existence of an armed conflict must, at a minimum, have played a substantial part in the perpetrator's ability to commit it, the manner in which it was committed or the

Deliberately attacking civilians in the conduct of hostilities is one of a number of war crimes perpetrated against the civilian population. Some of these are laid down in the 1949 Geneva Convention IV[13] or the 1977 Additional Protocol I. The International Committee of the Red Cross (ICRC), which made a detailed study of customary IHL in the 1990s and early 2000s, identified a number of war crimes under customary law that concern the targeting of civilians, including the following:[14]

- making the civilian population or individual civilians, not taking a direct part in hostilities, the object of attack;
- making persons involved in a humanitarian assistance or peacekeeping mission in accordance with the UN Charter the object of attack (as long as they are entitled to the protection given to civilians under the law of armed conflict);[15] and
- launching an indiscriminate attack resulting in loss of life or injury to civilians.

These war crimes are applicable in all armed conflict. War crimes may be committed by members of State armed forces and by members of organised armed groups (and even potentially by individual civilians).

The Statute of the International Criminal Court gives the Court jurisdiction over the war crime of 'intentionally directing attacks against the civilian population as such or against individual civilians not taking direct part in hostilities' in both international and non-international armed conflict.[16] It also has similar jurisdiction over the war

purpose for which it was committed. Hence, if it can be established ... that the perpetrator acted in furtherance of or under the guise of the armed conflict, it would be sufficient that his acts were closely related to the armed conflict.

ICTY, *Prosecutor v. Kunarac and others*, Judgment (Appeals Chamber) (Case No. IT-96-23 & IT-96-23/1-A), 12 June 2002, para. 58. The ICTR required that the act of the perpetrator be committed 'in conjunction with the armed conflict' or the existence of a 'direct link between the crimes committed and the hostilities'. For an overview of this issue, see H. van der Wilt, 'War Crimes and the Requirement of a Nexus with an Armed Conflict', *Journal of International Criminal Justice*, Vol. 10 (2012), 1113–28, at pp. 1117–20. Here, the author underlines the importance of the perpetrator's traits, such as being part of the military power apparatus or have access to employ the methods and means of warfare. According to van der Wilt, the nexus needs to denote a deviation from the perpetrator's tasks with respect to the conflict. According to Cassese, instead, the violation must have been (i) perpetrated against persons who do not take part in hostilities or who no longer take part in such hostilities; and (ii) committed to pursue the aims of the conflict or, alternatively, it must have been carried out with a view to somehow contributing to attaining the ultimate goals of a military campaign or, at a minimum, in unison with the military campaign. See P. Gaeta, L. Baig, M. Fan, C. Gosnell, and A. Whiting (eds.), *Cassese's International Criminal Law*, 3rd ed., Oxford University Press, Oxford, 2013, chapter 4.

13 Art. 247, Convention (IV) relative to the Protection of Civilian Persons in Time of War; adopted at Geneva, 12 August 1949; entered into force, 21 October 1950.

14 ICRC, Customary IHL Rule 156 ('Definition of War Crimes'), at: http://bit.ly/32HjZb2.

15 The ICRC notes that in the case of 'attack on troops [e.g. UN peacekeepers], the act would only be criminal if, at the time, the troops had not become involved in hostilities and had not thereby lost the protection afforded to civilians under international humanitarian law'.

16 Art. 8(2)(b)(i) and (e)(i), Rome Statute of the International Criminal Court. The scope of the war crime of directly attacking civilians under the Rome Statute differs from its Additional Protocol I grave breach counterpart. In the former, the subjective element (*mens rea*) requires 'intent' rather than 'wilfulness'. For an analysis of the difference, see P. Gaeta, 'Serious Violations of the Law on the Conduct of Hostilities: A Neglected Class of War Crimes?', in F. Pocar, M. Pedrazzi, and M. Frulli (eds.), *War Crimes and the Conduct of Hostilities: Challenges to Adjudication and Investigation* Edward Elgar, Cheltenham, 2013, 20–37, at pp. 32–5.

crime in all armed conflict of intentionally directing attacks against personnel involved in a humanitarian assistance or peacekeeping mission in accordance with the Charter of the United Nations, as long as they are entitled to the protection given to civilians or civilian objects under IHL.[17]

For each of the crimes falling within its jurisdiction, there is a set of 'elements of crime' that detail the *actus reus* and *mens rea* elements that the prosecution must prove beyond reasonable doubt. Thus, for the war crime in international armed conflict of 'intentionally directing attacks against the civilian population as such or against individual civilians not taking direct part in hostilities', the International Criminal Court must be satisfied as to the following five cumulative requirements:

Article 8 (2) (b) (i): War crime of attacking civilians

Elements

1. The perpetrator directed an attack.
2. The object of the attack was a civilian population as such or individual civilians not taking direct part in hostilities.
3. The perpetrator intended the civilian population as such or individual civilians not taking direct part in hostilities to be the object of the attack.
4. The conduct took place in the context of and was associated with an international armed conflict.
5. The perpetrator was aware of factual circumstances that established the existence of an armed conflict.

Elements 1 and 2 are the *actus reus* elements of the war crime of attacking civilians. Elements 3 and 5 are the *mens rea* elements of the war crime of attacking civilians.[18] The nexus to armed conflict, which the prosecution must also prove, is covered by Element 4.

The Statute of the International Criminal Court does not specifically provide for prosecution of indiscriminate attacks in any armed conflict. In its 2019 judgment in the *Ntaganda* case, however, a Trial Chamber of the Court held that the crime under the Statute of attacking civilians 'may encompass attacks that are carried out in an indiscriminate manner, that is by targeting an area, as opposed to specific objects, or not targeting specific military objects or persons taking a direct part in hostilities, ... so long as the perpetrator was aware of the presence of civilians in the relevant area'.[19] The Trial Chamber further held that the crime 'may also include attacks that are launched without taking necessary precautions to spare the civilian population or individual civilians'.[20]

[17] Art. 8(2)(b)(iii) and (e)(iii), Rome Statute of the International Criminal Court.
[18] The fifth element does not require that the perpetrator understand from a legal perspective whether an armed conflict exists, just the facts that underpin the existence of that armed conflict.
[19] International Criminal Court (ICC), *Prosecutor v. Bosco Ntaganda*, Judgment (Trial Chamber) (Case No. ICC-01/04-02/06), 8 July 2019, para. 921.
[20] Ibid. The paucity of cases within the jurisprudence of international tribunals and ICC on the war crime of attacking civilians (or civilian objects) shows, however, the difficulty to charge individuals for having committed such crimes due to both legal and practical reasons. For an analysis on this, see, for instance,

Acts of murder, torture, rape,[21] or other sexual violence against civilians, particularly when they are in the power of the enemy, are all war crimes under customary law in all armed conflict. They are also subject to the jurisdiction of the International Criminal Court in both international and non-international armed conflict.[22] Starvation of the civilian population is a war crime under the jurisdiction of the Court, not only in international armed conflict[23] but also, since an amendment to the Statute in December 2019, in non-international armed conflict.[24]

Attacks on civilian objects are also war crimes under customary law. Thus, the ICRC Study of Customary IHL concluded that, in all armed conflict, 'making civilian objects, that is, objects that are not military objectives, the object of attack' is a war crime.[25] Also a war crime is the launching of an indiscriminate attack 'resulting in damage to civilian objects'.[26] Under the Statute of the International Criminal Court, however, attacking civilian objects is only made a crime within the Court's jurisdiction in international armed conflict.[27] Attacks on a limited set of civilian objects are subject to prosecution in non-international armed conflict, in particular: 'Intentionally directing attacks against buildings dedicated to religion, education, art, science or charitable purposes, historic monuments, hospitals and places where the sick and wounded are collected, provided they are not military objectives.'[28]

The ICRC has identified the intentional launching of a disproportionate attack as a war crime under customary law. Its proposed formulation in an international armed conflict is, though, narrow. According to the organisation, it is a war crime in such an armed conflict to: 'Launch ... an attack in the knowledge that such attack will cause incidental loss of civilian life, injury to civilians or damage to civilian objects which

---

C. Wuerzner, 'Mission Impossible? Bringing Charges for the Crime of Attacking Civilians or Civilian Objects before International Criminal Tribunals', *International Review of the Red Cross*, Vol. 90 (2008), 907.

[21] In the *Furundžija* case, the ICTY reaffirmed that the prohibition of rape and other sexual assaults in armed conflict exists in customary international law as a war crime. ICTY, *Prosecutor v. Furundžija*, Trial Judgment, paras. 168–9 and 105. The *Delalić* case was the first time the ICTY had convicted an accused for rape as the war crime of torture. See: C. E. A. Ward, *Wartime Sexual Violence at the International Level: A Legal Perspective*, Brill, Leiden, 2018, pp. 72–3. The author claims that opportunistic and sporadic instances of rape committed in wartime also need to be treated as international crimes to fill the gap left by the lack of prosecution at the domestic level. Others, however, reject the argument that the ability or willingness of the perpetrator's own State to conduct investigations should play a role in determining what amount to war crimes. See, for example, van der Wilt, 'War Crimes and the Requirement of a Nexus with an Armed Conflict'.

[22] Art. 8(2)(a)(i), (ii), and (iii), (2)(b)(xxii), (2)(c)(i), and (2)(d)(vi), Rome Statute of the International Criminal Court.

[23] Art. 8(2)(b)(xxv), Rome Statute of the International Criminal Court.

[24] Art. 8(2)(e)(xix), Rome Statute of the International Criminal Court, relating to intentionally using starvation of civilians as a method of warfare by depriving them of objects indispensable to their survival, including wilfully impeding relief supplies.

[25] ICRC Study of Customary IHL, Rule 156 ('Definition of War Crimes'), '(ii) Other serious violations of international humanitarian law committed during an international armed conflict'; and '(iv) Other serious violations of international humanitarian law committed during a non-international armed conflict', respectively.

[26] Ibid.

[27] Art. 8(2)(b)(ii), Rome Statute of the International Criminal Court.

[28] Art. 8(2)(e)(iv), Rome Statute of the International Criminal Court.

would be clearly excessive in relation to the concrete and direct military advantage anticipated.'[29]

In contrast, in the context of a non-international armed conflict, the ICRC believes the crime is broader: 'launching an indiscriminate attack resulting in death or injury to civilians, or an attack in the knowledge that it will cause excessive incidental civilian loss, injury or damage'.[30] Here, the word 'clearly' is omitted, suggesting (improbably) that the standard for the customary law war crime of a disproportionate attack is lower in a non-international armed conflict than it is in an international armed conflict.[31]

Under the Statute of the ICC, disproportionate attacks are only crimes within the Court's jurisdiction in international armed conflict.[32] The narrow standard – 'clearly excessive' – and the broad one concerning the military advantage – 'overall' – are used for the formulation of the crime.[33] This makes the prosecution of the war crime of a disproportionate attack very challenging.[34]

6.3 CRIMES AGAINST HUMANITY

Crimes against humanity are punishable before the ICC where acts of violence are perpetrated 'as part of a widespread or systematic attack directed against any civilian population, with knowledge of the attack'.[35] The essence of crimes against humanity is therefore an attack[36]

---

[29] ICRC Study of Customary IHL, Rule 156 ('Definition of War Crimes'), '(ii) Other serious violations of international humanitarian law committed during an international armed conflict', point (ii).

[30] Ibid., '(iv) Other serious violations of international humanitarian law committed during a non-international armed conflict', point (ii).

[31] See on this issue Casey-Maslen with S. Haines, *Hague Law Interpreted: The Conduct of Hostilities Under the Law of Armed Conflict*, p. 192.

[32] Although the war crime of disproportionate attacks has not been applied to situations of non-international armed conflict, it is nonetheless submitted that such attacks can still be prosecuted by the ICC as the war crime of 'destroying or seizing the property of an adversary unless such destruction or seizure be imperatively demanded by the necessities of the conflict', for what concerns objects, and the war crime of murder or cruel treatment, with respect to civilians. See H. Olásolo, *Unlawful Attacks in Combat Situations*, Brill, Boston, 2008, pp. 87–90.

[33] Art. 8(2)(b)(iv), Rome Statute of the International Criminal Court. The Rome Statute provision criminalising disproportionate attacks requires a stricter mental element than does customary law. See, among others, Olásolo, *Unlawful Attacks in Combat Situations*, p. 85.

[34] The difficulty of clearly defining the constitutive elements of such crime makes prosecution even more unlikely. The jurisprudence of the ICTY, in particular with respect to the NATO Bombing Campaign, shows that prosecuting the war crime of a disproportionate attack brings to light all the challenges connected to the application of the proportionality rule under IHL, such as the balancing of two incomparable elements, the retrospective nature of the assessment, the context-dependent nature of the rule, and the question of the inclusion of one's party's own forces within the notion of 'military advantage'. See F. Moneta, 'Direct Attacks on Civilians and Indiscriminate Attacks as War Crimes', in Pocar et al., *War Crimes and the Conduct of Hostilities*, 59–77, at pp. 74–5. For an overview of the proportionality rule, see supra Chapter 2.

[35] Art. 7, Rome Statute of the International Criminal Court.

[36] Within the ICC jurisprudence, what amounts to 'attack' for the purpose of the prosecution of an alleged crime against humanity remains controversial, however. On the one hand, it is upheld that an 'attack' implies 'a course of conduct involving the multiple commission of acts' and that 'more than a few isolated incidents' is necessary. On the other hand, it has been claimed that an 'attack' may entail a 'campaign, an operation or a series of actions', but also that 'a single event may well constitute an attack'. Other doubts remain as to the definition of 'civilian', the requisite *mens rea*, and who must possess the requisite intent as perpetrator of the

that is made against civilians.[37] Crimes against humanity may be committed either in a situation of armed conflict or during peacetime.[38] The perpetrator may be a State official or a member of an armed group, where there is a governmental or organisational policy to commit such an attack.[39]

An attack is widespread if it is conducted on a large scale and results in many victims,[40] although there is no specific 'numerical threshold'.[41] The ICTY defined 'systematic' as 'the organised nature of the acts of violence and the improbability of their random occurrence'[42] and found that evidence of a pattern or a methodical plan establishes that an attack was systematic.[43]

The core elements of 'a widespread or systematic attack directed against any civilian population, with knowledge of the attack' and the associated crimes are part of customary law but there is no specific treaty that exists to prevent and repress crimes against humanity. An array of acts may be prosecuted as crimes against humanity. These include murder, enslavement, unlawful deprivation of liberty, torture, rape or sexual slavery, enforced disappearance, and other inhumane acts intentionally causing great suffering or serious bodily injury.[44]

crime. See R. Dubler and M. Kalyk, *Crimes against Humanity in the 21st Century*, Brill, Boston, 2018, pp. 317–20.

[37] The notion of 'directed against' a civilian population entails that the civilian population needs to be the 'primary object' of the attack 'rather than an incidental object' ICC, *Prosecutor v. Bemba Gombo*, Decision Pursuant to Article 61(7)(a) and (b) of the Rome Statute on the Charges (Case No. ICC-01/05–01/08), 15 June 2009 (Bemba Gombo – Confirmation), para. 76; and ICC, *Prosecutor v. Katanga and Chui*, Decision on the Confirmation of Charges (Case No. ICC-01/04–01/07–717), 13 October 2008 (Katanga – Confirmation), para. 399. According to Cassese, however, such a limitation is not reflected in customary international law, which rather covers acts perpetrated against military personnel. See A. Cassese, *International Criminal Law*, Oxford University Press, Oxford, 2003, pp. 85–91.

[38] International Law Commission (ILC), Draft articles on Prevention and Punishment of Crimes Against Humanity, with commentaries, in UN doc. A/74/10, 2019, at: https://bit.ly/30dgLXD, para. 45, commentary para. 1. When a crime against humanity is committed during an armed conflict, the same acts may also amount to war crimes.

[39] It is claimed, however, that the words 'organisational policy' do not refer to the policy of non-State actors, but rather to an organisation within the State, such as a State organ. See M. Bassiouni, 'Legal Nature', in *Crimes against Humanity: Historical Evolution and Contemporary Application*, Cambridge University Press, Cambridge, 2011, 1–50, at pp. 41–2. The author also argues that, despite the necessity of extending criminal responsibility to non-State actors, 'presently [such extension] may be a bridge too far'. See, ibid., p. 42.

[40] ICTY, *Prosecutor v. Blaškić*, Judgment (Trial Chamber) (Case No. IT-95–14-T), 3 March 2000, para. 206. More specifically, 'widespread' includes either an attack conducted over a large geographical area or an attack in a small geographical area but directed against a large number of civilians. This does not mean, however, that a single act cannot qualify as crime against humanity, but it implies that the overall conduct of the perpetrators 'is intended to generate a certain quantum of harm'. Dubler and Kalyk, *Crimes against Humanity in the 21st Century*, p. 316; Bassiouni, 'Legal Nature', p. 17.

[41] Stahn, *A Critical Introduction to International Criminal Law*, p. 57.

[42] ICTY, *Prosecutor v. Mrkšić*, Judgment (Trial Chamber) (Case No. IT95-13/1-T), 27 September 2007, para. 437.

[43] ICTY, *Prosecutor v. Kunarac*, Judgment (Appeals Chamber) (Case Nos. IT-96–23 & IT-96–23/1-A), 12 June 2002, para. 94. This approach was confirmed by the ICC. See ICC, Katanga – Confirmation, para. 397.

[44] See generally Art. 7(1)(a) to (k), Rome Statute of the International Criminal Court. These underlying offences must be linked to the attack, that is they must be committed in furtherance of the attack considering the 'nature, aims and consequences of such act'. See, ICC, Katanga – Confirmation, para. 400; ICC, Bemba Gombo – Confirmation, paras. 84, 86.

In the *Dragomir Milošević* case before the ICTY, the commander of the Bosnian Serbs in and around Sarajevo was accused of murder as a crime against humanity. As to the widespread nature of the attack, the Chamber found adequate evidence of 'a very large number of attacks by way of mortars, modified air bombs and sniping, spread out over the entire city of Sarajevo over a prolonged period of time'.[45] In addition, the circumstances were such, the Chamber held, 'that it must have been obvious' to the Bosnian Serb troops 'that they were targeting a civilian population'.[46] The requisite acts amounted to both murder and 'other inhumane acts' (where civilians were seriously injured but survived) as crimes against humanity.[47]

The frequent link between acts carried out with a view to terrorising civilians and crimes against humanity has been widely seen in Syria. In 2014, the UN Commission of Inquiry on Syria found that the Government had employed a military strategy targeting the civilian population, combining long-lasting sieges with continuous air and ground bombardment. In neighbourhoods around Damascus, civilians were targeted on the basis of their perceived opposition to the Government. Merely living in or originating from those neighbourhoods led to their being attacked.[48] The Commission concluded that the Syrian regime 'has carried out a widespread and systematic attack against the civilian population of Aleppo to punish and terrorize civilians for supporting or hosting armed groups, in an apparent strategy to erode popular support for those groups'.[49]

The Statute of the International Criminal Court contains 'one of the most modern and extensive lists of sexual and gender-based violence'.[50] These crimes are discussed in detail in the following chapter. In March 2016, the Court entered its first conviction relating to sexual violence, finding a former vice-president of the Democratic Republic of Congo guilty of rape as a crime against humanity and a war crime committed in the Central African Republic between 26 October 2002 and 15 March 2003.[51] Jean-Pierre Bemba, a trial chamber of the Court held, had failed to prevent and punish rapes, against both men and women, in his capacity as commander of the Movement for the Liberation of the Congo (MLC). The MLC was an armed opposition group that later became a political party. In 2018, however, Mr Bemba's conviction was overturned on appeal on the basis that he had taken measures to prevent and repress crimes by his soldiers

---

[45] ICTY, *Prosecutor v. Dragomir Milošević*, Judgment (Trial Chamber III) (Case No. IT-98-29/1-T), 12 December 2007, para. 927.

[46] Ibid., para. 930.

[47] Ibid., paras. 932, 934.

[48] Report of the Independent International Commission of Inquiry on the Syrian Arab Republic, UN doc. A/HRC/27/60, 13 August 2014, para. 104.

[49] Ibid.

[50] Stahn, *A Critical Introduction to International Criminal Law*, p. 63.

[51] ICC, *Prosecutor v. Jean-Pierre Bemba Gombo*, Judgment (Trial Chamber III) (Case No. ICC-01/05-01/08), 21 March 2016, para. 100. For an analysis on how the Trial Chamber departed from the notion of rape as developed in the previous jurisprudence, see J. N. Clark, 'The First Rape Conviction at the ICC: An Analysis of the Bemba Judgment', *Journal of International Criminal Justice*, Vol. 14 (2016), 667, at pp. 673–80.

which were deemed by a majority of the Appeals Chamber to be reasonable in the circumstances.[52]

6.4 GENOCIDE

Genocide, the so-called crime of crimes, which was formally outlawed by the 1948 Genocide Convention,[53] is also punishable as an international crime before the ICC. Genocide is the act of killing or seriously injuring or starving members of a minority where the act is committed 'with intent to destroy, in whole or in part' that group.[54] As is the case with crimes against humanity, genocide may be committed in a situation of armed conflict or in peacetime.

In 2004, the ICTY issued its judgment on appeal in the *Krstić* case, terming the killings in the aftermath of the fall of the Bosnian Muslim enclave of Srebrenica 'genocide'.[55] The Appeals Chamber accepted that genocide could occur in a localised area and with respect to a small percentage of the population of a national minority.[56]

Incitement to commit genocide, using the media, can also be prosecuted for using 'speech as a weapon'.[57] One of those prosecuted for the offence by the International

[52] ICC, *Prosecutor v. Jean-Pierre Bemba Gombo*, Judgment on the appeal of Mr Jean-Pierre Bemba Gombo against Trial Chamber III's 'Judgment pursuant to Article 74 of the Statute' (Case No. ICC-01/05-01/08 A), 8 June 2018, paras. 172–84 and 193–4.

[53] Convention on the Prevention and Punishment of the Crime of Genocide; adopted at Paris, 9 December 1948; entered into force, 12 January 1951 (hereinafter, 1948 Genocide Convention). As of 1 April 2022, 152 States were party to the Convention. In its judgment in *Bosnia v. Serbia and Montenegro*, the International Court of Justice interpreted the Convention as providing for 'a duality of responsibility' for genocide, according to which Article 1 would impose on States a duty to prevent and punish genocide *as well as* a duty to refrain from engaging in genocide; hence, State responsibility *and* individual criminal responsibility would be triggered. In the view of the Court, the same holds true with respect to the conduct addressed under Article 3 of the Convention, namely conspiracy, direct and public incitement, attempt to commit genocide, or complicity in genocide. For an overview, see generally A. Cassese et al., *Cassese's International Criminal Law*, 3rd ed., Oxford University Press, Oxford, 2013, pp. 112–13.

[54] Art. 6, Rome Statute of the International Criminal Court. See also Art. 2, 1948 Genocide Convention. This 'special' intent to destroy is what ultimately distinguishes crimes against humanity from genocide. As to this specific element, it is debated whether it is enough that the perpetrator merely 'believes' that with their act they can destroy the targeted group even if only one, isolated act is committed (as upheld by the ICTR in its judgment in the *Mpambara* case). Some – both in jurisprudence and among commentators – have claimed that a single act would not be enough and, on the contrary, that there must be a genocidal campaign or a pattern of collective violence of which the underlying offence was part. In its jurisprudence in *Al-Bashir*, the ICC seemed to reject the ICTR's approach, upholding that the act against the protected group may amount to genocide only if the threat it poses is 'concrete and real' rather than merely 'latent or hypothetical'. Therefore, it is claimed by some commentators that a single act may well amount to genocide provided that it poses a concrete risk to the group existence. Cassese et al., *Cassese's International Criminal Law*, 3rd ed., pp. 123–4.

[55] ICTY, *Prosecutor v. Krstić*, Judgment (Appeals Chamber) (Case No. IT-98-33-A), 19 April 2004, paras. 37–8.

[56] Stahn, *A Critical Introduction to International Criminal Law*, p. 40. In its judgment in *Akayesu*, a Trial Chamber of the ICTR adopted an even broader view, affirming that to amount to genocide it is enough that one of the relevant acts be committed against one member of a protected group. This approach has, however, been since deemed too broad and inconsistent with the text of the norms on genocide. Cassese et al., *Cassese's International Criminal Law*, 3rd ed., p. 117.

[57] Stahn, *A Critical Introduction to International Criminal Law*, p. 49.

Criminal Tribunal for Rwanda (ICTR) was the Chief Executive of *Radio Television Libre des Milles Collines*, Ferdinand Nahimana. The Tribunal told Mr Nahimana: 'Without firearm, machete or physical weapon, [you] caused the deaths of thousands of innocent civilians.'[58]

As of writing, a case was before the International Court of Justice with respect to genocide allegedly committed in Myanmar by the armed forces against Rohingya Muslims in Rakhine state.[59] The International Court of Justice hears cases between States, it does not try individuals, though it may call for the prosecution of senior State officials should it ultimately adjudicate that Myanmar has indeed engaged in acts of genocide. In this regard, in its Order of Provisional Measures issued in January 2020, the Court, by unanimous decision, declared that Myanmar 'shall take effective measures to prevent the destruction and ensure the preservation of evidence related to allegations of acts [of genocide]'.[60] In pleadings before the Court, one of the international lawyers hired by Myanmar had claimed that: 'Killing non-combatants in an armed conflict may violate the right to life. But 10,000 deaths out of a population of well over one million might suggest something other than an intent to physically destroy the group.'[61]

---

[58] ICTR, *Prosecutor v. Nahimana*, Judgment (Trial Chamber) (Case No. ICTR-99–52-T), 3 December 2003, para. 1099; see Stahn, *A Critical Introduction to International Criminal Law*, p. 49.
[59] ICJ, *Application of the Convention on the Prevention and Punishment of the Crime of Genocide (The Gambia v. Myanmar)*, at: http://bit.ly/2XWYrHy.
[60] ICJ, *Application of the Convention on the Prevention and Punishment of the Crime of Genocide (The Gambia v. Myanmar)*, Order, 23 January 2020, at: https://bit.ly/368lBPP, para. 86, dispositif 3.
[61] 'Professor William Schabas's Full Transcript in Myanmar's Defense in Genocide Trial', Eleven Media Group, 12 December 2019, at: http://bit.ly/3c1QXvf; see also A. Deutsch, 'Myanmar's Lawyer to Critics on Genocide Case: Everyone has Right to Defense', Reuters, 13 December 2019, at: http://reut.rs/3iQWXIJ.

7

The Prohibition of Sexual and Gender-Based Violence

7.1 INTRODUCTION

All civilians – men and boys as well as women and girls – are at risk of sexual and gender-based violence in peacetime and during armed conflict.[1] All are protected against such violence under international humanitarian law (IHL) during situations of armed conflict and by international human rights law. This protection applies at all times and in all circumstances.

The International Committee of the Red Cross (ICRC) has stated that: 'While the prohibition of sexual violence applies equally to men and women, in practice women are much more affected by sexual violence during armed conflicts.'[2] In its landmark resolution 1325 (2000) on women, peace, and security, the United Nations (UN) Security Council called on 'all parties to armed conflict to take special measures to protect women and girls from gender-based violence, particularly rape and other forms of sexual abuse, and all other forms of violence in situations of armed conflict'.[3]

Sexual violence primarily refers to sexualised acts of violence, including rape, sexual assault, and sexual abuse, while gender-based violence refers to acts of violence perpetrated against a victim based on their gender identity or expression. That said, the differences between the two are not clear cut, as one's gender is often a huge factor in issues surrounding sexual violence and vice-versa.[4] The term 'sexual and gender-based violence' thus covers the many types of sexual violence that are perpetrated against individuals, for whatever reason.[5]

---

[1] In 2013, the United Nations (UN) Security Council formally recognised for the first time that conflict-related sexual violence also affects men and boys. UN Security Council Resolution 2106, adopted by unanimous vote in favour on 24 June 2013, sixth preambular para.

[2] ICRC, Customary IHL Rule 134: 'Women', at: http://bit.ly/2Tj990S.

[3] UN Security Council Resolution 1325, adopted by unanimous vote on 31 October 2000, para. 10.

[4] C. Clemmer, 'Beyond the Definition: What Does "Sexual And Gender Based Violence" Really Mean?', WeWillSpeakOut.US, at: http://bit.ly/399Zhaq.

[5] One definition that is proposed for sexual and gender-based violence (SGBV) is as follows:

> any sexual or physical act, attempt to obtain a sexual act, unwanted sexual comments or advances, or acts to traffic, or otherwise directed, against a person's sexuality using coercion, by any person regardless of their relationship to the victim, in any setting. SGBV also includes any gender-motivated act that

International criminal law requires the prosecution of sexual or gender-based violence when it amounts to an international crime. In any armed conflict, sexual violence perpetrated by a belligerent on a member of the civilian population is a war crime. This covers rape, sexual slavery, enforced prostitution, forced pregnancy, and enforced sterilisation, and other serious forms of sexual violence.[6] Sexual violence may also amount to a crime against humanity.[7] The Statute of the International Criminal Court is said to contain 'one of the most modern and extensive lists of sexual and gender-based violence'.[8] The definition of gender in the Statute of the Court, discussed in Section 7.5 below, is relatively narrow, however.

7.1.1 *The Work of the Special Representative of the Secretary-General on Sexual Violence in Conflict*

As part of its system-wide approach to tackling the problem, in 2010 the United Nations appointed for the first time a Special Representative of the Secretary-General on Sexual Violence in Conflict.[9] The Office of the Special Representative, which is located within the UN Secretariat in New York, drafts the annual reports of the UN Secretary-General on 'conflict-related sexual violence'.[10] Each Annual Report includes detailed information on parties to armed conflict that are credibly suspected of committing or being responsible for acts of rape or other forms of sexual violence.[11]

Listed parties are required to engage with the Office in order to develop specific, time-bound commitments and action plans to address violations. Effective implementation of commitments is a key requirement for the de-listing of parties. All States repeatedly listed for conflict-related sexual violence are prohibited from participating in UN Peace Operations. In the Annual Reports of the UN Secretary-General, however, most of the listed parties are non-State actors, with six of these having been designated as terrorist groups pursuant to Security Council resolutions

---

       results in, or is likely to result in physical, sexual, or psychosocial harm or suffering, including threats of such acts, coercion, or arbitrary deprivation of liberty.

       Ibid.

6 Art. 8(2)(b)(xxii) and 2(e)(vi), Rome Statute of the International Criminal Court; adopted at Rome, 17 July 1998; entered into force, 1 July 2002. As of 1 April 2022, 123 States were party to the Statute.

7 Article 7(1)(g) of the Statute, as discussed below, concerns 'Rape, sexual slavery, enforced prostitution, forced pregnancy, enforced sterilization, or any other form of sexual violence of comparable gravity.'

8 C. Stahn, *A Critical Introduction to International Criminal Law*, Cambridge University Press, Cambridge, 2019, p. 63.

9 The Office of the Special Representative of the Secretary-General on Sexual Violence in Conflict was established by UN Security Council Resolution 1888 (2009).

10 The term 'conflict-related sexual violence' refers to rape, sexual slavery, forced prostitution, forced pregnancy, forced abortion, enforced sterilisation, forced marriage, and any other form of sexual violence of comparable gravity perpetrated against women, or against men, girls, or boys, where the act is directly or indirectly linked to a conflict.

11 The system of monitoring, analysis, and reporting on conflict-related sexual violence was established pursuant to UN Security Council Resolution 1960 (2010). UN Security Council Resolution 1960, adopted by unanimous vote in favour on 16 December 2010, operative para. 8.

1267 (1999), 1989 (2011), and 2253 (2015), the ISIL (Da'esh, i.e. Islamic State) and al-Qaeda sanctions list.[12]

7.2 THE PREVALENCE OF SEXUAL AND GENDER-BASED VIOLENCE IN ARMED CONFLICT

No one can possibly enumerate all the instances of perpetration of sexual and gender-based violence in any scenario but it can be said that every armed conflict sees heightened levels of such abuse, whether as part of a policy by parties to the conflict or as opportunistic attacks by individual belligerents. As of writing, the Office of the Special Representative was working in Afghanistan, Bosnia and Herzegovina, Burundi, the Central African Republic, Colombia, Côte d'Ivoire, the Democratic Republic of Congo, Iraq, Libya, Mali, Myanmar, Nepal, Nigeria, Somalia, Sri Lanka, South Sudan, Sudan (Darfur), Syria, and Yemen.[13]

This does not, of course, mean that such violence is limited to those countries. For instance, in January 2021, the Special Representative on Sexual Violence in Conflict, Ms Pramila Patten, urged all parties to prohibit the use of sexual violence in the Tigray region of Ethiopia.[14] The Special Representative recorded her great concern at serious allegations of sexual violence in the Tigray region, 'including a high number of alleged rapes in the capital, Mekelle'. There were also, she said, 'disturbing reports of individuals allegedly forced to rape members of their own family, under threats of imminent violence'. Some women had reportedly been forced by soldiers to have sex in exchange for basic commodities, while there were increasing reports of sexual violence being perpetrated against women and girls in a number of refugee camps.[15]

While all sexual violence is under-reported, a particular problem exists with respect to such violence when perpetrated against men or boys.[16] As Alice Priddy has reported, '[a]cute social stigma, lack of rehabilitation services, and lack of access to justice mean that male survivors continue to suffer the trauma of the abuse in silence, without treatment and reparation, while perpetrators remain free and enjoy impunity'.[17] In the early years of the Syrian conflict, the Independent International Commission of Inquiry on Syria reported the tying of genitals to be 'systematically perpetrated against men and boys in custody in Damascus, Homs and Aleppo', as well as electrocution of genitalia during

---

[12] Conflict-Related Sexual Violence, Report of the UN Secretary-General, UN doc. S/2019/280, 29 March 2019, paras. 4, 5.

[13] Office of the Special Representative of the Secretary-General on Sexual Violence in Conflict, at: http://bit.ly/2MofV3h.

[14] 'United Nations Special Representative of the Secretary-General on Sexual Violence in Conflict, Ms. Pramila Patten, urges all parties to prohibit the use of sexual violence and cease hostilities in the Tigray region of Ethiopia', Press statement, New York, 21 January 2021, at: http://bit.ly/3ohMMxI.

[15] Ibid.

[16] See in particular S. Sivakumaran, 'Sexual Violence against Men in Armed Conflict', *European Journal of International Law*, Vol. 18, No. 2 (2007), 253–76, at: https://bit.ly/39fQJid; and A. Priddy, 'Sexual Violence against Men and Boys in Armed Conflict', chapter 2 in S. Casey-Maslen (ed.), *The War Report: Armed Conflict in 2013*, Oxford University Press, Oxford, 2014, pp. 271–96.

[17] Ibid., p. 295.

interrogation.[18] The Commission also reported that in January 2013, at the Homs Security Branch, security agents beat and electrocuted the genitals of a seventeen-year-old boy and raped him while others watched.[19]

The UN Secretary-General has identified a clear nexus between sexual violence, trafficking, and terrorism. Radicalisation and violent extremism, the Secretary-General has affirmed, 'have contributed to the entrenchment of discriminatory gender norms that limit women's roles and their enjoyment of basic rights, for example in north-eastern Nigeria and Mali'. Sexual violence, he states

> has served strategic objectives of terrorism, including displacing populations, gaining information through interrogations, advancing extremist ideology and destabilizing social structures by terrorizing women and girls. Sexual violence has also been a recurrent feature of recruitment by terrorist groups, who may promise marriage and sexual slaves as forms of masculine domination and status to young men. Sexual violence can play a vital role in the political economy of terrorism, with physical and online slave markets and human trafficking enabling terrorist groups to generate revenue from the continuous abduction of women and girls.[20]

Another disturbing trend reported by the UN Secretary-General concerns sexual violence perpetrated against very young girls and boys in many countries, such as Afghanistan, Burundi, the Central African Republic, the Democratic Republic of Congo, Myanmar, Somalia, South Sudan, Sri Lanka, Sudan (Darfur), and Yemen. 'Girls and boys can be targeted in order to terrorize their communities, because of perceived affiliations of their parents or their perceived utility or market value. Those vulnerabilities are compounded when children are unaccompanied during migration or displaced with their families.'[21]

Sexual abuse has also been perpetrated by UN peacekeepers and officials and other military forces.[22] In June 2015, for instance, the UN Secretary-General, responding to allegations of sexual exploitation and abuse of children by foreign military forces not under UN command in the Central African Republic, appointed an external, independent review panel on sexual exploitation and abuse by international peacekeeping forces there.[23] The report of the Panel found that the manner in which the United Nations had responded to the allegations was 'seriously flawed'. In describing the response as 'fragmented', 'bureaucratic', and inadequate, the Panel recommended that the

---

[18]   Report of the Independent International Commission of Inquiry on the Syrian Arab Republic, UN doc. A/HRC/25/65, 12 February 2014, para. 65. See also '"I lost my dignity": Sexual and gender-based violence in the Syrian Arab Republic, Conference room paper of the Independent International Commission of Inquiry on the Syrian Arab Republic', UN doc. A/HRC/37/CRP.3, 8 March 2018.

[19]   Ibid.

[20]   Ibid., para. 14.

[21]   Ibid., para. 18.

[22]   See, for example, K. Grady, 'Sexual Exploitation and Abuse by UN Peacekeepers: A Threat to Impartiality', *International Peacekeeping*, Vol. 17, No. 2 (2010), 215–28.

[23]   Special measures for protection from sexual exploitation and sexual abuse, Report of the Secretary-General, UN doc. A/70/729, 16 February 2016, para. 83.

organisation acknowledge that sexual exploitation and abuse by peacekeepers, whether or not the alleged perpetrators were under UN command, is a form of conflict-related sexual violence 'to be addressed under United Nations human rights policy'.[24] The Panel further recommended that the United Nations negotiate with troop-contributing nations to ensure prosecution, 'including by granting host countries subsidiary jurisdiction to prosecute crimes of sexual violence by peacekeepers'.[25]

In 2020, the Secretary-General of the United Nations declared that the past decade had seen a 'paradigm shift' in global understanding of the impacts of conflict-related sexual violence, 'particularly in terms of its relevance to international peace and security, the multisectoral services needed by survivors, the imperative need for gender-responsive security sector reform, and the necessity of tackling gender inequality as a root cause in times of war or conflict, and in times of peace'.[26] More broadly, in 2019, the Secretary-General issued a Bulletin on discrimination and harassment, including sexual harassment, within the United Nations.[27] The Bulletin observes that sexual harassment is 'the manifestation of a culture of discrimination and privilege based on unequal gender relations and other power dynamics'. It may involve 'conduct of a verbal, non-verbal or physical nature' and may also constitute sexual exploitation or abuse.[28]

Although not related to armed conflict, the criminal actions of World Health Organization (WHO) staff during the tackling of the Ebola virus in Africa had come into the open as of writing. Staff at WHO knew of allegations back in early May 2019, but it was not until October 2020 that an independent commission was established. More than fifty women had reported being lured into sex-for-work schemes. Even the investigation appeared to be flawed, further victimising those who had suffered abuse. One woman victim said multiple investigators hounded her each day, asking her to relive details of the alleged abuse she suffered from a WHO worker.[29]

All told, reporters with *The New Humanitarian* and the independent commission's investigators interviewed some 150 victims. At least nine said they had been raped, including a thirteen-year-old girl. The allegations involved both national and international WHO staff. 'This is a dark day for WHO', Tedros Adhanom Ghebreyesus, the WHO's Director-General, told a press conference in Geneva in late September 2021. 'But by shining a light on the failures of individuals and the organisation, we hope that the victims feel that their voices have been heard and acted on.'[30]

---

[24] Ibid., para. 84(a) (Recommendation 1).
[25] Ibid., para. 84(h) (Recommendation 8).
[26] Conflict-Related Sexual Violence, Report of the United Nations Secretary-General, UN doc. S/2020/487, 3 June 2020, at: https://bit.ly/2KJs2RT, para. 10.
[27] 'Addressing Discrimination, Harassment, Including Sexual Harassment, and Abuse of Authority', Secretary-General's Bulletin, ST/SGB/2019/8, 10 September 2019, at: http://bit.ly/3pg7ZJB.
[28] Ibid., para. 1.7.
[29] R. Flummerfelt and P. Dodds, 'Sex Abuse Scandal Rocks World Health Organization, But What Now?', *New Humanitarian*, 29 September 2021, at: https://bit.ly/3D5xZy1.
[30] Ibid.

7.3 IHL RULES ON SEXUAL AND GENDER-BASED VIOLENCE IN ARMED CONFLICT

International humanitarian law has for a long time prohibited sexual violence, 'albeit implicitly and conservatively'; IHL treaties focus on sexual violence against women and in a number of instances the prohibitions are 'framed in rather archaic and discriminatory language'.[31] Thus, for example, in its regulation of international armed conflict, the 1949 Geneva Convention IV prohibits sexual violence against women, decreeing that: 'Women shall be especially protected against any attack on their honour, in particular against rape, enforced prostitution, or any form of indecent assault.'[32] It has been remarked that considering these acts of violence as attacks on women's 'honour' feeds the stereotype of women as weaker than their male counterparts and perpetuates discriminatory attitudes.[33]

More neutral is Common Article 3 to the 1949 Geneva Conventions, which applies to all civilians in non-international armed conflict that do not, or no longer, participate directly in hostilities. The provision encompasses sexual violence within the broad notion of 'outrages upon personal dignity, in particular humiliating and degrading treatment'; acts which are prohibited 'at any time and in any place whatsoever'. This language is largely reproduced as fundamental guarantees for all in international armed conflicts under the 1977 Additional Protocol I.[34]

The ICC remains an important forum for accountability for crimes of conflict-related sexual violence in States that are party to the Rome Statute or in situations referred to the Court by the UN Security Council.[35] The Elements of Crimes for the Statute defines sexual violence for the purpose of both war crimes and crimes against humanity as where a perpetrator

> committed an act of sexual nature against one or more persons or caused such person or persons to engage in an act of sexual nature by force, threat of force or coercion, such as that caused by fear of violence, duress, detention, psychological oppression or abuse of power, against such person or persons or another person, or by taking advantage of a coercive environment such person's or persons' incapacity to give genuine consent.[36]

In any international crime of sexual violence, the use or threat of force or other forms of coercion preclude the possibility of genuine consent.[37] Whether or not the victim physically resisted is thus not determinative, and consent cannot be inferred from the absence of a struggle by the victim.[38]

---

[31] Priddy, 'Sexual Violence against Men and Boys in Armed Conflict', p. 279.

[32] Art. 27, Convention (IV) relative to the Protection of Civilian Persons in Time of War; adopted at Geneva, 12 August 1949; entered into force, 21 October 1950. As of 1 April 2022, 196 States were party to the Convention.

[33] Priddy, 'Sexual Violence against Men and Boys in Armed Conflict', pp. 279–80 and note 65.

[34] Art. 75, Protocol Additional to the Geneva Conventions of 12 August 1949, and relating to the Protection of Victims of International Armed Conflicts; adopted at Geneva, 8 June 1977; entered into force, 7 December 1978 (hereinafter, 1977 Additional Protocol I).

[35] Conflict-Related Sexual Violence, Report of the UN Secretary-General, 2019, para. 27.

[36] See ICC Elements of Crimes, pp. 10, 30, 38.

[37] ICTY, *Prosecutor v. Kunarac*, Judgment (Appeals Chamber) (Case No. IT-96-23), 12 June 2002, para. 99.

[38] Ibid., para. 128; and Rule 70 of the International Criminal Court Rules of Procedure and Evidence, at: https://bit.ly/3qI8T1U.

7.4 SEXUAL AND GENDER-BASED VIOLENCE AS A WAR CRIME

'Controversially,' Priddy observes, 'rape and other forms of sexual violence are not explicitly deemed war crimes under the Geneva Conventions or the Additional Protocols thereto.'[39] Faced with the widespread use of rape in the armed conflicts in Bosnia and Herzegovina in the early 1990s, the ICRC issued an Aide-Mémoire to clarify that the grave breaches regime 'obviously not only covers rape, but also any other attack on a women's dignity'.[40] Furthermore, in its 2005 commentary to the customary rule on the definition of war crimes, the ICRC reiterated that although rape – of males or females – was not 'explicitly' listed as a grave breach, it would be a war crime 'on the basis that it amounts to inhumane treatment or wilfully causing great suffering or serious injury to body or health'.[41] Moreover, given that rape and sexual violence give rise to severe pain and/or suffering, these offences can also be prosecuted as torture.

Under the Statute of the International Criminal Court, sexual violence is explicitly punishable in connection with both an international and a non-international armed conflict. With respect to international armed conflict, the Court has jurisdiction over the war crimes of 'rape, sexual slavery, enforced prostitution, forced pregnancy,[42] ... enforced sterilization, or any other form of sexual violence also constituting a grave breach of the Geneva Conventions'.[43] In the context of non-international armed conflict, the same list of war crimes is applied but the catch-all phrase at the end concerns rather a 'serious violation' of Common Article 3 (to reflect the fact that the grave breaches regime only applies in international armed conflict).[44]

The *actus reus* (culpable act) element of crime of rape under the Statute of the International Criminal Court is that the perpetrator 'invaded the body of a person resulting in penetration however slight, of any part of the body of the victim or of the perpetrator with a sexual organ, or the anal or genital opening of the victim with any object or any part of the body'. The *mens rea* (culpable mental element) of the offence is that the invasion was 'committed by force, or by threat of force or coercion, such as that caused by fear of violence, duress, detention, psychological oppression or abuse of power, against such a person on another person, or by taking advantage of a coercive environment, or the invasion was committed against a person incapable of giving genuine consent'.[45]

The distinction between enforced prostitution and sexual slavery is, legally speaking, a little 'blurred'.[46] Sexual slavery occurs where the 'perpetrator exercised any or all of the

---

[39] Priddy, 'Sexual Violence against Men and Boys in Armed Conflict', p. 280.

[40] ICRC, Update on Aide-Memoire of 3 December 1992; see also T. Meron, 'Rape as a Crime under International Humanitarian Law', *American Journal of International Law*, Vol. 87 (1993), 427.

[41] ICRC, Customary IHL Rule 156 ('Definition of War Crimes') at: http://bit.ly/32HjZb2.

[42] Forced pregnancy means 'the unlawful confinement of a woman forcibly made pregnant, with the intent of affecting the ethnic composition of any population or carrying out other grave violations of international law'. Art. 7(2)(f), Rome Statute of the International Criminal Court.

[43] Art. 8(2)(b)(xxii), Rome Statute of the International Criminal Court.

[44] Art. 8(2)(e)(vi), Rome Statute of the International Criminal Court.

[45] Elements of Crimes, *Official Records of the Assembly of States Parties to the Rome Statute of the International Criminal Court, First session, New York, 3–10 September 2002* (hereinafter, ICC Elements of Crimes), p. 28.

[46] Priddy, 'Sexual Violence against Men and Boys in Armed Conflict', p. 285.

powers attaching to the right of ownership over one or more person, such as by purchasing, selling, lending or bartering such a person or persons, or imposing on them a similar deprivation of liberty' and causing that person 'to engage in one or more acts of a sexual nature'.[47] In turn, enforced prostitution occurs where the perpetrator

> caused one or more persons to engage in one or more acts of a sexual nature by force, or by threat of force or coercion, such as that caused by fear of violence, duress, detention, psychological oppression or abuse of power, against such person or persons or another person, or by taking advantage of a coercive environment or such person's or persons' incapacity to give genuine consent,

and the perpetrator or another person obtained or expected to obtain pecuniary or other advantage in exchange for or in connection with the acts of a sexual nature.[48] This latter requirement distinguishes the crime of enforced prostitution from that of slavery.[49]

7.5 SEXUAL AND GENDER-BASED VIOLENCE AS A CRIME AGAINST HUMANITY

Rape, sexual slavery, enforced prostitution, forced pregnancy, enforced sterilisation, and any other form of sexual violence 'of comparable gravity' are punishable by the International Criminal Court as crimes against humanity[50] if the underlying elements of a widespread or systematic attack against a civilian population and knowledge of the attack[51] can be established. The notion of a widespread attack comprises not only rape and other sexual violence occurring over a wide geographical area,[52] but also large numbers of rapes perpetrated in a localised area.[53] As Chapter 6 recounts, crimes against humanity can be committed in peacetime as well as in armed conflict.

The Prosecutor of the ICC is obligated by the Statute to appoint advisers with legal expertise on specific issues, 'including, but not limited to, sexual and gender violence and violence against children'.[54] In Article 7(3) of the Statute, with respect to the crime against humanity of persecution based on gender it is stipulated that, for the purpose of the Statute, 'the term "gender" refers to the two sexes, male and female, within the context of society'. In its consideration of the need for a Convention on the prevention and repression of crimes against humanity, the International Law Commission (ILC) observes that international understanding of the notion of gender has evolved since the Rome Statute was concluded, moving towards viewing gender as a socially constructed (rather than

---

[47]   ICC Elements of Crimes, p. 28.
[48]   Ibid., p. 29.
[49]   Priddy, 'Sexual Violence against Men and Boys in Armed Conflict', p. 285.
[50]   Art. 7(1)(g), Rome Statute of the International Criminal Court.
[51]   Art. 7(1) (chapeau), Rome Statute of the International Criminal Court.
[52]   ICC, *Prosecutor* v. *Jean-Pierre Bemba Gombo*, Decision pursuant to Article 61(7)(a) and (b) of the Rome Statute on the charges of the Prosecutor against Jean-Pierre Bemba Gombo (Pre-Trial Chamber II) (Case No. ICC-01/05-01/08), 15 June 2009, paras. 117–24.
[53]   ICTY, *Prosecutor* v. *Dario Kordić and Mario Čerkez*, Judgment (Appeals Chamber) (Case No. IT-95-14/2-A), 17 December 2004, para. 94.
[54]   Art. 42(9), Rome Statute of the International Criminal Court.

biological) concept.[55] This has been reflected, for instance, by the Inter-American Court of Human Rights in a 2017 Advisory Opinion.[56]

Trials before the International Criminal Court that have included charges of sexual violence are the *Ongwen*[57] and *Ntaganda* cases. Dominic Ongwen was a former Brigade Commander of the Sinia Brigade of the Lord's Resistance Army (LRA). He was convicted of, among other offences, rape, sexual slavery, and outrages upon personal dignity as war crimes; and sexual slavery, rape, enslavement, and forced marriage as an inhumane act as crimes against humanity.[58] The Court found that a female LRA attacker raped a civilian resident of a military camp with a comb and a stick used for cooking, while the victim's husband was forced to watch. 'The assault was committed with such force that the victim started to bleed.'[59] The Court held that the crimes of rape and sexual slavery could be concurrent:

> the crime of rape requires the invasion of the body of a person by conduct resulting in penetration, however slight, committed under certain specific circumstances, while for the crime of sexual slavery any act of a sexual nature in which the victim is caused to engage would suffice without the need for penetration; conversely, the crime of sexual slavery requires the exercise by the perpetrator of any or all of the powers attaching to the right of ownership over the victim – an element which is not required for the commission of the crime of crime of rape.[60]

In its judgment of 8 July 2019, the International Criminal Court found Bosco Ntaganda guilty of rape as a crime against humanity and a war crime, and guilty of sexual slavery as a crime against humanity and a war crime.[61] His conviction and sentence were confirmed on appeal.[62] One of the issues at trial was the 'delayed' reporting of rape by a number of victims. The Court relied heavily on the testimony of psychological expert Ms Maeve Lewis in this regard. Ms Lewis testified that delays in reporting of rape are 'extremely common', regardless of where the rape occurred, but that women are particularly reluctant to report their sexual assaults in conflict or post-conflict areas, where there is little trust in civil authorities, fear of stigmatisation, and fear of reprisals. The expert explained that one of the major reasons for delayed reporting of rape is the shame and stigma attached to it; the victims' fear that relationships will be broken; and their fear that they will be ostracised

---

[55] ILC, Draft articles on Prevention and Punishment of Crimes Against Humanity, with commentaries, in UN doc. A/74/10, 2019, at: https://bit.ly/3odgLXD, commentary, para. 41, on Draft Article 2(2).

[56] Inter-American Court of Human Rights, *Identidad de género, e igualdad y no discriminación a parejas del mismo sexo* ['Gender Identity, and Equality and Non-discrimination against Same-Sex Couples'], Advisory Opinion OC-24/17, 24 November 2017, at: http://bit.ly/3sN2dRY, para. 32.

[57] International Criminal Court (ICC), *Prosecutor v. Dominic Ongwen*, Case No. ICC-02/04-01/15, at: http://bit.ly/3iUZu4F.

[58] ICC, *Prosecutor v. Dominic Ongwen*, Judgment (Trial Chamber IX) (Case No. ICC-02/04-01/15), 4 February 2021.

[59] Ibid., para. 2885.

[60] Ibid., para. 3037.

[61] ICC, *Prosecutor v. Bosco Ntaganda*, Judgment (Trial Chamber IV) (Case No. ICC-01/04-02/06), 8 July 2019.

[62] ICC, *Prosecutor v. Bosco Ntaganda*, Judgment (Appeals Chamber) (Case No. ICC-01/04-02/06-2666-Red), 30 March 2021.

by their families. She further clarified that this fear is particularly prevalent in relation to female rape victims who fear rejection by their husbands.[63]

7.6 SEXUAL AND GENDER-BASED VIOLENCE AS GENOCIDE

In certain circumstances, sexual violence may amount to genocide, the so-called crime of crimes.[64] When the underlying crime is rape or forced pregnancy, in order for it to amount to an act also of genocide, the intent to destroy, in whole or in part, a minority group must accompany the intent to commit the underlying crime.[65] With respect to the International Criminal Court, the Elements of Crimes determine that the genocidal act of 'causing serious bodily or mental harm' under Article 6(b) of the Rome Statute may include rape and sexual violence.[66] The Court has, however, yet to prosecute any individual for rape as an act of genocide.[67] In Africa, the Statute of the African Criminal Court explicitly lists 'acts of rape or any other form of sexual violence' as genocidal acts, but it is not yet in force.[68]

---

[63] ICC, *Prosecutor* v. *Bosco Ntaganda*, Judgment (Trial Chamber IV), para. 187 and note 192.

[64] See, for example, W. A. Schabas, *Genocide in International Law: The Crime of Crimes*, 2nd ed., Cambridge University Press, Cambridge, 2009.

[65] G. Mettraux, 'Crimes against Humanity in the Jurisprudence of the International Criminal Tribunals for the Former Yugoslavia and for Rwanda', *Harvard International Law Journal*, Vol. 43 (2002), 237–316, at pp. 295–6; see also J. M. Short, 'Sexual Violence as Genocide: The Developing Law of the International Criminal Tribunals and the International Criminal Court', *Michigan Journal of Race and Law*, Vol. 8 (2003), 503–27, at pp. 505–6.

[66] Elements of Crime for Article 6(b) (Genocide by causing serious bodily or mental harm), Element 1, note 3. The Elements of Crimes are available at: https://bit.ly/3otajzl.

[67] See, for example, T. Altunjan, 'The International Criminal Court and Sexual Violence: Between Aspirations and Reality', *German Law Journal*, Vol. 22 (2021), 878–93.

[68] Art. 28B(f), Protocol on Amendments to the Protocol on the Statute of the African Court of Justice and Human Rights; adopted at Malabo, 27 June 2014; not yet in force. As of 1 April 2022, fifteen States had signed the Protocol but none had also ratified it.

PART II

Specific Protection of Certain High-Risk Groups

8

Protection of Women in Armed Conflict

8.1 INTRODUCTION

While women face a myriad of threats to their physical well-being in any situation of armed conflict, there is a particularly heightened risk of sexual or gender-based violence, including rape.[1] According to the Committee on the Elimination of Discrimination against Women, gender-based violence, 'which impairs or nullifies the enjoyment by women of human rights and fundamental freedoms under general international law or under human rights conventions', is discrimination within the meaning of Article 1 of the Convention on the Elimination of All Forms of Discrimination against Women (CEDAW). These rights and freedoms include the right to life; the right not to be subjected to torture or other forms of ill-treatment; the right to equal protection according to humanitarian norms in time of armed conflict; and the right to liberty and security of person.[2]

Armed conflict, including military occupation, often leads to increased prostitution, trafficking in women, and sexual assault of women, demanding 'specific protective and punitive measures'.[3] Within the United Nations (UN) Secretariat, the position of Special Representative of the Secretary-General on Sexual Violence in Conflict was established by UN Security Council Resolution 1888 (2009) to serve as the UN spokesperson and political advocate on conflict-related sexual violence.[4] As the Office has observed, such violence is no longer seen as an inevitable by-product of war, but rather a crime that is preventable and punishable under international human rights law and international criminal law.[5]

---

[1]   The United Nations defines violence against women as 'any act of gender-based violence that results in, or is likely to result in, physical, sexual or psychological harm or suffering to women, including threats of such acts, coercion or arbitrary deprivation of liberty, whether occurring in public or in private life'. UN General Assembly Resolution 48/104: 'Declaration on the Elimination of Violence against Women', adopted without a vote on 20 December 1993, Art. 1.

[2]   Committee on the Elimination of Discrimination against Women, 'Violence against Women', General Recommendation No. 19, adopted at the Committee's 11th session (1992), para. 7.

[3]   Ibid., para. 16.

[4]   Since 2017, Ms Pramila Patten of Mauritius has been the Special Representative of the Secretary-General on Sexual Violence in Conflict.

[5]   UN, 'The Office of the Special Representative of the Secretary-General on Sexual Violence in Conflict (OSRSG-SVC)', at: http://bit.ly/32qliN7.

During situations of armed conflict, women are both generally and specifically protected by international humanitarian law (IHL) and international human rights law. Their protection under IHL during the conduct of hostilities (i.e. amid the fighting) is first and foremost where they are civilians, although special protection is also afforded to all women against sexual violence when they are detained by an enemy or are otherwise in its power. International human rights law offers parallel protection to women in all circumstances and, of course, when IHL is not applicable, this will be the primary source of protection under international law. This protection exists alongside refugee law in the situation when a woman has crossed an international border and is seeking asylum from persecution.

There is no formal definition of a woman under international law. The term is not, for instance, defined in CEDAW to which 189 of 197 States were party as of 1 April 2022.[6] A woman may ordinarily be defined as any adult female as understood in accordance with international law pertaining to the child.[7] That said, the Committee on the Elimination of Discrimination against Women has often referred also to girls in its work. For instance, in its General Recommendation No. 24 (1999) on women and health, the Committee encouraged States Parties to address the issue of women's health throughout the woman's lifespan. For the purpose of that General Recommendation, the Committee stated, '*women* includes girls and adolescents'.[8]

8.2 IHL RULES ON THE PROTECTION OF WOMEN

The IHL principles of distinction and proportionality in attack apply to women civilians, just as they do to any other civilians. Thus, women will be protected by these fundamental principles unless and for such time as they participate directly in hostilities.[9] This is true under customary international law whether the conflict is international or non-international in character.

As Chapter 7 described, in international armed conflict, women, as 'protected persons' must be especially protected against any attack on their honour, in particular against rape, enforced prostitution, or any form of indecent assault.[10] Under the 1949 Geneva Convention IV, when they are detained, women in occupied territories must be confined in separate quarters from men and under the direct supervision of women.[11] Whenever it is

---

[6] Convention on the Elimination of All Forms of Discrimination against Women; adopted at New York, 18 December 1979; entered into force, 3 September 1981. In addition to the States Parties, Palau and the United States are signatories to the Convention.

[7] According to Article 1 of the Convention on the Rights of the Child, a child means every human being below the age of eighteen years unless under the law applicable to the child, majority is attained earlier. Art. 1, Convention on the Rights of the Child; adopted at New York, 20 November 1989; entered into force, 2 September 1990. As of 1 April 2022, 196 States were party to the Convention and the 197th, the United States, was a signatory.

[8] Committee on the Elimination of Discrimination against Women, 'Article 12: Women and Health', General Recommendation No. 24, adopted at the Committee's 20th session (1999), para. 8 [original emphasis].

[9] For a discussion of this concept, see Chapter 2.

[10] Art. 27, Convention (IV) Relative to the Protection of Civilian Persons in Time of War; adopted at Geneva, 12 August 1949; entered into force, 21 October 1950 (hereinafter, 1949 Geneva Convention IV).

[11] Art. 76, 1949 Geneva Convention IV.

necessary, as 'an exceptional and temporary measure', to accommodate women internees who are not members of a family unit in the same internment facility as men, 'the provision of separate sleeping quarters and sanitary conveniences for the use of such women internees shall be obligatory'.[12] This is a corresponding rule of customary IHL applicable to all armed conflicts.[13] Parties to an international armed conflict are further obligated to 'endeavour during the course of hostilities, to conclude agreements for the release, the repatriation, the return to places of residence, or the accommodation in a neutral country of pregnant women and mothers with infants and young children'.[14]

Article 3 common to the four 1949 Geneva Conventions, which formally applies in non-international armed conflict, but whose tenets constitute a minimum level of protection in all conflicts,[15] requires that anyone in the power of the enemy be treated humanely in all circumstances. This treatment must be ensured without any adverse distinction founded on 'race, colour, religion or faith, sex, birth or wealth, or any other similar criteria'. Under the 1977 Additional Protocol II, parties to the non-international armed conflict must, 'within the limits of their capabilities', detain women in quarters separate from those of men and under the immediate supervision of women. This is so except when men and women of the same family are accommodated together.[16]

It is also a customary rule in all armed conflicts that the specific protection, health, and assistance needs of women affected by armed conflict must be respected.[17] The International Committee of the Red Cross (ICRC) offers the following interpretation of this rule:

> The specific needs of women may differ according to the situation in which they find themselves – at home, in detention or displaced as a result of the conflict – but they must be respected in all situations. Practice contains numerous references to the specific need of women to be protected against all forms of sexual violence . . . While the prohibition of sexual violence applies equally to men and women, in practice women are much more affected by sexual violence during armed conflicts.[18]

Box 8.1 highlights the impact of food insecurity on the risk of sexual and gender-based violence.

---

[12]   Art. 85, 1949 Geneva Convention IV.

[13]   International Committee of the Red Cross (ICRC) Customary IHL Rule 119: 'Accommodation for Women Deprived of Their Liberty', at: http://bit.ly/32wGtxc: 'Women who are deprived of their liberty must be held in quarters separate from those of men, except where families are accommodated as family units, and must be under the immediate supervision of women.'

[14]   Art. 132, 1949 Geneva Convention IV.

[15]   International Court of Justice (ICJ), *Case Concerning Military and Paramilitary Activities In and Against Nicaragua (Nicaragua v. United States)*, Judgment (Merits) 27 June 1986, para. 218: 'There is no doubt that, in the event of international armed conflicts, these rules also constitute a minimum yardstick, in addition to the more elaborate rules which are also to apply to international conflicts; and they are rules which, in the Court's opinion, reflect what the Court in 1949 called "elementary considerations of humanity".'

[16]   Art. 5(2)(1), Protocol Additional to the Geneva Conventions of 12 August 1949, and relating to the Protection of Victims of Non-International Armed Conflicts; adopted at Geneva, 8 June 1977; entered into force, 7 December 1978 (hereinafter, 1977 Additional Protocol II).

[17]   ICRC, Customary IHL Rule 134: 'Women', at: http://bit.ly/2Tj990S.

[18]   Ibid.

BOX 8.1

Food insecurity may exacerbate some forms of GBV [gender-based violence]. For example, women and girls who are traditionally tasked with finding fuel to prepare food, may need to venture to unsafe areas to collect firewood and be exposed to risk of assault. Within households, domestic violence can rise during periods of food scarcity, and may decline as assistance fills the food gap. Women heads of households may engage in transactional sex to be able to meet food needs, and parents may push for early marriage for their daughters in the hope they will have their food needs met elsewhere. Food or cash assistance in itself may also unintentionally contribute to GBV. A food distribution site that is located in an unsafe area, or is far from where people live, may expose women to sexual violence. Cash delivered to women without taking into consideration gender roles and responsibilities may unintentionally increase domestic violence in a society that is strictly opposed to women having control over economic resources.

World Food Programme, Activities to End Violence Against Women, at: http://bit.ly/39znhnG

In any armed conflict, sexual violence is a war crime. This covers rape, sexual slavery, enforced prostitution, forced pregnancy, enforced sterilisation, or any other serious form of sexual violence.[19] Sexual violence may also amount to a crime against humanity, and even potentially genocide.[20]

A specific example of respect for the specific needs of women cited by the ICRC is the requirement that pregnant women and mothers of young children, in particular nursing mothers, be treated with particular care. 'This requirement is found throughout the Fourth Geneva Convention', as well as in the 1977 Additional Protocol I.[21] These provisions require special care for pregnant women and mothers of young children with regard to the provision of food, clothing, medical assistance, evacuation, and transportation.[22]

8.3 WOMEN AND THE DEATH PENALTY

In accordance with the 1966 International Covenant on Civil and Political Rights, the death penalty must not be *executed* on pregnant women who have been convicted of a capital crime.[23] This stipulation reflects customary international law applicable to all

[19] Art. 8(2)(b)(xxii) and 2(e)(vi), Rome Statute of the International Criminal Court; adopted at Rome, 17 July 1998; entered into force, 1 July 2002.
[20] See further on the issue of sexual and gender-based violence the details set out in Chapter 7.
[21] Arts. 16–18, 21–3, 38, 50, 89, 91, and 127, 1949 Geneva Convention IV; and Arts 70(1) and 76(2), Protocol Additional to the Geneva Conventions of 12 August 1949, and relating to the Protection of Victims of International Armed Conflicts (hereinafter, 1977 Additional Protocol I).
[22] ICRC, Customary IHL Rule 134: 'Women'.
[23] Art. 6(5), International Covenant on Civil and Political Rights; adopted at New York, 16 December 1966; entered into force, 23 March 1976 (hereinafter, ICCPR).

States and is valid whether the crime in question was committed in a situation of armed conflict or in peacetime. There is, however, no customary law prohibition on the *imposition* of the death penalty on a pregnant woman, nor its execution on her once her child has been born, at least after a period of nursing the baby. The African Commission on Human and Peoples' Rights has stated that the execution of pregnant or nursing women will always amount to a violation of the right to life.[24] The 2004 Arab Charter on Human Rights also prohibits the execution of the death penalty 'on a nursing mother within two years from the date on which she gave birth'.[25]

There is also no general prohibition on the imposition and execution of the death penalty on women who are not pregnant or nursing an infant.[26] This is despite the fact that, as the UN Secretary-General has reported:

> The application of the death penalty often also violates the right to equality and the principle of non-discrimination. The decision about whether to sentence a convict to death or to lesser punishment is often arbitrary and does not necessarily follow predictable, rational criteria. In that judicial lottery, the odds are often stacked against the poor, minorities and other common targets of discrimination, including women.[27]

The customary human rights law rule prohibiting the execution of pregnant or nursing women is also reflected in IHL treaties. Under the 1949 Geneva Convention IV, civilians in the territory of an adverse party to an international armed conflict, including in occupied territory, 'shall at all times be humanely treated, and shall be protected especially against all acts of violence or threats thereof'.[28] The 1977 Additional Protocol I requires that parties to an international armed conflict 'endeavour, to the maximum extent feasible' to avoid imposing the death penalty on pregnant women or mothers having dependent infants for any offence related to the armed conflict. In any event, the death penalty may not be executed on such women.[29] This rule applies to all persons convicted for an offence related to the armed conflict, whether or not they enjoy protected status under the Geneva Conventions and Additional Protocol 1.

In any non-international armed conflict, the death penalty 'shall not be carried out on pregnant women or mothers of young children'.[30] Unusually, this provision is stricter than the corresponding treaty provision pertaining to women in a situation of international armed conflict. In addition, under Common Article 3, 'the passing of sentences and the carrying out of executions without previous judgment pronounced by a regularly

[24] African Commission on Human and Peoples' Rights, General Comment No. 3 on the African Charter on Human and Peoples' Rights: The Right to Life (Article 4), adopted at Banjul (57th Ordinary Session), November 2015 (hereinafter, African Commission General Comment on the Right to Life), para. 25.

[25] Art. 7(2), Arab Charter on Human Rights; adopted at Tunis, 23 May 2004; entered into force, 15 March 2008.

[26] A woman will be protected in the same way as would a man if she had committed a capital offence while under eighteen years of age.

[27] 'Capital punishment and the implementation of the safeguards guaranteeing protection of the rights of those facing the death penalty: Yearly supplement of the Secretary-General to his quinquennial report on capital punishment', 2015, para. 55.

[28] Art. 27, 1949 Geneva Convention IV.

[29] Art. 76(3), Additional Protocol I.

[30] Art. 6(4), 1977 Additional Protocol II.

constituted court, affording all the judicial guarantees which are recognized as indispens-able by civilized peoples' is a serious violation of IHL. The imposition of a death sentence at the issue of an unfair trial is a war crime within the jurisdiction of the ICC.[31]

8.4 THE PROTECTION OF WOMEN IN A UN PEACEKEEPING MISSION

Senior Women's Protection Advisers are now incorporated within many UN peacekeep-ing missions. Advisers are deployed at the request of the UN Security Council to missions to support the implementation of a specific Council mandate. The 2019 Department of Peace Operations (DPO) Policy on the Protection of Civilians stipulates that the Senior Women's Protection Adviser will have the following responsibilities:

- Advising senior mission leadership on the implementation of the conflict-related sexual violence (CRSV) mandate and on relevant CRSV issues and actions to be taken, including during mediation and national reconciliation efforts
- Ensuring the integration of information and analysis of specific CRSV threats faced by women, men, girls and boys into PoC analysis and decision-making
- Providing advice on PoC activities and courses of action to ensure that they take into account risks and threats of CRSV
- Monitoring and analysing CRSV concerns with a view to provide up-to-date CRSV risk analysis and early warning for use by the mission in protecting civilians
- Engaging in dialogue with parties to conflict on the signing and implementation of commitments to halt and prevent CRSV, supporting parties to conflict in the implementation of commitments to address CRSV, and regularly reviewing progress with parties to conflict and the UN system
- Advocating for timely, dignified, and quality assistance for CRSV survivors
- Providing training, guidance, and expertise on CRSV prevention and response through PoC mechanisms
- Supporting the PoC adviser on the development of strategies to protect civilians, particularly from CRSV.[32]

---

[31] Art. 8(2)(c)(iv), ICC Statute. In the corresponding elements of crimes, the Court is asked to consider whether, 'in the light of all relevant circumstances, the cumulative effect of factors with respect to guarantees deprived the person or persons of a fair trial'. Elements of Crimes, *Official Records of the Assembly of States Parties to the Rome Statute of the International Criminal Court, First session, New York, 3–10 September 2002*, p. 34.

[32] DPO, *The Protection of Civilians in United Nations Peacekeeping*, Policy, New York, 1 November 2019, Annex, para. 27.

9

Protection of Children in Armed Conflict

9.1 INTRODUCTION

During situations of armed conflict, children are protected both generally (as persons) and specifically (as children) by international humanitarian law (IHL) and by international human rights law. Their protection under IHL during the conduct of hostilities (i.e. combat) is first and foremost in their capacity as civilians, although special protection is also afforded to children against recruitment, as well as when they are detained by an enemy or are otherwise in its power. International human rights law offers parallel protection to children and, of course, when IHL is not applicable, this will be the primary source of protection under international law. This protection exists alongside refugee law, in the situation when the child has crossed an international border and is seeking asylum from persecution.

9.1.1 *The Definition of a Child*

The Convention on the Rights of the Child[1] (CRC) is the most widely ratified human rights treaty in history. As of 1 April 2022, 196 States were party to the CRC, with only the United States – a treaty signatory – not yet a State Party. The Convention's definition of a child, which may be taken to reflect customary law, encompasses every human being below the age of eighteen, unless, under applicable domestic law, the age of majority is attained earlier.[2] Most States set the age of majority at eighteen, though some set it earlier, while in a very small minority of States children legally become adults at an age greater than eighteen years.

Worldwide, the lowest age of majority is set in Iran, where, in the words of the Committee on the Rights of the Child established to oversee implementation of the CRC, it 'remains set at predefined ages of puberty, namely 9 lunar years for girls and 15

---

[1] Convention on the Rights of the Child; adopted at New York, 20 November 1989; entered into force, 2 September 1990 (hereinafter, CRC).

[2] The age of majority is the age at which a child becomes an adult in the eyes of the law. In most cases, this coincides with the age at which a person is allowed to vote in national elections. The ages at which a child is allowed by law to, for instance, marry, enter into contracts, join the armed forces, or drink alcohol (where this is permissible for any person) may differ.

lunar years for boys'. This results, the Committee observes, in girls and boys above those ages 'being deprived of the protections under the Convention'.[3] Other national exceptions to an age of majority at eighteen years include Yemen, where it continues to be fifteen for both boys and girls. This is despite discussions in parliament in recent years about the possibility of raising the age to eighteen.[4] In Saudi Arabia, although legislation ostensibly defines a child as anyone under eighteen,[5] a judge has the power to set a different (lower) age.[6] Within Europe, only Scotland (a country within the United Kingdom and therefore not an independent State) sets the age of legal capacity below eighteen: at sixteen years of age.[7] Previously, Nepal's statutory age of majority was sixteen,[8] but in 2018 this was raised by law to eighteen years.[9]

9.2 THE APPLICATION OF THE CONVENTION ON THE RIGHTS OF THE CHILD IN ARMED CONFLICT

There is no provision for derogation from any of the rights set out in the CRC, including during armed conflict. That said, under Article 38(1) of the Convention, States Parties 'undertake to respect and to ensure respect for rules of international humanitarian law applicable to them in armed conflicts which are relevant to the child'. This provision has the indirect effect of introducing IHL as a means of interpreting certain rights of the child, such as to life[10] and to liberty.[11] In contrast, the prohibition under international human rights law of torture and other forms of ill-treatment[12] applies in situations of armed conflict just as it does in peacetime, without any exception or caveat. Moreover, a child detainee must be separated from adults unless it is considered in the child's best interest not to do so and he or she has the right to maintain contact with his or her family through correspondence and visits, 'save in exceptional circumstances'.[13]

Under Article 39 of the CRC, States Parties are obligated to take all appropriate measures to promote physical and psychological recovery and social reintegration of

---

[3]   Committee on the Rights of the Child, Concluding Observations on the combined third and fourth periodic reports of Iran, UN doc. CRC/C/IRN/CO/3–4, 14 March 2016, para. 27.
[4]   Committee on the Rights of the Child, Concluding Observations on the fourth periodic report of Yemen, UN doc. CRC/C/YEM/CO/4, 25 February 2014, paras. 9, 27.
[5]   See, for example, the Child Protection Act. Third and fourth periodic reports of Saudi Arabia under the CRC, UN doc. CRC/C/SAU/3–4, 8 April 2015, para. 70.
[6]   Committee on the Rights of the Child, Concluding Observations on the combined third and fourth periodic reports of Saudi Arabia, UN doc. CRC/C/SAU/CO/3–4, 25 October 2016, para. 13.
[7]   S. 1, 1991 Age of Legal Capacity (Scotland) Act.
[8]   S. 2(a) of the 1992 Children's Act states that every human being below the age of sixteen is a child. Third to fifth periodic reports of Nepal under the CRC, UN doc. CRC/C/NPL/3–5, 23 December 2013, para. 49.
[9]   S. 2(j), Act Relating to Children 2018, Act No. 23 of 2075 B.S.
[10] Art. 6, CRC.
[11] Art. 37(b), CRC.
[12] Art. 37(a), CRC. See also Art. 7, International Covenant on Civil and Political Rights; adopted at New York, 16 December 1966; entered into force, 23 March 1976 (hereinafter, ICCPR); and Art. 2, Convention against Torture and Other Cruel, Inhuman or Degrading Treatment or Punishment; adopted at New York, 10 December 1984; entered into force, 26 June 1987 (hereinafter, 1984 Convention against Torture).
[13] Art. 37(c), CRC.

a child victim of armed conflicts. This recovery and reintegration must take place 'in an environment which fosters the health, self-respect and dignity of the child'. There are corresponding obligations under a number of widely ratified disarmament treaties to assist child survivors of certain conventional weapons, most notably anti-personnel mines, cluster munition remnants, and other explosive remnants of war.[14] In addition, according to Article 38(4) of the CRC, in accordance with their obligations under IHL to protect the civilian population in armed conflicts, States Parties are obligated to take 'all feasible measures to ensure protection and care of children who are affected by an armed conflict'. This is a rule of customary international law.[15]

The impact of disability on children can be devastating. Children with disabilities have been found in certain research to be up to four times more likely to be subjected to violence than are other children.[16] In many countries, children with disabilities are frequently placed in institutions, where they are at heightened risk of abuse, exploitation, and neglect. Such facilities often have low standards of care and lack independent monitoring, with the result that perpetrators of violence and abuse are rarely held to account.[17] Placement in residential facilities also increases the risk of trafficking of children with disabilities. Studies have found that girls with disabilities are at particular risk of being trafficked because their impairments are presumed to limit their chances of escape.[18]

Children with disabilities who become separated from caregivers are especially endangered. Family members may have been the only persons to know how to care for a child's specific physical requirements or how to communicate with a child.[19] Children with disabilities may be unable to communicate information that is essential for family tracing and reunification. Unaccompanied children with disabilities may be excluded from traditional systems of care if local families do not accept them.

9.3 IHL RULES ON THE PROTECTION OF CHILDREN

The principles of distinction and proportionality in attack apply to protect child civilians, just as they do to any other civilians. As is the case with adults, children will be protected by these fundamental IHL principles unless and for such time as they participate directly in hostilities.[20] This is true under customary law whether the conflict is international or non-international in character.

---

[14]   See Chapter 5 for details of disarmament treaty obligations.

[15]   ICRC, Customary IHL Rule 135: 'Children affected by armed conflict are entitled to special respect and protection', at: http://bit.ly/2STHvQl.

[16]   K. Hughes et al., 'Prevalence and Risk of Violence against Adults with Disabilities: A Systematic Review and Meta-Analysis of Observational Studies', *The Lancet*, Vol. 379, No. 9826 (2012), 1621–9.

[17]   African Child Policy Forum, *The African Report on Violence against Children*, Addis Ababa, 2014, available at: https://bit.ly/3xsjHYB.

[18]   Leonard Cheshire Disability, *Still Left Behind: Pathways to Inclusive Education for Girls with Disabilities*, Report, 2017, at: https://bit.ly/3rm2Nag.

[19]   UNICEF, *State of the World's Children: Children with Disabilities*, New York, 2013.

[20]   For a discussion of this concept, see Chapter 3.

Article 3 common to the four 1949 Geneva Conventions, which formally applies in non-international armed conflict, but whose provisions constitute a minimum level of protection in all conflicts,[21] obligates humane treatment of persons in the power of the enemy (including children) in all circumstances. This treatment must be ensured without any adverse distinction founded on 'race, colour, religion or faith, sex, birth or wealth, or any other similar criteria'.

Under the 1977 Additional Protocol II, children must be provided with the care and aid they require, and in particular must receive an education, including religious and moral education, in keeping with the wishes of their parents or, in the absence of parents, of those responsible for their care.[22] In addition, all appropriate steps must be taken to facilitate the reunion of families temporarily separated.[23] Measures must further be taken, 'if necessary, and whenever possible with the consent' of their parents or guardians, 'to remove children temporarily from the area in which hostilities are taking place to a safer area within the country and ensure that they are accompanied by persons responsible for their safety and well-being'.[24]

9.4 ENLISTMENT IN ARMED FORCES OR GROUPS

During situations of armed conflict or other armed violence, including terrorist violence, children are vulnerable to recruitment. Under IHL, any recruitment (whether voluntary or coerced) or use in armed conflict of children under fifteen years of age, whether by armed forces or armed groups, is prohibited.[25] Under customary and conventional international criminal law, such recruitment or use of children is a war crime.[26]

The minimum age is higher under international human rights law, but the exact rule depends on whether the recruitment is by the State or by an opposition armed group. The legal situation with respect to non-State armed groups is straightforward: no children under eighteen years of age may be recruited by virtue of the 2000 Optional Protocol to the CRC on the involvement of children in armed conflict. According to Article 4(1) of the Protocol: 'Armed groups that are distinct from the armed forces of a State should not, under any circumstances, recruit or use in hostilities persons under

---

[21] International Court of Justice (ICJ), *Case Concerning Military and Paramilitary Activities In and Against Nicaragua (Nicaragua v. United States)*, Judgment (Merits) 27 June 1986, para. 218: 'There is no doubt that, in the event of international armed conflicts, these rules also constitute a minimum yardstick, in addition to the more elaborate rules which are also to apply to international conflicts; and they are rules which, in the Court's opinion, reflect what the Court in 1949 called "elementary considerations of humanity".'

[22] Art. 4(3)(a), Protocol Additional to the Geneva Conventions of 12 August 1949, and relating to the Protection of Victims of Non-International Armed Conflicts; adopted at Geneva, 8 June 1977; entered into force, 7 December 1978 (hereinafter, 1977 Additional Protocol II).

[23] Art. 4(3)(b), 1977 Additional Protocol II.

[24] Art. 4(3)(e), 1977 Additional Protocol II.

[25] Art. 77(2), Protocol Additional to the Geneva Conventions of 12 August 1949, and relating to the Protection of Victims of International Armed Conflicts; adopted at Geneva, 8 June 1977; entered into force, 7 December 1978 (hereinafter, 1977 Additional Protocol I); Art. 4(3)(c), 1977 Additional Protocol II.

[26] Article 8(2)(b)(xxvi) and Article 8(2)(e)(vii) of the ICC Statute provide that 'conscripting or enlisting children under the age of fifteen years' into armed forces or armed groups constitutes a war crime in international and non-international armed conflict, respectively.

the age of 18 years.'[27] Not so unequivocal as to the minimum age are the corresponding provisions governing voluntary recruitment into State armed forces. By virtue of Article 3(1), States Parties are obligated only to raise the minimum age to one that is greater than fifteen years, albeit 'recognizing that under the Convention persons under 18 are entitled to special protection'.

In its Resolution 2427 (2018), the UN Security Council strongly condemned 'all violations of applicable international law involving the recruitment and use of children by parties to armed conflict'.[28] The slightly awkward formulation of the censure reflected the fact that four of the five permanent members of the Council – China, France, the United Kingdom, and the United States – continue to recruit minors into their armed forces.[29] The Council stressed the need to pay 'particular attention to the treatment of children associated or allegedly associated with all non-State armed groups, including those who commit acts of terrorism, in particular by establishing standard operating procedures for the rapid handover of these children to relevant civilian child protection actors'.[30] It further emphasised that children 'who have been recruited in violation of applicable international law by armed forces and armed groups and are accused of having committed crimes during armed conflicts should be treated primarily as victims of violations of international law'.[31]

In his report on children and armed conflict for 2018, the UN Secretary-General stated that in Afghanistan the United Nations had 'verified the recruitment and use of 45 boys and 1 girl, with some of the children recruited as young as 8, who were used for combat, at checkpoints, to plant improvised explosive devices, to carry out suicide attacks or other violations, or for sexual exploitation. At least 22 boys were killed during their association.'[32] Most of the instances of recruitment and use of children as soldiers were in non-State armed groups, although the Afghan army continued to use a number of children to participate directly in hostilities.[33]

In Syria, the United Nations verified the recruitment and use of 806 children (670 boys, 136 girls), more than one fifth of whom were under 15 years of age. Of these child recruits,

---

[27] Optional Protocol to the Convention on the Rights of the Child on the involvement of children in armed conflict; adopted at New York, 25 May 2000; entered into force, 12 February 2002. As of 1 April 2022, 172 States were party to the Protocol.

[28] UN Security Council Resolution 2427, adopted by unanimous vote in favour on 9 July 2018, operative para. 1.

[29] For China, France, and the United States, the minimum age for voluntary recruitment is seventeen years. Other States that continue to accept the recruitment of children aged seventeen years into their armed forces include Algeria, Australia, Austria, Azerbaijan, Cabo Verde, Cuba, Cyprus, the Democratic People's Republic of Korea, Germany, Guinea-Bissau, Ireland, Israel, Italy, Luxembourg, Malaysia, New Zealand, the Philippines, São Tomé and Príncipe, Saudi Arabia, Turkmenistan, and the United Arab Emirates. The United Kingdom continues to recruit children at the age of sixteen years. Other States that continue to recruit children aged sixteen years into their armed forces include Brazil, Canada, Chile, the Dominican Republic, Egypt, El Salvador, India, Jordan, Pakistan, and Singapore. The situation with respect to Oman remains unclear. See: http://bit.ly/2SLXZKV. Iran, a signatory to the Optional Protocol, appears to allow voluntary enlistment into the Basij at fifteen years of age.

[30] UN Security Council Resolution 2427, operative para. 19.

[31] Ibid., operative para. 20.

[32] 'Children and Armed Conflict: Report of the Secretary-General', UN doc. A/73/907–S/2019/509, 20 June 2019, para. 18.

[33] Ibid., para. 28.

94 per cent were used in combat roles. The majority of the children (313) were recruited and used by Kurdish People's Protection Units (YPG/YPJ) operating under the umbrella of the Syrian Democratic Forces.[34] In most cases, the recruitment of children occurred without accountability, but in the Central African Republic, the UN Secretary-General reported that two anti-balaka leaders had been arrested and transferred to the International Criminal Court (ICC) for crimes including the recruitment and use of children under fifteen years of age.[35]

More generally, as the Committee on the Rights of the Child has observed in its General Comment No. 24:

> When under the control of such groups, children may become victims of multiple forms of violations, such as conscription; military training; being used in hostilities and/or terrorist acts, including suicide attacks; being forced to carry out executions; being used as human shields; abduction; sale; trafficking; sexual exploitation; child marriage; being used for the transport or sale of drugs; or being exploited to carry out dangerous tasks, such as spying, conducting surveillance, guarding checkpoints, conducting patrols or transporting military equipment. It has been reported that non-State armed groups and those designated as terrorist groups also force children to commit acts of violence against their own families or within their own communities to demonstrate loyalty and to discourage future defection.[36]

The Paris Principles, concluded in early 2007,[37] represent an important soft-law instrument governing association of children with armed forces and armed groups. The Principles stipulate that a child rights approach should underpin all interventions aimed at preventing recruitment or use, securing the release of, protecting, and reintegrating children who have been associated with an armed force or armed group. Measures to secure the reintegration of children into civilian life should not stigmatise or make any negative distinction between children who have been recruited or used and those who have not.[38] Measures must be taken to ensure the full involvement and inclusion of girls in all aspects of prevention of recruitment, release, and reintegration, and services should always respond to their specific needs for protection and assistance.[39]

Children who are accused of crimes under international law allegedly committed while they were associated with armed forces or armed groups should be considered primarily as victims of offences against international law; not only as perpetrators. They must be treated in accordance with international law in a framework of restorative justice and social

---

[34] Ibid., para. 174.
[35] Ibid., para. 40. On 20 February 2019, ICC Pre-Trial Chamber II decided to join the cases of *The Prosecutor v. Alfred Yekatom* and *The Prosecutor v. Patrice-Edouard Ngaïssona*. ICC, 'ICC Pre-Trial Chamber II joins Yekatom and Ngaïssona cases', Press Release No. ICC-CPI-20190220-PR143, 20 February 2019, at: http://bit.ly/2sKHmED.
[36] Committee on the Rights of the Child, General Comment No. 24 (2019) on children's rights in the child justice system, UN doc. CRC/C/GC/24, 18 September 2019 (hereinafter, Committee on the Rights of the Child, General Comment 24 on children's rights in the child justice system), para. 98.
[37] Principles and Guidelines on Children Associated with Armed Forces or Armed Groups (Paris Principles), Paris, February 2007.
[38] Ibid., para. 3.3.
[39] Ibid., para. 3.2.

rehabilitation, consistent with international law which offers children special protection through numerous agreements and principles.[40] This provision is often misquoted and misunderstood. It does not grant children a free pass for serious criminal offences committed, particularly when they amount to international crimes, but is, correctly, more nuanced: they should be considered '*primarily* as victims of offences against international law; *not only* as perpetrators'.

The 2007 Principles are now in need of revision and updating, in particular to deal with protection issues surrounding former members of non-State armed groups and terrorism offences. In this regard, in the UN Global Study on Children Deprived of Liberty, published in 2019, the independent expert Manfred Nowak recommended that States explicitly exclude children from national counterterrorism and security legislation 'and ensure that children suspected of national security offences are treated exclusively within child justice systems'.[41] He called on States to ensure that counterterrorism legislation with penal sanctions is never used against children peacefully exercising their rights to freedom of expression, religion, or assembly and urged an end to 'all administrative or preventive detention of children and extended pretrial detention for counterterrorism purposes'.[42]

Manfred Nowak further recommended that States should never use the gravity of an offence, even when linked to national security, as a justification for lowering the minimum age of criminal responsibility. States should, he stated, 'develop and apply a tailored and individual case management approach to children associated with non-State armed groups designated as terrorist'.[43]

In its Resolution 2427 of 2018, the UN Security Council stressed the need to establish standard operating procedures for the rapid handover of children associated or allegedly associated with all non-State armed groups, including those who committed acts of terrorism, to relevant civilian child protection actors. The Council emphasised that children who had been recruited in violation of international law by armed forces and armed groups and were accused of having committed crimes during armed conflicts should be treated primarily as victims of violations of international law.[44]

In her report to the Human Rights Council in December 2020, the Special Representative of the Secretary-General called 'anew' upon Member States to

> treat children allegedly associated with armed groups, including groups designated as terrorist by the Security Council, primarily as victims, prioritize their rehabilitation and reintegration, and address the especially detrimental impact of stigma on their reintegration.[45]

[40]   Ibid., para. 3.6.
[41]   'Global Study on Children Deprived of Liberty. Note by the Secretary-General', UN doc. A/74/136, 11 July 2019, para. 138.
[42]   Ibid., paras. 139, 140.
[43]   Ibid., paras. 141, 142.
[44]   See Committee on the Rights of the Child, General Comment 24 on children's rights in the child justice system, para. 100.
[45]   Children and Armed Conflict, Report of the Special Representative of the Secretary-General for Children and Armed Conflict, UN doc. A/HRC/46/39, 23 December 2020, para. 92.

She further reminded UN Member States that,

> if a child is accused of a crime during his or her association or alleged association, internationally recognized juvenile justice principles must be adhered to, including in relation to the minimum age of criminal responsibility and to ensuring that detention is used only as a measure of last resort and for the shortest possible period of time, as well as due process and international fair trial standards.[46]

The Special Representative called upon the Human Rights Council, treaty bodies, and relevant special procedure mandate holders 'to focus closely on the impact of violent extremism on children, including the issue of children with links to United Nations-listed terrorist groups'.[47]

9.5 THE SIX GRAVE VIOLATIONS

The United Nations has identified six grave violations committed against children during armed conflicts.[48] One is the prohibition on recruiting and using children as soldiers, as discussed above. The other five are as follows:

- Killing and maiming children
- Sexual violence against children
- Abduction of children
- Attacks against schools or hospitals
- Denial of humanitarian access for children.

In 2005, to document and report on these grave violations, the United Nations established the Monitoring and Reporting Mechanism (MRM)[49] pursuant to Security Council Resolution 1612.[50] On the basis of this information, the UN Secretary-General names parties to conflict who commit such acts in an annual report on children and armed conflict, with the goal of ending these violations. In addition to the Secretary-General's annual report to the UN Security Council, the Council's Working Group on Children and Armed Conflict reviews the country reports stemming from the MRM and makes recommendations on how to better protect children in specific country situations.

In his report to the Council covering 2018, the UN Secretary-General stated that more than 24,000 individual grave violations against children had been verified by the United Nations in twenty country situations.[51] Verified cases of the killing and maiming of children

---

[46] Ibid.

[47] Ibid.

[48] UN Security Council Resolution 1261, adopted by unanimous vote on 25 August 1999, para. 2; Report of the UN Secretary-General, UN doc. S/2004/72.

[49] United Nations Children's Fund (UNICEF), the UN Department of Peacekeeping Operations (DPKO), and the Office of the Special Representative of the Secretary-General for Children and Armed Conflict (OSRSG-CAAC) have launched a website dedicated to the MRM: www.mrmtools.org. See UNICEF, OSRSG-CAAC, and DPKO, *Monitoring and Reporting Mechanism (MRM) on Grave Violations against Children in Situations of Armed Conflict*, Field Manual, New York, June 2014.

[50] UN Security Council Resolution 1612, adopted unanimously on 26 July 2005, para. 3.

[51] Children and Armed Conflict: Report of the Secretary-General, UN doc. A/73/907–S/2019/509, 20 June 2019, para. 5. The twenty States concerned were Afghanistan, the Central African Republic, Colombia, the

reached record levels globally since the creation of the MRM, the Secretary-General reported. In Afghanistan, the number of child casualties 'remained the highest' (3,062) with children accounting for more than one in four of all civilian casualties. In Syria, air strikes, barrel bombs, and cluster munitions resulted in 1,854 child casualties, and in Yemen, 1,689 children were killed or injured by ground fighting and other military action.[52]

In more positive news, some 13,600 children benefited from release and reintegration worldwide in 2018.[53] In a subsequent briefing to the Security Council in February 2020, the Secretary-General announced that twelve parties to conflict had been removed from the list of those responsible for violations after complying with their commitments under an extant action plan. He further observed that sustained advocacy had led to changes in the law and better cooperation with government departments and the military. In Afghanistan, for example, child protection units have been established in every province, and the recruitment and use of children has been made a criminal offence.[54]

The credibility of the UN Secretary-General's reporting, though, came under intense scrutiny in 2017, after it emerged that Saudi Arabia had put pressure on the United Nations to keep its name off the list of those engaged in grave violations against children (in the context of the armed conflicts in Yemen).[55] Saudi Arabia threatened to pull funding to the UN, so, 'as a compromise', the Secretary-General's report now has two levels of actor, with one level outlining those committing grave violations and a second containing those actors that have put a plan in place to stop them from happening again.[56]

9.6 CHILDREN AND THE DEATH PENALTY

Under both the 1966 International Covenant on Civil and Political Rights and the CRC, the death penalty must not be imposed for crimes committed by those under eighteen years of age at the time of commission of the offence.[57] This stipulation reflects customary international law applicable to all States and is valid whether the crime in question is committed in a situation of armed conflict or in peacetime.

The 2004 Arab Charter of Human Rights is the only regional human rights treaty to infringe customary law with regard to the possibility of executing child offenders. Thus, Article 7(1) of the 2004 Charter provides that the death penalty 'shall not be inflicted on a person under 18 years of age, *unless otherwise provided by the law in force at the time of the*

Democratic Republic of the Congo, India, Israel, Lebanon, Libya, Mali, Myanmar, Nigeria, Pakistan, Palestine, the Philippines, Somalia, South Sudan, Sudan, Syria, Thailand, and Yemen.

52   Children and Armed Conflict: Report of the Secretary-General, 20 June 2019, para. 6.

53   Ibid., para. 7.

54   'UN Secretary-General Remarks to the Security Council Briefing on Children in Armed Conflict', 12 February 2020, at: http://bit.ly/2SSTRbu.

55   See, for example, 'UN again Blacklists Saudi-Led Forces for Yemen Child Killings: Coalition Blacklisted for Third Year Over Killing and Wounding of 729 Children but Critics Say Measure is Not Enough', *Aljazeera*, 28 July 2019, at: http://bit.ly/2worM9r.

56   See, for example, R. Blume, 'The "Children and Armed Conflict" Report on Grave Violations is Vital in Protecting Children, and Here's Why', *War Child*, 26 June 2018, at: http://bit.ly/32mLWX6.

57   Art. 6(5), ICCPR; Art. 37(a), CRC.

commission of the crime'. This provision allows a State to derogate in its national law from the customary prohibition on executing children and potentially also allows the execution of a death sentence once a convicted child has attained the age of eighteen. In January 2021, Saudi Arabia announced that it would no longer execute child offenders.[58]

The customary human rights law rule is also reflected, to a certain extent, in IHL treaties. Under the 1949 Geneva Convention IV, 'the death penalty may not be pronounced against a protected person who was under eighteen years of age at the time of the offence'.[59] This covers, in particular, children living in occupied territories. In contrast, the 1977 Additional Protocol I, which also applies only in international armed conflict, provides more narrowly that 'the death penalty for an offence related to the armed conflict shall not be *executed* on persons who had not attained the age of eighteen years at the time the offence was committed'.[60] This rule applies to all persons convicted for an offence related to the armed conflict, whether or not they enjoyed protected status under the Geneva Conventions and Additional Protocol 1. It is thus somewhat narrower than the rule that exists in customary law, but it does not act to derogate from it.

In any non-international armed conflict, Article 6(4) of the 1977 Additional Protocol II stipulates that the death penalty 'shall not be pronounced on persons who were under the age of eighteen years at the time of the offence'. In addition, under Common Article 3, 'the passing of sentences and the carrying out of executions without previous judgment pronounced by a regularly constituted court, affording all the judicial guarantees which are recognized as indispensable by civilized peoples' is a serious violation of IHL. The imposition of a death sentence at the issue of an unfair trial is a war crime within the jurisdiction of the ICC.[61]

9.7 CHILD PROTECTION IN A UN PEACEKEEPING MISSION

The UN policy on child protection in a UN peace operation states that one of the most effective ways of protecting children affected by armed conflict is for the Special Representative of the Secretary-General or Head of Mission (as the case may be) to ensure that principles and obligations on child protection are mainstreamed and integrated across all operational decisions, activities, and processes of the operation. 'This means including considerations in relation to child protection in core mission planning and mandate

---

[58] R. Jalabi, 'Saudis Vowed to Stop Executing Minors; Some Death Sentences Remain, Rights Groups Say', Reuters, 18 January 2021, at: http://reut.rs/3c9Tz12; see also Amnesty International, 'Saudi Arabia: Death Penalty Reform for Minors Falls Short, and Total Abolition Must Now Follow', 27 April 2020, at: http://bit.ly/3pg4Utl.

[59] Art. 68(4), 1949 Geneva Convention IV.

[60] Art. 77(5), Protocol Additional to the Geneva Conventions of 12 August 1949, and relating to the Protection of Victims of International Armed Conflicts; adopted at Geneva, 8 June 1977; entered into force, 7 December 1978.

[61] Art. 8(2)(c)(iv), Rome Statute of the International Criminal Court. In the corresponding elements of crimes, the Court is asked to consider whether, 'in the light of all relevant circumstances, the cumulative effect of factors with respect to guarantees deprived the person or persons of a fair trial'. Elements of Crimes, *Official Records of the Assembly of States Parties to the Rome Statute of the International Criminal Court, First session, New York, 3–10 September 2002*, New York, p. 34.

implementation documents and in the overarching documents guiding the work of the military, police and civilian components.'[62]

To assist in this process of mainstreaming and integration, many peacekeeping missions have a Senior Child Protection Adviser, whose function is to implement the child protection mandate of UN peace operations. The 2019 Department of Peace Operations (DPO) Policy on the Protection of Civilians stipulates that the Adviser will have the following responsibilities:

- Advising senior mission leadership on child protection issues and relevant actions to be taken
- Monitoring and sharing information on protection threats faced by children and grave violations committed against children in situations of armed conflict
- Engaging in dialogue with parties to the conflict on the signing and implementation of Security Council-mandated action plans to halt and prevent grave child rights violations
- Supporting the release and reintegration of children associated with armed forces and armed groups, as part of action plan dialogue; peace negotiations and peace agreements; Disarmament Demobilisation and Reintegration (DDR) programmes; or other relevant processes
- Advocating for protective, preventive, and remedial measures in relation to other violations of children's rights identified as key child protection concerns by the mission (i.e. security detention of children and use of schools for military purposes)
- Providing training, guidance, and expertise on child protection issues, tools, and methodologies to other components and sections of UN peace operations
- Advocating with host State governments, diplomatic and donor communities, regional and international organizations, including through the release of public advocacy reports on children affected by armed conflict.[63]

---

[62] DPKO, DFS and DPA *Policy on Child Protection in United Nations Peace Operations*, UN doc. 2017.11 (as updated in 2020), para. 12.

[63] DPO, *The Protection of Civilians in United Nations Peacekeeping*, Policy, New York, 1 November 2019, Annex, para. 26.

10

Protection of Persons with Disabilities in Armed Conflict

10.1 INTRODUCTION

This chapter addresses the protection of persons with disabilities in situations of armed conflict. There is no all-encompassing definition of a person with a disability under international law. According to the first article of the 2006 Convention on the Rights of Persons with Disabilities (CRPD), persons with disabilities 'include those who have long-term physical, mental, intellectual or sensory impairments which *in interaction with various barriers* may hinder their full and effective participation in society on an equal basis with others'.[1]

The phrase 'interaction with various barriers' marks a major departure from previous approaches to disability in that, according to the CRPD, disability derives not primarily from an individual's impairment and/or medical condition, but essentially as a consequence of environmental, social, cultural, and attitudinal barriers. Potentially the reference to impairments being of a 'long-term' nature significantly limits the personal scope of the term, although it is explicit in Article 1 of the CRPD that the definition is not exhaustive.[2] As of 1 April 2022, 185 States were party to the CRPD, making it one of the most widely ratified human rights treaties after the almost universal adherence to the Convention on the Rights of the Child[3] and the Convention on the Elimination of All Forms of Discrimination against Women (which had 189 States Parties, as of writing).

---

[1] Art. 1, Convention on the Rights of Persons with Disabilities; adopted at New York, 13 December 2006; entered into force, 3 May 2008 [added emphasis].

[2] Indeed, in the Preamble to the CRPD, it is stated that disability is an 'evolving concept and that disability results from the interaction between persons with impairments and attitudinal and environmental barriers that hinders their full and effective participation in society on an equal basis with others'. Moreover, in the 2018 Protocol to the African Charter on Human and Peoples' Rights on the Rights of Persons with Disabilities in Africa, the word 'long-term' is omitted. The Protocol was adopted at Addis Ababa on 29 January 2018 and will enter into force thirty days after the fifteenth ratification. As of 1 April 2022, eleven States had signed the Protocol and three had also ratified or acceded to it.

[3] Of 197 States recognised by the UN Secretary-General, only the United States is not a party to the Convention on the Rights of the Child.

10.1.1 *The Threats to Persons with Disabilities in Armed Conflict*

Persons with disabilities have been described as 'the largest minority group in the world'[4] while at the same time being largely sidelined in international discourse on violence.[5] In the words of the United Nations (UN) Committee on the Rights of Persons with Disabilities, they are all too often the 'forgotten victims of armed conflict'.[6] For instance, UN Security Council resolutions addressing situations of armed conflict have barely alluded to persons with disabilities over the years. Perhaps, though, that disregard is beginning to change.

It is certain that, as the UN Secretary-General reported in 2019, armed conflict has a disproportionate impact on persons with disabilities.[7] According to a survey in 2018 of Syrian refugees in Jordan cited by the Secretary-General in his report to the UN Security Council, almost one in four respondents had a disability, while three households in five reported at least one member with a disability.[8] 'Conflict', the UN Secretary-General recalled, 'heightens the risks for persons with disabilities because of destruction and other changes to the physical environment, stress and disruption of essential services. People with disabilities may be unable to flee attacks and are left abandoned and unprotected. Women and girls with disabilities are particularly at risk of violence, exploitation and abuse.'[9]

Disability-based violence, that is, violence and abuse targeted specifically at a person because of his or her disability, is all too common.[10] Targeted violence may include physical attacks, killings, denial of food and medicine, harassment, emotional abuse, profound neglect, shackling, and confinement. Following the entry into force of the CRPD, the UN Special Rapporteur on torture and other cruel, inhuman or degrading treatment or punishment called on the UN General Assembly, for the first time, to 'reframe violence and abuse perpetrated against persons with disabilities as torture or a form of ill-treatment'.[11]

---

[4] In 2011, the World Health Organization (WHO) and the World Bank estimated that persons with disabilities represented 15 per cent of the world's population. WHO and World Bank, *World Report on Disability*, Report, Geneva, 2011.

[5] WHO, *Violence against Adults and Children with Disabilities*, at: http://bit.ly/2Rck9o8.

[6] UN Enable Fact Sheet, cited in A. Priddy, *Disability and Armed Conflict*, Academy Briefing No. 14, Geneva Academy of International Humanitarian Law and Human Rights, Geneva, April 2019, p. 13. The UN Department of Peace Operations' 2019 Policy on the protection of civilians in UN Peacekeeping has a single reference to the need to plan for the needs of persons with disabilities. UN Department of Peace Operations, *The Protection of Civilians in United Nations Peacekeeping*, Policy, UN doc. Ref. 2019.17, New York, November 2019, para. 37.

[7] Protection of Civilians in Armed Conflict: Report of the Secretary-General, UN doc. S/2019/373, 7 May 2019, para. 49.

[8] Humanity and Inclusion, *Removing Barriers: The Path towards Inclusive Access*, Report, Jordan, July 2018.

[9] Protection of Civilians in Armed Conflict: Report of the Secretary-General, UN doc. S/2019/373, para. 49.

[10] See WHO, 'Prevalence and risk of violence against adults with disabilities: a systematic review and meta-analysis of observational studies', Report, Geneva, 2012; and WHO and World Bank, *World Report on Disability*, 2011.

[11] Interim Report of the Special Rapporteur on torture and other cruel, inhuman or degrading treatment or punishment, Manfred Nowak, UN doc. A/63/175, 28 July 2008, para. 45.

This, according to then Special Rapporteur Manfred Nowak, was owing to evidence he had received about 'different forms of violence and abuse inflicted against persons with disabilities – men, women and children'.[12] This concerned especially violence and abuse perpetrated in public institutions, private spheres, and medical settings, which comprised 'unspeakable indignities, neglect, severe forms of restraint and seclusion, as well as physical, mental and sexual violence'. The lack of reasonable accommodation in detention facilities, the Special Rapporteur further affirmed, 'may increase the risk of exposure to neglect, violence, abuse, torture and ill-treatment'.[13]

The UN/NGO Inter-Agency Standing Committee (IASC) and recent studies by Human Rights Watch have similarly asserted that persons with disabilities are more likely to experience violations if they are in institutions.[14] Such violations include inhuman and degrading treatment, unsanitary conditions, neglect, verbal, sexual and physical abuse, involuntary medication, and restraint.[15] Reasonable accommodation is defined by the CRPD as 'necessary and appropriate modification and adjustments, not imposing a disproportionate or undue burden, where needed in a particular case, to ensure to persons with disabilities the enjoyment or exercise on an equal basis with others of all human rights and fundamental freedoms'.[16]

In his 2019 report on the protection of civilians in armed conflict, the UN Secretary-General called for attention to be focused on 'a more comprehensive thematic approach across all relevant situations'; one that 'takes into account the role of conflict in both aggravating existing disabilities and causing new ones, and the need to ensure effective protection and assistance for persons with disabilities'.[17] In response to that report and subsequent discussions in the Council, in the preamble to its Resolution 2475, the UN Security Council expressed 'serious concern regarding the disproportionate impact that armed conflict has on persons with disabilities, including abandonment, violence, and lack of access to basic services'. It affirmed its 'commitment' to address that disproportionate impact.[18]

Previously, references by the UN Security Council to the protection of persons with disabilities during armed conflict had been scant and largely ad hoc in nature. In one such reference, in its Resolution 2406 (2018), the Security Council underlined the importance of the Government of South Sudan ensuring that the specific needs of children with disabilities are addressed, including access to health care, psychosocial support, and education programmes that contribute to the well-being of children.[19]

---

[12] Ibid., para. 37.

[13] Ibid., para. 38.

[14] IASC, *Inclusion of Persons with Disabilities in Humanitarian Action*, Guidelines, 2019, at: http://bit.ly /2wAok5E (hereinafter, 2019 IASC Guidelines), p. 145, citing WHO, *Promoting Rights and Community Living for Children with Psychosocial Disabilities*, 2015.

[15] Human Rights Watch, *They Stay There Until They Die*, Report, Washington, DC, 2018; Human Rights Watch, *Chained Like Prisoners*, Report, Washington, DC, 2015.

[16] Art. 2, CRPD.

[17] Protection of Civilians in Armed Conflict: Report of the Secretary-General, UN doc. S/2019/373, para. 49.

[18] UN Security Council Resolution 2475, adopted by unanimous vote in favour on 20 June 2019, first and second preambular paras.

[19] UN Security Council Resolution 2406, adopted by unanimous vote in favour on 15 March 2018, operative para. 25.

In its earlier Resolution 2217 (2015), the Council had expressed 'serious concern about the dire situation' of persons with disabilities in the Central African Republic, including 'abandonment, violence and lack of access to basic services'.[20] The Security Council emphasised the need to ensure that 'the particular needs of persons with disabilities are addressed in the humanitarian response'.[21] The Council specifically mandated the UN Multidimensional Integrated Stabilization Mission in the Central African Republic (MINUSCA) to monitor, help investigate, and report on violations and abuses committed against persons with disabilities, including rape and other forms of sexual violence in armed conflict. The Mission was also exhorted to 'contribute to efforts to identify and prosecute perpetrators, and to prevent such violations and abuses'.[22] But when the Security Council renewed MINUSCA's mandate in July 2016,[23] the language on persons with disabilities was omitted.

Indeed, the effectiveness of MINUSCA's work in protecting persons with disabilities has been questioned. In 2017, for instance, Human Rights Watch said that persons with disabilities in the Central African Republic 'have faced violent attacks, forced displacement, and ongoing neglect in the humanitarian response'.[24] The organisation stated that persons with disabilities 'are suffering disproportionately in the Central African Republic and then falling through the cracks'.[25] In its critique, Human Rights Watch referred to a 369-page Mapping Report issued by the United Nations in May 2017, which documented war crimes by all parties to the conflict from 2003 to 2015, but, a few briefing mentions aside, did not consider how persons with disabilities had been affected by the fighting.[26]

Access to water and sanitation services, such as latrines and showers, was said to be 'a daily struggle' for persons with disabilities in internally displaced camps. 'Without ramps, bars, and other support, some persons with physical disabilities must crawl on the ground to enter these areas, exposing them to health risks', Human Rights Watch noted. Emmanuel, a 38-year-old man who was injured when he fell while fleeing a Seleka attack in 2015 and now cannot walk, described to Human Rights Watch the obstacles to using the toilet at the Lazare IDP camp in Kaga-Bandoro. 'I have to sit on the ground where other people defecate,' he said. 'I don't have gloves so I just try to wash my hands afterward. I don't feel like a human being.'[27] Persons with disabilities often struggle to receive food aid, constrained to survive on scraps left behind by those with greater mobility.

---

[20] UN Security Council Resolution 2217, adopted by unanimous vote in favour on 28 April 2015, thirty-third preambular para.

[21] Ibid.

[22] UN Security Council Resolution 2217, operative para. 32(e)(ii).

[23] UN Security Council Resolution 2301, adopted by unanimous vote in favour on 26 July 2016.

[24] Human Rights Watch, 'Central African Republic: People with Disabilities at High Risk. 4 Years into Conflict, More Support, Protection Needed', 21 June 2017, at: http://bit.ly/38sNpxs.

[25] Ibid.

[26] Ibid.

[27] Ibid.

10.2 THE GLOBAL NORMATIVE FRAMEWORK

The CRPD dedicates a provision to the protection of persons with disabilities during 'situations of risk and humanitarian emergencies'.[28] According to Article 11, States Parties to the CRPD are obligated to take 'all necessary measures to ensure the protection and safety of persons with disabilities in situations of risk, including situations of armed conflict'. This is a broad-based duty to protect, whose legal impact is substantively heightened by the requirement of taking all 'necessary' measures to ensure the protection of persons with disabilities. International human rights law tends to consider the duty to protect as one of due diligence: meaning that a State must undertake 'reasonable' or 'reasonably possible' measures. International humanitarian law (IHL) refers to a duty to take only 'feasible' precautions in this regard during the conduct of hostilities.[29]

An Optional Protocol to the CRPD[30] allows individuals, groups, and/or their representatives who believe their rights under the Convention have been violated to take a case before the UN Committee on the Rights of Persons with Disabilities. As of 1 October 2021, 100 of the 184 States Parties to the CRPD had also adhered to the Optional Protocol. This includes States embroiled in armed conflicts, such as Afghanistan, the Central African Republic, the Democratic Republic of Congo, Nigeria, Palestine, Saudi Arabia, Syria, Turkey, Ukraine, and Yemen.

According to Alice Priddy, that the CRPD applies to a State Party's extraterritorial conduct 'is not controversial and is consistent with the approach of international courts and human rights treaty bodies'.[31] Working methods of the Committee on the Rights of Persons with Disabilities[32] provide for a special mechanism for 'early-awareness and urgent-action procedures' with the aim of 'preventing existing problems within States parties from escalating into full-fledged conflicts or preventing the revival of pre-existing problems'.[33] These mechanisms are also meant to address issues requiring 'immediate attention in order to avoid serious violations of the Convention or to reduce the number or degree of such violations'.[34]

The IASC Task Team on the Inclusion of Persons with Disabilities in Humanitarian Action has drafted guidelines to address the experiences of persons with disabilities in humanitarian disasters. The Guidelines, which were elaborated over the course of three

---

[28] Although not defined in the CRPD, in Article 1 of the 2018 Protocol to the African Charter on Human and Peoples' Rights on the Rights of Persons with Disabilities in Africa the term is defined as 'any situation that poses grave risk to the general population, including disasters and all forms of armed conflict'.

[29] Article 11 of the CRPD refers to the duty to take all necessary measures being 'in accordance with their obligations under international law, including international humanitarian law and international human rights law'. This does not diminish the extent of the duty.

[30] Optional Protocol to the Convention on the Rights of Persons with Disabilities; adopted at New York, 13 December 2006; entered into force, 3 May 2008.

[31] Priddy, *Disability and Armed Conflict*, Geneva Academy of International Humanitarian Law and Human Rights, p. 36.

[32] Committee on the Rights of Persons with Disabilities, *Working methods of the Committee on the Rights of Persons with Disabilities*, adopted at its fifth session (11–15 April 2011).

[33] Ibid., para. 26.

[34] Ibid.

years, were endorsed by the IASC in October 2019 and published in November 2019. They are, the United Nations proclaims,

> the first humanitarian guidelines to be developed with and by persons with disabilities and their representative organizations in association with traditional humanitarian stakeholders. Based on the outcomes of a comprehensive global and regional multi-stakeholder consultation process, they are designed to promote the implementation of quality humanitarian programmes in all contexts and across all regions, and to establish and increase both the inclusion of persons with disabilities and their meaningful participation in all decisions that concern them.[35]

The content of the Guidelines is discussed in Section 10.2.3 below.

10.2.1 *IHL Rules on the Protection of Persons with Disabilities*

Persons with disabilities are protected under IHL first and foremost in their capacity as civilians.[36] The principles of distinction and proportionality in attack apply to persons with disabilities, just as they do to any other civilians. This is true under customary law whether the armed conflict is international or non-international in character. Thus, for example, in its Resolution 2475, the UN Security Council urged all parties to armed conflict to 'take measures, in accordance with applicable international law obligations to protect civilians, including those with disabilities'. The Council referred specifically to killing and maiming; abduction and torture; and rape and other forms of sexual violence in conflict.[37]

Persons (civilians) with disabilities will be protected by IHL unless and for such time as they participate directly in hostilities.[38] In IHL, the term 'disabled' is employed in the 1949 Geneva Convention III only in relation to prisoners of war (POWs), that is to say predominantly members of armed forces who are captured by the enemy in an international armed conflict.[39] Under Article 30, '[s]pecial facilities shall be afforded for the care to be given to the disabled, in particular to the blind, and for their rehabilitation, pending repatriation'. In the relatively rare case that an embedded journalist within an armed force or a civilian contractor is a person with a disability, he or she will also be entitled to POW status and this protection. In the 1977 Additional Protocol I, however, the definition of 'wounded' and 'sick'

---

[35] 'IASC Guidelines, Inclusion of Persons with Disabilities in Humanitarian Action, 2019', Posted on 19 November 2019, at: http://bit.ly/2SIR58J.

[36] The Geneva Academy publication is highly critical of IHL's treatment of persons with disabilities, stating that: 'When viewed as a whole, IHL largely reflects the medical and charity approaches to disability by framing persons with disabilities as passive, weak, defective and vulnerable and, as such, in need of special, paternalistic protection.' Priddy, *Disability and Armed Conflict*, Geneva Academy of International Humanitarian Law and Human Rights, p. 52. At the same time, they concede that this is 'unsurprising considering the time at which most IHL instruments were drafted, long before disability rights discourse had begun to develop'. Ibid. Therefore, it is stated, 'terminology such as "the infirm" should be read as "a person with a disability", cases of mental disease should be read as "persons with psychosocial or intellectual disabilities" and "the blind" as "persons with visual impairments"'. Ibid., p. 53.

[37] UN Security Council Resolution 2475, operative para. 1.

[38] For a discussion of this concept, see Chapter 2.

[39] Art. 4, Convention (III) relative to the Treatment of Prisoners of War; adopted at Geneva, 12 August 1949; entered into force, 21 October 1950.

is explicitly understood to apply to all persons, 'whether military or civilian, who, because of trauma, disease or other physical or mental disorder or disability, are in need of medical assistance or care and who refrain from any act of hostility'.[40]

Article 3 common to the four 1949 Geneva Conventions, which formally applies in non-international armed conflict, but which constitutes a minimum level of protection in all conflicts,[41] obligates humane treatment of persons in the power of the enemy in all circumstances. This treatment must be ensured without any adverse distinction founded on 'race, colour, religion or faith, sex, birth or wealth, or any other similar criteria'. While disability is not specifically cited, this falls within the reference to 'other similar criteria' and therefore discrimination in the treatment of persons with disabilities (such as with respect to protection from violence or the provision of food, water, and shelter) would be unlawful. In contrast, special protection of persons with disabilities would not amount to adverse distinction as already well established under international human rights law jurisprudence.[42]

There are also obligations under IHL and disarmament treaties to assist the survivors of certain conventional weapons, most notably anti-personnel mines, cluster munition remnants, and other explosive remnants of war.[43]

10.2.2 *Protection under International Human Rights Law*

The need for a dedicated human rights treaty to protect persons with disabilities led to the negotiation of the CRPD. Prior to this, persons with disabilities were of course protected both by the substantive rights (including to life, to freedom from inhumane treatment, to liberty, and to security) as well as by the general prohibition on discrimination, though they were subsumed within unnamed categories of 'at risk' or 'vulnerable' groups. The CRPD continues to apply during armed conflict, alongside IHL, 'and may inform the content of the legal regulation of the given situation'.[44] Furthermore, where a State Party is engaged in armed conflict abroad, 'its CRPD obligations follow it'.[45]

Under the 1966 International Covenant on Civil and Political Rights, discrimination in the respect and ensuring of human rights is outlawed on a number of grounds.[46] While disability is not specifically referenced, it falls within the reference to 'other status'. In its Resolution

---

[40] Art. 8(a), Protocol Additional to the Geneva Conventions of 12 August 1949, and relating to the Protection of Victims of International Armed Conflicts (Protocol I), 8 June 1977; adopted at Geneva, 8 June 1977; entered into force, 7 December 1978 (1977 Additional Protocol I).

[41] International Court of Justice (ICJ), *Case Concerning Military and Paramilitary Activities In and Against Nicaragua (Nicaragua v. United States)*, Judgment (Merits) 27 June 1986, para. 218: 'There is no doubt that, in the event of international armed conflicts, these rules also constitute a minimum yardstick, in addition to the more elaborate rules which are also to apply to international conflicts; and they are rules which, in the Court's opinion, reflect what the Court in 1949 called "elementary considerations of humanity".'

[42] See, for example, Committee on the Rights of Persons with Disabilities, *General Comment No. 6 (2018) on equality and non-discrimination*, UN doc. UNCRPD/C/GC/6, paras. 28 and 29.

[43] See Chapter 5 above for details on disarmament treaty obligations.

[44] Priddy, *Disability and Armed Conflict*, Geneva Academy of International Humanitarian Law and Human Rights, p. 76.

[45] Ibid.

[46] International Covenant on Civil and Political Rights; adopted at New York, 16 December 1966; entered into force, 23 March 1976.

2475, the UN Security Council cited the 'need for persons with disabilities, including those with physical, intellectual, psychosocial and sensory disabilities and those marginalized on the basis of their disability, to be guaranteed their full enjoyment without discrimination'.[47]

10.2.3 *IASC Guidelines on Inclusion of Persons with Disabilities in Humanitarian Action (2019)*

The 2019 IASC Guidelines represent an important step forward by the United Nations towards guaranteeing and mainstreaming the protection of persons with disabilities within social and humanitarian protection. The guidance is divided into eighteen chapters, eight of which cover different thematic areas, including protection: camp coordination and camp management; education; food security and nutrition; livelihoods; health; protection; shelter and settlements; and water, sanitation, and hygiene. In his foreword to the 2019 Guidelines, Mark Lowcock, the then UN Under-Secretary-General for Humanitarian Affairs and Emergency Relief Coordinator, said that the humanitarian response 'becomes more effective as we give voice to the voiceless and leave no one behind'.[48] He noted that the Guidelines are 'a key contribution of the humanitarian sector' to the 2019 UN Disability Inclusion Strategy (UNDIS).[49]

The 2019 IASC Guidelines are 'underpinned by principles that guarantee that the rights of persons with disabilities will be respected, protected and promoted throughout humanitarian preparedness, response and recovery'.[50] The Guidelines give valuable examples of environmental barriers and enablers in a humanitarian context[51] (reproduced in Table 10.1), noting that while some environmental barriers are likely to be present already, humanitarian actors and local populations may unintentionally create others.

The Protection chapter of the 2019 Guidelines refers to 'Must do' actions, that is to say actions that must be undertaken 'in all phases of humanitarian action' when implementing protection programming for persons with disabilities.[52] These are participation; addressing barriers; empowerment and capacity development; and data collection and monitoring.

10.2.3.1 Participation

Action must be taken to ensure that persons with disabilities and organisations of persons with disabilities actively participate in identifying protection risks and barriers to accessing protection.[53] Persons with disabilities must be fairly represented in formal and informal protection mechanisms including community-based protection mechanisms (camp leadership mechanisms as well as women's, youth, and older persons' groups), taking into account all forms of disability as well as age, gender, and diversity. Concerted efforts must

---

[47] UN Security Council Resolution 2475, sixth preambular para.
[48] Foreword to the 2019 IASC Guidelines, p. xi.
[49] UNDIS, adopted at New York in March 2019, at: http://bit.ly/2T78neC.
[50] 2019 IASC Guidelines, p. 7.
[51] Ibid., pp. 13–14.
[52] Ibid., pp. 144–5.
[53] See, for example, Preamble, paras. e, k, m, and o; and Art. 3(c), CRPD.

TABLE 10.1 *Barriers and enablers in a humanitarian context*

Examples of barriers	Examples of enablers
Registration and distribution points are located far away, uphill, across difficult terrain; transport is inaccessible.	Place registration and distribution points in locations everyone can access. If this is not possible, provide transport or deliver services to individuals who cannot reach distribution points.
Food packages are too heavy to be carried by persons with disabilities.	Identify support people to collect and carry the food packages of persons with disabilities.
The latrine blocks are too narrow to accommodate a wheelchair and support person.	Design and procurement documents foresee latrines that are wheelchair accessible.
Tents and temporary shelters have steps and narrow entrances.	Design and procurement documents foresee temporary shelters that are wheelchair accessible.
Water points have elevated pumps that are difficult to operate.	Design and procurement documents foresee accessible water pumps. (Note that support may be required even for accessible designs.)
Coordination meetings take place in inaccessible buildings that fail the 'Reach, Enter, Circulate and Use' principle.	The response makes sure that coordination meetings are convened in buildings and at sites that are accessible.
Information about humanitarian assistance is provided using only one medium of communication (for example, oral or written messages or posters).	Information about humanitarian assistance is provided in multiple accessible formats (e.g. oral, print, sign language, easy-to-read/plain language). Human assistance is provided to those who need it to access information.
Humanitarian frameworks, codes of conduct and other key documents are not available in multiple accessible formats, including easy-to-read/plain language formats.	Key documents are made available in multiple accessible formats, including easy-to-read /plain language formats.
Consultations with the community (through focus group discussions, feedback, and complaint mechanisms, etc.) are not conducted in multiple formats, and persons with hearing, psychosocial or intellectual disabilities are not supported to understand or participate in them.	Consultations are conducted in a range of formats, and persons with hearing, psychosocial or intellectual disabilities are supported to participate in community consultations, focus group discussions, feedback, and complaint mechanisms.

be made to promote under-represented groups, such as persons with intellectual and psychosocial disabilities, indigenous persons, persons with albinism, women, and girls.

10.2.3.2 Addressing Barriers

Barriers that impede persons with disabilities from accessing protection must be identified and monitored and steps taken to make protection systems and services accessible to them.

Outreach and 'other reasonable accommodations' must be undertaken to reach persons with disabilities who are unable to leave their homes. All protection-related information must be communicated in multiple accessible formats, taking into account persons with hearing, visual, intellectual, and psychosocial disabilities. Sectoral policies, guidelines, and tools must be reviewed to ensure they clearly affirm the right of persons with disabilities to access and inclusion.[54]

10.2.3.3 Empowerment and Capacity Development

When persons with disabilities, including those with intellectual and psychosocial disabilities, need to take personal decisions, procedures must always require their informed consent.[55] Training should ensure that protection actors become more conscious of the rights of persons with disabilities and the specific protection risks they face.[56]

Local and national organisations for persons with disabilities should be assessed for their capacity to work in protection mainstreaming, and training and support provided where required. They should be involved in the work of protection coordination mechanisms. Persons with disabilities and their representative organisations should be involved in all community mobilisation and outreach activities. Their capacity to identify and refer persons at risk of violence or abuse should be enhanced with appropriate steps taken to protect the rights of persons with disabilities and address violations.

10.2.3.4 Data Collection and Monitoring

Protection data on persons with disabilities should be collected, analysed, and disaggregated by sex, age, and disability.[57] This should occur systematically across the humanitarian programme cycle in all protection information management systems, including the Gender-Based Violence Information Management System, the Child Protection Information Management System, and national reporting databases.

Data and information should be collected on barriers to claiming rights and on barriers that impede access to protection services. When so doing, data ethics and protection principles (including confidentiality, provision of information, informed consent, and security) must be respected.[58]

Information on the cross-sectoral needs of persons with disabilities should be shared in interagency coordination mechanisms (water, sanitation and hygiene (WASH), health, education), cross-disability, and cross-sectoral coordination ensured. Finally, there should

---

[54] See, for example, Art. 9, CRPD.

[55] See International Committee of the Red Cross (ICRC), *Professional Standards for Protection Work Carried Out by Humanitarian and Human Rights Actors in Armed Conflict and Other Situations of Violence*, Geneva, 2018. See also Art. 25(d), CRPD.

[56] The CRPD recognises 'supported' decision-making and outlaws 'substituted' decision-making in its Article 12(3) and (4).

[57] Art. 31, CRPD.

[58] Art. 22(2), CRPD.

be a general monitoring of violations of the rights of persons with disabilities during situations of armed conflict.

10.2.3.5 Gender-Based Violence

Women and girls with disabilities disproportionately experience gender-based violence (GBV); they are said to be victims of domestic violence twice as frequently as other women.[59] Owing to the discrimination and stigma associated with both gender and disability, this violence also takes unique forms. For example, women and girls with disabilities are more likely to be subjected to forced medical treatment, including forced sterilisation and other reproductive health procedures, without their consent.[60]

These risks can be reduced by the following actions:

➤ Recruiting persons with disabilities as staff, volunteers, and community mobilisers
➤ Integrating and mainstreaming content about persons with disabilities in core GBV training packages
➤ Training of local organisations for persons with disabilities, in particular women-led organisations, in how to safely identify and refer gender-based violence survivors
➤ Strengthening national policies and protocols, including standard operating procedures, case management systems, and referral systems
➤ Establishing safe, accessible, and confidential complaint mechanisms that comply with protection from sexual exploitation and abuse standards.[61]

10.2.3.6 Child Protection

Children with disabilities have been found in certain research to be three to four times more likely to be survivors of violence than children without disabilities.[62] In many countries, children with disabilities are frequently placed in institutions, where they are at risk of abuse, exploitation, and neglect. Such facilities often have low standards of care and lack monitoring. Perpetrators of violence and abuse are rarely held to account.[63] Placement in residential facilities also increases the risk of trafficking of children with disabilities. Studies have found that girls with disabilities are at risk of being trafficked because their impairments are presumed to limit their chances of escape.[64]

---

[59] Arts. 3(g) and 6, CRPD.
[60] 2019 IASC Guidelines, p. 149.
[61] See UN doc. 3ST/SGB/2003/13, 9 October 2003.
[62] K. Hughes et al., 'Prevalence and Risk of Violence against Adults with Disabilities: A Systematic Review and Meta-analysis of Observational Studies', *The Lancet*, Vol. 379, No. 9826 (2012), 1621–9.
[63] African Child Policy Forum, *The African Report on Violence against Children*, Addis Ababa, 2014, available at: https://bit.ly/3xsjHYB.
[64] Leonard Cheshire Disability, *Still Left Behind: Pathways to Inclusive Education for Girls with Disabilities*, Report, 2017, at: https://bit.ly/3rm2Nag.

Children with disabilities who have become separated from caregivers are especially endangered. Family members may have been the only persons to know how to care for a child's specific physical requirements or how to communicate with a child.[65] Children with disabilities may be unable to communicate information that is essential for family tracing and reunification. Unaccompanied children with disabilities may be excluded from traditional systems of care if local families do not accept them.

These risks can be reduced by the following actions:

➤ Increasing the capacity of staff and volunteers to understand and apply a rights-based approach to disability

➤ Giving training and support to foster carers and interim caregivers on the needs of children with disabilities

➤ Training all child protection staff in disability

➤ Choosing locations for child protection activities that are physically accessible; where this is not possible, necessary adjustments and 'reasonable accommodations' should be made

➤ Awareness of the rights of children with disabilities should be raised with their families, and with community leaders, religious leaders, traditional healers, education and health staff, and the wider community

➤ The safety concerns of children with disabilities, such as bullying or risk of injury, and physical or sexual abuse should be identified and steps taken to remove or mitigate these risks

➤ Adolescents and youth with disabilities should be involved in activities that help build their resilience

➤ Mentors with disabilities should be encouraged to use their leadership, skills, and capacities to counter negative attitudes to disability

➤ Children with disabilities living in residential facilities, including children who have been separated and abandoned when communities flee

➤ The requirements of unaccompanied and separated children with disabilities who are in respite or alternative care should be considered

➤ Any actions to prevent and respond to the worst forms of child labour should include children with disabilities

➤ Case management systems must be inclusive

➤ Mobile outreach teams should be used to reach children with disabilities who cannot travel to registration sites or child-friendly spaces

➤ Children in residential facilities, including detention centres, must be visited

➤ Work with communities to include children with disabilities and their parents in community-based child protection mechanisms

➤ Support should be provided to enable families and caregivers of children with disabilities to access assistance

➤ Monitoring mechanisms, including the Monitoring and Reporting Mechanism on Grave Violations against Children (MRM), should contain information on violations

---

[65]   UNICEF, *State of the World's Children: Children with Disabilities*, Report, New York, 2013.

of the human rights of children with disabilities, while also being cognisant of the possibilities of abuse by family members, guardians, or caregivers themselves.[66]

10.2.4 *Camp Coordination and Camp Management*

Camp coordination and camp management (CCCM) concerns standardised coordination mechanisms that may be applied in refugee and IDP operations. The CCCM sector's primary objective is to protect the rights of populations affected by forced displacement.

Risks can be mitigated through the following actions:

➤ Involving persons with disabilities and organisations for persons with disabilities in site planning and improvement meetings and seeking their advice on how to remove barriers and reduce protection risks

➤ Supporting or establishing governance mechanisms that ensure persons with disabilities can participate in formal and informal processes of consultation and decision-making

➤ Ensuring information campaigns and complaint and feedback mechanisms are accessible to all, independent of disability

➤ Monitoring the degree to which persons with disabilities successfully obtain access to general services and to services targeting persons with disabilities

➤ Ensuring that camp infrastructures (latrines, water, shelter) are maintained and accessibility improved

➤ Involving persons with disabilities in all activities and decision-making processes related to durable solutions.[67]

10.2.5 *Food Security and Nutrition*

Disability can adversely affect household food security and nutrition, with research indicating that households that include persons with disabilities are more likely to experience food insecurity, because they possess fewer economic resources and fewer work opportunities, require more health services, and spend extra time on care work. When the person with disabilities heads the household and is its primary income earner, the chances of falling into food insecurity are generally higher. Malnutrition rates may also be higher among persons with disabilities when they have difficulty eating and swallowing, are frequently ill, or are neglected.

These risks can be reduced by the following actions:

➤ Ensuring that the contingency plan that sets out the initial response strategy and the operational plan to meet urgent food and nutrition needs during the first three to four

---

[66] African Child Policy Forum (ACPF), *Violence against Children with Disabilities in Africa: Field Studies from Cameroon, Ethiopia, Senegal, Uganda and Zambia*, Addis Ababa, 2011.

[67] 2019 IASC Guidelines, pp. 80–81.

weeks of an emergency includes persons with disabilities and covers transport and food rations

➤ Involving organisations for persons with disabilities and other actors who work with persons with disabilities in designing and delivering an inclusive food security and nutrition assessment

➤ Assessing the capacity of staff with respect to disability inclusion

➤ Providing training to staff and partners, including emergency managers and first responders, which explain the rights and requirements of persons with disabilities and make clear that disability needs to be integrated in food security and nutrition-related preparedness plans

➤ Finding ways to reach marginalised and isolated affected populations, including persons with psychosocial disabilities, who are not mobile, or who face other barriers (e.g. through outreach and community-based distribution for the preparation and delivery of food)

➤ Developing a community approach and identifying staff who will support persons with disabilities to access food rations (on site and via outreach)

➤ Training local and national staff on good nutrition practices for persons with disabilities

➤ Working with national systems that have responsibility for food security and nutrition, including social protection systems, to put in place arrangements for supporting persons with disabilities after the emergency ends

➤ Establishing clear referral mechanisms for persons with disabilities who require food security and nutrition-related support

➤ Advising government counterparts and other national stakeholders on how to integrate disability-inclusive practices in relevant national food security and nutrition programmes and trainings

➤ Advising on accessibility compliance during the construction, reconstruction, and repair of nutrition-related infrastructure.[68]

---

[68] Ibid., pp. 98–100.

11

Protection of Older Persons in Armed Conflict

11.1 INTRODUCTION

This chapter describes the protection of the elderly in situations of armed conflict, a group that are said to be 'neglected' by the humanitarian sector.[1] There is no set international legal definition of the elderly or of 'older persons', the term that is more often used today in international human rights law. At regional level, the 2016 Protocol to the African Charter on Human and Peoples' Rights on the Rights of Older Persons in Africa defines older persons as those aged sixty years and above.[2] The United Nations (UN) also has a rule of thumb of sixty years[3] but its origin dates back decades when life expectancy was far lower than it is today.

The International Committee of the Red Cross (ICRC) has noted that international humanitarian law (IHL) 'says nothing about the age at which an individual is considered to be elderly'.[4] The ICRC Commentary on the Fourth Geneva Convention of 1949 states as follows:

---

[1] Age International and HelpAge International, *If Not Now, When? Keeping Promises to Older People Affected by Humanitarian Crises*, Report, 25 November 2020, at: http://bit.ly/3pukv8L.

[2] Art. 1, Protocol to the African Charter on Human and Peoples' Rights on the Rights of Older Persons in Africa; adopted at Addis Ababa, 31 January 2016; not yet in force. Under its Article 26(1), the Protocol will enter into force thirty days after the fifteenth ratification by an African Union Member State. As of 1 April 2022, there were six ratifications (Benin, Ethiopia, Kenya, Lesotho, Malawi, and Rwanda) and eighteen signatory States. In 2002, a World Health Organization (WHO) project on the elderly in Africa proposed to use fifty years as the definition of an older person. WHO, 'Proposed Working Definition of an Older Person in Africa for the MDS Project', 2002, at: http://bit.ly/3nzdz9D.

[3] Thus, for instance, the Political Declaration adopted at the Second World Assembly on Ageing in Madrid in April 2002 noted that:

> We recognize that the world is experiencing an unprecedented demographic transformation and that by 2050 the number of persons aged 60 years and over will increase from 600 million to almost 2 billion and that the proportion of persons aged 60 years and over is expected to double from 10 to 21 per cent. The increase will be greatest and most rapid in developing countries where the older population is expected to quadruple during the next 50 years.

Art. 2, Political Declaration; adopted at Madrid, April 2002, at: http://bit.ly/3iPgsj3. The Declaration further noted the determination of States 'to enhance the recognition of the dignity of older persons and to eliminate all forms of neglect, abuse and violence'. Art. 5, 2002 Political Declaration.

[4] F. Krill, 'The Elderly in Situations of Armed Conflict', *Address by the ICRC Deputy Director of Operations*, Helsinki, September 1999, at: http://bit.ly/34L8TVE.

No limit was fixed for 'aged persons'. Should this expression be taken to mean those over 65, as stipulated in the Stockholm Draft? The Conference refrained from naming a definite age, preferring to leave the point to the discretion of Governments. The age of 65 seems, however, to be a reasonable limit. It is often the age of retirement, and it is also the age at which civilian internees have usually been released from internment by belligerent Powers.[5]

11.2 THE THREATS TO OLDER PERSONS IN ARMED CONFLICT

The elderly are at obvious risk in armed conflict as they may not be either able or indeed willing to flee zones of combat. The ICRC has suggested that: 'The presence of elderly people among the victims of armed conflict is a relatively recent phenomenon, dating back only to the Second World War.'[6] That said, the ICRC has noted also that the 'plight of the aged has long been neglected', while observing that 'For a very long time the International Red Cross and Red Crescent Movement has been concerned about the plight of older persons. This concern gave rise to a number of resolutions adopted by various International Conferences of the Red Cross and Red Crescent since 1921.'[7] The elderly, the organisation has recalled, 'are often left without any means of subsistence' and 'may also be subjected to all sorts of abuse – looting, destruction of their property, threats, physical violence, including rape and sometimes murder – because they belong to a minority or live in particularly remote villages or isolated places'.[8]

11.3 PROTECTION UNDER INTERNATIONAL HUMAN RIGHTS LAW

While all the main global and regional human rights treaties offer general legal protection to all, including older persons, and encompassing their right to life, they do not, for the most part, specifically protect the rights of the elderly. The most notable exception is the 2016 Protocol to the African Charter mentioned above, a treaty which had not yet entered into force as of writing. Under Article 14(1), States Parties must ensure that, in situations of armed conflict 'Older Persons shall be among those to enjoy access, on a priority basis, to assistance during rescue efforts, settlement, repatriation and other interventions.' It is further stipulated that older persons must 'receive humane treatment, protection and respect at all times and are not left without needed medical assistance and care'.[9]

States Parties are also obligated to '[e]nsure the protection of the rights of Older Women from violence, sexual abuse and discrimination based on gender'.[10] Similarly, the Protocol to the African Charter on the Rights of Women in Africa, a treaty which is in force,

---

[5]   J. Pictet, Commentary on Article 14(1) of 1949 Geneva Convention IV, ICRC, Geneva, 1958, at: http://bit.ly/3lBHr3n, p. 125.

[6]   Krill, 'The Elderly in Situations of Armed Conflict', 1999.

[7]   Ibid.

[8]   Ibid.

[9]   Art. 14(2), Protocol to the African Charter on Human and Peoples' Rights on the Rights of Older Persons.

[10]   Art. 9(1), Protocol to the African Charter on Human and Peoples' Rights on the Rights of Older Persons.

provides for the special protection of 'elderly women' (although the term elderly is not defined).[11]

That fundamental human rights, including the right to life, apply to all without discrimination as to age was confirmed by the Inter-American Court of Human Rights in its 2005 judgment in the *Yakye Axa Indigenous Community* case against Paraguay.[12] The Court declared that, with respect to the 1969 American Convention on Human Rights:[13]

> As regards the special consideration required by the elderly, it is important for the State to take measures to ensure their continuing functionality and autonomy, guaranteeing their right to adequate food, access to clean water and health care. Specifically, the State must provide care for the elderly with chronic diseases and in terminal stages, to help them avoid unnecessary suffering.[14]

In that case, lack of water and food had caused the death of many elderly persons, as the Court had explicitly recalled.[15]

The best set of standards currently pertaining to the inclusion of older persons in the humanitarian system are the Humanitarian Inclusion Standards for Older People and People with Disabilities, published by non-governmental organisations in 2018.[16] On the issue of protection, the standards call for protection assessment and monitoring tools to be adapted in order to collect information on the protection concerns and capacities of older people.[17]

In seeking to ensure that older people with protection concerns have access to protection services, and are protected from risks of physical and psychological harm, the Humanitarian Inclusion Standards recommend training on communicating and on recognising the heightened risks of abuse they may face. These are not only physical, verbal, and emotional, but also sexual, financial, and of neglect. It should not be assumed that older persons are safe in their own homes.[18]

The risks to older persons are exacerbated by the prevalence of poverty. While poverty is not an issue exclusive to the older population, older people are often among the poorest members of a community. An estimated 100 million older people live on less than a dollar a day, and 80 per cent of older people in the developing world have no regular income.[19] It is also important to recognise the link between older people's poverty at household level and the impact on child protection, health, and well-being, as many older people are carers of children.[20]

[11] Art. 22, Protocol to the African Charter on the Rights of Women in Africa; adopted at Maputo, 1 July 2003; entered into force, 25 November 2005. As of writing, forty-two African States were party to the Protocol and a further ten States were signatories.

[12] Inter-American Court of Human Rights, *Yakye Axa Indigenous Community* v. *Paraguay*, Judgment (Merits, Reparations and Costs), 17 June 2005, para. 175.

[13] American Convention on Human Rights; adopted at San José, 22 November 1969; entered into force, 18 July 1978.

[14] Inter-American Court of Human Rights, *Yakye Axa Indigenous Community* v. *Paraguay*, Judgment, para. 175.

[15] Ibid., para. 50.15.

[16] *Humanitarian Inclusion Standards for Older People and People with Disabilities*, Age and Disability Consortium, Bensheim, 2018, at: https://bit.ly/2Mj7C2Q.

[17] Ibid., p. 96, para. 1.1.

[18] See also on this issue A. Allaire, *Protection Interventions for Older People in Emergencies*, HelpAge International, London, 2013.

[19] Ibid., p. 8.

[20] Ibid.

11.4 OLDER PERSONS AND THE DEATH PENALTY

There is no prohibition under general international law on the imposition and even the execution of the death penalty on older persons. The situation appears to be distinct under regional standards in Africa. In this regard, the African Commission on Human and Peoples' Rights has stated that, under the African Charter on Human and Peoples' Rights,[21] the execution of the 'elderly' will always amount to a violation of the right to life.[22]

In its 2019 judgment in *Madison* v. *Alabama*,[23] the United States (US) Supreme Court held that the Eighth Amendment to the US Constitution may permit executing a prisoner even if they cannot remember committing the crime for which they have been sentenced, but it may prohibit executing a prisoner who suffers from dementia or another disorder other than psychotic delusions.[24]

11.4.1 *The Death Penalty under IHL*

In a situation of military occupation, no sentence shall be pronounced by the competent courts of the Occupying Power except after a regular trial.[25] Under Article 75(4) of the 1977 Additional Protocol I, which governs all international armed conflict: 'No sentence may be passed and no penalty may be executed on a person found guilty of a penal offence related to the armed conflict except pursuant to a conviction pronounced by an impartial and regularly constituted court respecting the generally recognized principles of regular judicial procedure.'

In a situation of non-international armed conflict, Common Article 3 to the four 1949 Geneva Conventions expressly prohibits 'the passing of sentences and the carrying out of executions without previous judgment pronounced by a regularly constituted court, affording all the judicial guarantees which are recognized as indispensable by civilized peoples' as a serious violation of IHL. This applies to all persons, including older persons. The imposition of a death sentence at the culmination of an unfair trial is a war crime within the jurisdiction of the International Criminal Court.[26]

---

[21] African Charter on Human and Peoples' Rights; adopted at Nairobi, 27 June 1981; entered into force, 21 October 1986.

[22] African Commission on Human and Peoples' Rights, General Comment No. 3 on the African Charter on Human and Peoples' Rights: The Right to Life (Article 4), adopted at Banjul (57th Ordinary Session), November 2015 (hereinafter, African Commission General Comment on the Right to Life), para. 25.

[23] US Supreme Court, *Madison* v. *Alabama*, Judgment (Docket No. 17–7505), 27 February 2019.

[24] M. Ford, 'The Cruelty of Executing the Sick and Elderly: Two Controversial Cases in Alabama Reveal a Disturbing Trend in the Death Penalty in America', *New Republic*, 27 February 2018, at: http://bit.ly/39wPTuD.

[25] Art. 71, 1949 Geneva Convention IV.

[26] Art. 8(2)(c)(iv), Rome Statute of the International Criminal Court; adopted at Rome, 17 July 1998; entered into force, 1 July 2002 (ICC Statute). In the corresponding elements of crimes, the Court is asked to consider whether, 'in the light of all relevant circumstances, the cumulative effect of factors with respect to guarantees deprived the person or persons of a fair trial'. Elements of Crimes, *Official Records of the Assembly of States Parties to the Rome Statute of the International Criminal Court, First session, New York, 3–10 September 2002*, New York, p. 34.

11.5 PROTECTION OF OLDER PERSONS UNDER IHL

In its study of customary IHL, the ICRC determined that: 'The elderly, disabled and infirm affected by armed conflict are entitled to special respect and protection.'[27] The rule ostensibly applies to all armed conflict (although evidence for its application in non-international armed conflict is scant). Specific provisions are made under the Fourth Geneva Convention of 1949 for their protection whereby: 'The Parties to the conflict shall endeavour to conclude local agreements for the removal from besieged or encircled areas, of wounded, sick, infirm, and aged persons.'[28] Under Article 9 of the 2002 Madrid Declaration, States pledged 'to protect and assist older persons in situations of armed conflict and foreign occupation'.

But overall, there remains a remarkable dearth of practical guidance on assistance to the elderly during situations of armed conflict. In 2005, Global Action on Aging and HelpAge International cooperated to prepare a short checklist for the UN Secretary-General's Special Representative to Internally Displaced Persons, Walter Kälin. Walter Kälin had noticed a preponderance of older persons in some of the first internally displaced person (IDP) camps he visited. The checklist covers demographic data, health, nutrition, distributions, inclusion, and social support.[29]

[27]   ICRC, Customary IHL Rule 138: 'The Elderly, Disabled and Infirm', at: http://bit.ly/36PpM4a.
[28]   Art. 17, 1949 Geneva Convention IV.
[29]   Checklist for Older Persons in Internally Displaced Persons Camps, Submitted to the Representative of the UN Secretary-General on the Human Rights of Internally Displaced Persons Mr Walter Kälin by Global Action on Aging and HelpAge International, August 2005, at: http://bit.ly/3lTP9WL.

Protection of Medical and Humanitarian Personnel

12.1 INTRODUCTION

Medical personnel are granted special protection under international humanitarian law (IHL).[1] Military medics in an international armed conflict are non-combatants, not civilians, while civilian medical personnel are protected first and foremost through their civilian status. There is also specific protection afforded to other humanitarian personnel engaged in impartial humanitarian action. Attacking medical personnel (or medical facilities) or attacking humanitarian personnel engaged in their duties during a situation of armed conflict is a war crime. That is so, whether the conflict is international or non-international in character.

One debated question concerns whether military medical personnel, who benefit from special protection against direct attacks, are also to be considered in the application of the proportionality rule; that is whether in assessing the proportionality of an attack one should take into consideration also the potential harm to military medical personnel and objects.[2] From the perspective of the protection of civilians, it can be argued that the attacker should do so since military medical personnel and objects may serve to treat civilians.

12.1.1 The Definition of Medical Personnel

Under IHL, the term medical personnel refers to personnel assigned by a party to an armed conflict exclusively to the search for, collection, transportation, diagnosis, or treatment, including first-aid treatment, of the wounded, sick, and shipwrecked, and the prevention of disease. This work may be either permanent or temporary. The term encompasses the following:

- medical personnel of a party to an armed conflict, whether military or civilian, including those assigned to civil defence organisations;

---

[1] The rule, which goes back to the very first Geneva Convention of 1864, applied for more than a century only to military medical personnel. Its scope was expanded in the 1977 Additional Protocol I to cover also civilian medical personnel in all circumstances.

[2] See R. Kolb and F. Nakashima, 'The Notion of "Acts Harmful to the Enemy" under International Humanitarian Law', *International Review of the Red Cross*, Vol. 101, No. 912 (2019), 1171–99, at pp. 1175–7. For a useful literature review of the key issues see A. Sari and K. Tinkler, 'Collateral Damage and the Enemy', *British Yearbook of International Law*, 2019. See also L. Gisel, 'Can the Incidental Killing of Military Doctors Never be Excessive?', *International Review of the Red Cross*, Vol. 95, No. 889 (2013), 215–30.

- medical personnel of national Red Cross or Red Crescent societies and other voluntary aid societies duly recognised and authorised by a party to the conflict, including the International Committee of the Red Cross (ICRC); and
- medical personnel provided by a neutral or other State that is not a party to the conflict or by an impartial international humanitarian organisation.

This definition is set out in the 1977 Additional Protocol I[3] and is widely used in State practice, according to the ICRC.[4]

12.2 THE PROTECTION OF MEDICAL PERSONNEL

In broad terms, and within the context of an international armed conflict, a combatant is any member of the armed forces of a party to the conflict, except medical or religious personnel.[5] Medical personnel within the armed forces[6] are formally termed 'non-combatants',[7] that is to say, they do not have the right to participate directly in hostilities. They are not considered as civilians under IHL.

Medical personnel in the armed forces may carry small arms for their own protection and for the protection of their patients and medical facilities. If they are captured they do not have the status of prisoner of war but must be given the same treatment and equivalent protections. Should they use their weapon other than in self-defence or defence of other medical personnel or their patients who are under direct attack, they commit acts harmful to the enemy and may themselves be targeted.[8]

In the 1977 Additional Protocol I, protection is extended to all civilian medical personnel.[9] As the ICRC explains, in non-international armed conflicts, the protection of medical personnel is implicit in Common Article 3 to the 1949 Geneva Conventions, which requires that the wounded and sick be collected and cared for, 'because the protection of medical personnel is a subsidiary form of protection granted to ensure that the wounded and sick receive medical care'.[10] The rule that medical personnel must be respected and protected is explicitly stated in the 1977 Additional Protocol II.[11]

---

[3]   Art. 8(c), Protocol Additional to the Geneva Conventions of 12 August 1949, and relating to the Protection of Victims of International Armed Conflicts; adopted at Geneva, 8 June 1977; entered into force, 7 December 1978 (hereinafter, 1977 Additional Protocol I).

[4]   ICRC, Customary IHL Rule 25: 'Medical Personnel', at: http://bit.ly/2TbuZe8.

[5]   See ICRC, Customary IHL Rule 3: 'Definition of Combatants', at: http://bit.ly/2GYnRfC.

[6]   See Art. 33, Convention (III) relative to the Treatment of Prisoners of War; adopted at Geneva, 12 August 1949; entered into force, 21 October 1950 (hereinafter, 1949 Geneva Convention III).

[7]   Art. 43(2), 1977 Additional Protocol I.

[8]   'The protection to which fixed establishments and mobile medical units of the Medical Service are entitled shall not cease unless they are used to commit, outside their humanitarian duties, acts harmful to the enemy.' Art. 21, Convention (I) for the Amelioration of the Condition of the Wounded and Sick in Armed Forces in the Field; adopted at Geneva, 12 August 1949; entered into force, 21 October 1950 (hereinafter, 1949 Geneva Convention I).

[9]   Art. 15, 1977 Additional Protocol I.

[10]   ICRC, Customary IHL Rule 25: 'Medical Personnel'.

[11]   Art. 9, Protocol Additional to the Geneva Conventions of 12 August 1949, and relating to the Protection of Victims of Non-International Armed Conflicts; adopted at Geneva, 8 June 1977; entered into force, 7 December 1978 (hereinafter, 1977 Additional Protocol II).

It is a rule of customary international law that medical personnel 'exclusively assigned to medical duties must be respected and protected in all circumstances'. The rule clarifies that medical personnel 'lose their protection if they commit, outside their humanitarian function, acts harmful to the enemy'.[12] In addition, under the Rome Statute of the International Criminal Court,[13] intentionally directing attacks against medical personnel and medical facilities and transport that are using the distinctive emblems of the Geneva Conventions (i.e. red cross, red crescent, red crystal) in conformity with international law is a war crime in both international and non-international armed conflict.[14]

However, only medical personnel assigned to medical duties by a party to an armed conflict enjoy such protected status. Other persons performing medical duties enjoy protection against attack purely as civilians (and as long as they do not participate directly in hostilities). Such persons, the ICRC recalls, are not medical personnel and as a result have no right to display the distinctive emblems. The ICRC cites Canada's Code of Conduct, which explains that:

NGOs such as CARE and Médecins Sans Frontières (Doctors Without Borders) might wear other recognisable symbols. The symbols used by CARE, MSF and other NGOs do not benefit from international legal protection, although their work in favour of the victims of armed conflict must be respected. Upon recognition that they are providing care to the sick and wounded, NGOs are also to be respected.[15]

In its Resolution 2286 (2016), the United Nations (UN) Security Council expressed its deep concern that despite obligations under customary and conventional international law, 'acts of violence, attacks and threats against medical personnel and humanitarian personnel exclusively engaged in medical duties, their means of transport and equipment, as well as hospitals and other medical facilities, are being perpetrated in situations of armed conflicts and that the number of such acts is increasing'.[16] The Council further recalled that 'locally recruited medical personnel and humanitarian personnel exclusively engaged in medical duties account for the majority of casualties among such personnel in situations of armed conflict'.

The Council strongly urged States to conduct, 'in an independent manner, full, prompt, impartial and effective investigations within their jurisdiction' of violations of IHL related to the protection of medical personnel and humanitarian personnel exclusively engaged in medical duties, their means of transport and equipment, as well as hospitals and other medical facilities in armed conflict.[17] It further expressed its intention to ensure that the mandates of relevant UN peacekeeping operations 'can, where

---

[12] ICRC, Customary IHL Rule 25: 'Medical Personnel'.

[13] Rome Statute of the International Criminal Court; adopted at Rome, 17 July 1998; entered into force, 1 July 2002.

[14] Art. 8(2)(b)(xxiv) and (2)(e)(ii), Rome Statute of the International Criminal Court.

[15] ICRC, Customary IHL Rule 25: 'Medical Personnel', citing Canada, *Code of Conduct for CF Personnel*, Office of the Judge Advocate General, Ottawa, 4 June 2001, Rule 10.

[16] UN Security Council Resolution 2286 (2016), adopted by unanimous vote in favour on 3 May 2016, tenth preambular para.

[17] Ibid., operative para. 9.

appropriate and on a case-by-case basis, help to contribute to a secure environment to enable the delivery of medical assistance, in accordance with humanitarian principles'.[18]

In a 2019 report to the Security Council,[19] the UN Secretary-General stated that in 2018 there was further violence against medical personnel and other interference with the provision of medical care in conflict. 'Incidents included direct attacks against medical workers and facilities; the removal of medical supplies from humanitarian convoys and warehouses; and the use of medical facilities for military purposes.' The World Health Organization (WHO) recorded 705 attacks against medical facilities and workers in 2018, resulting in 451 deaths and 860 injuries in just eight conflicts: Afghanistan, Iraq, Libya, Mali, Nigeria, the Occupied Palestinian Territory, the Syrian Arab Republic, and Yemen. Explosive weapons were used in 38 per cent of those attacks.[20]

In Syria, 139 attacks on medical facilities were recorded in 2018, resulting in 101 deaths and 189 injuries. In Afghanistan, there were 90 attacks on medical facilities, killing 17 health-care workers. Seven facilities were destroyed in aerial attacks. An estimated 4.1 million people have been directly or indirectly denied medical services as a result of these incidents. The Secretary-General was also concerned at the continued criminalisation, in Syria and elsewhere, of 'the provision of medical care to wounded and sick civilians and fighters', despite the protection to these tasks afforded by IHL.[21]

The Secretary-General welcomed the launch in 2018 by Geneva Call of its Deed of Commitment on protecting health care in conflict, which provides non-State armed groups 'with an important opportunity to commit themselves to respecting the relevant rules and publicly account for their implementation'.[22] The Deed of Commitment – Geneva Call's fourth – aims to ensure, maintain, and provide access for affected populations to essential health care facilities, goods, and services, without adverse distinction; and to facilitate the provision of health care by impartial humanitarian organisations.[23]

12.3 THE PROTECTION OF HUMANITARIAN PERSONNEL

Humanitarian personnel are, in general, ordinary civilians and protected as such, unless and for such time as they participate directly in hostilities. United Nations' personnel delivering humanitarian aid in the context of a UN peacekeeping operation, however, enjoy specific protection under the 1994 Convention on the Safety of United Nations Personnel.[24] The distribution of humanitarian relief is not an act of direct participation in hostilities, even if it goes to enemy fighters. And as the ICRC has remarked, the safety and

---

[18] Ibid., operative para. 10.
[19] Protection of Civilians in Armed Conflict: Report of the Secretary-General, UN doc. S/2019/373, 7 May 2019.
[20] Ibid., para. 42.
[21] Ibid., para. 43.
[22] Ibid., para. 44.
[23] 'Geneva Call Launches an Innovative New Deed of Commitment on Protecting Health Care in Armed Conflict', Geneva, 23 November 2018, at: http://bit.ly/3ahM2ST. The text of the Deed of Commitment is available at: http://bit.ly/3cdSufs.
[24] Convention on the Safety of United Nations and Associated Personnel; adopted at New York, 9 December 1994; entered into force, 15 January 1999. As of 1 April 2022, there were 95 States party to the Convention.

security of humanitarian personnel 'is an indispensable condition for the delivery of humanitarian relief to civilian populations in need threatened with starvation'.[25]

With respect to international armed conflicts, an obligation to respect and protect humanitarian relief personnel is set out in the 1977 Additional Protocol I.[26] This means each party to the conflict must not just refrain from attacking humanitarian personnel, they must also take all reasonable measures to ensure that others do not do so. Under the Statute of the International Criminal Court, intentionally directing attacks against personnel involved in a humanitarian assistance mission in accordance with the UN Charter is a war crime in international armed conflicts, as long as such personnel are entitled to the protection given to civilians under IHL.[27] Hence, the ICRC observes, members of armed forces delivering humanitarian aid are not covered by this rule.[28]

The same problem could arise if a UN peacekeeping mission had become a party to an armed conflict, such as occurred in the Democratic Republic of Congo as a result of the actions of the Intervention Brigade within the UN Organization Stabilization Mission in the Democratic Republic of the Congo (MONUSCO).[29] Arguably, therefore, any national contingent within MONUSCO could be attacked by an adverse party to the non-international armed conflict in which the UN peacekeeping force was engaged. The personnel of UN agencies, of course, fully retain their civilian immunity and special protection under the 1994 Convention[30] and its Optional Protocol[31] even in such circumstances.

In non-international armed conflicts, the 1977 Additional Protocol II requires that relief actions for the civilian population in need be organised, but does not specifically protect humanitarian personnel.[32] Under the Rome Statute, however, intentionally directing attacks against personnel involved in a humanitarian assistance mission in accordance with the UN Charter is also a war crime in non-international armed conflicts, as long as such personnel are entitled to the protection given to civilians under IHL.[33]

In his 2019 report to the UN Security Council on the protection of civilians, the UN Secretary-General recorded that '[w]idespread and persistent constraints on humanitarian

---

[25]   ICRC, Customary IHL Rule 31: 'Humanitarian Relief Personnel', at: http://bit.ly/2Tf6a12.

[26]   Art. 71(2), 1977 Additional Protocol I.

[27]   Art. 8(2)(b)(iii), Rome Statute of the International Criminal Court.

[28]   ICRC, Customary IHL Rule 31: 'Humanitarian Relief Personnel'.

[29]   '"Intervention Brigade" Authorized as Security Council Grants Mandate Renewal for United Nations Mission in Democratic Republic of Congo', UN doc. SC/10964, 28 March 2013, at: http://bit.ly/2r8WZ8b.

[30]   Art. 7(1), Convention on the Safety of United Nations and Associated Personnel.

[31]   Optional Protocol to the Convention on the Safety of United Nations and Associated Personnel; adopted at New York, 8 December 2005; entered into force, 19 August 2010. The Optional Protocol expands the scope of protection to include operations conducted under UN authority and control that deliver 'humanitarian, political or development assistance in peacebuilding' or 'emergency humanitarian assistance'. As of 1 April 2022, there were thirty-three States party to the Optional Protocol.

[32]   Art. 18(2), 1977 Additional Protocol II. The ICRC observes that while the two 1977 Additional Protocols provide that the protection of humanitarian relief personnel applies only to 'authorised' humanitarian personnel as such, 'the overwhelming majority of practice does not specify this condition'. The notion of authorisation refers to the consent received from the party to the conflict concerned to work in areas under its control. ICRC, Customary IHL Rule 31: 'Humanitarian Relief Personnel'.

[33]   Art. 8(2)(e)(iii), Rome Statute of the International Criminal Court.

access jeopardized humanitarian operations in several conflicts in 2018'.[34] Violence against, or the detention or abduction of, humanitarian personnel, in particular national staff, continued to impede humanitarian operations in Afghanistan, the Central African Republic, the Democratic Republic of Congo, Mali, Somalia, and South Sudan, among others. In Afghanistan, for example, thirty humanitarian workers were killed in 2018 and fifty-three were injured in attacks and eighty-eight abducted. Somalia saw 130 violent incidents affecting humanitarian workers, including ten fatalities, while in South Sudan there were 760 security incidents in which fifteen humanitarian workers were killed in 2018 and 576 were relocated for security reasons, disrupting the provision of assistance for prolonged periods.[35]

The Secretary-General's 2019 report on the protection of civilians followed a report the previous year dedicated to the safety and security of humanitarian personnel and protection of UN personnel, in which he said that early warning, situational awareness, and the capacity to analyse security threats and risks remained a core priority.[36] Despite more encouraging figures, he noted that with continuing attacks against civilians and humanitarian workers in conflict areas, disregard for international humanitarian law and human rights law remains endemic. Humanitarian personnel face significant threats, including harassment, intimidation, criminality, and direct and indirect attacks, especially against front-line workers.[37]

---

[34] Protection of Civilians in Armed Conflict. Report of the Secretary-General, 2019, para. 38.
[35] Ibid., para. 40.
[36] Safety and Security of Humanitarian Personnel and Protection of United Nations Personnel. Report of the Secretary-General, UN doc. A/73/392, 24 September 2018, para. 42.
[37] Ibid., para. 7.

13

Protection of Internally Displaced Persons

13.1 INTRODUCTION

Chapter 5 addressed the protection of those who fled from persecution to seek asylum in another country, that is to say refugees under international law. This chapter concerns the prohibition on forced displacement and the protection of internally displaced persons (IDPs) who remain within their own country. Thus, IDP is a term that encompasses any civilian who has fled his or her home due to armed conflict – as well as violations of human rights and natural or human-made disasters – but who remains within the country of his or her nationality.[1]

Despite a widespread perception, IDPs do not always end up in camps for, as the Office for the Coordination of Humanitarian Affairs (OCHA) has observed, most IDPs are taken in by host families, while some find temporary shelter on the move or settle in urban areas. Moreover, IDPs often move several times during their displacement.[2] The Secretary-General of the United Nations (UN) has cited displacement as one of the world's greatest humanitarian challenges.

13.2 THE NORMATIVE FRAMEWORK

Under international human rights law, the primary responsibility for the respect and protection of IDPs, including during armed conflict, lies with the national authorities.[3] Too often, however, the State fails to meet its obligations, either wilfully or because it is unable, in the prevailing circumstances, to do so. Armed groups are bound to at least

---

[1] According to the 1998 United Nations (UN) Guiding Principles on Internal Displacement, IDPs are

> persons or groups of persons who have been forced or obliged to flee or to leave their homes or places of habitual residence, in particular as a result of or in order to avoid the effects of armed conflict, situations of generalized violence, violations of human rights or natural or human-made disasters, and who have not crossed an internationally recognized State border.

UN Guiding Principles on Internal Displacement, concluded in 1998, para. 2.

[2] OCHA, OCHA on Message: Internal Displacement, 2010, at: http://bit.ly/2wMZEXx.

[3] See, for example, *Protecting Internally Displaced Persons: A Manual for Law and Policymakers*, Brookings Institution and Bern University, United States, October 2008, p. 11.

respect the fundamental human rights of IDPs, in the view of agencies and bodies of the United Nations.[4]

Under international humanitarian law (IHL), the forced displacement of civilians is prohibited for States and non-State armed groups that are party to an armed conflict, unless the security of the civilians involved or imperative military reasons demands it. This is a rule of customary as well as conventional law.[5] The articulation of the rule by the International Committee of the Red Cross (ICRC) in its 2005 Study of Customary IHL depends on whether the conflict in question is international or non-international in character:

Rule 129.
A. Parties to an international armed conflict may not deport or forcibly transfer the civilian population of an occupied territory, in whole or in part, unless the security of the civilians involved or imperative military reasons so demand.
B. Parties to a non-international armed conflict may not order the displacement of the civilian population, in whole or in part, for reasons related to the conflict, unless the security of the civilians involved or imperative military reasons so demand.

Moreover, in each case, a serious violation of the rule attracts individual criminal responsibility under international criminal law as a war crime.[6] That said, as Erin Mooney observes, the prohibition in non-international armed conflict appears to be broader in scope than is the case in international armed conflict, wherein it is limited to situations of military occupation.[7] In addition, the deportation or forcible transfer of civilians is punishable as a crime against humanity when it is committed as part of a widespread or systematic attack directed against any civilian population, with knowledge of the attack.[8] In March 2014, Islamic State's order to all Kurdish residents to leave Tal Akhder village (Ar Raqqah) was deemed to be both a war crime and a crime against humanity by the Independent International Commission of Inquiry on Syria.[9]

In both international and non-international armed conflicts, State practice, the ICRC observes, 'establishes an exception to the prohibition of displacement in cases where the security of the civilians involved or imperative military reasons (such as clearing a combat

---

[4] See, for example, UN Assistance Mission in Afghanistan (UNAMA) Human Rights Service, *Afghanistan, Protection of Civilians in Armed Conflict: 2018 Annual Report*, UNAMA and OHCHR, Kabul, February 2019, p. 55. UN Mission in the Republic of South Sudan (UNMISS), 'Conflict in South Sudan: A Human Rights Report', 8 May 2014, p. 12, para. 18.

[5] International Committee of the Red Cross (ICRC), Customary IHL Rule 129: 'The Act of Displacement', at: http://bit.ly/2Vue9Kj.

[6] ICRC, Customary IHL Rule 156: 'Definition of War Crimes', at: http://bit.ly/32HjZb2; and Art. 8(2)(b)(viii), and (e)(viii), Rome Statute of the International Criminal Court; adopted at Rome, 17 July 1998; entered into force, 1 July 2002. See also Art. 8(2)(a)(vii), Rome Statute of the International Criminal Court.

[7] E. Mooney, 'Displacement and the Protection of Civilians under International Refugee Law', chapter 8 in H. Willmot, R. Mamiya, S. Sheeran, and M. Weller (eds.), *Protection of Civilians*, 1st ed., Oxford University Press, Oxford, 2016, p. 188.

[8] Art. 7(1)(d), Rome Statute of the International Criminal Court.

[9] Report of the Independent International Commission of Inquiry on the Syrian Arab Republic, UN doc. A/HRC/27/60, 13 August 2014, paras. 133–5; see Mooney, 'Displacement and the Protection of Civilians under International Refugee Law', p. 191.

zone) require the evacuation for as long as the conditions warranting it exist. This exception is contained in the Fourth Geneva Convention [of 1949] and [the 1977] Additional Protocol II."[10] It did not apply to Islamic State's actions in Syria, which amounted to serious violations of IHL.[11]

13.2.1 *The Guiding Principles on Internal Displacement*

Outside the African continent, there is no dedicated international treaty that concerns the protection of IDPs. The Guiding Principles on Internal Displacement were developed in the 1990s under the aegis of Francis Deng, the then Representative of the UN Secretary-General on internally displaced persons, and with the encouragement of the erstwhile UN Commission of Human Rights[12] and of the UN General Assembly. The Guiding Principles are a soft-law instrument (and are therefore not legally binding per se), though many of the principles espoused therein reflect existing rules of international human rights law and IHL. The Guiding Principles on Internal Displacement,[13] which were drafted by a team of international legal scholars chaired by Walter Kälin, were presented to the Commission on Human Rights in 1998. Today, they may generally be considered an authoritative statement of international law.[14]

Following a short introduction, the Guiding Principles comprise five sections. Section I concerns general principles. Section II addresses principles relating to protection *from* displacement. Section III pertains to principles relating to protection *during* displacement. Section IV covers principles relating to humanitarian assistance. Finally, Section V relates to principles relating to return, relocation, and reintegration. The Guiding Principles are reproduced in an Annex to this chapter but the core rules are summarised below.

13.2.1.1 General Principles

It is reiterated that IDPs enjoy, 'in full equality', the same rights and freedoms under international and domestic law as do other persons in their country. Discrimination on the basis that a person is internally displaced is unlawful. It is stated that the Principles do not restrict in any way human rights under international or domestic law or IHL rules.

Internally displaced persons have the right to request and to receive protection and humanitarian assistance from the authorities and must not be persecuted or punished for making such a request. In addition, certain IDPs (e.g. children, especially unaccompanied minors; expectant mothers; mothers with young children; female heads of household;

---

[10] ICRC, Customary IHL Rule 129: 'The Act of Displacement'.
[11] Report of the Independent International Commission of Inquiry on the Syrian Arab Republic, UN doc. A/HRC/27/60, para. 135.
[12] Commission of Human Rights Resolution 1996/52, operative para. 9. In 2010, the Commission was replaced by the Human Rights Council.
[13] UN doc. E/CN.4/1998/53/Add.2.
[14] See generally S. Bagshaw, *Developing a Normative Framework for the Protection of Internally Displaced Persons*, Transnational Publishers, Ardsley, 2005.

persons with disabilities; and older persons) are entitled to special protection and assistance and to treatment that takes account of their special needs.

13.2.1.2 Principles Relating to Protection from Displacement

Every person has the right to be protected against being arbitrarily displaced from his or
her home or place of habitual residence. Such arbitrary displacement includes displacement based on policies of *apartheid*, ethnic cleansing, or similar practices; when used as
a collective punishment; or during armed conflict, unless the security of the civilians
involved or imperative military reasons so demand. When it is not arbitrary at the outset,
displacement must last no longer than required by the circumstances and all feasible
alternatives must be explored in order to avoid displacement altogether.

The authorities undertaking displacement must ensure 'to the greatest practicable
extent' that proper accommodation is provided to the displaced persons, that such dis-
placements are effected in satisfactory conditions of safety, nutrition, health, and hygiene,
and that members of the same family are not separated. In any event, displacement must
not be carried out in a manner that violates the rights to life, dignity, liberty, and security of
those affected. States are under a particular obligation to protect against displacement
indigenous peoples, minorities, peasants, and pastoralists, among others.

13.2.1.3 Principles Relating to Protection during Displacement

The prohibition on arbitrary deprivation of life applies to every IDP. In particular, IDPs
must be protected against direct or indiscriminate attacks or other acts of violence;
starvation as a method of combat; use as human shields during hostilities; attacks against
their camps or settlements; and the use of anti-personnel mines.[15]

Every IDP also has the right to dignity and physical, mental, and moral integrity.
Accordingly, IDPs must be protected in particular against rape, mutilation, torture, or
other cruel, inhuman, or degrading treatment or punishment, and other outrages upon
personal dignity, such as acts of gender-based violence, forced prostitution, and any form
of indecent assault; slavery or any contemporary form of slavery; and acts of violence
intended to spread terror among IDPs.

Every IDP has the right to liberty and security of person. No one shall be subjected to
arbitrary arrest or detention. Accordingly, IDPs must not be interned in or confined to
a camp. If, in exceptional circumstances, such internment or confinement is absolutely
necessary, it must not last longer than required by the circumstances. In no case shall
internally displaced persons be taken hostage. Displaced children must be protected
against recruitment and participation in hostilities. Other IDPs must be protected against
discriminatory practices of recruitment into any armed forces or groups as a result of their
displacement.

---

[15]   By analogy, protection should also be provided against cluster munition remnants (in particular unexploded
submunitions) and other explosive remnants of war.

Every IDP has the right to liberty of movement and freedom to choose his or her residence. In particular, they have the right to move freely in and out of camps or other settlements. They also have the rights to seek safety in another part of the country; to leave their country; to seek asylum in another country; and to be protected against forcible return to or relocation in any place where their life, safety, liberty, or health would be at risk.

Every IDP has the right to respect of his or her family life. Accordingly, family members who wish to remain together must be allowed to do so. Families separated as a result of displacement should be reunited as quickly as possible. All appropriate steps must be taken to expedite the reunion of such families, particularly when children are involved.

At a minimum, regardless of the circumstances, and without discrimination, the authorities must provide internally displaced persons with essential food and potable water; basic shelter and housing; appropriate clothing; and essential medical services and sanitation. Special efforts should be made to ensure the full participation of women in the planning and distribution of these basic supplies.

All wounded and sick IDPs as well as those with disabilities must receive, to the fullest extent practicable and with the least possible delay, the medical care and attention they require, without distinction on any grounds other than medical ones. When necessary, internally displaced persons must have access to psychological and social services. Special attention should be paid to the health needs of women, including access to female health care providers and services, such as reproductive health care, as well as appropriate counselling for victims of sexual and other abuses. Special attention should also be given to the prevention of contagious and infectious diseases, including HIV/AIDS, among IDPs.

Every IDP has the right to recognition everywhere as a person before the law. Accordingly, the authorities concerned must issue IDPs all documents necessary for the enjoyment and exercise of their legal rights, such as passports, personal identification documents, birth certificates, and marriage certificates. In particular, the authorities must facilitate the issuance of new documents or the replacement of documents lost in the course of displacement, without imposing unreasonable conditions, such as requiring the IDP return to his or her area of habitual residence.

No IDP shall be arbitrarily deprived of property and possessions. Property and possessions left behind by internally displaced persons should be protected against destruction and arbitrary and illegal appropriation, occupation, or use.

Every IDP has the right to education. Accordingly, the authorities concerned must ensure that IDPs, in particular displaced children, receive education that is free and compulsory at the primary level. Education should respect their cultural identity, language, and religion. Special efforts should be made to ensure the full and equal participation of women and girls in educational programmes. Education and training facilities must be made available to internally displaced persons, as soon as conditions permit, in particular to adolescents and women, whether or not they are living in camps.

13.2.1.4 Principles Relating to Humanitarian Assistance

All humanitarian assistance for IDPs must respect the principles of humanity and impartiality, without discrimination. The primary duty and responsibility for providing humanitarian assistance to IDPs again lies with national authorities. Consent to international humanitarian organisations must not be arbitrarily withheld, particularly when the authorities are unable or unwilling to provide the required assistance. Those engaged in humanitarian assistance to IDPs, as well as their transport and supplies, must be respected and protected. Thus, they must not be the object of attack or other acts of violence.

13.2.1.5 Principles Relating to Return, Relocation, and Reintegration

The authorities have the primary duty and responsibility to establish conditions, as well as provide the means, to allow IDPs to return voluntarily, in safety and with dignity, either to their homes or to a place of habitual residence, or to relocate voluntarily in another part of the country. The authorities must seek to facilitate the reintegration of returned or resettled IDPs. Special efforts should be made to ensure the full participation of IDPs in planning and managing their return or relocation and reintegration. The authorities must grant and facilitate for international humanitarian organisations rapid and unimpeded access to IDPs to assist in their return or relocation and reintegration.

Internally displaced persons who have returned to their homes or places of habitual residence or who have relocated in another part of the country shall not be discriminated against as a result of their having been displaced. They have the right to participate fully and equally in public affairs at all levels and to have equal access to public services.

13.2.2 *The Kampala Convention*

The African Union Convention for the Protection and Assistance of Internally Displaced Persons in Africa (Kampala Convention) was adopted on 23 October 2009 and entered into force on 6 December 2012.[16] It is the only regional treaty dedicated to the protection of IDPs. The Kampala Convention applies the definition for IDPs set out in the Guiding Principles on Internal Displacement. The treaty is devised in an unusual manner insofar as it appears to impose human rights obligations directly on armed groups in addition to those on States. Strictly speaking, however, that is not the case: the State remains the duty bearer under the Convention.

Article 3 of the Convention sets out the general obligations upon its States Parties. In undertaking to 'respect and ensure respect' for the Convention, each State must:

a. Refrain from, prohibit and prevent arbitrary displacement of populations
b. Prevent political, social, cultural and economic exclusion and marginalisation, that are likely to cause displacement of populations or persons by virtue of their social identity, religion, or political opinion

---

[16] As of 1 April 2022, thirty-three of fifty-five African States were party to the Kampala Convention.

c. Respect and ensure respect for the principles of humanity and human dignity of internally displaced persons

d. Respect and ensure respect and protection of the human rights of internally displaced persons, including humane treatment, non-discrimination, equality, and equal protection of law

e. Respect and ensure respect for IHL regarding the protection of internally displaced persons

f. Respect and ensure respect for the humanitarian and civilian character of the protection of and assistance to IDPs, including ensuring that such persons do not engage in subversive activities

g. Ensure individual responsibility for acts of arbitrary displacement, in accordance with applicable domestic and international criminal law

h. Ensure the accountability of non-State actors concerned, including multinational companies and private military or security companies, for acts of arbitrary displacement or complicity in such acts

i. Ensure the accountability of non-State actors involved in the exploration and exploitation of economic and natural resources leading to displacement

j. Ensure assistance to IDPs by meeting their basic needs as well as allowing and facilitating rapid and unimpeded access by humanitarian organisations and personnel

k. Promote self-reliance and sustainable livelihoods among IDPs, provided that such measures shall not be used as a basis for neglecting the protection of and assistance to IDPs, without prejudice to other means of assistance.

Article 7 is entitled 'Protection and Assistance to Internally Displaced Persons in Situations of Armed Conflict'. It is stated in paragraph 3 that the protection and assistance to IDPs under the article is governed by international law and in particular IHL. The article continues as follows:

4. Members of armed groups shall be held criminally responsible for their acts which violate the rights of IDPs under international law and national law.

5. Members of armed groups shall be prohibited from:

   a. Carrying out arbitrary displacement

   b. Hampering the provision of protection and assistance to IDPs under any circumstances

   c. Denying IDPs the right to live in satisfactory conditions of dignity, security, sanitation, food, water, health, and shelter; and separating members of the same family

   d. Restricting the freedom of movement of IDPs within and outside their areas of residence

   e. Recruiting children or requiring or permitting them to take part in hostilities under any circumstances

   f. Forcibly recruiting persons, kidnapping, abduction, or hostage taking, engaging in sexual slavery and trafficking in persons, especially women and children

g. Impeding humanitarian assistance and passage of all relief consignments, equip-ment and personnel to IDPs

h. Attacking or otherwise harming humanitarian personnel and resources or other materials deployed for the assistance or benefit of IDPs and shall not destroy, confiscate or divert such materials

i. Violating the civilian and humanitarian character of the places where IDPs are sheltered and shall not infiltrate such places.

In fact, the formulations 'shall be held criminally responsible for their acts' and 'shall be prohibited from' mean that the obligations under the Kampala Convention remain on the States Parties to prohibit the acts of armed groups and do not directly bind the armed groups themselves. That said, the text of Article 7 of the Kampala Convention certainly moves towards imposing human rights obligations directly on such groups.

In 2016, the ICRC conducted a study of the practice of twenty-five African nations in which the organisation was operating (both States Parties and States not party to the Kampala Convention) who have taken action on internal displacement in the form of normative, policy, or concrete measures. The focus was on those obligations that are grounded in IHL.[17] With respect to the protection of IDPs, the ICRC made a set of five recommendations, four directed to States and the fifth to 'other actors'.

The ICRC called on States to ensure that all relevant public authorities – including their armed and security forces – are fully informed of their obligations and instructed to facilitate freedom of movement and residence of IDPs. Public authorities should further develop adequate capacities at central and local levels to create and maintain an updated register of all IDPs with a view to generating an agreed-upon baseline for all the actors concerned. The authorities should seek to allocate adequate efforts and resources to ensure that IDPs are able to obtain personal identity documents and other official documents, within a reasonable time. Finally, the authorities should also 'strengthen their laws, policies and concrete measures to ensure that the civilian and humanitarian character of IDP sites is maintained'.[18]

The ICRC also recommended that international and humanitarian actors should provide coordinated support to States to ensure a practical and effective system to address family tracing and family reunification needs.

In fact, taken in the round, the ICRC's recommendations appear rather ancillary to the protection of IDPs: potentially valuable, but rather indirectly so. Moreover, there was no recommendation addressed to armed groups on the protection of IDPs, although the ICRC explains that the report's focus on States meant 'it was not possible' to examine the obligations of non-State armed groups, defined as 'armed groups' and 'non-State actors' in the Kampala Convention. 'These obligations were clearly considered important by Member States when negotiating and adopting the Convention, and remain so today.'[19]

---

[17] ‘Translating the Kampala Convention into Practice: A Stocktaking Exercise’, *International Review of the Red Cross*, Vol. 99, No. 1 (2017), 365–420, at p. 365.

[18] Ibid., p. 372.

[19] Ibid., p. 380.

The ICRC concluded its assessment of the implementation of the Kampala Convention with the following statement:

> The comprehensive legal framework of the Kampala Convention offers African States the opportunity to improve the daily quality of life for IDPs across the continent by addressing their protection and assistance needs effectively. States can prevent, address and reduce displacement by methodically and comprehensively implementing the Convention. They can ensure that, when displacement occurs, IDPs are provided with assistance and treated with respect for their human dignity and their rights.[20]

The challenge is certainly there. In December 2019, the Internal Displacement Monitoring Centre (IDMC) launched a report that declared that internal displacement in Africa had reached unprecedented levels, with nearly 17 million people living in a situation of displacement within their own countries in Africa by the end of 2018. 'This is the highest figure ever recorded for the continent, and around 40 per cent of the global total.' The scale of displacement, the IDMC declared, 'is likely to continue unabated'.[21]

---

[20] Ibid., p. 419.
[21] IDMC, 'Internal Displacement in Africa Has Reached Unprecedented Levels', Geneva, 6 December 2019, at: http://bit.ly/39kZo1K.

14

Protection of LGBTI Civilians

14.1 INTRODUCTION

Lesbian, gay, bisexual, trans, and intersex (LGBTI) persons are at particular risk of being targeted in situations of violence because of their gender or sexual preference. Discrimination against LGBTI persons could be based on sexual orientation (to whom someone is attracted); gender identity (how people define themselves, irrespective of biological sex); gender expression (how gender is expressed, through clothing, hair, or make-up); or sex characteristics (for example, genitals, chromosomes, reproductive organs, or hormone levels.)[1]

A person's sexual orientation refers to who they are attracted to and with whom they form relationships. Sexual orientations include lesbian (women who are attracted to women); gay (usually men who are attracted to other men); bisexual (attracted to men and women); pansexual (attracted to individuals, regardless of gender); and asexual (not sexually attracted to anyone). Transgender (or trans) people are individuals whose gender identity or gender expression is different from typical expectations of the gender they were assigned at birth. Not all transgender people identify as male or female: some identify as more than one gender or no gender at all. Being transgender has nothing to do with a person's sexual orientation: you can be a trans man and be gay, or be a trans woman and be lesbian. When someone is born with sex characteristics that differ from what is typically seen as female or male traits, they are known as intersex.[2]

The United Nations (UN) Special Rapporteur on extrajudicial, summary, or arbitrary executions has observed that LGBT persons are 'especially vulnerable' to extrajudicial killings.[3] The human rights duty of due diligence requires States to do all they reasonably can to ensure the protection of those at particular risk of violence, including those targeted because of their sexual orientation and gender identity.[4]

---

[1] Amnesty International, 'LGBTI Rights', undated but accessed 24 October 2020, at: http://bit.ly/3jsdAZA.
[2] Ibid.
[3] Report of the Special Rapporteur on extrajudicial, summary or arbitrary executions, Addendum: Follow-up country recommendations: Colombia, UN doc. A/HRC/20/22/Add.2, 15 May 2012, para. 51.
[4] Office of the United Nations High Commissioner for Human Rights (OHCHR), 'Discrimination and Violence against Individuals Based on Their Sexual Orientation and Gender Identity', Report of the Office of the United Nations High Commissioner for Human Rights, UN doc. A/HRC/29/23, 4 May 2015, para. 20.

In a 2015 report to the Human Rights Council, the Office of the United Nations High Commissioner for Human Rights (OHCHR) noted that hate-motivated killings of LGBT individuals have been documented in all regions.[5] Such violence may be physical (including murder, beatings, kidnapping, and sexual assault) or psychological (including threats, coercion, and the arbitrary deprivation of liberty, including forced psychiatric incarceration). These attacks, the OHCHR has affirmed, 'constitute a form of gender-based violence, driven by a desire to punish individuals whose appearance or behaviour appears to challenge gender stereotypes'.[6] 'Violence motivated by homophobia and transphobia is often particularly brutal, and in some instances characterized by levels of cruelty exceeding that of other hate crimes.' Violent acts reported by the OHCHR include 'deep knife cuts, anal rape and genital mutilation, as well as stoning and dismemberment'.[7]

In 2020, the UN Independent Expert on protection against violence and discrimination based on sexual orientation and gender identity, Victor Madrigal-Borloz, told the UN General Assembly that information he had received corroborated the view that the response to the global COVID-19 pandemic 'reproduces and exacerbates the patterns of discrimination, social exclusion and violence' against LBGTI persons.[8] The Independent Expert is tasked with investigating attacks on lesbian, gay, bisexual, trans, intersex, and gender diverse individuals.

The position of the Independent Expert was created by the UN Human Rights Council in 2016.[9] In the resolution that established the position, supportive States strongly deplored the 'acts of violence and discrimination, in all regions of the world, committed against individuals because of their sexual orientation or gender identity'.[10] As the Expert has established, 'the structural vulnerability of LGBT and gender-diverse persons may be compounded by their status as migrants, asylum seekers and refugees. As they flee discrimination and violence at home, they may be at particular risk of violence, abuse and exploitation at all stages of their journey and at the hands of immigration officers, traffickers and smugglers.'[11]

14.2 ATTACKS AGAINST LGBTI CIVILIANS IN ARMED CONFLICT

While information on attacks against LGBTI civilians in armed conflict is sporadic and specific protection efforts continue to be relatively limited – a 'blind spot', in the view of

---

[5] Ibid., para. 36.
[6] Ibid., para. 21.
[7] Ibid., para. 23.
[8] Statement by Victor-Madrigal Borloz, UN Independent Expert on protection against violence and discrimination based on sexual orientation and gender identity at the 75th UN General Assembly.
[9] Human Rights Council Resolution 32/2, adopted on 30 June 2016 by twenty-three votes in favour to eighteen (Algeria, Bangladesh, Burundi, China, Congo, Côte d'Ivoire, Ethiopia, Indonesia, Kenya, Kyrgyzstan, Maldives, Morocco, Nigeria, Qatar, Russian Federation, Saudi Arabia, Togo, and United Arab Emirates), with six abstentions, operative para. 3.
[10] Ibid., operative para. 2.
[11] Report of the Independent Expert on protection against violence and discrimination based on sexual orientation and gender identity, UN doc. A/74/181, 17 July 2019, para. 52.

one expert[12] – it seems clear that the existence of an armed conflict acts as an exacerbatory factor for such violence.[13] This is especially the case with certain terrorist groups, such as Islamic State, which manifested an egregious approach to the treatment of, especially, homosexuals within its sphere of influence.[14] Gay men were targeted on the basis of their sexuality and killed, with reports indicating that such conduct was 'indicative of a broader pattern' of the group's treatment of homosexual men. Islamic State courts claimed to punish sodomy with stoning, firing squads, beheadings, and by pushing men off tall buildings.[15] As the Independent International Commission on Syria stated: 'Such killings constitute murder as a war crime, and a crime against humanity.'[16]

In addition to men perceived as gay, trans-identified people and lesbians were among those who faced threats of rape and murder at the hands of Islamic State.[17] In July 2020, Human Rights Watch published a report on sexual violence against men, boys, and transgender women in the Syrian conflict.[18] The report observed that in detention centres, detainees were subject to intensified interrogation or torture if their sexual or gender identity was exposed. Sexual violence also took place within the ranks of the Syrian army. Interviewees described being subject to rape, genital violence, threat of rape, forced nudity, and sexual harassment. The survivors who fled to Lebanon told Human Rights Watch they found limited services and inadequate support from humanitarian organisations that are often poorly funded and not equipped to meet the needs of male survivors of sexual violence. Service providers often lack training in response to male survivors and some belittle them, which contributes to poor treatment and re-traumatization of those seeking help.[19]

Violence against LGBTI civilians has also been perpetrated in other conflicts and situations of violence. Thus, for example, as of writing, a number of cases were pending before the European Court of Human Rights for alleged ill-treatment in violation of Article 3 of the European Convention on Human Rights against LGBTI persons in Chechnya. The case of *Lapunov* v. *Russia* concerns allegations of abduction, imprisonment, and ill-treatment by State agents in the region in March 2017 on the grounds of his homosexuality.[20] During detention, he alleges that guards

---

[12]   A. Margalit, 'Still a Blind Spot: The Protection of LGBT Persons during Armed Conflict and Other Situations of Violence', *International Review of the Red Cross*, Vol. 100, Nos. 1–3 (2018), 237–65, at: https://bit.ly/3qQRHY2.

[13]   Ibid., p. 238.

[14]   J. Stern, 'The UN Security Council's Arria-Formula Meeting on Vulnerable Groups in Conflict: ISIL's Targeting of LGBTI Individuals', *New York University Journal of International Law and Politics*, Vol. 48, No. 4 (Summer 2016), 1191.

[15]   Ibid., p. 1195.

[16]   Independent International Commission on Syria, UN doc. A/HRC/28/69, 5 February 2015, para. 189.

[17]   Stern, 'The UN Security Council's Arria-Formula Meeting on Vulnerable Groups in Conflict: ISIL's Targeting of LGBTI Individuals', p. 1196.

[18]   Human Rights Watch, '"They Treated Us in Monstrous Ways": Sexual Violence Against Men, Boys, and Transgender Women in the Syrian Conflict', 29 July 2020, at: http://bit.ly/3t53Bjc.

[19]   Ibid.

[20]   European Court of Human Rights, *Lapunov* v. *Russia* (Appl. no. 28834/19), Communicated on 14 November 2019, at: http://bit.ly/2HvuJVh.

armed with water pipes beat him up saying that they were punishing him for his homosexuality and for him having sexual intercourse with Chechens. One of the perpetrators tried to abuse him sexually, but the applicant resisted. Dozens of strokes with water pipe had been administered by the perpetrators on the applicant, particularly on his buttocks. The perpetrators hit his hand with a piece of water pipe. The blood from the hand stained the cell wall.[21]

14.3 LGBTI PERSONS AND THE DEATH PENALTY

The Human Rights Committee has made it explicit that: 'Under no circumstances can the death penalty ever be applied as a sanction against conduct the very criminalization of which violates the Covenant.' This includes not only homosexuality, but also sexual activities by other LGBTI persons.[22] States Parties that retain the death penalty for such 'offences', the Committee affirms, violate their obligations to respect and protect the right to life under International Covenant on Civil and Political Rights.[23] The prohibition on executing LGBTI persons on the basis of their gender or sexual identity is not only a customary rule, but it is also a peremptory norm of international law.[24]

Amnesty International has stated that it has had no reports of executions under anti-homosexuality laws in the past few years.[25] In April 2019, Brunei introduced a law that made sex between men a crime punishable by stoning to death. The following month, however, Sultan Hassanal Bolkiah extended a moratorium on the death penalty to cover the new legislation.[26] In October 2019, Ugandan members of parliament pressed for the death penalty to be imposed for homosexual acts.[27]

---

[21] Ibid., para. 20.

[22] Human Rights Committee, General Comment 36 on the right to life, para. 36.

[23] Ibid.

[24] S. Casey-Maslen, *The Right to Life under International Law: An Interpretive Manual*, Cambridge University Press, Cambridge, 2021, para. 24.14.

[25] BBC, 'Brunei Stoning: Which Places Have the Death Penalty for Gay Sex?', 3 April 2019, at: http://bbc.in/3dQrKTm.

[26] BBC, 'Brunei Says it Won't Enforce Death Penalty for Gay Sex', 6 May 2019, at: http://bbc.in/3dTLsNR. Lesbian sex carries a penalty of forty strokes of the cane and/or a maximum of ten years' imprisonment.

[27] J. Burke and S. Okiror, 'Ugandan MPs Press for Death Penalty for Homosexual Acts', *Guardian*, 15 October 2019, at: http://bit.ly/3eos1mH.

State and Institutional Policies on the Protection of Civilians

The third part of the book describes and reviews policies on the protection of civilians by international and regional organisations and key States. Policy within the United Nations is considered first, looking at both the mandates to protect civilians in peace operations and the protection work and policies of key UN agencies and bodies. Subsequently, specific and related policies and practices of the North Atlantic Treaty Organization (NATO), the African Union (AU), and the European Union (EU) on the protection of civilians are addressed in turn.[1] The key role of the International Committee of the Red Cross (ICRC), the largest humanitarian organisation in the world, in the promotion of international humanitarian law (IHL) and protection is then described.

Leading States' policies and positions on the protection of civilians are then analysed. Only two States – Switzerland and the United Kingdom – have specific policies on the protection of civilians (PoC). These policies are useful political signals that Switzerland and the United Kingdom take the protection of civilians seriously and that they are focusing their efforts in this regard. Both policies, however, tend to represent an overall direction without specifying and prioritising concrete measures. The United States does not have a specific or overarching policy on the protection of civilians yet has a well-established framework and practice to mitigate civilian harm. Besides these States, Brazil, India, and Norway have issued positions on or related to the protection of civilians, in particular at the UN Security Council. The following chapters analyse these positions, mainly relying on the States' statements at the debate on the protection of civilians at the Security Council in 2020, which are indicative of current positions yet also informative of potential future directions of the concept of protection of civilians.

---

[1] While international organisations such as the Arab League, the Association of Southeast Asian Nations (ASEAN), the Organization of American States (OAS), and the Organisation of Islamic Cooperation (OIC) have all condemned attacks on civilians and supported compliance with IHL, as of writing none had a formal, dedicated strategy or policy in place on the protection of civilians. See, for example, OAS, 'Department of International Law: International Humanitarian Law', at: http://bit.ly/3oxAC48; OIC, 'OIC Strongly Condemns Continued Targeting of Civilians in Aleppo by Syrian Government and its Allies', 3 August 2016, at: https://bit.ly/3cqXPlM; M. Caballero-Anthony, 'Developing a "Protection of Civilians" Agenda for Southeast Asia', Center for Non-Traditional Security Studies, Issue No. 5, 2011, at: https://bit.ly/2YmfHWV; and M. Caballero-Anthony, 'The Responsibility to Protect in Southeast Asia: Opening Up Spaces for Advancing Human Security', The Pacific Review, Vol. 25, No. 1 (2012), pp. 113–34.

15

The United Nations and the Protection of Civilians

15.1 INTRODUCTION

This chapter outlines and discusses the policies and practices relating to the protection of civilians within the United Nations (UN) system. First, it reviews the policy work of the Department of Peace Operations (DPO) with respect to UN peace operations.[2] It then considers efforts to protect civilians by a range of UN agencies and bodies. These include, in particular, the Office for the Coordination of Humanitarian Affairs (OCHA), which is responsible for drafting the Secretary-General's reports to the Security Council on the protection of civilians; the Office of the High Commissioner for Human Rights (OHCHR), which engages in protection at field level as well as providing guidance on international standards; the United Nations Children's Fund (UNICEF), which seeks to protect children affected by armed conflict; the Office of the High Commissioner for Refugees (UNHCR); and the World Food Programme (WFP).

Despite the critical involvement of UN organs, agencies, and bodies in the protection of civilians, there is no system-wide dedicated strategy on how the UN system and the international community should act to protect civilians. As the DPO has observed, no UN-wide definition of what constitutes 'protection of civilians' exists.[3] Experts have suggested that the absence of an overarching strategy is, in large part, due to the politicisation of the issue,[4] especially as a consequence of the controversies surrounding the North Atlantic Treaty Organization (NATO) operation in Libya in 2011. There are also broader concerns in certain non-aligned States about the concept as a manifestation

---

[2] The DPO provides political and executive direction to UN peacekeeping operations around the world and maintains contact with the UN Security Council, troop and financial contributors, and parties to the conflict in the implementation of Security Council mandates. It was formally created in 1992 as the Department of Peacekeeping Operations (DPKO) when Boutros Boutros-Ghali took office as UN Secretary-General. UN, 'Department of Peace Operations', at: http://bit.ly/3iUkPel. For a history of the protection of civilians in UN peacekeeping, see C. Foley, *UN Peacekeeping Operations and the Protection of Civilians: Saving Succeeding Generations*, 1st ed., Cambridge University Press, Cambridge, 2017.

[3] DPO, *The Protection of Civilians in United Nations Peacekeeping*, Policy, New York, 1 November 2019 (hereinafter, 2019 DPO Policy on the Protection of Civilians in UN Peacekeeping), para. 14.

[4] That said, terrorism also remains a highly contested issue, with no agreement among States as to even the definition of terrorism, and yet a global strategy was adopted in 2006. UN Global Counter-Terrorism Strategy, adopted by UN General Assembly Resolution 60/288, adopted by consensus on 8 September 2006.

of Western hegemony.[5] Some question the value of such a strategy. But others decry the focus on use of force in UN peacekeeping to protect civilians, to the apparent detriment of political approaches,[6] or, worse, suggest that the desire to protect civilians is little more than tokenistic. The latter claim is wrong, even if the rhetoric often surpasses the practice.

15.2 THE PROTECTION OF CIVILIANS IN UN PEACEKEEPING MISSIONS

After the disasters in Rwanda and Bosnia and Herzegovina in the 1990s, and the criticism of the 'lessons-learned' reports that followed, the Brahimi Report, published in 2000, proposed a new understanding of the notion of impartiality in UN peacekeeping. The Report identified key areas in which the UN, specifically in its peacekeeping missions, had been either too slow or too fragmented to tackle the conflicts efficiently.[7] In particular, it identified the need for clear, credible, and achievable mandates as well as the need for improved consultation and cooperation between countries.[8]

The Report stated clearly that:

> Impartiality for United Nations operations must . . . mean adherence to the principles of the Charter: where one party to a peace agreement clearly and incontrovertibly is violating its terms, continued equal treatment of all parties by the United Nations can in the best case result in ineffectiveness and in the worst may amount to complicity with evil. No failure did more to damage the standing and credibility of United Nations peacekeeping in the 1990s than its reluctance to distinguish victim from aggressor.[9]

Following the Report, the Security Council emphasised the need for peacekeeping operations to be mandated in a manner appropriate to the situation on the ground, including when considering factors such as 'the potential need to protect civilians' in Resolution 1327.[10]

This new 'robust' impartiality was articulated in the 'Capstone Doctrine' – the Principles and Guidelines for UN peacekeeping issued in 2008.[11] This document is, in Paddon Rhoads' words, 'the first and only attempt' by the UN to develop a comprehensive peacekeeping doctrine.[12] The Capstone Doctrine makes it manifest that force may – and indeed should – be used 'proactively' to implement the duty to protect civilians:

> The environments into which United Nations peacekeeping operations are deployed are often characterized by the presence of militias, criminal gangs, and other spoilers who may actively seek to undermine the peace process or pose a threat to the civilian

---

[5]   See on this issue E. Paddon Rhoads, *Taking Sides in Peacekeeping, Impartiality and the Future of the United Nations*, Oxford University Press, Oxford, 2016, p. 101.

[6]   Ibid., pp. 102–3.

[7]   UN Press Release, GA/AB/3414, 30 November 2000.

[8]   C. Gray, 'Peacekeeping After the Brahimi Report: Is There a Crisis of Credibility For the UN?', *Journal of Conflict and Security Law*, 2001, 267–88, at p. 269.

[9]   'Report of the Panel on United Nations Peace Operations', UN docs. A/55/305 and S/2000/809, 31 August 2000, at: https://bit.ly/2MdpEn7, p. ix.

[10]   UN Security Council Resolution 1327, Annex II.

[11]   United Nations Peacekeeping Operations Principles and Guidelines ('the Capstone Doctrine'), New York, 2008, at: https://bit.ly/3aaJxDq.

[12]   Paddon Rhoads, *Taking Sides in Peacekeeping, Impartiality and the Future of the United Nations*, p. 65.

population. In such situations, the Security Council has given United Nations peacekeeping operations 'robust' mandates authorizing them to 'use all necessary means' to deter forceful attempts to disrupt the political process, protect civilians under imminent threat of physical attack, and/or assist the national authorities in maintaining law and order. By proactively using force in defense of their mandates, these United Nations peacekeeping operations have succeeded in improving the security situation and creating an environment conducive to longer-term peacebuilding in the countries where they are deployed.[13]

Impartiality is described in the Capstone Doctrine as 'crucial to maintaining the consent and cooperation of the main parties, but should not be confused with neutrality or inactivity'.[14] Thus, the Doctrine refocused the use of force, not as a tool to defeat belligerent parties, but with the purpose of protecting peacekeepers, the mission mandate and, importantly, the civilian population,[15] introducing the concept of 'robust peacekeeping'. However, the Doctrine was criticised for not according sufficient attention to the means by which civilians could be protected. From a practical standpoint, the type of capacities the UN would have at its disposal to meaningfully protect civilians – techniques, tactics, and procedures – were omitted from the document.[16] The result has thus been called 'a collective denial of the mismatch between the doctrine and practice'.[17]

The Kigali Principles, which emanate from the 2015 High-Level International Conference on the Protection of Civilians, aim to promote the effective implementation of the protection of civilians in UN peacekeeping.[18] In particular, under Principle 3 the signatories pledge: 'To be prepared to use force to protect civilians, as necessary and consistent with the mandate. Such action encompasses making a show of force as a deterrent; interpositioning our forces between armed actors and civilians; and taking direct military action against armed actors with clear hostile intent to harm civilians."[19] Similarly, Principles 8 and 13, respectively, require peacekeepers 'not to hesitate to take action to protect civilians'; while calling for 'disciplinary action' against UN personnel 'if and when they fail to act to protect civilians'.[20] According to critics, this assumes that UN

[13] Capstone Doctrine, p. 34.

[14] At: http://bit.ly/2VTa7t6.

[15] B. Gerchicoff, 'Keeping Capstone in Context: Evaluating the Peacekeeping Doctrine', *Strategic Analysis*, 2013, 729–41, at p. 738.

[16] C. de Coning, J. Detzel, and P. Hojem, 'UN Peacekeeping Operations Capstone Doctrine: Report of the TfP Oslo Doctrine Seminar, 14 and 15 May 2008, Oslo, Norway', Report, *Norwegian Institute of International Affairs*, 2008, 5.

[17] M. Peter, 'Between Doctrine and Practice: The UN Peacekeeping Dilemma', *Global Governance*, 2015, 351–70, at p. 352.

[18] The Kigali Principles on the Protection of Civilians are a non-binding set of eighteen pledges for the effective and thorough implementation of the protection of civilians in UN peacekeeping. The Principles emanated from the High-Level International Conference on the Protection of Civilians held in Rwanda on 28–9 May 2015. The text of the Principles is available at: http://bit.ly/3kaQFDA.

[19] The Kigali Principles had been endorsed, as of 13 April 2020, by the following UN Member States: Australia, Austria, Bangladesh, Belgium, Bulgaria, Burkina Faso, Canada, Djibouti, Egypt, Estonia, Ethiopia, Finland, France, Germany, Ghana, Guinea, Ireland, Italy, Kenya, Latvia, Lithuania, Malawi, Montenegro, Nepal, the Netherlands, Niger, North Macedonia, Norway, Poland, Romania, Rwanda, Senegal, Slovenia, Sri Lanka, Sweden, Tanzania, Thailand, Togo, Ukraine, Uganda, the United Kingdom, the United States, Uruguay, and Zambia.

[20] Kigali Principles, Principles 8 and 13.

peacekeeping forces will be more effective if they use greater or more proactive force when protecting civilians.[21] In practice, however, the reality of peacekeeping missions is that force is only rarely used to protect civilians under attack.[22]

From a legal perspective, all current UN peacekeeping missions have the explicit or implicit mandate to protect civilians.[23] The *Leuven Manual on the International Law Applicable to Peace Operations* asserts that peace operations have the legal obligation to protect civilians even when the mission does not have the mandate to do so.[24] Indeed, protecting civilians is the central rationale of most current peace operations.[25] As such, peacekeepers may use force in self-defence, defence of others, and in defence of the mandate, although the delimitations of these legal constructs are not perfectly clear.[26] Unless international humanitarian law is applicable, such use of force needs to be in conformity with the law-enforcement paradigm according to international human rights law.

Overall, the legitimacy of peacekeeping operations has been increasingly linked to the ability to protect civilians. Indeed, it has been argued that there is 'no more compelling or credible stance for a mission than to advocate for the most vulnerable'.[27] This extends to the need to strengthen action to prevent UN personnel from preying on the very civilians they are supposed to be protecting.[28] Yet also more generally, peace operations continue to face major challenges in their efforts to protect civilians. In July 2018, thirty-two States wrote to UN Secretary-General António Guterres to urge him to do more to ensure that UN peace operations act to protect civilians.[29] In this vein, peace operations' ability to effectively protect civilians remains debated and continues to be examined.[30]

---

[21] L. Howard, 'Peacekeeping is Not Counterinsurgency', *International Peacekeeping*, 2019, 545–8, at p. 545.

[22] See, for example, the Report of the Office of Internal Oversight Services, UN doc. A/64/787, 7 March 2014.

[23] T. Gill, D. Fleck, W. Boothby, and A. Vanheusden (eds.), *Leuven Manual on the International Law Applicable to Peace Operations*, 1st ed., Cambridge University Press, Cambridge, 2017, pp. 176, 178.

[24] Ibid.

[25] F. Mégret, 'The "Protection of Civilians": Peacekeeping's New *Raison d'Être*?', in A. Barros and M. Thomas (eds.), *The Civilianization of War: The Changing Civil–Military Divide, 1914–2014*, 1st ed., Cambridge University Press, Cambridge, 2020.

[26] T. Vestner and A. Amoroso, 'Book Review: The *Leuven Manual on the International Law Applicable to Peace Operations*', *International Review of the Red Cross*, Vol. 100, No. 907–9 (2019), 429–36, at pp. 433–4.

[27] V. Holt and G. Taylor, with M. Kelly, Protecting Civilians in the Context of UN Peacekeeping Operations: Successes, Setbacks and Remaining Challenges, Independent study jointly commissioned by DPKO and OCHA, New York, 2009, at: https://bit.ly/3Fb3k42, p. 16; see also C. T. Hunt, 'Analysing the Co-Evolution of the Responsibility to Protect and the Protection of Civilians in UN Peace Operations', *International Peacekeeping*, 2019, 630–59, at p. 651.

[28] T. Donais and E. Tanguay, 'Protection of Civilians and Peacekeeping's Accountability Deficit', *International Peacekeeping*, 2021, 553–78, at p. 555.

[29] Letter of 31 July 2018 to the UN Secretary-General, signed by Australia, Austria, Belgium, Benin, Burkina Faso, Canada, Côte d'Ivoire, Djibouti, Estonia, Finland, France, Ireland, Latvia, the Former Yugoslav Republic of Macedonia (now North Macedonia), Malawi, Montenegro, the Netherlands, New Zealand, Norway, Poland, Portugal, Romania, Rwanda, Slovakia, Slovenia, Sweden, Togo, Uganda, Ukraine, the United Kingdom, the United States, and Uruguay.

[30] See, for example, A. Carnegie and C. Mikulaschek, 'The Promise of Peacekeeping: Protecting Civilians in Civil Wars', *International Organization*, Vol. 74, No. 4 (2020), 810–32; I. Bode and J. Karlsrud, 'Implementation in Practice: The Use of Force to Protect Civilians in United Nations Peacekeeping', *European Journal of International Relations*, Vol. 25, No. 2 (2018), 458–85; A. Shesterinina and B. L. Job,

15.2.1 *The 2019 DPO Policy*

The DPO's latest policy on the protection of civilians in UN peacekeeping[31] was published in November 2019, with the aim of providing the conceptual framework, guiding principles, and key considerations for the implementation of protection of civilians mandates by UN peacekeeping operations. The 2019 Policy updates and replaces the first UN Department of Peacekeeping Operations (DPKO) Policy on the Protection of Civilians in United Nations Peacekeeping, which was issued in 2015.[32] Compliance with the new DPO Policy is stipulated to be mandatory for all UN personnel, whether civilian or uniformed, who are working in any UN peacekeeping operation with a mandate to protect civilians.[33]

The Policy considers protection narrowly – considerably narrower than the longstanding Inter-Agency Standing Committee (IASC) definition of protection – as being limited to an (imminent) threat of physical violence against civilians.[34] According to paragraph 23 of the DPO Policy:

> Such threats encompass all hostile acts or situations which are likely to lead to death or serious bodily injury of civilians, including sexual violence, regardless of the source of the threat. This includes, inter alia, threats posed by non-state armed groups, self-defence groups, domestic and foreign State defence and security forces and other State agents and State-sponsored armed actors, as well as extremist groups and communities. It includes both direct and indiscriminate attacks, and attempts to kill, torture, maim, rape or sexually exploit, forcibly displace, starve, pillage, abduct or arbitrarily detain, kidnap, disappear or traffic persons or recruit and use children. It also includes harm associated with the presence of explosive ordnance including mines, explosive remnants of war and improvised explosive devices. 'Threat' includes both violence against civilians which has materialised and is ongoing and violence which has the realistic potential to occur. The threat need not be imminent, unless the specific Security Council mandate requires this.

That said, the protection provided by a UN peacekeeping operation includes, 'where necessary, the use of force, up to and including deadly force'.[35] In line with the definition under international humanitarian law (IHL), for the purposes of the DPO Policy, civilians are considered to be every person except a member of State armed forces.[36] Further excluded from the definition of a civilian, however, are 'members of an organized armed group with continuous combat function'; and 'civilians directly participating in

---

'Particularized Protection: UNSC Mandates and the Protection of Civilians in Armed Conflict', *International Peacekeeping*, Vol. 23, No. 2 (2016), 240–73; L. Hultman, 'UN Peace Operations and Protection of Civilians: Cheap Talk or Norm Implementation?', *Journal of Peace Research*, Vol. 50, No. 1 (2012), 59–73.

[31] DPO, *The Protection of Civilians in United Nations Peacekeeping*, Policy, New York, 1 November 2019 (hereinafter, 2019 DPO Policy on the Protection of Civilians in UN Peacekeeping).

[32] 2019 DPO Policy on the Protection of Civilians in UN Peacekeeping, para. 10.

[33] Ibid., para. 2.

[34] Ibid., para. 16.

[35] Ibid.

[36] See International Committee of the Red Cross (ICRC), Customary IHL Rule 5: 'Definition of Civilians', at: http://bit.ly/34KPPVO.

hostilities, for such time as they do so'.[37] Appropriately, the DPO Policy clarifies that the definition it employs is without prejudice to the definition of 'civilian' under IHL, as the obligation of UN forces to comply with the principles of distinction, proportionality, and precaution is 'independent of the PoC mandate'.[38]

15.2.1.1 General Principles of Action

As general principles of action, the DPO Policy emphasises that the approach to the protection of civilians must be both 'comprehensive' and 'integrated'. By this is meant that UN action must address short- and long-term factors which influence and underpin threats to civilians, including political, security, and economic factors. This comprehensive approach is, in turn, facilitated by internal UN coordination, combining the efforts of all the components of a peacekeeping mission (civilian, police, and the military), along with, 'where relevant and appropriate', coordination with other UN actors, including the UN Country Team.[39]

This approach seeks to embrace the engagement of the international community as a whole. The Policy thus recognises that peacekeepers will be judged on their success in protecting civilians, noting that: 'This challenging mandate is often the yardstick by which the international community, and those whom we endeavour to protect, judge our worth as peacekeepers.'[40]

According to the new Policy, the most effective form of protection is by addressing the root causes of armed conflict. This ambitious aim explicitly encompasses action to promote gender equality, with the Policy suggesting that 'proactive' protection of civilians by peacekeeping operations 'can enable inclusive political processes and facilitate meaningful participation, including by women and youth, in decision-making and peace and security processes'.[41] It can also, the Policy asserts, 'mitigate harm to civilian populations while those processes may be stalled'.[42]

At the same time, the Policy recognises that UN action is only feasible within the available capacities of the peacekeeping operations and its area of deployment. Nonetheless, the Policy stipulates,

> missions must always prevent and respond, if possible, to threats of physical violence against civilians where they have the capability to do so effectively, including where this can be done through advocacy and political engagement activities which may not require physical presence in the area at risk. Where a threat to civilians is in proximity to a mission presence or base, the mission must intervene within its capabilities.[43]

---

[37] 2019 DPO Policy on the Protection of Civilians in UN Peacekeeping, para. 21.
[38] Ibid., para. 22.
[39] Ibid., para. 8.
[40] UN DPO, Webpage on protection of civilians, available at: https://bit.ly/3uqia1S.
[41] 2019 DPO Policy on the Protection of Civilians in UN Peacekeeping, para. 13.
[42] Ibid.
[43] Ibid., para. 25.

15.2.1.2 Principles of Implementation of Protection of Civilians Mandates

A series of principles for action guide more specifically the protection of civilians by a UN peacekeeping mission. The list of principles is long, with the application of each likely to prove challenging in practice. The policy states that:

> ➤ Action taken must comply with both the letter and spirit of IHL, international human rights law, and international refugee law 'and related standards'
> ➤ The protection of civilians must be prioritised in decisions on the allocation and use of capabilities and resources
> ➤ The host State 'always' has the primary responsibility to protect civilians on its territory. When supporting host State security forces or other non-UN security forces, peacekeeping operations must respect the UN Human Rights due diligence policy on UN Support to State security forces
> ➤ Peacekeeping operations must comply with three inter-related and mutually reinforcing principles: consent of the parties, impartiality, and non-use of force (except in self-defence and defence of the mandate)
> ➤ Senior leaders in missions and in UN Headquarters are ultimately accountable for the implementation of the protection of civilians mandate
> ➤ There is an 'active duty to protect': all mission components must constantly work to prevent, pre-empt, and respond to threats to civilians, and not just react to attacks[44]
> ➤ The protection of civilians is a 'whole-of-mission' activity: all components must mainstream and prioritise protection activities
> ➤ The approach must be coordinated within and outside the mission
> ➤ Do no harm! All mission components must seek not to expose civilians to risk or to cause harm
> ➤ Action must be taken in cooperation with humanitarian and development actors and must respect humanitarian principles: humanity, neutrality, impartiality, and operational independence
> ➤ The approach must be community-based and consider the protection needs and threats faced by different groups of civilians (women, men, children, the elderly, youth, people with disabilities, ethnic, religious and minority groups, as well as displaced populations)
> ➤ Action must meaningfully integrate women, peace, and security priorities. This includes how gender inequality and discrimination impact threats to civilians and how participation and empowerment can address those threats
> ➤ Protection of civilians action must be undertaken with mainstreamed child protection concerns. This must be done in cooperation with the mission's Senior Child Protection Adviser and the UN policy on child protection (most recently reviewed in 2020).[45]

---

[44] This includes dialogue and engagement, presence in areas under greatest threat, creating a credible deterrent posture, and supporting national protection capacities.

[45] DPO/Department of Field Support/Department of Political Affairs, *Child Protection in United Nations Peace Operations Policy*, UN doc. 2017.11, effective as of 1 June 2017 (reviewed June 2020), at: https://bit.ly/39oIGQ4. See 2019 DPO Policy on the Protection of Civilians in UN Peacekeeping, paras. 28–39.

15.2.1.3 The Three Tiers of Protection of Civilians Action

More concretely, the DPO Policy distinguishes three tiers of action to protect civilians. Tier I pertains to protection through dialogue and engagement. Tier II concerns the provision of physical protection. Tier III is the establishment of a protective environment.[46] The three tiers are said to be 'mutually accommodating and reinforcing and are implemented simultaneously and strategically in accordance with the mission mandate, mission phase and the circumstances on the ground. There is no inherent hierarchy or sequencing between the tiers.'[47] The main thrust of the three tiers is as follows.

TIER I PROTECTION THROUGH DIALOGUE AND ENGAGEMENT. Tier I activities focus on dialogue with perpetrators or potential perpetrators of violence against civilians and conflict resolution and mediation between parties to the conflict. Tier I also comprises investigation, advocacy, and reporting on human rights and protection concerns. It is explicit that engagement may be conducted directly with non-State armed actors, and through the use of disarmament, demobilisation, and reintegration (DDR) programmes, 'where mandated and appropriate'.

The 'good offices' function of the mission must be used to prevent and mitigate threats to civilians. Advocacy and dialogue should immediately be used to prevent threats of attacks on civilians before they become imminent, or to end them once they occur. Engagement with communities should, the policy states, 'be an inclusive, two-way exercise which begins with listening to communities about their protection needs and capacities'.[48]

All UN support to host government security forces, including in the context of fulfilling the protection of civilians mandate, must, as noted above, be implemented in compliance with the UN Human Rights Due Diligence Policy on UN support to non-United Nations security forces.[49] This policy reiterates that the UN is obligated under international law to respect, promote, and encourage respect for IHL, international human rights law, and international refugee law.[50] Consistent with these obligations, UN support may not be provided where there are 'substantial grounds for believing' a real risk exists of the recipients committing 'grave violations of international humanitarian, human rights or refugee law', at the very least where the authorities 'fail to take the necessary corrective or mitigating measures'.[51]

TIER II PROVISION OF PHYSICAL PROTECTION. Tier II encompasses activities by mission components to physically protect civilians, 'whether through protective presence,

---

[46] 2019 DPO Policy on the Protection of Civilians in UN Peacekeeping, para. 40.
[47] Ibid.
[48] Ibid., paras. 43–4, 46, 47, and 50.
[49] UN, 'Human Rights Due Diligence Policy on UN Support to Non-United Nations Security Forces', UN doc. A/67/775-S/2013/110, 5 March 2013.
[50] Ibid., para. 1.
[51] Ibid.

interpositioning, the threat or use of force, or facilitating safe passage or refuge'.[52] According to the 2019 Policy, the protection of civilians 'must be prioritised in decisions on location, posture, length and type of deployment and patrolling and must be systematically included in operational orders'.[53]

With respect to the use of force, every reasonable effort must be made to resolve the situation by other means. Where armed force is used, it must be 'limited in its intensity and duration' to that deemed necessary to ensure that civilians are protected and civilian casualties avoided or at least minimised. The use of force should also be graduated, 'unless this would place the civilians to be protected or mission personnel themselves at risk of death or serious bodily injury, or clearly be ineffective in the circumstances'.[54] At the same time, the level of force used by the mission 'may be higher than the level of the force threatened or used by the attacker, if necessary to achieve the authorized objective'. Peacekeepers must be 'ready at all times to act swiftly and decisively', employing 'the full degree of force which is needed to protect civilians and avoid or minimize casualties among them'.[55] These rules are a combination of IHL rules on the conduct of hostilities and international law applicable to law enforcement, reflecting the grey zone within which UN peacekeepers are often operating.

The DPO Policy states that when IHL applies to UN forces, 'they must comply with it'.[56] This includes respect for the principles of distinction, proportionality, and precaution – an obligation stated to be 'independent' of the protection of civilians mandate.[57] What is more debated is how application to UN forces is unit- or brigade-specific and whether civilian personnel involved in the mission planning and operational implementation also lose immunity from attack.[58] In general, the United Nations also tends to argue that their peacekeeping operations are not parties to the given armed conflicts, thereby asserting that IHL does not apply to the missions.[59]

A particular challenge arises when the threat to civilians comes from the security forces of the host State, as the Policy explicitly recognises. While UN peacekeeping operations are mandated to protect civilians regardless of the source of the threat, 'it is recognised that a robust response to threats posed by the host State may be beyond the mission's capabilities, may result in insecurity for peacekeepers and can affect the host State's strategic consent to the mission'.[60] A preferable response to specific threats to civilians posed by host

---

[52]   2019 DPO Policy on the Protection of Civilians in UN Peacekeeping, para. 54.

[53]   Ibid., para. 55.

[54]   Ibid., para. 57.

[55]   Ibid.

[56]   This was set out in the Secretary-General's Bulletin of 1999 on 'Observance by United Nations Forces of International Humanitarian Law' (UN doc. ST/SGB/1999/13). 'Guidance' on whether IHL applies to a specific peacekeeping operation 'will be developed on a case-by-case basis and as required by the Office of Legal Affairs, in consultation with DPO and the relevant Mission'. 2019 DPO Policy on the Protection of Civilians in UN Peacekeeping, para. 22.

[57]   2019 DPO Policy on the Protection of Civilians in UN Peacekeeping, para. 22.

[58]   Paddon Rhoads, *Taking Sides in Peacekeeping, Impartiality and the Future of the United Nations*, p. 32.

[59]   See R. Mamiya and T. Vestner, 'Revisiting the Law on UN Peace Operations Support to Partner Forces', *Journal of Conflict and Security Law*, forthcoming.

[60]   2019 DPO Policy on the Protection of Civilians in UN Peacekeeping, para. 61. See, with respect to (in)action by MONUSCO: Paddon Rhoads, *Taking Sides in Peacekeeping, Impartiality and the Future of the United Nations*, p. 186.

State security forces 'should normally include political engagement, early and at the highest levels', and may even seek to involve the UN Security Council.[61]

In cases of credible threats of physical violence against individuals, such as notable personalities or figures, community workers, journalists, or other civil society representatives, 'missions may consider instituting specific measures to protect individuals'. This may extend, in certain cases, to the deployment of armed units outside the individual's residence or the regular patrolling of its environs. 'Guidance' on such measures must, though, be sought in advance from UN Headquarters.[62] 'In extremis', where the mission has insufficient military or police capacity to secure a site outside the mission compound, civilians may be admitted to UN premises. A decision to do so 'must be taken by the Head of Mission, in consultation, if time permits', with the DPO Under-Secretary-General.[63]

The DPO Policy states that UN peacekeeping operations 'may be obliged to temporarily detain individuals in the course of carrying out their protection of civilians mandates'.[64] This is a contested area of international law, with predominant opinion holding that IHL does not constitute the legal basis for detention in a situation of non-international armed conflict, but rather domestic law of the territorial State or international human rights law. The Policy states that any detention must be in accordance with the successor to the 2010 Interim Standard Operating Procedures on Detention by United Nations Peace Operations (adopted in 2020 and effective as of 1 January 2021),[65] as well as any safeguards relating to the detention of children. The Standard Operating Procedure provides as follows:

13. Any person detained by a United Nations field mission shall be handed over to the host State authorities or released as soon as possible and, in any case, within 96 hours of the time that he or she was first apprehended.

14. Where a handover takes place, all requirements for handover shall be met within this timeframe. If the requirements for handover are not met within 96 hours from the time that the person was apprehended, the detained person shall be released.

In an Annex with respect to the detention of children, it is stipulated that:

Any child detained by United Nations personnel should be handed over to the Host State child protection authorities or, if this is not possible, to humanitarian child protection actors for interim care within 48 hours from the moment of his or her apprehension, until such time as family reunification or other durable solution occurs.[66]

---

[61] 2019 DPO Policy on the Protection of Civilians in UN Peacekeeping, para. 62.

[62] Ibid., para. 63.

[63] Ibid., para. 65.

[64] Ibid., para. 69.

[65] UN Department of Peace Operations, UN Department of Political and Peacebuilding Affairs, and UN Department of Safety and Security, *The Handling of Detention in United Nations Peacekeeping Operations and Special Political Missions, Standard Operating Procedure*, UN ref. 2020.13. Effective 1 January 2021, at: https://bit.ly/3ocRqR8.

[66] Ibid., Annex B: 'Special Considerations for Children in Relation to the Standard Operating Procedures on the Handling of Detention in United Nations Peacekeeping Operations and Special Political Missions', para. 7 [original emphasis]. The Annex states, in a footnote, that the document 'should be read in conjunction with the DPKO/DFS/DPA Policy on Child Protection in United Nations Peace Operations (2017) and with the

TIER III ESTABLISHING A PROTECTIVE ENVIRONMENT. Tier III activities focus on peacebuilding and conflict prevention or resolution. They include programmatic interventions to build the capacity of the host State to protect civilians, such as through security sector reform, and support for the 're-establishment' of the rule of law and criminal justice.[67] Possible interventions are broad in scope, potentially encompassing, on the one hand, improvements to prison conditions and, on the other, building the capacities of civil society, journalists, and human rights defenders.[68] A possible avenue for action is rehabilitation of basic infrastructure through Quick Impact Projects (QIPs).[69]

Establishing a protective environment comprises support to political processes, such as the meaningful participation of women. It includes DDR of former fighters, the promotion and protection of human rights, survey and clearance of explosive ordnance, and the prevention of proliferation and trafficking of small arms and light weapons.[70]

Tier III activities can be undertaken at any time, but are 'particularly relevant in areas where conflict may be prevented, has subsided or when most imminent threats to civilians have decreased but protection gains need to be consolidated and future outbreaks of violence prevented'.[71] The DPO Policy recommends that Tier III be given priority 'as soon as conflict has subsided in a given area and conditions are conducive'.[72]

Overall, the three tiers address two different kinds of protection, namely *structural* and *proximate* protection, implicating different UN actors and, consequently, requiring different criteria for accountability.[73] Tiers I and III address more *structural* protection strategies, encompassing primarily non-coercive activities in order to address the underlying conflict. These can either be short-term, such as mediation at the local level, or long-term, through the promotion of the rule of law – overall constituting peacebuilding strategies.[74] However, this structural protection requires strong institutional resources in order to effectively link interventions and long-term structural transformation, which, at present, seem to be lacking within the UN system.[75] In contrast, Tier II focuses more on *proximate* protection by determining what peacekeepers can or cannot do when civilians face imminent threat of physical violence.[76] While structural protection is hard to achieve and measure, proximate protection remains politically sensitive and challenging at the operational level.

ensuing DPO Special Procedures and Safeguards for Children Deprived of Liberty by United Nations Peace Operations Personnel'.

[67] 2019 DPO Policy on the Protection of Civilians in UN Peacekeeping, paras. 71 and 74.

[68] Ibid., paras. 76 and 77.

[69] Ibid., para. 77.

[70] Ibid., para. 75.

[71] 2019 DPO Policy on the Protection of Civilians in UN Peacekeeping, para. 72.

[72] Ibid.

[73] Donais and Tanguay, 'Protection of Civilians and Peacekeeping's Accountability Deficit', p. 17.

[74] T. Donais, 'Protection through Peace Building: The Future of UNMISS Protection of Civilians Mandate in South Sudan', *Center for Security Governance (CSG)*, 2020, available at: https://bit.ly/39GW3e3.

[75] A. Gorur, 'The Need for Monitoring and Evaluation in Advancing Protection of Civilians', *International Peace Institute Global Observatory*, 2019, available at: https://bit.ly/3oigLto.

[76] Donais and Tanguay, 'Protection of Civilians and Peacekeeping's Accountability Deficit', p. 18.

15.2.1.4 The Operationalisation of the DPO Policy

To complement DPO Policy, the department issued *The Protection of Civilians in United Nations Peacekeeping Handbook* in 2020.[77] The Handbook is structured in six parts and includes valuable case studies for illustration and better application of the guidance.

Part I provides guidance on how to interpret the protection of civilians mandate given to a mission by the UN Security Council, including key mandate language. It also identifies contextual and systemic constraints that may hamper missions in implementing these mandates and suggests how these constraints may be addressed, circumvented, or overcome.

Part II provides guidance for mission leaders and managers on ensuring that the protection of civilians is at the heart of a mission's political strategy, providing strategic vision, deciding on resource allocation, and mainstreaming the protection of civilians in strategic planning and performance processes. It also provides guidance on how to develop a communication and influence plan on protection of civilians, including dialogue, engagement, public information, and advocacy in support of a mission's political approach to the issue.

Part III provides guidance for civilian, police, and military components on how to identify and prioritise protection of civilians threats and risks in planning and action. It also indicates how these components can engage with communities to understand protection threats faced by the population to inform the mission approach to protection of civilians and support local protection efforts.

Part IV provides guidance on how to integrate protection of civilians issues into mission operational planning, preparedness, and coordination. It also suggests how peacekeeping missions can balance the different options available to respond to threats to civilians.

Part V provides guidance on how to ensure a gendered approach to the protection of civilians, as well as recommendations for protection of civilians advisers on how to advise and support mission leaders on activities and operations to protect civilians.

Part VI provides guidance on responding when civilians are threatened, with simple scenarios followed by a list of 'dos' and 'don'ts'. The Handbook stresses the need for 'engaged and supportive leadership'. In this regard, the Special Representative of the Secretary-General should initiate action and 'personally tackle' the most complex and strategic protection of civilians threats, 'particularly through engagement and/or coordination with high-level host State officials'. At the strategic level, should the Special Representative lack time to lead all protection of civilians operations, he or she 'should designate and empower a dedicated senior mission lead', which will normally be his or her deputy. At operational and tactical levels, the protection of civilians adviser or focal point will ensure that each threat has a designated lead.[78]

At the same time, it is clarified that missions 'are not expected to prevent or intervene to stop all instances of violence'. Thus, peacekeeping missions 'may have to focus their resources on strategic threats, in particular violence that may result in mass civilian

---

[77]   DPO, *The Protection of Civilians in United Nations Peacekeeping Handbook*, New York, 2020, at: https://bit.ly/3oynVGg.

[78]   Ibid., p. 32.

casualties or lead to broader instability'. But, echoing the DPO Policy, missions 'should intervene to stop physical violence against civilians taking place in proximity of a mission presence, regardless of the level of violence'. Failure to respond to these threats, the Handbook acknowledges, 'undermines the credibility of the mission with the local population, perpetrators and other stakeholders'.[79]

Where the Handbook is at its weakest is on targeting and tailoring protection to specific at-risk groups. A formulaic list of such groups is recounted (e.g. women, men, girls, boys, different ethnic and religious groups, persons with disabilities, and internally displaced persons (IDPs)), but without giving guidance on how to tailor protection to them. More detailed advice is given on how to prevent and tackle sexual violence and child recruitment, but even these are limited nonetheless, covering only one-and-a-half pages and one page, respectively. Nothing is offered on how to practically protect or assist persons with disabilities, described by the World Health Organization (WHO) as the largest minority group in the world,[80] and a group considered by some as the forgotten victims of armed conflict.[81]

15.2.1.5 Institutional Issues and Accountability

Overall, the DPO Policy and its 2020 Handbook provide for a substantial body of guidance for the protection of civilians in UN peace operations, particularly when integrated with several other sector-specific guidelines, for example dealing with child or gender considerations. In practice, it is key for these new developments (both the Policy and Handbook) to stay clear of what has been called a 'diplomatic theatre, unlikely to translate into concrete field-level improvements'.[82]

This also requires certain levels of accountability.[83] In this regard, the States that wrote to the Secretary-General calling for action to protect civilians better stressed the importance of holding accountable those who fail to protect civilians in line with their mission's mandate. The letter concludes as follows:

> When there are substantial grounds to believe that troops have failed to uphold protection of civilians mandates, we encourage you to consider taking further action, including repatriation and exploring possible financial penalties, to ensure accountability. We understand that these are difficult decisions, and should be made with full consideration of a mission's unique needs and capacity to implement its mandate. However, such

---

79 Ibid., p. 83. There is also, though, a risk that the presence of a UN (or other) peacekeeping force will raise expectations. Emily Paddon Rhoads recounts that, in the Democratic Republic of Congo, civilians were emboldened to take 'even greater risks'. Paddon Rhoads, *Taking Sides in Peacekeeping, Impartiality and the Future of the United Nations*, p. 7.

80 UN Department of Economic and Social Affairs, 'Factsheet on Persons with Disabilities', at: http://bit.ly/3ckFoAT.

81 The 2019 DPO Policy has only a single reference to the need to plan for the needs of persons with disabilities. 2019 DPO Policy on the Protection of Civilians in UN Peacekeeping, para. 37.

82 Donais and Tanguay, 'Protection of Civilians and Peacekeeping's Accountability Deficit', p. 2.

83 Ibid.; H. Bourgeois, 'Failure to Protect Civilians in the Context of UN Peace Operations: A Question of Accountability?', *EJIL: Talk!*, 5 September 2018, at: https://bit.ly/2TfPabr.

decisions are necessary when civilian lives are at stake; and we, as supporters of the Kigali Principles,[84] stand behind you in making them.

We are ready to work in partnership with you to uphold our joint responsibility to ensure that peacekeeping operations protect civilians, particularly the vulnerable, from violence.[85]

Currently, the system might provide for accountability when addressing misconduct, for instance, by adopting zero-tolerance policies for sexual exploitation or abuse, but, on the other hand, may still fail to provide guidance as to what accountability might look like in practice. As such, the 2019 Policy calls for the establishment of protection of civilians advisors and focal points to support the mission leadership in coordinating all protection of civilians activities and to liaise and engage with humanitarian protection actors and coordination mechanisms, including the UN protection cluster[86] usually chaired by the Office of the UN High Commissioner for Refugees (UNHCR). Protection of civilians advisors on women and children have become mainstays of UN peacekeeping operations in recent years. Action must be supported by a specific protection of civilians strategy and a 'forward-looking' strategic threat assessment.[87] Gender and age-specific considerations shall be included in all plans, policies, analyses, and reports and women stakeholders must fully participate in all decision-making processes.[88]

In a peacekeeping operation, the Head of Mission is accountable to the UN Secretary-General, through the Under-Secretary-General for Peace Operations, for the implementation of the mission's protection of civilians mandate. 'In turn, the Head of Mission will delegate the relevant responsibility, authority and accountability.'[89] In situations where civilians have been killed or subject to physical violence, including sexual violence, either close to a UN base or where the mission knew 'or should have known' about an imminent threat to civilians and failed to respond within their capabilities, an inquiry or after-action review must be undertaken as soon as possible.[90]

In reality, however, the end result of several different actors either dealing with or delegating responsibility has led to contradictory practices in terms of chains of accountability,[91] with a disjuncture between those who set a budget, those who establish a mandate, and those who implement it.[92] As such, accountability relationships tend to be confusing, as well as lack clear standards and sanction regimes.[93]

---

[84]   The Kigali Principles on the Protection of Civilians are a non-binding set of eighteen pledges for the effective and thorough implementation of the protection of civilians in UN peacekeeping. The Principles emanated from the High-Level International Conference on the Protection of Civilians held in Rwanda on 28–9 May 2015. The text of the Principles is available at: http://bit.ly/3kaQFDA.

[85]   Letter of 31 July 2018 to the UN Secretary-General.

[86]   2019 DPO Policy on the Protection of Civilians in UN Peacekeeping, para. 79.

[87]   Ibid., paras. 79 and 83.

[88]   Ibid., para. 85.

[89]   Ibid., para. 90.

[90]   Ibid., para. 96.

[91]   T. Donais and E. Tanguay, 'Doing Less with Less? Peacekeeping Retrenchment and the UN's Protection of Civilians Agenda', *International Journal: Canada's Journal of Global Policy Analysis*, 2020, 65–82, at p. 80.

[92]   M. Lipson, 'Performance under Ambiguity: International Organization Performance in UN Peacekeeping', *Review of International Organizations*, 2010, 249–84, at p. 259.

[93]   Donais and Tanguay, 'Protection of Civilians and Peacekeeping's Accountability Deficit', p. 7.

15.3 PROTECTION OF CIVILIANS BY UN AGENCIES AND BODIES

15.3.1 *Protection of Civilians and the Global Protection Cluster*

The protection of civilians in armed conflict by UN agencies is coordinated at country level by the UN Humanitarian Coordinator and the Protection Cluster. Internationally, the coordination is entrusted to the Global Protection Cluster. Led by UNHCR, the Global Protection Cluster is divided into four subsidiary bodies with designated lead agencies with particular expertise: gender-based violence (the United Nations Population Fund, UNFPA); child protection (UNICEF); mine action (the United Nations Mine Action Service, UNMAS); and housing, land, and property rights (Norwegian Refugee Council).[94]

The Global Protection Cluster's Strategic Framework for 2020–4, entitled *Protection in a Climate of Change*, stresses that all humanitarian actors have a responsibility to place protection at the centre of humanitarian action 'through a system-wide commitment to preparedness and immediate and life-saving activities throughout the duration of a crisis and beyond, driven by the needs and perspectives of affected persons'.[95] But the Strategy remains fairly generic. Statements such as 'Priority should be given to ensuring the needs of persons at the greatest risk are not overlooked', are too general to promote focus or guide effective action. There are also gaps. The protection of LGBTI persons is mentioned only once in the strategy while the protection of persons with disabilities is mentioned only three times. This results in topic-oriented clusters that mostly rely on a top-down approach, failing to account for cross-cutting issues such as disability.[96] For instance, humanitarian actors have reported that persons with disabilities can only access 30–40 per cent of their activities, although consultations in this area could lead to better humanitarian responses.[97]

The Global Protection Cluster establishes five strategic priorities:

1) We will put basics of coordination and collaboration in place in all our operations.
2) We will ensure voices of crisis-affected persons and communities are heard, especially the forgotten ones.
3) We will meet the challenges to make protection actions contextually appropriate and complementary.
4) We will champion and advance durable solutions that meet protection standards through a nexus of humanitarian, peace and development action.
5) We will continue adapting to the shifting operational environment and keep looking forward.[98]

The reality within the UN system is more complicated. Humanitarian actors engage with peacekeeping missions but may fail to efficiently coordinate, sometimes reluctant to

---

[94] OCHA, *OCHA on Message: Protection*, New York, January 2020, p. 1.
[95] Global Protection Cluster, *Protection in a Climate of Change, Strategic Framework 2020–2024*, at: https://bit.ly/3os8DCD, p. 15.
[96] A. Perry and A. Héry, 'Disability in the UN Cluster System', *Forced Migration Review*, 2010, 38–9.
[97] Handicap International Federation (now rebranded as Humanity and Inclusion), 'Disability in Humanitarian Contexts', Report, 2015.
[98] Ibid., p. 14.

undertake joint planning with other parties to the conflict.[99] Systemic failures to promote and protect human rights, for instance, came to a head following the denouement of the armed conflict in Sri Lanka, and the deaths of thousands of Tamils, many of whom were civilians, in the military operations that crushed the Tamil Tigers (LTTE).

The silence of the UN while this was ongoing led to the launch of the (Human) Rights Up Front initiative by the UN Secretary-General in 2013. The initiative aims to help the UN to act more coherently across the pillars of the organisation's work – peace and security, development, and human rights – to meet its responsibilities to prevent and respond to serious violations of international human rights law and IHL. Human Rights Up Front aims to achieve this by three types of change. 'It seeks cultural change to make sure that UN staff understand their prevention responsibilities and pursue them, operational change to ensure that the UN works on the basis of shared analysis, and enhanced engagement with Member States.'[100] The challenge remains significant, with interaction with other key actors no more than a work in progress.[101]

Indeed, it was noted in a 2018 review of the Global Protection Cluster that despite 'many efforts of the Protection Cluster', protection 'may not always have been a priority of decision-making platforms'. There have 'also been weaknesses within the response and a disconnect between humanitarian, government and development actors'.[102] With respect to the protection of civilians, the review noted that protection staff on the ground 'are progressively faced with more complex dilemmas, such as humanitarian evacuations, cross-border relief operations, so called "safe zones", and military attacks against sites and settlements hosting IDPs, as well as schools and medical facilities'.[103]

In 2020, the Overseas Development Institute – Humanitarian Policy Group (HPG) announced an 'advocacy scoping study' on the Global Protection Cluster.[104] The scoping study reviews current practice in protection advocacy by the Global Protection Cluster and field protection clusters as the first step towards developing a Global Protection Cluster Advocacy Strategy.[105] Advocacy is useful within the UN organisation itself as well as externally: whereas the Global Protection Cluster has mostly prioritised indirect, that is through other humanitarian actors, and private advocacy, that is through its tools, further development of the Cluster's advocacy approach is commendable, particularly in providing support to the various field protection clusters and their work.[106]

---

[99]   D. Lilly, 'The Changing Nature of the Protection of Civilians in International Peace Operations', *International Peacekeeping*, 2012, 637.

[100]   '"Human Rights up Front" Initiative Ever More Vital to Strengthen UN's Preventive Work, Says Deputy UN Chief', UN News, 28 January 2016, at: http://bit.ly/3r0HOar.

[101]   IASC & OCHA, 'Civil-Military Guidelines & Reference for Complex Emergencies', *United Nations Humanitarian Civil–Military Coordination*, Report, UN, New York, 2008.

[102]   Global Protection Cluster, *Centrality of Protection in Humanitarian Action*, GPC 2018 Review, at: https://bit.ly/3r2DXK1, p. 16.

[103]   Ibid., p. 38.

[104]   D. Lilly with A. Spencer, *Global Protection Cluster: Advocacy Scoping Study*, ODI, London, July 2020, at: https://bit.ly/36nWmZU.

[105]   ODI – HPG, 'Global Protection Cluster: Advocacy Scoping Study', Analysis, *ReliefWeb*, Posted 26 July 2020, at: http://bit.ly/3r2C009.

[106]   Lilly and Spencer, *Global Protection Cluster: Advocacy Scoping Study*, p. 8.

15.3.2 *The Role of the Office of the UN High Commissioner for Human Rights*

The OHCHR has probably the biggest operational role in protecting civilians among UN agencies. More than the DPO, which primarily focuses on security aspects, the OHCHR understands the protection of civilians in terms of legal protection linked to international humanitarian law and human rights law, and, consequently, to armed conflict.[107] The OHCHR's twin roles of engagement with national authorities and monitoring of respect for civilians by parties to armed conflict and by actors in other situations of violence are critical. For instance, in the case of Afghanistan, mistakes in targeting led to many avoidable civilian casualties, an issue on which the Office engaged directly with the Afghan government and its security forces, the international coalition, and the Taliban. This led to changes in policy and a noticeable reduction in such casualties over time.[108] Key, in this change, was the OHCHR's field presence in Afghanistan, which allowed its staff to understand the political context of the country as well as coordinate with other actors on the ground.[109]

This advocacy role is directly related to the Office's work on monitoring respect for civilians by parties to armed conflict or other armed actors. With respect to such monitoring, the OHCHR often works with the local UN mission to compile dedicated reports on the protection of civilians. For instance, the Office and the UN Assistance Mission in Afghanistan (UNAMA) jointly compile regular reports on the protection of civilians in Afghanistan, which are of an exceptionally high standard. Their 2019 annual report found that the armed conflict continued to take a heavy toll on the civilian population in Afghanistan, with more than 10,000 civilian casualties recorded for the sixth year in a row. 'Since UNAMA began systematic documentation in 2009, it has documented more than 100,000 civilian casualties, with more than 35,000 killed and 65,000 injured.'[110] This report, and others before, have proved essential in analysing the human rights situation in Afghanistan as well as placing international attention on the abuses perpetrated in the area.[111]

In Iraq, while reports on the protection of civilians have not been issued since 2015,[112] reports on compliance with human rights continue to be published. For instance, intense and widespread violence against demonstrators was used by the security forces and other 'armed actors' in 2019 and 2020, as documented in *Human Rights Violations and Abuses in the Context of Demonstrations in Iraq, October 2019 to April 2020*.[113] Credible reports of the death of 487

---

[107] A. Ø. Stensland and O. J. Sending, 'Unpacking the "Culture of Protection": A Political Economy Analysis of OCHA and the Protection of Civilians', Report, *Norwegian Institute of International Affairs*, Oslo, 2011, 36, 31.

[108] Interview with Danielle Bell, OHCHR, Iraq, 14 December 2020.

[109] S. Samar, 'The Role of the High Commissioner in Protecting and Promoting Human Rights in Afghanistan and Sudan', in F. D. Gaer and C. L. Broecker (eds.), *The United Nations High Commissioner for Human Rights*, Brill, Leiden, 2013, p. 315.

[110] UNAMA, Annual Report on the Protection of Civilians in Armed Conflict in 2019, Kabul, February 2020, Executive Summary, at: http://bit.ly/3j5wJAE.

[111] Samar, 'The Role of the High Commissioner in Protecting and Promoting Human Rights in Afghanistan and Sudan', pp. 316–17.

[112] OHCHR and UN Assistance Mission in Iraq (UNAMI), *Report on the Protection of Civilians in the Armed Conflict in Iraq: 1 May–31 October 2015*, Baghdad, 2015, at: https://bit.ly/2YpUfjQ.

[113] OHCHR and UNAMI, *Human Rights Violations and Abuses in the Context of Demonstrations in Iraq, October 2019 to April 2020*, Baghdad, August 2020, at: https://bit.ly/34TIoPF.

protesters and the injury of 7,715 at protest sites were documented by UNAMI/OHCHR. Those killed included at least thirty-four children and one woman.[114] The level of violence employed against unarmed protesters across Iraq would seem to meet at least some of the criteria for crimes against humanity. To date, there has been little evidence of accountability for those responsible for the shootings, despite efforts in this regard by the OHCHR.[115]

Working with UNAMA, the OHCHR has produced a valuable manual to guide UN staff in Afghanistan on issues pertaining to the protection of civilians.[116] According to the Manual, every incident of alleged conflict-related harm must be investigated and relevant cases must be verified according to the set minimum methodological standards.[117] Members of organised armed groups are not counted as civilian casualties nor are civilians while they are directly participating in hostilities. However, civilians who have previously done so but who are killed or injured when no longer doing so are considered civilian.[118] Leaders of field teams are responsible for ensuring 'regular advocacy and outreach' with Government, Afghan security forces, international military forces, the Afghanistan Independent Human Rights Commission, as well as civil society and non-governmental organisations at regional, provincial, district, and village levels.[119]

Many elements in the Manual are clearly of broader utility beyond Afghanistan. Indeed, in its 2019 Report, the Secretary-General highlighted that 'efforts to strengthen protection [of civilians] cannot substitute for political processes aimed at preventing or ending conflict and building sustainable peace'.[120] In these processes, evidence-based advocacy represents an essential step for the identification of factors contributing to civilian casualties, informing adjustments to future UN operations.[121]

15.3.3 *The Role of UNICEF in Child Protection in Armed Conflict*

The UN Children's Fund (UNICEF) remains the key operational UN agency focused on the protection of children in armed conflict. Although its leading role has been recognised internationally,[122] the organisation has been less prominent in normative and policy development in recent years. In particular, as discussed in Chapter 9, the Paris Principles on children associated with armed forces or armed groups, adopted in 2007, appear to need an overhaul.

---

[114] Ibid., p. 6.

[115] This might be the result of OHCHR's work generally focusing on law and human rights monitoring, without, however, a deeper understanding of important political aspects; as argued by: H. Hannum, 'Human Rights in Conflict Resolution: The Role of the Office of the High Commissioner for Human Rights in UN Peacekeeping and Peacebuilding', *Human Rights Quarterly*, 2006, 1–85, at pp. 58–9.

[116] 'UNAMA Protection of Civilians Guidance for Field Teams', Kabul, March 2018.

[117] In particular, the field team investigating the incident must be satisfied that there exists 'clear and convincing evidence for each element and conclusion'. This is 'the minimum standard of proof' though it is further noted that field teams 'normally obtain greater certainty for most elements of an incident'. Ibid., p. 6.

[118] 'UNAMA Protection of Civilians Guidance for Field Teams', p. 11.

[119] Ibid., p. 4.

[120] UN Security Council, 'Protection of Civilians in Armed Conflict: Report of the Secretary-General', UN doc. S/2019/373, para. 8.

[121] Ibid., para. 11.

[122] In the 1990s and 2000s, UNICEF was at the forefront of UN agencies promoting action at an international on landmines, small arms and light weapons, and of course child soldiers.

The Principles provided important steps forward at the time of their writing. For instance, their recharacterisation of 'child soldiers' as the more broadly encompassing 'children associated with armed forces or armed groups' recognised that children in armed conflict can play roles much more intricate than simply being on the front line as fighters.[123] However, a revised and amended version of the 2007 Paris Principles would be necessary to take account of detention in the context of counterterrorism operations among other issues. Indeed, counterterrorism is not mentioned in the 2007 instrument.

UNICEF continues to actively support the field-based Monitoring and Reporting Mechanism on Grave Violations against Children in Situations of Armed Conflict (the MRM) and is also heavily involved in the elaboration and promotion of implementation of 'Action Plans' with both State and non-State armed groups to protect children, particularly child soldiers. In general, UNICEF is considered to follow a rights-based approach, working towards the creation of a 'child-safe' space for recovery and reintegration, during and after armed conflicts.[124]

Certainly, the Special Representative of the Secretary-General on Children in Armed Conflict has taken on some of the advocacy mantle previously assumed by UNICEF.[125] But that does not fully explain the relative absence of UNICEF from the normative arena, notably in light of the organisation's press release issued at the end of 2019 whereby it recognised that '2019 concludes a "deadly decade" for children in conflict, with more than 170,000 grave violations verified since 2010'.[126] Indeed, UNICEF has been criticised for failing, in practice, to marry its normative stances with its policy aspirations and advocacy role.[127] It has long been argued by some that it would be commendable, for UNICEF and humanitarian interventions generally, to re-think their models of childhood, conflict, and relief in order to include larger child populations indirectly affected by conflict – moving away from previous focuses on 'spectacular' groups of children, such as child soldiers, orphans, and refugees.[128]

15.3.4 *The UNHCR and the Protection of Refugees*

Based on the 1951 Refugee Convention, the UNHCR's 'core mandate is to ensure the international protection of uprooted people worldwide'. The UNHCR 'promotes the basic human rights of refugees and ensures they will not be returned involuntarily to a country where they face persecution'.[129] The fundamental UNHCR protection activity

---

[123] M. Drumbl, 'Children, Armed Violence and Transition: Challenges for International Law & Policy', *Georgia Journal of International and Comparative Law*, 2015, 623–7, at p. 623.

[124] S. Shenoda et al., 'Children and Armed Conflict', *Pediatrics Perspectives*, 2015, 1–3.

[125] UN, 'The Special Representative of the Secretary-General for Children and Armed Conflict', at: http://bit.ly/31E10PI.

[126] UNICEF, '2019 Concludes a 'Deadly Decade' for Children in Conflict, with More Than 170,000 Grave Violations Verified Since 2010', Press Release, New York, 29 December 2019, at: http://uni.cf/2vohBuL.

[127] P. W. Jones, 'Elusive Mandate: UNICEF and Educational Development', *International Journal of Educational Development*, 2006, 591–604.

[128] J. Boyden, 'Children's Experience of Conflict Related Emergencies: Some Implications for Relief Policy and Practice', *Disasters*, 1994, 254–67, at p. 254.

[129] UNHCR, 'Legal Protection', at: https://bit.ly/3cpEscW.

is ensuring that refugees and others in need of international protection are recognised and granted asylum. When national authorities cannot or will not implement procedures to identify refugees, UNHCR's staff are often deployed to assess individual cases.[130] The UNHCR further directly contributes to the protection of civilians through, for instance, monitoring, capacity-building (by providing advice and support on the incorporation of international law into national laws and policies), and supporting community-based conflict resolution.[131]

A paper published by the organisation in January 2020 observes that the UNHCR 'unequivocally instructs' that the 1951 Convention is applicable to civilians displaced by armed conflict and violence, as 'the "majority of these situations engender political, religious, ethnic, social, or gender persecution"'.[132] As of end 2019, an estimated 30–34 million (up to 43 per cent) of the 79.5 million forcibly displaced persons were children below eighteen years of age. Developing countries host 86 per cent of the world's refugees while the least developed countries provide asylum to 28 per cent of the total.[133] As of writing, this ratio was changing as States such as Moldova and Poland were hosting huge numbers of refugees from Ukraine.

In 2007, then UN High Commissioner for Refugees António Guterres (later UN Secretary-General, of course) launched the first in a series of 'Dialogues on Protection Challenges'. This annual event in Geneva discusses new or emerging global protection issues and helps the UNHCR to identify ways of strengthening the protection of people of concern.[134] Given the situation with COVID-19, the theme of the Dialogue in 2020 was entitled 'Protection and Resilience during Pandemics'. The Concept Note for the Dialogue observed that the COVID-19 outbreak had 'heightened the vulnerabilities of individuals with specific protection needs, such as individuals at increased risk of sexual- and gender-based violence (SGBV), women and girls as well as men and boys in vulnerable situations, and people who are elderly, have disabilities, or are in detention'.[135] In the Outcome Document, key recommendations included engaging refugees, IDPs, and stateless persons not just as recipients, but as providers of support; adapting protection responses to become, for instance, gender-inclusive; as well as adapting humanitarian and development programmes.[136]

Yet still missing from the UNHCR's work is a more in-depth analysis of how its strategies do not just attempt to tackle conflict in general, but also different levels of violence and threats. As the protection of civilians in armed conflict has its foundation in both IHL and international refugee law, which both have at their basis the principles of neutrality and impartiality, the

[130] UNHCR, 'Protection', at: https://bit.ly/3r2VFwZ.
[131] UNHCR Toolkit: Protection in Armed Conflict, *Protection of Civilians: The Role of UNHCR*, 2019.
[132] S. Weerasinghe, 'Refugee Law in a Time of Climate Change, Disaster and Conflict', Legal and Protection Policy Research Series, Division of International Protection, UNHCR, Geneva, January 2020, at: http://bit.ly/3rfpZon, pp. 82–3.
[133] UNHCR, 'Refugee Data Finder', 8 December 2020, at: http://bit.ly/39tMsHZ.
[134] UNHCR, 'High Commissioner's Dialogue', at: http://bit.ly/3r6xoHF.
[135] UNHCR, 'High Commissioner's Dialogue on Protection Challenges: Protection and Resilience during Pandemics', Concept Note, 11 November 2020, at: http://bit.ly/3j9ENSF.
[136] UNHCR, 'High Commissioner's Dialogue on Protection Challenges 2020 Theme: Protection and Resilience during Pandemics', Outcome Document, December 2020.

UNHCR has always highlighted the importance of neutrality in conducting its work.[137] However, exactly because of this heavy reliance on international law, the organisation has been criticised for failing to treat legal protection and public policy changes as means to ensure the protection of civilians, and instead treating them as ends in themselves.[138]

15.3.5 *WFP and the Protection of Civilians*

The World Food Programme has long recognised its commitment to protect civilians, seeking to 'constantly refine and deepen [our] understanding of the contexts where we work, assess the root causes of violence and rights violations, and think through steps to being part of the solution'.[139] Stemming from this commitment, the WFP has implemented a 'concentric circles' model of protection; starting with an inner circle – on protection issues within the WFP's traditional activities, such as core food-assistance activities; a middle circle – on causes of food insecurity and assistance-related violence, looking at not only humanitarian but also political issues; and an outer circle – on protection issues that are not directly related to hunger but are present in the WFP's operational context.[140]

The WFP has a protection and accountability policy, most recently issued in 2020.[141] This policy evidences a 'deliberate shift from the centrality of assistance in the 2012 WFP Humanitarian Protection Policy to the centrality of protection'. This means that the WFP has to focus 'not only on how it provides assistance, but also on how WFP decision making and related programming is strategically designed, received and perceived by affected populations – what impact it has on addressing protection risks'.[142]

The policy uses the IASC definition of protection but then qualifies it by stating that: 'More specifically, protection is understood as aiming to prevent, reduce, mitigate and respond to the risks and consequences of violence, coercion, deprivation and abuse for persons, groups and communities.'[143] Moreover, protection 'outcomes' are stated to include 'alleviating human suffering'; 'reducing risks and threat levels'; and 'improving the safety and dignity of individuals'. These outcomes 'will be measured by a reduction in risks to the enjoyment of nutrition and food security'.[144]

---

[137] R. Mamiya, 'A History and Conceptual Development of the Protection of Civilians', in H. Willmot et al., (eds.), *Protection of Civilians*, 1st ed., Oxford University Press, Oxford, 2016, pp. 67–8.

[138] M. Bradley, *Protecting Civilians in War: The ICRC, UNHCR, and Their Limitations in Internal Armed Conflicts*, Oxford University Press, Oxford, 2016.

[139] N. Crawford and G. Pattugalan, 'Protection in Practice, Food Assistance with Safety and Dignity', Report, World Food Programme, Rome, 2013, Foreword.

[140] Ibid., pp. 17–19.

[141] WFP Protection and Accountability Policy 2020, Third informal consultation, 24 July 2020, at: https://bit.ly/30xPrno. This new policy built on the 2012 WFP Humanitarian Protection Policy.

[142] Ibid., para. 7.

[143] Ibid., p. 5.

[144] Ibid. [footnotes omitted].

The Policy stipulates four protection mainstreaming principles, as follows:

- ➤ **Prioritise safety and dignity and avoid causing harm**: Prevent and minimize as much as possible any unintended negative effects of an intervention that can increase people's vulnerability to both physical and psychosocial risks.[145]
- ➤ **Meaningful Access**: Arrange for people's access to assistance and services – in proportion to need and without any barriers (e.g. discrimination). Pay special attention to individuals and groups who may be particularly vulnerable or have difficulty accessing assistance and services.[146]
- ➤ **Accountability**: Set up appropriate approaches, processes, and mechanisms through which affected populations can measure the adequacy of interventions, influence decision making and make informed decisions.[147]
- ➤ **Participation and empowerment**: Support the development of self-protection capacities and assist people to claim their rights, including – not exclusively – the rights to information, shelter, food, water and sanitation, health, and education.[148]

Gender and disability are specifically highlighted as issues of concern,[149] though age barely merits a mention. That said, it is stipulated that accountability to affected populations 'is a particularly important area of focus', which involves

> ensuring that affected populations, their families and diverse community organizations representing young people, older people, indigenous peoples, people living with HIV/ AIDS and persons with disabilities participate in the decisions that affect their lives, receive the information they need to make decisions and have access to safe and responsive mechanisms for providing feedback.[150]

From a practical perspective, the Policy does not go into depth as to what concrete steps the WFP will take to achieve its goals.[151] The document does observe, however, that because the WFP operates in 'volatile, complex and insecure environments its ability to establish and maintain principled and safe access is often challenged'. Nonetheless, it is stated that the organisation's 'planning for access-sensitive programmes and operations

---

[145] Indeed, the WFP has been frequently encouraged to 'strengthen its capacity to conduct conflict and contextual analysis that enables the development of strategies geared to avoiding harm to civilians and enhancing their protection'. See N. Niland, 'WFP Wins the Nobel! Is This an Opportunity to Enhance Protection? (WFP Nobel Series, 3)', Report, *Norwegian Centre for Humanitarian Studies*, at: https://bit.ly/3CQSSwB.

[146] A particularly relevant goal in the aftermath of COVID-19. See, for instance, J. Phumaphi et al., 'A Crisis of Accountability for Women's, Children's and Adolescent's Health', *The Lancet*, 2020, 222–4.

[147] The organisation has been encouraged to take action on accountability in particular related to starvation-related issues as well as issues of sexual exploitation, abuse, and harassment, a 'frequent reality in situations of humanitarian concern'. Niland, 'WFP Wins the Nobel! Is This an Opportunity to Enhance Protection? (WFP Nobel Series, 3)'.

[148] WFP Protection and Accountability Policy 2020, p. 5.

[149] Ibid., paras. 24–5 and 26–7.

[150] Ibid., para. 38.

[151] See, for example, W. Cameron, 'Public Accountability: Effectiveness, Equity, Ethics', *Australian Journal of Public Administration*, 2004, 59–67; and A. Davis, 'Concerning Accountability in Humanitarian Action', Report, Humanitarian Practice Network, 2007.

and negotiation of access with official and de facto authorities must be grounded in the centrality of protection'.[152] Indeed, the WFP has often been criticised for worsening, rather than ameliorating, the situation in countries in which it intervenes, precisely as a result of local actors taking advantage of its initiatives.[153] While this issue is not entirely addressed by the WFP in its 2017–21 Strategic Plan, the organisation has incorporated programmes of feedback from affected communities into its strategy, although limiting their scope to programme design and delivery.[154]

---

[152] WFP Protection and Accountability Policy 2020, para. 21.
[153] For instance, it has been claimed that WFP aid increases corruption as local politicians steal the aid and use it to bribe voters or sell it on the black market, or that the supply of food by the WFP in practice reduces production by local farmers who cannot compete with the programme. In this context, see, for instance, S. Ross, *The World Food Programme in Global Politics*, FirstForumPress, Boulder, 2011, p. 191.
[154] Word Food Programme, *WFP Strategic Plan (2017–2021)*, 2017, available at: https://bit.ly/3ANAoMR.

16

NATO and the Protection of Civilians

16.1 INTRODUCTION

The North Atlantic Treaty Organization (NATO) Policy for the Protection of Civilians was adopted in 2016.[1] The 2016 Policy defines the protection of civilians as including 'all efforts taken to avoid, minimize and mitigate the negative effects that might arise from NATO and NATO-led military operations on the civilian population and, when applicable, to protect civilians from conflict-related physical violence or threats of physical violence by other actors, including through the establishment of a safe and secure environment.'[2] The 2016 Policy's 'added value' is said to be 'not so much the novelty of any particular aspect of its content, but rather its overarching and comprehensive character'.[3] Indeed, the policy is said by one commentator to be 'noticeably still in the operationalization phase'.[4]

In 2021, NATO adopted the *Protection of Civilians Allied Command Operations Handbook*, an additional document aimed at advancing the protection of civilians (PoC) agenda within the Organization.[5] The Handbook clearly states that its aim is that 'of building a strong Protection of Civilians mind-set' and contains the pledge to integrate the 2016 NATO Policy for the Protection of Civilians in the planning and conduct of Alliance operations.[6] Indeed, the respective efforts stem from the understanding that NATO missions need to take civilian protection into account, not just from a humanitarian standpoint, but also as a strategic imperative.[7]

---

[1] NATO *Policy for the Protection of Civilians*, endorsed by the Heads of State and Government participating in the meeting of the North Atlantic Council in Warsaw, 8–9 July 2016 (hereinafter, 2016 NATO Policy on Protection of Civilians), at: http://bit.ly/2T8g842.

[2] Ibid., para. 9.

[3] S. Hill and A. Manea, 'Protection of Civilians: A NATO Perspective', *Utrecht Journal of International and European Law*, Vol. 34, No. 2 (2018), 146–60, at p. 146.

[4] B. Godefroy, 'NATO's New "Human Security" Umbrella: An Opportunity for Better Civilian Protection?', Blog post, Center for Civilians in Conflict (CIVIC), 4 December 2019, at: http://bit.ly/39WWbnK.

[5] NATO, *Protection of Civilians Allied Command Operations Handbook*, Brussels, 2021 (hereinafter, 2021 Handbook), at: https://bit.ly/3ydsxa8.

[6] Ibid., Foreword.

[7] This was emphasised in the webinar held by Stimson on 'Unfinished Business: NATO's Protection of Civilians Policy and the Way Forward' on 19 March 2021, and specifically by speaker K. Dock. See

Other related NATO policies and guidelines are the 2018 Policy and Action Plan on Women, Peace and Security,[8] the 2012 Military Guidelines on Children and Armed Conflict,[9] the 2015 *Policy on Protection of Children in Armed Conflict: The Way Forward*,[10] and the 2015 Military Guidelines on Conflict-related Sexual and Gender-based Violence.[11] The different sectoral approaches taken together are said to constitute an 'holistic approach to human security across NATO'.[12]

16.2 THE POLICY FRAMEWORK

The North Atlantic Treaty Organization's 2016 Policy for the Protection of Civilians describes the Organization's approach as being based on legal, moral, and political imperatives.[13] In particular, according to the policy, to ensure physical protection for civilians, NATO operations need to play a triad role: (i) before operations, by adopting standing policy and tools, developing a robust threat assessment process, and adopting civilian harm mitigation policies; (ii) during operations, by understanding civilians' reality during conflict through small advisory teams and tracking databases, and addressing civilian harm by attributing and investigating violations; and (iii) after operations, by learning the lessons of past conflicts.[14]

'Applicable' international law 'may include international human rights law and international humanitarian law, as applicable'.[15] It is recognised by NATO that 'all feasible measures' must be taken to avoid, minimise, and mitigate harm to civilians. These measures comprise 'a range of activities up to and including the use of force, as appropriate, to prevent, deter, pre-empt, and respond to situations in which civilians suffer physical violence or are under threat of physical violence'.[16] Indeed, Chapter 4 of the 2021 *Allied Command Operations Handbook* focuses specifically on mitigating harm, extending the scope of NATO's protection of civilians as encompassing both harm caused by NATO's own operations and harm inflicted by other actors.[17]

As such, the protection of civilians comprises duties to both respect and protect civilians.[18] According to the NATO Policy, when planning and implementing protection of

https://bit.ly/3veVbay; see also K. H. Dock, 'Origins, Progress, and Unfinished Business: NATO's Protection of Civilians Policy', Report, The Stimson Center, Washington DC, 2021.

[8] NATO/Euro-Atlantic Partnership Council (EAPC) Policy on Women, Peace and Security, first issued in December 2007, and revised and endorsed by Heads of State and Government at the Brussels Summit in July 2018, at: http://bit.ly/38LVwFo.

[9] NATO Military Guidelines on Children and Armed Conflict, 2012.

[10] *Protection of Children in Armed Conflict: The Way Forward*, Policy endorsed by the North Atlantic Council in March 2015.

[11] NATO Military Guidelines on the Protection of, and Response to, Conflict-Related Sexual and Gender-Based Violence, 2015.

[12] NATO/EAPC Policy on Women, Peace and Security 2018, para. 6.

[13] 2016 NATO Policy on Protection of Civilians, para. 4.

[14] M. Keenan and A. W. Beadle, 'Operationalizing Protection of Civilians in NATO Operations', *Stability: International Journal of Security & Development*, Vol. 4, No. 1 (2015), 1–13.

[15] 2016 NATO Policy on Protection of Civilians, para. 5.

[16] Ibid., para. 11.

[17] 2021 Handbook, p. 23.

[18] 2016 NATO Policy on Protection of Civilians, paras. 15, 16.

civilians measures, it 'should give consideration to those groups most vulnerable to violence within the local context'.[19] It is further recognised that, 'in general, children constitute a particularly vulnerable group during conflict and women are often dispropor- tionately affected by violence'.[20] There is also a commitment to learning: 'NATO shall identify and implement lessons learned on protection of civilians, including through a gender-sensitive approach, in all relevant areas of operations and missions, as well as in training and education.'[21] This might address a key lacuna in NATO's gender approach, namely the need to develop a more precise understanding of the 'operational relevance of gender'.[22] How this is to be achieved in practice remains unclear, and clarification on this issue is not provided in the 2021 Handbook, which only clarifies that the 'Gender Perspective' should be 'thoroughly considered'.[23]

In an 'OPEN' review within NATO[24] of the protection of civilians issue after the adoption of the 2016 Policy, Sarah Williamson argued for both an 'evolutionary' and a 'cautionary [sic]' approach to the concept of protection of civilians within NATO.[25] She considers the three main (and overlapping) components to the concept: mitigate harm (MH), facilitate a safe and secure environment (SASE), and facilitate access to basic needs (FABN). The first component concerns physical protection of civilians (also includes the principle of 'do no harm').

Facilitating a safe and secure environment is about a broader secure environment, through such actions as demobilising parties to the conflict, securing weapons stock- piles, demining, security sector reform, support to transitional justice mechanisms, supporting elections, and rebuilding public infrastructure such as electricity and telecommunications. In this pillar, Williamson criticises NATO for its omission of one of the fundamental tenets of the UN approach to protecting civilians: protection through dialogue and engagement. This includes persuading governments and other armed actors to protect civilians and reporting attacks on civilians 'to the relevant authorities'.[26] Perhaps to overcome this lacuna, the 2021 Handbook, alongside MH, SASE and FABN, included 'UHE', or Understanding the Human Environment. This claims to provide a 'population-centric' perspective – including 'culture, history, demographics, strengths, informal power structures such as religious and non-govern- mental leaders and influencers, resiliencies and vulnerabilities' – essential if civilians are to be protected.[27]

---

[19] Ibid., para. 7.
[20] Ibid.
[21] Ibid., para. 18.
[22] J. M. Prescott, 'Moving from Gender Analysis to Risk Analysis of Failing to Consider Gender', *The RUSI Journal*, Vol. 165, No. 5 (2020), 46–56, at p. 51.
[23] Ibid.
[24] OPEN publications are produced by Allied Command Transformation Operational Experimentation but are not formal NATO documents and do not represent the official opinions or positions of NATO or individual nations.
[25] S. Williamson, Overcoming Protection of Civilian Failures: The Case for an Evolutionary Approach Within NATO, OPEN Publications, NATO Allied Command Transformation, Vol. 1, No. 4 (Spring 2017), pp. 1, 2.
[26] Ibid., p. 13.
[27] 2021 Handbook, p. 15.

Potentially, facilitating access to basic needs is an even more ambitious aim, but in practice this component is likely to be limited to enabling the provision of humanitarian aid by others as and when necessary. Williamson affirms that facilitating access to basic needs is an important aspect of 'Contributing to a Safe and Secure Environment (C-SASE)', but argues that the provision of aid should not be 'a military objective'.[28] Indeed, the 2021 Handbook clarifies that one of the main processes when applying the C-SASE lens during the planning of an operation includes operation assessment for NATO forces encompassing non-military activities.[29]

Overall, Katie Dock identifies several areas in which NATO's ability to protect civilians should be improved. These include, for instance, the need to ensure that NATO's plans and missions encompass the protection of civilians, including in its next Strategic Concept and through specific action plans. This would further require for NATO to define its understanding of human security, clarifying how the protection of civilians fits into such a framework, and develop a military understanding of the concept, encompassing both evolving threats – including hybrid warfare and near-peer conflict – and traditional missions. As part of this process, the organisation should ensure that both lessons learned from missions as well as national policies, doctrines, trainings, and capabilities on the protection of civilians are mapped and assessed. Indeed, the concept needs to be integrated through mandatory training and education, including at headquarters, and on the basis of adequate staffing and other resources.[30]

Similar conclusions were reached in a series of workshops held by the Stimson Center to assess the implementation of NATO's 2016 Policy, where experts further suggested the need for NATO to: (i) build support for allies to adopt a more precise PoC roadmap or work together towards the progress of a PoC policy; (ii) establish a Centre for Excellence on PoC or integrate it into the Comprehensive Crisis and Operations Management Centre ('CCOMC'), in order to ensure research and thinking on implementation; and (iii) increase expertise, including through the deployment of PoC experts in future operations and by tailoring operations based on threat assessments.[31]

A remaining shortcoming of the 2016 policy document is the lack of references to remedial action, such as compensation, for NATO's own actions.[32] It was tackled during the operation of ISAF in Afghanistan, 'to a certain extent, through the adoption in August 2010 of a set of Non-Binding Guidelines on Monetary Payments to Civilian Casualties in Afghanistan'.[33] While the payments were made *ex gratia* and without any admission of responsibility, this was an important, positive measure by NATO.[34] However, it has not

---

[28]   Ibid.

[29]   2021 Handbook, p. 50.

[30]   Dock, 'Origins, Progress, and Unfinished Business: NATO's Protection of Civilians Policy'.

[31]   V. K. Holt and M. B. Keenan, 'NATO & The Protection of Civilians: Toward Implementation', *The Stimson Center*, 2021.

[32]   The same is true for the 2021 Handbook – 'access to justice and effective remedies' is mentioned only once, in reference to Security Council Resolution 2475 on the protection of persons with disabilities in armed conflict. Ibid., p. 16 (in footnote 17).

[33]   2021 Handbook, p. 154.

[34]   NATO, 'NATO Nations Approve Civilian Casualty Guidelines', 6 August 2010, at: http://bit.ly/2PdZGxW.

been standardised for other NATO military operations, including in Libya.[35] Ultimately, the Libyan Council provided reparations through its Ministry of Finance and Oil to victims of the conflicts that erupted in 2011. The Ministry registered more than 5,000 victims from all parties to the conflict, but NATO was not involved in the process.[36]

16.3 NATO AND INTERNATIONAL HUMANITARIAN LAW

Steven Hill and Andreea Manea recall that, although NATO is 'anchored in self-defence' and therefore within the law on inter-State use of force (*jus ad bellum*), NATO has affirmed on numerous occasions that good-faith compliance also with international humanitarian law (IHL) and international human rights law 'is at the heart of all NATO activities'.[37] Not all NATO Member States are party to the same IHL instruments (the United States has not ratified the two 1977 Additional Protocols to the Geneva Conventions, for instance), nor do they necessarily agree upon the content of customary IHL. Indeed, the references in the same sentence in Paragraph 5 of the 2016 Policy to 'applicable' international law including IHL 'as applicable' demonstrate the legal entanglements that may occur in practice[38] as well as the need for legal interoperability.[39] In this context, the need for NATO to 'maintain strict adherence to international humanitarian law' as well as 'build added capabilities for protection' – including a proactive stance rather than simple restraint – has been recognised.[40]

The first NATO combat action was in Bosnia in late February 1994, when NATO aircraft operating under Operation Deny Flight shot down four Bosnian Serb fighter aircrafts for violating a no-fly zone instituted by the United Nations (UN) Security Council. Beginning on 30 August 1995, major air strikes were conducted against Bosnian Serb forces under Operation Deliberate Force, following the genocide at Srebrenica (a UN-designated 'safe area')[41] and continued commission of crimes against humanity against Bosnian Muslims in Sarajevo. The collapse of the Srebrenica safe area significantly decreased the credibility of the peacekeeping mission and the involved states,[42] the UN, and NATO. However, this also led to international negotiations[43] in

---

[35]   Hill and Manea, 'Protection of Civilians: A NATO Perspective', p. 155.
[36]   K. Younus, and M. Pennington, *Libya: Protect Vulnerable Minorities & Assist Civilians Harmed*, Report, CIVIC, Washington, DC, November 2011.
[37]   Hill and Manea, 'Protection of Civilians: A NATO Perspective', p. 146.
[38]   The same is true for the 2021 Handbook, which mentions that 'the legal framework will be derived from IHL, customary international law and IHRL, *as applicable*' [emphasis added]. At p. 12.
[39]   M. Newton, 'The Interoperability of the Laws of Armed Conflict', in R. Geiß and H. Krieger (eds.), *The 'Legal Pluriverse' Surrounding Multinational Military Operations*, 1st ed., Oxford University Press, Oxford, 2020; K. Abbott, 'A Brief Overview of Legal Interoperability Challenges for NATO Arising from the Interrelationship between IHL and IHRL in Light of the European Convention on Human Rights', *International Review of the Red Cross*, Vol. 96, No. 893 (2015), 107–37.
[40]   Holt and Keenan, 'NATO & The Protection of Civilians: Toward Implementation', p. 2.
[41]   On 4 June 1993, the UN Security Council adopted Resolution 836 authorising use of force to protect designated safe zones.
[42]   D. S. Gordon, 'A Recipe for Making Safe Areas Unsafe', in D. S. Gordon and F. H. Toase (eds.), *Aspects of Peacekeeping*, Routledge, Abingdon, 2001, p. 213.
[43]   As analysed by R. Hering, 'Safe Areas for the Protection of Civilians: An Overview of Existing Research and Scholarship', *Z Friedens und Konfforsch*, Vol. 9 (2020), 283–303, at p. 288.

which NATO military action was determinant in ensuring the conclusion of the Dayton Peace Agreement, signed in Paris on 14 December 1995,[44] and hence in ensuring the protection of civilians.

The bulk of NATO's early learning on the protection of civilians, however, came later when seeking to implement its International Security Assistance Force (ISAF) mandate in Afghanistan following the US-led attack on the Taliban government in response to the terror attacks on 11 September 2001. There, from October 2006, NATO found itself conducting high-intensity ground combat operations for the first time in its history. While protecting the civilian population was said to be 'one of the most important military-strategic goals of the mission',[45] lessons were slow to be learned and civilian casualties resulting from NATO military action were, for many years, relatively high. The reasons, while multiple and complex, are often ascribed to the context. As Steven Hill and Andrea Manea have observed, it was and remains NATO's 'most challenging mission' to date[46] (the more politically controversial Libya operation is discussed in Section 16.5 below). Indeed, initially, civilians were considered to be only protected 'indirectly', meaning NATO focused on avoiding killing civilians rather than protecting them.[47] Yet, ultimately, the avoidance of civilian casualties was considered of strategic relevance to reduce 'the risk of strategic defeat by pursuing tactical wins that cause civilian casualties or unnecessary collateral damage'.[48]

Civilian casualties were significantly reduced thereafter. Williamson ascribes this success to the establishment by ISAF in 2008 of a Civilian Casualty Tracking Cell (CCTC) to gather data of reported casualties, which it then used to change tactics, resulting in an 80 per cent reduction in ISAF-related casualties by 2014.[49] It is noteworthy, in this regard, that ISAF commanders later recognised that mere compliance with IHL could not, in itself, sufficiently reduce the civilian harm caused by the coalition.[50] More restraint and pro-active measures were necessary.

The NATO ISAF mission in Afghanistan transitioned to its non-combat successor, the Resolute Support Mission, on 1 January 2015, following the handover of security responsibility to Afghan National Defence and Security Forces in December 2014. In response to the UN Assistance Mission to Afghanistan report for 2018, NATO stated that all feasible precautions were being taken to minimise the likelihood of civilian casualties and that all allegations were investigated. Based on detailed operational records, NATO confirmed its forces were responsible for sixty-two dead and fifty-five injured civilians but contested a further sixty-eight killed and sixty-six injured alleged by the United Nations. Nonetheless,

44   *NATO Handbook*, chapter 5: The Alliance's Operational Role in Peacekeeping, updated 18 December 2002, at: http://bit.ly/2PhRblw.
45   Keenan and Beadle, 'Operationalizing Protection of Civilians in NATO Operations', p. 2.
46   Hill and Manea, 'Protection of Civilians: A NATO Perspective', p. 147.
47   A. W. Beadle, 'Protection of Civilians in Theory: A Comparison of UN and Nato Approaches', Report, Norwegian Defence Research Establishment (FFI), 2010, p. 24.
48   *COMISAF's Initial Assessment*, Headquarters ISAF, Kabul, 2009, pp. 1–2.
49   Williamson, *Overcoming Protection of Civilian Failures: The Case for an Evolutionary Approach Within NATO*, p. 8, citing NATO Joint Analysis and Lessons Learned Center (JALLC), *Protection of Civilians: How ISAF Reduced Civilian Casualties*, June 2015.
50   Dock, 'Origins, Progress, and Unfinished Business: NATO's Protection of Civilians Policy', p. 5.

the NATO Resolute Support Mission acknowledged that the casualties were too high.[51] Overall, Afghanistan showed NATO the importance of preparedness 'where war meets crisis management, and where humanitarian law (the law of armed conflict) meets human rights law', leading to the NATO policy in 2016.[52]

Since then, NATO has been actively seeking to adapt to new challenges to the protection of civilians posed by changing security environments. For instance, after recognising urban warfare as a relevant humanitarian concern, NATO developed in 2021 a 'quad model' for urban warfare. This maps out the interaction between a population of a significant size, which comprises varying socio-cultural groups (physical systems), and the prevailing information system. This serves to understand how these elements interact and how such interaction can enable the protection of civilians in the urban context. The development of such guidelines for civilian protection in an urban environment would continue to fall under the protection umbrella of IHL, while at the same time providing for added standards by, for instance, enabling evacuations and humanitarian corridors for civilian aid, or prohibiting or restricting the use of certain weapons that can disproportionately affect the civilian population, such as certain explosive weapons.[53] With the war between Russia and Ukraine, renewed reflection on the protection of civilians in conventional warfare and collective defence has also gained in relevance.[54]

16.4 NATO AND INTERNATIONAL HUMAN RIGHTS LAW

The application of international human rights law to operations abroad is contentious because of jurisdictional elements. The United States, for instance, does not accept that the 1966 International Covenant on Civil and Political Rights[55] applies extraterritorially, while EU Member States are largely protected from application of the European Convention on Human Rights[56] to aerial attacks outside Europe by the 2001 decision on admissibility in the *Banković* case[57] and within Europe by the recent judgment in *Georgia v. Russia (II)*.[58] In

[51] UN Assistance Mission in Afghanistan (UNAMA), *2018 Annual Report on the Protection of Civilians in Armed Conflict in Afghanistan*, Kabul, February 2019, Annex VIII: NATO Resolute Support Response to the 2018 Afghanistan Annual Report on Protection of Civilians in Armed Conflict.

[52] S. Rynning, 'Rethinking NATO Policy on the Protection of Civilians', *Parameters*, Vol. 47, No. 3 (2017), 39–49, at p. 39.

[53] D. Kilcullen and G. Pendleton, 'Future Urban Conflict, Technology and the Protection of Civilians: Real-World Challenges for NATO and Coalition Missions', Report, The Stimson Center, Washington, DC, 2021, p. 7.

[54] See A. Atkinson, 'The Protection of Civilians within Collective Defense', Report, The Stimson Center, Washington, DC, 2021.

[55] International Covenant on Civil and Political Rights; adopted at New York, 16 December 1966; entered into force, 23 March 1976 (ICCPR). As of 1 April 2022, 173 States (including all NATO Member States) were party to the ICCPR.

[56] Convention for the Protection of Human Rights and Fundamental Freedoms; adopted at Rome, 4 November 1950; entered into force, 3 September 1953.

[57] European Court of Human Rights, *Banković and others v. Belgium and others*, Decision as to Admissibility (Grand Chamber), 12 December 2001.

[58] European Court of Human Rights, *Georgia v. Russia (II)*, Judgment (Grand Chamber), 21 January 2001, para. 137. The Court attached 'decisive weight to the fact that the very reality of armed confrontation and fighting between enemy military forces seeking to establish control over an area in a context of chaos not only means

addition to different understandings of the extraterritoriality of international human rights law, applicable domestic law also differs among NATO Member States, which contributes to the complexity of what is the 'applicable legal framework' for the protection of civilians during NATO operations.[59]

Certainly, NATO and the concerned Member State(s) will in any event be bound by customary international human rights law in any ground operations, in particular the *jus cogens* prohibitions on arbitrary deprivation of life and on torture. Non-refoulement and the prohibition on arbitrary deprivation of liberty – also arguably *jus cogens* norms[60] – means that holding a person against their will for any significant length of time or handing over detained persons to national authorities where there is a serious risk of them being unlawfully harmed would amount to a violation by NATO and the concerned Member State(s) of international human rights law. 'Catch and release' may not be a popular policy, but it is one that has been widely used in the context of counter-piracy operations, including by NATO naval forces during Operation Ocean Shield in 2009–16.[61]

Last, as outlined above, the 2016 Policy refers to applicable legal frameworks, including IHL and IHRL. Indeed, the Policy focuses on the right to life and physical integrity – in line with the Organization's focus on military operations – and the importance of actively engaging with key actors, such as civil society organisations.[62] However, what remains to be addressed is NATO's partners understanding of the protection of civilians, which at the moment remains fractured depending on each State's policies and approach towards international law.[63]

16.5 OPERATION UNIFIED PROTECTOR IN LIBYA

In 2011, when the emerging civil war in Libya threatened the lives of numerous civilians, NATO intervened with military means. Aerial intervention by NATO in Libya was indirectly authorised by the UN Security Council under Resolution 1973 with the use of force specifically authorised to protect civilians.[64] It remains the most controversial operation NATO has yet mounted – even NATO Member Germany had abstained from voting in favour of the resolution – and is considered to have politicised the notion of the protection of civilians. This is notably because Operation Unified Protector evolved

that there is no "effective control" over an area ... but also excludes any form of "State agent authority and control" over individuals'.

[59] Hill and Manea, 'Protection of Civilians: A NATO Perspective', p. 150.
[60] International Law Commission (ILC), Fourth report on peremptory norms of general international law (*jus cogens*) by Dire Tladi, Special Rapporteur, UN doc. A/CN.4/727, 31 January 2019, paras. 131–4.
[61] See, for example, NATO, 'Counter-Piracy Operations (Archived)', last updated 19 December 2016, at: http://bit.ly/2VzZqNL.
[62] Hill and Manea, 'Protection of Civilians: A NATO Perspective', pp. 156–7.
[63] As highlighted in the webinar held by Stimson on 'Unfinished Business: NATO's Protection of Civilians Policy and the Way Forward', and specifically by both Dock and Keenan in their presentations.
[64] UN Security Council Resolution 1973, adopted on 17 March 2011 by ten votes in favour to nil, with five abstentions (Brazil, China, Germany, India, Russian Federation). The insertion of ground troops was expressly excluded by operative paragraph 4 of the Resolution.

from a protective air campaign into one that effectively supported the removal of Muammar Gaddafi's forces.

The motivation for the passage of Security Council Resolution 1973 was a fear that genocide and/or crimes against humanity would be committed by Gaddafi's forces, specifically in Benghazi. Indeed, Security Council Resolution 1970, adopted by unanimous vote on 26 February 2011, had expressed 'grave concern' at the situation in Libya and condemned 'the violence and use of force against civilians'.[65] The Council had even considered that 'the widespread and systematic attacks currently taking place in the Libyan Arab Jamahiriya against the civilian population may amount to crimes against humanity', a rare pronouncement by the Security Council on the possible commission of international crimes.[66] Whether the risk of perpetration of such crimes was overblown by the opponents to Gaddafi's regime continues to be debated. Previous conflicts had indeed witnessed even the provocation of violence by those who sought foreign intervention.

Regardless, scholars have argued that, whereas the protection of civilians was fully within the Security Council mandate, this was not the case for the overthrowing of Gaddafi. Indeed, they aver, NATO's 'misinterpretation' of Resolution 1973 left several countries 'with a sense of betrayal', which later led to demands for an investigation into the legality of the whole operation.[67]

Rob Weighill and Florence Gaub's narration of the NATO campaign in Libya described in *The Cauldron*[68] notes that initially the use of force in Libya was not planned to be delivered through NATO. Indeed, the first military action after the adoption of Resolution 1973 came from France acting independently of the organisation in an operation code-named Harmattan.[69] It was only ten days afterwards, on 27 March 2011, that NATO's Secretary-General announced that the Organization would implement all aspects of the resolution.[70] Following suggestions that certain NATO Member States, such as the United Kingdom, were considering arming the rebels, Russia, which had not blocked the resolution, warned NATO of 'excessive creativity' in interpreting Resolution 1973.[71]

That said, an advisor to Allied Joint Force Command (JFC) in Naples described the difficulty of operationalising the language in the UN Security Council authorisation.[72] 'PoC does not indicate an end state to be achieved, nor does it identify an enemy ... concrete indications needed to be found that would point to effectively protected

---

[65]   UN Security Council Resolution 1970, adopted by unanimous vote in favour on 26 February 2011, first preambular para.

[66]   Ibid., sixth preambular para.

[67]   See, for instance, E. Ebrahim, 'Lecture by Deputy Minister of International Relations and Cooperation on the occasion of the Speakers Meeting at the South African Institute of International Affairs', *International Relations & Cooperation*, 2011, available at: https://bit.ly/3wuQni9.

[68]   R. Weighill and F. Gaub, *The Cauldron: NATO's Campaign in Libya*, Hurst, London, 2018. The authors' international legal analyses are flawed at times (for instance, mixing IHL and *jus ad bellum*), but their political analysis is persuasive.

[69]   Ibid., p. 71.

[70]   Ibid., p. 80.

[71]   Ibid., pp. 94, 95.

[72]   Williamson, *Overcoming Protection of Civilian Failures: The Case for an Evolutionary Approach Within NATO*, p. 5.

civilians.' Joint Force Command Naples developed three criteria for success: all attacks and threats against civilians and civilian populated areas have ended; the regime has verifiably withdrawn all military forces from all populated areas they have forcibly entered; and the regime has permitted humanitarian access to all people in need of assistance.[73]

The mission requirement that a strike would result in no civilian casualties at all goes considerably beyond IHL obligations of distinction and proportionality in attack – significantly reducing the possible targets and the weapons that could be used.[74] The civilian casualties caused by NATO air strikes were indeed exceptionally low, but, almost inevitably, they were not zero.[75] Indeed, NATO's decision not to deploy ground troops, relying instead on a 'no-fly-zone' and aerial bombardment, was criticised from a protection standpoint,[76] as the former is generally recognised to be a more effective method for protecting civilians in armed conflict.[77] This resulted, according to some sources,[78] in several indiscriminate attacks in violation of IHL. Moreover, NATO may have turned a blind eye to attacks on civilians and other serious violations of IHL by rebel forces.[79]

In the end, the intervention to protect civilians ultimately led to regime change. Some have argued that regime change was necessary to effectively protect civilians. The more common view, however, asserts a partial or even inaccurate application of Security Council Resolution 1973, shifting NATO's military objective and, ultimately, its choice of means and methods when intervening in Libya.[80]

It was further argued that NATO should have done more to monitor and investigate civilian casualties, a key step for identifying violations of international law and providing for reparations at the conclusion of the conflict.[81] In fact, perhaps the most significant error was in the failure by all concerned to plan adequately for the aftermath of the Libyan forces' defeat. The lessons from Iraq should have been uppermost in the minds of all those engaged in using force: these included controlling critical infrastructure, providing reception facilities, accommodation and medical services, and managing non-combatant evacuation, including of internally displaced people.[82] The chaos that is Libya today is

[73] Ibid., citing F. Gaub, *NATO and Libya: Reviewing Operation Unified Protector*, The Letort Papers, US Army War College Strategic Studies Institute, United States, June 2013, available at: http://bit.ly/2vXeY3k.
[74] *The Cauldron: NATO's Campaign in Libya*, pp. 161–2.
[75] See, for example, ibid., pp. 178–9.
[76] J.-M. Iyi, 'The Duty of an Intervention Force to Protect Civilians: A Critical Analysis of NATO's Intervention in Libya', *Conflict Trends*, No. 2, 2012, 41–8, at p. 44.
[77] T. B. Seybold, *Humanitarian Military Intervention: The Conditions for Success and Failure*, Oxford University Press, Oxford, 2008, p. 185.
[78] Notably, reports by Amnesty International (*Libya: The Forgotten Victims of NATO's Strikes*, London, 2012, p. 7); and Human Rights Watch (*Libya: Country Summary*, Washington, DC, 2012, p. 5).
[79] Seybold, *Humanitarian Military Intervention: The Conditions for Success and Failure*, p. 225.
[80] Iyi, 'The Duty of an Intervention Force to Protect Civilians: A Critical Analysis of NATO's Intervention in Libya', p. 48.
[81] I. Davis, 'How Good is NATO after Libya?', Briefing Paper, NATO Watch, 2011, available at: https://bit.ly/3NYfH8d, p. 4.
[82] As argued by Kilcullen and Pendleton when analysing the 'lessons learned' from the battle of Mosul in Iraq (2014–17) and the battle of Marawi in the Philippines (2017). Kilcullen and Pendleton, 'Future Urban Conflict, Technology and the Protection of Civilians: Real-World Challenges for NATO and Coalition Missions'.

testament to their individual and collective failures: the intervention left behind a large gap to fill in terms of foreign assistance, both to account for the number of civilians and migrants caught up in the conflict, as well as to collect and secure the large amount of weaponry still circulating in the country.[83]

---

[83] Davis, 'How Good is NATO after Libya?', p. 4. See also I. Martin, *All Necessary Measures? The United Nations and International Intervention in Libya*, Hurst, London, 2022.

17

The African Union and the Protection of Civilians

17.1 INTRODUCTION

With respect to the protection of civilians, the African Union (AU) has largely focused on elaborating guidelines for its peacekeeping operations. Its 'Draft' Guidelines, concluded in 2010 and published in 2012,[1] define the protection of civilians as

> includ[ing] activities undertaken to improve the security of the population and people at risk and to ensure the full respect for the rights of groups and the individual recognised under regional instruments, including the African Charter of Human and Peoples' Rights, the AU Convention for the Protection and Assistance of Internally Displaced Persons, and the Convention Governing the Specific Aspects of Refugee Problems in Africa, and international law, including humanitarian, human rights and refugee law.[2]

This is a broad definition, mirroring the international definition of protection, and not one that is restricted to situations of armed conflict.

17.2 'TIERED' PROTECTION OF CIVILIANS UNDER THE AU GUIDELINES

The 2012 Guidelines are largely generic in nature, providing for a view of protection of civilians as a broad and all-encompassing issue that goes beyond peace support operations.[3] At one point, with respect to the 'mainstreaming' of the protection of civilians 'within the African peace and security architecture', the Guidelines call for each protection of civilians mandate for an operation to be described 'in precise and detailed terms' and for the relationship between the protection mandate and other mandated tasks to be made clear.[4] In particular, the threats to, and vulnerabilities of, civilian populations

---

[1] *Draft Guidelines for the Protection of Civilians in African Union Peace Support Operations*, African Union, Addis Ababa, 2012.

[2] Ibid., para. 1.

[3] It includes IHL, human rights, humanitarian action, legal protection, and gender issues; see G. De Carvalho and A. Ø. Stensland, 'The Protection of Civilians in Peacekeeping in Africa: Context and Evolution', *Conflict Trends*, No. 2, 2012, 3–10, at p. 7.

[4] *Draft Guidelines for the Protection of Civilians in African Union Peace Support Operations*, para. 8.

should, the Guidelines stipulate, inform the scope of protection mandates. A protection strategy requires 'the collection and analysis of timely, reliable and widely-sourced information in order to understand the threats against, and vulnerabilities of, civilians'.[5] Once a protection mandate is provided to a peace support operation, the operation must be 'appropriately resourced, configured and equipped' in order to ensure it has the capacity to fulfil that mandate.[6]

Protection is organised into four 'tiers': protection through political process; physical protection; rights-based protection; and establishing a secure environment. These 'tiers' are broadly similar to the structure of the UN's Operational Concept of the time.[7]

The first tier – that of protection as *part of the political process* – is crucial to the success of a peace support operation, and 'lies at the centre of an operation's work to ensure that a State emerging from conflict can establish lasting and sustainable peace'.[8] As the Guidelines recall, a well-managed peace process that provides for justice and accountability is potentially the best form of protection for a civilian population.[9]

Within the context of the multi-tiered protection of civilians, *protection from physical violence* is given special attention in the Guidelines.[10] This second tier can, the Guidelines explain, be broken down into four phases although the phases 'may not be sequential and may co-exist across the mission area'.[11]

> Phase 1 is termed 'Prevention'. It encompasses activities to discourage groups from engaging in hostile activities, such as by means of patrols, and 'hearts and minds' activities.[12]
>
> Phase 2 is termed 'Pre-emption' and concerns measures 'to preclude or defeat an imminent threat[13] or to gain advantage over a spoiler group before it launches a designed violent activity'. This may be achieved through the tactical redeployment of troops.
>
> Phase 3 covers a forcible 'Response', which involves the 'proportionate use of force to neutralise or render ineffective a spoiler group' after violence has occurred.[14] The Guidelines observe that 'higher authorisation for certain activities may be required'.

---

[5]   Ibid., para. 16.

[6]   Ibid., para. 9.

[7]   E. A. Weir, 'Policies That Protect: The African Union and the Protection of Civilians', *NUPI Policy Brief*, Norwegian Institute of African Affairs, Oslo, 2013.

[8]   Thus, protection of civilians also entails ensuring a safe environment both during a conflict and post-conflict. De Carvalho and Stensland, 'The Protection of Civilians in Peacekeeping in Africa: Context and Evolution', p. 4.

[9]   *Draft Guidelines for the Protection of Civilians in African Union Peace Support Operations*, para. 20.

[10] In contrast to UN peacekeeping operations, within the AU protection of civilians rests predominantly on military protection – without civilian or police components – as the available AU civilian capacity is still 'embryonic'. A. Appiah-Mensah and R. Eklou-Assogbavi, 'The Protection of Civilians: A Comparison Between United Nations and African Union Peace Operations', *Conflict Trends*, No. 2, 2012, 11–16, at p. 15.

[11] *Draft Guidelines for the Protection of Civilians in African Union Peace Support Operations*, para. 20.

[12] This should include identifying what protection should look like in practice and from whom civilians should be protected: indeed, peacekeepers themselves can become a threat to civilians. De Carvalho and Stensland, 'The Protection of Civilians in Peacekeeping in Africa: Context and Evolution', p. 10.

[13] An imminent threat is based on an assessment of time (i.e. about to happen) and indication (i.e. factual information).

[14] In MONUSCO, for instance, Community Alert Networks (CANs) were established, distributing mobile telephones to alert the troops in case of imminent threat to the security of villagers. B. Martin, 'The Protection of Civilians in the Democratic Republic of the Congo', *Conflict Trends*, No. 2, 2012, 33–40, at p. 39.

Phase 4 is termed 'Consolidation'. In this phase, action to manage a post-conflict situation may include 'denying threatening groups the ability to restore fighting capability'. The example of disarmament, demobilisation, and reintegration (DDR) is given as a possible activity.

Rights-based protection must, the Guidelines stipulate, 'be applicable to both individuals and groups and must be mainstreamed from the outset'. This third tier may involve 'the monitoring and reporting of human rights violations in the mission area and the development of local capacity to promote and protect human rights (for example: conducting investigations into human rights abuses and supporting the establishment of transitional justice mechanisms)'.[15]

The *establishment of a protective environment*, the fourth and final tier, is 'comprehensive and broad, and includes a peace building dimension'.[16] It begins with early recovery 'and should lead to self-sustainable solutions'. It can include capacity-building measures and broad-based reform measures.[17]

The four tiers provide a framework within which protection mandated activities can be planned, conducted, and reported on.[18] The Guidelines underline that the tiers and the activities falling within each tier 'must be pursued in a continuous, concurrent and mutually supporting manner': the protection activities under each tier need to be conducted in a parallel and holistic manner.[19] They further gave the issue of protection of civilians a certain momentum within the AU, although major challenges remain. For instance, it had been pointed out that no clear definition of 'protection of civilians' yet exists in the AU. This is ascribed to diverging interpretations but also 'frequent miscommunication and a lack of coordination'.[20]

17.3 MANDATES TO PROTECT CIVILIANS

Between 2003 and 2017, the African Union mandated or authorised ten peace support operations, three multinational coalitions, and one hybrid mission with the United Nations (UN) in Darfur (AU-UN Mission in Darfur: UNAMID). Of these, six of the ten AU-led operations had protection of civilians dimensions to their mandates, as did two of the three multinational coalitions, along with the hybrid mission in Darfur. Both the AU

[15] *Draft Guidelines for the Protection of Civilians in African Union Peace Support Operations*, para. 20.
[16] This is an addition to the UN guidelines, which provide for three tiers. It stems from the conviction that the AU can give most meaning to the protection of civilians through peace support operations, according to M. Dembinski and B. Schott, 'Converging Around Global Norms? Protection of Civilians in African Union and European Union Peacekeeping in Africa', *African Security*, Vol. 6, Nos. 3–4 (2013), 276–96, at p. 286.
[17] As African institutions are understood as the competent first resort for gross human rights abuses, this might implicitly challenge the UN Security Council's primary responsibility for international peace and security. L. Gelot, 'Civilian Protection in Africa: How the Protection of Civilians is Being Militarized by African Policymakers and Diplomats', *Contemporary Security Policy*, Vol. 38, No. 1 (2017), 161–73, at p. 165.
[18] This four-tiered approach has clarified the context of protection of civilians within the AU; however, they still require further clarification to have practical significance in AU operations. De Carvalho and Stensland, 'The Protection of Civilians in Peacekeeping in Africa: Context and Evolution', p. 9.
[19] Ibid.
[20] Ibid., p. 8.

Mission in Burundi (AMIB) and the AU Mission in Somalia (AMISOM) gave their peacekeepers explicit authorisation to use force to protect local civilians, despite the fact that this task was not listed in the mission's official mandate as agreed upon by the AU.[21] Since the AU drafted its protection of civilians guidelines, all newly mandated AU-led operations, and the multinational coalitions it has authorised to fight the Lord's Resistance Army (LRA) and Boko Haram, have been explicitly mandated to protect civilians.[22]

Practice in protecting civilians has, however, been mixed. The original African Mission in Sudan (AMIS) had limited resources. Despite having a mandate to protect civilians, 'massacres, rapes and large movements continued in the presence of the monitoring troops' and, for the most part, 'AMIS forces stood by and recorded but did not stop attacks on civilians and the destruction of villages'.[23] John Ahere and colleagues suggest that the mission's leadership used lack of resources as an excuse for inaction.[24] Moreover, as Paul Williams observes, no official 'lessons learned' study was conducted either of AMIS as a whole or of the AU's efforts to protect civilians in Darfur.[25] A 2016 report on the challenges of peacekeeping in Darfur by the International Refugee Rights Initiative was headlined with the quote from an internally displaced person: 'No one on the earth cares if we survive except God and sometimes UNAMID.'[26]

Although UN intervention in the AU mission was encouraged by the international community, as the humanitarian crisis in Darfur deepened, the intervention effectively vilified the work AMIS had undertaken.[27] Protection of civilians action was undermined by several factors, including lack of adequate capacities, widespread corruption,[28] and the absence of operational and tactical guidelines on the implementation of the protection mandate,[29] effectively leaving the interpretation of the mandate up to each troop-providing State.[30]

---

[21] J. M. Okeke and P. D. Williams, 'Introduction', in J. M. Okeke and P. D. Williams (eds.), *Protecting Civilians in African Union Peace Support Operations: Key Cases and Lessons Learned*, Accord, South Africa, 2017, p. 16.

[22] Ibid., p. 18.

[23] L. S. Bishai, 'Darfur', in D. P. Forsythe (ed.), *Encyclopedia of Human Rights*, Vol. 1, Oxford University Press, Oxford, 2009, p. 477. See also J. Ahere, O. Davies, and I. Limo, 'Recounting the African Union's Efforts to Protect Civilians in Darfur: From AMIS to UNAMID', chapter 1 in Okeke and Williams (eds.), *Protecting Civilians in African Union Peace Support Operations: Key Cases and Lessons Learned*, p. 36.

[24] Ahere et al., 'Recounting the African Union's Efforts to Protect Civilians in Darfur: From AMIS to UNAMID', p. 37.

[25] P. D. Williams, 'The Ambiguous Place of Civilian Protection in the African Union Mission in Somalia', chapter 2 in Okeke and Williams (eds.), *Protecting Civilians in African Union Peace Support Operations: Key Cases and Lessons Learned*, p. 54.

[26] L. Hovil and O. Bueno with A. Lambe, 'The Challenges of Peacekeeping in Darfur', *International Refugee Rights Initiative*, July 2016, at: http://bit.ly/3j4V7SY.

[27] P. Kangwanja and P. Mutahi, 'Protection of Civilians in African Peace Missions: The Case of the African Union Mission in Sudan, Darfur', *Institute for Security Studies*, 2007, p. 14.

[28] A. de Waal and J. Flint, *Darfur A New History of a Long War*, Zed Books, London, 2008, p. 194.

[29] African Union, *Report of the Strategic Retreat of the African Union Interdepartmental Working Group on the Protection of Civilians*, 2011, p. 8.

[30] Dembinski and Schott, 'Converging Around Global Norms? Protection of Civilians in African Union and European Union Peacekeeping in Africa', p. 289.

Deployed to Mogadishu in March 2007, the African Union Mission in Somalia (AMISOM) was authorised by the AU Peace and Security Council and only later 'endorsed' by the UN Security Council.[31] It was, however, not until late May 2013 that AMISOM officially adopted a mission-wide strategy on the protection of civilians.[32] In addition, AMISOM 'was not a peacekeeping mission in the UN sense of the term' but more of a peace operation involving combat and counterinsurgency operations 'that went well beyond the levels of force and tempo of operations generally expected in UN-led peacekeeping missions'.[33] In Mogadishu, the UN-backed Transitional Federal Government 'lacked even rudimentary capabilities, and its armed forces routinely harmed civilians'.[34]

There was no legal adviser to AMISOM until 2010 and the Mission had insufficient numbers of police officers or civilian personnel to implement a protection of civilians mandate effectively. It also had 'no means to collect and analyse the type of information that is crucial for both ensuring compliance with IHL [international humanitarian law] and for more proactive PoC initiatives'.[35] Indeed, the mission was alleged to have presented 'mixed messages' on the protection of civilians, both at the tactical level – where AMISOM troops did not have a specific protection of civilians mandate for several years – and even at the strategic level.[36] According to Matthias Dembinski and Berenike Schott, the protection of civilians was not high on the agenda of the mission, whose core task changed from protection of the government to fighting al-Shabaab,[37] shifting from a peace support to a peace enforcement operation.[38]

Al-Shabaab exploited the opportunities provided by what it perceived as an 'invasion force'. In 'a typical scenario' in Mogadishu 'for much of 2009 and 2010', its militia would fire mortar rounds at AMISOM positions from the main market area and then withdraw. Fire would be returned by AMISOM with heavy weapons, without being able to observe where the shot fell, oftentimes inflicting significant civilian casualties.[39] Indirect fire from AMISOM units became a major source of civilian harm. Also AMISOM troops sometimes fired on civilians who they had mistaken for enemy fighters. 'In one such incident in 2009, a passenger bus was accidentally fired upon by AMISOM troops after they were ambushed by a combination of a roadside bomb and machine-gun fire.'[40]

---

[31] Williams, 'The Ambiguous Place of Civilian Protection in the African Union Mission in Somalia', p. 48.

[32] Ahere et al., 'Recounting the African Union's Efforts to Protect Civilians in Darfur: From AMIS to UNAMID'.

[33] Ibid., p. 54.

[34] Ibid.

[35] Ibid., pp. 55–56.

[36] P. D. Williams, 'The African Union Mission in Somalia and Civilian Protection Challenges', *Stability: International Journal of Security & Development*, Vol. 2, No. 2 (2013), 1–17, at p. 4.

[37] Dembinski and Schott, 'Converging Around Global Norms? Protection of Civilians in African Union and European Union Peacekeeping in Africa', p. 289.

[38] W. Lotze and Y. Kasumba, 'AMISOM and the Protection of Civilians in Somalia', *Conflict Trends*, No. 2, 2012, 17–24, at p. 19.

[39] Ahere et al., 'Recounting the African Union's Efforts to Protect Civilians in Darfur: From AMIS to UNAMID', p. 58.

[40] Ibid.

To reduce casualties, AMISOM hired international public relations expertise and invited in outside technical expertise. The outcome was the '3A strategy': Avoid, Attribute, and Amend:

> Where possible, AMISOM should avoid the use of indirect fire; where casualties occur, AMISOM should attribute responsibility to the perpetrator(s) by assessing and investigating incidents; and AMISOM should assist those who have been injured through emotional redress, medical care and/or material assistance, and make amends for civilian harm caused unintentionally by AMISOM, thus helping to build local support for the mission over the longer term.[41]

But even with these 'remedial initiatives, AMISOM was unable to eradicate all sources of civilian harm from among its own ranks and operations'. Instances of lethal force used against local civilians and accusations that some AMISOM personnel engaged in the sexual exploitation of local women and girls are two examples. 'The most prominent example of AMISOM personnel killing civilians came on 31 July 2015, when the AU acknowledged that Ugandan members of AMISOM killed seven civilians in the town of Marka. Three AMISOM personnel were subsequently indicted for this incident.'[42] Overall, the mission was considered to have revealed the weakness of the AU peacekeeping, as well as its inadequacy for tackling the complex situation in Somalia.[43] It revealed three important gaps, namely the need (1) to re-affirm IHL as the basis for AU operations as well as debates on the protection of civilians; (2) to finalise the Draft Guidelines with expectations for AU troops clearly set out; and (3) to provide AU commanders and troops with better training and equipment.[44]

Following the crisis in Libya – on February 2011 – the AU Peace and Security Council 'expressed deep concern with the situation'[45] and the African Court of Human and Peoples' Rights ordered provisional measures against Libya, calling on the authorities to 'refrain from any action that would result in loss of life'.[46] As intervention in Libya is generally agreed to have led to chaos within the country and outside, with arms being trafficked across the Sahel region,[47] this might impact future interventions in Africa.[48] In particular, it highlighted the need to determine 'how future protection missions should be carried out'.[49]

---

[41] Ibid., p. 60. Other policies, such as the rules governing detention by AMISOM forces, have not been made public.

[42] Ibid., p. 62.

[43] C. N. Oguonu and C. C. Ezeibe, 'African Union and Conflict Resolution in Africa', *Mediterranean Journal of Social Sciences*, Vol. 5, No. 27 (December 2014), 325–32, at p. 330.

[44] Weir, 'Policies That Protect: The African Union and the Protection of Civilians', p. 4.

[45] African Union Peace and Security Committee CCLXI (2011), AU doc. PSC/PR/COMM (CCLXI), para. 17(a).

[46] African Court of Human and Peoples' Rights, *African Commission on Human Rights and Peoples' Rights v. The Great Socialist Libyan Arab Jamahiriya*, Judgment, 2011, para. 25(1).

[47] UN Security Council, 'Report of the Assessment Mission on the Impact of the Libya Crisis on the Sahel Region, 7 to 23 December 2011', UN doc. S/2012/42, 2012, paras. 4, 15–17, and 32–62.

[48] M. Miramon, 'Jean Ping: "Western Countries Didn't Let the African Union Play a Role"', *l'Humanité in English*, 2014, available at: https://bit.ly/3F2otu8.

[49] B. Kioko and L. Wambugu, 'The African Union and the Protection of Civilians', in H. Willmot et al. (eds.), *Protection of Civilians*, 1st ed., Oxford University Press, Oxford, 2016, p. 290.

Nevertheless, human rights observers were deployed in Mali from 1 April 2013: the first time that human rights observers had been deployed in an AU peace support operation.[50] In the AU Mission in Central African Republic (MISCA), the absence of an effective joint operations centre and joint mission analysis centre was considered significant. In addition, due to the lack of police, 'military units were faced with public order functions, for which they had not been properly trained and equipped'.[51] These more recent crises have demonstrated the importance for African actors to be prepared in countering violent extremism, or international actors will exercise external influence either by financial assistance, political legitimising, or military means.[52] The lack of resources and equipment indeed remains a persistent theme in AU peace support operations.

17.4 THE POWER OF THE AU TO INTERVENE TO PROTECT CIVILIANS

Various mechanisms and instruments relate to the protection of civilians in Africa, namely the Constitutive Act of the African Union;[53] the African Peace and Security Architecture;[54] the African Human Rights System;[55] and the African Governance Architecture.[56] The 2000 Constitutive Act of the African Union[57] gives the Union the power to intervene in a Member State to put an end to genocide, crimes against humanity, or war crimes, as well as in other, unspecified 'grave' circumstances. While aggression is not explicitly mentioned, this may be considered as such a grave circumstance. The AU has not yet used this power, however, which must in any event be authorised by both the Assembly of the African Union[58] and the UN Security Council.[59] The threat of intervention was made in the case of Burundi but was not actualised.[60]

---

[50] M. D. Mbow and I. K. Souaré, 'Protecting Civilians in Mali and Central African Republic', chapter 3 in Okeke and Williams (eds.), *Protecting Civilians in African Union Peace Support Operations: Key Cases and Lessons Learned*, p. 75.

[51] Ibid., p. 78.

[52] Gelot, 'Civilian Protection in Africa: How the Protection of Civilians is being Militarized by African Policymakers and Diplomats', p. 165.

[53] Empowering the Union to intervene militarily in a Member State pursuant Article 4(h).

[54] Designed to provide the necessary tools for conflict prevention. Kioko and Wambugu, 'The African Union and the Protection of Civilians', p. 278.

[55] Centred on the African Charter on Human and Peoples' Rights.

[56] Designed to implement the African Peace and Security and Architecture – see: G. M. Wachira, 'Consolidating the African Governance Architecture', Policy Briefing 96, South African Institute of International Affairs, Johannesburg, July 2014, at: https://bit.ly/37FFnWz.

[57] Art. 4(h), Constitutive Act of the African Union; adopted 1 July 2000; entered into force, 26 May 2001.

[58] The Assembly of Heads of State and Government is the supreme organ of the African Union. AU, 'Assembly of Heads of State and Government', at: http://bit.ly/32w5Df4. In practice, such a decision has been ceded to the AU Peace and Security Council since 2004, and a validation of the decision by the Assembly is made *ex post facto*.

[59] Art. 53(2), Charter of the United Nations; signed at San Francisco, 26 June 1945; entered into force, 24 October 1945.

[60] On 17 December 2015, the AU Peace and Security Council authorised the deployment of the African Prevention and Protection Mission in Burundi (MAPROBU) with a mandate to 'contribute, within its capacity and in its areas of deployment, to the protection of civilian populations under imminent threat' (para. 13(a)(ii)). The decision was 'unprecedented' because of the inclusion of an option for 'unauthorised' or 'unilateral' intervention to fulfil the mandate of MAPROBU if the Government of Burundi refused to give its

The AU Peace and Security Council may, though, mandate a commission of inquiry into alleged serious violations of international law in a Member State without recourse to the Assembly. This it did, notably, in 2013 in the case of South Sudan.[61] The report was submitted in January 2015,[62] presenting findings on human rights violations and other abuses committed as well as recommendations for accountability, reconciliation, and healing.[63]

---

consent for the deployment of this mission. Okeke and Williams, 'Introduction', p. 20, citing AU Peace and Security Council Communiqué, AU doc. PSC/PR/COMM.(DLXV), 17 December 2015.

[61] B. Kioko and L. Wambugu, 'The African Union and the Protection of Civilians', in Willmot et al., *Protection of Civilians*, pp. 280–1.

[62] Communiqué of the 484th meeting of the PSC on the situation in South Sudan, 2015, available at: https://bit.ly/3ocoyZt.

[63] Kioko and Wambugu, 'The African Union and the Protection of Civilians', pp. 280–1.

18

The European Union and the Protection of Civilians

18.1 INTRODUCTION

The European Union (EU) does not have a single or comprehensive policy document on the protection of civilians. Rather, its interest and involvement in the protection of civilians (PoC) are reflected across a number of standards and policy documents.[1] Its Concept on Protection of Civilians in EU-led Military Operations was elaborated in 2015.[2] Described as 'excellent' by Béatrice Godefroy and Daniel Chinitz,[3] the Concept was based on the overarching EU Guidelines for the Protection of Civilians in its Common Security and Defence Policy (CSDP) missions and operations.[4] Also of value is the 2016 Policy Document issued by the European Commission Directorate-General for Humanitarian Aid and Civil Protection (DG ECHO), 'Humanitarian Protection: Improving Protection Outcomes to Reduce Risks for People in Humanitarian Crises'.[5]

More specific guidance is contained in a number of referential documents. The EU Guidelines on Children and Armed Conflict were concluded in 2008.[6] The DG ECHO gender policy, 'Gender in Humanitarian Aid: Different Needs, Adapted Assistance', issued in 2013, outlines a reinforced policy approach to gender and gender-based violence in humanitarian settings.[7] The EU Strategic Approach to Women, Peace and Security was

---

[1] For several aspects, the EU approach towards protection of civilians seems to be leaning towards, and interlinked with, that of the United Nations (UN). The EU has been an influential actor for the promotion of the protection of civilians in UN discourses. S. Kjeksrud et al., 'Protection of Civilians in Armed Conflict: Comparing Organisational Approaches', Report, Norwegian Defence Research Establishment, Oslo, 2011, p. 18.

[2] European External Action Service (EEAS), *Concept on Protection of Civilians (PoC) in EU-led Military Operations*, EU doc. CSDP/PSDC 114, Brussels, 2 March 2015, at: https://bit.ly/3t4EoHc.

[3] B. Godefroy and D. Chinitz, 'More Good Than Harm: Why the EU Must Learn From Others' Mistakes to Ensure Better Protection of Civilians through European Peace Facility (EPF) Activities', Blog post, Center for Civilians in Conflict (CIVIC), 29 August 2019, at: http://bit.ly/2HK81p2.

[4] Council of the European Union Revised Guidelines on Protection of Civilians (PoC) in CSDP Missions and Operations, EU doc. 15091/10, 15 October 2010.

[5] DG ECHO, *Humanitarian Protection: Improving Protection Outcomes to Reduce Risks for People in Humanitarian Crises*, Thematic Policy Document No. 8, May 2016, at: https://bit.ly/2MoyXAl.

[6] EU Guidelines on Children and Armed Conflict, 2008, at: https://bit.ly/3onqOJG.

[7] DG ECHO, *Gender: Different Needs, Adapted Assistance*, Thematic Policy Document No. 6, July 2013, at: https://bit.ly/3sVMgZX.

published in 2018. In 2019, DG ECHO issued its Operational Guidance on the Inclusion of Persons with Disabilities in EU-funded Humanitarian Aid Operations.[8] This is an important contribution to an area that has been significantly under-addressed in both the protection of civilians agenda and humanitarian action more broadly.[9]

There is also broad-based support for the promotion and implementation of international humanitarian law (IHL), including through the EU Guidelines on Promoting Compliance.[10] The EU Global Strategy and the Integrated Approach, which underline the importance of the protection of civilians, promote respect for international law, in particular IHL and international human rights law.[11]

18.2 THE 2015 CONCEPT ON PROTECTION OF CIVILIANS IN EU-LED MILITARY OPERATIONS

The leading policy document on the protection of civilians within military operations led by the European Union was, as of writing, the 2015 Concept on Protection of Civilians in EU-led Military Operations.[12] The Policy recalls that the protection of civilians in armed conflict 'has become increasingly important in recent years, particularly during international peacekeeping efforts, such as during UN peacekeeping operations and during EU CSDP military operations'.[13] A failure to ensure civilians are protected during an operation could, the Policy warns, have 'strategic consequences' due to the negative impact of media influence on public opinion. Potentially, this could lead to loss of credibility and even the ultimate success of a military operation 'due to failed expectations and resultant reduction in public support'.[14] Thus, Member States are keen to see CSDP missions achieving their goals, allowing for a certain level of commitment on their part. However, EU Members can have markedly differing opinions as to when CSDP missions should be deployed and under which mandate,[15] potentially undermining the effectiveness of the mission and thereby the concomitant efforts to protect civilians.

---

[8] DG ECHO, Operational Guidance on the Inclusion of Persons with Disabilities in EU-funded Humanitarian Aid Operations, Brussels, January 2019, at: https://bit.ly/3t1p78p.

[9] As has been emphasised by Rolfe, protection 'cannot be a military task alone'; issues such as child protection and gender need to be included in policies of protection in order to be effectively addressed. J. Rolfe, 'Partnering to Protect: Conceptualizing Civil–Military Partnerships for the Protection of Civilians', *International Peacekeeping*, Vol. 18, No. 5 (2011), 561–76, at p. 567.

[10] See, for example, *Report on the EU Guidelines on Promoting Compliance with International Humanitarian Law*, Council of the European Union General Secretariat, Brussels, June 2019.

[11] More specifically, the EU Integrated Approach reiterates the importance of adherence to IHL and reaffirms the EU's role in 'taking a strong stand to promote the respect for IHL and the protection of civilians in all conflict situations'. See EU Council Conclusions on the Integrated Approach to External Conflicts and Crises, 22 January 2018, at: https://bit.ly/2MuNpqF, para. 4.

[12] Previously, and perhaps still to a certain extent, the EU had been criticised for lacking a comprehensive conceptual and practical approach to protection of civilians. Kjeksrud et al., 'Protection of Civilians in Armed Conflict: Comparing Organisational Approaches', p. 34.

[13] *Concept on Protection of Civilians (PoC) in EU-led Military Operations*, para. 3.

[14] Ibid., para. 5.

[15] T. Tamminen, 'Civilian CSDP: Responding to Challenges and Meeting Expectations', in T. Tardy (ed.), *Recasting EU Civilian Crisis Management*, EU Institute for Security Studies, Paris, 2017, p. 24.

The 2015 Policy outlines a series of challenges to be faced when seeking to ensure that civilians are protected against harm. It notes that the military can contribute, together with police services, to the establishment of a 'Safe and Secure Environment (SASE)' where civilians can be protected from imminent threats of violence, but recalls that 'until the root causes of the conflict are solved over the longer term, this will constitute only a temporary solution, in which the resumption of violence is always possible'.[16] In addition, in EU-led military operations where the protection of civilians is a mandated task, 'an enormous array of actors in theatre have to be identified and, where appropriate and possible, coordinated with'. In such circumstances, military forces 'need to be extremely flexible, possibly swiftly shifting from non-kinetic to kinetic actions and vice versa as the situation requires'.[17]

When protecting civilians through the use of 'all necessary force' to prevent, pre-empt, or respond to violence, EU military forces will act in accordance with the following principles:

Mitigate protection of civilians risks by adopting a proactive rather than a passive posture
Comprehensively engage with all other actors to ensure the implementation of a defined framework of coordination with them
Contribute to a protective environment conducive to the protection of civilians; and
Ensure conflict sensitivity based on a deep understanding of the context, including civilian population insecurities/security concerns and implications for the military operation.[18]

The potential risks for civilians caused by EU forces when conducting military operations will further be mitigated through the principle of 'Do no harm'; by avoiding and minimising civilian casualties; and by using an 'ample spectrum' of non-lethal (less-lethal) capabilities.[19] However, the EU approach to security had been criticised as focusing exclusively on military force and military institutions, without strengthening or including civilian counterparts into their security approach.[20]

In this regard, the Policy calls for early analysis of the role and mandate of different protection actors, 'in order to plan for greater coordination of efforts and complementarity in the field'.[21] Proper planning has in fact been highlighted as one of the key factors to prevent, minimise, and halt violence against civilians caused by other actors, or potentially even EU partners themselves. As such, coordination and oversight must apply 'to all areas of security force assistance measures', including the sale of arms.[22] Such analysis should feed into planning, which should in turn be informed by senior experts on human rights,

---

[16]   *Concept on Protection of Civilians (PoC) in EU-led Military Operations*, para. 12.
[17]   Ibid., para. 13.
[18]   Ibid., para. 15.
[19]   Ibid., para. 16.
[20]   M. Drent and D. Zandee, *Breaking Pillars: Towards a Civil-Military Security Approach for the European Union*, Netherlands Institute of International Relations, The Hague, 2010, p. 6.
[21]   Ibid., para. 30.
[22]   B. Godefroy and D. Chinitz, 'More Good Than Harm: Why the EU Must Learn From Others' Mistakes to Ensure Better Protection of Civilians through European Peace Facility (EPF) Activities', *Center for Civilians in Conflict*, 2019, available at: http://bit.ly/2HK81p2.

gender, children affected by armed conflict, IHL, and conflict sensitivity, in order 'to ensure effective implementation' of the protection of civilians.[23]

During an EU operation, capabilities required in military operations to fully address the protection of civilians in the 'Joint Operation Area (JOA)' includes the following:

(1) Expert legal advisor(s) and political advisor(s) to support Commanders
(2) Conflict Advisors, cultural advisor(s), human rights, gender advisor(s) and children affected by armed conflict advisors to support commanders
(3) Very well trained officers (possibly gender balanced) and well informed with respect to human rights and local culture and customs, who can detect and address sexual and gender-based violence (both in medical staff and patrol teams)
(4) A robust communication plan to engage with and manage the level of expectations of the local population . . .
(5) Intelligence . . .
(6) Strong Civil-Military Co-operation (CIMIC) capability to ensure interaction and enhance coordination with all the protection of civilians actors in the planning and conduct of protection of civilians tasks.[24]

Engagement with the local communities is essential for the protection of civilians, as the Policy underlines.[25] Rules of Engagement should define precisely when and how use of force is allowed, though it is noted that use of force in the protection of civilians may 'compete' with force protection.[26] In adjudging the success of a protection of civilians operation, in addition to a reduced level of violence and threats against civilians, feedback from the population is critically important.[27] Indeed, the EU has been often criticised for its lack of contribution to the protection of civilians in practice, and particularly its failure to focus on this issue within its documents – and specifically the documents related to the CSDP – thereby engendering a gap between EU's provision of humanitarian aid and its interest to protect.[28]

Specific recommendations are directed to EU military forces with respect to the prevention and minimising of civilian casualties:

• Avoid contacts between civilians and manoeuvre units
• Because perpetrators may be located among civilians and may even attempt to use civilians as shields, it is vital to envisage modifying or delaying operations when civilians are at risk
• When time and resources permit, clear and repair damaged infrastructure, such as buildings, bridges, and roads, to help prevent civilian casualties

---

[23] *Concept on Protection of Civilians (PoC) in EU-led Military Operations*, para. 33.
[24] Ibid., para. 40.
[25] Ibid., para. 43.
[26] Ibid., paras. 44, 45.
[27] Ibid., para. 50.
[28] C. Churraca, 'EURFOR Chad/CAR Mission on the Protection of Civilians: A Distinctive EU Way to Peace Operations', in M. G. Galantino and M. R. Freire (eds.), *Managing Crises, Making Peace*, Palgrave Macmillan, London, 2015, p. 231.

- Remove unexploded ordnance and/or take other measures to avoid casualties (e.g. markings and warnings)
- Establish a local civilian casualties prevention working group to meet periodically
- Establish systematic procedures in advance to respond to civilian casualty incidents (reporting, tracking, investigation, and public response)
- Establish good personal relationships in advance with key host nation leaders.[29]

According to the Policy, a mechanism should be put in place to address complaints and, 'where appropriate', to compensate any civilian who may have suffered harm or damages as a result of EUFOR (EU Force) actions. This action is 'without prejudice' to the Status of Forces Agreement for the operation and to other applicable law. This could, the Policy states, 'turn out to be a critical aspect in mitigating the effects of collateral damages [*sic*], in particular those which involve civilian casualties'.[30]

18.3 DG ECHO THEMATIC POLICY DOCUMENT ON HUMANITARIAN PROTECTION

The 2016 policy document on humanitarian protection is a valuable contribution to the corpus of EU documentation on the protection of civilians.[31] The document views protection as 'a single sector' that encompasses all aspects of protection, such as child protection; action on gender-based violence (GBV); housing, land, and property (HLP); and mine action.[32] It refers to the Inter-Agency Standing Committee definition of protection but notes that while 'generally accepted', it 'has continued to cause debate and criticism for being too open to interpretation and for not providing a clear, common and operational framework'.[33] The paper observes that:

> the fundamental purpose of protection strategies in humanitarian crises is to enhance physical and psychological security or, at least, to reduce insecurity, for persons, groups and communities under threat, to reduce the risk and extent of harm to populations by seeking to minimise threats of violence, coercion and deliberate deprivation, reduce vulnerability to such threats, and strengthen (self-protection) capacities as well as enhancing opportunities to ensure safety and dignity.[34]

Based on this, the European Commission defines humanitarian protection as addressing '*violence, coercion, deliberate deprivation and abuse for persons, groups and communities in*

---

[29] *Concept on Protection of Civilians (PoC) in EU-led Military Operations*, Annex A.
[30] Ibid., para. 35.
[31] In previous research, ECHO's challenges had been identified as encompassing the management of difficult relationships with Member States, maintaining its position within the Commission, and establishing itself as a credible player in the humanitarian field. T. Mowjee, 'The European Community Humanitarian Office (ECHO): 1992–1999 and Beyond', *Disasters*, Vol. 22, No. 3 (1998), 250–67, at p. 265. The new thematic policy document discussed here addresses some of these challenges.
[32] DG ECHO, *Humanitarian Protection: Improving Protection Outcomes to Reduce Risks for People in Humanitarian Crises*, p. 4.
[33] Ibid., p. 5.
[34] Ibid., p. 6.

the context of humanitarian crises', in compliance with the humanitarian principles of humanity, neutrality, impartiality, and independence and within the framework of international law and in particular international human rights law, IHL, and refugee law.[35] These principles should lead to coordination and complementarity when responding to emergencies. However, the Commission has emphasised in the past that coherence should not jeopardise the necessary conditions for a neutral, impartial, and non-discriminatory delivery of humanitarian assistance.[36] Nevertheless, as Helen Versluys puts it, the 'question remains to what extent such humanitarian isolation is advisable'.[37]

The principal objective for the European Commission in humanitarian protection is to prevent, reduce/mitigate, and respond to the risks and consequences of such harm through three specific objectives:

- To *prevent, reduce, mitigate and respond to protection threats* against persons, groups and communities affected by on-going, imminent or future humanitarian crises
- To reduce the protection vulnerabilities and increase the protection capacities of persons, groups and communities affected by humanitarian crises
- To *strengthen the capacity of the international humanitarian aid system* to enhance efficiency, quality and effectiveness in reducing protection risks in humanitarian crises.[38]

Careful risk analysis is integral to the work supported by the European Commission. The policy document usefully highlights issues of social exclusion/structural discrimination as issues often forgotten in protection analysis. It notes that while who is ignored will depend on the specific context, certain groups tend to be overlooked to a larger degree than others. These include:

- Persons with disabilities
- Lesbian, Gay, Bisexual, Transgender, and Intersex (LGBTI) persons
- Very marginalised social groups, such as the untouchables (Dalits) in South Asia; the Roma in Europe; the Pygmies, San or Bella in Africa; and indigenous populations.[39]

These can be addressed, the policy indicates, through targeted approaches and/or mainstreaming in programming.[40]

---

[35] Ibid.

[36] European Commission, 'Communication from the Commission to the Council, the European Parliament, the European Economic and Social Committee and the Committee of the Regions "Reinforcing EU Disaster and Crisis Response in Third Countries"', COM, Brussels, 2005, p. 9.

[37] H. Versluys, 'Coherence in EU External Action: the Case of Humanitarian Aid', Paper presented at the 10th Biennial EUSA Conference, Panel Session on Development Aid and Economic Partnership Agreements, Montreal, 2007, p. 26.

[38] DG ECHO, *Humanitarian Protection: Improving Protection Outcomes to Reduce Risks for People in Humanitarian Crises*, p. 6.

[39] Ibid., p. 13.

[40] In 2017–18, the EU allocated €62 million for the prevention of sexual and gender-based violence, recognising as 'absolutely imperative' the need to include a gender perspective in humanitarian action. This was emphasised in the 2019 EU Statement at the UN Security Council, available at: https://bit.ly/3kOKNmg.

Persuasion, mobilisation, and denunciation are all described in the policy. These are different means of 'applying pressure to ensure the compliance and cooperation of the relevant authorities in line with standards of protection of civilians laid down in international law'.

> Persuasion requires a discreet engagement with duty-bearers to let them know about their duties in protection and to promote their fulfilling their protection obligations. Mobilisation involves engaging (often in a non-public way) with other key stakeholders so that they themselves put some pressure on duty-bearers. Both persuasion and mobilisation require a certain degree of confidentiality, but if they do not work, sometimes it is possible and necessary to resort to the third means, denunciation, in which information is put in the public realm, so that the duty-bearers feel compelled to take action (provided they are moved by shame).[41]

The policy document explains that: 'Any requests for funding denunciation activities will be thoroughly analysed by the European Commission, as they would imply public disclosure of international law violations and likely create an adversarial relationship, which may be detrimental to responding to people's protection and assistance needs and contrary to the European Commission's principled approach.'[42] If the more consensual approach has been effective in practice deserves a closer examination.

18.4 THE EUROPEAN UNION AND INTERNATIONAL HUMANITARIAN LAW

More broadly, the European Union is committed both to respecting IHL in its own military operations and to promoting respect by others.[43] The EU military Concept on Effective Civil-Military Coordination in Support of Humanitarian Assistance and Disaster Relief[44] provides operational guidance to EU military mission commanders, including in relation to issues that touch upon humanitarian civil-military coordination and IHL. The concept also includes concrete IHL-related best practices and lessons learnt from operations and missions, while underlining the need to keep IHL 'high on the agenda and conveying it early on (including during CSDP planning),[45] as well as to higher political and military levels'.

---

[41] DG ECHO, *Humanitarian Protection: Improving Protection Outcomes to Reduce Risks for People in Humanitarian Crises*, p. 59.

[42] Ibid., p. 60.

[43] In its 2019 statement at the UN Security Council, the EU stated that: 'Promoting compliance with IHL and respect of the humanitarian principles has always been, and remains, a top priority for the EU and its Member States.' The full text of the speech is available at: https://bit.ly/3kOKNmg.

[44] EU military Concept on Effective Civil-Military Coordination in Support of Humanitarian Assistance and Disaster Relief, Brussels, 30 January 2019, at: https://bit.ly/2KRmOno.

[45] Under the CSDP umbrella, the EU has been developing an ambitious approach to peace and stabilisation operations, demonstrating its ability to showcase complex civil-military structures in operations such as the Balkans and the Democratic Republic of Congo. Kjeksrud et al., 'Protection of Civilians in Armed Conflict: Comparing Organisational Approaches', p. 30.

Consistent with the undertaking that the Union respect international law in its external relations,[46] the EU and its Member States recognise that if EU-led forces become engaged in an armed conflict, IHL 'will fully apply' to them.[47] In fact, as Frederik Naert has observed, 'this is likely to be the case in only a few EU operations'.[48] Indeed, since the EU's first military operation – Operation Concordia in 2003 in the then former Yugoslav Republic of Macedonia (now renamed North Macedonia) – the Union has undertaken a total of twelve military operations under its CSDP[49] and in none of these has the relevant EU force become party to an armed conflict.[50] If and when it does so, there would potentially be challenges of legal interoperability, although IHL obligations in EU military operations 'seem to be primarily conceived as resting on the participating States'[51] and many, if not most, of the IHL and disarmament law treaty obligations upon Member States are the same. Nevertheless, possible disparities within EU Member States might challenge the organisations' coherence: overlapping humanitarian programmes could lead to overlapping humanitarian policies, effectively hindering EU crisis responses.[52] That said, the European Union 'may also have its own IHL obligations, especially under customary IHL'.[53]

18.5 THE EUROPEAN UNION AND INTERNATIONAL HUMAN RIGHTS LAW

When IHL does not apply to EU action, the Union 'primarily looks towards human rights law as the appropriate standard for the conduct of EU military operations'.[54] Although the European Union is still not formally a party to the European Convention on Human Rights, its accession thereto is expected in the near future.[55] Indeed, EU organs such as the European Commission are already generally recognised to uphold the rule of law and

---

[46] Arts. 3(5) and 21(1) and (2)(b), Treaty on European Union; adopted at Maastricht, 7 February 1992; entered into force, 1 November 1993 (hereinafter, TEU); and F. Naert, 'The Application of International Humanitarian Law and Human Rights Law in CSDP Operations', in E. Cannizzaro, P. Palchetti, and R. Wessel (eds.), *International Law as Law of the European Union*, Martinus Nijhoff, Leiden, 2011, pp. 189–212.

[47] F. Naert, 'Observance of International Humanitarian Law by Forces under the Command of the European Union', *International Review of the Red Cross*, Vol. 95, Nos. 891/892 (2013), 637–43, at p. 639.

[48] Ibid.

[49] T. Palm and B. Crum, 'Military Operations and the EU's Identity as an International Security Actor', *European Security*, Vol. 28, No. 4 (2019), 513–34, at p. 513.

[50] Perhaps its operation in Chad is the closest it has come to being a party to an armed conflict. See, for example, C. Churucca, 'EUFOR Chad/CAR Mission on the Protection of Civilians: A Distinctive EU Way to Peace Operations', chapter 11 in M. G. Galantino and M. R. Freire (eds.), *Managing Crises, Making Peace: Towards a Strategic EU Vision for Security and Defence*, Palgrave Macmillan, London, 2015.

[51] Naert, 'Observance of International Humanitarian Law by Forces under the Command of the European Union', p. 641.

[52] Versluys, 'Coherence in EU External Action: The Case of Humanitarian Aid', pp. 26–7.

[53] Ibid.

[54] Naert, 'Observance of International Humanitarian Law by Forces under the Command of the European Union', p. 639.

[55] Council of Europe, 'EU Accession to the ECHR', 2020, at: http://bit.ly/2PdjUrC.

human rights, particularly when trying to address the root causes of fragility in their conflict prevention strategies.[56]

In any event, the EU is bound by customary human rights law, including *jus cogens* norms on the prohibitions on arbitrary deprivation of life and on torture. Non-refoulement and arbitrary deprivation of liberty – also arguably *jus cogens* norms[57] – means that holding a person against their will for any significant length of time as well as handing over detained persons to national authorities where there is a serious risk of their being unlawfully harmed would amount to a violation by the European Union of international human rights law.

Frederik Naert has called for each Operation Plan (OPLAN) adopted for EU forces to clarify as much as possible the applicable law and specify whether IHL and/or human rights law applies. This does not, he notes, always occur. References merely to 'applicable' rules of IHL or human rights law, he observes, 'do not clarify whether, when or which of those rules actually are applicable and may require an Operation Commander to determine the applicable rules, with the assistance of legal advice at his/her level'.[58] Indeed, whereas the EU and its Member States have long emphasised their respect for international law, this has generally been the result of generalised statements, with open questions on how protection of civilians would in practice be prioritised and operationalised.[59]

18.6 THE 2020 UN SECURITY COUNCIL DEBATE ON THE PROTECTION OF CIVILIANS

The EU issued a statement at the UN Security Council's debate on the protection of civilians in 2020. The observer delegation of the European Union stated that the protection of civilians in armed conflict 'remains of utmost concern for the EU and its Member States'.[60] The EU expressed its grave concern at the 'ever-growing number of deliberate violations of international humanitarian law and the continued high prevalence of civilian deaths and injury, as well as the destruction or damage caused to civilian objects such as schools and health infrastructure, including maternities, and religious sites'. The Union was also concerned by the 'growing number of attacks on humanitarian personnel as well as those on medical personnel and facilities'. It pledged to continue its

[56] C. Boutillier, 'Development Cooperation and Crisis Management', in Tardy (ed.), *Recasting EU Civilian Crisis Management*, p. 41.

[57] International Law Commission (ILC), Fourth report on peremptory norms of general international law (*jus cogens*) by Dire Tladi, Special Rapporteur, UN doc. A/CN.4/727, 31 January 2019, paras. 131–4.

[58] Naert, 'Observance of International Humanitarian Law by Forces under the Command of the European Union', p. 643.

[59] M. Dalton, et al., *The Protection of Civilians in U.S. Partnered Operations*, Report, CIVIC, CSIS, and Interaction, Washington, DC, 2018, p. 4.

[60] Letter dated 29 May 2020 from the President of the Security Council addressed to the Secretary-General and the Permanent Representatives of the members of the Security Council, UN doc. S/2020/465, 2 June 2020, at: http://bit.ly/3qPVTYa, Annex 32: 'Statement by the Permanent Delegation of the European Union to the United Nations'.

efforts to strengthen the protection of humanitarian workers and health care facilities from attacks.[61]

According to the statement, IHL and the protection of civilians are included in the planning and conduct of all civilian and military EU crisis-management missions and operations that promote peace and security in the context of the CSDP. In particular, the EU promotes increased systematisation of IHL training within the armed forces. The EU also recognises that training on IHL to non-State armed groups is 'key' to ensuring compliance with the law 'and should be pursued'. Similar to other trainings, the incorporation of practical approaches improves IHL trainings.[62]

The EU further underlined that the protection of civilians must be at the core of peacekeeping mandates. It endorses the three-tiered approach to protection outlined in the Department of Peace Operations 2019 Policy on the Protection of Civilians in UN Peacekeeping. It also recalled the earlier adoption of the Kigali Principles on the Protection of Civilians, which are 'an important tool' for strengthening the effective implementation of protection mandates in peacekeeping.

The EU also expressed its commitment to better addressing the needs of persons with disabilities in armed conflicts and to promoting their empowerment and meaningful participation in decision-making processes in all phases of humanitarian action. The Union welcomed the Inter-Agency Standing Committee Guidelines on Inclusion of Persons with Disabilities in Humanitarian Action, adopted in 2019, 'and fully supports their implementation'. However, the overall debate was criticised for only discussing people with disabilities 'in broad strokes', and more generally for failing to incorporate 'substantive' gender lenses as in previous years.[63]

---

[61] Ibid.

[62] Godefroy and Chinitz, 'More Good Than Harm: Why the EU Must Learn From Others' Mistakes to Ensure Better Protection of Civilians through European Peace Facility (EPF) Activities'.

[63] Peace Women, 'Security Council Debate on Protection of Civilians in Armed Conflict, May 2020', 2020, available at: https://bit.ly/3igYoT7.

19

The ICRC and the Protection of Civilians

19.1 INTRODUCTION

Besides international and regional organisations, the International Committee of the Red Cross (ICRC) is one of the most important actors for protecting civilians. Founded in 1863, the ICRC 'strives to ensure that those involved in the fighting comply with their obligations under international humanitarian law' (IHL). Its mission is to protect the lives and dignity of victims of armed conflict and other situations of violence and to provide them with assistance. The ICRC also endeavours to prevent suffering 'by promoting and strengthening humanitarian law and universal humanitarian principles'.[1] Central to this mission is the protection of civilians. Respective difficulties in today's conflicts 'cannot be attributed to shortcomings' in IHL, according to the organisation. The 'real problem', it believes, 'is the failure by the parties to the conflict to comply' with the fundamental rules of IHL.[2]

19.2 ICRC POLICY ON PROTECTION

In 2008, the ICRC adopted its Policy on Protection. The Policy notes that the four Geneva Conventions of 1949 refer to 'protection' several times without actually defining the term. The Statutes of the International Red Cross and Red Crescent Movement introduced the notions of 'protection' and 'assistance' in 1952. These two terms are, it is said, 'intrinsically linked'. They are also 'inseparable elements of the ICRC's mandate'. Broadly speaking, the organisation says, 'four spheres of action are involved in protection: political, military or security, legal (including judicial), and humanitarian. Every actor with a role in protecting persons, or an obligation to do so, belongs to one of them'.[3]

The ICRC Policy stipulates that protection aims to ensure that authorities and other actors, such as armed groups and other non-State actors, 'respect their obligations and the rights of individuals in order to preserve the safety, physical integrity and dignity of those

---

[1] 'ICRC Protection Policy: Institutional Policy', *International Review of the Red Cross*, Vol. 90, No. 871 (September 2008), 751–75, at: http://bit.ly/3aRPVyi.
[2] ICRC, 'Protection', undated but accessed 1 October 2021, at: http://bit.ly/2VdnxAl.
[3] 'ICRC Protection Policy: Institutional Policy', pp. 751–2.

affected by armed conflict and other situations of violence'.[4] Protection relates firstly to the causes of, or the circumstances that lead to, violations and secondly to their consequences. 'This definition of protection also includes activities that seek to make individuals more secure and to limit the threats they face, by reducing their vulnerability and/or their exposure to risks, particularly those arising from armed hostilities or acts of violence.'[5]

The individual remains the primary concern of the ICRC and the basis of all protection activities.[6] In implementing its policy on protection, four general principles guide the organisation's actions:

- A neutral and independent approach
- Dialogue and confidentiality
- The 'holistic' and multidisciplinary character of ICRC action
- The search for results and impact.

19.2.1 *Guiding Principle 1: A Neutral and Independent Approach*

The ICRC adopts a neutral and independent approach in all phases of its work, which, it affirms, gives the organisation the credibility it needs to conduct its operations. 'Its neutrality and independence enable the ICRC to avoid becoming instrumentalized by some and rejected by others.' This approach guarantees that its activities 'will be implemented without discrimination and based solely on needs'. Moreover, by being neutral and independent, the ICRC 'is able to play the role of neutral intermediary and to offer its mediation and good offices whenever required'.[7]

19.2.2 *Guiding Principle 2: Dialogue and Confidentiality*

Confidential dialogue is the ICRC's preferred method of working 'and a strategic choice'. Dialogue that takes place in confidence 'usually' facilitates access to victims.[8] However, the confidentiality of the ICRC's dialogue with authorities and other actors is not without limits. The ICRC 'reserves the right', should confidential dialogue not have the desired impact, 'to resort to other action, including public denunciation'.[9] This it rarely does, however.

19.2.3 *Guiding Principle 3: The Holistic and Multidisciplinary Character of ICRC Action*

The ICRC affirms that its protection strategies 'are based on comprehensive analyses of protection problems and on their causes and consequences'.[10] The organisation cautions,

---

[4]   Ibid., p. 752, para. 2.1.1.
[5]   Ibid.
[6]   'ICRC Protection Policy: Institutional Policy', p. 757, para. 2.2.2.
[7]   'ICRC Protection Policy: Institutional Policy', p. 758.
[8]   Ibid.
[9]   Ibid., pp. 758–9.
[10]   Ibid., p. 759.

though, that this does not mean that the ICRC will respond to all protection needs in a given situation. Priorities are set on the basis of the following criteria: the nature and gravity of the violations or risks; the effects of the violations or risks on victims; the impact on victims that the ICRC can reasonably expect its action to have; and the ICRC's capacities and the means at its disposal.[11]

19.2.4 *Guiding Principle 4: Search for Results and Impact*

Protection activities are carried out by the ICRC in conformity with the highest ethical and professional standards. A protection strategy is developed by 'selecting and integrating various modes of action' in a balanced approach. The ICRC's three complementary modes of action are: raising awareness of responsibility (persuasion, mobilisation, and denunciation); support; and substitution (direct provision of services).[12] The ICRC uses information that is collected either by its own delegates or through a network of contacts. It is, though, 'mindful of the specific difficulties of analysing the conduct of hostilities, for instance, their impact – direct and indirect – on civilians'.[13]

19.2.5 *Ethical and Professional Standards for Protection*

The ICRC has adopted professional standards for protection, which reflect shared thinking and common agreement among humanitarian and human rights practitioners, including the United Nations, non-governmental organisations (NGOs), and the various components of the International Red Cross and Red Crescent Movement.[14] The latest edition of the standards (the third) was adopted in 2018 following an ICRC-led consultation process.[15]

The three humanitarian principles that must always be respected during protection work are humanity, impartiality, and non-discrimination. Further principles of action include the duty to avoid harmful effects that could arise from their work and an approach that puts affected populations, communities, and individuals at the centre of protection activities.[16]

19.2.6 *The Principle of Humanity*

The principle of humanity holds that all people must be treated humanely in all circumstances. It demands that priority be given to protecting life and health, alleviating

---

[11]   Ibid.
[12]   Ibid., p. 760.
[13]   Ibid., p. 771, para. 5.3.1.
[14]   ICRC, 'Professional Standards for Protection Work', undated but accessed 1 October 2021, at: http://bit.ly /3e2vIb5.
[15]   *Professional Standards for Protection Work Carried Out by Humanitarian and Human Rights Actors in Armed Conflict and Other Situations of Violence*, 3rd ed., ICRC, Geneva, 2018.
[16]   Ibid., chapter 1.

suffering, and ensuring respect for the rights, dignity, and mental and bodily integrity of all individuals in situations of risk.[17]

19.2.7 *The Principle of Non-Discrimination*

The principle of non-discrimination prohibits adverse distinction in the treatment of different groups or individuals, on the basis of race, colour, sex, age, language, religion, political or other opinion, national or social origin, property, birth, disability, health, sexual orientation, gender identity, or other status.[18] Of course, the application of this and the other humanitarian principles does not preclude taking account of particular elements (including, notably, gender, age, or disability) as factors that may require a targeted response. Children, for example, tend to be disproportionately affected by armed conflicts 'and are usually at greater risk owing to their stage of development and dependence on adults, especially when separated from their families or habitual caregivers'.[19]

19.2.8 *The Principle of Impartiality*

The principle of impartiality aims to ensure that a protection activity addresses 'all relevant rights and obligations, as well as the specific and most urgent protection needs of communities and individuals affected that are at risk of or subject to violations and abuses'. The principle of impartiality also requires that all duty bearers be held 'to similar standards with regard to their obligations and responsibilities, and possible breaches thereof'.[20] These understandings constitute a broad interpretation of the principle of impartiality.

19.2.9 *'Do No Harm'*

The principle of 'do no harm' emerged from medical practice that traces its origins back to the Hippocratic Oath. It was developed for humanitarian action by Mary Anderson in the 1990s as an approach to working effectively in conflict-affected situations.[21] As the Professional Standards for Protection Work recall, 'Poorly conceived or carelessly implemented protection activities can aggravate or even generate additional protection risks for populations at risk or subject to violations and abuse.'[22]

---

[17]   Ibid., p. 24.
[18]   Ibid.
[19]   Ibid., p. 25.
[20]   Ibid.
[21]   See, for example, F3E, 'Incorporating the Principle of "Do No Harm": How to Take Action Without Causing Harm: Reflections On a Review of Humanity & Inclusion's Practices', Project evaluation, 2018, at: http://bit.ly /2Rj3Vtj.
[22]   *Professional Standards for Protection Work Carried Out by Humanitarian and Human Rights Actors in Armed Conflict and Other Situations of Violence*, p. 27.

19.2.10 *Participation of Affected Communities*

Measures to respect, safeguard, and promote the dignity of persons at risk are not limited to engaging with them in a respectful manner. These measures, the Professional Standards for Protection Work observe, 'also include facilitating their access to accurate and reliable information, ensuring their inclusion and meaningful participation in decision-making processes that affect them, and supporting their independent capacities, notably those of making free and informed choices, and of asserting their rights'.[23] The 'Participation Revolution' holds that people receiving aid must be included in making the decisions which affect their lives.[24] No longer is community engagement a largely one-way process – participation puts the emphasis on inclusion of the most vulnerable, especially important during protection work.

Actively engaging populations at risk in protection activities also provides a means for them to evaluate the performance of protection actors, which serves in turn to increase the accountability of these actors. In reality, however, this accountability can be elusive, as the Professional Standards for Protection Work explicitly acknowledge.[25] The spread of communication technologies has enabled many individuals and communities to mobilise public opinion and, directly or indirectly, humanitarian and human rights organisations, when violations of fundamental rights are being committed, including during armed conflict. This helps to recalibrate the relationship between communities and individuals at risk and protection actors, which is ordinarily characterised by a marked imbalance of power.[26]

19.3 PARTICULAR CHALLENGES FOR THE ICRC

The ICRC has exceptional expertise in protection work, especially through its right to visit detainees during an international armed conflict and its right to offer its services during a non-international armed conflict. Perhaps its greatest challenge in the protection of civilians occurs during the conduct of hostilities since there is a widespread perception that it is loath to denounce publicly the commission of serious violations of IHL, including war crimes, for fear of losing access to populations for the purpose of providing them with humanitarian aid.

The organisation has sometimes appeared reluctant to tackle this perception overtly. For instance, its 2017 reference work, *Enhancing Protection for Civilians in Armed Conflict and Other Situations of Violence*, hardly acknowledges the existence of such trade-offs, which are central to the organisation's ability to perform its protection mandate adequately during the conduct of hostilities by parties to armed conflict. Arguably, a 1998 opinion piece by the then head of the Legal Division was more open, accepting that the ICRC exercises 'restraint' in criticising those violating IHL 'because it wants to maintain its access to the victims'. Indeed, denouncing the actors responsible for violations 'involves the risk of bringing the whole operation to an end, either because the ICRC's presence

---

[23] Ibid., p. 28.
[24] See, for example, VOICE, 'The Grand Bargain', undated but accessed 1 April 2022 at: http://bit.ly/2XhvdnN.
[25] *Professional Standards for Protection Work Carried Out by Humanitarian and Human Rights Actors in Armed Conflict and Other Situations of Violence*, p. 30.
[26] Ibid.

might be declared undesirable or because its delegates would no longer be safe'.[27] Even stronger were the words of the President of the ICRC, Jakob Kellenberger, who in rejecting criticisms of the organisation he then headed, declared in 2001 that: 'The age in which we live – loquacious, swift to pass judgment and ever ready to express an opinion – tends to overestimate the impact of speaking out.'[28]

Such practice and supporting statements can leave the organisation open to the charge that, despite its role of 'guardian' of IHL it 'fiddles while Rome burns'. For instance, during the genocide in Rwanda, in the view of the one commentator otherwise supportive of the ICRC, 'there is no disputing the fact that ... the core element of the ICRC's approach – diplomatic persuasion – failed'.[29] As he notes, 'there are natural limits to a strategy of civilian protection based on persuasion'.[30] Similarly, Steven Ratner's reasoned critique concluded in 2011 that 'persuading to comply with the law is not always the best course of action for law-interested institutions'.[31]

Steven Ratner explicitly considers whether, when the ICRC acts on its humanitarian imperative to save as many lives as possible through access to victims – the utilitarian course – it creates a moral wrong if, for example, it then refuses to address an episode of torture (an act clearly illegal under IHL) of which it is aware.[32] He cautions that if the ICRC 'consistently chooses a particular set of victims over another, or always acts in a utilitarian way, the targets of its action will know what they can get away with, and that the ICRC no longer stands for certain principles'.[33] In this vein, while studying the organisational history, functioning, and culture of the ICRC, Miriam Bradley has suggested that the ICRC tends to address 'new problems' with 'old solutions', which ultimately limits the protection that the ICRC can provide.[34]

Besides these issues and lines of work, the ICRC has been innovative and pro-active regarding diplomatic initiatives. The ICRC was a crucial driver of recent disarmament treaties regarding anti-personal landmines, cluster munitions, the arms trade, and nuclear weapons.[35] Most recently, it has also launched, developed, and supported campaigns and guidance on the prevention of attacks against healthcare, investigations in situations in armed conflict, and partnered operations, among others. This line of work may indirectly help protect civilians.

[27] Y. Sandoz, 'The International Committee of the Red Cross as Guardian of International Humanitarian Law', Geneva, 31 December 1998, at: http://bit.ly/3e4rr7a.
[28] J. Kellenberger, 'Reflections on Speaking Out or Remaining Silent in Humanitarian Activity', Paper presented to the Second Zurich Denkpause, Zurich, 27 June 2001, at: http://bit.ly/2RjBImi.
[29] N. Lamp, 'Conceptions of War and Paradigms of Compliance: The "New War" Challenge to International Humanitarian Law', *Journal of Conflict & Security Law*, Oxford University Press, 2011, at: http://bit.ly/39MIW8J, p. 257.
[30] Ibid., p. 258.
[31] S. R. Ratner, 'Law Promotion Beyond Law Talk: The Red Cross, Persuasion, and the Laws of War', *European Journal of International Law*, Vol. 22, No. 2 (2011), 459–506, at: http://bit.ly/2V5vUxE, p. 506.
[32] Ibid., p. 503.
[33] Ibid., p. 505.
[34] M. Bradley, *Protecting Civilians in War: The ICRC, UNHCR, and Their Limitations in Internal Armed Conflicts*, Oxford University Press, Oxford, 2016.
[35] See, for example, C. Carpenter, 'Vetting the Advocacy Agenda: Network Centrality and the Paradox of Weapons Norms', *International Organization*, Vol. 65, No. 1 (2011), 69–102.

20

Switzerland and the Protection of Civilians

20.1 INTRODUCTION

Switzerland has a long humanitarian tradition and has been strongly supportive of many initiatives to protect civilians, especially in its central role in the development of international humanitarian law (IHL). The Swiss Federal Council (the government of Switzerland) is the depositary of the four 1949 Geneva Conventions[1] and of the Additional Protocols thereto,[2] reflecting its critical role in the elaboration of these instruments. Switzerland is one of the very few States which have adopted a dedicated strategy on the protection of civilians.[3] It was also the first State to conclude such a document in 2009, which is in line with its broader engagement for global peace and security.[4]

20.2 THE SWISS STRATEGY ON THE PROTECTION OF CIVILIANS

Switzerland revised its strategy in 2013. The 2013 Strategy on the protection of civilians notes that protecting people from armed violence and armed conflict 'is a Swiss tradition'. It was, the Foreword to the Strategy recalls, 'a Swiss national, Henry Dunant, who in the

---

[1] The Swiss Federal Council has delegated the task of depositary to the Directorate of International Law of the Federal Department of Foreign Affairs. International Committee of the Red Cross (ICRC), Commentary on 1949 Geneva Convention I, 2016, at: http://bit.ly/30k1KDm, para. 3118.

[2] Art. 93, Protocol Additional to the Geneva Conventions of 12 August 1949, and relating to the Protection of Victims of International Armed Conflicts (Protocol I); adopted at Geneva, 8 June 1977; entered into force, 7 December 1978.

[3] 'Strategy on the Protection of Civilians in Armed Conflicts', Swiss Federal Department of Foreign Affairs, Bern, 2013, at: https://bit.ly/3ceiGsM.

[4] According to Mason and Sguaitamatti, the nation's 'values and interests converge and build on each other'. Accordingly, Switzerland's humanitarian values or long tradition of neutrality reflect specific security, political, and economic interests, including mitigating indirect threats to the Swiss population and assets, ensuring access to key political players, and building a safe global environment for trade. Graf and Lanz argue that what sets Switzerland apart from other – mainly Western – States, is its focus on civilian rather than military peacebuilding, which is today 'fully institutionalised and broadly recognised as an important area of foreign policy activity'. Such an approach would be the result of Swiss domestic politics, which limits high levels of military engagement abroad. S. J. A. Mason and D. A. Sguaitamatti, 'Mapping Mediators: A Comparison of Third Parties and Implications for Switzerland', Center for Security Studies, 2011, 29; A. Graf and D. Lanz, 'Conclusions: Switzerland as a Paradigmatic Case of Small-State Peace Policy?', *Swiss Political Science Review*, Vol. 19, No. 3 (2013), 410–24.

19th century put forward the idea of codifying the law of war, which led to the signing of the First Geneva Convention in 1864'.[5] Switzerland's role 'is recognised by the international community, as demonstrated by the fact that it chairs the Group of Friends on the Protection of Civilians in New York'.

The 2013 Strategy is oriented around three general axes:

Axis 1 – Achieve greater compliance with the normative framework
Axis 2 – Consolidate actions taken in favour of persons to be protected
Axis 3 – Lend support to international peacekeeping missions.

As part of these actions, Switzerland articulated seven broad 'areas of activities':

- Clarify or develop the normative framework if and where needed
- Ensure greater understanding of the normative framework
- Ensure greater compliance with the normative framework and bring the alleged perpetrators of violations to justice
- Reinforce the action of organisations working to protect people on the ground
- Reinforce the direct action by Switzerland in favour of persons to be protected
- Consolidate support given to peacekeeping operations
- Contribute even more actively to the elaboration of mandates and standards.

The Strategy is particularly valuable to signal Switzerland's commitment to the protection of civilians, thereby fostering the concept at the international level and strengthening Switzerland's ability to lead and influence international efforts on the matter. It also fosters a whole-of-government approach regarding Switzerland's actions. Yet, the strategy tends to be abstract and general, thereby not specifying concrete measures and priorities.

Indeed, the articulation of the general areas of activities offers scant guidance as to the main programmatic approaches that are to be adopted as a consequence. For instance, the Strategy notes that Switzerland has 'extensive experience' in the protection of women, children, and internally displaced persons (IDPs) 'and will continue to pursue these activities'[6] but offers no indication as to what those activities are.

It also evidences some omissions. For instance, no mention is made of the Convention on Cluster Munitions, even though Switzerland has played an important role in promoting the Convention, such as, more recently, presiding over the Second Review Conference in 2020–1 and leading the development of the Lausanne Action Plan for the five years of work by the States Parties in 2021–5.[7] There is also no mention of the threat from explosive weapons in populated areas nor of the attacks on health care that

[5]   PoC Strategy, foreword.
[6]   'Strategy on the Protection of Civilians in Armed Conflicts', p. 17.
[7]   In 2018, for instance, Switzerland deployed around CHF18.4 million (some £14.5 million) to 'efforts to clear mines, raise awareness, strengthen local capacities, and facilitate the implementation of existing conventions at the international level'. See, the Swiss Confederation, 'Mine Action Strategy of the Swiss Confederation 2016–2019: 2018 Annual Report', Confédération suisse, 2018.

bedevil many contemporary conflicts,[8] suggesting that an updated version of the Strategy could be worth considering.

In sum, after almost ten years since its last update, the Strategy could benefit from revision, including in its use of terminology. References to 'the handicapped' are both outdated and inappropriate and should be replaced, along with the addition of considerably greater attention to the protection of persons with disabilities, for instance. Moreover, such a revision could give new impetus for future diplomatic and programmatic efforts as well as guidance for strengthened military engagement in peace operations.

20.3 THE 2020 UN SECURITY COUNCIL DEBATE ON THE PROTECTION OF CIVILIANS

Switzerland participated at the Security Council's debate on the protection of civilians in 2020. In delivering a statement, Switzerland was speaking on behalf of the members of the Group of Friends on the protection of civilians in armed conflict, which it has led since 2007, namely Australia, Austria, Belgium, Brazil, Canada, Côte d'Ivoire, France, Germany, Indonesia, Ireland, Italy, Kuwait, Liechtenstein, Luxembourg, the Netherlands, Norway, Poland, Portugal, Sweden, Switzerland, the United Kingdom, and Uruguay.[9] The statement noted that protection challenges 'are as acute as ever, and the protection of civilians becomes even more crucial in the time of coronavirus disease (COVID-19). The pandemic poses a threat to human security and exacerbates the vulnerability of people living in conflict situations. It magnifies existing protection challenges.'[10]

The Group of Friends affirmed that: 'Our international legal framework on protection of civilians is sound; the challenge lies in its implementation.' In this regard, it welcomed the adoption by the Assembly of States Parties to the Rome Statute of the International Criminal Court (in December 2019) of the amendment to the Statute to include the war crime of intentionally using starvation of civilians as a method of warfare in non-international armed conflicts.[11] Reflecting possible divergences within the Group of

---

[8] Brehm, for instance, claimed that the Swiss position in this regard is inconsistent. See, M. Brehm, 'Protecting Civilians from the Effects of Explosive Weapons: An Analysis of International Legal and Policy Standards', Report, UNIDIR, Geneva, 2012, p. 149.

[9] Letter dated 29 May 2020 from the President of the Security Council addressed to the Secretary-General and the Permanent Representatives of the members of the Security Council, UN doc. S/2020/465, 2 June 2020, at: http://bit.ly/3qPVTYa, Annex 66: Statement by the Permanent Mission of Switzerland to the United Nations.

[10] Ibid. As emphasised by Dicker and Paterson, COVID-19 might be a global problem, but 'its effects are not equally distributed'. Switzerland has long been hosting negotiations for conflict resolution in and for countries such as Syria; talks that, with the spread of the pandemic, have come to a halt. L. K. Dicker and C. Danae Paterson, 'COVID-19 and Conflict: The Health of Peace Processes During a Pandemic', *Harvard Negotiation Law Review*, Vol. 25 (2020), 214–49; and see also N. Cumming-Bruce and L. Jakes, 'Syria Peace Talks to Open After a Long, Strange Month', *The New York Times*, 28 October 2019.

[11] Ibid. Indeed, this amendment could have a significant impact on the ability of prosecutors to charge perpetrators of starvation as a war crime in situations such as Yemen, a conflict in which several Western States have been directly or indirectly involved (such as France and the United Kingdom). L. Graham,

Friends, however, the statement only took 'note' of the 'process towards developing a political declaration to enhance the protection of civilians in urban warfare, including protection from the possible humanitarian impacts of the use of explosive weapons in populated areas'.[12]

The Group of Friends reiterated the importance it attached to the 'full and effective implementation of protection of civilians mandates' by UN peace operations, and noted the 2019 Department of Peace Operations Policy on the Protection of Civilians. It stressed that the Security Council must ensure that UN peace operations have 'clear and realistic mandates' and called on the General Assembly to allocate resources 'consistent with those mandates'.[13]

The year 2022 marked the twentieth anniversary of Switzerland joining the United Nations as a full member. At the time of writing, Switzerland was for the first time in its history a candidate for a non-permanent seat on the UN Security Council for 2023–4. In advocating for its election to this position, Switzerland has reiterated its commitment to 'a strong, effective multilateral system'.[14] A workshop organised by civil society has suggested that Switzerland makes the protection of civilians a priority theme.[15]

'Prosecuting Starvation Crimes in Yemen's Civil War', *Case Western Reserve Journal of International Law*, Vol. 52 (2020), 267–86. See also F. D'Alessandra and M. Gillet, 'The War Crime of Starvation in Non-International Armed Conflict', *Journal of International Criminal Justice*, Vol. 17 (2019), 815–47, at pp. 845–6.

[12] Annex 66: Statement by the Permanent Mission of Switzerland to the United Nations.

[13] Ibid.

[14] 'Why Support Switzerland?', at: http://bit.ly/3iPUwpF.

[15] M. Fegert, 'Ein Plus für den Frieden: Wie sich die Schweiz im UNO-Sicherheitsrat für Frieden und Sicherheit einsetzen kann', Policy Brief, *foraus*, 2021, 5.

21

The United Kingdom and the Protection of Civilians

21.1 INTRODUCTION

Besides Switzerland, the United Kingdom (UK) is the only State to have elaborated a national strategy on the protection of civilians (PoC). A formal 2010 *UK Government Strategy on the Protection of Civilians in Armed Conflict*[1] has been supplemented by an August 2020 Policy Paper, *UK Approach to Protection of Civilians in Armed Conflict*.[2] The Policy Paper was the joint work of the Department for International Development, the Foreign & Commonwealth Office, and the Ministry of Defence. Since the Paper's promulgation, the Department for International Development has been incorporated within a revamped Foreign, Commonwealth & Development Office (FCDO).[3]

The protection of civilians in armed conflict is, the 2010 Strategy declares, 'central to the achievement of UK Government policy to prevent, manage and resolve conflict and to improve the effectiveness of the humanitarian system'.[4] It affirms that the protection of civilians matters from both a moral and a legal perspective. Everyone has the right not to be arbitrarily deprived of their life and the right not to be tortured. In addition, the United Kingdom has specific obligations concerning the protection of civilians 'in situations where it is involved in military action'.[5]

The United Kingdom has, the Strategy declares, a number of different roles in promoting and protecting civilians in armed conflict, including:

- As a member of international organisations, and as a permanent member of the United Nations (UN) Security Council
- As a party to international humanitarian law (IHL) treaties
- As a donor to intergovernmental organisations and other humanitarian actors operating in situations of armed conflict

---

[1] UK Foreign and Commonwealth Office (FCO), *UK Government Strategy on the Protection of Civilians in Armed Conflict*, London, 2010 (hereinafter, 2010 UK Strategy on the Protection of Civilians).

[2] 'UK Approach to Protection of Civilians in Armed Conflict' Policy Paper, 27 August 2020, at: http://bit.ly/3iPRZLY.

[3] The FCDO 'unite[s] development and diplomacy in one new department'. FCDO, 'About Us', at: http://bit.ly/36ftbbn.

[4] 2010 UK Strategy on the Protection of Civilians, p. 2.

[5] Ibid.

- As a provider of international military forces, including peacekeepers, and sometimes as a party to an ongoing conflict
- Training foreign military, civilian and police peacekeepers.[6]

The following summarises the content of the 2010 Strategy as well as the 2020 Policy Paper supplement.

21.2 THE 2010 UK STRATEGY

The 2010 Strategy sets out four policy areas:

1. Political engagement
2. Protection by peace support operations
3. Humanitarian action
4. State capacity.

The Strategy employs the broad definition of 'protection' adopted by the Inter-Agency Standing Committee: 'all activities aimed at ensuring full respect for the rights of the individual in accordance with the letter and the spirit of the relevant bodies of law, i.e. human rights law, international humanitarian law and refugee law'.

21.2.1 *Policy Area 1: Political Engagement*

The United Kingdom commits to working bilaterally not only on resolution of an armed conflict, but also to ensure that the parties involved respect their obligations under international law: 'We will make protection issues an integral part of our work to prevent, manage and resolve conflicts.'[7]

At international level, the United Kingdom believes that the UN Security Council 'should be prepared to act quickly and concertedly to prevent and respond to protection crises: holding governments to account and where necessary considering sanctions as well as referrals to the International Criminal Court'.[8] Furthermore, when protection 'fails and civilians become victims of war crimes or human rights violations, there need to be mechanisms and processes to combat impunity and to allow victims and survivors to seek justice and redress'.[9]

The UK Government 'recognises that a comprehensive approach to transitional justice is needed. Religion, ethnicity and the overall demands of the community should be considered when defining the strategies to be used.'[10]

---

[6] Ibid., p. 3.
[7] Ibid., p. 7.
[8] Ibid.
[9] Ibid., p. 9.
[10] Ibid. The United Kingdom as well as other countries' approach to transitional justice had been criticised for being understood too strictly as legal accountability or truth commission without integrating the need to prevent future abuses. C. L. Sriram, 'Justice as Peace? Liberal Peacebuilding and Strategies of Transitional Justice', *Global Society*, Vol. 21, No. 4 (2007), 579–91, at p. 585.

21.2.2 *Policy Area 2: Protection by Peace Support Operations*

The United Kingdom seeks improved action by international and regional peace operations in protection crises.[11] One aspect of this concerns better reporting on protection issues by peace operations. The United Kingdom believed, writing in 2010, that reports from the UN Secretary-General to the UN Security Council covered protection issues in an inconsistent manner: 'Improved coverage of protection in the Secretary-General's reporting is important, as is better coverage of protection in oral reporting to the Council.'[12]

Execution of protection tasks within a peace operation, according to the Strategy, 'varies widely depending on the resources available, the approach of the mission leadership – including military commanders, and the capability, ethos and training of the troop and police contributing countries'. At the time of drafting the Strategy, the United Kingdom criticised the fact that: 'None of the major international or regional organisations running peace operations has a fully formed doctrine on the execution of protection tasks.'[13] Moreover, the Strategy affirmed, 'At a very practical level, it is not always clear to troops and police what is expected of them.'[14] As developed in the previous chapters, the UN and regional organisations have evolved in this regard.

21.2.3 *Policy Area 3: Humanitarian Action*

In this third policy area, the UK priority is an improved international humanitarian response to protection crises. The UN 'Cluster' Approach is, the United Kingdom believes, a key element of the international response. Accordingly, it has pledged to 'continue to support and monitor the capacity of UNHCR [Office of the UN High Commissioner for Refugees] to lead the Protection Cluster at the global level, and promote the roll-out of appropriate protection coordination mechanisms in all humanitarian emergencies, in accordance with the Cluster Approach'.[15] The United Kingdom

---

[11]   In this ambit, the Oxford Research Group listed several recommendations for the UK at the strategic, operational, and oversight levels. The Group argued that the UK Government should increase its expertise in peace operations as well as effective institutional mechanisms. The Group also argued for a more coherent strategy, along with flexible and sustainable funding mechanisms. At the operational level, cooperation at both the international level – within the UN – and at regional level – notably with European partners – was advocated, along with systematic and comprehensive studies of lessons learned. Lastly, at the oversight level, a wider scrutiny of UK commitments to UN peace operations was considered necessary. D. Curran and P. D. Williams, 'The UK and UN Peace Operations: A Case for Greater Engagement', Report, Oxford Research Group, Oxford, 2016, pp. 2–3.

[12]   2010 UK Strategy on the Protection of Civilians, p. 10.

[13]   Ibid.

[14]   Ibid. In the past, the United Kingdom, along with other States such as the United States, had been criticised for emphasising the importance of civilian security without, in practice, providing guidance on how troops should actually implement this task. This is particularly relevant when distinct approaches are necessary depending on whether the operation is one of peacekeeping or one of peace enforcement. D. Lilly, 'The Changing Nature of the Protection of Civilians in International Peace Operations', *International Peacekeeping*, Vol. 19, No. 5 (2012), 628–39, at p. 635.

[15]   2010 UK Strategy on the Protection of Civilians, p. 13.

committed to 'continue to work with the cluster to monitor its effectiveness in responding to the protection needs of affected populations'.[16]

21.2.4 *Policy Area 4: State Capacity*

This final policy area focuses on building the capacity of States to protect civilian populations. This is consonant with the second pillar of the 'Responsibility to Protect' doctrine. Accordingly, where a State does not have the capacity to integrate protection duties and concerns into its action, external assistance may be effective. As the Strategy observes:

> Protection requires legitimate, accountable and capable national security and justice institutions (military, police, prisons, courts) that provide equitable and effective security and justice services in accordance with the rule of law. They need to be responsive to citizens' needs; be able to understand and meet domestic and international human rights and humanitarian law obligations; and be particularly responsive to gender-based and sexual violence as women and children are disproportionately affected in conflict and post-conflict situations.[17]

A key element in the UK approach is also to support the work of local human rights non-governmental organisations (NGOs) to conduct and support human rights monitoring in situations of conflict and political or social unrest.[18]

21.3 THE DEVELOPMENT OF THE 2020 POLICY PAPER

The 2010 UK Strategy was a leading first construction of a national policy on protection of civilians issues. As the summary above indicates, it tends to be generic in nature (an issue shared with the Swiss Strategy; see Chapter 20). A formal review was commissioned by the UK Government with a view to elaborating a new Strategy; the task of critiquing the original strategy was contracted to the Royal United Services Institute (RUSI) and Save the Children. Their work was summarised in a report published in 2019.[19]

The report affirmed: 'Two central challenges stood out in the research as key when considering the drafting of a new UK strategy on PoC in armed conflict: competing definitions of what the protection of civilians encompasses, and the format and style the new strategy should take.'[20] With respect to the definition of protection, some advocated the broad definition incorporated in the 2010 Strategy, while other consulted stakeholders preferred the narrower focus on the protection of civilians from the (imminent) threat of physical violence. With respect to the format of the new document, several interlocutors

---

[16] Ibid.
[17] Ibid., p. 14.
[18] Ibid.
[19] A. B. Tabrizi, A. Brydon, and E. Lawson, *The UK Strategy on Protection of Civilians: Insights for the Review Process*, RUSI Whitehall Report 2–19, Royal United Services Institute (RUSI) and Save the Children, London, September 2019.
[20] Ibid., p. 3.

within government, 'particularly those with experience in implementation' in the Ministry of Defence, 'favoured a short strategy, which, unlike the previous document, outlines clear roles, responsibilities and implementation targets for the various actors'.[21] Policymakers, on the other hand, the report notes, 'stressed the need for any text to be flexible given that "the more you go into detail, the more it can tie up in knots"'.[22]

A gap in the original strategy picked up upon by those engaged in its review is the lack of detail on the protection needs of specific groups. As the report observes: 'Within the PoC mandate, there is a risk that the protection needs of specific vulnerable groups get lost in political discussions and are then missed in the implementation of activities on the ground.'[23] The past two decades, the report notes, 'have seen significant progress in the development and visibility of parallel agendas, championing the different experiences gender and age can have for people in conflict through the Women, Peace and Security ... and the Children and Armed Conflict agendas'.[24]

The report does not fully develop, however, the issue of responding to new challenges. The report made the assertion that during the past decade 'conflict environments have changed', citing a general debate on the issue in the British Parliament.[25] Key issues, the report affirms, include:

the increasing complexity in the number and nature of actors; second- and third-order (reverberating) effects;[26] increased reliance on remote warfare and partnered operations; deliberate targeting of civilians; the regulation of private security contractors; and the impact of new technologies, including cyber warfare.

In today's battlefields, there has been a proliferation of non-State actors, with conflicts becoming more protracted and increasingly fought in urban areas using explosive weapons that have wide-area effects.[27]

These assertions are valid. It is worth recalling, however, that the targeting of civilians was a major element throughout the history of the second half of the twentieth century and many of those conflicts involved the use of explosive weapons in urban areas.[28]

[21] Ibid., p. 4.
[22] Ibid.
[23] Ibid., p. 8.
[24] Ibid., pp. 8–9. See also in this regard Reaching Critical Will (Women's International League for Peace and Freedom), 'Women and Explosive Weapons', Report, New York, 2014; M. Butcher, 'The Gendered Impact of Explosive Weapons Use in Populated Areas in Yemen', Report, Oxfam International, 2019; R. Williamson, 'Children and Armed Conflict: Towards a Policy Consensus and Future Agenda – Ten Years After the Machel Study', Report, Wilton Park, 2007.
[25] Ibid., p. 10.
[26] These include damage to infrastructure, and the distribution of food, water, and health supplies.
[27] 2010 UK Strategy on the Protection of Civilians, p. 10.
[28] Furthermore, Save the Children UK has gathered evidence that in conflicts such as Iraq and Afghanistan, civilian casualties have often included a substantial number of children, with schools often being intentionally targeted. See, among others, K. Smith, *Devastating Impact: Explosive Weapons and Children*, Save the Children UK, London, 2011; B. Rappert et al., 'The Case for Addressing Explosive Weapons: Conflict, Violence and Health', *Social Science & Medicine*, 2012, 2052.

The report rightly notes the 'significant' protection concerns from the use of aerial targeting to support the advance of host nation troops in populated areas,[29] in light of the consequences of the loosening of restrictions on targeting in such cases by the United States[30] and the appalling – though improving – respect for civilians and civilian objects by the Saudi Arabian Air Force, which is supported in its targeting endeavours by the United Kingdom.[31] That said, the reference to the UK obligations under the Arms Trade Treaty (see Chapter 5) is timely and welcome, as is the stated requirement for 'a strong component for ensuring that weapons, material or financial services from the UK are not transferred to parties where they could be used to commit or facilitate serious violations of international law, including deliberate, indiscriminate or disproportionate attacks on civilians'.[32]

The issue of operationalisation of the new strategy is justly raised as a specific concern. As the 2019 report observed, the 2010 Strategy on the Protection of Civilians 'was perceived by some interviewees, especially those with a military background, as failing to translate into a document with specific guidance for implementers and MoD [Ministry of Defence] personnel working on the ground. Instead, it was perceived as a policy document with too few elements on how it was to influence operational design.'[33]

To avoid the same outcome, the report argued, the new strategy 'must entail the involvement by operational staff in the strategic design and framing of the action plans to ensure that it is translated into policy, guidance, and for the armed forces, doctrine, as well as training on the various scenarios troops will face'.[34] Relevant in this regard, as the report states, are the Safe Schools Declaration and Guidelines (signed by the United Kingdom); the 2007 Paris Principles on children associated with armed forces or armed groups (see Chapter 9); and the 2019 Vancouver Principles on Peacekeeping and the Prevention of the Recruitment and Use of Child Soldiers promulgated by the Canadian government.[35]

21.4 THE 2020 POLICY PAPER

The UK government decided not to produce a revised strategy on the protection of civilians, but instead to issue a new Policy Paper. The introduction to the 2020 Policy Paper states that the 'update' to the 2010 Strategy was written before the outbreak of the COVID-19 pandemic but the key principles referred to in the Paper on adherence

---

[29]   2010 UK Strategy on the Protection of Civilians, p. 11.
[30]   Perhaps, though, the reference to 'commitments to ensure allies respect' IHL may be read as an oblique reference to this major protection problem, especially in the context of Iraq.
[31]   A. Merat, 'The Saudis Couldn't Do It Without Us': The UK's True Role in Yemen's Deadly War', *Guardian*, 18 June 2019, at: http://bit.ly/32NsNOx.
[32]   2010 UK Strategy on the Protection of Civilians, p. 12. For a discussion of related issues in practice, see K. Hartley, 'The Benefits and Costs of the UK Arms Trade', *Defence and Peace Economics*, 2007, 447.
[33]   2010 UK Strategy on the Protection of Civilians, p. 14.
[34]   Ibid.
[35]   Ibid., pp. 14–15.

to IHL and 'international human rights laws' were not affected.[36] The structure of the Policy Paper comprises, in addition to a brief introduction, seven main areas of action:

1. Political engagement
2. Strengthening accountability
3. Peace support operations
4. Ensuring respect for IHL in UK military operations
5. Strengthening State and non-State capacity
6. Humanitarian action
7. Offering refuge to those in need of protection.[37]

The seven main areas are illustrated by twelve text boxes describing UK action on a range of issues: arms control treaties, conventions, and regimes; the UK National Action Plan on Women Peace and Security 2018–22; children and armed conflict; persons with disabilities and armed conflict; the Responsibility to Protect (R2P); the Preventing Sexual Violence in Conflict Initiative; sexual exploitation and abuse; the protection of cultural heritage; domestic implementation of IHL; humanitarian principles; hunger and conflict; and sexual and gender-based violence.

The Paper retains the definition of protection agreed upon by the IASC. With respect to arms control, the 2020 Policy Paper highlights the 1997 Anti-Personnel Mine Ban Convention, the 2008 Convention on Cluster Munitions, and the 2013 Arms Trade Treaty, to all of which the United Kingdom is a State Party.

The UK National Action Plan on Women Peace and Security 2018–22 involves putting women and girls at the centre of efforts to prevent and resolve conflict in order to promote peace and stability.[38] The Plan covers all fragile and conflict-affected States but focuses on nine countries for reporting annually to Parliament (Afghanistan, the Democratic Republic of Congo, Iraq, Libya, Myanmar, Nigeria, Somalia, South Sudan, and Syria) 'where there is potential for the UK to have a substantial impact'.

In January 2019, the Ministry of Defence published Joint Service Publication 1325: 'Human Security in Military Operations'.[39] Published in two parts – the first normative

---

[36] Introduction', 'UK Approach to Protection of Civilians in Armed Conflict', Policy Paper, 27 August 2020, at: http://bit.ly/3iPRZLY.

[37] Compared with the 2010 Strategy, three new areas are singled out for attention: accountability; respect for IHL by the United Kingdom in its military operations; and offering refuge to those in need of protection (i.e. asylum seekers).

[38] The United Kingdom enacted its national action plan in 2006 but did not set a specific timeframe for the implementation of the plan. The plan lacks a set of priorities on how the gender perspective would be integrated in its policies and programmes, and roles were not clearly assigned to those who involved in the implementation process. Yet the United Kingdom identified key outcomes for each objective and ensured the plan would be a living document to be evaluated regularly, with a reporting and feedback process and guidance on assessing performance. C. Achilleos-Sarll and Y. Chilmeran, 'Interrogating the "Local" in Women, Peace and Security: Reflections on Research on and in the UK and Iraq', *International Feminist Journal of Politics*, Vol. 22, No. 4, 2020, 596–605.

[39] UK Ministry of Defence, *JSP 1325: Human Security in Military Operations*, Part 1: Directive, London, January 2019, at: https://bit.ly/2Ykvx4c.

and the second comprising more detailed guidance[40] – the policy is founded on the participation of women both in negotiations and peace talks and provides a 'population-centric lens' to military operations. Within the UN Security Council, the United Kingdom is the 'pen-holder' for Security Council resolutions linked to the Women, Peace and Security agenda.

With respect to children in armed conflict, the United Kingdom is part of the UN Working Group that leads the international response on child protection in armed conflict, supporting the work of the Special Representative of the Secretary-General for children and armed conflict by applying diplomatic pressure to listed governments and armed groups. In 2018, the United Kingdom endorsed the Safe Schools Declaration and the Vancouver Principles. In conjunction with the UK's endorsement of the Paris Principles and Commitments and ratification of the Optional Protocol to the UN Convention on the Rights of the Child on the involvement of children in armed conflict in 2003, the United Kingdom 'supports and adheres to a set of instruments that constitute a vital compendium of safeguards to the rights of children in armed conflict'.

The Paper highlights Security Council Resolution 2475 on the impact of armed conflict on persons with disabilities, which is a valuable normative reference, but does not indicate how the United Kingdom (which drafted the resolution jointly with Poland) intends to implement its recommendations. In this regard, the Joint Service Publication 1325 on Human Security in Military Operations does not refer to persons with disabilities in its normative document and only three brief mentions are included in the detailed guidance.

On peace agreements, the 2020 Policy Paper stresses the importance of incorporating human rights standards within peace agreements, and ensuring the ability to monitor them, 'including through national human rights mechanisms'. The UK supports the inclusion of international human rights and IHL standards, with supporting national mechanisms, in peace agreements as well as their subsequent implementation.

The Paper endorses the R2P doctrine and reiterates the UK pledge never to vote against a 'credible' draft Security Council resolution that seeks to prevent or halt mass atrocities. The UK uses tools to promote R2P, which include:

- early warning mechanisms to identify countries at risk of instability, conflict, and atrocities
- development and programmatic support to help States address the root causes of conflict and the drivers of instability
- defence and policing tools, which may include deployments of UK armed forces, to support training and capacity building in the security sector.

When protection fails and civilians become victims of war crimes or human rights violations, the Paper emphasises that mechanisms and processes must be in place to

---

[40]   UK Ministry of Defence, *JSP 1325: Human Security in Military Operations*, Part 2: Guidance, London, January 2019, at: https://bit.ly/3sXoxWa.

combat impunity and to allow victims and survivors to seek justice and redress. The UK Government recognises that a comprehensive approach to transitional justice is needed and that any approach 'must be contextual and based on the needs and objectives of the people of the country concerned'.

The Prime Minister's Special Representative on Preventing Sexual Violence in Conflict leads the Preventing Sexual Violence in Conflict Initiative across the UK government. The aim of the initiative is to raise awareness and rally global action to:

- strengthen justice for survivors of sexual violence and hold the perpetrators to account
- tackle the stigma faced by survivors of sexual violence
- prevent and respond to sexual violence in conflict, including through using the military and police.

Tackling sexual exploitation and abuse is 'a central plank' of the UK's peacekeeping reform work. The UK led in the Security Council on Resolution 2272, which mandated reporting on sexual exploitation and abuse and demanded that contingents guilty of persistent and widespread sexual offences are repatriated.[41]

The UK's approach to humanitarian protection is found in its Humanitarian Reform Policy 2017.[42] Example areas that have subsequently been developed include:

- Supporting the development of guidance/research on working with non-State armed groups (NSAGs). The number and complexity of NSAGs has increased exponentially since the 2010 UK protection of civilians strategy. Finding ways to encourage NSAGs to recognise and abide by IHL has become increasingly important.
- Supporting the establishment of a UN High-Level Panel on Internally Displaced Persons (IDPs). The UK notes the absence of 'concrete, effective and lasting solutions for IDPs, without the same rights and protections afforded under international law to refugees. The response to IDPs is a political and development challenge as much as a humanitarian one.'
- Encouraging UN Humanitarian Country Teams to produce quality protection strategies for conflict contexts and to improve their implementation. These strategies are key to ensuring a cohesive and longer-term approach to the protection of civilians in humanitarian contexts.[43]

The United Kingdom works closely with other States and the Red Cross Movement to promote compliance with IHL. The UK encourages States to adopt national legislation to enforce IHL and works to ensure that non-State armed groups understand and comply with their obligations in conflict situations.

[41] This is an important contribution as the UN policy system towards sexual 'misconduct' had been criticised for suffering from 'staff, funding, and enforcement deficiencies'. Nduka-Agwu argued back in 2009 that UN policies on gender awareness needed to be reviewed and furthered through field research. A. Nduka-Agwu, '"Doing Gender" After the War: Dealing with Gender Mainstreaming and Sexual Exploitation and Abuse in UN Peace Support Operations in Liberia and Sierra Leone', *Civil Wars*, 2009, 179.
[42] UK Government, *Humanitarian Reform Policy*, Policy Paper, 2017, at: https://bit.ly/3sZzlGm.
[43] 2020 Policy Paper.

Finally, as a 'signatory' to the 1951 Refugee Convention,[44] the UK pledges to fully consider all claims to asylum made in the UK in accordance with its international obligations under the Convention. The Policy Paper states that:

> Those who are determined as having a well-founded fear of persecution for one of the five Convention reasons will normally be granted refugee status for a five-year period. If there is a well-founded fear of persecution or risk of serious harm for a non-Convention reason, the UK will consider granting Humanitarian Protection under the European Convention on Human Rights.

21.5 THE 2020 UN SECURITY COUNCIL DEBATE ON THE PROTECTION OF CIVILIANS

In delivering a statement at the Council's debate on the protection of civilians in 2020, the United Kingdom called for greater efforts to protect civilians in Syria.[45] The protection of civilians was also 'of paramount importance', it said, in Yemen. 'The ongoing conflict has claimed more than 100,000 lives, and we must all continue to push the parties to the conflict to uphold international humanitarian law and protect human rights'. The United Kingdom has been assisting Saudi Arabia in its targeting procedures in accordance with IHL.[46]

The United Kingdom urged an immediate cessation of hostilities in Rakhine and Chin states in Myanmar. 'Those who commit human rights violations, including against the Rohingya, must be held to account, and there must be unhindered humanitarian access to protect all communities from the effects of COVID-19.'[47] The 'potentially catastrophic impacts' of COVID-19 'mount on top of the challenges facing civilians living amid armed conflict. We must now redouble our efforts to protect them, including from those who would seek to use the pandemic to their advantage.'[48]

---

[44] In fact, the United Kingdom is a State Party to the Convention relating to the Status of Refugees; adopted at Geneva, 28 July 1951; entered into force, 22 April 1954.

[45] Letter dated 29 May 2020 from the President of the Security Council addressed to the Secretary-General and the Permanent Representatives of the members of the Security Council, UN doc. S/2020/465, 2 June 2020, at: http://bit.ly/3qPVTYa, Annex 14: Statement by the Special Representative of the Prime Minister of the United Kingdom of Great Britain and Northern Ireland on Preventing Sexual Violence in Conflict and Minister of State for the Commonwealth and the United Nations, Lord Ahmad.

[46] Merat, '"The Saudis Couldn't Do It Without Us": The UK's True Role in Yemen's Deadly War'.

[47] Annex 14: Statement by the Special Representative of the Prime Minister of the United Kingdom.

[48] Ibid.

The United States and the Protection of Civilians

22.1 INTRODUCTION

The United States (US) does not have a federal policy or strategy document on the protection of civilians. Instead, elements of relevant policy can be found across a range of government documents issued over the past decade. In general, the US tends to address the issue at the national level through the prism of 'civilian harm mitigation',[1] which suggests a more limited and legalistic approach than the broad concept of protection of civilians. Several documents specifically refer to the protection of civilians as well as develop and apply the concept.[2]

In June 2015, the US Department of Defense issued a new Manual on the Law of War (the body of international law also called international humanitarian law (IHL) or the law of armed conflict). The Manual, which was subsequently revised and updated in December 2016, observes that the 'protection of civilians against the harmful effects of hostilities is one of the main purposes of the law of war'.[3] The Manual 'generally uses "civilian" to mean a member of the civilian population, i.e., a person who is neither part of nor associated with an armed force or group, nor otherwise engaging in hostilities'.[4] The notion of 'association', which is not part of IHL, is not defined but is potentially very broad in scope (and far wider than the notion of membership, potentially meaning that civilians may be targeted by US forces). In a similar vein, by 'engaging in hostilities', it is assumed that this refers only to 'direct' participation in hostilities.[5]

On 1 July 2016, US President Barack Obama issued Executive Order 13732 detailing the 'United States Policy on Pre- and Post-Strike Measures to Address Civilian Casualties in

---

[1] See, for example, the webinar series 'Civilian Casualties: The Law of Prevention and Response' organised by the American Society of International Law, 2020.

[2] It had been noted that although various instruments cumulatively provide for a framework of protection, none of these contains a systematic treatment of protection of civilians (PoC). G. Stuart, 'The Protection of Civilians: An Evolving Paradigm?', *Stability: International Journal of Security and Development*, Vol. 2, No. 2 (2013), 1–16, at 5.

[3] US Department of Defense, *Department of Defense Law of War Manual*, June 2015 (updated December 2016), Washington, DC, 2016, §5.2 (footnote omitted).

[4] Ibid., §4.8.1.5.

[5] See on this issue Chapter 2.

US Operations Involving the Use of Force'.[6] The Presidential Document stated that the protection of civilians 'is fundamentally consistent with the effective, efficient, and decisive use of force in pursuit of US national interests. Minimizing civilian casualties can further mission objectives; help maintain the support of partner governments and vulnerable populations, especially in the conduct of counterterrorism and counterinsurgency operations; and enhance the legitimacy and sustainability of US operations critical to our national security'. As a matter of policy, the Document stipulates, the United States 'routinely imposes certain heightened policy standards that are more protective than the requirements of the law of armed conflict that relate to the protection of civilians'.[7]

In 2018, the US Army War College's Peacekeeping and Stability Operations Institute issued a second edition of its valuable and detailed *Protection of Civilians Military Reference Guide*.[8] The Guide states that the protection of civilians 'must be considered and integrated during all military operations, including peace operations and operations during armed conflicts'. Civilians are protected persons under international law, the Guide recalls, and parties to a conflict 'have a legal obligation to protect civilians from the conflict's effects'.[9] The Guide defines protection of civilians as 'efforts to reduce civilian risks from physical violence, secure their rights to access essential services and resources, and contribute to a secure, stable, and just environment for civilians over the long-term'.

Also in 2018, the Center for Strategic and International Studies (CSIS), published a report entitled *The Protection of Civilians in US Partnered Operations*.[10] The report, which treated north-east Nigeria and Syria as case studies, recommended that in early planning stages, partnerships be designed that 'incorporate and prioritize protection of civilians and civilian objects'. It further called upon the Department of Defense and the Department of State to ensure they have 'a common framework to assess benefits, risks, and opportunities for partnered operations and potential effects on civilian populations, along with dedicated and adequately resourced capabilities for developing and implementing mitigation plans and programs'.[11] The report, however, did not recommend the elaboration of a national US strategy for the protection of civilians.

On 23 October 2018, the US Under Secretary of Defense for Policy, John Rood, designated the Deputy Under Secretary of Defense for Policy (DUSDP), David Trachtenberg, as the civilian official in the Department of Defense responsible for developing, coordinating, and overseeing compliance with the Department's future policy related to civilian casualties. In a 2019 report to Congress, the Department of Defense

---

[6] *United States Policy on Pre- and Post-Strike Measures To Address Civilian Casualties in US Operations Involving the Use of Force*, A Presidential Document by the Executive Office of the President, Executive Order 13732, Federal Register, Vol. 81, No. 130 (7 July 2016), at: https://bit.ly/36doq1N.

[7] Ibid., §1 ('Purpose').

[8] *Protection of Civilians Military Reference Guide*, 2nd ed., Army Peacekeeping and Stability Operations Institute, Army War College, Carlisle, PA, January 2018, at: http://bit.ly/3dDcPMa.

[9] Ibid., Executive Summary.

[10] M. Dalton, et al., *The Protection of Civilians in US Partnered Operations*, Report, CSIS, Washington, DC, 2018, at: https://bit.ly/3a2WsXQ.

[11] *Protection of Civilians Military Reference Guide*, 2nd ed., p. 19.

described the development of the civilian casualty policy which will govern US military operations and defence security cooperation activities.[12] As of writing, the policy had not been finalised, but the Department has created a website so people can report information on civilian casualties directly.[13]

Subsequently, InterAction (one of the partners on *The Protection of Civilians in US Partnered Operations* report) issued a short list of recommendations on the protection of civilians for consideration by the US Congress and key US departments and officials.[14] The organisation called for enhanced US government transparency regarding civilian casualties resulting from US government or US-led coalition operations,[15] including through the monthly release of estimates of civilian casualties caused by such operations. It recommended that the Secretaries of Defense and of State 'assure staffing to adequately support the protection of civilians, particularly to support the new senior Department of Defense official responsible for civilian casualty policy'. It further called on the government to prohibit the sale, license, or export of defence articles[16] or services to foreign security services 'until it is certified that the recipient has not engaged in violations of IHL or human rights'.[17]

Also in 2019, the United States issued its national strategy on women and peace and security,[18] implementing the Women, Peace, and Security Act of 2017, a legislative act signed into law by US President Donald Trump on 6 October 2017. The Strategy identified as the 'strategic challenge' the fact that conflict and disasters around the world 'adversely and disproportionately affect women and girls, yet women remain under-represented in efforts to prevent and resolve conflict, and in post-conflict peacebuilding or recovery efforts'.[19]

Yet, according to Sarah Holewinski, 'there is still nobody with the Department of Defense that is specifically looking at civilian protection across the board'. Although the documents analysed in this chapter will support effective implementation of protection of civilians, while the US's operational experience in the last twenty years has led to

---

[12]   *Department of Defense Report on Civilian Casualty Policy*, Submitted pursuant to Section 936 of the National Defense Authorization Act for Fiscal Year 2019, 2019, at: https://bit.ly/3iPVOkt; see also 'Creation of a Unified Civilian Casualty Policy', Blog entry, NDIA, 16 October 2019, at: http://bit.ly/2MolpeI.

[13]   J. Garamone, 'DOD Posts Webpage to Aid in Reporting Civilian Casualties', US Department of Defense, 23 October 2020, at: http://bit.ly/39kiBSb.

[14]   InterAction, *Protection of Civilians in Conflict*, Washington, DC, 2019, at: https://bit.ly/39ohPUc.

[15]   US military interventions have been criticised for their limited transparency and lack of accountability when 'collateral damage' in armed conflict occurs. For instance, in the war in Afghanistan, the UN and NGOs did not have access to the relevant information compiled by military investigations, thereby were not able to provide external accountability. A. Suhrke, 'From Principle to Practice: US Military Strategy and Protection of Civilians in Afghanistan', *International Peacekeeping*, Vol. 21, No. 5 (2015), 1–19.

[16]   The sale should be further suspended where there exists credible information that the recipient is 'committing violations, violates the end-user agreement, or fails to provide appropriate information thereto'. See: https://bit.ly/2XYy47a.

[17]   Ibid.

[18]   *United States Strategy on Women, Peace, and Security*, US Department of State, Washington, DC, June 2019, at: https://bit.ly/2Mr7XAb.

[19]   Ibid., p. 4.

'incredible insights' into the protection of civilians, those lessons learned have still to be institutionalised.[20]

A first step in this direction is the *Best Practices Handbook for Civilian Harm Mitigation and Response in US Military Operations* published in 2021 by the Center for Excellence in Disaster Management and Humanitarian Assistance (CFE-DM), a US Department of Defense organisation.[21] Intended as an introductory reference for US military personnel at all levels, the Handbook consolidates two decades of unclassified best practices for mitigating and responding to civilian harm. Furthermore, the US Department of Defense released a memorandum from Secretary of Defense Lloyd Austin, outlining a roadmap – not yet published as of writing – for tackling concerns about civilian casualties.[22] A report from the RAND Corporation served as background for the memorandum.[23]

22.2 THE US DEPARTMENT OF DEFENSE *LAW OF WAR MANUAL*

The *Law of War Manual* is a comprehensive review and guidance on the IHL obligations recognised or accepted by the United States. Covering almost 1,200 pages, the Manual addresses all aspects of IHL, not only those pertaining to the protection of civilians during situations of armed conflict.[24] The revised Manual of December 2016 recalls the language of the July 2016 Presidential Policy in noting that US military operations 'are routinely subject to more restrictions and apply standards that are more protective of civilians than required by the law of war'.[25]

The Manual recalls that under IHL parties to an armed conflict must take feasible precautions to reduce the risk of harm to the civilian population and other protected persons and objects. Such precautions must be taken when planning and conducting attacks. It is specifically provided that feasible precautions must be taken in connection with certain types of weapons.[26]

[20] In a discussion for the online event 'Improving Civilian Protection in Conflict' by the Center for Strategic and International Studies, held by CSIS expert Jacob Kurtzer and featuring Sarah Holewinski and Larry Lewis (2021), available at: https://bit.ly/3EYoz6e.
[21] Center for Excellence in Disaster Management and Humanitarian Assistance, *Best Practices Handbook for Civilian Harm Mitigation and Response in US Military Operations*, 2021, at: https://bit.ly/3vrmHla.
[22] *Department of Defense Releases Memorandum on Improving Civilian Harm Mitigation and Response*, US Department of Defense, Washington, DC, January 2022. For a short commentary, see L. Hartig, 'A Big Step Forward or Running in Place? The Pentagon's New Policy on Civilian Casualties', *Just Security*, 8 February 2022, at https://bit.ly/3PBPNrN.
[23] M. J. McNerney, G. Tarini, K. M. Sudkamp, L. Lewis, M. Grisé, and P. Moore, *U.S. Department of Defense Civilian Casualty Policies and Procedures: An Independent Assessment*, Report, RAND Corporation, Santa Monica, 2022, at https://bit.ly/3wvb11E.
[24] The need for a new Manual had become apparent as extensive developments in the law took place in the last few decades, making a completely new manual a necessity. See S. Carvin, 'The US Department of Defense Law of War Manual: An Update', in M. N. Schmitt et al. (eds.), *Yearbook of International Humanitarian Law*, 2010, p. 356.
[25] US Department of Defense, *Department of Defense Law of War Manual*, December 2016, §5.1.2.1.
[26] Ibid., §5.2.3.

In explaining its understanding of the term 'feasible', the Manual states that the obligation to take feasible precautions 'does not require everything that is capable of being done – a standard that would be almost impossible to meet if interpreted literally and that is inconsistent with the definition of feasible precautions that provides for taking into account humanitarian and military considerations'.[27] The standard for what precautions must be taken is, the Manual stipulates, 'one of due regard or diligence, not an absolute requirement to do everything possible'. That said, a 'wanton disregard for civilian casualties or harm to other protected persons and objects is clearly prohibited'.[28]

An important change was made between the first edition of the new Manual in 2015 and the second edition issued the following year.[29] As Chapter 2 describes, the challenge in applying the customary rule of proportionality in attack concerns the inherent imprecision of the term 'excessive'. In the 2015 edition of the Manual it was stated, correctly, that the 'weighing or comparison between the expected incidental harm and the expected military advantage does not necessarily lend itself to empirical analyses'.[30] On the one hand, the Manual continued, 'striking an ammunition depot or a terrorist training camp would not be prohibited because a farmer is plowing a field in the area'. On the other hand, 'a very significant military advantage would be necessary to justify the collateral death or injury to thousands of civilians'.[31]

The assertion that no more than 'very significant' military advantage could justify the incidental death of, or injury to, thousands of civilians was deliberately narrowed in the revised *Law of War Manual* in December 2016. In coming closer to the state of the law, it was now affirmed that 'an *extraordinary* military advantage would be necessary to justify an operation posing risks of collateral death or injury to thousands of civilians'.[32]

Overall, however, the changes made to the Manual in 2016 have been 'modest'.[33] Indeed the Manual has been criticised for failing to understand and address the needs of the US military personnel 'for definitive, and accessible, legal guidance[34] due to its critical shortcomings in both substantive content and form'.[35] Specifically, it has been argued that the Manual fails to be authoritative, concise, and a stand-alone publication.[36] For

[27] Ibid., §5.2.3.1.

[28] Ibid., §5.2.3.2.

[29] According to Haque, the Manual's approach to proportionality and precaution was subject to criticism – which is why the December 2016 version focused on this issue, acknowledging the responsibility to take feasible precautions to reduce civilian collateral damage. Nevertheless, the revised Manual still did not provide for a clear definition of proportionality. A. A. Haque, 'Off Target: Selection, Precaution, and Proportionality in the DoD Manual', *International Law Studies*, Vol. 92 (2016), 32–84.

[30] US Department of Defense, *Department of Defense Law of War Manual*, June 2015, §5.12.4.

[31] Ibid.

[32] US Department of Defense, *Department of Defense Law of War Manual*, December 2016, §5.12.3.

[33] D. Glazier et al., 'Failing Our Troops: A Critical Assessment of the Department of Defense Law of War Manual', *Yale Journal of International Law*, Vol. 42 (2017), 221.

[34] Contrary to what is auspicated by Carvin, who argued that 'there is hope' that the Manual would make 'a significant contribution to the understanding of the laws of war'. Carvin, 'The US Department of Defense Law of War Manual: An Update', p. 362.

[35] Glazier et al., 'Failing Our Troops: A Critical Assessment of the Department of Defense Law of War Manual', p. 216.

[36] Ibid., p. 226.

instance, it never claims to be of any authoritative standing, as an official manual should be,[37] but is only described as a 'resource' in its preface.[38]

22.3 THE 2016 EXECUTIVE ORDER

The 2016 Executive Order observes that civilian casualties are 'a tragic and at times unavoidable consequence of the use of force in situations of armed conflict or in the exercise of a State's inherent right of self-defense'. The US Government, the document stipulates, 'shall maintain and promote best practices that reduce the likelihood of civilian casualties, take appropriate steps when such casualties occur, and draw lessons from our operations to further enhance the protection of civilians'.[39]

The document does not seek to restrict the use of force in armed conflict beyond the dictates of IHL. Thus, for instance, it requires that the United States 'take feasible precautions in conducting attacks to reduce the likelihood of civilian casualties, such as providing warnings to the civilian population (unless the circumstances do not permit), adjusting the timing of attacks, taking steps to ensure military objectives and civilians are clearly distinguished, and taking other measures appropriate to the circumstances'.[40]

The document does require, though, that the United States 'review or investigate incidents involving civilian casualties, including by considering relevant and credible information from all available sources, such as other agencies, partner governments, and non-governmental organizations,[41] and take measures to mitigate the likelihood of future incidents of civilian casualties'.[42] It also states that the US Government will 'acknowledge responsibility for civilian casualties and offer condolences, including ex gratia payments, to civilians who are injured or to the families of civilians who are killed'.[43] In September 2021, for instance, the United States admitted that a drone attack in Afghanistan's capital mistakenly killed ten members of a family, when targeting a suspected suicide bomber from Islamic State Khorasan Province (ISIS-K). General Frank McKenzie, head of US Central Command, called the attack a 'tragic mistake',

---

[37] W. H. Boothby, 'Addressing the Realities, Development and Controversies Regarding the Conduct of Hostilities', in N. Hayashi (ed.), *National Military Manuals on the Law of Armed Conflict*, Torkel Opsahl Academic EPublisher, Oslo, 2008, p. 125.

[38] US Department of Defense, *Department of Defense Law of War Manual*, December 2016, p. iii. For further analysis and commentary, see M. Newton, *The United States Department of Defense Law of War Manual: Commentary and Critic*, 1st ed., Cambridge University Press, Cambridge, 2019. See also W. Boothby and H. von Heinegg, *The Law of War: A Detailed Assessment of the US Department of Defense Law of War Manual*, 1st ed., Cambridge University Press, Cambridge, 2018.

[39] *United States Policy on Pre- and Post-Strike Measures to Address Civilian Casualties in US Operations Involving the Use of Force*, §1 ('Purpose').

[40] Ibid., §2(a)(iv).

[41] Improving the conduct of partner forces was one of the key recommendations provided by NGO alliance InterAction, which specifically argued the US should both call for an independent review of such forces and invest resources to enhance institution-building programmes.

[42] *United States Policy on Pre- and Post-Strike Measures to Address Civilian Casualties in US Operations Involving the Use of Force*, §2(b)(i).

[43] Ibid., §2(b)(ii).

and said that the United States was considering making reparation payments to the family of the victims.[44]

22.4 THE ARMY WAR COLLEGE MILITARY REFERENCE GUIDE

The *Protection of Civilians Military Reference Guide* sets out in detail the steps that the armed forces can take to protect civilians. As the Guide recalls, there is 'often a lack of clarity and common understanding' about the protection of civilians and 'how to achieve it'.[45] Military forces, the Guide explains, support the protection of civilians in two general ways:

- *Avoidance of Civilian Harm.* Military forces act in accordance with the law of armed conflict/IHL and other relevant bodies of law to minimise civilian harm. Additionally, military forces avoid actions that undermine efforts by other actors that improve human security.
- *Deliberate Protection of Civilians Actions.* Military forces conduct offensive, defensive, and stability activities expressly intended to mitigate harm to civilians, including operations intended to create an environment conducive to the protection of civilians.[46]

Three 'fundamental' areas of action govern the protection of civilians by the armed forces:

- Understand civilian risks
- Protect civilians during operations
- Shape a protective environment.[47]

The three areas are summarised as 'UNDERSTAND – PROTECT – SHAPE'.

The Guide sets out a list of no fewer than forty-five tasks within these general areas of action, each of which is presented alongside a discussion of the task description, its relevance to the protection of civilians, how the task is accomplished, and task challenges. The list clearly enumerates the tasks to be performed, almost akin to a set of standing operating procedures.[48]

---

[44] 'Apology "Not Enough", Say Survivors of US Drone Attack in Kabul', *Aljazeera*, September 2021, at: https://bit.ly/3a3Vk6C.

[45] *Protection of Civilians Military Reference Guide*, 2nd ed., p. vii.

[46] Ibid.

[47] Ibid., pp. viii–x. The Trump administration withdrew the requirement to release data on deaths related to US drone strikes. J. Bonino, 'Transparency into Darkness: How the United States Use of Double-Tap Drone Strikes Violates IHL Principles of Distinction and Proportionality', *Law School Student Scholarship*, 2021, pp. 13–18.

[48] The tasks are, in chronological order, as follows: understand the operational environment; understand the actors; understand the dynamics; understand civilian vulnerabilities and threats; understand the protection of civilians strategy; conduct intelligence activities; manage multi-source information; conduct assessments; protect civilians during operations; plan for the protection of civilians; prepare for the protection of civilians; conduct patrols; establish checkpoints, guard posts, and observation posts; conduct cordon and search operations; neutralize or defeat perpetrators; secure vulnerable civilians; evacuate vulnerable civilians; conduct interposition operations; mitigate civilian casualties; respond to reported incidents of civilian harm; protect the force; provide command and control; provide administration and logistics; integrate fire

The Guide has a useful final section on 'trade-offs', drawing attention to some of the many trade-offs that military leaders can expect to encounter. These include peace and stability versus a just environment in which human rights are protected and perpetrators are held accountable; host-State ownership and capacity versus host-State government and security forces as a threat to civilians; mandate implementation (for peacekeepers) versus the perception of impartiality; and security/secrecy versus transparency.[49]

22.5 THE NATIONAL STRATEGY ON WOMEN, PEACE, AND SECURITY

The 2019 National Strategy on Women, Peace, and Security is also relevant in the context of the protection of civilians. The Strategy sets three strategic objectives:

- Women are more prepared and increasingly able to participate in efforts that promote stable and lasting peace
- Women and girls are safer, better protected, and have equal access to government and private assistance programmes, including from the United States, international partners, and host nations
- United States and partner governments have improved institutionalisation and capacity to ensure women, peace, and security efforts are sustainable and long-lasting.[50]

Four 'lines of effort' are detailed in the 2019 National Strategy on Women, Peace, and Security to achieve these strategic objectives.[51]

The first line of effort is to 'support the preparation and meaningful participation of women around the world in informal and formal decision-making processes related to conflict and crisis'.

The second line of effort is to 'promote the protection of women and girls' human rights, access to aid, and safety from violence, abuse, and exploitation around the world'.

The third line of effort is to 'adjust United States international programs to improve outcomes in equality for, and the empowerment of, women'.

support; support the protection of children; support the elimination of conflict-related sexual violence; conduct combined operations; support relief for displaced persons; support humanitarian assistance; contain public unrest; protection of civilians military reference guide; manage expectations; conduct information activities; conduct engagements with key leaders and the population; support the political settlement; coordinate with other actors; build partner capacity; establish and maintain a safe and secure environment; support good governance; support the rule of law; support social well-being; support a sustainable economy; maintain protection of civilians during transitions; support security sector reform; support disarmament, demobilization, and reintegration; support transitional justice; and support community building.

[49] *Protection of Civilians Military Reference Guide*, 2nd ed., pp. 157–9.
[50] *United States Strategy on Women, Peace, and Security*, 2019, p. 5.
[51] These 'lines of efforts' are comparable to the 'Women, Peace and Security' Agenda at the UN, based particularly on UN Security Council Resolution 1325. According to O'Rourke, the Agenda focuses on women's participation in peace and security and, as argued by Otto, it provides for a platform for women to voice their opinions. However, the Agenda has often been overshadowed by domestically more urgent matters. This attitude has been reflected in State practice, not just in the United States, but also in European countries and within the EU system. C. O'Rourke, 'Walking the Halls of Power: Understanding Women's Participation in International Peace and Security', *Melbourne Journal of International Law*, Vol. 15, No. 1 (2015), 1–27.

The fourth line of effort is to 'encourage partner governments to adopt policies, plans, and capacity to improve the meaningful participation of women in processes connected to peace and security and decision-making institutions'.

To track progress towards women's ability to participate meaningfully in and contribute to preventing, mediating, and resolving conflict and countering terrorism, the Administration committed to 'rigorously track and report on metrics across the interagency on an annual basis', and to seek meaningful change in all three strategic objectives by 2023.[52]

22.6 THE 2020 UN SECURITY COUNCIL DEBATE ON THE PROTECTION OF CIVILIANS

At the Security Council's debate on the protection of civilians in 2020,[53] the United States recalled that the global COVID-19 pandemic 'has the potential to devastate conflict-affected countries and overwhelm already weak health-care systems'. The statement explicitly endorsed support for the UN Department of Peace Operations' revised Policy on the Protection of Civilians. In addition, to better protect civilians in conflict, 'the United States and 46 Member States have endorsed the Kigali Principles on the Protection of Civilians. We encourage all Member States to join us so that we can help peacekeepers effectively implement their protection of civilian mandates.'

The United States Strategy on Women, Peace, and Security supports efforts to ensure that US assistance 'includes local strategies to mitigate COVID-19's acute risks to women and girls, including conflict-related sexual and gender-based violence'. The United States 'believes that efforts to protect civilians and build peace cannot be achieved without the full, equal and meaningful participation of women. Peace is more durable when women are at the table for peace talks.'[54] Additionally, the United States said, 'increasing women's meaningful participation in peacekeeping improves operational effectiveness and a mission's ability to fulfil protection of civilian mandates'. Nevertheless, the debate failed to discuss some relevant topics related to women in security policies, including the need for stronger resourcing of the humanitarian work of local civil society led by women, as well as the importance of a survivor-centred and non-discriminatory access to services such as sexual health.[55]

How such initiatives will be realised in practice remains to be seen. Indeed, Sarah Holewinski has called on the Biden administration to 'course correct' previous US policies. She argues that the United States has, up until this moment, failed to uphold

---

[52]   *United States Strategy on Women, Peace, and Security*, p. 15.

[53]   Letter dated 29 May 2020 from the President of the Security Council addressed to the Secretary-General and the Permanent Representatives of the members of the Security Council, UN doc. S/2020/465, 2 June 2020, at: http://bit.ly/3qPVTYa, Annex 15: Statement by the Permanent Representative of the United States of America to the United Nations, Kelly Craft.

[54]   Ibid.

[55]   Peace Women, 'Security Council Debate on Protection of Civilians in Armed Conflict, May 2020', 2020, at: https://bit.ly/3igYoT7.

several elements essential for effective protection of civilians. These include the payment of compensation, collecting and publishing correct data relating to civilian harm and casualties, investigating such harm in a standard and all-encompassing way (for instance, by including media coverage and civil society information), improving precautionary measures and the accuracy of targeting, and, importantly, building capacity through human rights units.[56] Larry Lewis raises similar issues and problematises the case of US support to the Saudi-led coalition in Yemen, conducting airstrikes that have killed thousands of civilians.[57]

In response, John Cherry and colleagues explain that besides the *Law of War Manual*, guidance on civilian protection is provided through rules of engagement, such as the US *Operational Law Handbook*, targeting directives, no-strike lists, and restricted target lists. Respective tools – such as the Collateral Damage Estimation Methodology, developed to identify the extent of civilian harm – and technologies are also applied to mitigate civilian harm. Nevertheless, they recognise that 'the mere existence' of these processes 'does not, in itself, solve the tragedy of collateral damage' but that the 'US and allied forces take exceptional measures to reduce the pain inflicted by war.'[58] Indeed, historical and more recent cases tend to confirm that civilian harm cannot be fully avoided even when mitigation measures and new technologies are applied.[59] Further challenges arise from modern partnered operations.[60]

---

[56] S. Holewinski, 'The Progress Not Made on Protecting Civilians', *Just Security*, 2021, at: https://bit.ly/2XYznTC.

[57] L. Lewis, 'Why We Haven't Made Progress on Civilian Protection', *Just Security*, 2021, at: https://bit.ly/3CThvJk.

[58] K. Cherry, et al., 'Avoiding Collateral Damage on the Battlefield', *Just Security*, 2021, at: https://bit.ly/2YTTa7W.

[59] B. Conin, *Bugsplat: The Politics of Collateral Damage in Western Armed Conflicts*, 1st ed., Oxford University Press, Oxford, 2018; J. Tirman, *The Death of Others: The Fate of Civilians in America's Wars*, 1st ed., Oxford University Press, Oxford, 2012. See also A. Suhrke, 'From Principle to Practice: US Military Strategy and Protection of Civilians in Afghanistan', *International Peacekeeping* Vol. 11, No. 1 (2015), 100–18; C. H. Kahl, 'In the Crossfire or the Crosshairs?: Norms, Civilian Casualties, and US Conduct in Iraq', *International Security* Vol. 32, No. 1 (2007), 7–46.

[60] See above referring to Melissa Dalton et al., 'The Protection of Civilians in US Partnered Operations'.

23

Brazil and the Protection of Civilians

23.1 INTRODUCTION

In the past, Brazil has been one of the States most concerned that the concepts of 'responsibility to protect' and the 'protection of civilians' are not used as a cover for regime change by Western nations. This concern was most acute during and following the North Atlantic Treaty Organization (NATO) intervention in Libya following the passage of United Nations (UN) Security Council Resolution 1973.[1] Brazil, a member of the Security Council at that time, was one of five States to abstain on the vote (the other four were China, Germany, India, and Russia).

Following the adoption of the resolution, Brazil stated that: 'We are not convinced that the use of force ... will lead to the realization of our common objective – the immediate end of violence and the protection of civilians.' Indeed, Brazil feared that the measures approved in Resolution 1973 might have the unintended effect of 'causing more harm than good to the very same civilians we are committed to protecting'. Brazil argued that protecting civilians, ensuring a lasting settlement, and addressing the legitimate demands of Libyan citizens demanded a political process.[2]

---

[1] UN Security Council Resolution 1973, adopted on 17 March 2011 by ten votes to nil with five abstentions (Brazil, China, Germany, India, and Russia).

[2] UN, 'Security Council Approves "No-Fly Zone" over Libya, Authorizing "All Necessary Measures" to Protect Civilians, by Vote of 10 in Favour with 5 Abstentions', UN doc. SC/10200, 17 March 2011, at: http://bit.ly/3qSy2Hn. On the other hand, Kenkel and Stefan have argued that it was the Libyan intervention that provided Brazil the opportunity to launch a 'normative initiative', namely RWP. According to the authors, the intervention had increased the growing tensions towards UN-backed use of force and the overall idea of a 'responsibility to protect', thus creating a normative gap, and allowing Brazil to fill it. Passarelli Hammann suggested that the Libyan crisis showed an irregularity within the Brazilian position towards intervention: although Brazil generally focuses on prevention and the use of non-coercive measures, the country generally tends to not vote against the use of force when considered at the UN Security Council. See, K. M. Kenkel and C. G. Stefan, 'Brazil and the Responsibility While Protecting Initiative: Norms and the Timing of Diplomatic Support', *Global Governance*, Vol. 22 (2016), 41–58; E. Passarelli Hammann, 'Brazil and R2P: A Rising Global Player Struggles to Harmonise Discourse and Practice', in *The Responsibility to Protect: From Evasive to Reluctant Action? The Role of Global Middle Powers*, Hanns Seidel Foundation, Johannesburg, 2012, pp. 79–80.

23.2 RESPONSIBILITY WHILE PROTECTING

Brazil is credited with devising – and then not further pursuing – the phrase 'Responsibility While Protecting' (RWP). In a Concept Note issued in 2011,[3] Brazil reaffirmed that violence against civilian populations 'must be repudiated wherever it takes place'.[4] Recalling the international community's 'failure to act in a timely manner to prevent violence on the scale of that observed in Rwanda',[5] it further acknowledged that there 'may be situations in which the international community might contemplate military action to prevent humanitarian catastrophes'.[6] But, it cautioned, there was a 'growing perception that the concept of the responsibility to protect might be misused for purposes other than protecting civilians, such as regime change'. This perception, Brazil affirmed, 'may make it even more difficult to attain the protection objectives pursued by the international community'.[7]

Prevention of conflict has been the mainstay of Brazil's approach to the protection of civilians, along with a call for a 'higher level of responsibility on the part of the international community' to protect vulnerable civilians in situations of conflict.[8] The 'key value added' from the Concept Note was the set of guidelines for the Security Council and other involved States in contemplating and setting up an intervention based on 'responsibility to protect'.[9] Brazil stressed the need to follow the three pillars of the responsibility to protect (R2P) doctrine in strict sequencing order (State responsibility,

---

[3] 'Responsibility while Protecting: Elements for the Development and Promotion of a Concept', Annex to the letter dated 9 November 2011 from the Permanent Representative of Brazil to the United Nations addressed to the Secretary-General, UN doc. A/66/551–S/2011/701, 11 November 2011, at: http://bit.ly/3sZYJeU.

[4] Ibid., para. 8.

[5] It had been argued that, previously, Brazil was reluctant to use force in a humanitarian crisis, even when arguing that it would act otherwise. E. Diniz, 'Brazil: Peacekeeping and the Evolution of Foreign Policy', in J. T. Fishel and A. Saenz (eds.), *Capacity Building for Peacekeeping: The Case of Haiti*, National Defense University Press, Washington, DC, 2007, 74–88; Passarelli Hammann, 'Brazil and R2P: A Rising Global Player Struggles to Harmonise Discourse and Practice', pp. 76–7.

[6] 'Responsibility while Protecting: Elements for the Development and Promotion of a Concept', Annex to the letter dated 9 November 2011 from the Permanent Representative of Brazil to the United Nations addressed to the Secretary-General.

[7] Ibid., para. 10. According to Kenkel, Brazil's opposition towards the idea of responsibility to protect ('R2P') was grounded on 'an absolutist interpretation of State sovereignty as the inviolability of borders', which would be – in contrast to the view of many Western countries – a way of protection against interference from larger powers. For instance, Article 4 of the 1988 Brazilian Constitution places on equal footing the principles of national independence and non-intervention along with human rights and cooperation. Indeed, Brazil's emphasis on the use of force as always the last resort was particularly welcomed by States that rejected R2P as a concept and especially its potential for regime change. Brazil's later step back as proponent of RWP was, according to McDougall, due to possible political costs at the international level. K. M. Kenkel, 'Brazil and R2P: Does Taking Responsibility Mean Using Force?', *Global Responsibility to Protect*, Vol. 4, No. 1 (2012), 5–31; D. McDougall, 'Responsibility While Protecting: Brazil's Proposal for Modifying Responsibility to Protect', *Global Responsibility to Protect*, Vol. 6, No. 1 (2014), 64–87.

[8] E. P. Hamann, 'The Protection of Civilians in Armed Conflict and Brazil's "Responsibility While Protecting"', NOREF Policy Brief, October 2012, pp. 3, 4.

[9] C. Harig and K. M. Kenkel, 'Are Rising Powers Consistent or Ambiguous Foreign Policy Actors? Brazil, Humanitarian Intervention and the "Graduation Dilemma"', *International Affairs*, Vol. 93, No. 3 (2017), 625–41, at: https://bit.ly/36d8Vak, at p. 632.

capacity-building, and timely and decisive response),[10] with resort to the use of force, avowedly a last resort:

> The international community must be rigorous in its efforts to exhaust all peaceful means available in the protection of civilians under threat of violence, in line with the principles and purposes of the Charter and as embodied in the 2005 World Summit Outcome;
>
> The use of force, including in the exercise of the responsibility to protect, must always be authorized by the Security Council, in accordance with Chapter VII of the Charter, or, in exceptional circumstances, by the General Assembly, in line with its resolution 377 (V);
>
> The authorization for the use of force must be limited in its legal, operational and temporal elements and the scope of military action must abide by the letter and the spirit of the mandate conferred by the Security Council or the General Assembly, and be carried out in strict conformity with international law, in particular international humanitarian law and the international law of armed conflict;
>
> The use of force must produce as little violence and instability as possible and under no circumstance can it generate more harm than it was authorized to prevent;
>
> In the event that the use of force is contemplated, action must be judicious, proportionate and limited to the objectives established by the Security Council. ...
>
> The Security Council must ensure the accountability of those to whom authority is granted to resort to force.[11]

The initiative, Christoph Harig and Kai Michael Kenkel suggest, 'remains perhaps the most prominent instance of Brazilian norm entrepreneurship at the global level'. Its later withdrawal, however, meant that it 'did not develop its full potential, despite later endorsement from broad sections of the R2P community, practitioners and academics alike'.[12]

Despite this, Brazil's caution with respect to the use of force to protect civilians has persisted. In January 2016, Brazil's Permanent Representative to the UN, Ambassador Antonio de Aguiar Patriota, spoke at the Security Council debate on protection of civilians in the following terms:

> Preventing and resolving conflict through peaceful means is the most effective way to shield civilians from the miseries of war. Conversely, the ill-advised notion that the protection of civilians is better guaranteed through the use of force finds no evidence in reality, and more often than not exacerbates the suffering of innocents and leads to negative humanitarian consequences.[13]

---

[10] Ibid.

[11] 'Responsibility While Protecting: Elements for the Development and Promotion of a Concept', para. 11(b) to (f) and (i). As highlighted by Österdahl, this mixes *jus ad bellum* and international humanitarian law (*jus in bello*), which is – contrary to Österdahl's claims – not of significant relevance, however. I. Österdahl, 'The Responsibility to Protect and the Responsibility While Protecting: Why Did Brazil Write a Letter to the UN?', *Nordic Journal of International Law*, Vol. 82 (2013), 459–86.

[12] Harig and Kenkel, 'Are Rising Powers Consistent or Ambiguous Foreign Policy Actors? Brazil, Humanitarian Intervention and the "Graduation Dilemma"', p. 632.

[13] Statement of Brazil delivered by its Permanent Representative to the United Nations, Ambassador Antonio de Aguiar Patriota, at the Security Council debate on protection of civilians, New York, 19 January 2016.

23.3 THE 2020 UN SECURITY COUNCIL DEBATE
ON THE PROTECTION OF CIVILIANS

In its statement before the Council's debate on the protection of civilians in 2020, Brazil did not address the issue of the use of force per se. Instead, it cautioned that when 'protection of civilians' mandates are authorised by the Security Council, 'they should be clear enough so that peacekeepers on the ground, especially commanders, understand precisely what is expected of them, without hampering the autonomy that leaders in the field require'. It was important, Brazil stated, 'to provide realistic mandates, with feasible tasks from the military, political and legal perspectives'.[14]

Brazil also emphasised the duty to comply with international humanitarian law (IHL) and to investigate 'impartially alleged' violations, and hold accountable the perpetrators.[15] It singled out the threat to civilians from the use of explosive weapons in urban warfare, noting it had endorsed the 2018 Santiago Declaration ('Communiqué'), supported by Latin American and Caribbean States, in favour of a political declaration on the use of explosive weapons in populated areas. (Under the Declaration, endorsing States also commit to: 'Avoid the use of explosive weapons with wide area effects in populated areas'.)[16]

---

[14] Letter dated 29 May 2020 from the President of the Security Council addressed to the Secretary-General and the Permanent Representatives of the members of the Security Council, UN doc. S/2020/465, 2 June 2020, at: http://bit.ly/3qPVTYa, Annex 25: 'Statement by the Permanent Mission of Brazil to the United Nations'. According to Kenkel, Brazil has been promoting a different approach to peacekeeping, focused on peace, security, and development to solve conflicts rather than merely military force or 'soft peacekeeping'. The aim is that of stabilisation and conflict mediation, for instance through close contact with local populations, focusing on peacebuilding rather than security aspects, and exporting successful domestic policies for combating poverty and hunger. For Chatin, this shows Brazil's desire to become a 'committed and responsible' actor by tackling 'high-level global peace and security challenges'. In contrast, Santos and Cravo argue that Brazil has more recently reoriented its foreign policy considerations, participating in UN missions but through a symbolic presence, without major contributions of personnel or funding. The consequence, they believe, has been the legitimisation of traditional powers' interests, by conforming to their vision of the world, while at the same time contesting that same international power structure by advocating for the Global South and 'endorsing a peace and development agenda'. K. Kenkel, 'Brazil's Peacekeeping and Peacebuilding Policies in Africa', *Journal of International Peacekeeping*, Vol. 17, Nos. 3–4 (2013), 272–92; M. Chatin, 'Brazil: Analysis of a Rising Soft Power', *Journal of Political Power*, Vol. 9, No. 3 (2016), 369–93, at p. 376; R. Santos and T. A. Cravo, 'Brazil's Rising Profile in United Nations Peacekeeping Operations since the End of the Cold War', Report, Norwegian Peacebuilding Resource Centre, March 2014, p. 5; and see also M. Hirst, 'Emerging Brazil: The Challenges of Liberal Peace and Global Governance', *Global Society*, Vol. 29, No. 3 (2015), 359–72.

[15] Letter dated 29 May 2020 from the President of the Security Council addressed to the Secretary-General and the Permanent Representatives of the members of the Security Council, UN doc. S/2020/465.

[16] International Network on Explosive Weapons (INEW), Communiqué from Regional Meeting on Protecting Civilians from the Use of Explosive Weapons in Populated Areas (Santiago, Chile), December 2018, at: https://bit.ly/2MprAsm. Brazil has, in fact, been at the forefront of efforts to regulate the use of explosive weapons. Among other legal and policy positions, Brazil has argued that the 'post-conflict' effects of cluster munitions should be considered part of the proportionality and precaution assessments of the legality of an attack, as the weapons can cause casualties long after their use. I. Robinson and E. Nohle, 'Proportionality and Precautions in Attack: The Reverberating Effects of Using Explosive Weapons in Populated Areas', *International Review of the Red Cross*, Vol. 98, No. 1 (2016), 107–45.

At the same time, Brazil cautioned against the expansion 'ad infinitum' of the 'already comprehensive protection-of-civilians agenda, particularly with issues that fall outside the mandate of the Security Council'. It cited, as an example – perhaps mindful of the situation in the Amazon – the impact of armed conflict on the environment and climate change, issues raised by the UN Secretary-General in his report to the Council in 2020. In Brazil's view: 'we must be wary of proposals to address non-military challenges through security lenses'.[17]

Brazil has not adopted a protection of civilians strategy at national level. Brazil has not been a member of the Security Council since 2011.[18]

---

[17] Annex 25: 'Statement by the Permanent Mission of Brazil to the United Nations'.

[18] Until then, Brazil had what some call a 'semi-permanent status' on the Security Council, having a seat for about 30 per cent of the Council's existence. Thus, Brazil was present during several humanitarian crises, including Rwanda, Kosovo, Darfur, and Libya. Nevertheless, Brazil has long called for reform of the UN Security Council, defending the expansion of the number of permanent seats and presenting itself as a candidate for one of them. Passarelli Hammann, 'Brazil and R2P: A Rising Global Player Struggles to Harmonise Discourse and Practice', p. 76; G. Fonseca Jr., 'Notes on the Evolution of Brazilian Multilateral Policy', *Global Governance*, Vol. 17, No. 3 (2011), 375–97.

24

India and the Protection of Civilians

24.1 INTRODUCTION

India, the world's most populous democracy, has, like Brazil, a nuanced position towards international efforts to protect civilians. India does not have a formal national strategy or policy on the protection of civilians. The issue is, though, of particular concern to India owing to insurgencies within its own borders[1] and the politically sensitive issue of Kashmir.[2] The use of force by United Nations (UN) peacekeepers is also a major concern given the significant contribution of troops and other personnel that India makes to the blue helmets. As of December 2020, India was the fourth largest troop contributor to the United Nations, with more than 5,000 soldiers engaging in UN peacekeeping operations.[3] Thereby, India plays a large part in the protection of civilians by the UN.

[1] Rule of Law in Armed Conflict (RULAC), 'India', last updated 15 October 2020, at: http://bit.ly/3peQlWN. Goswami argues that, ever since India's independence, the country has been 'suffering' from various insurgencies, particularly in the Northeast region – including the Nagalim-Isak-Muvah, the United Liberation Front of Asom, the People's Liberation Army and the People's Front. According to Cline, India faces a significant threat to its internal stability due to the continued existence of these groups, although the country made progress in dealing with some of these groups. N. Goswami, 'Escalation and De-escalation of Violence in Insurgencies: Insights from Northeast India', *Small Wars and Insurgencies*, Vol. 24, No. 1 (2013), 28–56; and L. E. Cline, 'The Insurgency Environment in Northeast India, *Small Wars and Insurgencies*, Vol. 17, No. 2 (2006), 126–47.

[2] The conflict, dating back to the partition of the subcontinent in 1947, resurged in the late 1980s, with ethnic, religious, and territorial division claims being raised by both India and Pakistan. Majid and Hussain assert that both States have arguable claims of sovereignty over the territory, and both face challenges in the region. But it has been increasingly difficult to 'quarantine problems such as Kashmir from international concern'. Indeed, India's peacekeeping role has been described as 'paradoxical' exactly because of its approach towards the situation in Kashmir: whereas India has 'one of the longest and most consistent records of participation in UN peacekeeping operations', it does not recognise nor support the presence of the UN Military Observer Group in India and Pakistan (UNOGIP) in the region. This stands in contrast to the Pakistani position, which instead views it as 'the road to peace'. According to Krishnasamy, this might be explained due to India's general reluctance in supporting peace missions that aim at ethnic separatism, a stance it held in East Timor as well as in the Kashmir region. A. Majid and M. Hussain, 'Kashmir: A Conflict between India and Pakistan', *A Research Journal of South Asian Studies*, Vol. 31, No. 1 (2016), 149–59; S. Ganguly and K. Bajpai, 'India and the Crisis in Kashmir', *Asian Survey*, Vol. 34, No. 5 (1994), 401–16, at p. 410; K. Krishnasamy, 'The Paradox of India's Peacekeeping', *Contemporary South Asia*, Vol. 12, No. 2 (2003), 263–80.

[3] UN, 'Contributors to UN Peacekeeping Operations by Country and Post Police, UN Military Experts on Mission, Staff Officers and Troops', New York, 2020, at: https://bit.ly/3ckDoag. See on this issue E. Paddon Rhoads, *Taking Sides in Peacekeeping, Impartiality and the Future of the United Nations*, Oxford University

India's stated position is that the protection of civilians is the primary responsibility of national governments.[4] This is consistent with Pillar 1 of the responsibility to protect (R2P) doctrine. Thus, in addressing the UN Security Council open debate on protection of civilians in armed conflict in 2019, India's Deputy Permanent Representative to the UN Ambassador K. Nagaraj Naidu said: 'The general tendency is to wrongly assume that protection of civilians is the responsibility of the parties to the conflict, peacekeepers, and humanitarian organisations. However, this responsibility primarily rests with the national governments.'[5]

Ambassador Naidu also recalled the 'stellar example' of Captain Gurbachan Singh Salaria, who led an Indian Infantry Brigade Group as part of the UN Operation in the Congo in November 1961. The mission's objective was to restore the peace and unity of the Congo and to protect the lives of the civilian population in Elizabethville. However, it resulted in the maximum number of casualties suffered by India in any UN operation – thirty-nine personnel laid down their lives. 'This was at a time when "Protection of Civilians" was not part of peacekeeping mandate,' he said.[6]

24.2 RESPONSIBILITY TO PROTECT

As is the case with Brazil, India has been 'wary' of any coercive role by the international community in the exercise of the R2P doctrine.[7] India is said to 'demand' that those who authorise action and those who act on the basis of such a mandate should be held

Press, Oxford, 2016, p. 94. According to Hansel and Möller, this is why India has been called the 'backbone of peacekeeping': after the Cold War, as Western countries became more reluctant to contribute to UN peace operations, India represented an essential resource for the success of peacekeeping missions. Banerjee emphasises that the motivation behind such a presence in peacekeeping is political, economic, and normative: India has been aspiring for a larger role in the UN system – in particular, the chance of gaining a permanent seat on the UN Security Council – and it receives compensation for its participation in missions and promotes international peace and security. In Africa, India's involvement in peacekeeping has been explained as being a part of India's objective to promote world peace. It can also be a way to expand its economic and commercial linkages with Africa, as well as its energy cooperation with African countries such as Sudan and Mauritius. M. Hansel and M. Möller, 'House of Cards? India's Rationales for Contributing to UN Peacekeeping', *Global Change, Peace & Security*, Vol. 26, No. 2 (2014), 141–57; D. Banerjee, 'Contributor Profile: India', *Institute of Peace and Conflict Studies*, Vol. 27 (2013), 1–6; R. Beri, 'India's Role in Keeping Peace in Africa', *Strategic Analysis*, Vol. 32, No. 2 (2008), 197–221.

[4] 'Protection of Civilians is Primary Responsibility of National Governments: India', *Economic Times*, May 2019, at: http://bit.ly/39kijLc.

[5] Ibid. Although India and the other BRICS countries (Brazil, Russia, China, and South Africa) are often seen as unsupportive of the R2P doctrine due to their concern about its Pillar 3 (intervention). Stuenkel argues that they support the importance of protecting civilians in their peacekeeping but with an emphasis on prevention. O. Stuenkel, 'The BRICS and the Future of R2P: Was Syria or Libya the Exception?', *Global Responsibility to Protect*, Vol. 6 (2014); and see also A. Bullion, 'India and UN Peacekeeping Operations', *International Peacekeeping*, Vol. 4, No. 1 (1997); and Banerjee, 'Contributor Profile: India'.

[6] 'Protection of Civilians is Primary Responsibility of National Governments: India'.

[7] C. S. R. Murthy, 'India's Approach to the Protection of Civilians in Armed Conflicts', NOREF Policy Brief, November 2012, at: https://bit.ly/2MnkaGe, p. 2. India had in fact almost rejected out of hand a 'responsibility to protect' in the early development of the concept on the basis that the concept advanced similar arguments to colonialism. Stuenkel, 'The BRICS and the Future of R2P: Was Syria or Libya the Exception?'; and see also A. J. Bellamy, *Global Politics and the Responsibility to Protect: From Words to Deeds*, Routledge, London, 2011, .p. 23; M. M. Jaganathan and G. Kurtz, 'Singing the Tune of Sovereignty? India and the Responsibility to

accountable for any resulting unacceptable outcomes. This stance aligns with the Brazilian idea of 'Responsibility While Protecting' as a complement to R2P.

India recognises that the international community, through the UN Security Council, has an obligation to provide technical assistance to States in order to help build their institutions. But it rejects military intervention as an 'obligation' of the world community. In its view, the trigger for the invocation of the responsibility to protect has to be mass atrocities. Nonetheless, it has made the claim that common agreement has yet to be reached on what constitute war crimes and crimes against humanity.

This is despite the existence of the provisions in the Rome Statute of the International Criminal Court,[8] to which India is not a signatory much less a State Party. Indeed, although India has long provided support for the international criminal justice system, it voiced several objections when the International Criminal Court was being designed, including the Court's jurisdiction over internal armed conflicts, the non-inclusion of terrorism and use of nuclear weapons as crimes within its jurisdiction, and the modes triggering the Court's jurisdiction.[9]

24.3 THE 2020 UN SECURITY COUNCIL DEBATE ON THE PROTECTION OF CIVILIANS

In its statement before the Security Council's debate on the protection of civilians in 2020, India maintained its sceptical view on the use of force in the protection of civilians. While accepting that it is 'well understood' that protecting civilians is 'a multidimensional and cross-cutting issue', India stated that 'an attempt to view and interpret every conflict situation as requiring United Nations protection is not just misleading but could have unintended consequences. The presumption that every conflict situation requires a United Nations intervention is not only too ambitious but could encroach upon the sovereignty of national Governments, which have the primary responsibility for protecting civilians'.[10]

India again recalled the example of Captain Salaria, asserting that 'even before the protection of civilians was a part of the peacekeeping mandate, India was in the forefront of

---

Protect', *Conflict, Security and Development* Vol. 14, No. 4 (2014); S. Ganguly, 'India and the Responsibility to Protect', *International Relations* Vol. 30, No. 3 (2016).

[8] Rome Statute of the International Criminal Court; adopted at Rome, 17 July 1998; entered into force, 1 July 2002. As of 1 October 2021, 123 States were party to the Statute.

[9] Ramanathan best summarises India's objections, stating that the ICC Statute 'would have been more acceptable to India if it had contained an opt-in provision whereby a State could accept the jurisdiction of the ICC by declaration . . . . The lack of such a provision, and the inherent jurisdiction which replaced it, are perceived as representing a violation of the consent of States, and thus a threat to sovereignty.' U. Ramanathan, 'India and the ICC', *Journal of International Criminal Justice*, Vol. 3 (2005), 627. On the concern as to the inclusion of war crimes in non-international armed conflict in Article 8 of the Statute, see also H. Jamil, 'Critical Evaluation of India's position on the Rome Statute', *Indian Journal of International Law*, Vol. 57, Nos. 3–4 (2017), 411.

[10] Letter dated 29 May 2020 from the President of the Security Council addressed to the Secretary-General and the Permanent Representatives of the members of the Security Council, UN doc. S/2020/465, 2 June 2020, at: http://bit.ly/3qPVTYa, Annex 36: Statement by the Permanent Mission of India to the United Nations.

protecting civilians'.[11] Later in its statement, India stated that: 'The expectation that United Nations peacekeepers can effectively ensure the protection of civilians in the absence of clear and prioritized mandates is not realistic.' That said, India expressed its belief that increasing women's participation in peacekeeping 'improves operational effectiveness and a mission's potential to implement protection of civilian mandates. In that context, we support efforts to reduce barriers to women's participation and promote greater participation through incentivization.'[12]

Going forward, India called for consideration of the development of 'a normative architecture for protection of civilians in armed conflict as part of a broad endeavour'. India believes that a framework 'that is politically attuned, but not politicized, and clearly defined and that strengthens capacities of national Governments, enhances community engagement, protects those who need it and abides by the do-no-harm principle with a strong gender lens can be a workable solution.'[13] India has not been a member of the Security Council since 2012.

---

[11] Ibid.

[12] Ibid. For instance, as pointed out by Dharmapuri, India has been one of the most prominent UN Member States in increasing their contributors of female police by deploying, in Liberia in 2007, the first all-female formed police unit. The goal, according to the author, is that of obtaining a 'gender perspective' on mandates, which should enhance the operations' effectiveness, for instance by providing for a more nuanced understanding of the area of operation. According to the unit commander, the all-female police unit influenced Liberian women to increasingly join the police force. S. Dharmapuri, 'Not Just a Numbers Game: Increasing Women's Participation in Peacekeeping', International Peace Institute, New York, 2013; But see also L. Klossek and E. Johannson-Nogués, 'The Female "Boot on the Ground": Indian Ambivalence over Gender Mainstreaming in UN Peacekeeping Operations', *International Peacekeeping*, Vol. 28, No. 4 (2021), 527–52.

[13] Annex 36: Statement by the Permanent Mission of India to the United Nations.

25

Norway and the Protection of Civilians

25.1 INTRODUCTION

Norway has been at the forefront of several major initiatives to protect civilians. It hosted the diplomatic conference in September 1997 that adopted the Anti-Personnel Mine Ban Convention,[1] and led the elaboration of the Convention on Cluster Munitions in 2008.[2] The Safe Schools Declaration is a joint initiative led by Norway and Argentina and endorsed by governments at the Oslo Conference on Safe Schools convened by the Royal Norwegian Ministry of Foreign Affairs on 29 May 2015.[3]

While Norway does not have a formal strategy or policy specifically dedicated to the protection of civilians, protection against violence both in situations of armed conflict and in natural disasters is one of three main priorities in Norway's Humanitarian Strategy for 2019–23.[4] 'Norway's Humanitarian Strategy: An Effective and Integrated Approach' details Norway's commitment to 'work actively to promote compliance with international humanitarian law and to counter attempts to weaken international humanitarian law obligations'.[5]

---

[1] Convention on the Prohibition of the Use, Stockpiling, Production, and Transfer of Anti-Personnel Mines and on their Destruction; adopted at Oslo, 18 September 1997; entered into force, 1 March 1999. As of 1 April 2022, 164 States were party to the Convention.

[2] Convention on Cluster Munitions; adopted at Dublin, 30 May 2008; entered into force, 1 August 2010. As of 1 April 2022, 110 States were party to the Convention.

[3] 'Safe Schools Declaration', at: https://bit.ly/2YiQSeg. As of 1 April 2022, 114 States had endorsed the Declaration. List at: http://bit.ly/2k3LOtS. The Declaration stems from the increased military use of education institutions, a practice that not only deprives children of their right to access education, but further puts them at risk of attack. As such, countries were encouraged to implement the 'Guidelines for Protecting Schools and Universities from Military Use during Armed Conflict' into domestic policy and operational frameworks. See, for example, the Global Coalition to Protect Education from Attack, 'Submission to the Committee on the Rights of the Child's pre-session working group for the adoption of a list of issues to be taken up in connection to the consideration of the State Report of Estonia' (1–6 February 2016). The Guidelines' text was not opened up for negotiation, meaning no changes could be made. This led to several States' reluctance to sign the guidelines, along with the fact that it was an NGO-led initiative. Article 36, 'Reflections from the Safe Schools Declaration Process for Future International Political Commitments on Civilian Protection', 2019.

[4] Royal Norwegian Ministry of Foreign Affairs, 'The Protection of Civilians and Health Workers in Conflict Situations', Article, last updated 11 April 2019, at: http://bit.ly/3plFXN5.

[5] Further, as a troop-contributing nation for the UN, NATO, and the EU, these organisations' protection of civilians policies (discussed in previous chapters) are relevant and inform Norway's humanitarian strategies. See S. Kjeksrud, J. A. Ravndal, A. Ø. Stensland, C. de Coning, W. Lotze, and E. A. Weir, 'Protection of

Norway pledges political engagement in situations where international humanitarian law (IHL) is violated, and 'help to ensure that these violations are documented and prosecuted'. Norway also seeks to ensure that international action against terrorism complies with IHL and international human rights law.[6]

Norway pledged that in the period 2019–23 it would increase its focus on protection in situations of crisis and conflict, with special priority to be given to the protection of women, children, and youth.[7] Protection against sexual and gender-based violence (SGBV) is to be given high priority in Norway's humanitarian efforts. Norway will increase its support for operational measures to prevent this kind of violence and to provide psychosocial support to the survivors.[8] Norway also noted the challenge faced by international efforts to improve the protection of internally displaced people, in particular within the United Nations (UN), given the 'multilateral climate' where more States are citing sovereignty 'as grounds for not expanding the international protection regime, despite the immense scale of humanitarian needs in areas where internally displaced people are living'.[9]

Norway participated actively in the military effort in Libya authorised by UN Security Council Resolution 1973 (2011). Indeed, it was reported in the media that Norwegian and Danish combat aircraft had bombed the most targets in Libya in proportion to the number of planes involved.[10] Norwegian planes dropped a total of 588 bombs, accounting for between 15 and 18 per cent of the NATO bombing before, under domestic political pressure, the Norwegian government put an end to the operation. A Commission established to evaluate Norway's role in the Libya operation reported in 2018.[11] It concluded that regime change was a natural consequence of the operation.[12]

25.2 THE 2020 UN SECURITY COUNCIL DEBATE ON THE PROTECTION OF CIVILIANS

In its statement before the Council's debate on the protection of civilians in 2020,[13] Norway declared that it was 'deeply troubled about the effects that the use of explosive weapons with wide-area effects in populated areas have had on the civilian population in

Civilians in Armed Conflict: Comparing Organisational Approaches', Report, Norwegian Defence Research Establishment, Oslo, 2011.

[6] 'Norway's Humanitarian Strategy: An Effective and Integrated Approach', at: https://bit.ly/3a6wFOA, p. 14.

[7] Ibid., p. 19.

[8] Ibid., p. 20.

[9] Ibid., p. 22.

[10] 'Norske fly bomber mest i Libya', *Dagbladet*, 31 May 2011, at: http://bit.ly/2MuMWVu.

[11] *Evaluering av Norsk Deltakelse i Libyaoperasjonene i 2011*, 2018, at: https://bit.ly/30ilMhB.

[12] K. Berg Harpviken, 'The Norwegian Libya Commission: An Important Report, But We're Still Missing Answers', Blog entry, PRIO, 25 September 2018, at: http://bit.ly/39kBoOS. See further D. Henriksen, 'The Political Rationale and Implications of Norway's Military Involvement in Libya', chapter 9 in D. Henriksen and A. K. Larssen (eds.), *Political Rationale and International Consequences of the War in Libya*, Oxford University Press, Oxford, 2016.

[13] Letter dated 29 May 2020 from the President of the Security Council addressed to the Secretary-General and the Permanent Representatives of the members of the Security Council, UN doc. S/2020/465, 2 June 2020, at: http://bit.ly/3qPVTYa, Annex 52: Statement by the Permanent Mission of Norway to the United Nations.

many conflicts'.[14] It therefore supported the development of a political declaration aimed at enhancing the protection of civilians in urban warfare. Norway also declared the need to increase UN capacity to prevent and resolve conflicts. United Nations peacekeeping and political missions 'must have the protection of civilians firmly embedded in their mandates and operationalized on the ground as a mission-wide responsibility, ranging from preventive measures to institutional reform and direct physical protection', Norway stated.[15]

Norway has highlighted the exacerbated protection risks for people in conflict zones as a result of the COVID-19 pandemic. It has supported the efforts of the International Committee of the Red Cross (ICRC) and the World Health Organization (WHO) to identify best practices to protect health care and document attacks. 'It is paramount that humanitarian organizations get safe, timely and unhindered access to populations in need everywhere."[16]

As part of its commitment to prevent and tackle the prevalence and impact of SGBV in conflict, Norway called for the implementation of Security Council Resolution 2467 (2019), 'with a focus on justice, accountability and a survivor-centred approach in the prevention and response to conflict-related sexual violence' and recalled the pledges made at the international conference on sexual and gender-based violence held in Oslo in 2019.[17]

Norway was one of a number of delegations to pay particular attention in their statements to the Council on the protection of persons with disabilities. Noting the disproportionate impact of armed conflicts on persons with disabilities, Norway emphasised their particular needs in humanitarian responses. 'Member States should take all the

---

[14] Ruys notes that Norway had previously showed support for weapons – such as the 12.7 mm multi-purpose bullets – which had shown to frequently explode, with the International Committee of the Red Cross (ICRC) expressing 'deep concern' about their legality and the risk of their proliferation. Norway argued that these bullets were compliant with international humanitarian law (IHL), although it accepted they should not be used against personnel, but only for anti-vehicle purposes. T. Ruys, 'The XM25 Individual Airburst Weapon System: A "Game Changer" for the (Law on the) Battlefield? Revisiting the Legality of Explosive Projectiles under the Law of Armed Conflict', *Israel Law Review*, Vol. 45, No. 3 (2012), 401–49. In the last decade, Norway has taken a stronger stance against explosive weapons. It was one of the main States engaging on the issue of explosive weapons, funding the Norms on Explosive Weapons project launched by UNIDIR (UN Institute for Disarmament Research) in 2011, for instance, with the aim of raising awareness of the consequences of the use of explosive weapons in populated areas. M. Brehm, 'Protecting Civilians from the Effects of Explosive Weapons: An Analysis of International Legal and Policy Standards', Report, UNIDIR, Geneva, 2012.

[15] Annex 52: Statement by the Permanent Mission of Norway to the United Nations.

[16] Ibid.

[17] For the goals put forward in the UN Security Council resolutions on women, peace, and security (WPS) to be reached, True specifically recommends Norway to follow three core principles: (1) embed WPS provision in its post-conflict strategy and planning; (2) prioritise conflict-affected and post-conflict countries in its national action plan; and (3) realise gender equality through support and financing for post-conflict countries. On the other hand, Schia and de Carvalho also point to the importance of avoiding gender dichotomies that are often the result of representing 'women and children' as especially vulnerable groups without considering the different range of roles these groups can play. See, J. True, 'Women, Peace and Security in Post-Conflict and Peacebuilding Contexts', Report, Norwegian Peacebuilding Resource Centre, Oslo, 2013; N. N. Schia and B. de Carvalho, 'Being Peacekept? The Implicit Assumptions that Hamper the Protection of Civilians', Policy Brief No. 42, Norwegian Institute of International Affairs, Oslo, 2016.

appropriate measures to eliminate discrimination and marginalization of persons based on disability in situations of armed conflict,' Norway said.[18]

Norway was elected as a member of the UN Security Council in 2001–2 and 2021–2. Norway's Foreign Minister, Ine Eriksen Søreide, emphasised the country's commitment to strengthening the protection of civilians in armed conflicts in her speech addressing Norway's membership of the Security Council in 2020. In particular, the protection of civilians was one of the four thematic areas of priority for the country – alongside peace diplomacy, inclusion of women, and climate change and security – on which work was needed to ensure that the Council 'promotes full compliance with international humanitarian law and human rights and thereby enhances the protection of civilians in practice'.[19] This focus was confirmed on other occasions.[20]

---

[18] Annex 52: Statement by the Permanent Mission of Norway to the United Nations.
[19] Statement by Minister of Foreign Affairs Ine Eriksen Søreide, 'Address on Norway's Membership of the Security Council', 8 December 2020, at: http://bit/ly.2YQPIKK.
[20] A. De Lauri, with contributions from S. Turunen, A. Suhrke et al., 'Protection of Civilians: Norway in the Security Council', Chr. Michelsen Institute (CMI) Report R 2021:01, Bergen, 2021.

26

South Africa and the Protection of Civilians

26.1 INTRODUCTION

South Africa does not have a formal protection of civilians strategy in place although it has played an important role in the elaboration of doctrine and policy on the issue, especially at regional level. Before the responsibility to protect framework was endorsed at the World Summit in 2005, South Africa was 'active in negotiating the move from non-intervention to non-indifference, the latter regarded as a forerunner of R2P, in Africa'.[1] It was thus 'instrumental' in ensuring that the 2000 Constitutive Act of the African Union included a provision that refers to 'the right of the Union to intervene in a Member State pursuant to a decision of the Assembly in respect of grave circumstances, namely: war crimes, genocide and crimes against humanity'.[2]

---

[1] Landsberg argues that South Africa's history of *apartheid* shaped its stance towards R2P – prioritising engagement and the promotion of a new value system throughout the continent – and points specifically to Nelson Mandela, Thabo Mbeki, and Jacob Zuma as 'leaders' in the promotion of R2P. Indeed, according to Mabera and Dunne, South Africa's support for R2P is a direct result of its memory of a violent State, which has shaped the country's understanding of sovereignty as responsibility. However, more recent developments have raised questions over South Africa's commitment to this principle. Mamdani links this 'discomfort' to the inconsistent application of R2P, following which certain countries are seen as sovereign States and others as 'territories whose populations are . . . in need of external protection'. As such, Smith concludes that South Africa is not 'categorically opposed to the use of force' but only to its use as a pretext for regime change, instead of favouring a more moderate and regional approach focused on conflict prevention and resolution. C. Landsberg, '*Pax South Africana* and the Responsibility to Protect', *Global Responsibility to Protect*, Vol. 2, No. 4 (2010), 436–57; F. Mabera and T. Dunne, 'South Africa and the Responsibility to Protect', *Asia Pacific Centre for the Responsibility to Protect*, Vol. 3, No. 6 (2013), 1–11; M. Mamdani, 'Responsibility to Protect or Right to Punish?', *Journal of Intervention and State Building*, Vol. 4, No. 1 (2010), 53–67, at p. 53; K. Smith, 'South Africa and the Responsibility to Protect: From Champion to Sceptic', *International Relations*, Vol. 30, No. 3 (2016), 391–405, at p. 401.

[2] Art. 4(h), Constitutive Act of the African Union; adopted at Lomé, 7 November 2000; entered into force, 26 May 2001. Indeed, according to Mwanasali, Article 4(h) of the Constitutive Act was one of three instrumental mechanisms in the establishment of R2P, along with the UN World Summit outcome document of 2005 and the protection mandates issued by the Security Council, including for Sierra Leone, the Democratic Republic of Congo, Sudan, and Darfur. Under Article 4(h), the Assembly of the AU can decide whether intervention is required with respect to war crimes, genocide, and crimes against humanity. M. Mwanasali, 'The African Union, the United Nations, and the Responsibility to Protect: Towards an African Intervention Doctrine', *Global Responsibility to Protect*, Vol. 2, No. 4 (2010), 388–413. Kioko argues

South Africa's position during the consideration at the UN Security Council of the situation in Libya in 2011 is more complex. South Africa voted in favour of the adoption of UN Security Council Resolution 1973[3] (despite widespread opposition to the use of force in Libya within the African Union), but subsequently President Jacob Zuma was critical of the NATO intervention in Libya. 'The intention was not to authorise a campaign for regime change or political assassination,' he said.[4] While supporting efforts to improve the protection of civilians, South Africa remains sceptical about the use of force to protect civilians, in part as a consequence of the longer-term outcome of resultant armed intervention.[5]

26.2 THE 2020 UN SECURITY COUNCIL DEBATE ON THE PROTECTION OF CIVILIANS

In its statement before the Security Council's debate on the protection of civilians in 2020,[6] South Africa, a Council member at the time, reiterated its 'full support for the call by the Secretary-General for a global ceasefire in order to focus on the fight against the COVID-19 pandemic'. But recalling the Council's mandate to maintain international peace and security, South Africa declared that: 'If innocent children, women and men continue to suffer on our watch and the Council fails to take meaningful action, we will be failing in the responsibility entrusted to us.' It regretted that the plight of civilians in protracted conflict situations, 'such as in Palestine and Western

---

that, by introducing this Constitutive Act's provision, the African Union (AU) has moved away from non-interference and non-intervention and enforced new standards of democracy, accountability, and good governance. B. Kioko, 'The Right of Intervention under the African Union's Constitutive Act: From Non-interference to Non-intervention', *International Review of the Red Cross*, Vol. 85, No. 852 (2003), 807–24. Amvane notes that, in theory, the AU would always be required to seek such authorisation when intervening in a country. However, he also argues, controversially, that when genocide, war crimes, and crimes against humanity take place in an AU Member State, and where the Security Council is unable to act, the AU might have a right to intervene in accordance with Article 4(h) even without prior Council authorisation. G. Amvane, 'Intervention Pursuant to Article 4(h) of the Constitutive Act of the African Union without United Nations Security Council Authorisation', *African Human Rights Law Journal*, Vol. 15 (2015), 282–98.

[3] UN Security Council Resolution 1973, adopted on 17 March 2011 by ten votes to nil with five abstentions (Brazil, China, Germany, India, and Russia).

[4] R. Weighill and F. Gaub, *The Cauldron: NATO's Campaign in Libya*, Hurst, London, 2018, p. 180.

[5] K. Smith, 'R2P and the Protection of Civilians: South Africa's Perspective on Conflict Resolution', Policy Brief 133, South African Institute of International Affairs, March 2015, p. 3. According to Africa and Pretorius, the case of Libya had the result of raising concerns among the international community, in particular South Africa, regarding the doctrine of 'responsibility to protect'. S. Africa and R. Pretorius, 'South Africa, the African Union and the Responsibility to Protect: The Case of Libya', *African Human Rights Law Journal*, Vol. 12, No. 2 (2012), 394–416; see also A. Beresford, 'A Responsibility to Protect Africa from the West? South Africa and the NATO Intervention in Libya', *International Politics*, Vol. 52, No. 3 (2015), 288–304.

[6] Letter dated 29 May 2020 from the President of the Security Council addressed to the Secretary-General and the Permanent Representatives of the members of the Security Council, UN doc. S/2020/465, 2 June 2020, at: http://bit.ly/3qPVTYa, Annex 12: Statement by the Permanent Representative of South Africa to the United Nations, Jerry Matjila.

Sahara',[7] seems 'not to receive adequate attention and that accountability for violations against civilians in these territories is lacking'.[8]

'If the Council is going to issue mandates to protect civilians,' South Africa continued, 'we have to provide the necessary resources to those executing the mandate.' Its statement concluded with a plea for greater cooperation between the United Nations and regional organisations, in particular the African Union:

> Finally, greater coordination and cooperation between the United Nations and regional organizations, such as the African Union, which continues to develop its framework on the protection of civilians for its own peace support operations, are necessary to create an enabling environment for the protection of civilians. The comparative advantage of regional organizations can enable closer collaboration and coordination with local communities, including creating the necessary environment for the return of refugees and internally displaced persons on a voluntary basis and in accordance with the principle of non-refoulement.[9]

South Africa was a member of the UN Security Council in 2019–20. Throughout its membership, South Africa expressed several times the importance that it attributes to the protection of civilians.

---

[7] The conflict in Western Sahara tends to be considered one of self-determination between the people of Western Sahara and the Moroccan occupiers. According to Zunes, South Africa aligns with this view as it was one of the most recent countries to recognise the Sahrawi Arab Democratic Republic (SADR) as an independent country, joining now more than eighty other governments. The SADR has also been a member of the African Union since 1984. Zunes further compares the situation in Western Sahara with that of both the Palestinian territories and South Africa itself, arguing that what these struggles have in common is a shift from 'military and diplomatic initiatives of an exiled armed movement' towards 'a larger unarmed popular resistance from within'. S. Zunes, 'Western Sahara, Resources, and International Accountability', *Global Change, Peace & Security*, Vol. 27, No. 3 (2015), 285–99, at p. 296.

[8] Annex 12: Statement by the Permanent Representative of South Africa to the United Nations, Jerry Matjila.

[9] Ibid.

27

The Future of Protecting Civilians

In a speech delivered in New York in September 2021, Peter Maurer, the President of the International Committee of the Red Cross (ICRC), said: 'Parties to some conflicts continue to flout the most basic rules of international humanitarian law on a scale that is cause for global alarm.' Moreover, he declared, the harm inflicted on populations is not confined to loss of life or to injuries, for protracted armed conflicts 'are damaging entire social systems, essential services and economies'.[1]

It is not, however, happenstance that the level of respect for civilians in armed conflict is so dire. Nor is the failure to respect and protect civilians in situations of armed violence necessarily a new occurrence. Indeed, in his 2019 report to the UN Security Council, the Secretary-General of the United Nations deemed it 'the cause of considerable concern' that 'the state of the protection of civilians today is tragically similar to that of 20 years ago'.[2] But nothing justifies acceptance of the status quo, much less a persistent political, legal, and military inertia. For without mandating effective measures to redress the situation, expressing 'outrage' that civilians 'continue to account for the vast majority of casualties in situations of armed conflict',[3] as the UN Security Council has done on numerous occasions over past years, constitutes little progress. As of writing, the conflict in Ukraine was still raging, with strong evidence that both war crimes and crimes against humanity had been committed against civilians by Russian forces.[4]

Accordingly, this final chapter of the book offers a *vade mecum*: analysis and reflections on law and policy, and associated operational practice that may contribute to improve protection of civilians. For, as the Secretary-General went on to say in his 2019 report on the protection of civilians in armed conflict, attacks on civilians, indiscriminate bombing, sexual and gender-based violence (SGBV), forced displacement, and a myriad of other

---

[1] 'International Humanitarian Law: Enhancing Monitoring, Improving Compliance', Speech by Mr Peter Maurer, President of the ICRC, during the United Nations (UN) General Assembly, New York, 22 September 2021.

[2] Protection of Civilians in Armed Conflict, Report of the Secretary-General, UN doc. S/2019/373, 7 May 2019, para. 4.

[3] Statement by the President of the Security Council, UN doc. S/PRST/2018/18, 21 September 2018, para. 3.

[4] See Report on Violations of International Humanitarian and Human Rights Law, War Crimes and Crimes Against Humanity Committed in Ukraine Since 24 February 2022, Report of the OSCE Moscow Mechanism's Mission of Experts, ODIHR.GAL/26/22/Rev.1, 13 April 2022.

abuses will 'continue for another 20 years, and beyond, without urgent action to grapple with the central challenge of enhancing and ensuring respect for international humanitarian law and international human rights law, in particular in the conduct of hostilities'.[5] This much is true, improved respect for civilians will not happen by chance, even as it is clear that warfare will always lead to a certain measure of civilian suffering. Yet specific, tailored, and sustained analysis and action can effect change.

27.1 ENHANCING THE PROTECTION
OF CIVILIANS THROUGH THE LAW

International law is the most fundamental normative framework for the protection of civilians. As has been reviewed in the previous chapters, the complexities of the applicable rules tend to be difficult to navigate. It is noteworthy, though, that international law has not greatly evolved over the last decades. Calls for better 'respect' and 'implementation' of international humanitarian law (IHL) and other international law have oftentimes not provided concrete results, in the absence of concomitant strategies as to how this will or could be achieved. In a similar vein, the claim that the 'humanitarian space' in complex emergencies has shrunk have rarely been followed by suggestions as to how it can be enlarged. Yet concrete, targeted development of both law and policy could strengthen operational practice to protect civilians.

27.1.1 *Clarity and Normative Development of IHL*

The two Additional Protocols to the Geneva Conventions were a great normative breakthrough when they were concluded in 1977. Since then, however, technology has significantly evolved, and customary law does not always – or indeed effectively – fill the gap. In situations of non-international armed conflict, which represent the bulk of armed conflicts today, far too much is left to customary law when detailed codification of the law is also required. And much clearer interpretation of fundamental IHL norms, particularly the conduct of hostilities rules set forth in the First Additional Protocol, is vital. Today no one doubts the legal application of the principles of distinction and proportionality in attack to all armed conflicts, but precisely *how* those principles are to be applied remains unclear, leaving a large measure of *manoeuvre* in their application.

First and foremost, it is unclear how accurate an attack must be to comply with the rule of distinction. This is the most basic of all IHL rules for warfare, yet we do not know precisely what is lawful and what is unlawful. International jurisprudence suggests that missing a lawful military objective by several hundred metres when conducting bombing from the air or firing from long-range artillery may not be unlawful. This is critical to the interest of civilian protection in a populated area and such lack of accuracy should be more tightly restrained. Smart ('precision-guided') munitions can ensure that, in the overwhelming majority of cases, the targets are effectively hit so that mistakes are reduced.

---

[5] Ibid., para. 5.

Second, the proportionality rule in IHL is specifically intended to protect civilians, but what amounts to 'excessive' civilian harm in application of the rule is unclear. Even close military allies seem to have markedly differing interpretations of what amounts to lawful incidental death or injury to civilians or destruction of civilian objects. A formulaic application of the rule may be neither appropriate nor achievable. But vectors for assessment, to adjudge what the 'reasonable' commander would do, are surely attainable.

Third, the notion of direct participation in hostilities continues to bedevil discussions around the protection of civilians in both international armed conflict and, especially, in non-international armed conflict. Clarifying when protection is lost as a matter of law is critical to ensuring that civilians are not killed or seriously injured for what should be considered as *indirect* acts of participation. In this regard, terrorism highlights one of the major challenges of modern warfare and conflict, namely the blurring of the line between combatants and civilians. And outside armed conflict, when terrorism often exists, the two terms are neither meaningful nor helpful. Civilians are the main victims of terrorism. But too often they can also be the principal victims of counterterrorism.[6] Law enforcement rules only allow for intentional lethal use of force when it is strictly unavoidable in the circumstances to protect life.

In each of the three areas of contention in IHL rules on the conduct of hostilities, consensus on interpretation will most likely not be achieved. Increased clarity on how States interpret, implement, and comply with these rules which have direct relevance on civilian harm, however, would allow to better understand, coordinate, and improve States' approaches. New treaty law – although hard to achieve – could also allow progress in certain areas, particularly with respect to the means of warfare.

The 1997 Anti-Personnel Mine Ban Convention is an example of a treaty that was designed to increase civilian protection. In the early 1990s, the ICRC was warning of an 'epidemic' of anti-personnel mine injuries, as rural poor in Afghanistan and Cambodia, especially returnees, were being killed and maimed at a high rate. Each year, more than twenty thousand women, children, and most of all men were being victimised by these weapons at that time. Notably, thanks to the comprehensive prohibition on use and the requirement for the destruction of stockpiles under the 1997 Convention, this number has reduced by more than three quarters in the last twenty-five years. Major military powers – China, Russia, and the United States – have remained outside its purview, but the norms set forth in the Convention have proved robust and influential, at least among States.

Today, the greater threat from these largely indiscriminate weapons comes from anti-personnel (and anti-vehicle) mines of an improvised nature, which have been produced by non-State armed groups such as Islamic State. But while progress has been made on eliminating anti-personnel mines, the need for a corresponding treaty prohibition on anti-vehicle mines becomes apparent. Anti-vehicle mines are just as indiscriminate in effect as are anti-personnel mines, failing to distinguish between the armoured vehicle or the tank and the school bus or the civilian lorry. In Cambodia, for instance, such mines have killed

---

[6] In this regard, it is recommended that UNICEF and key States revise and update the Paris Principles on Children Associated with Armed Forces or Armed Groups to take account of the needs and protection of children suspected of terrorism.

more civilians than have anti-personnel mines in several of the past years. In Mali in 2019, as was the case in recent years, as well as in Burkina Faso, only vehicles were involved in mine incidents and no casualty occurred while individuals were on foot.[7]

Another issue of concern exists with respect to the use of 'heavy' weapons or weapons with 'wide-area' effects in populated areas. As the ICRC stated in 2019: 'The use of heavy explosive weapons in populated areas directly impacts civilians, leading to death, grave injury, and severe mental trauma to thousands of men, women and children.'[8] In March 2020, Ireland circulated a draft Political Declaration on Strengthening the Protection of Civilians from Humanitarian Harm arising from the use of Explosive Weapons in Populated Areas.[9] The Draft Political Declaration recalls 'the obligations on all States and parties to armed conflict to adhere to International Humanitarian Law when conducting hostilities in populated areas, including the requirements to distinguish between combatants and civilians as well as between military objectives and civilian objects; the prohibitions against indiscriminate and disproportionate attacks and the obligation to take all feasible precautions in attack'.[10]

While the attention being paid to the issue is appropriate, the Draft Declaration does not suggest that any weapons either are, or will be, prohibited for use in populated areas. The International Criminal Tribunal for the former Yugoslavia held that artillery-delivered cluster munitions fired into a city (Zagreb) from the limit of their operational range were indiscriminate[11] as too were adapted aerial bombs, also delivered by artillery, into Sarajevo.[12] The UN Commission of Inquiry on the 2014 Gaza conflict reported that most of the projectiles fired by Palestinian armed groups were rockets 'that at best were equipped with only rudimentary guidance systems and in the vast majority of cases had none at all'. The rockets available to armed groups in Gaza at the time 'were unguided and inaccurate'.[13]

To buttress their IHL obligations, States could, for instance, conclude a binding disarmament treaty under which they committed not to develop, produce, or transfer heavy explosive weapons that could not be lawfully used in populated areas, and undertook to destroy any such weapons within their arsenals. To clarify issues of accuracy, a maximum circular error probable (CEP) – the area within which 50 per cent of the

---

[7]   *Landmine Monitor Report 2020*, International Campaign to Ban Landmines – Cluster Munition Coalition (ICBL-CMC), November 2020, at: https://bit.ly/3ixCJob, p. 37.

[8]   Statement by Judith Kiconco, Humanitarian Affairs Adviser, Delegation to the African Union of the ICRC, Open Session of the African Union Peace and Security Council on the Protection of Civilians against Use of Explosive Weapons in Populated Areas, Addis Ababa, 17 July 2019, at: http://bit.ly/3c2ctzT.

[9]   See Irish Ministry of Foreign Affairs, 'Protecting Civilians in Urban Warfare', at: http://bit.ly/39aeDM9.

[10] Irish Ministry of Foreign Affairs, Draft Political Declaration on Strengthening the Protection of Civilians from Humanitarian Harm arising from the use of Explosive Weapons in Populated Areas, March 2020, at: https://bit.ly/2MiRLAP, para. 2.3.

[11] International Criminal Tribunal for the former Yugoslavia (ICTY), *Prosecutor* v. *Milan Martić*, Judgment (Appeals Chamber) (Case No. IT-95-11-A), 8 October 2008, para. 247.

[12] ICTY, *Prosecutor* v. *Dragomir Milošević*, Judgment (Trial Chamber III) (Case No. IT-98-29/1-T), 12 December 2007, paras. 912, 1001.

[13] Report of the detailed findings of the independent commission of inquiry established pursuant to Human Rights Council resolution S-21/1, UN doc. A/HRC/29/CRP.4, 22 June 2015, para. 97.

weapons fired are likely to fall from the intended target – could be agreed upon as a legal limit by the negotiating States.[14]

27.1.2 *Making Refugee Law More Protective of Those Fleeing Armed Conflict*

The displacement of civilians that is deliberately wrought during armed conflict or which exists as a coping strategy exposes civilians to danger. Children may be separated from their families amid the panic and mayhem. Displaced women are at greater risk of harassment, domestic violence, rape, trafficking, and forced prostitution.[15] Yet, despite the toll hostilities wreak on civilians, for those who flee over an international border, refugee law remains largely individualised. In terms of the right to seek and enjoy asylum from persecution, civilians fleeing armed conflict continue to have to prove the likelihood of being targeted – the risk of being shot, bombed, raped, or tortured is not enough.

As Vanessa Holzer wrote a decade ago: 'The assessment of whether a well-founded fear of being persecuted is *for reasons of* a 1951 Convention ground is probably the most crucial and the least clear aspect of refugee status determination in contexts of armed conflict and other situations of violence."[16] She argues, on the basis of the 1951 Convention's object and purpose, for an 'inclusive and dynamic interpretation that provides protection to people fleeing armed conflict and other situations of violence without confronting them with higher hurdles'. Given inconsistencies in jurisprudence,[17] a 'clear, authoritative guidance on the interpretation of the 1951 refugee definition in the context of armed conflict and other situations of violence' would be helpful for harmonisation of States' actions.[18]

---

[14] A CEP of 135 metres would seem to be a reasonable figure for medium and long-range bombing and shelling. This would mean a 3 CEP – the area within which 95 per cent of munitions fired would fall – of 405 metres. Imagine a city or town and how much civilian harm can be inflicted even then, by a bomb that lands more than 400 metres away from its intended target.

[15] Oxfam, 'The Gendered Impact of Explosive Weapons Use in Populated Areas in Yemen', *Oxfam Briefing Paper*, 2019, pp. 8–9.

[16] V. Holzer, 'The 1951 Refugee Convention and the Protection of People Fleeing Armed Conflict and Other Situations of Violence', Division of International Protection, UNHCR doc. PPLA/2012/05, Geneva, September 2012, p. 43 (original emphasis). UNHCR recognises that '[p]ersons compelled to leave their country of origin as a result of international or national armed conflicts are not normally considered refugees under the 1951 Convention or 1967 Protocol'. Yet, it also recognises that one of the problems in such circumstances 'is the often automatic denial of refugee status to persons who happen to come from a civil war situation, often on the grounds that even excessively cruel treatment is merely the inevitable by-product of generalized violence', and clarifies that 'persons become refugees when they flee or remain outside a country for reasons pertinent to refugee status, whether these reasons arise in a civil war situation, in an international conflict or in peace time' UNHCR Handbook, at 164; and UNHCR, 'International Protection', UN doc. A/AC.96/750, 27 August 1990. See on this issue J. Hathaway and M. Foster, *The Law of Refugee Status*, Cambridge University Press, Cambridge, 2014, 91–181, at p. 177.

[17] For an overview of domestic jurisprudence on this issue, see, for example, Hathaway and Foster, *The Law of Refugee Status*, pp. 177–81.

[18] Holzer, 'The 1951 Refugee Convention and the Protection of People Fleeing Armed Conflict and Other Situations of Violence', p. 43.

27.1.3 *More Force or Less?*

To seek to protect civilians, both in general and in the particular framework of peace operations, dialogue, technical assistance, persuasion, and sanctions can and must play their part in influencing greater respect for IHL and human rights.[19] But time and again, the limitations of a purely non-coercive approach have also been exposed. An arms embargo and repeated Security Council resolutions did not end the armed conflict in Bosnia and Herzegovina – only the use of force by NATO and sustained, allied political pressure did that – nor did sanctions and the declaration of 'safe areas' by the Security Council prevent the genocide at Srebrenica.

In this regard, NATO action in Libya – even if well-intentioned – has done the advocates of the Responsibility to Protect (R2P) doctrine no good. The chaos that is Libya today, and the knock-on effects on its neighbours of weapons proliferation, illustrate the dangers of initiatives to use force for humanitarian purposes on a broad scale. Moreover, civilian protection should have meant military action limited to halt and prevent atrocities. A small peacekeeping force inserted in Benghazi, for instance, could have averted crimes against humanity while not subverting the humanitarian purpose of the endeavour, although sending foreign troops into (emerging) civil wars for humanitarian purposes remains dangerous. The conflict in Syria has illustrated once again that this also remains a practice that is hard to achieve.

In an article published back in 2001, the ICRC's Legal Division wrote that

> in deciding to order armed intervention under Chapter VII of the UN Charter, the Security Council cannot ignore the fact that its primary role is to restore peace. It cannot take such a decision without drawing up a consistent and comprehensive plan of action that addresses the situation as a whole and, in particular, deals with the underlying causes. In addition, adequate resources and facilities must be provided to those sent on such missions, in order to ensure that genuine protection is provided for those groups who are supposed to be protected.[20]

Twenty years on, these remarks remain as apposite as they were then.

Within UN peace operations, mandates to protect civilians from an imminent threat of violence are routinely authorised by the Security Council. This is, in and of itself, normative progress. But operational guidance on judicious use of force is too often lacking at mission level, although the Department of Peace Operations' 2019 Policy on the Protection of Civilians and the associated Handbook provide overarching guidance. When force is to be used, and with what purpose, needs to be just as clear to every blue helmet as it is to the force commander. Indeed, there is also the risk that UN peacekeepers, who have suffered high levels of casualties, restrain themselves for their own safety reasons.[21]

[19] For an analysis of different means of influence in peacekeeping, see Lise Morjé Howard, *Power in Peacekeeping*, 1st ed., Cambridge University Press, Cambridge, 2019.
[20] A. Ryniker, 'The ICRC's Position on "Humanitarian Intervention"', *International Review of the Red Cross*, Vol. 83, No. 842 (June 2001), at: https://bit.ly/3kKEv6W, 527–32, at pp. 531–2.
[21] See in this regard C. A. dos Santos Cruz, W. Phillips and S. Cusimano, *Improving Security of United Nations Peacekeepers: We Need to Change the Way We Are Doing Business*, Improving Security Peacekeeping Project Report, 2017.

The Kigali Principles may be contentious in some of their detail, but their conclusion is evidence of the demands for systemic change.

In extremis, is there also a role for 'humanitarian intervention' in protecting civilians, when the situation is acute and the Security Council is unable or unwilling to act? In terms of controversies, the purported existence of the permissibility of unilateral use of force for humanitarian purposes remains perhaps the most disputed legal issue in contemporary *jus ad bellum*. Certainly, there are significant dangers and consequences when the Security Council is sidelined. Still, it is hard to argue that inaction is always better than action when the Security Council is blocked in the face of atrocities, in particular genocide, such as the one in Rwanda in 1994.

27.2 ENHANCING THE PROTECTION OF CIVILIANS THROUGH POLICY

Policy represents what, when, and how international organisations, States, and other actors intend to act to protect civilians, thereby implementing and complementing their legal obligations. Interestingly, in this regard, is the Martens Clause in IHL, which stipulates that, in cases not covered by international treaties, civilians (and combatants) remain protected not only by customary international law but also by the 'principles of humanity' and the 'dictates of public conscience'.[22] Seen through this lens, policy can serve to apply the principles of humanity by going beyond what the law requires. Most importantly, policy defines organisational objectives and directs resources and efforts accordingly.

27.2.1 *State Policy on the Protection of Civilians*

Despite the prominence of the concept of protecting civilians at the multilateral level, very few States have elaborated a national policy on the issue. Switzerland, the first to do so in 2009, and the United Kingdom, which followed a year later in 2010, are the exceptions that prove the general rule. Their policies are valuable political and programmatic signals. Although room exists for substantive improvement in both cases, these policies may inspire other States to adopt their own policies on the protection of civilians.

Indeed, States with a military that engages in fighting or peacekeeping should conclude and implement a clear policy on the protection of civilians. Such policies can support compliance with international law. Policies may also concert and enhance military and non-military measures that go beyond legal requirements for the purpose of better protecting civilians. Indeed, protection must not necessarily have strategic benefits in warfare, but oftentimes does – notably in non-international armed conflicts where 'winning hearts and minds' can contribute to achieving strategic and military objectives. Besides, policies may further strengthen States' diplomatic efforts and their international

---

[22] Art. 1(2), 1977 Additional Protocol I.

cooperation on the issue. Even the process of elaboration may bring benefits as different units and policymakers are brought together with a single purpose, raising awareness and committing to action regarding key issues and challenges across government.

27.2.2 *Organisational Policy on the Protection of Civilians*

The same logic applies to both global and regional organisations that are concerned by the protection of civilians. Each and every one should have an overriding and overarching policy for their conduct that seeks to protect civilians. Each should refer to and support the attainment of the UN Sustainable Development Goals, in particular SDG 16 on the promotion of peaceful and inclusive societies.[23] Over the last years, organisations dedicated to protecting civilians have made significant progress at the policy level. This is particularly relevant for defining overarching objectives and frameworks, streamlining efforts, and enabling oversight and accountability. Naturally, challenges and room for improvement remain.

The United Nations pioneered the development and implementation of the concept of the protection of civilians. Currently, the absence of a UN-system-wide policy on the protection of civilians is a weakness given the numerous missions, agencies, and departments involved in protecting civilians. The manifold reasons advanced for this normative gap seem to boil down to the challenges that would be confronted in the development and adoption of such a policy. But individual UN agencies have been able to issue policies on the protection of civilians. A common policy could help coordinate system-wide action and rectify some of the omissions in those policies, most notably with regard to the protection of certain at-risk groups of civilians (children, women, persons with disabilities, older persons, and the internally displaced come readily to mind).

Persons with disabilities have been described by the World Health Organization (WHO) as the largest minority group in the world,[24] and as a group are considered as the forgotten victims of armed conflict.[25] They are both the victims of armed conflict and of insufficient responses to the protection of civilians. It is an important omission that the 2019 UN Department of Peace Operations (DPO) policy on the protection of civilians does not tackle the issue, and indeed mentions them only once. The more detailed operational guidance provided by *The Protection of Civilians in United Nations*

---

[23] Key targets for SDG 16 include the following:

- Significantly reduce all forms of violence and related death rates everywhere (Target 16.1)
- End all forms of violence against and torture of children (Target 16.2)
- Promote the rule of law at national and international levels and ensure equal access to justice for all (Target 16.3)
- By 2030, significantly reduce illicit financial and arms flows (Target 16.4).

[24] UN Department of Economic and Social Affairs, 'Factsheet on Persons with Disabilities', at: http://bit.ly/3ckFoAT.

[25] DPO, *The Protection of Civilians in United Nations Peacekeeping*, Policy, New York, 1 November 2019, Annex, para. 37.

Peacekeeping Handbook, issued by DPO in 2020,[26] also does not tackle the issue. Nothing is offered on how to practically protect or assist persons with disabilities.

More detailed advice is given on how to prevent and address sexual violence and child recruitment, but even in these cases, guidance covers only one-and-a-half pages and one page, respectively. With respect to older persons, again the 2019 DPO policy on the protection of civilians mentions them only once, in an itemised list of groups that, it is stated, need a tailored approach.[27] Similarly, the World Food Programme (WFP)'s 2020 policy on the protection of civilians cites the needs of older persons only once, in relation to accountability to affected populations.[28]

Where the United Nations has shown particular progress and achievement is in monitoring successes and failures regarding the protection of civilians. A consistently high standard for such monitoring has been the work of the UN Assistance Mission in Afghanistan (UNAMA) and the Office of the United Nations High Commissioner for Human Rights (OHCHR) on the protection of civilians in Afghanistan, even though the reports make sober reading. In reporting on the protection of civilians during 2020, it was observed that:

> For a seventh consecutive year, UNAMA documented more than 3,000 civilians killed in a single year, with Afghanistan remaining among the deadliest places in the world to be a civilian. . . . A distressing feature of the conflict remains the shocking and disproportionate impact on Afghan women and children. They make up 43 per cent of all civilian casualties: child casualties numbered 2,619 (30 per cent) and women 1,146 (13 per cent). More women were killed in the conflict in 2020 than any year since UNAMA began systematic documentation in 2009.[29]

The 2021 report made a series of recommendations to the different parties, including an end to indirect fire by mortars, rockets, and grenades in populated areas by all anti-government elements, and an end to use of victim-activated improvised explosive devices (IEDs) such as pressure-plate IEDs, which are de facto and de jure landmines. With the Taliban now the national authority of Afghanistan, they are bound under the 1997 Anti-Personnel Mine Ban Convention never under any circumstances to use anti-personnel mines, including of an improvised nature. Ensuring the Taliban respects its international disarmament law obligations will demand sustained effort by the United Nations, the States Parties to the 1997 Convention, and other key stakeholders.

A number of regional organisations have adopted institutional policies on the protection of civilians, as this book has illustrated, most notably the African Union, the European Union, and the North Atlantic Treaty Organization (NATO). Each is to be welcomed for its efforts. But each could be strengthened. The EU still lacks an overarching policy and it

---

[26] DPO, *The Protection of Civilians in United Nations Peacekeeping Handbook*, New York, 2020, at: https://bit.ly/3oynVGg.

[27] 2019 DPO Policy on the Protection of Civilians in UN Peacekeeping, para. 37.

[28] WFP Protection and Accountability Policy 2020, para. 38.

[29] UNAMA and OHCHR, *Afghanistan: Protection of Civilians in Armed Conflict: Annual Report 2020*, Kabul, February 2021.

is not easy to navigate the different relevant documents. Yet the concept of protection of civilians in EU-led military operations is an appropriate guidance for military action.

With respect to the African Union policy on the protection of civilians, there is a need for broadening to encompass all parts of the Union not merely its peacekeeping. Ben Kioko and Lydia Wambugu argue that while the African Union has put in place a normative framework and mechanisms that could support efforts towards effective civilian protection, they have not worked as a coherent whole and require better coordination to enhance effectiveness and delivery.[30] Jide Martyns Okeke and Paul Williams call for increased reflection on the underlying strategy and understanding of what the role of the African Union is, and should be, in the protection of civilians.[31]

Armed AU peace operations now consistently include a protection of civilians mandate. But the 'draft' Guidelines are already a decade old and need revision and expansion, in order that they go beyond generic statements of concern to detail what an AU peace support operation should ideally – and realistically – do to protect civilians in armed conflict. For now, the AU is seemingly allying its understanding of the protection of civilians to that of the UN, particularly on the required degree of force deployed for a mission. However, when analysed in practice, the missions undertaken by the AU have not seemed to converge with UN norms nor significantly increased effectiveness at the local level. In this regard, it has noted that 'convergence of doctrines should not be confused with convergence in practice'.[32]

The North Atlantic Treaty Organization has also played a leading role in the conceptual development of the protection of civilians. The NATO policy on the protection of civilians is succinct yet allows a common denominator among its members. References in the same sentence in the 2016 Policy to 'applicable' international law, including IHL 'as applicable', demonstrate the challenges of legal interoperability. Within NATO, besides further efforts for implementation measures, continued prioritisation of the issue – notably in light of new military challenges, war at its border, and great power competition – is necessary.[33]

Consideration of the needs of specific civilian groups tends to be unspecified. A key lacuna in NATO's gender approach is thus the lack of a precise understanding of the 'operational relevance of gender'.[34] No clarification is provided in NATO's 2021 Handbook, which only clarifies that the 'Gender Perspective' should be 'thoroughly considered'.[35]

[30] B. Kioko and L. Wambugu, 'The African Union and the Protection of Civilians', in H. Willmot et al. (eds.), *Protection of Civilians*, 1st ed., Oxford University Press, Oxford, 2016, p. 275.

[31] J. M. Okeke and P. D. Williams, 'Conclusion: Lessons Identified and Recommendations for the African Union', in J. M. Okeke and P. D. Williams (eds.), *Protecting Civilians in African Union Peace Support Operations: Key Cases and Lessons Learned*, Accord, South Africa, 2017, pp. 91–3.

[32] M. Dembinski and B. Schott, 'Converging Around Global Norms? Protection of Civilians in African Union and European Union Peacekeeping in Africa', *African Security*, 2013, p. 291.

[33] Andrew Hyde, 'A Political and Diplomatic Case for Protection of Civilians at NATO', *The Stimson Center*, 2021.

[34] J. M. Prescott, 'Moving from Gender Analysis to Risk Analysis of Failing to Consider Gender', *The RUSI Journal*, 2020, p. 51.

[35] NATO, *Protection of Civilians Allied Command Operations Handbook*, Brussels, 2021 (hereinafter, 2021 Handbook), at: https://bit.ly/3ydsxa8, p. 51.

27.3 NEW CHALLENGES TO THE PROTECTION OF CIVILIANS

Besides conceptual issues at the legal and policy level, developments in security and military affairs, new conflict scenarios, and emerging weapons technologies may bring further challenges to the future protection of civilians. Urban warfare, cyber operations, great power competition, and hybrid warfare are all expected to pose such challenges to the protection of civilians, along with the increasing need to protect the environment amid warfare. It is too soon to say whether the military application of artificial intelligence (AI) will have positive or negative ramifications for civilian protection, although some actors have already taken clear positions.[36]

27.3.1 *Urban Warfare*

Urban warfare and siege warfare are not new phenomena by any stretch of the imagination, as the sieges of Stalingrad and Berlin demonstrated graphically in World War II. But in recent years, prolonged fighting in cities and towns has increasingly become a humanitarian concern given the severe adverse consequences for civilian protection.[37] Casualties in urban warfare in the conflicts in Syria and Libya, for instance, were reportedly eight times higher than in other types of conflicts.[38] Sieges of cities such as Mariupol in southern Ukraine in March and April 2022 were visiting devastating harm upon civilians. Urban environments present specific characteristics that differentiate them from warfare in the countryside. It is forecast that most of the world's population will live in cities by 2035, which will further increase their relevance for civilian protection in future conflicts.[39]

Various challenges exist for ensuring the protection of civilians in urban warfare. First, given the interconnectedness of systems providing for essential services in cities, such as electricity, hospitals, and water, attacks need to take into consideration the so-called reverberating effects. These include the long-term displacement that often results from large-scale destruction. A second challenge in urban warfare is how to protect civilians in 'dual use' objects where a building could serve both military and civilian purposes, thus rendering it (or at least parts of it) targetable under IHL. Third, where troops are involved in firefights or fire support operations, ensuring incidental civilian harm given the urgency of these situations continues to prove particularly challenging.[40]

---

[36] The Campaign to Stop Killer Robots, formed in 2012, is a coalition of non-governmental organisations (NGOs) which seek a pre-emptive ban on lethal autonomous weapons. The campaigners believe that there must always be human control over the use of force. Campaign to Stop Killer Robots, 'About Us', at: https://bit.ly/3ovni3D.

[37] S. Adamczyk, 'Twenty Years of Protection of Civilians at the UN Security Council', *Humanitarian Policy Group*, Policy Brief 74, 2019.

[38] ICRC, 'New Research Shows Urban Warfare 8 Times More Deadly for Civilians in Syria and Iraq', 2018, at: https://bit.ly/3oAUzL3.

[39] D. Kilcullen and G. Pendleton, 'Future Urban Conflict, Technology and the Protection of Civilians: Real-World Challenges for NATO and Coalition Missions', *The Stimson Center*, 2021.

[40] ICRC, 'International Humanitarian Law and the Challenges of Contemporary Armed Conflicts: Recommitting to Protection in Armed Conflict on the 70th Anniversary of the Geneva Convention', 2019.

The main debate surrounding the protection of civilians in urban warfare has been whether IHL provides for an adequately encompassing framework of protection. The ICRC 'believes that the challenges posed to IHL by asymmetric and urban warfare cannot *a priori* be solved by developments in treaty law',[41] and can instead be regulated – at least to a certain extent – by reference to the core principles of IHL. In contrast, Alvina Hoffman argues that existing 'codified' IHL is ineffective in limiting the effects of warfare in urban environments, and that a development of the law could ensure a better framework of protection by focusing on the progressive interpretation of the rules of precaution and proportionality in attack to render attacks on dual-use infrastructure unlawful and by prohibiting the use of indiscriminate weapons.[42]

It is clear today that the Siege of Sarajevo in the early 1990s was not a unique event. Siege warfare played a persistent and significant role in the conflicts in Syria, engendering appalling humanitarian suffering. Yet the siege of Mosul has shown that even when the most advanced military powers are involved, civilian casualties tend to be high. In this regard, Andrew Bell has argued that the United States and other concerned militaries have failed to properly integrate the protection of civilians in urban operations, treating the presence of civilians 'as a secondary complication that can be adequately mitigated through campaign planning and execution'.[43] For supporting such action, the ICRC developed a commander's handbook for reducing civilian harm in urban warfare.[44]

In their analysis of lessons learned from the battle for Mosul in Iraq in 2014–17 and for Marawi in the Philippines in 2017, David Kilcullen and Gordon Pendleton offer important recommendations for improved civilian protection. Among others, they call for the provision of reception facilities, accommodation, medical services, trauma and psychological support services, and life-saving medical and humanitarian supplies for displaced civilians; the need for specifically targeted messaging for civilians within a besieged area; and especial care when targeting critical infrastructure because of the knock-on effects in surrounding areas.[45] Dedicated urban rules of engagement (ROE) could help to reduce civilian casualties by, for instance, identifying densely populated areas within cities where higher restrictions on the use of force might be imposed, or enabling safe evacuation and humanitarian corridors to provide civilian aid. As noted above, prohibiting or restricting the use of heavy explosive weapons can prevent their disproportionate impact on the civilian population.[46]

---

[41] ICRC, 'International Humanitarian Law and the Challenges of Contemporary Armed Conflicts', Document prepared for the 30th International Conference of the Red Cross and Red Crescent, Geneva, 26–30 November 2007, *International Review of the Red Cross*, Vol. 89, No. 867 (2007), p. 734.

[42] A. Hoffmann, 'The Urbanization of Warfare: Historical Development and Contemporary Challenges for International Humanitarian Law', *St Antony's International Review*, Vol. 12, No. 2 (2017).

[43] A. Bell, 'Civilians, Urban Warfare, and US Doctrine', *The US Army War College Quarterly: Parameters*, Vol. 50, No. 4 (2020), p. 34.

[44] ICRC, 'Reducing Civilian Harm in Urban Warfare: A Commander's Handbook', 2021, at https://bit.ly/3yGLJjV.

[45] Kilcullen and Pendleton, 'Future Urban Conflict, Technology and the Protection of Civilians: Real-World Challenges for NATO and Coalition Missions', pp. 10–13.

[46] Ibid.

Starvation of the civilian population in a besieged area is unlawful as a method of warfare.[47] Yet siege operations with the predictable consequences of civilian starvation along with combatants is a favoured strategy for some attacking forces in armed conflict.[48] In Syria, according to the World Food Programme (WFP), seven million people became food-insecure as a result of the conflict.[49] In certain cases, such as eastern Ghouta, this was the result of a deliberate policy by the Syrian regime to block most of the food and other humanitarian supplies from entering the city. Such endangerment of food security inside a city or town by besieging forces needs to be avoided and strongly condemned.

27.3.2 Cyber Operations

Cyber operations have become an increasingly relevant tool in conflicts, and will likely become even more relevant in the future, raising important political and legal questions, including for the protection of civilians. Cyber tools have grown in importance for armed forces and they offer the possibility to achieve military objectives without necessarily causing direct harm to civilians or physical damage to civilian infrastructure.[50] However, ensuring that these operations comply with international law is a demanding task. Recent cyber operations have shown that malware – malicious software – can spread fast and greatly affect civilians. This was, for instance, the case of 'WannaCry', a malware that spread in UK health clinics a few years ago, cancelling 19,000 appointments, including urgent ones.[51] In addition, cyber tools pose challenges as they make the attribution of an attack difficult.[52] The development of artificial intelligence, Internet of Things (IoT), and quantum computing could 'dramatically increase computational power available' while further complicating the protection of civilians.[53]

The ICRC affirms that IHL applies to cyber operations and, as such, it can restrict cyberattacks to minimise humanitarian concerns linked to them. Although no definition of cyber warfare is provided for under international law, cyber operations during an armed conflict are widely understood as encompassing action against any connected device as means or method of warfare.[54] Many States and commentators, including the ICRC, have aligned themselves with the definition of a cyberattack set in the *Tallin Manual*, namely

---

[47] ICRC, Customary IHL Rule 53: 'Starvation as a Method of Warfare', at: http://bit.ly/2BNHBAi.

[48] N. Hägerdal, 'Starvation as Siege Tactics: Urban Warfare in Syria', *Studies in Conflict & Terrorism*, 2020.

[49] J. Kern, 'Humanitarian Food Assistance: Syria 2017', *World Food Program*, 2017.

[50] L. Gisel, T. Rodenhäuser, and K. Dörmann, 'Twenty Years On: International Humanitarian Law and the Protection of Civilians against the Effects of Cyber Operations during Armed Conflicts', *International Review of the Red Cross*, Vol. 102, No. 913 (2020), p. 293.

[51] W. Smart, 'Lessons Learned Review of the WannaCry Ransomware Cyber Attack', *UK Government*, 2018.

[52] Gisel, Rodenhäuser, and Dörmann, 'Twenty Years On: International Humanitarian Law and the Protection of Civilians against the Effects of Cyber Operations during Armed Conflicts'.

[53] E. Lawson and K. Mačák, 'Avoiding Civilian Harm from Military Cyber Operations During Armed Conflicts', ICRC Expert Meeting, 2020, p. 33.

[54] International Humanitarian Law and Cyber Operations during Armed Conflicts', ICRC Position Paper, *International Review of the Red Cross*, Vol. 102, No. 913 (2020).

that a cyberattack can be considered as such when it interferes with functionality, requiring the replacement of physical components.[55] Such an interpretation would require compliance with the principles of distinction, proportionality, and precautions in attack.

If this is the case, cyberattacks must never target civilians or civilian objects or cause indiscriminate or disproportionate harm or damage. Cyberattacks may never have as a primary purpose the spreading of terror among the civilian population. Those launching cyber operations must ensure that objects indispensable for the survival of the civilian population are not damaged, and that medical facilities and personnel are fully respected – as customary IHL demands.[56]

International human rights law also impose constraints upon cyberattacks. A cyberattack affecting civilian services might undermine a person's right to health[57] and potentially even violate their right to life,[58] depending on the disruptiveness of the attack.[59] Some, however, particularly in the United States, are reluctant to accept the application of human rights law where the harm is caused extraterritorially. The *Tallin Manual* itself requires 'physical control over territory or the individual before human rights law obligations are triggered'.[60] The International Court of Justice takes a different view on extraterritoriality, affirming that even the use of intercontinental ballistic nuclear missiles would fall within human rights obligations, albeit as interpreted through an IHL lens.[61]

To minimise civilian harm during cyber operations, Michael Schmitt calls for the granting of special protection status to 'essential civilian functions or services' that, if targeted by cyber operations, could damage civilian infrastructure and data. These would include services for the delivery of social services or financial institutions.[62] Eric Boylan argues that States should conduct a thorough analysis before initiating a cyberattack, subjecting it to a proportionality review, while prioritising intelligence gathering and reconnaissance operations over cyberattacks.[63] Yet States are only starting to formally recognise that IHL applies to cyber activities. Their views regarding the protection of civilians amid cyber warfare remain to be further developed.

---

[55] Gisel, Rodenhäuser, and Dörmann, 'Twenty Years On: International Humanitarian Law and the Protection of Civilians against the Effects of Cyber Operations during Armed Conflicts'.

[56] Rules 2, 54, and 25, 28, and 29 of the ICRC Study of Customary IHL.

[57] Art. 12(1), 1966 International Covenant on Economic, Social and Cultural Rights.

[58] Art. 6, 1966 International Covenant on Civil and Political Rights.

[59] R. Geiss and H. Lahmann, 'Protecting Societies: Anchoring a New Protection Dimension in International Law in Times of Increased Cyber Threats', Working Paper, Geneva Academy of International Humanitarian Law and Human Rights, Geneva, 2021, at: https://bit.ly/3ivdGSQ.

[60] M. N. Schmitt (ed.), *Tallin Manual 2.0 on the International Law Applicable to Cyber Operations*, 2nd ed., Cambridge University Press, Cambridge, 2017, para. 11.

[61] ICJ, *Legality of the Threat or Use of Nuclear Weapons*, Advisory Opinion, 8 July 1996, para. 25.

[62] M. Schmitt, 'Wired Warfare 3.0: Protecting the Civilian Population during Cyber Operations', *International Review of the Red Cross*, Vol. 101, No. 1 (2019).

[63] E. Boylan, 'Applying the Law of Proportionality to Cyber Conflict: Suggestions for Practitioners', *Vanderbilt Journal of Transnational Law*, Vol. 50, No. 1 (2017).

27.3.3 *Great Power Conflict and Hybrid Warfare*

Global power shifts have led to increased tension between the Great Powers, which may lead to increased hybrid warfare or even conventional warfare at a large scale. The international system is most likely being transformed into a bi- or multipolar international system, where China has joined the longstanding competition between the United States and Russia.[64] States may avoid open warfare by recourse to both conventional and non-conventional means in what are termed 'hybrid conflicts'.[65] The high levels of complexity of actors, means of warfare, and tactics typical to hybrid warfare are likely to make the efficient use of protection measures for civilians more difficult than is currently the case in asymmetrical warfare.[66]

For, if engaged in combat against near-peer competitors in future,[67] the United States is emphasising 'the speed and decisiveness needed to survive first contact with a major military power'. This will inevitably have consequences for civilians. Not only at the outbreak but also during large-scale conflict, since military casualties are likely to be high, warfighting parties are likely to tolerate high levels of civilian harm in consequence. While such a logic would be in accordance with the proportionality rule under IHL, this would suggest that the protection of civilians would be reduced to the legal requirements under IHL. In this sense, the war between Russia and Ukraine, a conventional inter-state war, has led to high civilian casualties, albeit also due to the disrespect of the fundamental principles of IHL by the attacker.

But, to date, little assessment of the impact of great power conflict on civilian harm has been undertaken. The presence of civilians, or their behaviour in future scenarios, continue to be omitted in the training and planning of actual operations.[68] Accordingly, the US Department of Defense has been called upon to institutionalise policies aimed at preventing civilian harm, including through planning and intelligence preparation; through cells responsible for assessing and responding to civilian harm; as well as through real-time learning and adaptation. Such policies should be buttressed through effective investigation practices, public acknowledgements of harm, and other forms of reparation.[69]

[64] A. Klieman, 'Pushing Back: The Balance and Balancing of Power', in A. Klieman (ed.), *Great Powers and Geopolitics: International Affairs in a Rebalancing World*, Springer, 2015; K. Schake in the Webinar 'Great Power Competition', *Center for Strategic and International Studies*, 2019.

[65] B. Card, D. R. Mahanty, D. Polatty, A. Shiel, and P. Wise, 'Anticipating the Human Costs of Great Power Conflict', *Just Security*, 2020, at: https://bit.ly/3Ff90Kv.

[66] On PoC related to the counterterrorism and asymmetric warfare, see S. Kaempf, *Saving Soldiers or Civilians? Casualty-Aversion versus Civilian Protection in Asymmetric Conflicts*, 1st ed., Cambridge University Press, Cambridge, 2020; V. Badalič, *The War Against Civilians: Victims of the War on Terror in Afghanistan and Pakistan*, 1st ed., Palgrave Macmillan, London, 2019.

[67] In this regard, see as first related analysis A. Atkinson, 'The Protection of Civilians within Collective Defense', Report, The Stimson Center, Washington, DC, 2021.

[68] Ibid.

[69] NGO Recommendations for DoD Policy on Civilian Harm, 'Applying the DoD Policy on Civilian Harm to Protection of Civilians in Large-Scale Combat Operations (LSCO)', InterAction, 2020.

27.3.4 *Protection of the Environment*

Climate change affects people's lives around the globe and in conflict-prone regions, thereby reinforcing the link between the protection of the environment and the protection of civilians. As Principle 24 of the 1992 Rio Declaration on Environment and Development states: 'Warfare is inherently destructive of sustainable development. States shall, therefore, respect international law providing protection for the environment in times of armed conflict and cooperate in its further development, as necessary.'

The protection of the environment – understood broadly as 'the complex of physical, chemical, and biotic factors that act upon an organism or an ecological community and ultimately determine its form of survival'[70] – contributes to the protection of civilians during armed conflict.[71] The environment can, however, also be 'an amplifier for conflict', notably due to the poor management of water and other natural resources, droughts, and climate change.[72] Abdulkarim Umar, for instance, highlights the over-exploitation of natural resources as a result of local populations becoming unable to grow crops during a conflict, or following the intentional removal of vegetation to facilitate the greater mobility of troops.[73]

Environmental protection is embedded in IHL. Under customary law, no part of the natural environment may be attacked, unless it is a military objective and its destruction is required by imperative military necessity, and only if the attack is not expected to cause excessive incidental damage to the environment compared to the concrete and direct military advantage expected.[74] In addition, the prohibition or restriction of use of specific conventional weapons and all weapons of mass destruction represents an important element of the environmental protection envisaged by IHL.[75]

International human rights law also protects the environment. Several human rights concern, in part, environmental protection, including the right to an adequate standard of living (including adequate food);[76] the right to be free from hunger;[77] and the right to the highest attainable standard of physical and mental health.[78] These same rights are also found in regional human rights treaties, including the European Convention on Human Rights and the American Convention on Human Rights.[79]

---

[70] The Britannica Encyclopedia, at: https://bit.ly/3mni33p.

[71] Z. M. Jaffal and W. F. Mahameed, 'Prevent Environmental Damage during Armed Conflict', *BRICS Law Journal*, Vol. 5, No. 2 (2018).

[72] J. L. Roesch, 'Making the Environment an Ally for Peace: Q&A with Erik Solheim', *International Peace Institute Global Observatory*, 2017, at: https://bit.ly/2WCe7CY.

[73] A. Umar, 'Environmental Consequences of Armed Conflict: A Case of the Northeastern Nigeria', *International Journal of Humanities & Social Sciences*, Vol. 19, No. 6 (2020).

[74] ICRC Customary IHL Rule 43: 'Application of General Principles on the Conduct of Hostilities to the Natural Environment', at: https://bit.ly/3vfV1iI.

[75] J. Islam, 'The Protection of the Environment during Armed Conflict: A Review of IHL', *Society & Change*, Vol. 11, No. 3 (2017).

[76] Art. 11(1), 1966 International Covenant on Economic, Social, and Cultural Rights.

[77] Art. 11(2), 1966 International Covenant on Economic, Social, and Cultural Rights.

[78] Art. 12, 1966 International Covenant on Economic, Social, and Cultural Rights.

[79] U. Mammadov and T. Huseynov, 'Protecting Environmental Human Rights in Armed Conflict Situations', *Environmental Policy and Law*, Vol. 49, Nos. 2–3 (2019).

Overall, however, it is generally acknowledged that the current international legal framework regulating the protection of the environment during armed conflict still lacks application, and even fails to provide for an all-encompassing protection. For instance, whereas IHL treaties do include rules addressing environmental protection, four main difficulties remain, relating to definitional vagueness, discordant paradigms, normative lacunae, and goal dissonance.[80] As Aaron Walayat puts it: 'While major steps have been taken within the current regime to remedy the problems of warfare in the natural environment, a wider legal regime, including considerations outside of the context of armed conflict, is necessary to address the current international obligation to protect the environment for future generations.'[81]

---

[80] M. N. Schmitt, 'War and the Environment: Fault Lines in the Prescriptive Landscape', in J. E. Austin and C. E. Bruch (eds.), *The Environmental Consequences of War: Legal, Economic, and Scientific Perspectives*, Cambridge University Press, Cambridge, 2007.

[81] A. J. Walayat, 'From Restraint to Obligations: Protection of the Environment in Armed Conflict', *Charleston Law Review*, Vol. 14, No.3 (2020), 465, at p. 486.

Conclusion

To conclude, the protection of civilians has become a well-established concept consisting of international law, policies, and practices. The legal framework, notably the content and form of international humanitarian law (IHL), human rights law, disarmament law, and refugee law, offers protection to civilians, particularly in situations of armed conflict. At the level of *jus ad bellum* and the primary role of the United Nations (UN) Security Council, the last two decades have witnessed a higher priority being accorded to the protection of civilians. That violations of IHL and especially attacks against civilians or indiscriminate attacks constitute a threat to international peace and security, as that term is understood in Chapter VII of the UN Charter, is a major normative shift.

International and regional organisations especially have shaped the practice and conceptualisation of the protection of civilians at the policy level. Notably the UN, NATO, the African Union, and the EU have driven the protection of civilians by both non-military and military means. The last decade has witnessed the adoption of several new or revised institutionalised policies, which indicates progress and the effort towards further improvement.

States have been reluctant to adopt national policies or strategies, thereby suggesting that the protection of civilians is more an issue for international, regional, and non-governmental organisations. This, however, would not be true, in particular as States are bound by the legal framework applicable to the protection of civilians and the implementation of the organisations' policies when engaged in their missions. To advance global efforts for civilian protection, to foster national efforts, but also to create more clarity on national views and priorities, it would be highly valuable if more States developed national policies on the protection of civilians.

Indeed, attention to and care for the protection of civilians must continue to be fostered, as the tragedies of Syria, Ukraine, and Yemen have demonstrated. Considerable efforts have been devoted to the issue in recent years, as illustrated by the High-Level Conference on the Protection of Civilians organised in Rwanda in 2015, the conclusion of new institutional policies, and the regular debates on the topic at the UN Security Council. States, international organisations, and other actors need to keep up the political momentum both for maintaining and enhancing conceptual developments and commitment. Other political priorities and challenges should not overshadow the issue. New security challenges, political trade-offs, and possible legal justifications should not serve as excuses to neglect civilian protection. Independently of what the future holds, civilians must be protected.

APPENDIX 1

Overview of Relevant International Law

A1.1 INTRODUCTION

This chapter provides an overview of the fundamental tenets of public international law. International law focuses primarily on regulation of the conduct of States (the main 'subjects' of international law), although it also addresses acts and omissions by international organisations, armed non-State actors, corporations, and individuals. All of these different entities are relevant to the protection of civilians.

A1.1.1 *The Definition of a State*

There is no universally accepted definition of a State under international law. The 1933 Montevideo Convention on the Rights and Duties of States provides that a State is an entity with a permanent population, a defined territory (even if there exist border disputes with neighbours), a government, and the ability to enter into international relations with other States.[1]

As of 1 April 2022, the Secretary-General of the United Nations (UN) considered that there were a total of 197 States in the world: all 193 UN member States (see Box A1.1), the two UN observer States (Holy See and the State of Palestine), and two other States (Cook Islands and Niue). This list may change in the future, for example should Kosovo's secession from Serbia,[2] or the existence of the Sahrawi Arab Democratic Republic (Western Sahara),[3] be recognised by the UN General Assembly, or should either be admitted as a member of a UN specialised agency.[4] As of writing, Bougainville, a chain of islands, was on course to secede lawfully from Papua New Guinea and become a State by 2025, following a referendum.

---

[1] Art. 1, Montevideo Convention on the Rights and Duties of States; signed at Montevideo, 26 December 1933; entered into force, 26 December 1934: 'The State as a person of international law should possess the following qualifications: a. a permanent population; b. a defined territory; c. government; and d. capacity to enter into relations with the other States.'

[2] The Republic of Kosovo is a member of the World Customs Organization (WCO).

[3] The Sahrawi Arab Democratic Republic is a Member State of the African Union.

[4] In 2015, Kosovo fell three votes short of the two-thirds majority vote it needed in the United Nations Educational, Scientific and Cultural Organization (UNESCO) General Assembly to be able to join the organization.

BOX A1.1 THE LIST OF UN MEMBER STATES (OFFICIAL SHORT FORMS)

Afghanistan, Albania, Algeria, Andorra, Angola, Antigua and Barbuda, Argentina, Armenia, Australia, Austria, Azerbaijan, Bahamas, Bahrain, Bangladesh, Barbados, Belarus, Belgium, Belize, Benin, Bhutan, Plurinational State of Bolivia, Bosnia and Herzegovina, Botswana, Brazil, Brunei Darussalam, Bulgaria, Burkina Faso, Burundi, Cabo Verde, Cambodia, Cameroon, Canada, Central African Republic, Chad, Chile, China, Colombia, Comoros, Congo, Costa Rica, Côte d'Ivoire, Croatia, Cuba, Cyprus, Czech Republic, Democratic People's Republic of Korea, Democratic Republic of the Congo, Denmark, Djibouti, Dominica, Dominican Republic, Ecuador, Egypt, El Salvador, Equatorial Guinea, Eritrea, Estonia, Eswatini, Ethiopia, Fiji, Finland, France, Gabon, Republic of The Gambia, Georgia, Germany, Ghana, Greece, Grenada, Guatemala, Guinea, Guinea Bissau, Guyana, Haiti, Honduras, Hungary, Iceland, India, Indonesia, Islamic Republic of Iran, Iraq, Ireland, Israel, Italy, Jamaica, Japan, Jordan, Kazakhstan, Kenya, Kiribati, Kuwait, Kyrgyzstan, Lao People's Democratic Republic, Latvia, Lebanon, Lesotho, Liberia, Libya, Liechtenstein, Lithuania, Luxembourg, Madagascar, Malawi, Malaysia, Maldives, Mali, Malta, Marshall Islands, Mauritania, Mauritius, Mexico, Federated States of Micronesia, Monaco, Mongolia, Montenegro, Morocco, Mozambique, Myanmar, Namibia, Nauru, Nepal, Netherlands, New Zealand, Nicaragua, Niger, Nigeria, Republic of North Macedonia, Norway, Oman, Pakistan, Palau, Panama, Papua New Guinea, Paraguay, Peru, Philippines, Poland, Portugal, Qatar, Republic of Korea, Republic of Moldova, Romania, Russian Federation, Rwanda, Saint Kitts and Nevis, Saint Lucia, Saint Vincent and the Grenadines, Samoa, San Marino, Sao Tome and Principe, Saudi Arabia, Senegal, Serbia, Seychelles, Sierra Leone, Singapore, Slovakia, Slovenia, Solomon Islands, Somalia, South Africa, South Sudan, Spain, Sri Lanka, Sudan, Suriname, Sweden, Switzerland, Syrian Arab Republic, Tajikistan, Thailand, Timor-Leste, Togo, Tonga, Trinidad and Tobago, Tunisia, Turkiye, Turkmenistan, Tuvalu, Uganda, Ukraine, United Arab Emirates, United Kingdom of Great Britain and Northern Ireland, United Republic of Tanzania, United States of America, Uruguay, Uzbekistan, Vanuatu, Bolivarian Republic of Venezuela, Viet Nam, Yemen, Zambia, and Zimbabwe.

A1.1.2 *The Definition of an International Organisation*

An international organisation is defined simply as an *intergovernmental* organisation.[5] This includes global organisations such as the United Nations, and regional organisations such as the African Union, the European Union, the North Atlantic Treaty Organization, and the Organization of American States.

---

[5]   Art. 2(1)(h)(i), Vienna Convention on the Law of Treaties between States and International Organizations or between International Organizations, adopted at Vienna, 21 March 1986; not yet in force.

An international organisation can negotiate a treaty (see the definition of a treaty in A1.2.1) with States and can also become party to a treaty where this is expressly allowed by a provision of the treaty. For instance, the International Atomic Energy Agency (IAEA) has a generic Comprehensive Safeguards Agreement (CSA) that it concludes with States. Under a CSA, the IAEA has the right and obligation to ensure that safeguards are applied on all nuclear material in the territory, jurisdiction, or control of each State for the exclusive purpose of verifying that such material is not diverted to nuclear weapons or other nuclear explosive devices.[6]

A1.1.3 *The Definition of a Corporation*

A corporation is an organisation that is authorised by a State to act as a single entity and which has an existence in law separate from its shareholders and employees. A corporation includes, but is not limited to, a company. A corporation, called a 'body corporate' in many national laws, may sue and be sued and in many countries can be held responsible for certain acts in the criminal law. In a treaty, the term typically used to describe a corporation is a 'legal person'.

It is disputed whether public international law, in particular international human rights law, binds corporations directly. The *Guiding Principles on Business and Human Rights: Implementing the United Nations 'Protect, Respect and Remedy' Framework* were developed by the Special Representative of the UN Secretary-General on human rights and transnational corporations. These Principles refer to a 'responsibility' of corporations to respect human rights. Principle 11 states as follows: 'Business enterprises should respect human rights. This means that they should avoid infringing on the human rights of others and should address adverse human rights impacts with which they are involved.' The UN Human Rights Council endorsed the Guiding Principles in 2011.[7]

A1.1.4 *The Definition of a Non-State Actor*

A non-State actor is not formally defined under international law. In UN Security Council Resolution 1540 (2004), the following definition was offered, for the purpose of the resolution alone: 'individual or entity, not acting under the lawful authority of any State in conducting activities which come within the scope of this resolution'.[8] The term *non-State actor* is often used to denote a non-State armed group. In the 2000 Optional Protocol to the Convention on the Rights of the Child, a provision concerns 'armed groups that are distinct from the armed forces of a State'.[9]

---

[6] IAEA, 'Comprehensive Safeguards Agreements', 2019, at: http://bit.ly/2UvGxeL.
[7] Human Rights Council Resolution 17/4 (Human rights and transnational corporations and other business enterprises), adopted without a vote on 16 June 2011, para. 1.
[8] Footnote to UN Security Council Resolution 1540 (2004); adopted unanimously on 28 April 2004.
[9] Art. 4(1), Optional Protocol to the Convention on the Rights of the Child on the involvement of children in armed conflict; adopted at New York, 25 May 2000; entered into force, 12 February 2002.

It is generally agreed that armed groups can become 'parties' to an armed conflict and that they are bound by the rules of international humanitarian law (IHL).[10] The means by which this occurs under international law, though, is disputed. It is not settled whether armed groups are bound by customary international human rights law, but the United Nations increasingly takes the view that they are at the least obligated by fundamental norms, such as the prohibition on arbitrary deprivation of life, the prohibition on torture and other inhumane treatment, the prohibition on discrimination, and the prohibition on arbitrary deprivation of liberty.

A1.2 THE SOURCES OF INTERNATIONAL LAW

This section explains where we find the rules of international law, discussing the 'primary' and 'subsidiary' sources.

There are three primary sources of international law according to the 1945 Statute of the International Court of Justice (ICJ).[11] These are *treaties*;[12] *custom*;[13] and *general principles of law*.[14] Particularly important in the protection of civilians are treaties and custom, although a number of general principles of law are also relevant. This is where one must look first in order to identify a rule of international law.

Also of great significance to international law, though, are the two 'subsidiary means' for the determination of rules of international law: judicial decisions (case law, whether at national, regional, or global level) and the writings of 'publicists' (meaning the world's leading public international lawyers).[15] Soft law – politically binding instruments as well as rules or principles elaborated by experts in a particular area – may also be influential in determining norms that are in the process of becoming international legal rules.

A1.2.1 *Treaties*

Many international rules protecting civilians are found in treaties. A treaty is broadly defined in international law as an international agreement between States[16] that is made in writing and which is intended to be regulated by international law.[17] If it meets these three criteria, it does not matter whether a particular text is called a treaty or a charter,[18] a

---

[10] See, for example, Special Court for Sierra Leone, *Prosecutor* v. *Hinga Norman*, Decision on Jurisdiction (Appeals Chamber), 31 May 2004, para. 22.
[11] Statute of the International Court of Justice; adopted at San Francisco, 24 October 1945.
[12] Art. 38(1)(a), ICJ Statute. The provision in the ICJ Statute refers to 'international conventions' while in international law, the generic term used today is 'treaty'. A 'convention' is, though, a common form of treaty. This is reflected in the title of the 1969 'Vienna *Convention* on the Law of *Treaties*' (emphasis added).
[13] Art. 38(1)(b), ICJ Statute.
[14] Art. 38(1)(c), ICJ Statute.
[15] Art. 38(1)(d), ICJ Statute.
[16] A treaty may also be made between a State and an international organisation.
[17] Art. 2(1)(a), Vienna Convention on the Law of Treaties; adopted at Vienna, 23 May 1969; entered into force, 27 January 1980 (1969 Vienna Convention on the Law of Treaties, or VCLT).
[18] Such as the Charter of the United Nations.

convention,[19] a covenant,[20] a protocol,[21] a declaration,[22] a statute;[23] or even a memorandum of understanding.[24] Of course, the converse is also true: calling a document a declaration or a protocol, for instance, does not mean that it is a treaty. As examples, the Geneva Declaration on Armed Violence and Development is not a treaty (even though is it signed by representatives of States), nor is the *Minnesota Protocol on the Investigation of Potentially Unlawful Death (2016)*.[25]

A treaty enters into force after a set number of negotiating States have indicated their consent to be bound (adherence). It then binds all of these States Parties (but not other States). Signature is rarely enough to amount to adherence (see Box A1.2). Any States that subsequently adhere become parties in accordance with the provisions of the treaty.

Multilateral treaties generally specify a threshold of ratifications necessary for entry into force and a certain period after the last ratification. Certain treaties, such as the 1996 Comprehensive Nuclear-Test-Ban Treaty (CTBT),[26] require ratification by specific States. The CTBT is not yet in force as several of the States named in a legally binding annex have not yet ratified the treaty.[27]

A1.2.2 Soft-Law Instruments

Soft-law instruments are political declarations or agreements that do not have the legal status or direct binding effect of a treaty but may nonetheless be influential in changing policy or identifying trends in the practice of States. Some soft-law instruments call for limitations on weapons to protect civilians. Examples include the 2001 UN Programme of Action on Small Arms and Light Weapons.

A principal advantage of soft-law instruments is that they are easier to negotiate than treaties. This is because there is less political cost or burden to their adoption and States may therefore be willing to show greater flexibility than they would in a diplomatic conference negotiating a legally binding instrument. Enforcement is also not a core feature of a soft-law instrument. Soft-law instruments may also apply to other actors

---

[19] Such as Convention on the Prohibition of the Use, Stockpiling, Production and Transfer of Anti-Personnel Mines and on their Destruction; adopted at Oslo, 18 September 1997; entered into force, 1 March 1999.

[20] Such as the International Covenant on Civil and Political Rights; adopted at New York, 16 December 1966; entered into force, 23 March 1976.

[21] Such as the Protocol Additional to the Geneva Conventions of 12 August 1949 and relating to the Protection of Victims of International Armed Conflicts (Protocol I); adopted at Geneva, 8 June 1977; entered into force, 7 December 1978.

[22] Such as the Declaration Renouncing the Use, in Time of War, of Explosive Projectiles Under 400 Grammes Weight; adopted at Saint Petersburg, 11 December 1868; entered into force, 11 December 1868.

[23] Such as the Rome Statute of the International Criminal Court; adopted at Rome, 17 July 1998; entered into force, 1 July 2002.

[24] See Office of Legal Affairs, *Treaty Handbook*, rev. ed., UN, New York, 2012, para. 5.3.2.

[25] *Minnesota Protocol on the Investigation of Potentially Unlawful Death (2016)*, Office of the UN High Commissioner for Human Rights, Geneva/New York, 2017.

[26] Comprehensive Nuclear-Test-Ban Treaty; adopted at New York, 10 September 1996; not yet in force.

[27] As of 1 October 2021, the following States named in an annex to the treaty had all still to ratify (or sign and ratify) the CTBT in order to trigger the treaty's entry into force: China, Egypt, India, Iran, Israel, North Korea, Pakistan, and the United States.

BOX A1.2 SIGNATORY STATES AND STATES PARTIES TO TREATIES

Becoming a *State Party* to a treaty is normally achieved by the separate acts of signature and ratification* or by the singular act of accession. A State that ratifies or accedes to a disarmament treaty typically becomes party to it after a set period of time (as long as the treaty itself has entered into force). A State Party is one that is fully bound by all of the provisions of the treaty. This is so, unless it is possible to enter 'reservations' to some of the provisions. Global disarmament treaties typically prohibit reservations.

Instruments of ratification or accession are sent to – "deposited with" – the treaty depositary. This is often the Secretary-General of the United Nations: the UN Secretary-General is the depositary of, for instance, the 1997 Anti-Personnel Mine Ban Convention and the 2008 Convention on Cluster Munitions. The depositary may also, however, be an individual state (Switzerland is the depositary for the 1949 Geneva Conventions and their Additional Protocols) or a small group of states. For instance, the depositaries of the 1968 Treaty on the Non-Proliferation of Nuclear Weapons (NPT) are the Russian Federation (as successor State to the Soviet Union), the United Kingdom, and the United States of America.

A *signatory State* – meaning a State that has signed but not become a party to the treaty – has more limited obligations under international law. These comprise a duty to 'refrain from acts which would defeat the object and purpose' of the treaty.** These are acts that are fundamental to the treaty. The term signatory State is often used incorrectly, particularly in the media, to denote a state party, but legally they are very different.

* Certain states, based on their domestic constitutional processes, 'approve' or 'accept' a treaty rather than ratify it. This has the same legal effect as ratification. See: http://bit.ly/2D5h3N7. For instance, Japan accepted the 1997 Anti-Personnel Mine Ban Convention while Slovakia approved it.
** Art. 18, 1969 Vienna Convention on the Law of Treaties.

beyond States, such as non-State armed groups, corporations, and non-governmental organisations.

The obvious disadvantage of soft-law instruments is that they do not have the force of treaties at international or domestic level.[28] That said, however, a soft-law instrument may precede the adoption of a treaty. Certain provisions in soft-law instruments may also become legally binding on all States by becoming customary international law.

[28] G. C. Shaffer, M. A. Gregory, and M. Pollack, 'Hard vs. Soft Law: Alternatives, Complements, and Antagonists in International Governance', *Minnesota Law Review*, Vol. 94 (June 2009), pp. 706–99. See also: K. Abbott and D. Snidal, 'Hard and Soft Law in International Governance', *International Organization*, Vol. 54, No. 3 (2000), 421–56.

A1.2.3 *Customary International Law*

Customary international law applies to States irrespective of whether they are party to a treaty that contains a particular rule. For a rule of customary law to exist, specific conduct (called 'State practice')[29] must be widespread among States and must be supported by a belief that the practice is obligated by a rule of international law (often referred to by the Latin phrase '*opinio juris*'). To become custom, a rule needs to be generally accepted by States, including what are termed 'specially affected States',[30] but does not need to reflect the views or actions of every single one.[31]

It is also widely argued that where a rule of customary law comes into existence, a State or small group of States can hold 'persistent objector' status to it, meaning that such States are not bound by the rule if they consistently objected to it during its formation and if they sustain their objection thereafter.[32]

Customary international legal rules are especially important in the realm of international humanitarian law (IHL, also called the law of armed conflict). The International Committee of the Red Cross (ICRC) dedicated ten years of research to identify the rules of customary IHL. The very first rule in the list of 161 recorded by the ICRC ('The Principle of Distinction between Civilians and Combatants') pertains to the protection of civilians: 'The parties to the conflict must at all times distinguish between civilians and combatants. Attacks may only be directed against combatants. Attacks must not be directed against civilians.'[33] The ICRC records that State practice establishes this rule as a norm of customary international law applicable in both international and non-international armed conflicts.[34] It is so fundamental – 'peremptory' in nature (*jus cogens*) – that it is never possible to override the rule by treaty.

A1.2.4 *General Principles of Law*

General principles of law comprise principles of international and domestic law that are found in most States.[35] The international legal duty on States to respect treaties to which

---

[29] When assessing State practice, more emphasis is placed on what States *say* they do, then what they *actually* do (or are alleged to do).

[30] These are States that have a particular interest in the rule. In the *Marshall Islands* case, the ICJ suggested in its 2016 judgment of preliminary objections that 'it considered the Marshall Islands specially affected with regard to whether customary international law requires States to affirmatively pursue nuclear disarmament'. ICJ, *Obligations Concerning Negotiations Relating to Cessation of the Nuclear Arms Race and to Nuclear Disarmament* (*Marshall Islands* v. *United Kingdom*), Judgment (Preliminary Objections), 5 October 2016, para. 44.

[31] In the 1969 *North Sea Continental Shelf Cases*, the ICJ explained the criteria necessary to establish State practice: widespread and representative (though not necessarily universal) participation by States, but including States that were specially affected by the proposed customary rule. ICJ, *North Sea Continental Shelf Cases* (*Germany/Denmark* and *Germany/The Netherlands*), Judgment, 20 February 1969, para. 73.

[32] See, for example, H. Thirlway, 'Sources of International Law', in M. D. Evans (ed.), *International Law*, 4th ed., Oxford University Press, Oxford, 2014, p. 103; and M. N. Shaw, *International Law*, 8th ed., Cambridge University Press, Cambridge, 2017, p. 67.

[33] ICRC Study of Customary IHL, Rule 1, at: http://bit.ly/32rIER0.

[34] Ibid.

[35] See, for example, J. Crawford, *Brownlie's Principles of Public International Law*, 8th ed., Oxford University Press, Oxford, 2012, p. 37; Shaw, *International Law*, pp. 73–8.

they are party (referred to by the Latin, *pacta sunt servanda*), and the allied principle that each State must evidence good faith in its interpretation and application of treaty obligations, underpin all treaties.[36] These general principles of law support the functioning of the international legal system. While many general principles apply to the entire international legal system, some are related to particular branches of international law, for example the principle of humanity in the law of armed conflict.[37]

A1.3 APPLICABLE INTERNATIONAL LEGAL REGIMES

There are many branches of international law that are relevant to the protection of civilians in armed conflict and other situations of armed violence as this work has sought to highlight. That complexity is one of the reasons for this book, to help to ensure that all relevant international rules are understood by the key stakeholders.

First and foremost, the rules of the law on inter-State use of force (often referred to as *jus ad bellum*) are important because they seek to minimise the risk of recourse to the use of military force. The UN Charter introduced a general prohibition on inter-State use of force that is the cornerstone of *jus ad bellum*. In recent years, inter-State conflicts have become the exception rather than the rule. Preventing armed conflicts from occurring is obviously a critical way of preventing harm to civilians. Non-international armed conflicts on the territory of a State (particularly internal conflicts, such as insurrections and insurgencies, that pit the State armed forces against non-State armed groups) are not regulated by *jus ad bellum*.[38]

In addition to, and in parallel with the rules of *jus ad bellum* (when it applies), *international humanitarian law* (IHL) governs the conduct of parties to armed conflicts during those conflicts. The law applies to each party to a conflict irrespective of whether the rules of *jus ad bellum* have been complied with. This branch of law protects civilians when they are in occupied territory and when they are detained for reasons related to the conflict, as well as during combat between parties (termed the conduct of hostilities under IHL). This is so whether the parties to a conflict are States or non-State actors (or both). Civilians and civilian property are protected from direct and indiscriminate attack and the risk of civilians being incidentally harmed is the key balancing factor in the rule of proportionality. Major challenges in interpreting or applying IHL today include determining when a non-international armed conflict exists and when a civilian is 'directly participating in hostilities' (making him or her a legitimate target for the period of his or her participation).

International human rights law applies at all times: peacetime and armed conflict. It protects civilians whether they are at home or outside or have been displaced. During

---

[36] See Art. 26 ('*Pacta sunt servanda*'), VCLT: 'Every treaty in force is binding upon the parties to it and must be performed by them in good faith.' See also, for example, Shaw, *International Law*, p. 77.

[37] M. Kohen and B. Schramm, 'General Principles of Law', *Oxford Bibliographies*, last updated 27 March 2019, at: http://bit.ly/2BwybtD.

[38] This is so, unless the 'non-State' armed group is trained, equipped, and/or financed, and *directed* in its operations by another State.

armed conflict, the interpretation of certain fundamental human rights, in particular the right to life and to freedom from torture, is heavily influenced by the content of the rules of IHL during the conduct of hostilities. The enjoyment of certain other fundamental rights, such as the right of peaceful assembly, may be limited during armed conflict.

Disarmament law applies at all times: peacetime and armed conflict. Disarmament treaties prohibit the use of certain weapons that are particularly dangerous to civilians: anti-personnel mines, biological weapons, chemical weapons, and cluster munitions. Some of the rules in disarmament treaties also reflect customary law; others are only applicable to States Parties.

International criminal law (ICL) is the branch of international law that requires the punishment of individuals for international crimes: genocide and crimes against humanity (attacks against civilians which can be committed outside or within an armed conflict), war crimes (which can only be committed during and in connection with an armed conflict), and aggression (a serious violation of the rules of *jus ad bellum*). International criminal law seeks to ensure individual accountability for past crimes as well as to deter future serious violations of international law.

Refugee law is the branch of international law that protects those seeking asylum from persecution. Refugees retain their human rights but are given specific protections under the 1951 Refugee Convention[39] and other global and regional treaties, as well as under customary international law.

Finally, *counterterrorism law* may be relevant to the protection of civilians in situations of armed violence. During armed conflict, however, acts of State armed forces or non-State armed groups that are regulated by IHL are generally excluded from the rules of counter-terrorism law. This is explicitly the case, for instance, under the 1997 Terrorist Bombings Convention.[40]

A1.4 THE RELATIONSHIP BETWEEN INTERNATIONAL AND DOMESTIC LAW

The notion of State responsibility reflects the fact that a State is responsible under international law for its own conduct when it violates international law. The details of State responsibility are set out in the International Law Commission (ILC)'s 2001 Draft Articles on the Responsibility of States for Internationally Wrongful Acts.[41] Many of these provisions represent customary international law.

Under the law of treaties, a State cannot use its domestic law as an excuse for failing to respect international legal obligations.[42] In some States, treaties are

[39] Convention relating to the Status of Refugees; adopted at Geneva, 28 July 1951; entered into force, 22 April 1954.
[40] See, for example, Art. 19(2), International Convention for the Suppression of Terrorist Bombings; adopted at New York, 15 December 1997; entered into force, 23 May 2001.
[41] ILC, *Draft articles on Responsibility of States for Internationally Wrongful Acts, with commentaries*, UN doc. A/56/10, New York, 2001.
[42] According to Article 27 of the VCLT: 'A party may not invoke the provisions of its internal law as justification for its failure to perform a treaty.'

automatically part of the law of the land and are therefore justiciable before domestic courts. In other States, treaties must be implemented in domestic legislation before a national court will apply the rules they contain. This may lead to domestic law in certain States not being in compliance with that State's international legal obligations.

APPENDIX 2

The Two Types of Armed Conflict under International Humanitarian Law

Two (and only two) classifications of armed conflict exist under international humanitarian law (IHL): international armed conflict and non-international armed conflict.[1] Once either type of armed conflict exists, IHL is applicable.[2] Other categorisations of armed violence sometimes referred to in academic literature, such as 'internal' armed conflict, 'civil war', 'transnational' armed conflict, or 'internationalised' armed conflict have no legal status and confuse more than they clarify. Moreover, political science definitions of armed conflict, such as the one conceived by Uppsala University,[3] have no basis in international law and do not trigger the application of IHL.

A2.1 INTERNATIONAL ARMED CONFLICT

An international armed conflict exists first and foremost where one State uses force against another State. This may occur, for instance, through bombardment or occupation of part of sovereign territory (without that State's express consent),[4] or through military action against another State's armed forces in any other place, including on the high seas. A major international armed conflict between Ukraine and Russia was ongoing as of writing.

The amount of force necessary to trigger an international armed conflict is 'fairly low'. According to the ICRC, for example, 'factors such as duration and intensity are

---

[1] The official term, as set out in Common Article 3 to the 1949 Geneva Conventions, is 'armed conflict not of an international character', but 'non-international armed conflict' or 'NIAC' are more commonly used to describe these conflicts.

[2] Certain IHL provisions exist outside armed conflict, such as the duty to adopt national legislation or to disseminate and teach the law to a State's armed forces as well as to the general public.

[3] The Uppsala Conflict Data Program defines an armed conflict as 'a contested incompatibility that concerns government and/or territory over which the use of armed force between the military forces of two parties, of which at least one is the government of a State, has resulted in at least 25 battle-related deaths each year'. Definitions, sources, and methods for Uppsala Conflict Data Program Battle-Death estimates, Uppsala Conflict Data Program, Department of Peace and Conflict Research, Uppsala University, Sweden, at: http://bit.ly/2z7GTLV.

[4] In its judgment in the *Nicaragua* case, the ICJ observed that (military) intervention was 'already allowable at the request of the government of a State'. ICJ, *Case Concerning Military and Paramilitary Activities in and Against Nicaragua (Nicaragua v. United States of America)*, Judgment (Merits), 27 June 1986, para. 246.

generally not considered to enter the equation'.[5] Indeed, in the ICRC's view, 'the mere capture of a soldier or minor skirmishes between the armed forces of two or more States may spark off an international armed conflict and lead to the applicability of IHL', at least 'insofar as such acts may be taken as evidence of genuine belligerent intent'.[6]

An international armed conflict exists even if the State being attacked or invaded does not respond with any military action of its own.[7] Thus, IHL both applies to and restricts the force that is being used unilaterally and in such a case both States are still 'party' to an international armed conflict. Moreover, the fact that, in an armed conflict, a regime in place in one State is not recognised by the government of its enemy also does not preclude the application of IHL.[8]

In rare circumstances, there may also be an international armed conflict when one State actively supports a non-State armed group that is engaged in armed violence against another State. Ordinarily, as discussed in Section A2.2 below, such a case is a non-international armed conflict. But where the non-State armed group is, in effect, fighting one State on behalf of another – operating as a 'proxy' for that foreign State – an international armed conflict exists between the two States.[9] This international armed conflict exists in addition to, and side-by-side with, the non-international armed conflict between the non-State armed group and the State it is fighting (see Section A2.3 below).

Exceptionally, where a State is party to the 1977 Additional Protocol I, and is deemed to be engaged in either 'colonial domination' or foreign ('alien') occupation, or where the government is a 'racist' regime (such as was the case in *apartheid* South Africa), a national liberation movement fighting against it may make a formal declaration to the Swiss Federal Council that it will respect the Additional Protocol I and the 1949 Geneva Conventions. If the Swiss Federal Council accepts the declaration as valid, this transforms what would otherwise be a non-international armed conflict into an international armed conflict.[10] This possibility has only been successfully invoked once in the history of the Protocol, in the case of Morocco and Western Sahara, where the longstanding conflict between the two has, as a consequence, been considered an international armed conflict since 2015.[11] The provision in the 1977 Additional Protocol I is not reflective of customary international law.

---

5   ICRC, 'International Humanitarian Law and the Challenges of Contemporary Armed Conflicts', Report for the 32nd International Conference of the Red Cross and Red Crescent, Geneva, October 2015, at: http://bit.ly /2Mzrxch, p. 8.
6   Ibid.
7   Art. 2 common to the 1949 Geneva Conventions.
8   Art. 4(3), Convention (III) relative to the Treatment of Prisoners of War; adopted at Geneva, 12 August 1949; entered into force, 21 October 1950 (1949 Geneva Convention III). In October 2001, for instance, the Taliban was recognised as the legitimate government of Afghanistan by only three States (Pakistan, Saudi Arabia, and the United Arab Emirates) but when the United States started bombing Afghanistan, an international armed conflict came into existence between the two nations.
9   This occurs where the non-State armed group pursues a military strategy under the foreign State's instruction and where the foreign State provides funding, weapons, and/or military training. This is known as 'overall control' of the non-State armed group by the external State.
10   Arts. 1(4) and 96(3), 1977 Additional Protocol I.
11   K. Fortin, 'Unilateral Declaration by Polisario under API accepted by Swiss Federal Council', Armed Groups and International Law blog, 2 September 2015, at: http://bit.ly/2NcAolb.

A2.2 NON-INTERNATIONAL ARMED CONFLICT

A non-international armed conflict exists where there is intense armed violence either between State authorities and an organised armed group, or between two organised armed groups.[12] The concept was first incorporated by States in Article 3 common to the four 1949 Geneva Conventions.

The first criterion for a non-international armed conflict, that of the intensity of the violence, excludes 'situations of internal disturbances and tensions, such as riots, isolated and sporadic acts of violence and other acts of a similar nature'.[13] A 'genuine' non-international armed conflict must therefore be distinguished from 'a mere act of banditry or an unorganized and short-lived insurrection'.[14] In its judgment in one case, the International Criminal Tribunal for the former Yugoslavia (ICTY) stated that indicative factors for the existence of a non-international armed conflict comprise 'the number, duration and intensity of individual confrontations'.[15] Individual terrorist attacks do not meet the threshold of armed violence.[16]

The second criterion, that of organisation, limits the application of IHL to 'organised' armed groups. This concerns armed groups that are: imbued with a military-style command-and-control structure; where their members typically possess and use effectively a variety of weapons; and whose logistical capacities give them the ability to sustain military operations. When an organised armed group is engaged in intense armed confrontations with State armed forces, such an armed group is 'party' to a non-international armed conflict.[17] When one organised armed group is engaged in intense armed confrontations with another such group, both groups are party to a non-international armed conflict.

All non-international armed conflicts are regulated by Common Article 3 to the 1949 Geneva Conventions as well as by customary law rules on the conduct of hostilities.[18] The 1977 Additional Protocol II to the Geneva Conventions regulates certain, but not all non-international armed conflicts. These are where the non-State armed group controls territory within a State against which it is fighting and which is a State Party to the Protocol. This instrument codifies rules that are all today also reflected in customary law for all armed conflicts, so Additional Protocol II's contemporary importance is arguably less than would otherwise be the case.

---

[12] International Criminal Tribunal for the former Yugoslavia (ICTY), *Prosecutor v. Dusko Tadić*, Decision on the Defence Motion for Interlocutory Appeal on Jurisdiction (Appeals Chamber) (Case No. IT-94-1), 2 October 1995, para. 70, at: http://bit.ly/2JkqZ5z.

[13] Art. 1(2), 1977 Additional Protocol II.

[14] J. Pictet (ed.), *Geneva Convention for the Amelioration of the Condition of the Wounded and Sick in Armed Forces in the Field: A Commentary*, ICRC, Geneva, 1952, p. 50.

[15] ICTY, *Prosecutor v. Haradinaj*, Judgment (Trial Chamber) (Case No IT-04-84-T), 3 April 2008, para. 49.

[16] ICTY, *Prosecutor v. Tadić*, Judgment (Trial Chamber) (Case No IT-94-1-T), 7 May 1997, para. 562.

[17] S. Casey-Maslen with S. Haines, *Hague Law Interpreted: The Conduct of Hostilities Under the Law of Armed Conflict*, Hart, Oxford, 2018, pp. 62–3.

[18] ICRC, 'Customary International Humanitarian Law', Article, 29 October 2010, at: http://bit.ly/33UmyIL. For the ICRC's view on the customary rules applicable to international armed conflict and non-international armed conflict, see: http://bit.ly/2ZecVG4.

A2.3 ARMED CONFLICTS MAY EXIST IN PARALLEL

Separate armed conflicts can exist on the same territory in parallel.[19] Each armed conflict is regulated by the respective rules applicable to it, depending on whether it is international or non-international. This potentially makes for a complex legal analysis, although in fact most of the rules governing the conduct of hostilities are the same in non-international armed conflict as they are in international armed conflict.

A non-State armed group acts on behalf of a foreign State where its operations are coordinated by that State, and not just being supported financially or with military equipment or training. In such a circumstance, there may be not only a non-international armed conflict between that group and the State against which it is fighting, there may also be an international armed conflict between that State and the foreign State that is using the group as its proxy to do its fighting for it. Figure A2.1 describes the process of determining the existence and type of an armed conflict.

A2.4 THE KEY DIFFERENCES IN APPLICABLE RULES IN ARMED CONFLICTS

International armed conflicts have become much rarer in recent decades than non-international armed conflicts. But, paradoxically, there are far more IHL rules regulating international armed conflicts than apply in non-international armed conflicts. This is especially the case in IHL treaties; but in terms of customary law, the gap in regulation between the two classifications of armed conflict is much narrower.

Perhaps the greatest difference between the rules applicable in international armed conflicts and those governing non-international armed conflicts pertains not to the protection of civilians but to the protection of soldiers. This concerns, in particular, the right of combatants to prisoner-of-war status upon capture. This affords them immunity from prosecution for the fact of having taken up arms (participated directly in hostilities) against the enemy. This 'combatants' privilege' against prosecution includes situations where the former combatant (now prisoner of war) has killed enemy soldiers, as long as the killings complied with IHL rules.[20] The summary execution of a prisoner or the wilful killing of a soldier rendered *hors de combat* by wound or sickness is a war crime.

A2.5 THE PREVALENCE OF INTERNATIONAL AND NON-INTERNATIONAL ARMED CONFLICTS

The relative infrequency of active international armed conflicts does not mean that the applicable rules of IHL are unimportant. Military occupations – where one State occupies part or all of another without its consent – are international armed conflicts too. As of

---

[19] ICTY, *Prosecutor v. Tadić*, Judgment (Appeals Chamber) (Case No IT-94-1-A), 15 July 1999, para. 84; International Criminal Court (ICC), *Prosecutor v. Thomas Lubanga Dyilo*, Judgment (Trial Chamber I), 14 March 2012, para. 540.

[20] See, for example, 'Combatants and POWs', ICRC, at: http://bit.ly/2ZGz8fk. But see also J. D. Ohlin, 'When Does the Combatant's Privilege Apply?', 1 August 2014, at: http://bit.ly/2PwKzlT.

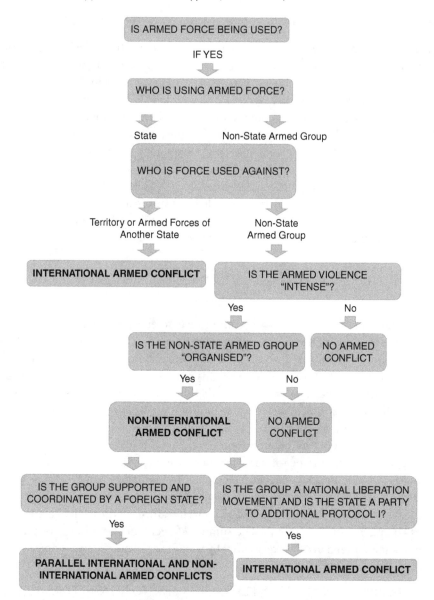

FIGURE A2.1 Determining the existence of armed conflicts

1 April 2022, a total of ten were occurring in Africa,[21] in Asia,[22] and in Europe.[23] Civilians will be at great risk during any military occupation as, typically, their government armed

[21]   Morocco's occupation of part of Western Sahara.
[22]   Israeli occupations of parts of Lebanon, Palestine, and Syria; and Turkey's occupation of part of Syria.
[23]   Armenian occupation of part of Azerbaijan; and Russian occupation of parts of Georgia, Moldova, and Ukraine; and Turkish occupations of northern Cyprus. See the Rule of Law in Armed Conflict (RULAC) project of the Geneva Academy of International Humanitarian Law and Human Rights, at: http://bit.ly/2ZoIDLO.

forces have been pushed out from the occupied areas. The police may remain, but they are not in place to resist an occupation.

In September–November 2020, an active international armed conflict between Armenia and Azerbaijan concerning the territory of Nagorno-Karabakh was ended by an agreement instigated by Russia. In 2019, a short-lived armed conflict between India and Pakistan,[24] both nuclear-armed powers, threatened to spill out of control. In addition, in 2018, there were short-lived armed conflicts between Turkey and Iraq as a result of Turkish forces attacking Kurdish forces inside Iraq without the Iraqi government's consent.[25] Arguably, Saudi Arabia's warfare in Yemen against the de facto Houthi authority continues to be an international armed conflict. The war between Russia and Ukraine, which started on 24 February 2022, is clearly an international armed conflict.

Non-international armed conflicts have existed in dozens of countries worldwide, including in Afghanistan (between the ruling Taliban and the Islamic State Khorasan Province (ISIS-K), Burkina Faso, Cameroon, Colombia, the Democratic Republic of the Congo, Egypt, Ethiopia, India, Libya, Mali, Mexico, Mozambique, Myanmar, Nigeria, Pakistan, Somalia, South Sudan, Syria, and Thailand. Finally, it is specified in Article 3 to the 1949 Geneva Convention IV that the parties to a non-international armed conflict should 'endeavour to bring into force, by means of special agreements, all or part of the other provisions of the . . . Convention'. This means that the broader protection to civilians afforded by the 1949 Geneva Convention IV, which would normally apply only to international armed conflicts, may also be made applicable to a non-international armed conflict if a special agreement is made between the parties to that conflict to do so.

---

[24] See, for example, '2019 India-Pakistan War', *History Guy*, at: http://bit.ly/2MOt7qS.
[25] See, for example, D. Butler, 'Turkish Military Strikes against Kurdish Militants in Iraq', *Reuters*, 28 May 2019, at: http://reut.rs/2HztDos.

Index

1864 Geneva Convention, 30
1868 Saint Petersburg Declaration, 11, 30
1899 Hague Convention II, 30
1899 Hague Declaration on the Use of Asphyxiating Gases, 75
1899 Hague Regulations, 31
1907 Hague Regulations, 44
1925 Geneva Gas Protocol, 75
1934 Monaco Convention, 4
1934 Tokyo Convention, 4, 31
1945 Charter of the United Nations, 12, 19
  Article 2(4), 20
  Chapter V, 21
  Chapter VI, 22
  Chapter VII, 14, 21, 22, 84
  Preamble, 20
1948 Universal Declaration of Human Rights, 67
1949 Geneva Convention III, 37, 131
1949 Geneva Convention IV, 4, 12, 31, 32, 43, 62, 70, 89, 102, 110, 113, 124, 140, 144, 153
1949 Geneva Conventions, 64
1950 European Convention on Human Rights, 58, 196
1951 Refugee Convention, 67, 69, 186, 238, 269
1954 Hague Convention on Cultural Property, 43
1966 International Covenant on Civil and Political Rights (ICCPR), 10, 51, 60, 63, 112, 132, 163, 196
1967 Protocol on the Status of Refugees, 67
1969 American Convention on Human Rights, 58
1969 Organization of African Unity (OAU) Refugees Convention, 67, 72
1977 Additional Protocol I, 4, 5, 32, 39, 43, 47, 71, 89, 102, 112, 113, 124, 131, 143, 146, 149
  Fundamental guarantees, 46
1977 Additional Protocol II, 32, 111, 118, 124, 149, 153
1979 Convention on the Elimination of All Forms of Discrimination against Women, 110
1980 Convention on Certain Conventional Weapons (CCW), 78
1984 Convention against Torture, 60
1989 Convention on the Rights of the Child, 115

Article 38(1), 116
Article 38(4), 117
1990 UN Basic Principles on the Use of Force and Firearms, 53
  Basic Principle, 9, 53
1992 Chemical Weapons Convention, 74, 75
1992 Rio Declaration on Environment and Development, 280
1994 Convention on the Safety of United Nations Personnel, 148
1996 CCW Protocol on Landmines, 78
1996 International Covenant on Civil and Political Rights (ICCPR), 50
1997 Anti-Personnel Mine Ban Convention, 74, 77, 267, 273
1997 Terrorist Bombings Convention, 38
1998 Guiding Principles on Internal Displacement, 153
1999 Istanbul Protocol, 61
2000 Constitutive Act of the African Union, 207
2000 Optional Protocol to the Convention on the Rights of the Child, 48, 118
2004 Arab Charter on Human Rights, 113, 123
2006 Convention on the Rights of Persons with Disabilities (CRPD), 126, 132
  Article 11, 130
2007 Paris Principles, 120, 184, 234
2008 Convention on Cluster Munitions, 74, 81, 226, 258
2009 Kampala Convention, 156
2013 Arms Trade Treaty, 75, 84
2015 Nelson Mandela Rules, 55
2016 Protocol to the African Charter on Human and Peoples' Rights on the Rights of Older Persons in Africa, 140, 141
2017 Minnesota Protocol on the Investigation of Potentially Unlawful Death (2016), 56
2018 Global Compact, 68

2018 Humanitarian Inclusion Standards for Older
People and People with Disabilities, 142
2019 IASC Guidelines on Inclusion of Persons with
Disabilities in Humanitarian Action, 133
2019 IASC Guidelines on the Inclusion of Persons with
Disabilities in Humanitarian Action, 131
2019 Vancouver Principles on Peacekeeping and the
Prevention of the Recruitment and Use of
Child Soldiers, 234

actus reus, 87, 103
Afghanistan, 79, 81, 82, 83, 100, 119, 123, 130, 148, 150,
183, 193, 195, 244
African Commission on Human and Peoples' Rights,
56, 113
African Court of Human and Peoples' Rights, 206
African Criminal Court, 106
African Union (AU), 273
2012 Guidelines, 201
Protection of civilians, 201
Aggression, 21, 86, 207
All necessary means, 22
All necessary measures. *See also* All necessary means
al-Shabaab, 205
American Civil War, 11
AMISOM, 205, 206
Amnesty International, 2, 163
Annan, Kofi, 14
Anti-personnel mines, 77, 117, 132
Clearance, 80
Definition, 79
Anti-vehicle mines, 267
Armed forces, 6
Artificial intelligence (AI), military application of, 275

Barrel bombs, 123
Belgium, 28, 76
Bellingcat, 2
Bemba, Jean-Pierre, 94
Bombardment, 21
Bosnia and Herzegovina, 13, 23, 24, 83, 88, 103, 194
Brahimi Report (2000), 168
Brazil
Protection of civilians, 249
Brunei, 163
Burkina Faso, 268
Burundi, 207

Cambodia, 13, 267
Canada, 78
Capstone Doctrine, 168
Center for Civilians in Conflict (CIVIC), 2
Central African Republic, 100, 120, 129,
130, 150
Chamberlain, Neville, 12

Chemical weapons, use of, 28, 75
Child
Definition, 115
Detainee, 116, 176
Child soldiers, 6, 48, 118
children, 115
and the death penalty, 123
Protection of, 115
Special Protection, 48
with disabilities, 117, 136
China, 15, 85, 119, 249
Civilian object, 33, 41
Definition, 41
Civilian population, 33
Definition. *See also* Civilians
Civilians
Definition, 2, 5
direct attack on, 33
in the power of the enemy, 46
Clapham, Andrew, 66
Cluster munition
Definition, 82
Cluster munitions, 117, 123, 132
Cold War, xvii, 22, 74
Combatant, 33, 36
Definition, 5
Commission on Human Rights. *See also* Human
Rights Council
Committee on the Elimination of Discrimination
against Women, 109, 110
Committee on the Rights of Persons with Disabilities,
127, 130
Committee on the Rights of the Child, 120
Common Article 3, 31, 64, 102, 111, 113, 118, 124, 132,
143, 146
Conduct of hostilities, 31, 32, 42, 52, 54, 115
Conference on Disarmament, 76
Consent to use of force, 20
Continuous combat function, 6
Core Humanitarian Standard, 7
Coupland, Robin, 9
COVID-19, 161, 186, 238, 247, 260
Crimes against humanity, 8, 25, 84, 92, 98, 104, 152, 184,
194, 198, 207, *See also* International criminal
law (ICL)
Definition, 92
Cultural objects
Special protection, 43
Customary international law, 10, 32, 65, 68, 110, 117, 147
Cyber operations, 277

Dallaire, Roméo, 23
Darfur, 15, 203
Dayton Peace Agreement, 195
Democratic Republic of the Congo, 94, 100, 130, 150

Deng, Francis, 24, 153
Detainees
    Treatment of, 47, 55
Direct participation in hostilities, 5, 33, 36, 48, 52
Disarmament, demobilisation, and reintegration
        (DDR), 125, 174
Disarmament law, 74
    Definition, 74
Distinction, rule of, 33, 54, 117, 131
Dunant, Henry, 30, 225
Duty to investigate, 56, 61
    During armed conflict, 57
Duty to prosecute, 57
Duty to respect and ensure respect, 58

Ebola virus, 101
Education, 118
    right to, 155
Elderly. *See* Older Persons
Environmental protection, 280
Ethiopia, 73, 99
Ethnic cleansing, 25, 154
European Court of Human Rights, 52, 53, 56, 58
    A and others v. *United Kingdom*, 62
    al-Skeini case, 58
    Aydin case, 61
    Banković case, 196
    Finogenov case, 54
    Georgia v. Russia (II) case, 59, 196
    Jaloud case, 59
    Lapunov case, 162
    McCann case, 53
European Union (EU), 273
    Concept on Protection of Civilians in EU-led
        Military Operations, 210
    Protection of civilians, 209
Exploding bullets, 30
Explosive Weapons in Populated Areas, 268

Ferrière, Frédéric, 3
Firearms, 53
Force, definition of, 20
Force, use in detention facilities, 55
France, 76, 78, 85, 119

Gadhafi, Muammar, 26, 198
Gaza, 64
Geneva Academy of International Humanitarian Law
        and Human Rights, 130
Geneva Call, 2, 148
Geneva Centre for Security Policy (GCSP), xviii
Genocide, 8, 13, 15, 25, 84, 95, 106, 198, 207, 271, *See
        also* International criminal law (ICL)
    Definition, 95
Germany, 197, 249

Glover, Jonathon, 12
Great power conflict, 279
Greminger, Thomas, xvi
Guatemala, 13, 61
Guterres, António, 32, 170, 186

Halabja, 76
HIV/AIDS, 155
Holzer, Vanessa, 269
Hospitals
    Special protection, 42
Human Rights Committee, 10, 51, 54, 63
    General comment, 37
        (on peaceful assembly), 63
Human Rights Council, 121, 122
Human Rights Up Front, 182
Human Rights Watch, 2, 77, 129, 162
Human shields, 34
Humane treatment
    Duty of, 46
Humanitarian intervention, right of, 27
Humanitarian personnel, 36
    Protection, 148
Humanity, principle of, 156, 221

ICBL, 79
Immunity from attack, loss of, 5
Impartiality, principle of, 156, 222
India, 79, 249
    Protection of civilians, 254
Indiscriminate attack. *See also* Indiscriminate
        bombing
Indiscriminate bombing, prohibition of, 12
Insurrection, 19
InterAction, 241
Inter-Agency Standing Committee, 171
Inter-Agency Standing Committee (IASC), 7, 128
Inter-American Court of Human Rights, 60
        2017 Advisory Opinion, 105
    Urrutia case, 60
    Yakye Axa Indigenous Community case, 142
Internal Displacement Monitoring Centre
        (IDMC), 159
Internally displaced persons (IDPs), 151
International armed conflict, 5, 37, 145, 294
International Commission on Intervention and State
        Sovereignty, 24
International Committee of the Red Cross (ICRC), 2,
        5, 7, 30, 34, 39, 55, 63, 64, 77, 89, 97, 111, 140,
        146, 152, 158, 265
    2008 Policy on Protection, 219
    Protection of civilians, 219
International Court of Justice, 15, 29, 50,
        54, 96
    Oil Platforms case, 29

International Criminal Court, 15, 86, 89, 98, 102, 103, 104, 106, 124, 143, 147, 149, 256
  Ntaganda case, 90, 105
  Ongwen case, 105
International criminal law (ICL), 33, **86**, 98
International Criminal Tribunal for the former Yugoslavia (ICTY), 88, 93, 96, 268
  Dragomir Milosevic case, 94
  Tadic case, 88
International human rights law, 8, **50**, 97, 110, 115, 130, 151, 196, 216, 280
  Application in armed conflict, 51
  Application to non-State actors, 64
  Derogation, 51
  Relationship with IHL, 62
International humanitarian law (IHL), 5, **30**, 50, 54, 97, 102, 110, 115, 117, 130, 131, 140, 143, 144, 152, 171, 194, 210, 215
  and refugees, 70
International Institute for Strategic Studies (IISS), 15
International Law Commission (ILC), 104
International law, overview of, 284
International Military Tribunal, 87
International peace and security
  Threat to, 19
International Refugee Rights Initiative, 204
International Rescue Committee, 2
Inter-State use of force
  Prohibition of. *See also* jus ad bellum
Iran, 115
Iran–Iraq War, 76
Iraq, 22, 36, 76, 79, 82, 83, 86, 148, 183
Iraqi Civil Defence Corps, 59
Ireland, 268
Islamic State, 77, 79, 152, 162, 267
Islamic State Khorasan Province (ISIS-K), 244

Journalists, protection of, 37
jus ad bellum, 1, **19**, 53, 86, 271
jus cogens, 65, 70, 197, 217
Just War theory, 11
Juvenile justice, 122

Kälin, Walter, 144, 153
Kellenberger, Jakob, 224
Kigali Principles, 169, 271
Kosovo, 28
Kuwait, 22

Laos, 81, 83
Lattimer, Mark, 58
Law enforcement rules, 52
  Principle of necessity, 52
  Principle of precaution, 53
  Principle of proportionality, 53

Law of armed conflict. *See* International humanitarian law (IHL)
Lebanon, 83, 162
Leuven Manual on the International Law Applicable to Peace Operations, 170
Levée en masse, 6
LGBTI persons, 181
  and the death penalty, 163
  Protection, 160
Libya, 22, 26, 148, 167, 194, 195, 206, 249, 263, 270, 275
Lieber Code, 11
Lord's Resistance Army (LRA), 105, 204
Lowcock, Mark, 133

Mali, 148, 150
Mamiya, Ralph, 3
Martens Clause, 271
Maurer, Peter, 265
Médecins sans Frontières, 2, 147
Medical personnel
  Definition, 145
  Special protection, 145
mens rea, 87, 103
Military objective, 33
  Definition, 41
Military occupation, 44
Mine action, 213
MINUSCA, 129
Mogadishu, 205
MONUSCO, 149
Mooney, Erin, 69
Mortars, 33
Moses Okello, J. O., 72
Mosul, 276
Mousa, Baha, 58
Moynier, Gustave, 30
Myanmar, 15, 79, 96, 100, 238

Nahimana, Ferdinand, 96
NATO, 10, 27, 167, 190, 249, 273
  2016 Policy for the Protection of Civilians, 191
  Operation Deny Flight, 194
  Operation Unified Protector, 197
Nepal, 80, 116
Netherlands, the, 59
Nigeria, 79, 130, 148
Non-discrimination, principle of, 222
Non-international armed conflict, 5, 31, 46, 103, 294
Non-refoulement, principle of, 70, 72
Non-State actors. *See* Non-State armed groups
non-State armed groups, 31, 50, 65, 79, 119, 120, 267
North Macedonia, 216
Norway, 82
  Protection of civilians, 258

Norwegian People's Aid
   Mine Action Review, 80
Norwegian Refugee Council, 181
Nowak, Manfred, 128
Nuclear power stations
   Protection, 43

Obama, Barack, 239
Older persons, 140
   and the death penalty, 143
Organisation for the Prohibition of Chemical
        Weapons (OPCW), 77
Organised armed groups, 5
Overseas Development Institute, 182

Pacific settlement of disputes, 20
Paddon Rhoads, Emily, 168
Pakistan, 13, 79
Palestine, 130, 148
Participation Revolution, 223
Persons with disabilities, 117, 126, 179, 236, 260,
   272
Physicians for Human Rights, 77
Posner, Eric, 27
Power to detain, 63
Precautions in attack, rule of, 40
Precision-guided ('smart') munitions, 55
Priddy, Alice, 99
Propaganda, 34
Proportionality in attack, rule of, 33, 39, 43, 53, 54, 117,
   131, 145, 243
Protect
   Definition, 55
Protection
   Definition, 6
Protection of Civilians
   Definition, xvii, 1, 9
   Preventive measures, 9

Rape, 61, 94, 97, 99, 103, 104, 161, *See also* Sexual and
   Gender-Based Violence (SGBV)
Ratner, Steve, 224
Refugee, 15, 67, 99, 110
   Definition, 67
Regime change, 26
Reisman, W. Michael, 28
Respect
   Definition, 55
Responsibility to Protect (R2P), xvii, 24, 270
   Pillars, 26
Responsibility While Protecting (RWP), 250, 256
Rifles, 33
Right of peaceful assembly, 63, 183
Right of return, 156
Right to liberty, 51, 61, 109, 154

Right to life, 51, 59, 109, *See also* International human
        rights law
   Prohibition on arbitrary deprivation of life,
        51, 56
Right to security, 61
Right to seek asylum, 68
Rohingya, 15, 96
Roosevelt, Franklin D., 12
Royal United Services Institute (RUSI), 232
Russia, 27, 249
Rwanda, 13, 23, 24, 250, 271

Sarajevo, 94, 194, 276
Sarin, 75
Saudi Arabia, 85, 116, 123, 124, 130, 238, 248
Save the Children, 2, 232
Schools
   Protection, 44
   Safe Schools Declaration, 44, 234, 258
Scotland, 116
Second World War, 4, 12, 20, 31, 75, 86, 141, 275
Self-defence, 22, 29
Self-determination, right of peoples to, 1
Self-protection, 11
Sexual and Gender-Based Violence (SGBV), 97, 112,
        136, 186, 213, 237
Sexual violence
   Definition, 97
Sherman, William, 11
Shooting to kill, 53
Sieges, 35, 275
Sierra Leone, 14, 23
Small arms and light weapons (SALW), 177
Solferino, Battle of, 30
Somalia, 150, 205
South Africa
   Protection of civilians, 262
South Sudan, 66, 79, 100, 150, 208
Sovereignty, 19
Special Court for Sierra Leone, 64
Srebrenica, 13, 24, 194
Stahn, Carsten, 86
Starvation of civilians as a method of warfare,
        36, 91
Submunitions, 81
   Clearance, 83
Sudan, 15
Suez Canal, 22
Supreme Iraqi Criminal Tribunal, 76
Sweden, 82
Switzerland
   2013 Strategy on the Protection of Civilians, 225
   Protection of civilians, 225
Syria, 15, 28, 36, 76, 79, 94, 99, 119, 123, 130, 148, 153, 162,
        270, 275, 277

Taiwan, 80
Tear gas, 76
Terrorism, 8, 37, 100, 119, 121
Thakur, Ramesh, 26
Torture, prohibition of, 60
Tsar Alexander II, 30
Turkey, 79, 130

Uganda, 163
Uighurs, 15
Ukraine, 79, 130
UNHCR, 15, 69, 72, 180, 181, 185
UNICEF, 181, 184
United Kingdom, 28, 85, 116, 119
    House of Lords
        Adan case, 69
        R. v. Jones (Margaret), 86
    Protection of Civilians, 229
    Supreme Court
        Serdar Mohamed case, 62
United Nations
    Department of Peace Operations (DPO)
        2019 policy on the protection of civilians, 171
    Monitoring and Reporting Mechanism (MRM), 185
    Office of the High Commissioner for Human Rights
        (OHCHR), 183
    Security Council
        Resolution 1970, 198
    Special Representative of Secretary-General for
        Internally Displaced Persons, 144
    UNAMSIL, 23
United Nations (UN), 50, *See also* Human Rights Up
        Front, UNHCR, UNICEF
    Assistance Mission in Afghanistan (UNAMA), 183
    Commission of Inquiry on Syria, 94, 99, 152
    Department of Peace Operations (DPO), 114
        2019 Policy on the Protection of Civilians, 125
        Three Tiers of Action, 174
    General Assembly, 25
        Resolution 63/308, 26
    Global Study on Children Deprived of Liberty, 121
    High-Level Panel on Threats, Challenges and
        Change, 24
    Human Rights Due Diligence Policy on UN
        Support to Non-United Nations Security
        Forces, 174
    Independent Expert on protection against violence
        and discrimination based on sexual orientation
        and gender identity, 161
    Monitoring and Reporting Mechanism (MRM), 122
    Office for the Coordination of Humanitarian Affairs
        (OCHA), 151
    Office of the High Commissioner for Human Rights
        (OHCHR), 161
    Peacekeeping operations, 22, 124, 173

Policies on the protection of civilians, 167
Secretary-General, 13, 25, 77, 100, 123, 127, 149
Security Council, 13, 19, 32, 85, 121, 194, 217, 227, 261
    Authorisation to use force, 21
    Resolution 678, 22
    Resolution 1265, 14, 23
    Resolution 1270, 14, 23
    Resolution 1325, 97
    Resolution 1327, 168
    Resolution 1674, 25
    Resolution 1888, 109
    Resolution 1970, 26
    Resolution 1973, 26, 197, 249, 259
    Resolution 2217, 129
    Resolution 2272, 237
    Resolution 2286, 147
    Resolution 2406, 128
    Resolution 2427, 119
    Resolution 2475, 128, 131
    responsibility for the maintenance of inter-
        national peace and security, 21
    Working Group on Children and Armed
        Conflict, 122
Security Council Resolution 1612, 122
Six Grave Violations (against children), 122
Special Rapporteur on extrajudicial, summary or
    arbitrary executions, 160
Special Rapporteur on torture, 127
Special Representative of the Secretary-General on
    Children in Armed Conflict, 121, 185
Special Representative of the Secretary-General on
    Sexual Violence in Conflict, 98
Sustainable Development Goals (SDGs), 272
Under Secretary-General for Peace Operations, 180
United States, 85
    National Strategy on Women, Peace, and
        Security, 246
United States (US), 6, 15, 77, 81, 82, 115, 119, 194
    2016 Executive Order, 244
    Department of Defense, 239
        Law of War Manual, 242
    Department of State, 12
    Protection of civilians, 239
    Supreme Court, 143
Urban warfare, 275
Use of force, general prohibition of, 20

Victim assistance, 81
Vietnam War, 13, 81

War crime, 98
War crimes, 25, 48, 84, 87, 103, 145, 149, 207, *See also*
    International criminal law (ICL)
Wassenaar Arrangement, 84
Weapons of mass destruction (WMD), 74, 77

Williamson, Sarah, 192
Women
   and the death penalty, 112
   Protection of, 109
   Special Protection, 47
World Food Programme, 112, 187, 277
   2020 Protection Policy, 187

World Health Organization (WHO), 101, 148, 179,
   272
World Summit, 25
World War I, 3, 20, 75, 76

Yemen, 15, 79, 100, 116, 123, 130, 148, 238, 248
Yugoslavia, Federal Republic of, 28